Routledge Revivals

Nationalized Industry and Public Ownership

First Published in 1960, *Nationalized Industry and Public Ownership* is concerned with the state of nationalized industries in Britain in the context of the wider sphere of public enterprise in the world. It critically examines themes like the motives and background of nationalization; the state of public corporation in Britain; public utilities as monopoly; parliamentary debates and questions regarding government control; the idea of public accountability; the status of consumers' councils, and the link between labour relations and public ownership. This book is an important historical document for scholars and researchers of public administration, political economy, British economy, labour economics and British labour history.

Nationalized Industry and Public Ownership

William A. Robson

Routledge
Taylor & Francis Group

First published in 1960
by George Allen & Unwin Ltd.

This edition first published in 2022 by Routledge
2 Park Square, Milton Park, Abingdon, Oxon, OX14 4RN

and by Routledge
605 Third Avenue, New York, NY 10017

Routledge is an imprint of the Taylor & Francis Group, an informa business

Publisher's Note
The publisher has gone to great lengths to ensure the quality of this reprint but points out that some imperfections in the original copies may be apparent.

Disclaimer
The publisher has made every effort to trace copyright holders and welcomes correspondence from those they have been unable to contact.

A Library of Congress record exists under LCCN: 66034210

ISBN: 978-1-032-20297-6 (hbk)
ISBN: 978-1-003-26308-1 (ebk)
ISBN: 978-1-032-20298-3 (pbk)

Book DOI 10.4324/9781003263081

WILLIAM A. ROBSON
Professor of Public Administration
London School of Economics and Political Science
(University of London)

NATIONALIZED INDUSTRY AND PUBLIC OWNERSHIP

Ruskin House
GEORGE ALLEN & UNWIN LTD
MUSEUM STREET LONDON

FIRST PUBLISHED IN 1960
SECOND EDITION 1962

PRINTED IN GREAT BRITAIN
in 11 *on* 12 *pt. Bell type*
BY SIMSON SHAND LTD
LONDON, HERTFORD AND HARLOW

TO
SIR KELVIN SPENCER

INTRODUCTION TO THE SECOND EDITION

THE publishers have informed me of the need for a second edition of this book within a few months of its first publication.

I have not the time at my disposal to revise the text in detail. This would also involve much delay and heavy additional cost in resetting the type. The result would not, I think, justify the effort, delay, and expense because the general picture I have drawn of the nationalized industries remains substantially accurate. I have, therefore, done no more in this respect than correct a few literal inaccuracies to which my attention has been drawn.

The preparation of a new edition does, however, enable me to discuss in this Introduction a number of important matters of policy concerning the nationalized industries which have arisen since the book appeared.

THE SELECT COMMITTEE'S REPORT ON THE RAILWAYS

The principal focus of public interest has been the railways. In July 1960 the Select Committee of the House of Commons on Nationalized Industries presented their report on British Railways.[1] The British Transport Commission had taken the initiative in requesting, through their Chairman, the Select Committee to conduct an inquiry into the railways; and the Commission made every effort to reveal their position as fully as possible.

The report is in two parts. The first part considers the structure of the British Transport Commission and its relationship with the Ministry of Transport. It surveys in some detail the finances of British Railways, and then goes on to consider the Modernization and Re-equipment Plan in terms of its aims, assumptions and priorities, and its probable effects. The report looks briefly at the questions of manpower and productivity, technical resources, design and research. Finally, the performance of the railways is analysed in the light of the figures for wagon turn-round time, the passenger load factor, and the punctuality of trains.

In the second part of the report the Select Committee express their views and conclusions on these matters. The report is on the whole an unfavourable one though not pessimistic about the future; for while the

[1] BPP 254/1960. HMSO.

Select Committee recognize the severe difficulties which confront the railway system at the present time, they do not believe that any of these difficulties are insuperable. However, they criticize the Commission for not having grappled sooner or more vigorously with some of them, such as the slower turn-round of wagons in recent years. It is essential, they say, that improvements should be made, and made quickly.[1]

The Select Committee express regret that work study, which is urgently needed in every branch of railway operation, has not been more extensively applied, despite its success in improving efficiency at Reading Station.[2] Other aspects of management which receive adverse comment are a lack of vigour in recruiting technical staff and the failure to keep a careful watch on the relatively small number of professional engineers employed by the Commission; and the defective costing system which precludes any quantitative assessment of the profitability of individual Regions or services, and even any estimate of the profitability of the capital works embodied in the Modernization and Re-equipment Plan. The Ministry of Transport and the Treasury are also censured for their readiness to lend money to the Commission without adequate justification for its investment.

The Select Committee gave their general approval to the organization of the Commission, despite its complexity, apart from the fact that there was no one authority in the undertaking whose sole duty was to achieve an efficient railway system.[3] The Committee explicitly approved the general policy of the Commission in regard to central co-ordination and decentralization of managerial responsibility to the regions.[4]

On the economic aspects the report points out that both passenger fares and freight charges are substantially lower, in real terms, than they were in 1938.[5] Passengers in general, and especially commuters, have not been paying the full cost of their travel. In the first few years after the Second World War passengers were subsidized by revenue from freight; but more recently the taxpayer has met the deficit.[6] The Committee refer to the losses incurred by the British Transport Commission as a result of government control over fares and charges, to which I have drawn attention in this book;[7] and they express the view that in such cases the Government should reimburse the Commission for their losses. There is no longer any need for the Transport Tribunal or a similar body to approve fares and charges, in view of the heavy competition with which the Commission are now confronted, with the possible exception of fares for suburban services in Greater London

[1] Para. 366. [2] Para. 368. [3] Para. 358. [4] Para. 360. [5] Para. 375. [6] Para. 377.
[7] Paras. 407–8; *Post* pages 150–4.

and other places where large numbers of workers must use the suburban rail services.

The Select Committee, following the line adopted by the Committee of Inquiry into the Electricity Supply Industry, declare that the British Transport Commission should consider only what is economically right in making their decisions, leaving all questions of social policy or the national interest to the Minister.[1] The Commission have not followed this line in the past, nor did they consider it right or proper for a public transport undertaking to ignore public needs, interests and susceptibilities.

Despite these adverse comments the Select Committee did not take a pessimistic view of the future outlook. They explicitly stated that on the evidence they had received 'there is no doubt that a large-scale British railway system can be profitable'.[2]

Long before the publication of the Select Committee's Report the financial plight of the railways had become increasingly serious for reasons which are set out in Chapter XI of this book. The continuing and increasing deficits and the hand-to-mouth expedients devised to meet them made it abundantly clear that a major crisis had arisen which would require drastic remedies. The Government decided to appoint a Special Advisory Group of three business men under the chairmanship of Sir Ivan Stedeford to inquire into the needs of the situation. This decision was sharply criticized both inside and outside Parliament, mainly on the grounds that the proceedings were secret, that the British Transport Commission were not represented on the Group, and that its findings were not published. The Commission were thus unable to put forward publicly their own views about future policy or to comment on the recommendations of the Group.

THE GOVERNMENT'S PROPOSALS ON RAILWAY FINANCE

The proposals of the Government were formulated in a White Paper entitled *Reorganisation of the Nationalised Transport Undertakings*, issued in December 1960. These proposals fall under two heads: those affecting the capital structure of the undertakings; and those affecting their organization.

The financial position of the railways was acknowledged to be so serious that they could not carry on without heavy subsidization by the Exchequer. It was no longer realistic to believe that the British Transport Commission would be able unaided to meet fully their existing liabilities. Financial reconstruction was therefore essential and this

[1] Paras. 413–7; 423. [2] Para. 419.

would take the form of a drastic reduction in the burden of debt falling on the Commission.[1] The plan proposed in the White Paper is of an interim character only; but it clearly resembles the bankruptcy process normally applied to an insolvent business in the private sector.

The net capital liabilities of the Commission at the end of 1959 stood at about £2,000 million. Of this total, £1,400 million consisted of British Transport Stock owned by members of the public, while the remaining £600 million was made up of money advanced by the Minister of Transport.

About £1,600 million of the whole sum is attributable to the railways. Of this, a quarter (£400 million) represents the accumulated losses of recent years which have been financed by advances from the Exchequer. These losses are regarded as irrecoverable and will be written off the outstanding debt of the Commission.

A further £400 million, equal to the investment by the British Transport Commission in the modernization of the railways since 1955, will remain a liability of the Commission as an interest-bearing loan on normal terms.

The remaining £800 million of the railway debt is to be placed in a suspense account. It will carry neither fixed interest nor regular repayment obligations. The amount and treatment of this account will be reviewed from time to time, and the White Paper frankly admits that some of it may have to be written off to offset capital losses as they are revealed.

The balance of £400 million of the total capital liabilities of the Commission is attributable to undertakings other than railways. This sum will be apportioned among the various activities and transferred to the appropriate authorities responsible for them.

These drastic proposals will result in the railways being immediately relieved of responsibility for finding the interest and redemption charges on £1,200 million, amounting to more than £40 million a year. A third of this large sum is to be written off and two-thirds is put into the suspense account—a kind of 'wait and see' gesture. The Treasury will take over the obligations of the Commission to the owners of British Railway Stock.

When the White Paper was issued the railways were running at an annual operating loss of some £60 million a year. The obligations to be met out of their revenue will comprise interest on the capital liability of £400 million already incurred under the modernization plan; interest on new borrowings for additional capital expenditure; and interest on superannuation funds and savings bank deposits invested

[1] Cmnd. 1248/1960, HMSO, para. 35.

in the Commission's undertaking. By the end of 1965 the charges under these heads may amount to £60–£70 million a year; so the railways' revenue must increase by at least £120 million by that time if they are to break even. Thus, despite the immediate relief of about £40 million a year given by the White Paper proposals, the railways are still left with a very formidable task.

So much for the financial reconstruction contemplated by the Government, which is summarized in the following table:

	Railways	*Other Activities*	*Total*
	£m.	£m.	£m.
EXISTING CAPITAL LIABILITIES (after deducting Capital Redemption Fund investments)	1,600	400	2,000
PROPOSALS			
Debt to be written off on account of revenue losses	400	—	400
Interest-bearing capital liabilities to be retained	400	400	800
Debt to be carried in suspense ...	800	—	800
TOTAL	1,600	400	2,000

PROPOSALS FOR TRANSPORT REORGANIZATION

The Government's proposals regarding the organization of the nationalized transport undertaking are also exceedingly drastic. The British Transport Commission will be abolished and each of its main activities will be managed by a separate board.

Thus, there will be a British Railways Board responsible for administering the railways as a national system. Regional Railway Boards will replace the present Area Boards and will be responsible for the management and operation of their respective portions of the system. The London Transport Executive will resume its status as an independent Board. The ports and docks administered by the Docks Division of the British Transport Commission will be hived off to a new British Docks Board. Similarly, British Transport Waterways will be transferred to a new Inland Waterways Authority, to be set up by statute. Railway catering services will go to the Railway Boards, but the numerous hotels owned by the railways will be handed over to a new company to be called British Transport Hotels. This Company, together with the other publicly owned companies running British Road Services, the Tilling (Buses) Group, the Scottish Omnibuses Group, Road Freight Shipping Services, and Thomas Cook, will come under a new holding company.

The British Railways Board will consist of a chairman and vice-chairman, representatives of each of the Regional Railway Boards, some full-time members with special responsibilities, and one or two part-time members. This central body will deal with staff and wage negotiations, overall control of finance and investment, the future size and shape of the railway system, policy for safety, training, and research. The property and other assets of the railways will be vested in it, and it will be responsible for the capital debt of the entire railway system. Each Regional Board will be required to maintain a trading account for its region to serve as an index of efficiency and economy of operation.

The Regional Railway Boards will have few members and most of them will give their full time to the work. The Regional General Manager will be a member of his Regional Board.

The members of all these boards will be appointed by the Minister of Transport. The directors of the joint stock companies will be appointed by the Holding Company. The board of the holding company will be appointed by, and be responsible to, the Minister. Certain other appointments will require his approval.

The Minister will be responsible for co-ordinating the policies and activities of the boards, and he will also allocate funds for capital development. His chief task will be to secure the general efficiency of the undertakings. In this he will be assisted by a Nationalized Transport Advisory Council which will not have executive powers.

The Council will be composed of the Minister, who will preside, the Chairmen of the Boards of British Railways, London Transport, British Transport Docks, the Inland Waterways Authority and the Holding Company. Other persons from outside the nationalized transport undertaking will be appointed.

The White Paper declares that the restrictions which have prevented the British Transport Commission from adjusting their fares and freight charges quickly to meet rising costs are no longer justifiable in the competitive conditions which face the railways today. The statutory controls exercised by the Transport Tribunal will disappear except in regard to fares in the London Passenger Transport Area.

The legal restrictions on the development of land owned by the nationalized transport undertakings will also be relaxed in order to enable them to exploit valuable sites more fully. To this end specialized organizations will be set up to advise, and even to act on behalf of, the public transport boards. The restrictions which preclude inland transport competition with coastal shipping are to be reconsidered. And the railways are to be authorized to lease, provide and operate pipelines on their property.

The White Paper contains a hortatory paragraph emphasizing the crucial need for efficiency of operation and the most economic use of manpower. The importance of an extended use of work study is stressed. The report recognizes the special contribution which trade union officials can play in economizing manpower, and the Minister will bear this in mind in appointing the boards.

In appraising the proposals in the White Paper it is necessary to bear in mind two important facts. One is that railways are having great difficulty in making two ends meet in the great majority of countries today. In the United States alone as many as seventeen railway systems discontinued passenger services between 1945 and 1961 and 5,000 trains stopped running.[1] The decline in the economic position of railways is mainly due to the competition of motorbuses, private cars, and air services in the sphere of passenger transport; and to loss of freight because an increasing proportion of goods are carried by road.

The other fact is that Government policy since 1951 has undoubtedly increased the difficulties under which British Railways have laboured. I will mention in this connection only two instances. One was the decision to denationalize the road haulage industry and to repeal the powers of the Commission regarding passenger road services. It is possible to disapprove on rational grounds of one publicly-owned service subsidizing another; but it is incontestible that the railways were brought much nearer to the crisis which has occurred by the return to private enterprise of the great bulk of the nationalized road haulage industry.[2]

The other instance was the intervention by the Government in 1952 and 1956 to prevent the British Transport Commission from increasing their charges,[3] and repeated pressure by Ministers to raise wages above the level which the existing railway earnings could support. The much-vaunted commercial freedom which the Conservative Party promised to give the railways turned out in practice to be of a very limited kind;

[1] See 'End of the Line for Railways'. *The Times* newspaper, July 5, 1961

[2] *Post* page 284. [3] *Post* pages 150–3.

and it related only to the controls exercised by the Transport Tribunal. It certainly had no influence whatever on the actions or attitudes of Ministers, who have intervened more actively than ever since 1951.

The railway crisis could possibly not have been avoided, but it might have been delayed for several years by which time the modernization and re-equipment scheme will perhaps have substantially improved the position. But even that will depend on whether the low productivity has been raised, less wasteful use of manpower made on the railways, and uneconomic services drastically pruned. Whether these conditions are likely to be fulfilled is a matter on which opinions may differ. They will remain indispensable pre-requisites of a solvent railway undertaking, and the answer will emerge in the coming years.

The immediate removal of three quarters of the capital liabilities from the nationalized railways undertaking is an emergency relief operation which was unavoidable unless Parliament and the public were prepared to contribute a heavy annual subsidy to the railways for an indefinite period.

There is little in the reorganization proposals which seems likely to increase the efficiency of the railways or other parts of the nationalized transport undertaking. The British Transport Commission have not been an adverse factor in the conduct of the railways, though there are good reasons for detaching London Transport from the main line railways.[1] The assumption that the difficulties facing the railways are due even in part to the wide scope of the Commission's responsibilities or to the absence at headquarters of a body exclusively concerned with the railways, is a proposition which is unsupported by any published evidence. If the new organization proves to be better than the old, it will be an occasion for rejoicing; but the proposals set forth in the White Paper give the impression of a shot in the dark rather than a well-considered remedy for proved defects.

Of far greater importance than defective organization is the shortage of high-class ability in the railway management of this country. One of the inevitable causes and consequences of a momentum of decline in an industry is the failure to attract young men of brains and ability, and especially of young graduates from the universities. In this respect British Railways has suffered from a long tradition of inbreeding; a failure to recruit sufficient university graduates; and, above all, a neglect to make proper use of those who did enter its service. I know of several well-educated men of ability who left the railways because they were not given reasonable opportunities for promotion and responsibility. These shortcomings go back long before nationalization, and I believe

[1] *Post* p. 102–4.

the Commission have tried to overcome them in very unfavourable circumstances.

DR BEECHING'S APPOINTMENT: SALARIES DE LUXE

This particular shortage may explain Dr Beeching's appointment as chairman of the British Transport Commission and as the chairman designate of the British Railways Board when it comes into existence. Dr Beeching was previously an Executive Director of Imperial Chemical Industries, in which capacity he received £24,000 a year. The Government announced that he would continue to receive this remuneration as chairman of the Commission.

The salary paid to Dr Beeching was widely criticized both inside and outside Parliament. The most serious grounds of objection have no relation to the personal qualities of Dr Beeching.

In a volume of essays on public enterprise published in 1937 I pointed out the disadvantages of *Salaries de Luxe*. The chief instances then cited were the Chairman and Vice-Chairman of the London Passenger Transport Board, who received £12,500 and £10,000 a year respectively; the Chairman of the former Central Electricity Board, whose salary was originally fixed at £8,000 a year; and the Chairman of the Coal Mines Reorganization Commission who received £7,000. The equivalent amount of these salaries today would be at least three times as large as the above figures.

I asked why it should be considered necessary to pay these individuals two, three, or four times as much as the permanent secretary of one of the great departments of State, whose responsibilities are at least as great, if not much greater.

I pointed out that the payment of extremely high salaries to the occupants of official positions would have far-reaching consequences. 'First, it will tend to magnify the power and prestige of the recipient, not merely to the world generally, but also *vis-a-vis* his colleagues on the board. They become, in comparison, if not poor relations, at any rate humble participants in the enterprise.'[1] Furthermore, 'we run the risk of doing injury to the Civil Service if we permit posts on these public boards to be rewarded on a scale which bears no relation to the salaries paid to the men at the top of the Civil Service. How can we expect the Civil Service to remain the loyal, devoted, upright, and efficient body that it is today if we permit the members of it to find themselves surrounded with public boards controlled by men who are technically outside the Civil Service, but in fact very definitely within the public service, and who are remunerated on a scale far more lavish

[1] *Public Enterprise* (Ed. W. A. Robson) 1939. George Allen and Unwin, p. 372.

than anything offered to the civil servant. Discontent, jealousy, and envy are almost certain to arise, and when that occurs one of our most valuable national assets will have been damaged beyond repair.'[1] I referred to the High Court Judges as a standing demonstration of the possibility of persuading men accustomed to earning very large incomes to accept remuneration on a more modest scale on entering public life. And there is also the political argument that the establishment of public boards would seem to be a move away from socialism if they involve the stabilization or intensification of the inequalities of income which arise in private enterprise.

The table given elsewhere in this book[2] shows that the salaries paid to the members of the boards of the public corporations vary according to the size and importance attributed to the undertaking. Despite a few anomalies, considerable care has hitherto been taken to achieve a fair measure of consistency.

The terms of Dr Beeching's appointment completely disrupts this effort at consistency. Previously, the chairman of the three largest public corporations running the coal, electricity and transport undertakings, had received £10,000 a year. Now that rate for the job is abandoned in favour of a rate for a particular man.[3] What will be the effect on the Chairmen and members of the other boards, many of them men of equally high ability and qualifications?

The inflated salaries paid to the chairmen and executive directors of large commercial companies are not 'earned' in any meaningful sense. They are emblems of status, part of the insignia of office in a society in which affluence is rated above public service. The importation of this scale of values into the public sector is part of the Conservative tendency to mould—or to remould—public enterprise in the image of big business.

If the Government considered it to be essential to secure the services of Dr Beeching as Chairman of British Railways and he was unwilling to accept a lower salary, a less objectionable method should have been used at the very least. The Minister should have explained that the salary of the post was £10,000. Any additional remuneration which was required should have been paid to Dr Beeching by Imperial Chemical Industries, and reimbursed to them by the Government out of public funds.

THE ROLE OF THE MINISTER

An important consequence of the new set-up will be to bring the Minister of Transport into a much closer relationship with the national-

[1] *Ib.*, pp. 372–3. [2] *Post* p. 234–5.

[3] In August, 1961, the Minister of Transport appointed Mr P. H. Shirley of Unilever Ltd to the British Transport Commission at £16,000 a year.

ized transport undertakings. He will have the task of co-ordinating the policies of the several boards and of allocating funds among them for capital development projects. This seems to be right in principle since these functions should be exercised by a Minister.

The new organization is intended to provide for direct contact between the Minister and the main component parts of the nationalized transport industry. The Government state definitely that they do not propose to extend the Minister's existing statutory powers and responsibilities. His main concern will be to achieve overall co-ordination and the general efficiency of the undertakings. The real question, however, is whether the Minister intends to increase or diminish or continue unchanged the exercise of his non-statutory powers. This is a matter of great importance to which the Select Committee has drawn repeated attention.[1]

The danger which Mr Ernest Davies foresees is that the relations between the Minister and the transport undertakings will become so close in the new structure that the managerial and commercial independence of the public corporations will be diminished.[2] If that were to happen, he rightly says, the advantages of this institution would soon disappear and there would be no point in retaining the public corporation.

Mr A. H. Hanson has recently challenged the notion that the public corporation either can or should possess any substantial degree of independence. He believes that the Government cannot divest itself of responsibility for any aspect of the performance of a nationalized industry, whether it be categorized as one of 'general policy' or 'commercial judgement' or day-to-day administration.' On this assumption he contends that no limits can be placed on ministerial responsibility, and that any clear-cut division of reponsibility between Ministers and the public corporations is impracticable. In consequence Mr Hanson accepts and, indeed, advocates full ministerial answerability to Parliament for every aspect of the nationalized industries. He is even ready to abandon the whole concept of the public corporation, which in his view has become little more than an inconvenient and frustrating constitutional fiction.[3]

Having rejected the whole conceptual framework on which the public corporation is constructed Mr Hanson finds, however, that there are greater difficulties to overcome than he seems to have anticipated in

[1] *Post* p. 156. See also Report of the Select Committee on Nationalized Industries, British Railways, para. 79.

[2] Ernest Davies: 'Reorganization of Nationalized Transport', 32 *Political Quarterly* (April–June, 1961), pp. 188–90.

[3] A. H. Hanson: *Parliament and Public Ownership*, pp. 112, 214–5.

providing a suitable alternative method of administering the nationalized industries. He considers the case for direct departmental administration of the nationalized industries to be 'very much stronger than the original advocates of the public corporation were prepared to allow'.[1] Yet if a transformation of this kind were attempted, the established principles and practices both of executive departments and of Parliament would have to be radically changed. Mr Hanson is uncomfortably aware of this, for he concedes that, 'To impose detailed estimating and accounting procedures, to give the Treasury control of establishments, to introduce ordinary departmental rules about the making of contracts, etc., would be fatal. Moreover, a wide delegation of authority to some kind of internal board, composed of top managers, would be almost essential, for the simple reason that the organization to be managed would be too big and complex for one or two men only to hold the whole of it before their minds as an entity and at the same time to control it in the requisite detail. Theoretically, there is no reason why these necessary modifications should not be made.'[2] He admits that full ministerial responsibility, which is the *sine qua non* of departmentalization and indeed one of its purposes, would inevitably reduce commerical flexibility below the essential minimum.

I believe there are very great objections, both theoretical and practical, to introducing a departmental system of administration for the nationalized industries, while at the same time enabling them to escape from the restrictions on finance. personnel, and ministerial control which prevail in Government departments generally. It is scarcely surprising that Mr Hanson does not attempt to show how this could be done. In the end, he appears to reject the ordinary departmental type of administration and proposes some kind of a half-way house. He asks whether it would not be possible 'to preserve the form and something of the spirit of the public corporation and yet hold the nationalized industry entirely responsible to its Minister, thus abolishing the artificial distinction between general policy and day-to-day administration and putting an end to the present equivocal Board-Minister-Parliament relationship?'[3] Such a compromise clearly raises many questions of great difficulty and complexity which Mr Hanson does not examine. It would also have at least as many disadvantages as advantages.

RECENT CHANGES IN THE POST OFFICE

With these sweeping proposals in mind it will be of interest to consider recent changes in the position of the Post Office.

[1] *Ib.*, p. 217. [2] *Ib.*, p. 218. [3] *Ib.*, p. 221.

A White Paper published in 1960 on *The Status of the Post Office* contained a number of proposals designed to give the Post Office greater commercial and financial freedom while remaining under the direct control of the Postmaster-General.[1] These proposals were subsequently embodied in the Post Office Act, 1961.

Under the new system Post Office finances are separated from the Exchequer, and will no longer be dependent on money voted by Parliament in the annual estimates. Thus, the elaborate scrutiny and control exercised by the Treasury, by the Chancellor of the Exchequer, and by the Estimates Committee, will no longer apply to the Post Office. The justification for this is that the Post Office depends for its revenue not on taxation but on the money it receives from its customers.

Henceforth the Post Office will prepare and present only Commercial Accounts. The antiquated Appropriation Accounts and the cash accounts will be discontinued. A Post Office Fund will be established into which all revenue will be paid and from which all sums required for the purpose of ordinary Post Office business will be taken. Thus a further stage has been reached in the protracted struggle to secure self-contained finance for the Post Office.

Yet the Post Office has not by any means achieved financial autonomy. First, Treasury control will continue in respect of capital developments. This includes approval of the total amount proposed to be spent each year and of borrowing for the purpose of such investments. In the event of a struggle with rival claimants in the public sector for capital in short supply, the Post Office might have to justify its investment proposals in detail. In these respects the Post Office will be in the same position as the nationalized industries. Secondly, the Treasury will control the foreign exchange operations of the Post Office. And thirdly, the Treasury will regulate the pay, grading, and conditions of service of the Post Office staff, who will remain civil servants.

In my view it is right in principle that the Treasury should exercise these controls. The capital expenditure of the public sector is a matter of great importance to the whole economy, and the Chancellor, and ultimately the Cabinet, must have the final decision. But a much more liberal policy is needed on the part of the Treasury towards Post Office development, particularly in regard to telephones, than it has shown in the past. In this field we are far behind the standard set only not by the United States but by many European countries. This applies to the number of telephones in proportion to the population, the intensity of use, the standard of service, and the type of equipment in use. The disparity between the excellence of the postal service, in which the

[1] For the previous position see *Post* p. 283.

British Post Office leads the world, and the mediocrity of the telephone service, is striking and deserves investigation. The telephone service absorbs by far the greater share of capital investment—about 88 per cent, compared with 8 per cent for posts and 4 per cent for telegraphs. On the other hand, the telephones contributed nearly £17 million to the total surplus of about £21 million in 1959–60. It is frequently alleged that the Treasury is largely responsible for the stunted development of the telephone service in this country.[1]

Again, in the matter of pay, grading, and conditions of service, it is necessary that the Post Office staff should be kept broadly in line with the rest of the civil service, in so far as circumstances are comparable.

Another feature of the new arrangement which calls for comment is that the outstanding capital indebtedness of the Post Office to the Exchequer, which amounts to about £800 million, is to be repaid by twenty-five equal portions during a similar number of years. Hitherto the outstanding debt of the Post Office to the Exchequer has been perpetual; now there is to be an obligation to repay it unless it is renewed. Here is an example of the curious distinction which is often made in this country between public and private enterprise in the treatment of their capital liabilities. The capital of a company is represented by the assets of the business, and it is illegal to repay such capital to the stockholders without the permission of the High Court. In the case of a local authority or a public corporation, and now the Post Office, the capital liabilities are to be treated as a debt to be repaid within twenty-five years. Thus, a heavy obligation is laid on the shoulders of the Post Office for which there is no parallel in private enterprise, apart from debentures or loan stock, which are seldom used today. In practice, however, the outstanding debt will certainly have to be renewed when it falls due for repayment, so the obligation is likely to result only in a review of interest rates in the light of conditions prevailing at the time when repayment is due.

The new Post Office Act places a duty on the Postmaster-General to conduct the business of his department in such a manner as to secure that its revenue is not less than sufficient, taking one year with another, to meet outgoings properly chargeable to revenue account, including 'proper allocations' to the general reserve. This resembles the obligation placed on the nationalized industries.

The Postmaster-General will continue to be fully responsible to Parliament for the work of his department. The total amount of Post

[1] Lord Crook referred with some bitterness during a debate in the House of Lords on February 1, 1961, to the dead hand of Treasury control which has limited the ability of the Post Office to give us an up-to-date telephone service.

Office borrowings of new capital will be authorized by statute, as in the past, every two or three years. The Commerical Accounts will be audited by the Comptroller and Auditor-General and examined by the Public Accounts Committee of the House of Commons. The charges and tariffs of the Post Office for postal and other services will be fixed by or under Statutory Instruments, and these will be subject to a negative resolution of Parliament. This goes further than the present practice, as not all Statutory Instruments of the Post Office are at present subject to parliamentary control. MPs will have the same scope for parliamentary questions as they have today.

The salaries of the Postmaster-General and Assistant Postmaster-General will continue to be voted annually so that a Supply Day can be devoted to discussing and criticizing the work of the department. A House of Commons resolution will also be required before the beginning of each financial year to authorize expenditure from the Post Office Fund. Parliament will receive the annual reports and accounts of the Post Office after they have been examined and certified by the Comptroller and Auditor-General. Thus, all the safeguards necessary to preserve accountability to Parliament and ministerial responsibility will be maintained in full force.

The Post Office is at present financing about 70 per cent of its annual capital expenditure on renewals, modernization, and expansion from internal sources, i.e., from depreciation funds. This is undoubtedly the correct policy for all undertakings of this character to pursue; and we may hope that the proportion of capital expenditure raised from internal sources will increase with the greater financial independence of the Post Office in the future. The average figure for all the nationalized industries is about 30 per cent, though there are large variations among the industries. This is far less than the corresponding figure for private enterprise.

The reforms now being introduced are in general likely to prove beneficial to the Post Office and the services it provides to the public. The degree of financial independence which the new Act permits could bring the Post Office several steps nearer to the position of one of the public corporations as regards finance.

Nevertheless, even after the present reforms have been put into practice, large differences will still remain between the position of the Post Office and that of a nationalized industry. First, charges and tariffs will be fixed by statutory instrument, and these will be liable to discussion and rejection in Parliament. Second, the Comptroller and Auditor-General will audit the accounts of the Post Office, and this means that the staff of the Exchequer and Audit Department will have access to all its books and other documents. Third, a resolution of the House of Commons is required each year to empower the Post Office to spend money from the Post Office Fund. Fourth, the entire staff of the Post Office consists of civil servants whose terms and conditions of employment must be approved by the Treasury, and which will be kept in line with the rest of the civil service. Fifth, the Post Office is expected to follow the normal contracting procedures imposed on Government Departments. None of these requirements apply to the public corporations.

Finally, the Postmaster-General is answerable in the House of Commons for every act of every one of his officials, from the local postman delivering letters to the Director-General at headquarters.

Over and above all these constitutional and political differences is the economic fact that the Post Office enjoys a much nearer approach to an absolute monopoly in its mail and telephone services than any of the nationalized industries concerned with the fuel, power, and transport industries.

THE FINANCIAL OBLIGATIONS OF THE NATIONALIZED INDUSTRIES

A White Paper entitled *The Financial and Economic Obligations of the Nationalized Industries* was presented to Parliament by the Chancellor of the Exchequer in May 1961. This was based on a review of the experience in the past decade or so against the background of the Government's general policy concerning these industries. This policy assumes that the Government has the task of ensuring that the industries are carried on in an economical and efficient manner so that they can make their maximum contribution to the economic well-being of the country. Although public corporations have to discharge obligations based on non-economic considerations in order or to serve the national interests, the nationalized industries are not to be regarded as social services which do not require economic and commercial justification.[1]

The statutes which provide the legal framework prescribe that the revenues of the nationalized industries should be not less than sufficient to meet all items properly chargeable to revenue, including interest, depreciation, the redemption of capital and the provision of reserves. This is a minimum performance and does not in any way preclude the making of a surplus. Moreover, the White Paper explains, 'this performance is defined in terms of a surplus or deficit, which differs from the ordinary definition of profit or loss inasmuch as provision is re-

[1] Cmnd. 1337/1961, para. 2.

quired to be made from revenue for all the items mentioned above before a surplus in the statutory sense arises. The undertakings are thus expected to make some profits in the ordinary sense of that term in order to accumulate reserves from them.'[1]

The White Paper points out that the nationalization Acts impose an obligation to provide out of revenue for the maintenance of capital assets and also to repay the whole capital indebtedness. I have already drawn attention to this severe and unnecessary burden, which in practice has been greatly lightened with the connivance of successive Governments.[2]

The White Paper is mainly concerned with the financial performance of the nationalized industries in relation to their capital investment programmes. The total retained income of all the industries taken together, (or of each one singly in most cases), including capital redemption funds, reserves, and supplementary depreciation allowances, has not been large enough to replace the assets used up in the process of production. Thus in 1959, the public corporations and the Post Office invested about £810 million while their savings amounted to £240 million, leaving a balance of £570 million to be provided from external sources.[3]

In private enterprise in Britain the average return on capital in recent years has been at the rate of about 15 per cent. A publicly owned enterprise which was 'fully commercial in its nature and engaged in the same type of business as private enterprise' might expect to obtain a similar rate of return; but the main nationalized industries are not in this position.[4]

One important difference which distinguishes the nationalized industries is that several of them belong to the public utility category, in which the yield on capital has always been lower, partly because the risk of loss is less than in general industry and partly because the prices and profits of public utilities are regulated by the State in order to prevent them from fully exploiting the monopolistic position they enjoy. In the second place, the nationalized industries have been under heavy pressure from Ministers, the Press and the public to keep their prices at an unrealistically low level, regardless of the trend of rising costs or the movement of prices in the private sector. The smallest increase of underground, bus or rail fares in London, for example, becomes front-page news in popular newspapers which do not pay any attention to much steeper price increases in other parts of the economy. This has had a highly detrimental effect on the financial position of the public corporations. Third, for several reasons the nationalized industries are unable

[1] *Ib.*, para. 5–7. [2] *Post* pp. 312–3. [3] Para. 10–11. [4] *Ib.*, para. 13.

to adjust their expenditures as easily or as quickly as other industries to changes in economic conditions.

These basic facts have for long been obvious to disinterested observers; but they have not hitherto been officially acknowledged or stated. Their belated recognition is long overdue but is none the less welcome. One hopes it may have some effect in quieting, if not stilling, the shallow or ill-intentioned voices which have drawn unfavourable comparisons between the public and private sectors of economy.

The relatively low return on the capital invested in the nationalized industries is fully accounted for by the considerations set out above, according to the White Paper. But the present situation produces certain disadvantages both to the economy as a whole and to the public sector. The White Paper contends that 'If the profitability of capital development is assessed on different (and easier) financial criteria from those adopted in industry generally, there is a risk that too much of the nation's savings will be diverted into the nationalized industries. Again, if the prices of the goods and services which the nationalized industries provide are uneconomically low, demand for them (and for investment to produce more of them) may be artificially stimulated.'[1] This leads to the conclusion that to allow the nationalized industries to operate on an 'unduly' low rate of return on capital compared with private enterprise would eventually damage the economy as a whole.

The remedies proposed do not affect the basic financial and economic principles which the public corporations are required to follow. Only a clarification and a more precise interpretation is given to them.

The nebulous phrase 'taking one year with another' should in future be interpreted to mean that surpluses on revenue account should be at least sufficient to cover deficits over a five year period. Interest and depreciation on the historic cost basis should be charged before arriving at a surplus or deficit. The difference between historic cost and replacement cost should also be provided from revenue. Adequate sums must be set aside in a reserve fund to contribute *inter alia* to capital development, premature obsolescence, and other contingencies.[2]

The White Paper points out the need of the nationalized industries to accumulate adequate reserves to cope with contingencies of all kinds. Furthermore, they should be required to make a substantial contribution from their earnings towards the cost of their own capital development, thus reducing their claims on the nation's savings and their demands on the Exchequer. The amount of reserves should where possible be related to the amount of capital invested in the undertaking. To achieve these objectives capital must earn a higher rate of return than the rate

[1] *Ib.*, para. 15. [2] Para. 19.

which the Exchequer has to pay in raising the money. These views coincide closely with those expressed in this book.[1] They are directly opposed to those of the Herbert Committee on the electricity supply industry.[2]

The procedure for discussing and approving the capital investment proposals of, and the borrowing of money by, the nationalized industries will be continued more or less on the same lines as hitherto, except that a tighter control will be kept by the Government on proposals to engage in new capital projects from which a relatively low return is expected. The main stages of the procedure are clearly formulated in the White Paper. Where the financial performance and prospects of an industry are so poor that it cannot meet its statutory obligations, as now defined, the Board will be asked to propose specific measures to remedy the situation. A similar demand may be made where the rate of return on capital investment is inadequate.

All this presupposes that the nationalized industries will enjoy much greater freedom than they have had in the past to raise their prices, whenever this will provide a net increase in their revenues. The White Paper skims lightly over this unavoidable necessity and talks airily of other methods of meeting the prescribed financial obligations, such as improved commercial efficiency, increased productivity, and reduction in costs. In the end, however, the Government frankly recognize that industries must be free to raise their prices, particularly where they have been kept artificially low. But there is no intention of abandoning ministerial influence in this sphere. The chairman of each public corporation will continue to ascertain the views of the appropriate Minister before introducing substantial changes in the level of prices. Then comes this statement: 'If a Board decided to modify their own proposals by reason of views expressed by the Minister it would be open to them to require a written statement of those views, which could be published by the Minister or the Board, and to propose an appropriate adjustment of their financial objectives where, in their opinion, this modification would significantly impair their ability to meet them.'[3] No mention is made of what would happen if the Board decided to go ahead with their original proposals. The assumption is that the Minister's view must ultimately prevail in all cases. The new feature is that it should at last become known to Parliament and the public where responsibility for prices really lies.

If an undertaking is required to carry on commercially unprofitable services, such as some of the services provided by BEA, these will be taken into account in determining the financial target at which it must

[1] *Post*, pp. 317–8. [2] *Post*, pp. 307–11. [3] Para. 31.

aim. The suggestion which has often been made that a subsidy should be paid to a public corporation which is required by the Government to provide a service for social or political reasons is not mentioned and has evidently little chance of being adopted.

Taken as a whole, the White Paper is a carefully drafted and fairly clear document. The policies which it sets out are sound and reasonable; and the tone is moderate. This is shown particularly in the concluding paragraph, which points out that the nationalized industries are by their very nature bound to play a major role in the national economy. 'They cannot, however, be regarded only as very large commercial concerns which may be judged mainly on their commercial results: all have, although in varying degrees, wider obligations than commercial concerns in the private sector. The object of these proposals is to find for each industry or Board a reasonable balance between these two concepts. The Government believe that the closer definition now proposed for the financial and economic obligations of the industries should help improve their performance and morale. It should also reduce the occasion and need for outside intervention in the affairs of the industries and enable them to make the maximum contribution towards their own development and the well-being of the community as a whole.'[1]

AIR TRANSPORT POLICY

I have described in this book the change in Government policy on civil air transport which took place after the Conservative Party achieved power in 1951, a change in favour of commercial operators and against the nationalized airlines.[2] A further step of great importance in the same direction was taken with the passing of the Civil Aviation (Licensing) Act, 1960.

This statute set up the Air Transport Licensing Board in place of the Air Transport Advisory Council The latter body was originally intended to be mainly a consumers' council, but it had gradually assumed the functions of a licensing authority at the request of successive Ministers. While the decision to issue licences to operate scheduled air services lay with the responsible Minister, in practice he almost invariably accepted the recommendations of the Advisory Council.

The new Air Transport Licensing Board, as the name indicates, are primarily a licensing body, although they will have the ancillary function of considering representations or complaints about air services, including charges and facilities relating to such services. They will be a larger body than the Air Transport Advisory Council, consisting of not

[1] Para. 33. [2] *Post* pp. 428–30.

less than six and not more than ten members appointed by the Minister of Aviation, who will also appoint the chairman and deputy chairman from among them. The Board will have a comprehensive jurisdiction since the statute forbids the use of any aircraft on flights for reward, or in connection with any trade or business, unless the operator holds an air service licence issued under the Act and an air operator's certificate (which concerns matters of safety) under the Civil Aviation Act, 1949. One commendable result of the new Act is to bring all aircraft operating for commercial purposes under the rigorous safety code which has hitherto applied only to operators running scheduled air services.

But the main effect of the Act is to undermine the monopoly which the nationalized air corporations and their associates were granted by the Civil Aviation Act, 1946, to operate regular services within the United Kingdom and on international routes.[1] BOAC and BEA are now placed in the same position as every independent commercial company which operates, or wishes to operate, scheduled air services: namely, of having to apply to the Air Transport Licensing Board for a licence.[2]

The Act does not lay down any policy which the Board are to follow apart from the almost meaningless statement that they are to exercise their functions 'in such a manner as to further the development of British civil aviation'. It expressly declares that the Board may at their discretion either refuse an application for an air service licence or grant it as requested or with such modifications as they think fit.[3] The statute merely requires the Board to consider certain specified matters in exercising their functions. These are: (a) whether the applicant is competent, and a fit and proper person, to operate aircraft for the purposes for which he seeks an air service licence having regard to his experience and financial resources, his ability to provide satisfactory equipment, organization and staffing arrangements (b) the provision made or proposed to be made against liability for loss or damage to persons and property (c) any unfair advantage over other operators by reason of the terms and conditions of employment of his servants (d) the existing or potential need or demand for any air transport service proposed (e) in the case of any proposed service, the adequacy of any similar service authorized by any air service licence already granted and the tariff in respect of that similar service (f) the extent to which any proposed service would be likely to result in wasteful duplication of, or in material diversion of traffic from, any air transport service being

[1] *Post* pp. 33–4, 48.

[2] After a short initial period from the coming into force of the Act, during which standstill orders were issued continuing the existing position pending a review.

[3] Section 2 (1).

provided, or about to be started, under an air service licence already granted (g) any capital or other expenditure reasonably incurred, or any financial commitment or commercial agreement reasonably entered into, in connection with air services by anyone (including the applicant) who holds any air service licence already granted, (h) any objections or representations from various specified categories of interested persons.

Enactments which specify several matters to be considered in deciding a particular question place no serious check on the discretion of the body authorized to make the decision, nor have they necessarily much or even any influence on the policies adopted. Legislation of this kind usually results from mental laziness or from a deliberate refusal on the part of the Minister to formulate a policy. The Minister of Aviation, Mr Duncan Sandys, was pressed by the Opposition to include in the Bill a direction to the Licensing Board as to the policy they were to follow, but he refused to do so. In consequence, the Air Transport Licensing Board are virtually free to arrive at whatever decision they favour in respect of each application by giving such weight as they wish to any of the factors specified in the Act.

In opening the Second Reading debate the Minister said that the Civil Aviation (Licensing) Bill was 'not intended to undermine the position of BOAC or BEA. Those two corporations are our main flag carriers on the air routes of the world. Large sums of public money have been invested in them and they have to face fierce competition from foreign rivals. They therefore deserve, and will get, our full support and encouragement.'[1] Within a remarkably short time the truthfulness and sincerity of these words were to be put to the test.

In the summer of 1961 more than seventy major applications for licences were made by commercial operators which, if granted, would undoubtedly have a disastrous effect on the financial position and the development of BEA and BOAC.

THE CUNARD EAGLE AND THE NEW LINER

The most notorious application was that submitted by Cunard Eagle Airways to run a scheduled passenger service from London to New York for a period of fifteen years. The application was strenuously opposed by BOAC, who maintained that the proposed service on the leading air route of the world would inevitably result in a material diversion of traffic from their own service to Cunard Eagle, if the latter were to operate successfully. In that event the position of BOAC on

[1] House of Commons Deb. 455, 1959–60, March 2, 1960, Col. 1231/2.

the North Atlantic would be undermined. The Air Transport Licensing Board agreed that the advent of a Cunard Eagle service would lead to a diversion, and probably a material diversion, of traffic from BOAC, but they did not regard this as a necessary bar to the grant of a licence because: (1) to do so would lead to an automatic 'freezing' of the situation on any route already served by a United Kingdom operator; (2) where traffic is likely to increase rapidly, as on the North Atlantic route, BOAC should be able to increase their present earnings even despite the diversion of traffic to a rival British operator; (3) the advent of Cunard Eagle may generate new traffic and attract other traffic from foreign carriers. The Board therefore granted the licence.

Cunard Eagle is a wholly-owned subsidiary of the Cunard Steam Ship Company, which had recently applied to the Government for a large subsidy towards building a new giant passenger liner to replace the *Queen Mary*. The proposal to build another liner of this size with the aid of £18 million of public money was strongly opposed by British shipping interests, by a number of Conservative MPs, by the Labour Party in Parliament, by some of the shareholders of the Cunard Company, and by *The Times* newspaper. Out of a total estimated cost of £30 million for the new ship, the Company were willing to find only £12 million, while at the same time they were investing £6 million in their new Cunard Eagle airline.

The North Atlantic Shipping Bill which authorized the loan had a stormy passage through the House of Commons. Despite very strong criticism from their own supporters as well as from the Opposition and the Press, the Government refused to reconsider their decision. They also refused to adopt the suggestion that they should acquire a share in the equity of the Cunard Steamship Company and the right to nominate directors on the Board, in exchange for the public money being advanced to the Company. No financial house would loan a sum of this magnitude for such a purpose without demanding a share in the equity. The Minister of Transport's reply was that the Government wanted security rather than a share of the profits; though it is widely believed that the whole enterprise is of a highly uncertain and risky nature.

The decision of the Air Transport Licensing Board to grant the Cunard Eagle permission to run a daily air service to New York was announced a few days before the North Atlantic Shipping Bill passed through the committee stage in the House of Commons. Mr George Strauss MP, speaking for the Opposition, pointed out that the Cunard Eagle air service was estimated to reduce BOAC's gross revenue by £5 million a year. He therefore asked the Minister to make it a condition for subsidizing the liner that the company should not use its resources which were liberated as a result of the Government's loan for the new ship, to damage the interests of the taxpayer.[1]

It would appear that no attempt was made by the Government to relate their policy towards the Cunard Steamship Company to the latter's policy towards BOAC. When financial aid was first given to the *Queen Mary*, the Government of the day made it a condition that competition between Cunard and White Star should cease and the companies be merged. This has been of immense benefit to Cunard. Now the company has suddenly become eager to compete in the air regardless of the effect on the airways corporations.

The outcome now rests with the Minister of Aviation, to whom an appeal lies from decisions of the Air Transport Licensing Board. It will be interesting to see how far Mr Duncan Sandys will be prepared in practice to give BOAC the 'full support and encouragement' which he promised when the Bill was before Parliament. What is at stake is more than the solvency of the nationalized air lines: the whole future of British air transport is in jeopardy if ill-considered rivalry is permitted between British operators.

The Times, in a leading article on the Licensing Board's decision in the Cunard Eagle case, said that 'the probable immediate check to BOAC is slurred over', despite the fact that a competing British service might take a fifth of BOAC's business on the route. BOAC is already facing new foreign competitors on the North Atlantic this year. So far the British nationalized air line has obtained 'a surprisingly high proportion of the North Atlantic traffic from London, has taken optimistic views of the future, and planned for large increase of capacity'.[2] Its plans to acquire a considerable fleet of new VC10 aircraft may need revising in the light of the new threat to its trade.

The philosophy of the Conservative Party appears to be that the State may own and operate industries which are unprofitable or declining, such as railways and coal, but that it may not be left in undisturbed possession of those which are new, expanding, and profitable, such as television and air transport. This is a perverse and malign conception of public enterprise for which there is nothing to be said. As I have shown in the concluding chapter of this book,[3] the Labour Party's policy of nationalizing industries which are 'failing the nation' is no better as a guide to action, but this phrase has fortunately disappeared from the most recent statement of Labour Party policy.[4]

July, 1961.

[1] See the report in *The Times* newspaper, June 30, 1961.
[2] See the first leading article 'Free as Air', *The Times*, June 23, 1961.
[3] *Post* pp. 488–9. [4] *Signposts for the Sixties*.

PREFACE

THE present work is a successor to *Problems of Nationalized Industry*, which was published in 1952.[1] That book was a symposium. It consisted of several articles which had appeared in a special number of *The Political Quarterly*[2] together with a larger number of new essays written specially for the book. In addition to editing and writing three of the essays I contributed a long concluding Part comprising my general conclusions.

Despite this attempt to integrate the work of several contributors I was conscious that the book lacked the unity which can come only from an undivided authorship. When, therefore, the publishers informed me that *Problems of Nationalized Industry* was out of print I decided to write an entirely new book for whose contents I would alone be responsible. The present work is the result of my decision.

The position in 1960 is very different from what it was in 1950-2. More than a decade has passed since the main industries were nationalized and there is now a considerably longer experience on which to base one's statements and judgments. A vast mass of information is now available about the nationalized industries which must clearly be taken into account by anyone who ventures to present a serious study of the subject.

More important, in my opinion, than the garnering and assimilation of knowledge about the nationalized industries is the need to analyse and discuss some of the theories and conceptions which have emerged in recent years from several different quarters as to the manner in which public enterprise should be run and the purposes it should pursue. This task I have also attempted to perform in the following pages.

In the concluding chapter I have examined in some detail the ideas, views and proposals about the public ownership of industry which have in recent years been agitating the Labour Party, the trade unions, and the co-operative movement.

Public enterprise has for long been, and still remains, a highly controversial subject. This does not preclude rational discussion provided that those who take part in it are reasonably honest about the facts, and about their own prejudices. Unfortunately these conditions are often not fulfilled. An incredible amount of ignorance, distortion, and misrepresentation is displayed by persons who write and speak on this subject.

[1] London, George Allen and Unwin; New York, The Oxford University Press.
[2] April-June, 1950. Vol. XXI, No. 2.

I have made no attempt in this book to conceal my own views, or to present them as though they were part of the order of the Universe. I have, however, done my utmost to write an honest book, by which I mean one that does not shirk the facts, whether pleasant or unpleasant, and which endeavours to give a reasonably balanced view of the subject. The reader will not find in the following pages a picture in black and white, a simple story of success or failure. He will find statements and conclusions about some things which are favourable and about others which are unfavourable. I have never wavered in my belief that nationalization will not by itself bring about drastic changes in the operation of old established industries, although it may enable improvements to be subsequently made.

I have received much help from many people. First and foremost I wish to acknowledge my debt to the late Miss Jennifer Hines, MA, who acted as my Research Assistant for two years, from April 1954 to December 1956. During that time she was mainly engaged in assisting me to obtain material for this book; she also helped me to collect material for studies of public enterprise in Commonwealth and foreign countries. Miss Hines had an exceptional gift for research, which she combined with immense energy and devotion to the task in hand. After finishing her work for me she was appointed by the Royal Institute of Public Administration as their Research Officer in charge of an important research project on budgetary practices. In that capacity she won high praise for the remarkable ability with which she carried through the work to a successful conclusion. Her untimely death in a cycling accident in March 1959 removed, to the deep sorrow of all who knew her, a young worker of exceptional promise who would undoubtedly have made distinguished contributions to social research. From the beginning of 1958 until the summer of 1959 I received much valuable help for this and other work from Mr Alan Watkins, BA, LLB, to whom my thanks are due. I also wish to express my appreciation of the assistance I have had from Mr Alan Burns, barrister-at-law.

I have been greatly helped in particular parts of the book by discussion with friends and acquaintances whose work lies in the field of nationalized industry. I will not name them all, but I wish particularly to thank Sir Henry Self, former Chairman of the Electricity Council; Sir George Cribbett, Deputy Chairman of BOAC; Mr Ernest Long, a member of the Central Electricity Generating Board; Sir Kelvin Spencer, former Chief Scientist, Ministry of Power; Mr H. L. de Bourcier, former Secretary of the Industrial and Domestic Coal Consumers' Councils, and now a member of the latter body; Mr Leslie Hardern, public relations officer of the North Thames Gas Board; Mr C. C. Inglis, Chief Research Officer of the British Transport Commission; Mr S. G. Williams, Director of Television Administration of the British Broadcasting Corporation; and Mr D. R. Willson and Mr Le Cren of the Atomic Energy Authority. Among my colleagues I am specially indebted to Mr Gilbert Ponsonby, Sir Ernest Cassel Reader in Commerce (with special reference to Transport); Professor W. T. Baxter, Professor of Accounting in the University of London; Mr Idris Hicks of the Department of Accountancy and Financial Administration in the University of Sheffield; Mr B. C. Roberts, Reader in Industrial Relations, and Mr B. S. Yamey, Reader in Economics, in the University of London. I should also like to thank Professor G. Fua of ENI, and Professor Saraceno of IRI, for their kindness in giving me information about public ownership in Italy. I have inquired into the position there during the course of two recent visits to Rome.

In compiling the Bibliography I received substantial help from Dr M. Plant, Deputy Librarian, and Mr T. H. Bowyer, Assistant Librarian of our splendid library at the London School of Economics and Political Science, to whom I must extend my thanks. I also acknowledge the help given to me in the same connection by Dr L. N. Gupta, a graduate student from India who was working in this field at the School.

I wish also to thank Sir John Simpson, CB, Controller of Her Majesty's Stationery Office, for permission to quote from official reports and other publications published by the Stationery Office. It has been my intention to acknowledge in all cases the sources of these and any other extracts which I have used.

Finally, I should like to express my thanks to my secretary, Mrs J. Deal, for her unfailing and most efficient help in connection with this book and to Miss Vera Seal for kindly reading the page proofs.

WILLIAM A. ROBSON

London School of Economics
and Political Science

CONTENTS

Contents

CHAPTER I

Public Enterprise Today

THIS book is concerned with nationalized industry in Britain, but we may begin by taking a glance at the wider sphere of public enterprise in the world today, both as regards the scope of its activities and the nature of its institutions. By so doing we shall better understand our own experience, and see it in better perspective.

State intervention of a positive kind in the ownership, operation or regulation of industries and services is a vast movement of worldwide dimensions. It is to be found not only in the highly developed countries of the West but also in the underdeveloped countries of Asia and Africa. It is the leading characteristic of communist regimes. It is also an important feature of all political democracies, whether they claim to be based avowedly on private enterprise or on a mixed economy. The scale of this movement is vast; its diversity bewildering; its political, economic and social significance unquestionable.

The great mass of public undertakings may be divided into seven main categories so far as the scope and nature of the undertaking is concerned. Undertakings belonging to these categories exist in some or many or all countries. They are as follows:

PUBLIC UTILITIES

No one has ever defined a public utility in a satisfactory manner. The industries or services which are regarded as public utilities vary from one country to another; and even within each country the experts often disagree as to what types of undertaking should be brought under the heading. The public utility concept appears to involve two conditions: one is that the service should be considered to be so essential that it requires public regulation, ownership or operation; the other is that the service should be monopolistic. The first of these requirements raises the question of what is essential; and this is a matter which depends on circumstances of time and space, of economic and technological development, of social custom and popular psychology. The luxuries of one age become the necessities of the next; and the services which are today widely recognized as public utilities were for long the luxuries of the well-to-do. We can say, however, that water, gas, electricity, ports and harbours are indubitably public utilities. Some people may wish to include public transport services and telecommunications, but I find it better to place these under a separate heading.

TRANSPORT AND COMMUNICATIONS

This appears to be a coherent group of undertakings which include railways, motorbus, tramway and trolleybus services, airlines, airports, canal and inland waterways, shipping, ferries, telephone and telegraph services. The mail-carrying services can also be brought under this heading.

BANKING, CREDIT AND INSURANCE

This represents a well-established manifestation of public enterprise which includes central banks, commercial or business banks and savings banks. Leading examples are the four great nationalized banks in France (the Crédit Lyonnais, La Societé Générale, Le Comptoir d'escompte, and La Banque Nationale pour le Commerce et l'Industrie), and, of course, the Banque de France. In Italy, the three most important commercial banks are nationalized. They are the Banca di Roma, Credito Italiano, and Banca Commerciale Italiana. Other types of public enterprise coming under this heading are bodies intended to provide credit for agriculture, such as the Farm Land Banks, the Federal Intermediate Credit Banks, and the Production Credit Corporations of the United States, or the Land and Agricultural Bank of South Africa. This category also includes organs set up to provide commercial or industrial companies with capital, such as the Reconstruction Finance Corporation in the United States (1932–54) and the present Small Business Administration which has succeeded it; or to advance money to a particular industry, like the National Film Finance Corporation in Britain. It is possible to bring under this heading municipal pawnshops and state mortgage institutions; and also a body like the Conseil National du Credit in France which exercises very wide and important functions affecting the whole economy. International institutions for lending money derived from public revenues like the International Bank for Reconstruction and Development come under this heading.

So far as insurance is concerned, we may mention the nationalized insurance companies in France and India, the State Life insurance offices in New Zealand, the crop insurance carried out by the United States Federal Crop Insurance Corporation, the insurance of loans and mortgages effected by the Federal Housing Administration, and the guarantees to exporters provided by the Export Credit Guarantee Department in Britain. We are not concerned here with social insurance schemes, since these are more a social service financed by taxation masquerading as insurance rather than a form of public enterprise of an industrial or commercial character. It is permissible, however, to extend this category to include fiduciary activities of the State, such as those carried out on a large scale in England by the Public Trustee.

There is a surprisingly large amount of public enterprise in many countries coming under this heading, but very little study has been given to it. A wide variety of public undertakings engaged in banking, financial and insurance is to be found in Argentina, Brazil, Australia, France, Italy, Canada, Chile, Mexico, South Africa, Switzerland, and Western Germany—to name only a few countries out of many.

In the United States alone, there are about a hundred administrative organs owned by the Federal Government engaged in lending, guaranteeing and insurance business. Their activities include lending money, guaranteeing loans and deposits, life insurance, and the purchase and sale of farm produce.[1] The scope of these activities covers housing, agriculture, business, life insurance, insurance of bank deposits, and import and export arrangements negotiated with foreign governments.

The first Hoover Commission reported in 1949 that it was opposed to direct lending by government as giving opportunities for waste, favouritism, political or private pressure, and corruption. The second Hoover Commission assumed in 1955 that a number of weaknesses are inherent in government lending agencies, and both Commissions made recommendations leading to a reduction of public lending. These reports were coloured by the political convictions of the Commission. It is not clear at present what effect, if any, they will have on the future trend of events.

In general, public enterprise in these fields has come to be accepted in most countries, and is likely to expand.

MULTI-PURPOSE DEVELOPMENT PROJECTS

The Tennessee Valley Authority was the first modern example of a multi-purpose river valley project sponsored and initiated by the State. The aims originally specified for the TVA were flood control, improving the navigation of the Tennessee river, generation of electrical power, the proper use of marginal lands, reforestation, and promoting the economic and social well-being of the people living in the river basin. The main

[1] Second Hoover Commission. *Report on Lending Agencies* (1955) p. 1.

functions which have actually been performed by the TVA relate to water control, navigation, the generation and distribution of electric power, and the production of nitrate for fertilizer. But although the wide ranging purposes envisaged by President Roosevelt have dwindled under the pressure of resistance from lesser men, the TVA remains a pioneer multi-purpose project of great significance. It has served as a model for many river valley projects either constructed or under consideration in different parts of the world, particularly Asia and Africa. The Snowy-Murray project in Australia and the Damodar Valley undertaking in India were largely inspired by the TVA.[1]

The Volta River scheme for Ghana is an interesting example of a river valley project, although it is not certain that the entire plan will be carried out. This embraces the construction of a dam and a lake, the development of hydro-electric power, and the building of a smelting plant to produce aluminium from the local bauxite deposits. This vast scheme would transform the economic and social life of the people of Ghana. It would require the building of railways, roads, houses, schools, hospitals and other public works. It would involve education, industrial training, town and country planning, health services, and much else.[2]

Another type of multi-purpose undertaking is the Panama Canal Company, formerly known as the Panama Railway Company. This company, which is entirely owned and controlled by the United States Government, maintains and operates the Panama Canal. It also carries on a large number of business activities in the canal zone, including a railway and steamship line, docks, piers and terminal facilities, bunkering plant, cold storage facilities, hotels, restaurants, theatres, bowling alleys, electric power supply, water and telephone services, a printing plant, motor transport services, ship repairing, etc. The maintenance and operation of the canal is the major purpose, and everything else is ancillary to that predominant end.

The Development Corporations engaged in building the new towns in Britain are multi-purpose projects of a very different kind. They are urban and not rural. They are concerned with the control and use of land rather than of water. They are mostly located in or near over-developed conurbations rather than in under-developed or neglected areas. Their

[1] *TVA as a symbol of Resource Development in many countries.* A Digest and Selected Bibliography of Information compiled by TVA Technical Library. (January 1952.)

[2] *The Volta River Project. Report of the Preparatory Commission.* HMSO (1956). And the White Paper Cmd. 8702/1952. In October, 1958, the Kaiser Industries Corporation were engaged to carry out a reassessment of the project. In September, 1959, Dr Nkrumah, the Prime Minister of Ghana, announced that the construction of the dam and power installation would proceed as soon as possible, but no positive statement has so far been made about the development of the aluminium industry, which in the original project was to have been carried out by the British Aluminium Company and Aluminium Ltd of Canada.

comprehensive character is the distinguishing feature which places them under the same general heading as the river valley projects.

A further example of a multi-purpose undertaking is the Colonial Development Corporation. This is based on quite a different conception. It was originally established in order to investigate, formulate, and carry out 'projects for developing resources of colonial territories with a view to the expansion of production therein of foodstuffs and raw materials, or for other agricultural, industrial or trade development therein.'[1] The activities which have been promoted or supported by the Corporation include a considerable variety of enterprises in the Carribean, the Far East, and Africa. Among them are developments relating to agriculture, animal products, fisheries, forestry, mining, housing, highways, public utilities and manufacture. The Corporation were responsible *inter alia* for the new Fort George hotel in Honduras and for producing turtle soup in Jamaica.[2] The scope of the Corporation's activities has in recent years been considerably reduced and their powers are more closely defined by the Overseas Resources Development Act, 1956. So far as new projects are concerned, these are concentrated mainly on those likely to be financially self-supporting, in the long run at least. The Corporation endeavour to work in association with experienced private enterprise in the colonial territories in which they are operating.[3]

BASIC ESTABLISHED INDUSTRIES

In this category we should place industries or services of importance to the economy which have already been established by private enterprise and are subsequently transferred to the public sector in one form or another. (One must exclude, of course, industries coming in any of the other categories previously mentioned.) Coal mining, iron and steel, oil production or refining, and forestry are obvious examples, although in some countries some of these industries have been initiated by public enterprise. Here again we must consider not only national enterprises but also international undertakings.

In Britain, France, Italy and a number of other countries, nationalization has in the main signified the State taking over long-established industries such as coal mining, railways, gas, electricity supply, and engineering works of many different kinds. Some of the most difficult problems which have arisen in these countries in the sphere of nationali-

[1] Overseas Resources Development Act, 1948, s. 1 (1).

[2] S. 1 (1). For an account of the earlier activities see C.W. Dumpleton: *Colonial Development Corporation* (1957) (Fabian Research Series No. 186).

[3] *Colonial Development Corporation Report 1954*, HMSO, HC 113/1954-5, p. 7. *Ib. 1955.* HC 260/1955-6, pp. 7-9.

zation are due to the fact that the technology, organization, management, labour relations, and *morale* of the industries are largely influenced by the history and conditions which prevailed when the industries were under private enterprise. One of the most important distinctions in the realm of public enterprise is between industries which have been taken over at a late stage of their development and those which have grown up as public undertakings.

NEW INDUSTRIES OR SERVICES

In many countries public enterprise is an initiating force. This is particularly true in India, where recent nationalization policy (with the exception of the air lines and life assurance) has been directed towards the creation of new industries or undertakings. Thus, under the first five-year plan the industrial projects completed in the public sector included the Sindri fertilizer factory, the Chittaranjan locomotive factory, Indian Telephone Industries, a new aircraft factory in Bangalore, the National Instruments factory, the Hindustan shipyard, and factories for the manufacture of penicillin, DDT, and newsprint. These were all pioneer efforts in new spheres of industry so far as India is concerned.

India's second five-year plan envisages very important developments in steel production. Three new steel plants, each of one million tons ingot capacity, will be constructed in the public sector. Factories for the production of heavy electrical equipment will be established over a period which is estimated to take seven or eight years. The Integral Coach factory, which began production in 1955, will be completed. The first factory for the production of explosives for industrial purposes constructed by a subsidiary of Imperial Chemical Industries in partnership with the Indian Government, was opened in 1958. These are only a few of the more important new projects now under way.

The Indian National Industrial Development Corporation has also an ambitious programme of development to be carried out during the period of the second five-year plan. The Corporation will assist in modernizing the cotton, textile and jute industries. 'The greater part of their activities are, however, of a pioneering nature, being intended to promote the establishment of basic and heavy industries.'[1] The Corporation are considering the feasibility of establishing heavy foundries, forge and structural shops, refractories, chemical pulp and newsprint plant, dye-stuff factories, the making of printing machinery, and several other industries.

[1] Government of India. Planning Commission. *Second Five Year Plan: A Draft Outline* p. 115.

In Japan, government policy in the past was to establish by public enterprise key industries for which no private initiative was forthcoming, and then later to transfer these undertakings to private companies. This policy was carried out in regard to mining, silk and textile factories, shipping and shipbuilding, cement, glass, and paper manufacture. Iron and steel mills were started in this way and were transferred to private enterprise in the 1930's. Power undertakings were treated in a similar manner. Comparatively little public enterprise now exists in Japan, and most of it is in conventional spheres such as railways, telecommunications, and fiscal monopolies such as salt, tobacco, camphor and alcohol.

In several other countries of South and South-East Asia the governments have followed a policy of establishing new state-owned industries to supplement rather than supplant private enterprise; or to make up for the shortage of supplies from abroad. This has occurred in the Phillipines, in Thailand and in Ceylon.

CULTURAL ACTIVITIES

This heading includes a substantial number of functions or services in the realm of the arts and entertainment, or of science and learning, which the State has promoted, subsidized or fostered in various ways. Public service broadcasting and television belong to this category; and so too does the encouragement and support given to drama, music and the visual arts by a body like the Arts Council in Britain. Some of the most famous theatres, such as the Comedie Française in Paris and the Old Vic in London; great opera houses like the Scala in Milan, and national ballet companies are either run as forms of public enterprise or heavily subsidized by public money.[1] A wide range of municipal activities assisting local dramatic and musical performances, art exhibitions, festivals, and other forms of entertainment is to be found in many different countries.

There is a long tradition of state patronage of the arts which originated in the days of monarchical rule; and the State has inherited from princely rulers the responsibility for many great national art collections, museums and libraries. Many of the cultural activities mentioned above are, however, of more recent origin, and in general they require direction and management of a quite different kind from that needed for the administration of museums, art galleries and libraries. For this reason they may properly be classed with nationalized industries rather than with the social services.

In the light of this conceptual framework we can appraise the scope

[1] *Government and the Arts in Britain*, HMSO (1958).

and nature of the British nationalization movement up to the present time. Gas and electricity supply belong to the public utility group. Railways, the London passenger transport system, and the air lines fall under the heading of transport and communications. The Bank of England obviously belongs to the banking, credit and insurance group. The new towns and the Colonial Development Corporation are examples of multi-purpose development projects. Coal is a typical instance of a basic established industry which has been transferred to the public sector, while atomic energy is a new industry initiated by public enterprise. Broadcasting is a cultural activity.

This conceptual framework may be useful in reminding us of the immense differences in the purposes of public enterprise in different spheres, and in the character of the nationalized industries. It should prevent us from assuming that the undertakings are all alike merely because they happen to be publicly owned and administered.

THE TYPES OF INSTITUTIONS

The forms of public enterprise, no less than the directions, provide a variegated picture. The following represent the principal types of institution used to administer publicly-owned industries or services:

(i) *The Government Department or Ministry*

This is the instrument for conducting postal services in all countries, and telephone and telegraph services in most of them. Some Post Offices, like those of Switzerland and Britain, conduct a large banking and money order business. The Swiss Post Office also operate the entire motor-bus system on which many mountain villages depend for their sole method of public transportation.

Many people believe that a Government Department is not an appropriate organ for administering public enterprise of a modern kind; yet this contention is not everywhere accepted. The All-India radio system is under the direct control of a central Government Department with a Minister in charge of it. There appears to be little or no political interference with broadcasting programmes. Moreover, directors of the broadcasting stations in India are said to enjoy a substantial degree of freedom in regard to programmes.

(ii) *The Local Authority*

The public utility era, which began in the mid-nineteenth century, saw the town council (by whatever name it was called) invested with power to own and operate water, gas, electricity, and street transport undertakings, and a great deal of municipal trading in these spheres still exists in many countries. But in general the areas of administration needed for the most efficient operation of these services have expanded, whereas the areas of local government have remained static. In consequence, municipal enterprise is declining and public utility services are being projected on to a regional or national scale. Nationalization of these services in France and Britain, and their provincialization in Canada, are only municipal trading writ large.

(iii) *The Regulatory Commission*

This device emerged in mid-nineteenth century Britain as an instrument for regulating the railways in the public interest. It was Victorian capitalist democracy's notion of how to reconcile the public interest in a monopolistic service of primary importance with the profit-making incentive of joint stock enterprise. The idea quickly spread to the United States and the regulatory commission has come to occupy in that country a most significant place in both federal and state governments.[1] The independent regulatory commission is represented at the federal level by such massive and powerful institutions as the Interstate Commerce Commission, the Securities and Exchange Commission, the Civil Aeronautics Board, and perhaps twenty or more similar bodies which constitute what the President's Committee on Administrative Management described in 1937 as a fourth arm of government. In Canada the idea also took root and produced organs like the Board of Transport Commissioners and the Board of Grain Commissioners.

In Britain the Railway and Canal Commission managed to survive until they were abolished by the Transport Act, 1947. Other more recently established regulatory commissions include the now defunct Electricity Commission, the regional licensing authorities who regulate both road passenger services and the road haulage industry; and the Independent Television Authority.

The task of the regulatory commission is usually to control or supervise undertakings tinged with a public interest which are operating for private profit. Publicly owned undertakings can be and are controlled by other means. Hence we should expect the regulatory commission to decline in countries which have moved from regulated profit-seeking enterprise to public ownership and administration, and this in fact corresponds with experience, notably in Britain. Conversely, when the steel industry was denationalized, the Iron and Steel Board were established as a regulatory commission.

Recent experience of the Monopolies and Restrictive Practices Com-

[1] See E. Pendleton Herring: *Public Administration and the Public Interest* (New York 1936) Part III; R. E. Cushman: *The Independent Regulatory Commissions* (New York 1941); L. Sharfman: *The Interstate Commerce Commission* (New York 1935).

mission shows how essentially negative organs of this type tend to be, even when they are trying to investigate and abolish restrictive practices. The growing edge of state intervention in economic lite is in a positive direction and this may account in part for the general dissatisfaction with the regulatory commission. As an expression of this we may cite the interim report of the Trades Union Congress on Public Ownership published in 1953. The General Council of the TUC expressed the view in this report that there is need for public control over certain industries conducted by private enterprise but they rejected the idea of supervision by a public board of control because it has 'obvious disadvantages when what is required is to ensure that essential investment is undertaken'.[1]

(iv) *Mixed Enterprise*

By this we mean organs which combine public and private ownership and control. Mixed undertakings are today an extremely widespread form of public enterprise. They are to be found in Argentina, Chile, Mexico, New Zealand, Portugal, Spain, Italy, Denmark, and in many other countries. On the Continent *les sociétés d'économie mixte* are very numerous. In France alone the State participates in more than forty companies engaged in a wide range of activities, including mining for ore, film production, a news agency, the production and distribution of petroleum, the merchant marine, the railways, industrial research, river navigation, and broadcasting. In Germany, a great part of the public utility undertakings have taken the form of mixed enterprise. It has been exceedingly common for German municipalities to hold part of the stock of gas and electricity companies, and for the national government to be associated with private interests. In Belgium mixed enterprise is to be found in many activities, such as the railways, water supply, low cost housing, canal and maritime installations, etc.

Mixed enterprise has made much less headway in the English-speaking countries. In Britain the British Petroleum Company Ltd and the Manchester Ship Canal are leading examples, but there are tew others of importance. The Agricultural Mortgage Corporation also belongs to the category of mixed enterprise. Its purpose is to grant long-term loans against first mortgages of agricultural land and buildings in England and Wales either to facilitate farm purchase, or to finance improvements in farm buildings, electricity and water supplies, drainage, and equipment. Authority to form the Corporation was conferred by the Agricultural Credits Acts, 1928, but it was incorporated under the Companies Acts.

[1] Para. 206.

The funds of the Corporation consist partly of capital subscribed by various banks and partly of money raised on loan from the Government. The deputy chairman is nominated by the Treasury and two other directors (out of a total of eight) are nominated by the Minister of Agriculture.

The South African Iron and Steel Industrial Corporation, the Bank of Canada, and the Federal Home Loan Banks in USA are specimens of mixed enterprise from other English-speaking countries. In India, important new forms of joint enterprise consist of a vast new steel works which Krupps are building for the Indian Government, and another joint enterprise is the explosives factory which ICI have constructed in association with the Government and which they are now operating.

Two conditions must be fulfilled to create a genuine mixed enterprise. One is that the state or local authorities must own a substantial part of the capital, side by side with private ownership. The other is that public authorities must participate in the direction or administration of the enterprise, usually through representation on the board of directors. Some French writers[1] have also postulated that a mixed enterprise must be constituted under the ordinary law applying to joint stock companies; but this condition scarcely seems to be essential.

In view of the extensive use of mixed enterprise in many countries it is surprising that more is not known about it. In theory one may assume that it will produce the worst of both worlds; or one may equally well assume that it will combine the best features of capitalism and public enterprise. But assumptions are of small use here, and so little is known of its practical working that it is difficult to make an informed judgment of mixed enterprise. It would appear, however, that the existence of mixed enterprise arouses comparatively little criticism or protest.

(v) *The Representative Trust*

Some writers distinguish the representative trust in the shape of bodies like the Port of London Authority, the Mersey Dock and Harbour Board, or the Metropolitan Water Board. I scarcely think this is justified. These bodies are public corporations of a special type.

(vi) *The Joint Stock Company*

This can be and is used for public enterprise, notably in India at the present time. It was also used during the brief period of nationalization of iron and steel in Britain for the operating companies whose shares were acquired and transferred to the British Iron and Steel Corporation.

After the denationalization of the road haulage industry effected under the provisions of the Transport Act, 1953, and the consequent abolition of the Road Haulage Executive, three joint stock companies were

[1] Roger Bloch: *Les Applications en France de l'Economie Mixte* (Paris, 1941), pp. 2, 5, 6, 7-8.

formed to take over the road haulage services still permitted to the British Transport Commission.

The joint stock company compares unfavourably with the public corporation in almost every respect. It is not created by Parliament or in any way answerable to it. It is not directly under the control of the Government, except insofar as Ministers can control the membership of the board or influence their policy indirectly. Its activities and policies are sometimes carried on behind a thick smokescreen of secrecy which conceals much of what should be publicly known. Its policy is neither openly laid down in an Act of Parliament after public debate nor are there usually opportunities for discussing it in the legislature. Its reports and accounts are either not published or are no more informative than those of a commercial undertaking. Its corporate nature is often fictitious, since the ownership is usually vested in the Crown or in the Government. It is in no way an instrument of democratic socialism but is rather a device for avoiding public accountability and control.

(vii) *The Public Corporation*

The public corporation is the most important invention of the twentieth century in the sphere of government institutions. It is to be found in one form or another in many different countries all over the world; in Britain and the Commonwealth countries; in the United States;[1] in France, Belgium and many other continental countries.

Public authorities enjoying various degrees of autonomy have existed for centuries; but the public corporation of today has special characteristics which distinguish it from these older bodies. It was specially devised as an organ of public enterprise and it has become the chosen instrument for this purpose in many lands.

As it is the institution used for operating nearly all the industries and services which have been nationalized in Britain, a detailed account of its characteristics is given in chapter III. Indeed, the rest of this book is mainly concerned with the administration and management of the nationalized industries in Britain by public corporations.

The public corporation is now on trial on an extensive scale. It has solved a number of problems, but it has also created some new ones. Those which are proving most difficult concern its relations with the Government and the legislature. The right balance between independence and political control has not yet been struck in most countries, and the process of search and adjustment is still continuing. But of the broad result I have little doubt. The public corporation has come to stay.

[1] See John Thurston: *Government Proprietary Corporations in the English-Speaking Countries* (Harvard University Press, 1937) for a general survey.

CHAPTER II

The Motives and Background of Nationalization

THE BANK OF ENGLAND

THERE is much diversity in the historical and economic background of the nationalized industries. The Bank of England has been a chartered corporation for centuries, enjoying a position of great power and importance, and engaged in close and frequent relations with the Treasury and the Chancellor of the Exchequer. Its proper functions and purpose are so clearly recognized that no dispute on the subject occurred when the Labour Government came into power in 1945, pledged to nationalize the Bank. The only question was whether the Bank should be publicly owned and the Governor and Court of Directors appointed by the Government and subject to their ultimate control. In moving the second reading of the Bank of England Bill,[1] Mr Dalton, the then Chancellor of the Exchequer, put forward two reasons for nationalizing the Bank:[2] first, that, as there was close co-operation between the Treasury and the Bank, the Bill made the law fit the facts; secondly, that the Bill ensured 'an integrated and coherent system of financial institutions'.[3] Mr Gaitskell, though he acknowledged that the Government had effectively controlled the Bank during the war, and that in the eight or so years before the war control had increased, pointed out that the Bank had not always been so co-operative. He also gave two cases, both of 1939, when the Bank had exercised an independent influence.[4] The issue, he thought, was 'whether this country is to take control of the head and fount of financial power'.[5] The Conservative Party opposed the Bill on the ground that it was unnecessary.

COAL

The coal industry has a long history of state intervention. The aims of the early legislation were to safeguard the lives, health, and well-being of the miners, to prevent women and children from working under-

[1] 415 HC Deb. 5s., cols. 43 ff. (October 29, 1945.)
[2] *Ib.*, cols. 46 and 54.
[3] *Ib.*, col. 54.
[4] In regard to the Czech gold episode and the raising of the bank rate: *ib.*, cols. 83-5.
[5] *Ib.*, col. 88.

ground, to limit the working hours of men in the pits, to ensure that those paid according to the weight of mineral gotten should be able to check the weight, and cognate matters. In 1912 the minimum wages of miners were fixed under statute. During the period between the First and Second World Wars legislation took a new turn: it began to deal with the economic conduct of the industry. Legislation was passed to enable the unreasonable opposition of private owners to the working of coal to be overcome,[1] and to permit amalgamations to take place where some but not all the collieries concerned favoured such a course.[2] In 1930, the Labour Government persuaded Parliament to impose a stringent cartel system on the coalmines.

Under the Coal Mines Act, 1930, a Central Council of Mineowners fixed the maximum permitted output for the whole country each quarter. This in turn was translated into a maximum district output for each coalfield. Each district had an executive board, representing the colliery owners which divided the district allocation among the individual collieries. Every colliery had a right to produce not more than a specified tonnage of coal in any quarter. If it exceeded that amount it could be severely penalized in various ways. The only lawful means by which this figure could be exceeded by an efficient mine was to purchase quota rights from a less efficient colliery, which thereby received money for not producing. This obviously handicapped the more efficient mines by increasing their costs of production, and prevented the old and worn-out ones from closing down.

The executive boards were also permitted to impose minimum prices and district selling schemes on their collieries, and several of them did so.

This fantastic system of restrictive practices was intended to rescue the British coal industry from the wretched condition into which it had fallen owing to the backward technological state of the mines resulting from bad management and the owners' failure to introduce modern equipment or to embark upon adequate capital development.

The Act of 1930 also set up a Coal Mines Reorganization Commission to amalgamate collieries where to do so would be likely to increase the efficiency of the industry. Owing to the opposition of the owners and a House of Lords amendment to the Bill, the commission were unable in practice to carry out their task, and nothing except frustration resulted from its labours during seven long years of effort.[3] In 1938 the smouldering discontent of the miners led to the expropriation by the State of

[1] Mines (Working Facilities and Support) Act, 1923.
[2] Mining Industry Act, 1926.
[3] See Ivor Thomas: 'The Coal Mines Reorganization Commission' in *Public Enterprise*, ed. W. A. Robson (London: Allen & Unwin, 1937), p. 209.

the royalty owners' property rights. This meant that the coal reserves of the country passed into public ownership, but the colliery companies were left free to manage their undertakings as they thought fit.

By 1945 the coal industry was in a dangerous state from almost every point of view. It was technologically inefficient, particularly in regard to the loading and transportation of coal underground. The colliery companies had for many years been unable or unwilling to invest the large sums necessary to modernize the mines, improve the underground haulage systems, introduce power loading machinery, and generally apply the benefits of modern science to Britain's greatest basic industry. An inevitable consequence of the backward technological condition of the industry was that the earnings of the miners fell in a catastrophic manner compared with those of comparable grades of labour.[1] This led to embittered labour relations, to the calamitous strike of 1926, and to the futile restrictive legislation of 1930 referred to above. The exporting coalfields were severely handicapped in competitive markets by old-fashioned technology and an almost static output per man shift in comparison with rival producing countries; and this further weakened the resources of the industry.

Poor leadership, conservative management, backward technology and inadequate investment characterized the British coal industry during the twenty-five or thirty years prior to nationalization. Neither the public, nor Parliament, nor successive governments, showed any understanding of the underlying causes for the dangerous malaise which had gripped the industry most fundamental to the nation's economy. No one looked below the surface for the reasons which led the miners and their union to voice a demand for nationalization which in 1945 became so irresistible that no government, whatever its political convictions, could have allowed matters to continue as they were under private management. The fundamental reason which led to the public ownership of the coal industry was the need to arrest the momentum of decline which had set in during the past twenty-five or thirty years. All the subsequent difficulties which have faced the industry, and the problems which have still to be solved, arise from this essential circumstance. Many of the critics of the nationalized coal industry display gross ignorance of the situation prior to nationalization; they should at least become better informed if they wish to be taken seriously.

The nationalization of the coal industry which was effected by Parliament in 1946 was thus the culminating point in the evolution of state

[1] In 1938 the mineworker's earnings placed him in the 81st position on a list of about one hundred industries. See W. H. B. Court: *Coal* (1951), p. 266.

policy and had become inevitable. It was adopted only after numerous other expedients to improve the condition of the industry had been tried and failed. The elimination of private ownership was a surgical operation which had become necessary to save the life of the patient. But the removal of a diseased organ is not, by itself, necessarily sufficient to restore a sick patient to health.

TRANSPORT

Transport had a very different background. The railways have been regulated by public authorities of one kind or another since their inception. Their rates, fares, and charges were always liable to control; they were not permitted to show undue preference to one trader as compared with others; they could be required to afford reasonable services, facilities, and conveniences, including the provision of extensions and improvements; and in 1921 the multitude of separate railway companies were forced by Parliament to amalgamate into four large groups.

The railways found themselves in a position of increasing difficulty during the period between the First and Second World Wars. This was partly due to the great depression; but a more deep-seated cause was the competition of the road haulage industry and road passenger services. Instead of endeavouring to meet this competition by improved services and modern equipment, cheaper fares and rates, and better facilities, the railway companies invoked statutory authority to restrict the services provided by their competitors to the utmost possible extent. Another policy they pursued was to acquire an interest in road haulage and passenger undertakings, and also to promote railway-owned domestic air services. In the United States the undertakers of one form of transport are not permitted to operate rival forms of transport; but the British Parliament was more complaisant to the railway companies' demands. The result was that the companies were permitted to adopt expedients which enabled them to carry on without facing up to the fundamental problem of modernizing the railway system so that it could meet the competition of road and air transport.

In the Greater London region the whole complex of public transport facilities, comprising the group of Underground railways, the Metropolitan Railway, the motorbus companies, the tramway and trolleybus services, whether owned and operated by local authorities or by commercial companies, were handed over in 1933 to a public corporation known as the London Passenger Transport Board.[1]

[1] See Ernest Davies: 'The London Passenger Transport Board' in *Public Enterprise*, ed. W. A. Robson (1937), p. 155.

Motorbus and motorcoach services were subjected to a drastic system of regulation by the Road Traffic Act, 1930; and the road haulage industry was brought under state regulation in 1933. The object of the legislation in each case was to restrict road competition in the interests of the railways. This aim was achieved to a substantial degree.

The restriction of competition offered to railways by road vehicles, or the deprivation of the latter of their advantages to the user, is generally described as 'co-ordination'. This euphemism has always seemed less likely to offend the susceptibilities of business men or arouse the suspicions of the travelling community than a cruder expression such as 'the elimination of competition' or 'the handicapping of road transport'. But this is in fact what it has meant. The 'co-ordination', moreover, has so far always been one-sided. Railway services have never been restricted, or fares raised, in order to assist road operators.

The nationalization of the railways was part of the Labour Party's plan for transferring to public ownership the entire system of public transport, comprising railways, the long distance road haulage industry, passenger road services, canals and inland waterways, and the London passenger transport complex. By this means it was hoped to administer all these several elements as part of a comprehensive and co-ordinated whole; to shield the railways from financial disaster caused by competition from road vehicles; to bring about improvements of organization and operation which could not take place unless all the different types of transport were under a common ownership; and to enable the railways to modernize and re-equip themselves more adequately than they were able to do under the conditions of private enterprise.

AIR SERVICES

The other means of transportation which were nationalized are the British airlines operating regular services within the United Kingdom and between Britain and overseas countries. In this industry the form which state intervention took for many years before 1939 consisted of a substantial subsidy paid to Imperial Airways and other profit-making companies.[1] This brought with it a considerable degree of governmental control or influence over routes and services. The Empire Air Mail Scheme, initiated in 1938, also rendered substantial financial aid to Imperial Airways.[2]

Here governmental action was positive, fostering, expansive, in contrast to the negative and restrictive rôle of the State in relation to inland

[1] For details of the subsidies see W. A. Robson: 'General Conclusions' in *Problems of Nationalized Industry*, ed. W. A. Robson (Allen & Unwin, 1952), p. 281.

[2] *Ib.* See *Empire Air Mail Scheme*, HMSO, Cmd. 5414/1937, pp. 5-6.

surface transport. It involved, however, the payment of subsidies to a profit-making company for an indefinite period; and subsidies of this kind are unpopular in England.[1] The need to provide financial aid from public funds for several years to come undoubtedly played a considerable part in the nationalization of air services.

The decision to nationalize the overseas air services had been taken in 1939, when the British Overseas Airways Corporation was created by legislation on the eve of the Second World War. Post-war policy was, however, formulated on more ambitious lines, involving nationalized internal air services, a vastly expanded plan of operations for BOAC, the setting up of British European Airways and the short-lived British South American Airways Corporation. No new principle was involved. It was, however, generally recognized that for some time ahead no international air line could hope to maintain itself without a substantial subsidy of one kind or another; and if this was necessary, it would be better that the money should go to a public undertaking rather than into private pockets.

But apart from such considerations as these, the Second World War had a great influence on British public opinion concerning civil aviation. The massive achievements of the RAF, the vast aircraft industry which had been built up in the United Kingdom, and the immense air traffic—both friendly and hostile—which flew over Britain by day and by night, made people much more air conscious than they had been before. Millions of people came to feel that much of the destiny of Britain and the Commonwealth lies in the air; that the future holds great opportunities for a seafaring people with wings; and that much greater efforts should be taken to obtain a substantial slice of the world's air traffic. This required a pooling of national resources, and led, in fact, to nationalization.

GAS

The gas supply prior to nationalization was divided between municipal undertakings and commercial companies. Some 269 local authorities and five joint boards had entered the field, and many large cities owned and operated their own gas undertaking. Among them were Birmingham, Bradford, Coventry, Leeds, Leicester, Nottingham, Halifax, Huddersfield, Oldham and Rochdale. The municipalities accounted for about 37 per cent of the industry, reckoned in terms of sales. The remainder of the industry (apart from 264 non-statutory undertakings supplying less

[1] Imperial Airways paid a dividend of 6 per cent (plus a bonus of 2 per cent) in 1935-6; of 7 per cent (plus a bonus of 2 per cent) in 1936-7; and of 7 per cent in 1937-9.

than 2 per cent of the gas sold) was in the hands of 509 public utility companies.[1] The largest of them was the Gas Light & Coke Company of London which disposed of twelve per cent of the total gas sales. The companies were subject to stringent statutory provisions designed to restrict profits and regulate prices, and there were various ingenious devices to relate prices and profits in a manner which would be fair both to the stockholder and the consumer.

The reasons for nationalizing gas are set out in the Report of the Committee on the Gas Industry.[2] The chairman of this committee was Lord Heyworth, chairman of Unilever and Lever Brothers.

The Heyworth Report declared that the then existing structure of the industry restricted further progress in gas supply. The prevailing forms of organization were not suited to present-day conditions and even less likely to meet the needs of the future. Basic change in the structure of the gas industry was the only method which could produce really effective results quickly. The essential need lay in the grouping of gas undertakings into larger operating units. Such groupings would lower costs of production by raising the carbonizing efficiency, achieving a better use of labour, reducing the burden of maintenance, and improving the load factor. There would, however, be only a limited scope for improvement in these directions. It would result mainly from a reduction in the number of producing units and raising the technical efficiency of the small concerns. There was room for further progress through economizing in capital charges; through more intensive study of distribution problems; through a more vigorous sales policy to promote the use of improved appliances on attractive terms, to develop new uses for gas, and to experiment with tariffs; through an expanded research and development programme; and through the better grading and disposal of coke. The argument for nationalizing the industry was thus based on grounds of better organization, operating techniques and sales management.

ELECTRICITY

Electricity supply, like the gas industry, was divided between municipal undertakings and commercial companies. The proportion of the electricity supply industry in the hands of local authorities was, however, much larger than in the case of gas, and amounted to approximately two-thirds of the whole. Both the municipal and privately owned undertakings had been elaborately regulated by legislation and by governmental action.

[1] *The Gas Industry: Report of the Committee of Enquiry*, HMSO, Cmd. 6699/1945, para. 57.
[2] *Ib.*, paras. 227-39.

In 1919 the Electricity Commission was set up to promote, regulate and supervise the supply of electricity on a national scale. In 1926, the Electricity Supply Act introduced the ideas of an interconnected system of high pressure transmission known as the grid, into which electricity would be poured by large and up-to-date generating stations. This involved closing down many of the small and less efficient power stations. The objects of the plan were to concentrate generation in a few large interconnected stations operating under unified control; to standardize frequency throughout the country; to construct a network of transmission lines into which power could be fed from all available sources; to effect economy in fuel consumption; to lower capital expenditure through a reduction of reserve plant; and to improve the load factor.

This plan was carried out in less than a decade. It achieved an immense improvement in the generation, transmission and bulk supply of electricity. It is not too much to say that the British war effort of 1939–45 could not have succeeded without the grid.

The distributive side of the industry was not touched. Electricity was sold in bulk by the Central Electricity Board to the authorized undertakers (whether municipal or company) and distributed by them to individual consumers on the same lines as before. The McGowan Committee on Electricity Distribution was appointed in 1936 to consider this aspect of the problem. They recommended schemes of amalgamation, to be prepared by district commissions, which would bring the grouped undertakings under either company or local authority ownership, with provision for financial control of the companies and their eventual transfer to public ownership.[1] No action was taken on this report.

Thus, electricity supply was an industry in which a profound and beneficial advance had taken place on the generating and transmission side from 1926, in consequence of the setting up of the Central Electricity Board for the purposes already mentioned. But the distribution side of the industry was untouched by these improvements and the vested interests of distributors made it impossible to rationalize, or to pass on to consumers the economies of production resulting from the construction and operation of the grid. Much larger areas of distribution were required in order to obtain improved load factors. London was a confused tangle of diverse voltages and antiquated systems which threw a heavy expense on consumers who, in moving from one district to another, found it necessary to buy new domestic equipment. It was impossible to find a satisfactory basis for amalgamating municipally owned undertakings run in the public interest with those operated for profit by public

[1] See Graeme Haldane: 'The Central Electricity Board and other Electricity Authorities', in *Public Enterprise*, ed. W. A. Robson, p. 105.

utility companies. A solution was therefore sought by nationalizing the whole industry, including both generation and distribution.

The nationalization of gas and electricity meant, as regards a substantial part of each industry, a transfer from one form of public ownership to another form. Some extremely important changes in organization and control took place, but, from the proprietary angle, the nationalization of these industries was a much less drastic event than that of coal or steel.

Gas and electricity, and to some extent the railways, had been regulated as public utilities for many years. This was not true of iron and steel, or of raw cotton, which were nationalized by the Labour Government of 1945–50. The intervention of the State in the steel industry had been confined (except during the Second World War) to the use of a protective tariff as a means of inducing the industry to improve its organization and efficiency. In wartime, of course, the industry was closely controlled by the State, like all others essential to munition manufacture.

IRON AND STEEL

Iron and steel, the last industry to be nationalized by the Attlee Government, was in a class by itself. Here was an industry which was relatively progressive from a technological standpoint and with a good record of labour relations. Moreover, the prices of British steel compared favourably with those of most other countries. On what, then, did the case for nationalization rest?

The main argument advanced by Mr G. R. Strauss, the Labour Minister of Supply, in introducing the Bill was that iron and steel are essential to the British economy as a whole and must, therefore, be under public control. The national interest is so heavily involved in the products of this industry that it cannot safely be left in private hands. In particular, the vital decisions on planning and development should be taken by the Government.[1] This argument was reinforced by the high degree to which the industry was—and is—dominated by cartels, which exert a substantial control over prices and production. A serious ground of complaint against the industry was that during the inter-war period, when prices generally had fallen sharply, steel and iron prices had been kept up by the action of the trade associations.

The nationalization of iron and steel aroused more controversy and opposition than all the other nationalization measures of the Labour Government put together. The Conservative Party fought the Bill tooth

[1] *Public Enterprise* (1957), (Labour Party) p. 21.

and nail in Parliament and made its repeal an item in their subsequent election campaign. They had several motives for regarding the denationalization of steel as essential to the party's interests. First, it was —and is—an extremely prosperous industry, in which profits are high. Second, most of the plants taken over formed part of engineering or processing concerns for which they supplied the raw steel, but which were not nationalized. Hence the iron and steel industry has very wide ramifications which extend into almost every branch of metal-using manufacture. The transfer of the steel industry seemed like a challenge to the central citadel of private enterprise. If that fell, everything else was threatened. Third, Conservatives disliked immensely the idea that a highly prosperous industry should be taken over by the State. Nationalization might be tolerated—and perhaps even welcomed by some—in the case of derelict or declining industries which had ceased to be profitable and were no longer attractive to new capital investment, such as coal and the railways; but the outlook for the steel companies was a very bright one. And fourthly, while gas, electricity, transport and possibly even coal could be regarded as coming within the category of public utilities, it was impossible to apply this concept to the production of iron and steel.

The Conservative Government which took office in 1951 under Sir Winston Churchill therefore made the denationalization of iron and steel a major act of policy. The Iron and Steel Corporation of Great Britain was abolished and a new body called the Iron and Steel Holding and Realization Agency set up to dispose of the subsidiary companies and other interests which were transferred to it from the Corporation.[1] The task of the Agency has been to dispose of the companies and investments to the best advantage, offers from the former owners being given preferential consideration. Where the companies are offered for sale by public announcement, their capital structure has usually been re-organized.[2] It will take a few years to complete this task.[3]

[1] Iron and Steel Act, 1953.

[2] *Iron and Steel Holding and Realization Agency Annual Report 1954–5*, HMSO, HC 152/1955–6, paras. 9 and 11.

[3] On July 13, 1953, the number of subsidiaries in which the Agency had a direct holding was seventy-one. Of these, the Agency transferred eight to other subsidiaries and one was wound up. Of the remaining sixty-two, forty-nine had been disposed of at September 30, 1958. In terms of employment, production and sales, it is estimated that these forty-nine account for about five-sixths of the Agency's inheritance. In terms of value—computed on the basis of the Iron & Steel Act, 1949—the Agency took over from the Iron and Steel Corporation of Great Britain securities whose cost to the Corporation was £252·3 m. Of this, £42·0 m. was represented by the thirteen companies which were subsidiaries at September 30, 1958. (Richard Thomas & Baldwins, Ltd and Staveley Iron & Chemical Co Ltd accounted for £30·7 m. of this.) *Iron and Steel Holding and Realization Agency Annual Report 1957–8*, HMSO, HC 29/1958 paras 5–7.

As soon as the Conservative Government announced their decision to denationalize iron and steel, the Labour Party immediately declared that, when they returned to power, they would renationalize the industry. This was a political response to a political act which Labour politicians felt affected the prestige of their party. All the subsequent policy statements issued by the Labour Party have repeated the party's intention to take over the industry as soon as possible. *Industry and Society*, in which the Labour Party reject further nationalization in favour of public ownership of equity shares, declared that the case for the nationalization of iron and steel is 'as powerful today as it was when our programmes were first drafted'. It does not state what the case is, but denounces denationalization as harmful to the industries concerned and points out that, since its return to private ownership, it has yielded an increase of perhaps £10 millions a year to the shareholders.[1] The Labour Party declared their intention to reintroduce public ownership of iron and steel. The Trades Union Congress, in their 1953 report, stressed the importance of public ownership of the industry in order to ensure that sufficient steel producing capacity was available in case of need, even though it might involve some over-investment in steel plants.[2] The Labour Party's policy statement *Public Enterprise*, issued in 1957, repeats the arguments about the dangers of monopoly and cartels and the need to ensure adequate supplies of home-produced steel, as a justification of public ownership and control.[3]

A recent Fabian research pamphlet by John Hughes[4] makes an out-and-out attack on the steel industry, for which he has not a good word to say. The main grounds of his criticism are the failure of the industry to expand sufficiently to meet the needs of the home market in the post-war years or to assist the balance of trade problem by exporting steel. The iron and steel companies, he asserts, have persistently under-estimated home demand and have shown themselves indifferent to the national interest in increasing exports. They have neglected the development of plants which would use a higher proportion of home-produced ore, despite the efforts of the Iron and Steel Board to encourage it. They have delayed the introduction of new processes and the replacement of obsolete plant. Since denationalization, their profits have been excessive and prices have risen far in excess of costs. Finally, Mr Hughes alleges that the boards of the great steel companies represent concentrations of power which must be brought under social control. The Iron and Steel

[1] *Industry and Society* (1957) (Labour Party), p. 46.
[2] *TUC Interim Report on Public Ownership* (1953), para. 161.
[3] *Public Enterprise* (1957) (Labour Party), p. 21.
[4] *Plan for Steel Re-Nationalization* (1958) (Fabian Research Series No. 198).

Board, set up by the denationalization Act of 1953, is ineffective to control the industry. He concludes that, 'The conflict between the requirements of the national economy—both for growth and in foreign trade—and the narrow, restrictive attitudes of "the industry" cannot be overcome without public ownership. The steel industry's "leadership" has demonstrated clearly its inability even to think in terms of the national interest.'[1] The British Iron and Steel Federation categorically denied the truth of all these statements. The Labour Party continued to be sufficiently convinced of their truth to include the renationalization of steel in their manifesto for the 1959 election.

When the industry was nationalized in 1951, the least possible disturbance was made to the organization of the producing units. The previous structure of the industry was preserved almost intact in the form of ninety-six joint stock companies, whose stocks and shares were compulsorily acquired and transferred to the Iron and Steel Corporation of Great Britain, which thus became a gigantic holding company. Indeed, the reorganization of the capital structure and regrouping of units by the Steel Holding and Realization Agency has disturbed the industry far more than the process of nationalization.

Whatever policy one may favour for steel, no industry can continue to oscillate every few years between private ownership and public enterprise without suffering grave inconvenience, interruption of policy and a general feeling of unsettlement which can lead to stagnation.

There are two vital considerations to be borne in mind. One is that strong political convictions and political prestige have become involved in the future of iron and steel. The other is that national economic interests of the first importance are at stake. The wisest course of action for the Labour Party would be to stop trying to take over the whole industry. It should aim at nationalizing only a proportion of the industry. This would give the Government all the control it needs over the industry. If total capacity is insufficient, the nationalized firms can expand by building new plants. If prices are too high, they can reduce theirs. If technology is lagging, they can introduce whatever improved processes are available.

Furthermore, this policy would provide an opportunity for an element of competition to be introduced between public enterprise and private enterprise. And it would avoid the over-large monopolistic undertaking in the sphere of nationalized industry which Mr Gaitskell is anxious to avoid. The Labour Party statement *Industry and Society* remarks that, in the past, public ownership has meant the taking over and reorganizing of an entire industry under a single authority. 'This was the form best

[1] *Plan for Steel Re-Nationalization* (1958) (Fabian Research Series No. 198), p. 4.

suited to the basic industries in which a complete change of structure was called for. But there may be other cases where, if the needs of the nation are to be met, the public ownership of a single company or of a group of companies may be more appropriate.'[1] Iron and steel was never regarded as an industry which required a radical change of organization, and, as I have pointed out, it was one in which almost no fundamental alteration of structure was either contemplated or carried out.

ATOMIC ENERGY

Atomic energy is an industry which originated in state action during the Second World War for military purposes. Although much of the early pioneer work both on the scientific and development sides was due to British scientists and engineers, the making of the first atomic bombs was taken over by the American Government during the Second World War.

After the war, the research, development and manufacture of atomic weapons became a responsibility of the Ministry of Supply. Gradually, the immense potentialities of the peaceful uses of atomic energy became apparent and the Atomic Energy Authority was set up by the Churchill Government in 1954, to carry out Government policy both in the military and civil spheres.[2]

There has been no disagreement between the parties about the need for the nationalization of atomic energy development. The fearful possibilities of nuclear weapons for the destruction of civilization and the immense potentialities for good of nuclear power for civil purposes, combine to make atomic energy a subject which no Government dare leave to uncontrolled private enterprise.

The spearhead of the British effort on the peaceful side is the ambitious programme of nuclear electricity generating stations on which we have embarked and of which Calder Hall was a pilot project. This programme is being carried out by the Central Electricity Generating Board with technical advice and help from the Atomic Energy Authority. The actual work of construction is given under contract to groups of engineering companies who have formed themselves into teams capable of building complete nuclear generating stations at home or abroad.

[1] p. 50.

[2] See *The Future Organization of the UK Atomic Energy Project*. HMSO, Cmd. 8986/1953 and R. D'Arcy Best: 'The United Kingdom Atomic Energy Authority', XXXIV. *Public Administration* (1956), p. 1.

GENERAL SOCIALIST DOCTRINES

The Labour Party's nationalization policy in 1945–51 sprang from a conviction that socialism requires the public ownership and operation, in the interests of the whole community, of the basic industries concerned with fuel and power, transport and the essential raw materials on which the entire economy depends.[1] It was further held that a policy of full employment demands effective control of currency and credit through national ownership of the central bank. This general view was reinforced by bitter memories of Bank of England policy during the great depression in the 1920's and '30's, when industrial well-being was sacrificed to financial interests, capital expenditure restricted by high rates of interest and the misery of prolonged unemployment suffered by millions of men and women for nearly two decades. The Labour Party determined that never again should the Government and the people be at the mercy of a Bank of England intent on deflation at all costs. The financial crisis of 1931 was also remembered as an indication of the ease with which financiers can create a state of insecurity and bring about a political crisis by manipulating the instruments they control.

Finally, there was the conviction that control over these basic industries is essential to effective economic planning. The concept of central economic planning as a necessary factor in the socialist commonwealth had become part of the philosophy of Labour after the disastrous failure of the MacDonald administration in 1929–31. Public ownership of a substantial group of basic industries could contribute greatly to the effectiveness of central economic planning. Nationalization of such industries thus came to be considered as a means of placing in the hands of the State the levers which could control the whole economy.

There were several other strands in the thread from which the case for nationalization was woven. There was the argument that certain industries which are by their nature monopolistic must be taken over because it is too dangerous to leave them to be exploited by private enterprise for profit. There was the belief that competition leads to a waste of resources and that nationalization would avoid duplication in at least the basic industries which require very large capital expenditure. There was the dislike of the profit-motive on moral grounds, inculcated by such influential writers as R. H. Tawney in his *Sickness of an Acquisitive Society*. There was the hope that, if capitalist enterprise were replaced by public ownership and operation, an era of harmonious labour relations and greater equality would be ushered in.[2]

[1] *TUC Interim Report on Public Ownership* (1953), para. 7.
[2] C. A. R. Crosland: *The Future of Socialism* (1956), pp. 462-5.

These general doctrines played a very important part in prompting the Labour Governments of 1945–51 to launch a great programme of nationalization. But, as we have seen, there were solid reasons of a practical kind which led to the selection of the particular industries chosen for transfer to the public sector.

THE CONSERVATIVE PARTY'S ATTITUDE

What has been the Conservative Party's response to this extensive programme of collectivism? I have already recounted the denationalization of iron and steel. Another early measure was a Bill to denationalize the road haulage industry and to deprive the British Transport Commission of its powers to reorganize and acquire road passenger transport undertakings, and to prepare development and management schemes for trade ports and harbours.[1]

The return of the road haulage industry to private ownership was pressed on the Conservative Government of 1951–5 very hard by the associations representing the hauliers. This was a good instance of a pressure group at work.[2] The industry was represented by Ministers as one in which the small man, working his way up from little or nothing, became the hardworking and enterprising owner of his own lorries in a highly competitive business.[3] This particular measure turned out in the event to be something of a fiasco, since it was found impossible to dispose of all the road haulage units which the Act of 1953 required to be sold to private operators, and a later Act had to be passed increasing the number of vehicles which the British Transport Commission were authorized to retain.[4] Little use had been made of the Commission's powers regarding road passenger transport undertakings and trade harbours, but they were potentially important.

The Raw Cotton Commission, which possessed a monopoly in buying and selling raw cotton in bulk, first lost its monopoly and was subsequently abolished.[5]

[1] Transport Act, 1953.

[2] See S. E. Finer: 'Transport Interests and the Roads Lobby', XXIX *Political Quarterly* (1958), p. 47, and the same author's *Anonymous Empire* (1958), pp. 49, 59, 68, 71, 73, 85-8 and 96.

[3] For the Conservative Party's reasons for denationalizing road haulage, see *The Campaign Guide 1951* (Conservative Central Office), pp. 56-9, and *The Campaign Guide 1955* (Conservative Central Office), pp. 93-4 and 99-103.

[4] Transport (Disposal of Road Haulage Property) Act, 1956. Of 35,018 vehicles for disposal, the Board sold 19,303: *Seventh Report of the Road Haulage Disposal Board*, HMSO, HC 410/1955-6, para. 2. 'The work of the Board', says the Report (para. 14), 'has taken . . . considerably longer than some of the forecasts made before disposals started.'

[5] Cotton Act, 1954.

There were other signs of Conservative reaction against public ownership, such as the policy announced in 1952 of allowing private operators in civil aviation to compete with the nationalized air corporations in seeking permission to operate new scheduled services.[1] A more conspicuous change was the decision to introduce commercial television services in addition to those provided by the BBC[2]—a decision strongly opposed at the time by many leaders of opinion who would normally support the Conservative Party. A less controversial or surprising step was the dissolution of the Overseas Food Corporation, which had been responsible for the ill-fated groundnuts scheme, and the transfer of the remnant of that poorly planned and badly executed enterprise to the Tanganyika Agricultural Corporation under the direction of the Secretary of State for the Colonies.

At the same time, Sir Winston Churchill made it clear that, although the Conservative Party was opposed to the nationalization of industry and, to a lesser extent, to the nationalization of services, the Government of which he was the head accepted it in the case of the coal mines, the railways, the air lines, gas and electricity supply. Moreover, he said, in these instances, 'We have done and are doing our utmost to make a success of it, even though this may somewhat mar the symmetry of party recrimination.'[3] The Conservative and Union Central Office repeated this in *The Campaign Guide* for the 1955 General Election by declaring that, while opposing further nationalization, Conservatives would 'do everything possible to make a success of those industries remaining nationalized and to apply themselves to the many problems bequeathed to them by the Socialists. Such action is essential in the national interest'.[4] The Conservative Party manifesto for the 1959 election once again declared the party to be utterly opposed to any extension of nationalization, but said that a Conservative Government would 'review the situation in civil aviation'. They would make every effort to ensure improved commercial standards of operation in the industries already nationalized.

The extent to which the tidal wave of nationalization, which engulfed so considerable a proportion of British industry in 1946–51, has receded in consequence of the return to power of a Conservative Government in three successive General Elections is clear. What remains of the Labour programme is much larger and more important than what has been repealed. Nevertheless, the denationalization of steel and road haulage

[1] Statement by the Minister of Transport and Civil Aviation, May 27, 1952.
[2] Television Act, 1954.
[3] 520 H.C. Deb. 55, col. 23 (November 3, 1953).
[4] *The Campaign Guide 1955* (Conservative Central Office), p. 83.

were decisions of major importance. Some of the less spectacular tendencies to which we shall call attention in the following pages are also significant.

The attitude of the Labour Party and the Trade Union Movement towards nationalization has changed enormously in recent years; and this change is likely to have more far-reaching effects than the reversal of policy carried out by Conservative Governments since 1951. But this is a subject which I shall reserve for discussion in a later chapter.[1]

[1] *Post* Ch. XVI.

CHAPTER III

The Public Corporation in Britain

GENESIS OF THE PUBLIC CORPORATION

BRITAIN is at the present time engaged in an experiment on the outcome of which will depend the success or failure of her great effort at economic reform and social and physical reconstruction. That experiment is the nationalization of various major industries and services. The institution by which the policy of nationalization is in most cases being carried out is the public corporation.

The public corporation is not an entirely new institution. There have long existed numerous organs exercising official or governmental functions, yet possessing varying degrees of independence from the executive and distinguishable from the great departments of state under the direct control of Ministers of the Crown. There are bodies such as the Public Trustee,[1] the Charity Commission,[2] and Trinity House.[3] There are organs performing technical and specialist functions such as the Tithe Redemption Commission,[4] the Air Registration Board,[5] and the Medical Research Council.[6] There are bodies concerned with cultural activities such as the Arts Council,[7] the British Council,[8] the great national museums and scientific collections, and the Public Record

[1] Public Trustee Act, 1906.

[2] Charitable Trusts Act, 1853.

[3] 'The master, wardens, and assistants of the guild, fraternity, or brotherhood of the most glorious and undivided Trinity and of St. Clement in the parish of Deptford Stroud, in the County of Kent' (Merchant Shipping Act, 1894, s. 742). By the Merchant Shipping Act, 1854, s. 389, the superintendence and management of all lighthouses and beacons in England and the adjacent seas were vested in the Trinity House, subject to the existing jurisdiction of local lighthouse authorities.

[4] Tithe Act, 1936.

[5] Constituted under the Air Navigation Act, 1936, s. 2, and incorporated on February 28, 1937, under the Companies Act, 1929. The Air Registration Board is composed of representatives of the aviation industry. It performs functions relating to the airworthiness of aircraft delegated to it by the Secretary of State for Air and the Minister of Civil Aviation. It receives financial grants from the government.

[6] Originally established under the National Health Insurance Act, but incorporated by Royal Charter in 1928. See National Health Service Act, 1946, s. 16.

[7] Established by Royal Charter, August 9, 1946.

[8] Constituted by Royal Charter in 1940.

Office.[1] There are bodies which are ancillary to and almost integrated in the great departments of State such as the Prison Commissioners,[2] General Register Office, the Commissioners for Crown Lands,[3] and the State Management Districts for Liquor Control in Carlisle.[4] An essential feature of all these bodies is that they were created in order to undertake tasks of a specialized nature free from the direct executive control of Ministers, although often subject to their influence or decisions on matters of policy. These organs are, however, quite different from the new public corporations concerned with the operation of great socialized industries or services. The underlying reason for the creation of the modern type of public corporation is the need for a high degree of freedom, boldness and enterprise in the management of undertakings of an industrial or commercial character and the desire to escape from the caution and circumspection which is considered typical of government departments.[5]

The growth of the public corporation has been very rapid. The Port of London Authority, set up in 1908,[6] was virtually the only example prior to the war of 1914–18. The Haldane Committee on the Machinery of Government, in their famous report published in 1918, regarded the public corporation with disfavour, as not securing the safeguards which ministerial responsibility to Parliament alone provides.[7] This part of the report had no influence on the subsequent course of events. The following year saw the establishment of the Electricity Commission[8] and the Forestry Commission.[9] In 1926 the British Broadcasting Corporation and the Central Electricity Board were established.[10] In 1928 the Racecourse Betting Control Board was set up to instal, own and

[1] Public Record Office Act, 1838, s. 8. The Public Record Office, formerly under the supervision of the Master of the Rolls, is now under the supervision of the Lord Chancellor. The Master of the Rolls continues, however, to be responsible for Chancery Records: Public Records Act, 1958, ss. 1 and 7.

[2] Prisons Act, 1877, s. 6.

[3] Crown Lands Act, 1927, s. 1.

[4] Licensing Act, 1921, s. 16.

[5] The Post Office has been criticized by members of all political parties as an example of how the constitution of an ordinary government department is ill-designed to secure business efficiency in the services which it administers. Criticism culminated in a Memorial signed by some 320 M.Ps. and addressed to the Prime Minister in December, 1931. See the *Report of the Committee of Inquiry on the Post Office*, HMSO, Cmd. 4149/1932.

[6] Port of London Act, 1908, s. 1. See Lincoln Gordon: 'The Port of London Authority' in *Public Enterprise*, ed. W. A. Robson (1937), p. 13.

[7] HMSO, Cmd. 9230/1918, para. 31.

[8] Electricity (Supply) Act, 1919, s. 1. See Graeme Haldane: 'The Central Electricity Board and Other Electricity Authorities' in *Public Enterprise*, ed. W. A. Robson (1937), p. 105.

[9] Forestry Act, 1919, s. 1.

[10] The BBC was incorporated by Royal Charter; the Central Electricity Board was constituted under the Electricity (Supply) Act, 1926, s. 1.

operate the totalisator.[1] In 1933 the London Passenger Transport Board,[2] and in 1939 the British Overseas Airways Corporation[3] were created. These bodies represent the first phase of the movement. The second phase began with the return to power in 1945 of a Labour Government pledged to large measures of nationalization. These measures involved the establishment of many different kinds of organization. They all, however, belong to the species known as the public corporation.[4] All political parties now accept the public corporation as being the appropriate instrument for operating state-owned undertakings requiring management of a commercial or industrial character.

NATIONALIZATION AND DENATIONALIZATION LEGISLATION SINCE 1945

The Bank of England Act, 1946, transferred the capital stock of the Bank of England to public ownership, and brought the Bank under public control. The Coal Industry Nationalization Act of the same year brought about the public ownership and operation of the coal-mining industry and certain allied activities. For this purpose the Act established the National Coal Board, charged with the duties of working and getting the coal in Great Britain, securing the efficient development of the coal-mining industry, and making supplies of coal available in the manner which seems to the Board best suited to the public interest.

The Civil Aviation Act, 1946, established three airways corporations (in place of BOAC as a single unit) with exclusive rights to operate regular services within the United Kingdom or on international routes. By means of amalgamation the number of airways corporations has now been reduced to two.[5] The legislation also enabled the Minister of Transport and Civil Aviation to own and operate civil airfields, and his department has authority to manage airfields in Britain required for regular air services.

The Transport Act, 1947, nationalized forthwith the railways, canals and inland waterways, and also the chain of hotels and restaurants owned by the railways. In addition the entire London passenger transport system, which had been placed under public ownership and operation by

[1] Racecourse Betting Act, 1928, s. 2.

[2] London Passenger Transport Act, 1933, s. 1.

[3] British Overseas Airways Act, 1939, s. 1.

[4] For a discussion of the characteristics and nomenclature of public corporations see D. N. Chester: 'Public Corporations and the Classification of Administrative Bodies', I, *Political Studies* (1953), pp. 34–52.

[5] By the Airways Corporations Act, 1949, British South American Airways Corporation was merged with BOAC, so that there are now only two corporations, BOAC and BEAC. See, also, the Civil Aviation Act, 1949.

the London Passenger Transport Act, 1933, was transferred to the Transport Commission. In regard to road transport services a duty was imposed on the Commission to acquire undertakings engaged (in 1946) to a predominant extent in ordinary long-distance carriage of goods for hire or reward. This formula covered the road haulage industry other than that part of it which was engaged in purely local transport. Certain specialized types of vehicles were, however, excluded, such as tank vehicles engaged in the carriage of liquids, those used for furniture removals, the carriage of meat, livestock, felled timber, etc. Moreover, vehicles used by manufacturers, traders or other business concerns for the conveyance of goods in the conduct of their business were not nationalized, although when the Bill was originally presented they were included.

It was left to the commission to acquire those road haulage concerns which fell into the category mentioned above, and a commercial operator could require the Commission to take over his business if he fell into that category.

In regard to passenger road services, the British Transport Commission were authorized to prepare and submit at any time to the Minister of Transport schemes for passenger road transport services covering specified areas. A scheme was to promote or facilitate the co-ordination of the passenger transport services provided in the area, whether by road or by rail. They had also to secure the provision of adequate, suitable and efficient passenger road services to meet the needs of the area. The Transport Commission were required to review the existing road passenger services in Great Britain as soon as possible in order to decide which areas should have schemes.

Coast-wise shipping was not nationalized and the merchant marine was left untouched except for cross-Channel services to France and Ireland which formed part of the railway undertakings. Trade harbours, on the other hand, came within the ambit of the statute and were accorded somewhat similar treatment to that provided for motor bus and motor coach services. Thus, schemes of management and development of trade harbours could be prepared by the Commission and submitted to the Minister of Transport.

The Transport Act, 1953, repealed the Transport Commission's powers to prepare schemes of organization and management for passenger road services, and for the management and development of trade harbours. The Commission can no longer provide port facilities except where it was providing such facilities in July 1952, and had power to provide such facilities otherwise than by virtue of the Act of 1947.

The main purpose of the Act was to de-nationalize the road haulage industry. A duty was imposed on the British Transport Commission to dispose promptly of all the property they held for the purposes of the Road Haulage Executive, which was to be abolished. The Transport Commission were authorized to retain only vehicles or other road haulage property required for the efficient conduct of some other part of their undertaking, and even then ministerial permission was required. Vehicles belonging to the railway companies prior to nationalization might be retained and a slight increase was permitted over the 1947 figures. The unladen weight of vehicles retained was not to exceed five-fourths of that of all the vehicles possessed by the railway companies in 1947.

A new body called the Road Haulage Disposal Board was created to supervise and approve the manner in which the British Transport Commission disposed of their road haulage business in accordance with the provisions of the 1953 Act. The Disposal Board were appointed by the Minister of Transport. The members included, in addition to a chairman and deputy chairman, a nominee of the British Transport Commission and persons representing road haulage interests. The British Transport Commission were henceforth made subject as regards goods vehicles to the licensing system for road haulage services introduced by the Road and Rail Traffic Act, 1933, in the same manner as any other operator. The general licensing provisions of that statute were, however, modified in order to secure that the licensing authorities should in future have regard primarily to the interests of traders or other consumers requiring facilities rather than, as hitherto, to the interests of the transport undertakers.

The policy of denationalizing the road haulage undertakings acquired by the British Transport Commission under the 1947 Act was modified by a later statute. There were two reasons for the change. One was that it was found difficult, and indeed impossible, to dispose of all the vehicles. The other was that the Conservative Government of which Sir Anthony Eden was the head had discovered the great value to industry of the trunk service network which the Road Haulage Executive were running, and wished to preserve it.[1] Accordingly, the Transport Commission were authorized by another statute, the Transport (Disposal of Road Haulage Property) Act, 1956, to transfer to companies remaining under their control some 8,000 lorries, which was 4,500 more than had previously been authorized.

The Act of 1953 considerably reduced the scope of the general duties falling on the British Transport Commission. They are now limited to

[1] Statement by Mr J. Boyd-Carpenter, the Minister of Transport and Civil Aviation, in the House of Commons. 574 HC Deb. 5s., col. 573 (July 21, 1955).

the provision of railway services, an adequate and properly co-ordinated system of passenger transport services in the London Passenger Transport region, and the provision of other transport services and facilities for traffic on the inland waterways to the extent the Commission consider expedient. In performing these tasks the Commission are to pay due regard to 'efficiency, economy and safety of operation and to the needs of the public, agriculture, commerce and industry'.[1] This has replaced the much more ambitious duty formulated by the 1947 Act of providing 'an efficient, adequate, economical and properly integrated system of public inland transport and port facilities . . .'[2]

The Electricity Act, 1947, completed the movement toward the nationalization of electricity supply which began in 1926 when the Central Electricity Board was set up to construct and operate a nationwide system of interconnected generating stations known as the grid. The earlier legislation introduced a large measure of public ownership and control over the generation and distribution in bulk of electricity, but left the detailed distribution to consumers in the hands of 'authorized undertakers'. Approximately two-thirds of electricity distribution was owned and operated by local authorities and one-third by public utility companies. Now the whole mass of these undertakings has passed into national ownership and an integrated system of public management. The Central Electricity Generating Board[3] are the body responsible for generation of electricity, while twelve public corporations known as Area Electricity Boards are responsible for distribution. In Scotland there are two Scottish Electricity Boards which are responsible for both generation and distribution.

The Gas Act, 1948, transfers the entire gas industry to public ownership. Previously about a third of the industry was owned by town councils and two-thirds by public utility companies. It is now operated by a series of twelve area gas boards covering large regions with a National Gas Council in charge of a few central functions.

The New Towns Act, 1946, authorizes the Minister of Housing and Local Government to create new towns either on virgin land or on the sites of existing small towns or villages; and he can establish development corporations for this purpose. About 14 development corporations have so far been created.

The Overseas Resources Development Act, 1948, created the Colonial Development Corporation. The Act also set up the Overseas Food Corporation, which was formed to undertake the ill-prepared and ill-fated

[1] Transport Act, 1953, s. 25 (1).
[2] Transport Act, 1947, s. 53 (1) and (3).
[3] Electricity Act, 1957, s. 2.

groundnut project in Tanganyika. After the failure of the groundnut project the remainder of the Overseas Food Corporation's undertaking was transferred to the Tanganyika Agricultural Corporation and the Overseas Food Corporation dissolved.[1]

The work of the Colonial Development Corporation has been restricted since 1952, partly owing to the policy of the Conservative Government, and partly because several of the earlier schemes were not really sound and had to be abandoned. The Corporation announced in their report for 1952[2] that new projects would in future be taken up only on a strictly commercial basis, although this would exclude some types of desirable development, especially agricultural settlements. The Government stated in Parliament in July 1953[3] that the primary duty and principal purpose of the Corporation was unchanged, but that new projects must continue to show, after severe investigation, the likelihood of being at least self-supporting from a financial point of view if not definitely profitable. They would also be expected to enable commercial interests and the local governments of the territories concerned to be associated with the projects.[4]

In 1956 the statutory purpose of the Colonial Development Corporation was revised. They now have the more modest duty of 'assisting colonial territories in accordance with the provisions of this Act, in the development of their economies'.[5] The new enactment lists the specific powers of the Corporation in greater detail, and specifies the types of enterprise in which they may engage, with savings for activities on which they were already engaged. The Corporation are not now responsible for social services such as health or education, nor for the comprehensive planning of development, nor even for power and communications, which should be embodied in the plans of the colonial government. Their rôle is to assist in developments for which capital cannot be obtained elsewhere, if possible in association with the government of the territory and private enterprise.

The Iron and Steel Act, 1949, provided for the establishment of the Iron and Steel Corporation of Great Britain, and for the transfer to the Corporation of the securities of ninety-six named companies engaged in

[1] Overseas Food Corporation Act, 1954, s. 1. Overseas Food Corporation (Date of Transfer) Order, 1955, s. I. 1955. No. 311. For a good account of the groundunt project see Alan Wood: *The Groundnut Affair* (1950).

[2] HMSO, HC 158/1952-3, para. 7 (2) (a).

[3] 183 H.L. Deb. 5s., cols. 1226-37 (July 30, 1953); see also 176 HL Deb. 5s., cols. 1602-13 (May 28, 1952).

[4] *Colonial Development Corporation Annual Report 1953*, HMSO, HC 148/1953-4, para. 7; Annual Report and Accounts 1955, p. 9.

[5] Overseas Resources Development Act, 1956, s. 1 (1), now replaced by the consolidating Act of 1959.

the iron and steel industry. The general duty of the Corporation was to promote the efficient and economic supply of iron ore and the production of steel. This statute was repealed by the Iron and Steel Act, 1953, which was passed to carry out the Conservative Government's policy of denationalizing the industry. For this purpose all the property and rights of the Iron and Steel Corporation were transferred to an Iron and Steel Holding and Realization Agency, and the Corporation was dissolved. The Agency, whose chairman and members are appointed by the Treasury, had a duty imposed on them of securing the return to private ownership of the undertakings owned by the companies originally taken over by the Corporation. An adequate consideration was to be obtained for these valuable assets, and pending their disposal the Agency were to exercise the powers of a holding company in such a manner as to promote the efficient direction of the subsidiaries. The Agency were not obliged to dispose of the undertakings in the form in which they were taken over in the first instance, and a great deal of reorganization and 'dressing-up' of the iron and steel companies has actually taken place. An Iron and Steel Board were established by the 1953 Act to exercise supervisory and consultative functions in the iron and steel industry, particularly with regard to the provision of plant, the fixing of maximum prices, research and training, imports and the distribution of raw materials and steel products.

The Forestry Commission were originally set up under the Forestry Act, 1919, and therefore belonged to the earlier phase of the movement; but changes in the constitutional status and characteristics of the Commission introduced by the Forestry Act, 1945, have brought them into line with the more modern type of public corporation.

Several other public corporations have been created during the past fifteen years. There are, for example, the Regional Hospital Boards set up in connection with the National Health Service.[1] But these relate to a social service rather than a nationalized industry. The National Research Development Corporation[2] were established to secure the development or exploitation of inventions resulting from public research and of any other invention which is not being properly developed.

The most important recent example of a public corporation is the Atomic Energy Authority. During the initial period of public enterprise in this field, responsibility lay with the Ministry of Supply. As greater emphasis came to be placed on the industrial uses of atomic energy, the arguments in favour of 'a form of control of the project which is more akin to the structure of a big industrial organization than to that of a

[1] National Health Service Act, 1946, s. 11 and Sch. III.
[2] Development of Inventions Act, 1948, ss. 1 and 2.

government department'[1] became stronger. Moreover, they were likely to become even stronger as the need increased for closer contact and co-operation with both private industry and the nationalized industries. It was these considerations which led a Conservative Government to decide that the most swift and effective development of atomic energy would be achieved if responsibility were transferred from the Ministry of Supply to a public corporation carrying out an approved policy and subject to financial limitations. 'They believe,' said a White Paper entitled *The Future Organization of the UK Atomic Energy Project*, 'that the necessary flexibility and speed of decision can best be obtained from the Board of an organization run on industrial lines, and with no responsibility outside the field of atomic energy.'[2]

The Atomic Energy Authority Act was passed in 1954 to give effect to these conclusions. It provides for the establishment of the Atomic Energy Authority; for the transfer thereto of the powers of the Lord President of the Council in relation to atomic energy, and the acquisition, production and disposal of radioactive substances. The Authority may not develop or produce weapons of war except in accordance with arrangements made with the Minister of Supply, although they may carry out experimental work which may lead to improved types of explosive nuclear assemblies for atomic weapons.[3]

It was strange to find that the Labour Opposition criticized the proposal to set up the Atomic Energy Authority, since the Labour Party has been a strong advocate of entrusting nationalized industries to public corporations. Mr George Strauss, MP, a former Labour Minister of Supply, made the points that the existing arrangements had been successful; that a change of organization would inevitably have a disruptive effect and slow down progress; that there was a valuable relation between atomic energy and other scientific research and development work for military purposes carried on under the Ministry of Supply; that so many Ministers would be concerned with controlling the Authority that control would be cumbersome; and that the independent position of the Lord President as a Cabinet Minister free from departmental interests would be jeopardized.[4] In the House of Lords Lord Wilmot, who had also been a Labour Minister of Supply, declared that government control must be closer over atomic energy than over the other nationalized industries, and hence the Authority would embody

[1] *The Future Organization of the UK Atomic Energy Project*, HMSO, Cmd. 8986/1955, para. 8.

[2] HMSO, Cmd. 8986/1953, para. 9.

[3] Atomic Energy Authority Act, 1954, ss. 1 and 2.

[4] 521 HC Deb. 5s., cols. 2286-94 (December 10, 1953); 524 HC Deb. 5s., cols. 860-5 (March 1, 1957).

the worst features of a government department and a public corporation; that the salaries of scientists transferred from the Civil Service to the Authority would be increased, thus involving unnecessary expense and causing anomalies; and finally, that atomic energy was not really a commercial undertaking at all, since it was not financially self-supporting and would only have one important customer in the industrial sphere—namely, the Central Electricity Authority.[1]

It is true that the Authority possess certain special features which distinguish them from the other public corporations. Their commercial functions are at present limited to the sale of isotopes on a small scale, though the Authority may later earn part of their revenue from the sale of nuclear fuel elements. Their chief function is to design prototype nuclear power stations, such as the one at Calder Hall; the construction of successful prototypes will be taken up by leading commercial firms and they will be operated by the Central Electricity Generating Board.[2] The Authority's overall policy must be determined by the Government owing to the overwhelming importance of atomic energy, both for military and civil purposes.[3] And finally, the Authority will for a long time to come be mainly or wholly dependent on Government grants, with all that that involves in terms of Treasury and parliamentary control over finance. Lord Salisbury, Lord President of the Council, made the position abundantly clear when he said in the House of Lords that 'in view of the political, international and security aspects of atomic energy, and the complete financial dependence of the Authority on public funds, the relations between the Government and the Authority will have to be closer than is the case with corporations whose activities are mainly non-contentious, domestic, non-secret and financially self-supporting'.[4]

Despite these unusual features, the decision to establish the Atomic Energy Authority was justified. The Corporation are assured of freedom in the day-to-day management of their affairs, including their finances,[5] and this is a most valuable attribute possessed by a public corporation. The importance of atomic energy to the United Kingdom and the world is so vast and so manifest that large views are likely to prevail in regard to financial grants to the Authority; and the spectre of a parsimonious Treasury holding up the most promising developments for the sake of a few millions is unlikely to be a realistic one.

[1] 185 HL Deb. 5s., cols. 40-5 (December 14, 1953); 187 HL Deb. 5s., cols. 482-90 (May 11, 1934).

[2] R. D'Arcy Best: 'The UK Atomic Energy Authority', XXXIV *Public Administration* (1956), pp. 15-6.

[3] HMSO, Cmd. 8986/1953, para. 17.

[4] 187 HL Deb. 5s., col. 478 (May 11, 1954).

[5] HMSO, Cmd. 8986/1953, para. 17.

Another public corporation which may be mentioned is the Independent Television Authority, set up by the Television Act, 1954. This statute was passed to implement the Conservative Government's decision to introduce commercial television in addition to the services provided by the BBC. Very strong opposition was displayed in Parliament by the Labour Party, and outside Parliament by many leading Conservatives and by eminent men in various walks of life, and by almost the whole Press. Sponsoring came in for widespread objection and was ruled out; and in the House of Lords debate on the subject the elder statesmen of all parties, with one exception, were strongly in favour of public service broadcasting as exemplified by the BBC.[1]

The ITA are a body whose functions are in part constructional, in part negotiating, in part operational, and in part regulatory. Their task is to provide television services additional to those of the BBC for as much of the United Kingdom, the Isle of Man and the Channel Islands as is reasonably practicable. They must provide and use broadcasting stations, see that they are equipped, and arrange for the distribution of programmes from broadcast relay stations. The programmes are provided by programme contractors who operate under agreements made with the Authority. They are chosen by the ITA and pay money to the latter out of revenue derived from advertisements. The ITA may themselves provide programmes needed to secure a balanced presentation in the subject matter, or to fill in gaps between contracts, but their chief responsibility is to see that the provisions of the Act are carried out by the contractors in respect of the content and balance of the programmes, the broadcasting of advertisements, the inclusion of sufficient material of British origin and performance, the accuracy and impartiality of news bulletins, impartiality in matters of political or industrial controversy, the offer of prizes or gifts, religious services or propaganda, and the observance of standards of taste and decency.[2]

The public corporations with which we are concerned in this book are those established to administer nationalized industries. But public corporations have also been set up in recent years for quite different purposes. The British Council, for example, were created in 1934 to promote abroad a wider knowledge of the United Kingdom and of the English language, and to develop closer cultural relations with other countries. The Arts Council, established in 1946 by Royal Charter, have as their purpose to develop greater knowledge, understanding and practice of the fine arts. The Council are enjoined to make the fine arts more accessible to the public.

[1] Lord Simon of Wythenshawe: *The BBC from Within* (1953), pp. 41-4.
[2] Television Act, 1954, ss. 1-6.

Even in the purely economic sphere the public corporation has been used for a variety of purposes. The White Fish Authority are a public corporation charged with regulating, reorganizing and assisting the white fish industry. There has never been any intention of nationalizing the industry.

The Authority were appointed under the Sea Fish Industry Act, 1951, introduced by the second Attlee Government. The measure arose out of the failure of a White Fish Commission which had been established in 1938 to implement the recommendations of the Duncan Report of 1936 by means of marketing schemes covering different sections of the industry.[1] The near and middle water fishing fleets were in need of financial help to enable them to replace their boats and other equipment. There was also a need to bring about a better spacing of landings, and improvements in the stowage of catches and methods of preservation. The marketing arrangements could also be made more effective. All these reforms would assist the industry.

The White Fish Authority are a small body of five members, all of whom serve part-time, appointed by the relevant Ministers. They have power to regulate the handling and storage of white fish on fishing vessels, and after landing. They can order the timing of landings so as to secure regularity of supplies and prevent congestion in harbours. They can regulate the sale of white fish and determine the conditions of sale other than the price. They can prescribe standards of quality.[2] They can undertake research and experiment, establish selling agencies and storage facilities abroad in order to promote the export of white fish, provide and operate processing plants in Great Britain, and conduct publicity campaigns to encourage the consumption of white fish.

One of their most important functions is to make loans to fishing undertakings to enable them to acquire or improve their fishing vessels, gear or processing plants. In doing this they can take or acquire shares or other interests in any company engaged in the industry.[3]

The Authority are advised by the White Fish Industry Advisory Council, a large body representing all sections of the industry. The Authority receive loans from the Exchequer. This expenditure on current account is met mainly by a levy on landed fish; and there would seem to be no reason why money borrowed from the Exchequer should not in due course be repaid with interest.

One other public corporation we may note is the Sugar Board, con-

[1] See the speech by Mr T. Williams, Minister of Agriculture and Fisheries on the second reading of the Sea Fish Industry Bill 483 HC Deb. 5s., cols. 322 ff. (January 25, 1951).

[2] Sea Fish Industry Act, 1951, s. 5.

[3] *Ib.*, s. 4.

stituted under the Sugar Act, 1956. The background to this Act is a long history of state intervention in the British sugar-beet industry, including the payment of subsidies to sugar-beet growers and refiners. The history is too complicated to relate in detail here; however, in 1936 the British Sugar Corporation was formed by the amalgamation of the sugar-beet companies. The Corporation were, and are, a public limited company with private shareholders, but the chairman and two directors are nominated by the Government. The articles of association provide for Government control of the Corporation's policies.

The functions of the Sugar Board in relation to the British Sugar Corporation are financial. If the revenues of the Corporation for any financial year beginning after March 31, 1957, fall short of the total sums properly chargeable by the Corporation to revenue account, the Sugar Board must make good the deficiency; and if for any financial year the Corporation's revenues exceed the total sums properly chargeable to revenue account, the Corporation must pay the excess to the Sugar Board.[1] Any 'incentive payments' (i.e. efficiency payments) which are due to the Corporation must be paid by the Sugar Board;[2] and the Sugar Board may, with the consent of the Minister of Agriculture and the approval of the Treasury, advance sums not exceeding £30 millions in aggregate to the Corporation to provide working capital or to enable the Corporation to meet seasonal outgoings properly chargeable to revenue account.[3]

But more important are the Sugar Board's functions in relation to Commonwealth sugar. Agreements had been made with Commonwealth countries whereby the Government undertook to purchase sugar in bulk. In 1955 the Conservative Government announced their intention of bringing to an end the system of State trading in sugar which they disliked in principle. They wished, however, to continue in force the arrangements made under the Commonwealth sugar agreements.[4]

Prior to 1956 all imported sugar—most of it coming from Commonwealth countries—was purchased and transported by the Ministry of Agriculture, who sold it to refiners in Britain at a price sufficient to cover the average cost to the Ministry. The Sugar Board was established to act thenceforth as the buying agent and to sell the sugar at the

[1] Sugar Act, 1936, s. 20 (1).

[2] *Ib.*, s. 20 (2).

[3] *Ib.*, s. 21 (1) and (3). The Sugar Board must be distinguished from the now defunct Sugar Commission, who acted as an intermediary between the Government and the British Sugar Corporation. The Sugar Commission's powers are now exercised by the Minister of Agriculture and the Secretary of State for Scotland, acting jointly. *Ib.*, ss. 23 and 32; see also s. 18 (9).

[4] White Paper entitled *Future Arrangements for the Marketing of Sugar*, HMSO, Cmd. 9519/1955.

market price to the British refiner, who would be responsible for shipping the commodity to Britain. If the negotiated price is higher than the world market price the Sugar Board will sustain a loss. In that event they balance their revenue account by levying a surcharge on all imported and home-produced sugar which is to be consumed in Britain. If on the other hand the Commonwealth buying price is lower than the world price, the Board will make a profit, which is distributed to the sugar refiners, and no surcharge would then be levied. The Sugar Board was described by Mr Heathcoat Amory when Minister of Agriculture as merely an accountancy agency.[1] It is probably the least important example of a public corporation to be found in Britain, but it shows how diverse are the uses to which this institutional device can be applied.[2]

CONSTITUTIONAL STATUS OF THE PUBLIC CORPORATION

The original impetus to the movement for public corporations came from a twofold desire to secure freedom from parliamentary supervision over management on the one hand and Treasury control over personnel and finance on the other. Both these normal features of British government were regarded, rightly or wrongly, as likely to hamper efficiency and restrict initiative in undertakings of an industrial or commercial character. Earl Attlee, after serving as Postmaster-General in the second Labour Government of 1929, expressed the view in an article[3] that Treasury control is wholly incompatible with the flexibility necessary for the conduct of a business concern. While conceding the right of the Treasury to be consulted on such matters as the time for making capital issues, and while agreeing that the pay of Post Office employees must be related to the general standard of remuneration in the Civil Service, he stated: 'I am quite clear that Treasury control as now exercised should be abolished.' On the question of parliamentary control Earl Attlee observed that it was sometimes said that parliamentary interpellation keeps public administration at a high level. This, he said, is not true. 'It tends to timidity and centralization and has militated against the adoption of a public relations technique in the service . . . . The Minister and his principal officials, who ought to be concerned with major problems, are constantly diverted to deal with matters which owe their importance only to the status of those who bring them forward.'

[1] 545 HC Deb. 5s., cols. 2019 ff (November 10, 1955); HC Deb., Standing Committee A (December 6, 1955), col. 69, Mr Amory; December 13, 1955, col. 157, Mr Amory.

[2] For details of the Sugar Board see Sugar Act, 1956.

[3] 'Post Office Reform', *New Statesman and Nation*, November 7, 1931.

MINISTERIAL CONTROL

The elimination in whole or part of ministerial responsibility to Parliament for the day-to-day administration of the undertaking is a vital feature of the public corporation. Here we must be careful to avoid loose generalizations, since the position is by no means static or clearly defined.

The earlier generation of public corporations, ranging from the Port of London Authority to the Central Electricity Board or the London Passenger Transport Board, were largely immune from ministerial direction or control save in regard to a few matters which seldom included any of major importance. Even the British Overseas Airways Act, 1939, which was the last Act prior to the Second World War establishing a public corporation, gave the Secretary of State for Air no general power of direction.[1]

When we turn to the post-war legislation we find that the controlling powers of Ministers have become much wider and more general. Thus the Minister of Transport and Civil Aviation, after consultation with either of the airways corporations, may give to BEA or BOAC 'directions of a general character as to the exercise and performance by that corporation of their functions in relation to matters appearing to the Minister to affect the national interest; and the corporation concerned shall give effect to any such directions'.[2]

The Minister of Power possesses similar powers of giving directions of a general character to the National Coal Board,[3] to the Electricity Boards and Electricity Council,[4] and to the Gas Boards and Gas Council;[5] the Minister of Transport has similar powers in relation to the British Transport Commission.[6] This formulation of ministerial power over the public corporation may be regarded as the standard model in recent legislation.

The powers of the Prime Minister over the Atomic Energy Authority are, however, wider and more far-reaching than those possessed by other Ministers over the nationalized industries mentioned above. The reasons for this different treatment are to be found in the exceptional nature of atomic energy. It is at once the most dangerous and the most promising source of energy ever to be discovered by man. It contains

[1] Though certain activities of BOAC were prohibited under the Act except with the authority of a ministerial order (s. 4), and the Secretary of State was given certain specified powers of direction.

[2] Air Corporations Act, 1949, s. 5.

[3] Coal Industry Nationalization Act, 1946, s. 3.

[4] Electricity Act, 1947, ss. 5, 6; Electricity Act, 1957 s. 8.

[5] Gas Act, 1948, s. 7.

[6] Transport Act, 1947, s. 4.

within it the possibility of final disaster and of unlimited benefits to the human race. The exploitation and development of so vital a field of activity must inevitably be liable to governmental direction without reservation, to whatever extent the responsible Minister thinks fit. It was for this reason, and because of the dependence of atomic energy development on money voted by Parliament, that the Labour Party in Parliament opposed the establishment of the Atomic Energy Authority. They considered a public corporation unsuitable and favoured direct Government administration.

The relations between the Chancellor of the Exchequer and the Bank of England are formulated in somewhat different terms. The Treasury are authorized to give such directions to the Bank[1] as, after consultation with the Governor of the Bank, they think necessary in the public interest. The Bank of England Act then provides that subject to any such directions the affairs of the Bank shall be managed by the Court of Directors in accordance with the charter of the Bank and any by-laws which have been made under it. There is no express statutory obligation on the Bank to give effect to the directions of the Treasury; but such a duty is clearly implied. The directions need not necessarily be of a general character.

The Overseas Resources Development Act, 1948, gives the Secretary of State for the Colonies powers over the Colonial Development Corporation similar to those which apply to the corporations in Britain operating coal, gas, and electricity.[2]

The Forestry Commission, set up in 1919, have been brought under far greater ministerial control and direction by the Forestry Act, 1945, which requires the Commissioners to comply with such directions as may be given them by the responsible Ministers. The BBC, which was created by Royal Charter, is in an exceptional position, but the Postmaster-General exercises considerable powers over it. Thus he may require the Corporation to broadcast government announcements, and he has a power to require the Corporation to refrain from broadcasting any matter, either particular or general. Furthermore, the Corporation are dependent for revenue on a proportion of the receipts from the issue of wireless receiving licences by the Post Office. In time of emergency, the Postmaster-General can take over all or part of the wireless transmission stations of the BBC.

In addition to these general powers of direction Ministers are given specific powers over the public corporations in regard to particular matters of special importance. Thus, most of the public corporations, in

[1] Bank of England Act, 1946, s. 4.

[2] Overseas Resources Development Act, 1948, s. 9.

framing programmes of reorganization or development involving substantial capital outlay, are required to act on lines settled from time to time with the approval of the Minister. The same applies to their activities in respect of training, education, and research.[1] The Minister is to determine the form of the annual accounts and is to appoint the auditors each year.

There are large numbers of matters in regard to which Ministers have been given statutory powers and responsibilities. These cover a wide variety of topics, including the acquisition by the British Transport Commission of a controlling share in a motorbus or motorcoach undertaking; making regulations concerning pensions for employees of the Commission and of transferred undertakings; authorizing the compulsory acquisition of land; variations in the areas of Area Gas or Electricity Boards, the dissolution of existing Boards or the setting up of new ones; authorizing Gas Boards in special cases to charge for gas otherwise than by the therm, etc.[2]

PARLIAMENTARY RESPONSIBILITY

It has long been accepted that while a public corporation should be immune from parliamentary questioning on matters of day-to-day management, it should not be wholly free either from responsibility to Parliament or from ministerial control. The position was adumbrated in the Report of the Broadcasting Committee set up in 1925. 'We assume,' said the report, 'that the Postmaster-General would be the parliamentary spokesman on broad questions of policy, though we think it essential that the Corporation should not be subject to the continuing ministerial guidance and direction which apply to Government offices. The progress of science and the harmonies of art will be hampered by too rigid rules and too constant a supervision by the State.'[3] Shortly after the British Broadcasting Corporation was established by Royal Charter in 1927, the Postmaster-General stated in Parliament that he was responsible for questions of general policy but not for questions of detail and particular points of the service.[4]

The extent to which Ministers should be subject to parliamentary questioning in respect of public corporations has been debated at considerable length in the House of Commons. On December 4, 1947, Mr

[1] Coal Industry Nationalization Act, 1946, s. 3; Electricity Act, 1947, s. 5; Electricity Act, 1957, s. 8; Transport Act, 1947, s. 4; Iron and Steel Act, 1949, s. 4.

[2] A complete list is given in the *Special Report from the Select Committee on Nationalized Industries*, HMSO, HC 120/1955-6.

[3] HMSO, Cmd. 2599/1926, p. 13.

[4] 206 HC Deb. 5s., cols. 976 and 977 (May 17, 1927).

Herbert Morrison, Lord President of the Council and Leader of the House of Commons, declared in Parliament:

'A large degree of independence for the boards in matters of current administration is vital to their efficiency as commercial undertakings. A Minister is responsible to Parliament for action which he may take in relation to a board, or action coming within his statutory powers which he has not taken. This is the principle that determines generally the matters on which a Question may be put down for answer by a Minister in the House of Commons. Thus, the Minister would be answerable for any directions he gave in the national interest, and for the action which he took on proposals which a board was required by Statute to lay before him.

'It would be contrary to this principle, and to the clearly expressed intention of Parliament in the governing legislation, if Ministers were to give, in replies in Parliament or in letters, information about day-to-day matters. Undue intervention by the Minister would tend to impair the board's commercial freedom of action. The boards of socialized industries are under an obligation to submit annual reports and accounts which are to be laid before Parliament. In the Government's view, it is right that Parliament should from time to time review the work of the boards, on the basis of the reports and accounts presented to Parliament.'[1]

An important debate took place on this statement on March 3, 1948. In this debate[2] a considerable measure of agreement was shown both by supporters and by opponents of the Government that it is desirable to increase the rights of members to question Ministers about public corporations. This debate showed that members wished to avoid investigating day-to-day management, but that it was not possible to draw a rigid line between management and administration. The matter was further discussed in Parliament at a later date, and subsequently the Speaker made a proposal that he should exercise a greater latitude in admitting questions about nationalized industries which he considered of public importance.[3]

Under the rules of procedure of the House of Commons, if a Minister has once refused to answer a question, no further question dealing with the same class of matters can be admitted to the question paper. This had worked harshly and had played the largest part in excluding questions about nationalized industries. While leaving unchanged the rule which forbids questions on matters outside ministerial responsibility,

[1] 445 HC Deb. 5s., col. 566 (December 4, 1947).
[2] 448 HC Deb. 5s., cols. 391 ff. (March 3, 1948).
[3] 451 HC Deb. 5s., cols. 1635 and 1636 (June 7, 1948).

the Speaker proposed, if general approval were given, to modify the rule against repetition by allowing questions to be asked about matters on which information has previously been refused, if they are of sufficient public importance to justify the concession. The right of Ministers to refuse to answer still continues in this as in every other sphere of public affairs. Both the Government and the Opposition readily accepted this proposal.

This and other aspects of parliamentary responsibility will be discussed more fully in later chapters.[1]

LEADING PRINCIPLES

The first essential characteristic of the public corporation is, then, its freedom from parliamentary inquiry into the management of the concern as distinct from its policy. We cannot, however, say that the public corporation is in any sense immune from political interference since it is subject to a considerable degree of ministerial control. This involves responsibility to Parliament by the Minister for at least those matters on which he can control the corporation. Recent debates in Parliament have made it clear that there will be in each session full-dress debates on the work of at least some of the public corporations. The purpose of these debates will be to discuss the general policies which the corporations are pursuing and the efficiency and economy of their administration.

The second leading principle is disinterestedness. The statute or charter formulates in each case the public purpose which each corporation is to follow. Thus, the National Coal Board are charged by statute with the duty of securing the efficient development of the coal-mining industry and making coal available in such qualities and in such quantities and at such prices as may seem to them best calculated to further the public interest in all respects. The Central Electricity Generating Board are enjoined to develop and mantain an efficient, co-ordinated and economical system of supply of electricity in bulk for all parts of England and Wales, while the Area Electricity Boards are to plan and carry out an efficient and economical distribution of electricity supplies to consumers in their areas. Each of the nationalized air lines (BEA and BOAC) is to secure that the air services which they provide are developed to the best advantage and at reasonable charges. Analogous provisions are contained in the statutes relating to the other corporations, with the sole exception of the Atomic Energy Act, which imposes no general duty on the Authority.

A proposal was made when the Bill was before Parliament that the

[1] See chs. VII and VIII.

Authority should be given a general duty to develop the knowledge, production and use of atomic energy. This was rejected by the Government, on the ground that it might conflict with the overriding powers of the Lord President, who was at that time entrusted with general policy. (He has since been replaced in that capacity by the Prime Minister.) 'It is the Government's declared intention,' the Solicitor-General informed the House of Commons, 'to retain in their own hands the general policy in relation to development, that is, to the knowledge, production and use of atomic energy, and to delegate the execution of that policy to the Authority.'[1]

'The public corporation', wrote Mr Herbert Morrison in 1933, 'must be no mere capitalist business, the be-all and end-all of which is profits and dividends, even though it will, quite properly, be expected to pay its way. It must have a different atmosphere at its board table from that of a shareholders' meeting; its board and its officers must regard themselves as the high custodians of the public interest. In selecting the Board, these considerations must be in the mind of the Minister.'[2]

The principle of disinterestedness cannot, however, be considered apart from the question of profit-making and financial policy generally. Commercial companies may claim that they are in many instances providing goods or services in a manner which serves the public interest. They cannot, however, be regarded as disinterested for the simple reason that their main object is to make a profit for their proprietors. This is not the case with a public corporation, and here we strike a fundamental distinction between the joint stock company and the public corporation.

A public corporation has no shareholders in the ordinary sense of the term. Even in the case of the older types, such as the Port of London Authority or the London Passenger Transport Board, the stockholders were no more than creditors of the corporation possessing rights to interest on their holdings but without voting rights or control over the management.[3]

In the more recent examples the capital is provided in the form of assets taken over from private or municipal ownership and capitalized by means of stock bearing fixed rates of interest. In some instances it is Government stock.[4] In others it is stock issued by the corpora-

[1] 525 HC Deb. 5s., col. 1135 (March 23, 1954).

[2] *Socialization and Transport* (1933), pp. 156 and 157.

[3] The holders of London Passenger Transport stock could in certain circumstances apply to the High Court for a Receiver to be appointed. But this was the limit of their power. See London Passenger Transport Act, 1933, s. 39 (14).

[4] Coal Industry Nationalization Act, 1946, s. 21; Cable and Wireless Act, 1946, s. 1.

tion itself with a Treasury guarantee.[1] In either event there is no one corresponding to the private shareholder in a joint stock company, nor can there be any shareholders' meeting. Professor Friedmann rightly says, 'The public corporation has no shares and no shareholders, either private or public.'[2] The equity is owned by the nation.

The principle of disinterestedness is further emphasized by the fact that in no case is a public corporation required or enjoined to make a profit. The statutes require in the case of most of the public corporations, such as those concerned with coal, transport, electricity, and gas, that the corporation shall carry on their undertaking in such a manner as to pay their way out of revenue over a period of years.[3] Thus, while in any particular year there may be a surplus or a deficit, the general intention is that the undertakings shall not be run at a loss. There is no requirement of this kind applicable to the airways corporations, which received subsidies from the Exchequer for a few years after they were first set up, though these have now ceased.

There is, on the other hand, nothing to prevent a public corporation from operating at a profit, nor any legal limit to such profit. In the event of a profit being made, how is it to be disposed of in accordance with the principle of disinterestness? The word 'profit' is really inappropriate. 'Surplus' is a better term. The Electricity Act, 1957, enacts that any excess in the annual revenue of an Electricity Board is to be applied for such purposes of the Board as the Board may determine.[4] This provision applies both to the Generating Board and to each of the Area Boards. The Minister of Power is, however, empowered to give directions, with Treasury approval, concerning the application of any excess revenue. The National Coal Board have a similar obligation.[5] The Colonial Development Corporation are under similar obligations in regard to the balancing of their revenue account and the disposal of surplus revenue.[6] We can see from these provisions that the law precludes a public corporation from distributing profits among stockholders or proprietors; and that no payment to employees or executives may be made by way of commission on profits in the manner which is common in the case of managing directors or directors of joint stock companies. Any surplus will normally be ploughed back into the business, placed to re-

[1] Transport Act, 1947, ss. 89 and 90; Electricity Act, 1947, ss. 40 and 42; Gas Act, 1948, ss. 43 and 45.

[2] W. Friedmann: 'The New Public Corporations and the Law', X. *Modern Law Review* (1947), p. 235.

[3] Coal Industry Nationalization Act, 1946, s. 1 (4); Transport Act, 1947, s. 3 (4); Electricity Act, 1947, s. 36 (1); Gas Act, 1948, s. 41 (1).

[4] Electricity Act, 1957, s. 22 (1).

[5] Coal Industry Nationalization Act, 1946, s. 30.

[6] Overseas Resources Development Act, 1948, s. 15.

serve, or be devoted to reducing prices, improving the service, or giving the employees better working conditions. All the statutes which set up public corporations for nationalized industries provide for the creation of reserve funds. The management of these funds is left to the discretion of the corporation concerned, subject to an overriding ministerial power to give directions, of either a general or a specific character, about the management of the fund, or the payment of money into it or out of it.

While any excess revenue made by a nationalized industry which is required to be financially self-supporting must be applied at the board's discretion to the public purposes which are laid down in the Act, there is no similar restriction in the case of the airways corporations. In their case, while the Act provides that any excess revenue shall be applied by the corporations concerned in such manner as the Minister, with the approval of the Treasury, may direct, there is a further provision to the effect that such direction may require the whole or any part of such surplus to be paid into the Exchequer so long as the total amount paid into the Exchequer by each corporation does not exceed the total grants made by the Minister to that corporation.[1]

A third principle of the public corporation is that the personnel does not form part of the Civil Service. This applies not only to the members of the board, the chairman and deputy chairman, and the chief executive, but also to the salaried and wage-earning staff. The significance of this is that there is no control by the Treasury or the Civil Service Commission or even Parliament over remuneration, conditions of service, and establishment questions generally. We cannot assume from this that the Government will at all times be willing to leave the public corporations unfettered in regard to staff questions. It may well happen that large questions of policy will be determined by ministerial directions or intervention in this as in other fields. Indeed, a White Paper on broadcasting policy contained the following statement about the level of remuneration for employees of the BBC: 'The Government consider that, in staff matters, the Corporation should retain the general independence which it now possesses, and Government control should be restricted to laying down broad limits of policy within which it should work; nevertheless, the Corporation has been informed that, while it is not rigidly bound to relate the salaries and conditions of employment of its permanent staff to those ruling in the Civil Service, it should in fixing such salaries and conditions, pay proper regard to those of the Civil Service and to the greater security offered by employment in a public corporation, as compared with employment in most business concerns.'[2] This was little

[1] Air Corporations Act, 1949, s. 19.
[2] *Broadcasting Policy*, HMSO, Cmd. 6582/1946, p. 9.

more than a general directive, but it may be an indication of future possibilities. Occasional ministerial intervention of this kind is, however, an entirely different matter from subjection to detailed Treasury regulations applicable to civil servants and the requirements of the Civil Service Commission regarding recruitment of staff. It is incomparably less onerous.

A fourth leading principle of the public corporations is that they have self-contained finance. The finances of the public corporations are divorced from the national budget,[1] although there is a considerable degree of Treasury control over certain aspects of the financial operations of the public corporations. Nevertheless, capital development is usually financed out of public funds; and in a few instances annual subventions are given from parliamentary money in aid of current expenditure.

A fifth leading principle of the public corporation is that the members and chairman are normally appointed for a fixed term of years. They do not enjoy the permanent tenure of established civil servants, nor are they subject to the vicissitudes attaching to ministerial office. The posts are non-political in the sense that they are not vacated on the fall of the government or when a new government assumes office. The chairman and members of the board may be removed by the appropriate Minister, but the intention is that they shall normally serve until the expiration of their terms of office. This is of crucial importance in determining the constitutional status of the corporation.

We can see, therefore, that the public corporation of the modern type is a constitutional innovation. It reveals a tendency to enlarge the unit of administration to a national or regional scale; to divorce the administration of industrial or public utility functions or the conduct of certain bodies providing services of a cultural kind from the ordinary activities of government; to separate the finances of these boards from the national budget; to eliminate the profit-making incentive and to substitute the public service motive.

[1] This applies only to the corporations engaged in running nationalized industries and public utility services. It is not true of the public corporations which depend for their finance on government grants, such as the British Council, the Arts Council, the new town Development Corporations, the Regional Hospital Boards, and the Agricultural Land Commission. The Atomic Energy Authority is in this respect in an exceptional position, since it depends almost entirely for funds on money voted by Parliament. Payments are made to the Authority by the Atomic Energy Office, subject to Treasury consent. Payments are made under a number of subheads, and savings under one subhead may not be used to cover excess expenditure under another subhead without Treasury consent. Unspent balances must be handed over to the Exchequer by the AEA. Even revenue from non-parliamentary sources, such as the sale of isotopes, may not be appropriated by the Authority without Treasury approval and subject to the direction of the Prime Minister. The self-contained finance which is a typical feature of most British public corporations, is thus almost wholly lacking in the case of the AEA.

'We are seeking,' wrote Mr Herbert Morrison in 1933, 'a combination of public ownership, public accountability, and business management for public ends.'[1] In a later passage he declared: 'It is important that, from the beginning, the public corporation should be regarded by all, and should regard itself, as a public concern. Its first business is the competent conduct of the undertaking committed to its charge in the public interest. It must feel that it is responsible to the nation accordingly, and that it cannot be the instrument of this or that private or sectional interest.'[2] Twenty-one years later Mr Morrison, who had played a leading part as Lord President of the Council in carrying out the Labour Party's nationalization programme, expounded the aims of his party in somewhat broader terms.

> 'What we were seeking,' he said, 'was public ownership, public appointments, a sense of accountability to the nation—John Bull—together with efficiency of day-to-day business management on commercial lines. . . . We were seeking, in its day-to-day operations, whole detachment or partial detachment from one department or another of a public corporation free from political interference, because we did not wish to upset the commercial success of the undertaking. . . . It was for reasons such as this that Parliament . . . deliberately took the line that this was a different outfit from a State Department and that we were giving this greater degree of managerial autonomy in order that we could get a higher degree of business efficiency and less red tape and bureaucracy.'[3]

LEGAL STATUS

The statutes make it quite clear that the public corporations are subject to the ordinary law of the land. Prior to 1954, there was a limitation of three years for the period in which an action in tort or contract could be commenced against a public corporation. The Law Reform (Limitation of Actions) Act, 1954, applies the same periods of limitation to public corporations, other public authorities, and all other legal persons: namely, three years for personal injury actions and six years for other actions in tort or contract. Moreover, the nationalized undertakings are liable to criminal prosecutions for any offences they may commit under the criminal law.

The legal status of a public corporation was considered by the Court of Appeal in *Tamlin* v. *Hannaford*.[4] The question before the court was

[1] Herbert Morrison: *Socialization and Transport* (1933), p. 149.
[2] *Ib.*, p. 156.
[3] 523 HC Deb. 5s., cols. 849–50 (February 8, 1954).
[4] [1950] 1 K.B. 18.

whether or not the British Transport Commission is a servant or agent of the Crown, so as not to be bound by the Rent Restriction Acts, in accordance with the principle that the Crown is not bound by a statute unless there can be gathered from it an intention that the Crown should be bound. Lord Justice Denning (as he then was), in delivering the judgment of the court, said that whether or not the Commission was a servant or agent of the Crown depended on the true construction of the Transport Act, 1947. The British Transport Commission was, he said, a statutory corporation of a kind comparatively new to English law, but it had many of the usual qualities of corporations, including defined powers, which it might not exceed. But there was a significant difference: there were no shareholders to subscribe the capital and to have a voice in its affairs. The money needed by the corporation was obtained by borrowing, and was guaranteed by the Treasury, so that if it could not repay the loss fell on the Consolidated Fund; that meant the taxpayer—the universal guarantor of the corporation. Besides the taxpayer everybody who depended on the services which it provided was concerned to see that it was properly run, and the protection of their interests was entrusted by Parliament to the Minister of Transport. The fact that the Minister of Transport exercised control over the Commission was not sufficient to make it the Crown's servant or agent. 'In the eye of the law,' said the learned Lord Justice, 'the corporation is its own master and is answerable as fully as any other person or corporation. It is not the Crown and has none of the immunities or privileges of the Crown. Its servants are not civil servants and its property is not Crown property. It is as much bound by Acts of Parliament as any other subject of the King. It is, of course, a public authority, and its purposes, no doubt, are public purposes. But it is not a Government department, nor do its powers fall within the province of Government.'[1]

It is clear, therefore, that a public corporation like the British Transport Commission, which is not the servant or agent of the Crown, is liable under the ordinary law of the land in almost the same way as a commercial company or a private person, except in so far as special immunity is conferred upon it by the legislation which creates it. This is one of the good features of the legislation creating public corporations. It may be observed that some public corporations, for example, the Central Land Board,[2] were expressly stated to act on behalf of the Crown, and they presumably have the privileges still attaching to the Crown in litigation.

[1] [1950] 1 K.B. 24.

[2] Town and Country Planning Act, 1947, s. 3 (3). The Board was abolished by S.I. no. 530 of 1959. See Town and Country Planning Act, 1954, s. 63.

The Atomic Energy Authority are placed in the same position as the other public corporations in regard to the limitation of actions; and the Authority are not to be treated as a body exercising functions on behalf of the Crown, except where this is expressly laid down by the Atomic Energy Act, 1954. There are a few special enactments to this effect contained in the statute. Thus, the Official Secrets Acts apply to the members, employees and premises of the Authority; the Authority may employ and control their own special constables; their premises are to be treated as Crown property for the purposes of the Factories Acts; the Minister of Supply may supply stores and equipment to the Authority as though they were a government department; land occupied by the Authority is to be treated as Crown property for rating purposes, and so forth.[1]

The statutes dealing with nationalization confer powers in such general terms and formulate them in such language that it will be difficult, if not impossible, for the courts to apply the doctrine of *ultra vires*.[2] For this reason attempts to invoke the aid of the judicature in defining or limiting the power of the public corporations are unlikely to be successful. In some Acts the powers of the board are formulated in subjective terms. Thus, the Coal Industry Nationalization Act, 1946, after describing the board's functions in wide terms,[3] declares that they shall have power to do anything or to enter into any transaction which *in their opinion* is calculated to facilitate the proper discharge of their duties or the carrying on by them of the activities described or anything incidental or conducive thereto.[4] If the National Coal Board declare that in their opinion it is necessary for them to provide beauty parlours for miners' wives or holiday hotels in Switzerland for miners and their families, in order to facilitate the discharge of their duties or the carrying on of their authorized activities, it is difficult to see by what means their right to do so can be effectively challenged in the courts.[5] The formulation of powers in subjective terms is, indeed, an objectionable feature of the legislation creating public corporations. It is, however, a feature which

[1] Atomic Energy Authority Act, 1954, s. 6 (5), and Third Schedule.

[2] See, e.g. *Smith v. London Transport Executive*, [1951] AC 555.

[3] Coal Industry Nationalization Act, 1946, s. 1 (2).

[4] *Ib.*, s. 1 (3).

[5] Consider *Liversidge v. Anderson and Another*, [1942] AC 206; *Greene v. Secretary of State for Home Affairs*, (1942) AC 284; *Rex v. Secretary of State for Home Affairs, Ex parte Budd*, [1942] 2 KB 14; *Point of Ayr Collieries, Limited v. Lloyd George*, [1943] 2 All ER 546; *In re City of Plymouth (City Centre) Declaratory Order, 1946, Robinson v. Minister of Town and Country Planning*, [1947] KB 702. But see *Nakkuda Ali v. Jayaratine* [1951] AC 66 (PC) at pp. 76-7, where Lord Radcliffe denies that the 'subjective' approach in *Liversidge v. Anderson* is of general applicability. See also *DPP v. Head* [1958] 2 WLR 617 (HL) especially p. 632 *per* Lord Denning.

is not present in every case: the powers of the airways corporations, for example, are not formulated subjectively, being confined to the doing of things which are *calculated to facilitate* the discharge of the functions of the corporations, and whether or not they do so is a matter into which a court can presumably enquire.[1]

Although the powers of the public corporations are expressed in such wide terms as to make the doctrine of *ultra vires* almost inapplicable, Parliament has been careful to declare that the public corporations have no authority to commit unlawful acts. A typical formulation is found in the statute nationalizing the gas industry:

> 'For the avoidance of doubt it is hereby declared that the preceding provisions in this section, so far as they confer powers on Area Boards, relate only to the capacity of Area Boards as statutory corporations, and nothing in those provisions shall be construed as authorizing the disregard by any such Board of any enactment or rule of law.'[2]

The power of the appropriate Minister to give to the board of a public corporation directions of a general character as to the exercise and performance of their functions has already been mentioned. There is no limit to the ministerial power of giving directions, and the board have an unqualified statutory duty to give effect to them.[3] It seems possible, therefore, that the board might find themselves in a dilemma if the Minister gave them an order to commit an illegal act.

ACCOUNTS AND AUDIT

As one would expect in legislation setting up great public undertakings dealing with very large sums of money both for capital expenditure and for trading purposes, careful provision is made to ensure proper auditing and accounting.[4] Parliament has in certain instances insisted that the accounts shall distinguish between different activities of the corporations.[5] The corporations are required to keep proper accounts and other records, and must prepare an annual statement of accounts in such form as the Minister may direct. In most cases the form of this statement is to conform with the best commercial standards,[6] and usually separate ac-

1 Air Corporations Act, 1949, s. 3(2).
2 Gas Act, 1948, s. 1 (9).
3 See, e.g. Transport Act, 1947, s. 4 (1).
4 For a typical enactment see the Coal Industry Nationalization Act, 1946, s. 31 (1).
5 See, e.g. Air Corporations Act, 1949, s. 22 (1).
6 Coal Industry Nationalization Act, 1946, s. 31; Electricity Act, 1947, s. 46; Overseas Resources Development Act, 1948, s. 16; Gas Act, 1948, s. 50; Air Corporations Act, 1949, s. 22; Television Act, 1954, s. 15 (1).

counts are to be provided in respect of each of the main activities of the corporation.

In almost all cases where the form of the statement of accounts is required to conform with the best commercial standards the Minister is given power to appoint auditors, and he is required to lay the accounts, with a copy of the auditors' report thereon, before each House of Parliament. The Independent Television Authority appoint their own auditor with the approval of the Postmaster-General. In the case of the development corporations for new towns the Minister is empowered to appoint an auditor, but is required to submit the audited accounts to the Comptroller and Auditor-General for his examination, certification and report thereon to both Houses of Parliament.[1] No provision is made for the appointment by the Minister of auditors to audit the accounts of the Forestry Commission, and he is merely required to transmit the accounts to the Comptroller and Auditor-General, who must deal with them in the same manner as accounts of the development corporations.[2] In the case of the British Transport Commission there is no requirement that the statement of accounts should conform with the best commercial standards, but the Minister is empowered to appoint auditors and is required to 'lay the audited accounts before Parliament'.[3]

ANNUAL REPORTS

The annual report of a public corporation is a document which is or should be of first-class importance. It affords an opportunity to the board to explain and justify their policy and to show the results of their administration. It forms the main source of public information on which debates in Parliament can be founded. It will normally be required to contain any directions which the Minister has given to the board during the year under review, but in some statutes there is a proviso that ministerial directions shall not be disclosed if in the Minister's opinion it is against the national interest or national security to do so.[4] This proviso has aroused considerable criticism because it enables the Minister to give directions which the board are bound to obey, but which are kept secret from the public. In addition to the obligation to make an annual report, the public corporations are required to give to the appropriate Minister such information about the undertaking as he may from

[1] New Towns Act, 1946, s. 13.
[2] Forestry Act, 1945, s. 7.
[3] Transport Act, 1947, s. 94.
[4] See, e.g. Coal Industry Nationalization Act, 1946, s. 54 (2); Transport Act, 1947, s. 4 (7); Gas Act, 1948, s. 10 (2); Air Corporations Act, 1949, s. 23 (3); Atomic Energy Authority Act, 1954, s. 3 (5); Electricity Act .1957, s. 10 (3).

time to time require.[1] In most cases the Minister may prescribe the form which the reports are to take.[2]

A THEORY OF THE PUBLIC CORPORATION

In conclusion, I will attempt briefly to formulate a theory of the public corporation. This will inevitably involve matters which are dealt with at length in later chapters; but this anticipation is unavoidable.

The starting point of such a theory is the proposition that the nationalized industries or services, like all publicly owned undertakings, form part of the public domain. The object of bringing them into the public sector of the economy is to ensure that they are subject to political control by the Legislature and the Executive in their respective spheres.

The public corporations are organs of public administration. As such they are instruments of public policy just as much as the older departments exercising conventional functions. They are distinct from the regular departments under the control of Ministers; but they are subordinate to Parliament and the Executive.

The organization, assets, functions and powers of the public corporations spring from the creative act of the legislature; their purposes and property are given to them by Parliament. The public corporation cannot by its own authority modify these purposes; nor sell, terminate, liquidate, or pledge the undertaking with which it is entrusted.

To foster initiative and enterprise in the conduct of the nationalized industries the public corporation has had conferred upon it a substantially greater degree of independence in its daily working than is possessed by departments in charge of a Minister. In matters of finance and personnel, budgeting and accounting, production, distribution and development, it enjoys a large measure of freedom. The public corporation is, however, not an autonomous institution and was never intended to be.

The public corporation is based on the theory that a full measure of accountability can be imposed on a public authority without requiring it to be subject to ministerial control in respect of its managerial decisions and multitudinous routine activities, or liable to comprehensive parliamentary scrutiny of its day-to-day working. The theory assumes that policy, in major matters at least, can be distinguished from management

[1] See, e.g. New Towns Act, 1946, s. 13 (7); Coal Industry Nationalization Act, 1946, s. 3 (4); Transport Act, 1947, s. 4 (6); Gas Act, 1948, s. 7 (3); Air Corporations Act, 1949, s. 23 (6); Atomic Energy Authority Act, 1954, s. 3 (4); Electricity Act, 1957, s. 8 (5) and (6).

[2] See, e.g. Forestry Act, 1945, s. 7 (1) and (3); New Towns Act, 1946, s. 13 (1); Transport Act, 1947, s. 94 (1)(Ib); Gas Act, 1948, s. 10 (3); Television Act, 1954, s. 15 (1); Electricity Act, 1957, s. 10 (4).

Public Corporations: Parent Ministers and Approximate Numbers of Employees 1957–8

Parent Minister	*Corporation*	*Approx No. of Employees*	*Approx. No. of Employees under each Minister*
Minister of Power	National Coal Board	687,000	1,007,000
	Electricity Council and Generating Board plus Area Boards	187,000	
	Gas Council plus Area Boards	133,000	
Minister of Transport and Civil Aviation	British Transport Commission	806,000	837,000
	British Overseas Airways Corporation	19,000	
	British European Airways Corporation	12,000	
Prime Minister	Atomic Energy Authority	35,000	35,000
Secretary of State for Scotland	South of Scotland Electricity Board ...	12,000	26,000[1]
	North of Scotland Hydro-Electricity Board ...	2,861	
Postmaster-General	British Broadcasting Corporation	16,000	26,000
	Cable and Wireless	10,000	
	Independent Television Authority	Small no. (300)	
Ministry of Agriculture ...	Forestry Commission	15,000	11,000[2]
Chancellor of the Exchequer ...	Bank of England	7,000	7,000
Colonial Secretary	Colonial Development Corporation	Small no. (300)	—

Approximate Total Employees of Public Corporations 1,942,000
Less number employed abroad 14,000[3]

1,928,000

Approximate Number of persons in civil employment in this country 22,875,000
Approximate percentage employed by public corporations 8·42 per cent

Notes: [1] Includes 4,000 Scottish forestry workers. [2] Excludes 4,000 Scottish forestry workers.
[3] Cable and Wireless 9,000; BOAC 4,000; BEA 1,300.

Sources: Annual Reports and Economic Survey 1959.

or administration; and that a successful combination of political control and managerial freedom can be achieved by reserving certain powers of decision in matters of major importance to Ministers answerable to Parliament and leaving everything else to the discretion of the public corporation acting within its legal competence. The Government are further endowed with residual powers of direction and appointment which mark their unquestionable authority.

Approximate Gross Incomes of the Public Corporations 1958–9

Corporation	*Approx. Gross Income (£m.)*
National Coal Board	922·1
British Transport Commission	729·5
Electricity Council plus Boards	517·8
Gas Council plus Boards	389·6
Atomic Energy Authority	105·0
British Overseas Airways Corporation	57·9
British European Airways Corporation	37·3
South of Scotland Electricity Board	31·8
British Broadcasting Corporation	28·6
Cable and Wireless	15·8
Forestry Commission	12·1
North of Scotland Hydro-Electric Board	13·5
Colonial Development Corporation	2·5
Independent Television Authority	3·0
White Fish Authority	0·3
Total	2,866·8

Approximate gross national income £20,114 m.
Approximate gross incomes of the corporations as a percentage of this 14·3 %.
Sources: Annual Reports and Economic Survey 1959.

The theory leaves out of account the all-pervading influence which Ministers can exert over the activities of public corporations if they are so disposed. Where this occurs there is a danger of blurring the distinction between policy and management on which the theory rests; and a no-man's land emerges in which nominal responsibility does not coincide with the real power of decision-making. A clear allocation, recognition, and public acknowledgment of the respective spheres of Ministers, Parliament, and the public corporation is necessary; and an assurance that they will be respected.

The allocation of powers need not be static but may be altered if and when conditions change. But a re-allocation should be publicly announced in a formal manner.

The public corporations administering the British nationalized industries are conducting their affairs with a true sense of accountability to the Government, to Parliament, to their own employees, to the consumers, and to the nation. They constitute a creative achievement of high value on the part of our democracy. There is no doubt that the public corporation is the most important constitutional innovation which has been evolved in Great Britain during the past fifty years. It is destined to play as important a part in the field of nationalized industry in the twentieth century as the privately owned corporation played in the realm of capitalist organization in the nineteenth century.

CHAPTER IV

Organization and Management

A GREAT deal of diversity has been deliberately introduced into the forms and organization of nationalized undertakings. It was the intention of Parliament and the government to avoid uniformity in these and other matters. Even in regard to nomenclature there is great variety. We have the National Coal Board, the British Transport Commission, the Gas Council, the Electricity Boards, the Airways Corporations, the Atomic Energy Authority, to mention only a few. Yet all are public corporations. A more important reason for the diversity of organization is to be found in the economic conditions and political backgrounds of the several industries.

The Bank of England was taken over intact, and the organization remained virtually unchanged. The National Coal Board was created as a single giant monopoly embracing the entire coal industry except for a few small mines which are operated by private management under licence. This is a much larger undertaking, in terms of the numbers employed, than any other industrial undertaking in Britain except the British Transport Commission;[1] and its annual turnover is the greatest of any industrial or commercial organization. The National Coal Board represents the high-water mark of legal centralization, and much criticism has been expressed on the subject. Colonel C. G. Lancaster, MP, for example, in a pamphlet published by the Conservative Political Centre in 1948, declared the industry to be 'dangerously over-centralized'.[2] In his opinion the fact that so many members of the Board were engaged in executive duties emphasized the tendency to over-centralization; and this together with divided responsibility had profoundly affected Area General Managers and mine managers, whose personal authority was too small.

Other critics had declared the divisions to be a superfluous element in the structure; had denounced the increased functionalism within the industry on the ground that it produced a tendency to by-pass the operational management; and had deplored the inadequate authority given to mine managers, which was alleged to be insufficient for the proper dis-

[1] The British Transport Commission had about 806,000 employees in 1958 compared with the National Coal Board's 687,000.

[2] *The Organization of the Coal Board*, p. 6.

charge of their responsibilities. It was even suggested that the structure made for remoteness between management and the men, thus producing bad human relations, although embittered labour relations had been a characteristic feature of the British coal industry under private ownership during the whole inter-war period. Much of this type of criticism sprang from political hostility to the principle of nationalization; and the *legal* centralization of the nationalized coal industry gave ill will combined with ignorance a valuable target to attack.[1]

CENTRALIZATION, REAL AND APPARENT

The centralization to which objection has been taken by this and other critics is, however, legal or constitutional. It has always been regarded as essential that the public ownership and operation of the coal industry should be organized on a national basis, because only by that method could the fundamental questions of manpower, wages and conditions of employment, modernization and capital investment, scientific research and development, the co-ordination of prices and selling policy, the improvement of mechanical equipment, etc. receive the comprehensive consideration and action which they require. But this necessary condition does not rule out a great deal of managerial decentralization which has in fact taken place within the legally monolithic structure of the National Coal Board. The tendency almost from the beginning was to increase the discretionary powers of the Divisional Coal Boards and the Area General Managers.

Criticism of the kind mentioned above might have been avoided if Parliament had inserted into the Coal Industry Nationalization Act some provisions relating to the internal structure of the industry. But it would be quite wrong to assume that there has been more centralization in practice in the coal industry than there would have been if Parliament had made the Divisional Coal Boards separate corporations or required powers to be delegated to them.

In this connection it is instructive to read the report of the Fleck Committee appointed by the NCB to advise them on organization. Sir Alexander Fleck is chairman of Imperial Chemical Industries and therefore conversant with the practices of private enterprise in matters of organization and management.

The organization which Dr Fleck (as he then was) and his colleagues investigated is briefly as follows: There are about 840 collieries employing more than 700,000 mineworkers, including 38,000 colliery under-

[1] Cf. D. W. Kelly: 'The Administration of the National Coal Board', XXXI *Public Administration* (1953), pp. 1-11.

officials. (The rest of the Board's staff numbers about 55,000.) They produce well over 200 million tons of coal a year and the turnover exceeds £900 million. At the summit is the National Coal Board and the headquarters departments; next come nine coalfield divisions, in eight of which is a Divisional Coal Board appointed by the NCB; the South Eastern Division is too small to justify a Divisional Board and has instead a General Manager. The divisions are in turn (with the exception of the small Kent coalfield, which has only four collieries) broken up into areas, of which there are 51 in all, each being managed by an Area General Manager. The areas contain the collieries, which in the larger areas are sometimes grouped into sub-areas.

The divisions and areas contain the producing organizations, and therefore are located in the coalfields. In addition there are nine sales regions covering the whole country; each division is wholly within one region. There is a Regional Sales Manager in charge of each region who is directly responsible to the Headquarters Marketing Department. All coal used in a region is sold by the regional selling organization which is under the Regional Sales Manager.[1]

EXCESSIVE DECENTRALIZATION IN THE COAL INDUSTRY

Far from charging the NCB with over-centralization, the Fleck Committee criticized them for exercising insufficient authority over the Divisional Boards. The divisions are very large units, and on an average each one produces about 25 million tons of coal a year, worth about £70 million, and employing a labour force of nearly 90,000. The Committee considered and explicitly rejected the suggestion that the divisions can only perform their task effectively if they are given a high degree of autonomy or financial independence. By this they understood that each division would be given a statement of the broad aims it was to pursue, a budget indicating permitted expenditure, and then be left to get on with the task on its own lines, reporting progress from time to time to headquarters. 'We are satisfied that such a concept is neither right nor practicable.'[2] In the first place there are a number of matters in regard to which the industry must be dealt with as a single unit. These include the long term planning of the industry, prices, capital investment, and wages. Second, there are various fields in which the activities of the Board concern the whole industry. An example of this is scientific

[1] NCB Annual Reports: 1953, paras. 197-207; 1954, para. 144; 1955, para. 65.

[2] *Report of the Advisory Committee on Organization* (1955) (National Coal Board), para. 184.

research and development, the results of which must be utilized by the whole industry, and not left to the choice of each Divisional Board. The role of the division is therefore a managerial one. It should initiate and stimulate the areas, and not merely co-ordinate and supervise them.[1]

The Fleck Committee found that the divisions had been actually given far too much freedom in certain matters. Thus the organization and staffing of a division were left to the discretion of each Divisional Board, with the consequence that there was no common pattern and no consistency of standards in regard to staff. An essential function of the National Coal Board should be to see that each division is properly organized, and the committee made a recommendation that they should embark on this task forthwith.[2] Similarly it had been the policy of the National Board not to lay down any standard pattern of organization for the areas; and here again the committee considered there was unjustified decentralization. They urged the NCB to lay down a pattern of organization which each area would be required to adopt, subject only to variations called for by local conditions.[3]

Again, too much autonomy had been given to the divisions in regard to capital expenditure, and by the Divisional Boards to Area General Managers. Complaints had been made that the national headquarters took too long in approving schemes of capital development submitted to them for approval. Not only did the Fleck Committee find this complaint without foundation but they said that far from major capital projects being unduly delayed by meticulous examination at headquarters, they were not scrutinized there with sufficient closeness. They dismissed the notion that the preparation and submission to headquarters of large capital schemes was a burden of which Divisional Boards and Area General Managers might reasonably ask to be relieved. On the contrary, this task ought to be a serious burden on the lower formations and they had no right to complain of it. With capital in short supply the examination of large new developments should be tightened up rather than made easier.[4] Divisional Boards could authorize capital expenditure up to £250,000 on any one colliery project. The committee considered the powers delegated by some Divisional Boards to their Area General Managers in respect of capital development to be excessive, since they were authorized to sanction on their own responsibility an expenditure on any one colliery project of up to £100,000. 'This degree of delegation,' the Committee observed, 'cannot be matched in any well-run

[1] *Report of the Advisory Committee Organization* (1955) (National Coal Board), para. 186.

[2] *Ib.*, paras. 205–7. [3] *Ib.*, para. 225. [4] Paras. 337–40.

industrial undertaking within our knowledge,' and they recommended the figure should be reduced to £50,000.[1]

By contrast, there seemed to be some ground for regarding the Area General Managers as too strictly controlled in regard to appointments, promotions, and salary adjustments, and a relaxation of control was urged in this sphere. But the more important charge which had been made that Area General Managers had insufficient voice in the making of policy by their Divisional Boards was unfounded.

The Fleck report not merely disposed of the ill-informed criticism of Colonel Lancaster and others who had declared the industry to be over-centralized:[2] it explicitly urged the National Coal Board to exercise more central authority than they had done hitherto. The Committee found that the Board had been unwilling to insist on their policies being carried out and had tried to control their subordinate formations with too light a touch to secure effective compliance. The Board had not infrequently failed to require divisions to apply a policy they had adopted—a fatal sign of weakness. They had relied on exhortation to persuade reluctant divisions to carry out their decisions instead of issuing a firm instruction and enforcing it with disciplinary action if necessary.[3]

DECENTRALIZATION TRUE AND FALSE

In one of the most valuable parts of the report, the Committee expounds the meaning of decentralization in a large organization. They thought the weakness of the Board in failing to enforce its policy sprang from a wrong conception of decentralization.

Properly understood, decentralization means that each level of management clearly specifies the powers which the *échelon* below it may freely exercise. That *échelon* must then be left to exercise those powers as it thinks best without restraint. 'But each level of management must see that the policies which it lays down are punctually and effectively carried out by the level of management below it. No organization will work well unless the people who give the instructions and frame the policies also ensure that they are carried out. This should be done, not by interference in detailed or day-to-day matters, but by modern management techniques of approved programmes followed by periodical reports

[1] Para. 237.

[2] 'In the main, we find that the powers delegated by the Divisional Boards to their Area General Managers are satisfactory. We think it important that this point should be appreciated. There has been much ill-informed criticism, suggesting that Area General Managers have not been given adequate authority and responsibility. We are satisfied that this is not so, and the great majority of Area General Managers support this view.' Para. 235.

[3] Paras. 300–3.

and reviews of progress and by physical inspections. The Board appears to have assumed that decentralization means that they should not, or need not, impose their will on divisions and areas. We do not agree with this policy.'[1]

Several illustrations could be given of this confused and mistaken conception of decentralization. One example was the refusal to compel collieries to adopt modern methods of budgetary control combined with a system of standard costs. The Board had worked out the right methods and wanted to see them established throughout the industry, yet they felt it would be 'wrong' to force the more backward divisions to accept them. They therefore left the Divisional Boards free to decide the matter.

Similarly a false conception of decentralization has often prevailed in the divisions. Each level of management expects its orders to be obeyed by the lower formations while resisting the idea that it should itself carry out the decisions coming to it from a higher level: in short, each level expects to exert authority on the organs below it, but to be subject only to advice from those above.[2] Mr W. W. Haynes, an acute American observer of the British coal industry, has remarked that decentralization in the abstract is favoured by almost all NCB officials at every level. But their usual complaint is of too much centralization above themselves and too much autonomy below them. He cites the typical case of the Area General Manager who was an extreme centralizer in his own area but a strong opponent of centralization, by which he meant interference of any kind from the division or headquarters.[3]

A general directive on organization, issued by the National Coal Board to all divisions, areas and collieries, in October 1953, crystallized all the weaknesses inherent in the prevailing tendencies. In this directive the National Coal Board declared that in discharging its own responsibilities it regarded the Divisional Boards and headquarters departments as 'equally its advisers'; that the executive heads of the Board's departments were merely in the position of *primus enter pares* in dealing with similar departments in the divisions; that Divisional Boards were bound to consider but need not accept the advice or suggestions of headquarters' departments; that Divisional Boards should act in a supervisory and co-ordinating capacity in relation to the areas, which should be recognised as the main and vital management units; that members of a Divisional Board are collectively accountable for the conduct of affairs in their Division but individually responsible solely to their own Boards; and much else in similar vein. The Fleck Committee exposed the directive to the devastating criticism which its weak and muddled thinking deserved

[1] Para. 307. [2] Para. 309.
[3] W. W. Haynes: *Nationalization in Practice* (1953), pp. 289 and 300.

and urged that it should be withdrawn and replaced by one which would take account of their criticism and recommendations.[1]

The Fleck Committee accomplished their main task, which was to advise on organization, with great lucidity and distinction. (We shall refer elsewhere to other parts of their report, some of which were less satisfactory, but these need not detain us now.)[2] They expounded for the first time a coherent and reasonable structure for the nationalized coal industry, and defined an intelligible system of relationships on which it must rest. No longer will the National Coal Board be under the illusion that they can hope to carry responsibility for the entire industry without exercising effective central authority and control. The bubble of over-centralization has been pricked and the true fault shown to be that of excessive decentralization. I repeat here without qualification the statement which I made in 1952. 'It has not yet been proved that the National Coal Board is too large, too cumbersome, or too over-centralized for efficiency. But its ability to organize and manage the British Coal Industry in a satisfactory manner has also not yet been demonstrated.'[3]

It is satisfactory to note that most of the recommendations of the Fleck Report were accepted in principle by the reconstituted National Coal Board in March 1955. Many of them had been put into practice by the end of that year, while others were in process of being applied, in consultation with the coalfield managements and the trade unions. In particular, the NCB accepted the Committee's recommendations concerning the organization of divisions, areas and groups, departmental organization, and management policy and practice.[4]

A NEW DIRECTIVE

A new general directive was issued by the Board on July 5, 1955, to replace that of October 1953. It omits the provisions contained in the earlier document about decentralization and lays down new provisions about the use to be made of functional channels. The responsibilities of line authorities at each level are defined with greater precision. The section on 'Supervision and Accountability' in this reflects a new attitude which one hopes will be firmly carried out in practice, and which can be clearly attributed to the advice given by the Fleck Committee. 'Policy decisions of the Board', it says, 'must be properly and promptly carried out, and control must be firm: in this all levels of management must play

[1] The Directive is reprinted in the report of the Fleck Committee, App. D.

[2] *Post* pp. 220, 442.

[3] W. A. Robson: 'General Conclusions' in *Problems of Nationalized Industry*, ed. W. A. Robson (1952), p. 292.

[4] *National Coal Board Annual Report 1955*, HMSO, HC 263-I/1955, 6, vol. I, paras. 119-38.

their part. Policies must be expressed fully, specifically and, where necessary, in detail. Each level of management must avoid interfering in the day-to-day work of the level of management below it, but should exercise control by means of modern management techniques, including the use of approved programmes followed by periodical reports and reviews of progress. The National Board intend that the use of standards and budgets shall be fully developed throughout their organization. The authorities and functional heads at each level of management are responsible for ensuring that they obtain the information that is needed for supervising and guiding subordinate levels of management and for holding them to account. . . .'[1]

Standard patterns of organization have been laid down for all the main divisional departments and for area headquarters, and deviation from these patterns is permitted only where necessitated by local conditions, and subject to approval and control by headquarters.[2] A variety of intermediate levels of authority had previously existed between area headquarters and the pits. Sometimes there were two intermediate levels; and the nomenclature and organization of these intermediate organs varied indiscriminately. All this irrational diversity was cleared up and henceforth a group, with a group manager in charge, is to be the only intermediate level of management between an area and the collieries. There are about 200 of these groups now established, each comprising two or more collieries.[3] They will have only a small staff and will chiefly rely on the departmental staff of the area.

The powers of an Area General Manager to authorize capital expenditure on any one project were reduced substantially, and now vary between £15,000 and £50,000 according to the character of the area.[4] On the other hand, the powers of the Area General Managers in regard to staff appointments were enlarged, since these now relate to particular posts and not to appointments below a specified salary limit. The AGM is in future to have an assistant general manager to help him to shoulder some of his responsibilities; and the exclusion of anyone other than a mining engineer from appointment as AGM has been abandoned.[5]

A number of important changes in the organization of departments were also announced. Staff departments were set up at headquarters, in the divisions, and in the areas; these would be responsible not only for the work previously done by the Establishments Department but also for the vital function of training. An Industrial Relations Department (at headquarters and in each division) would be responsible for recruit-

[1] *National Coal Board Annual Report 1955*, HMSO, HC 263–I/1955, 6, vol. I, para. 120 and App. I.

[2] *Ib.*, paras. 132, 135. [3] *Ib.*, paras. 137-8. [4] *Ib.*, para. 133. [5] *Ib.*, paras. 134-5.

ment, training and welfare of industrial staff, thereby replacing the Labour Relations Department and the Manpower and Welfare Department. Purchasing and Stores would in future have their own department at all three levels of organization in place of the supplies sub-departments which formed part of the Production Department.[1] The latter would be strengthened by the appointment of Deputy Area Production Managers in most areas with the specific function of helping with planning and reconstruction. The medical service was raised to the level of a Department.[2]

A CLEAR ALLOCATION OF DUTIES NEEDED

One very important point in connection with so large an organization is the need for a high degree of clarity in the distribution of duties and the respective spheres of responsibility of officials who may be brought into continuous or intermittent co-operation as participants in a common task. Without a crystal-clear definition of duties and responsibilities it is quite possible for different officials to have differing views about their own position as well as that of others. Uncertainty or lack of precision in this matter can lead to disaster in mining operations, as was shown by the Knockshinnoch Castle Colliery accident in 1950, which resulted in the death of thirteen miners and the imprisonment for two days of 116 others by an inrush of peat. The disaster was the result of subsidence during the development of new works, owing to the support above being much less than had been anticipated. The report on the formal inquiry into the accident commented at length on the allocation of responsibilities in respect of the development plans for the mine between the sub-area planning department and the colliery management. Sir Andrew Bryan, HM Chief Inspector of Mines, said in his report that the functions and precise relations between the two departments were not very clearly defined, and some of the people concerned took differing views of them.[3]

While there was a considerable degree of co-operation between the planning department and the colliery management, there was a lack of effective liaison between the planning engineers and the management, and between the engineers and surveyors. The planner mainly concerned never made inquiries about the progress of the work after the plans had been agreed; and when the management found that the gradient in the

[1] *National Coal Board Annual Report 1955*, HMSO, HC 263–I/1955, 6, vol. I, paras. 124-7.

[2] *Ib.*, para. 130.

[3] Report by Sir Andrew Bryan on the Accident at Knockshinnoch Colliery, HMSO, Cmd. 8180/1950, pp. 23-31.

working where the disaster occurred was rising more steeply than they expected, they did not bring this fact to the notice of either the planner or the planning department. The Chief Inspector concluded that there was a weakness in the organization in that insufficient arrangements were made to keep the planning engineers properly informed of the changes which occurred as the workings progressed; and hence they were unable to check the accuracy of the forecasts in the development plan.[1] He recommended that in the NCB organization 'the status and responsibility of all planning engineers, planners and surveyors at all levels should be clearly defined in relation to those of colliery agents and managers'.[2]

With an accident like this to point the moral, Mr Haynes remarks that lack of clarity in the organization may have been more disturbing to colliery managers than their alleged loss of authority to tiers of specialists placed above them.[3] Effective communication is an essential element in good organization.

A somewhat different manner of expressing a similar thought is used by Mr G. Baldwin in his study of labour in the British coal industry when he says that administrative rather than structural over-centralization is the real problem. The depressing effects of centralization could, he believes, be relieved by closer attention to a more precise definition of executive responsibilities at the existing levels, without any need for structural decentralization which, without administrative reform, would leave the basic problem unresolved.[4] The depressing effects on labour relations are, according to this investigator, felt most intensely at the colliery level, and concern questions of administrative policy or procedure and personal relationships within the managerial hierarchy. Mr Baldwin cites among the typical grievances of colliery managers, their inability to regrade men or increase their remuneration without permission of the group manager, the failure or refusal of Area General Managers to provide them with financial information about their own pits, the great pressure of work, especially the obligation to prepare many reports without adequate assistance, and uncertainty as to whom they should approach with personal grievances.

Some of these matters are really questions of staffing and management rather than of organization or centralization, whether structural or

[1] Report by Sir Andrew Bryan on the Accident at Knockshinnoch Colliery, HMSO, Cmd. 8180/1950, p. 45.

[2] *Ib.*, p. 46. After the inquiry, the NCB issued a Directive on the status and responsibility of management and of planning and surveying staffs, designed to clarify their respective responsibilities under existing safety legislation. *National Coal Board Annual Report 1952*, HMSO, HC 157/1952-3, para. 102.

[3] W. W. Haynes: *op. cit.*, pp. 311-5.

[4] George B. Baldwin: *Beyond Nationalization* (1955), pp. 22-4.

managerial. The Fleck Report drew special attention to the fact that colliery managers are overburdened with work, especially on the administrative and personnel side of their job,[1] and it recommended they be given skilled staff of good calibre to help them. Questions of promotion and increases of pay cannot be left to purely local decision in any large organization, except within narrow and carefully defined limits, since any appearance of inconsistency or personal favouritism will quickly give rise to widespread discontent and resentment. As we have seen, a recent directive has enlarged the powers of the Area General Manager in regard to staff. The need to seek approval of the intermediate authority does not appear to disclose an excessive degree of control from above.

The question of financial information about a pit is less easy to decide. Some pits are making a profit while others are running at a loss. Is the profitability of a pit to be made a reason for upgrading the staff or increasing the pay of the miners working in it? If so, what conclusions are to be drawn from the figures relating to collieries showing a deficit? In general, all available information about every aspect of the industry should be supplied freely on request not only to managers but to everyone in the industry. But financial information can be misleading if it is used as a criterion of efficiency unless it is related to the system of standardized costs which the NCB have been trying for several years to introduce throughout the industry.

Lastly, one should appreciate that colliery managers have in the past been singularly deficient in knowledge of administration. In the words of the Fleck Committee, 'The colliery manager has been taught how to mine but not how to manage.'[2] It is scarcely surprising that he has often felt bewildered and frustrated at the complexity of the vast organization of which he is now a part. For an understanding of administrative organization and methods is far more essential in a large-scale undertaking than in a small one. Thus, some of the complaints of the kind mentioned by Mr Baldwin are due to the limited outlook and lack of training on the part of colliery managers rather than, or as much as, any administrative or structural over-centralization in the coal industry. If the NCB carry through a comprehensive programme of training courses for colliery managers in administration and management, as the Fleck Committee recommend,[3] most of their present grievances will be literally 'trained away'.

[1] *Report of the Advisory Committee on Organization* (1955) (National Coal Board), para. 285.

[2] *Ib.*, para. 283.

[3] *Ib.*, para. 292.

THE FRENCH NATIONALIZED COAL INDUSTRY

One alternative to the single national unit such as the National Coal Board is a system of interlocking regional and national organs. An example of this is the French nationalized coal industry. There one finds a central body called the *Charbonnages de France* which is charged with seeing that the programme of production is executed, with the direction of the industry as a whole, and with the control and co-ordination of activities in the coal fields. It must approve plans of development and production, make proposals concerning fuel prices, provide the finance for equipment, direct technical research and vocational training, and secure, by means of an equalization fund, the financial stability of the productive units. It is thus an organ of administration and supervision.

In each of the nine coalfields in which the mineral resources of the country are found, a separate coalmining corporation is established. These coalfield corporations are called *houillères de bassin*. On them falls the responsibility for the production, processing and disposal of coal. The nomination of their governing boards and chief executives is effected by decree under the same conditions as those which apply to the *Charbonnages de France*. This assures genuine autonomy for each coalfield and at the same time assists good commercial management. In order, however, to provide liaison between the national organization and the regional bodies, the chairmen of the governing boards of the *houillères de bassin* may attend in a consultative capacity the meetings of the governing board of the *Charbonnages de France*, whenever they are considering questions concerning their coalfields. Conversely, the governing board of each *houillère de bassin* includes six representatives of the *Charbonnages de France*.

An undertaking which is highly centralized from a legal or constitutional standpoint may be highly decentralized in its actual working arrangements. The French coal industry is more decentralized from a legal point of view than the British, because the coalfield corporations are separate legal entities whose governing boards are appointed independently and whose powers are conferred upon them directly by law, whereas the Divisional Boards were created by the NCB and could be abolished by the same body at will; and the Divisional Board members are appointed by the NCB. It must not, however, be assumed that there is more decentralization in practice in the French industry than in the British. Nevertheless, in my opinion, the formal decentralization of the French organization is to be preferred to the British model. The representation of the *Charbonnages de France* on the boards of the coalfield corporations is an interesting device which can have useful possibilities.

It has been copied to some extent in the composition of the Area Boards created to supervise the railways, since these contain one or more members of the British Transport Commission.[1]

THE ORGANIZATION OF ELECTRICITY SUPPLY

Electricity supply is another nationalized industry whose organization has recently been closely investigated by an independent committee, with very different premises and results from those relating to the coal industry.

The legislation which the Labour Government of 1945-50 introduced to nationalize transport, gas, electricity, and steel was based on the idea that the main principles of organization should be laid down by Parliament and that decentralization should be secured by law and not left, as in the case of the coal industry or the BBC, to managerial discretion.

Thus, the Electricity Act, 1947, established the Central Electricity Authority as the national organ responsible for the generation of electricity, while fourteen Area Boards (later reduced to twelve when two independent Scottish Electricity Boards[2] were set up) were entrusted with the distribution of electricity in their respective regions. Each of these Area Boards is a separate public corporation the members of which are appointed by the Minister of Power. The Area Boards had conferred upon them considerable powers and duties in their own right but the Central Electricity Authority were given a deciding voice on questions of policy and finance. There was, however, a federal element in its constitution, since four of the Area Board chairmen served in rotation on the central body. The task of the Central Electricity Authority was to develop and maintain an efficient, co-ordinated and economical system of electricity supply. For that purpose it was required to generate electricity and provide supplies in bulk to the Area Boards for them to distribute; to co-ordinate distribution by the Area Boards; and to exercise a general control over them in regard to policy and finance. The central authority had the exclusive right of borrowing money for the whole industry by the issue of stock. The Area Boards were required to purchase supplies of electricity from the central organ, and to plan and carry out in an efficient and economical manner the distribution of those supplies to individual consumers.

The balance of authority and responsibility between the centre and the regions appeared to be reasonably well maintained in the legal structure, but the Herbert Committee, which was appointed in 1954 by the Minister of [Fuel and] Power to inquire into the working of the

[1] *Post* pp. 98–101. [2] Electricity Reorganization (Scotland) Act, 1954.

electricity supply industry, took an unfavourable view of the organization in several important respects.

The enormous task which confronted the central authority and the Area Boards on vesting date was that of forging 560 separate supply undertakings into a unified national service. About a third of the industry was previously owned by commercial companies and the remaining two-thirds by municipal corporations. The areas of supply and the operating units were largely obsolete, and this indeed was one of the reasons for nationalizing the industry.

The organization set up by the 1947 Act performed this initial task with notable success. At the same time it embarked on a gigantic expansion of the industry on both its generating and distribution sides. In 1947–8 the installed capacity of generating plant was 11,680 megawatts; by 1954–5 it had risen to 18,950 megawatts, and is expected to reach 26,500 megawatts by 1959–60.[1] The annual capacity of plant commissioned was 566 megawatts in 1948 and 1,431 in 1954.[2] The number of consumers had risen from 10·8 millions in 1948 to 13·7 millions in 1954–5; and is expected to be 15·4 millions in 1959–60. Expansion on this scale is a remarkable achievement which would not have occurred if the industry had not been nationalized.

The Herbert Committee criticized the organization on two main grounds. First, that it was over-centralized; and second, that it was a mistake to entrust the Central Authority with both executive and supervisory functions.

The question of centralization was considered not only in relation to the Area Boards, but also in relation to the generating divisions into which the Central Authority had divided the country for the purpose of managing the power stations and the construction of new power stations and the main transmission system. These divisions have no statutory basis. They are administered by Divisional Controllers who are appointed by the Central Authority and responsible to them.[3] The divisions originally corresponded with the areas of the distribution boards; but in 1954 a very large division[4] was set up as an experiment consisting of the North Western, Merseyside and North Wales Divisions.

[1] *Report of the Committee of Inquiry into the Electricity Supply Industry*, HMSO, Cmd. 9672/1956, para. 83.

[2] *Ib.*, para. 114.

[3] *Ib.*, p. 67.

[4] This large division is controlled by a Committee of Management consisting of the Divisional Controller, his Deputy, and three part-time members appointed by the Central Authority (now the Central Electricity Generating Board). This division has had larger powers delegated to it than the other divisions, particularly in regard to expenditure contracts and staff. *British Electricity Authority Annual Report 1954–5*, HMSO, HC 72/1955–6, paras. 318–20.

The Herbert Committee accepted the principle that generation should be performed by a Central Authority and distribution by the Area Boards. They recommended that in exceptional circumstances, where an Area Board could use a power station both for generating electricity and for district heating, it should be permitted with central approval to construct and operate one for these purposes.

As regards the general relationship between the Central Authority on the one hand and the Area Boards and generating divisions on the other, the Herbert Committee considered that there was far too much interference by the central body. The headquarters staff had reached a figure of about 2,000, and they thought this too large, though no detailed analysis was made of the employees or their work in support of this view. The committee emphasized 'the undoubted *feeling* of most of the Area Boards that the Authority interferes too much in their affairs although under the Act they are quasi-autonomous statutory corporations. There is a similar *feeling* on the part of some Divisional Controllers that they are not given as much power and responsibility in relation to the design and operation of power stations as they could with advantage exercise and discharge. They *feel* that there is an unnecessary amount of duplication of work at headquarters and in the divisions which leads to expense and delay. As a result it appears very difficult to say where the actual responsibility for any particular decision with regard to the design of plant really lies.'[1] The chairman and two deputy chairmen of the Central Authority were loaded with a vast burden of work and responsibility; and much of their time and that of the members and chief officers of the regional bodies was occupied with attending committees and conferences at headquarters. This excessively heavy burden of day-to-day work left them with insufficient time to reflect on the larger problems of policy.

One of the unsatisfactory features of the situation was that the planning, preparation, and construction of a power station took as much as eight years, so that by the time it came into commission it was already obsolescent. This was in part due to excessive supervision by headquarters and the need for Divisional Controllers to obtain headquarters approval at too many stages of each project.[2]

Another and less valid criticism was directed at the obligation imposed on Area Boards to comply with a general pattern of organization laid down for the regions. Here the Herbert Committee took a diametrically opposite view of the matter to the Fleck Committee, who criticized the National Coal Board for failing to lay down the structure of the divisions and to require the Divisional Boards to observe it. My own

[1] Para. 239. My italics. [2] Para. 257.

opinion is that the Fleck Committee were right on this point. The Herbert Committee seems frequently to have taken the view that if an official of a subordinate formation disliked or resented the powers of the central organ, that by itself was sufficient reason for abolishing them. This is not a rational view of organization. I have already quoted a passage from their report in which a *feeling* by an Area Board that they should have more autonomy is repeatedly assumed to be proof of excessive interference from the centre. This is a quite unwarranted assumption. Few people ever agree with the need for authority to be exercised over them by a higher level: nearly everyone believes he would do better if he were left to his own devices. While there is every reason to remove unnecessary restraints at every point in an organization, dislike of authority must be balanced against the objective advantages of control, and this the Herbert Committee did not attempt to do.

The main recommendation of the Herbert Report was that a Central Electricity Generating Board should be set up to take over executive responsibility for the design, construction, and operation of power stations, the grid and the projected super-grid. It would plan the general development of electricity supply, and the main transmission system; it would be responsible for the siting of power stations; the design and possibly the construction of power stations using atomic energy and other advanced methods of generation; research and development; staff policy; financial policy; and load control over the entire system.[1] The design and construction of 'conventional' power stations would lie with the divisions, apart from approval of the site and a few other details.[2]

The Government accepted the Herbert Committee's recommendation that the functions of generating and delivering electricity in bulk should be separated from the functions of co-ordinating and controlling the whole system of generation and distribution; and they approved the proposal to set up a new Central Electricity Generating Board to take charge of the former tasks.[3] This was implemented by the Electricity Act, 1957, which requires the Minister of Power to establish the Board and to appoint the chairman, deputy chairman and members.

The Government also accepted the committee's recommendation that Area Boards should be given more autonomy. The White Paper which they published said that the Central Generating Board and each Area Board should in future be required to balance their accounts individually. Each legally distinct organ would have a self-contained financial system, including its own reserve fund. The Minister would no longer have a statutory obligation to consult the Central Authority before appointing

[1] Paras. 248-52. [2] Para. 267.
[3] *Proposals for the Reorganization of the Electricity Supply Industry*, HMSO, Cmd. 27/1956.

the members of the Area Boards. The Electricity Act, 1957, implements these decisions. It further permits Area Boards to generate electricity in the exceptional circumstances already mentioned, and authorizes them to engage in research.

The Herbert Committee considered that the Central Electricity Authority, denuded of executive responsibility for generation, should devote itself solely to considering the larger questions of policy. They conceived it as a body which would keep the industry alert by criticizing its shortcomings and stimulating its activities to higher standards of achievement.

The CEA would review the policies, programmes and finance of the Area and Generating Boards; and none of its members would be drawn from those Boards. The time and energy of the Central Authority would be devoted to discussing and thinking about such questions as development programmes, capital and revenue budgets, depreciation policy and reserve funds, bulk supply and retail tariffs, research and development.[1] Little would have been left to the Minister of Power beyond appointing the members of the Boards and the Central Authority, authorizing capital issues, and instructing the industry whenever it was required to act on other than purely economic grounds. He might also possibly have to determine a dispute within the industry. In general, he would have had little impact on the industry apart from the indirect effect of the power of appointment.

It is scarcely surprising that the Government were unwilling to accept the virtual elimination of ministerial control in favour of an independent and almost irresponsible policy-determining body such as the Herbert Committee wished the CEA to become. The concentration of such great powers of supervision and decision in the Central Authority would, moreover, militate against the growth of that sense of initiative and responsibility in individual boards which the committee had urged should be a major aim of a reformed structure.

In place, therefore, of the Central Electricity Authority proposed by the committee, the Government decided to establish an Electricity Council. This is intended to be a forum in which the generating and distributing sides of the industry can meet to discuss and settle their common problems under independent guidance.[2] The new body consists of a chairman and one or two deputy chairmen appointed directly by the Minister, together with the chairman and a second representative of the Generating Board, and the chairmen of the twelve Area Boards. The main functions of the Council are to advise the Minister on questions concerning the electricity supply industry, and to promote and assist the maintenance and development by the Boards of an efficient, co-ordinated

[1] Report, para. 255. [2] White Paper, Cmd. 27/1956, para 7.

and economical system of supply. The Council may act on behalf of the Boards, or at their request provide services for them in matters of common interest. The Council will advise the Minister on major measures of reorganization or development involving substantial capital outlay submitted by the several Boards for his approval. The Council will borrow money by the issuing of stock on behalf of the entire industry, and will manage a central guarantee fund. They will be consulted on the prices to be charged for supplies of electricity both by the Generating Board for bulk supplies and by the Area Boards for retail supplies. They are the negotiating body for setting up the machinery for settling terms and conditions of employment and the machinery for joint consultation. They are to draw up from time to time, in consultation with the Minister, a general programme of research and to arrange for it to be carried out either by their own research institutions or by the Boards or any other person or agency.

The Electricity Council is modelled on the pattern of the Gas Council. It is essentially a federal body, with the board chairmen forming a large majority of the members. It is mainly a consultative and deliberative organ, and is unlikely to assert itself except in matters on which the Boards are almost entirely or wholly agreed. It is, as the White Paper makes clear, not an 'authority' exercising powers of direction and control; not even a supervisory organ; but a convenient centre for focusing opinion and encouraging discussion in the industry as a whole.

THE ORGANIZATION OF TRANSPORT

An interesting lesson about policy-making bodies can be learned from the experience of the British Transport Commission. The Transport Act, 1947, embodied the most grandiose scheme of nationalization so far witnessed in Britain. It nationalized forthwith the railways, the hotels owned by the railway companies, the London passenger transport system, the canals and inland waterways, the road haulage industry, and gave the Commission power to reorganize and transfer to public ownership the principal trade harbours and the road passenger services throughout the country.

The Act of 1947 introduced a two-tier organization of a mainly functional character. The lower tier consisted of six public corporations known as executives, in charge of specialized services. Five of these executives were responsible for functional elements of the transport system. Thus, there were executives dealing respectively with railways, road haulage, road passenger transport,[1] hotels and catering, docks and

[1] The Road Passenger Executive was abolished as from October 1, 1952, by S.I. 1952 No. 1726. See *British Transport Commission Annual Report 1952*, HMSO, HC 190/1952-3, para. 161.

inland waterways. The remaining executive took over the entire London passenger transport undertaking from the London Passenger Transport Board. Above these specialized bodies was the British Transport Commission, which was intended to be mainly a policy-making, co-ordinating, and controlling organ.

I expressed considerable doubt about the soundness of this complex organization in a book published in 1952.[1] I pointed to the disadvantages in the use of tiers of semi-government bodies superimposed one upon the other: as the late Sir Arthur Street remarked 'they tend unduly to complicate the administrative pattern and may be said to make control of Parliament and the people too remote'.[2] A further criticism was that it was doubtful whether the co-ordination of road and rail, of which high hopes were entertained and which was a strong motive in nationalizing transport, would best be promoted by so sharp a separation, in terms of organization, of the railways and the road services. The co-ordination of motorbus, trolleybus, underground, and suburban rail services in London had been effected by a regional body controlling all forms of transport. And finally, there was the objection that the British Transport Commission had been entrusted with the kind of high-level policy decisions which the Minister of Transport should exercise. The co-ordination and general supervision of nationalized industries and the harmonization of conflicting interests among them are surely matters for the appropriate Minister rather than for an intermediate body interposed between the government department concerned and the operating organs. There is not much more reason for creating the Transport Commission than for setting up a Fuel and Power Commission, with the corporations responsible for coal, gas, and electricity as subordinate executives.[3]

In point of fact, the British Transport Commission carried out very little co-ordination of real importance between road and rail during the six years prior to the passing of the Transport Act, 1953, which provided for the denationalization of the road haulage industry and the repeal of the Commission's powers relating to road passenger services and trade harbours. By far the most important question which faced the Commission was the modernization of the antiquated railway system. But the Commission did nothing about this until the publication of its modernization plan in 1955—a quite inexcusable delay on the part of a

[1] W. A. Robson: 'General Conclusions' in *Problems of Nationalized Industry*, ed. W. A. Robson (1952), p. 293.

[2] Sir Arthur Street: 'Quasi-Government Bodies since 1918' in *British Government since 1918* (1950), p. 171.

[3] W. A. Robson: 'General Conclusions' in *Problems of Nationalized Industry*, ed. W. A. Robson (1952), p. 294.

body supposed to be devoting its whole energy to matters of major policy. At a time when the shortage of coal had been acute for several years, the British Transport Commission gave no indication that it recognized the need for a less wasteful system of traction than the coal-burning locomotive, which normally operates at about five per cent thermal efficiency.

The British Transport Commission, in its Annual Report for 1952, seemed to be dimly aware of the feeble progress it had made in the co-ordination and integration of the several forms of transport placed in its charge. The Commission referred to the schemes designed to produce a nationalized internal transport system which had been brought to a halt by the Conservative Government's policy announced in that year. The schemes which had to be put aside included the transfer of Railway Executive collection and delivery services to the Road Haulage Executive, with a view to their ultimate fusion with the latter's local services; the establishment of common commercial services for the carriage of freight by road and rail under unified control; a general plan for the integration of railway and road haulage motor engineering and stores organizations; the trunk haulage of Road Haulage Executive traffic by rail between certain main centres, such as London to Glasgow or Cardiff; the transfer of some railway trunk services to the Road Haulage Executive; and plans for speeding up the transit time of small parcels traffic sent by rail on cross-country routes by transferring them to road transport.[1]

There is no evidence that any of these 'plans' or 'schemes' or proposals had reached the stage of being put into practice, in whole or part, beyond a reference to a small-scale common commercial service which had been tried as an experiment in East Anglia and was to have been expanded. Nor were any firm dates announced for the carrying out of these schemes. It was generally known, however, that difficulties had arisen with the trade unions concerned over any proposal to transfer goods from road to rail, or *vice versa*. In any event, even if all these schemes had been fully put into practice, the basic problems confronting the railways and the road services would scarcely have been touched.

The Act of 1953[2] required the British Transport Commission to submit a scheme of administrative reorganization to the Minister of Transport within a year. This scheme was to provide for the establishment of area authorities in place of the Railway Executive, the publication of statements of operating costs and other statistics in respect of each area authority, and the co-ordination of area activities. The general control of finance and charges remained with the Commission.

[1] *British Transport Commission Annual Report 1952*, HMSO, HC 190/1952-3, para. 12.
[2] s. 16.

REORGANIZATION OF THE RAILWAYS

The Railways Reorganization Scheme 1954[1] was produced in compliance with this obligation. It divided England and Wales into five areas, with Scotland as a sixth. The London passenger transport system remained undisturbed under its executive; but elsewhere Area Boards were set up composed of a chairman and not more than six other members appointed by the Commission, of whom at least one is a member of the Commission. All the members of the Area Boards, including the chairman, are part-time and serve for a period of two years.

The Commission intend the Area Boards to exercise general supervision of the railways in their areas and ensure that policies laid down by the Commission are faithfully carried out. The Boards are to foster initiative in improving rail services and effecting economies; and they can make recommendations to the Commission in matters of general policy. They must submit budgets and forecasts of capital and revenue expenditure to the Commission, and exercise delegated powers in such matters as approving expenditure and making appointments. They will keep in close touch with railway users, seek to inculcate *esprit de corps* in the personnel, and see that proper attention is paid to staff welfare.[2]

The new scheme of organization is based on the idea that the supervision of the railways is a function of the Area Boards, subject to the observance of such policies, conditions and limitations as the Commission may impose.[3] There is in each area a Chief Regional Manager on whom executive responsibility rests. The Area Boards are not intended to be executive organs of day-to-day management but bodies corresponding to the boards of the companies which existed when the railways were privately owned. They will form policy at the area level, and supervise the Chief Regional Manager in a general way. Some matters requiring treatment on a national scale, such as the management of the wagon stock, negotiations with great industrial or trading organs, having nationwide interests, may be carried out at Commission level. The chain of responsibility runs from the Commission to the Area Board and from the latter to the Chief Regional Manager; but there will be much direct contact between the executive elements at Commission headquarters and the Regional Managers.[4]

This regional organization of the railways has a two-fold aim. In the first place it seeks to establish a much more decentralized system of

[1] HMSO, Cmd. 9191/1954.
[2] *Ib.*, Explanatory Statement, para. 27.
[3] *Ib.*, art. 5 (1).
[4] *Ib.*, pp. 2-3; see also 'Ten Years of Nationalized Transport', *Railway Gazette*, October 2, 1957, p. 391.

control and management than existed under the single Railway Executive. According to the BTC, although centralized management was necessary during the earlier stages of nationalization in order to unify the four groups of the former railway companies, it was never intended to be a permanent method of organization. Steps had therefore been taken even before 1951 to delegate additional responsibilities to the regions, so that when the change of government occurred in that year the time was approaching when departmental control could largely be delegated to Chief Regional Managers.[1]

In the second place the new form of organization seeks to encourage a strong spirit of emulation between different railway regions, though competition in the ordinary commercial sense is ruled out. The BTC have made the rather childish proposal to re-introduce distinctive uniorms and different colours for the locomotives and carriages of the several regions. Of greater importance is the intention to improve the compilation of statistics designed to stimulate comparison and emulation between the areas, and to provide both the area authorities and BTC with whatever measurements of efficiency can usefully aid managerial control. The Commission hope to evolve a costing system which will make it possible to compare the operating costs in each area.[2]

No attempt was made to integrate the other services provided by the Commission into the area plan. Docks and inland waterways have been handed over to a board of management composed of the three members of the former Docks and Inland Waterways Executive. Hotels and catering services have been placed under a chief officer who is the former chairman of the defunct Hotels and Catering Executive and now a member of the Transport Commission. Three companies, owned and controlled by the Commission, have been formed to take over the road haulage services which still remain with the Commission after denationalization. They are British Road Services Ltd, for general haulage business; British Road Services (Pickfords) Ltd, for special traffics; and British Road Services (Contracts) Ltd, which handles contract hire.

The reasons put forward in support of this disjunctive organization were that hotel management and the operation of docks and inland waterways, are specialized businesses which have little connection with railway transport. They should therefore be separated from the manage-

[1] *Railways Reorganization Scheme*, HMSO, Cmd. 9191/1954, para. 12.

[2] *Ib.*, paras. 31 and 37. It will not be possible, however, to show the net earnings of each region in a way which would significantly reflect either the revenues and expenditures attributable to each area or the relative efficiencies of the area managements, since much traffic is not confined to a single area.

ment of the railways.[1] On the other hand, the BTC Catering Services will attach a catering services officer to the staff of each Chief Regional Officer, who may ask him to make improvements in the services provided in his area. By this means it is hoped that railway refreshment rooms and the catering services on trains will be under the influence of the area railway management though not under its control. Neither the Chief Regional Manager nor the Area Board will have the power to override any instructions a catering services officer may receive from the head of his department.

Under the new set-up the British Transport Commission themselves handle a number of matters which formerly belonged to the Railway Executive and which should be decided at a national level. These include the design, manufacture, and standards of maintenance of locomotives, rolling stock, permanent way, and signalling; major matters concerning labour relations; higher appointments; the general level of charges; policies and principles of railway operation; the inter-regional distribution of wagons; and general commercial policy.[2]

It is difficult at this stage to prophesy how successful this complex system will prove to be in practice. The future of the British Transport undertaking depends on a number of factors which have little relation to organization as such. They include improved equipment, better technology, more up-to-date methods of operation, the attraction of men of greater ability, better qualifications and wider outlook to the industry, and more vigorous and aggressive management. The railways have been declining steadily in almost every respect during the past thirty-five years, and they made no serious effort under private ownership to arrest that decline, except by seeking to restrict the scope of their competitors' activities on the roads. During the first decade of nationalization their record has been singularly unimpressive. Good organization is obviously important; but by itself it cannot accomplish the transformation which is needed.

There is, however, some evidence to show that the new system is working well in practice; and in any case it is certainly better than the original structure of the Railway Executive. According to the *Railway Gazette*,[3] which is well-informed on such matters, the Area Boards are recognized by the railway staff as serving a useful purpose. When they were first established there was some doubt about the wisdom of removing one level of management—the Railway Executive—only in order to replace it by another—the Area Boards—which might prove to

[1] HMSO, Cmd. 9191/1954, Explanatory Memorandum, paras. 33-5.
[2] *Ib.*, para. 13.
[3] October 2, 1957, p. 391.

be a barrier between the Chief Regional Managers and the Commission. This has not proved to be the case. 'The good sense of the individuals concerned in this rather complicated and far from clear relationship between Commission, Boards, and Managers have succeeded in making it a reasonable working possibility.'[1]

It will be noted that in the new organization the members of the Area Boards are appointed by the British Transport Commission, whereas the members of the former Executives were appointed by the Minister of Transport. Moreover, one or more members of the Commission sits on each of the Area Boards. In consequence the Commission are firmly in control of the Area Boards. By contrast there were large differences of opinion between the Railway Executive and the British Transport Commission on several matters of importance. This created such friction that the Commission formally requested the Government to abolish the Railway Executive and to give the Commission full and undisputed control over the personnel and working of their undertaking.[2]

THE LONDON PASSENGER TRANSPORT SYSTEM

The position of the London passenger transport system in relation to the BTC raises some important problems of organization. The public ownership of this great undertaking was carried out in 1932 when it was placed in the charge of the London Passenger Transport Board.[3] It continued to be operated by that body until 1947, when the position was changed by the Transport Act, 1947. Thenceforth, it became part of the nationalized transport system and was made responsible to the British Transport Commission. Its finances were merged in those of the Commission. The London Transport Executive replaced the London Passenger Transport Board.

The passenger transport complex which serves the metropolis is an outstanding success. It is not only the largest but also the best system of public transport existing in any great city in the world.[4] Its principal architects were the late Lord Ashfield and Sir Frank Pick, while on the political side the chief credit goes to Mr Herbert Morrison. The British Transport Commission have contributed little or nothing to the London passenger transport system, and a recent inquiry conducted by the

[1] *Loc cit.*

[2] 509 HC Deb. 5s., col. 1042, Mr Lennox-Boyd, Minister of Transport and Civil Aviation (December 15, 1952).

[3] For an account, see Ernest Davies: 'The London Passenger Transport Board' in *Public Enterprise*, ed. W. A. Robson (1937), p. 155.

[4] See *Great Cities of the World*, ed. W. A. Robson (Allen & Unwin) (1954).

Chambers Committee has raised the question whether the present organic connection between the two bodies should continue.

The relationship is unsatisfactory, because while the BTC have ultimate responsibility for London transport, and especially for its finances, they do not appoint the members of the London Transport Executive[1] or possess the indisputable right to control the Executive which they exercise over the other bodies which they have set up to manage the several parts of the BTC undertaking. The Chambers Committee thought the state of semi-independence accorded to the LTE had prevented a clear definition of the responsibilities falling on the Executive and the Commission respectively, and they rightly considered this to be essential for the efficiency of a large organization.[2] They emphasized that the existence of the Commission in an intermediate position between the LTE and the Minister might lower the sense of financial responsibility felt by the Executive. A consciousness that any financial burdens would ultimately rest on the shoulders of the Commission may well have made the LTE less zealous than they otherwise might have been in pressing for the highway improvements which are so urgently needed and so long overdue in London. Moreover, the suburban services of the British railways are today no better co-ordinated with the road and rail services of the London Transport Executive than they were when the undertakings were under separate control.[3]

The Chambers Committee considered that the present unsatisfactory relationship could be cured by one of two remedies: one was to make LTE completely independent of the Commission; the other would be to abolish the London Transport Executive as a separate legal entity and to give BTC complete control of, and responsibility for, London transport. If the latter course were adopted, the Commission would probably appoint a management board which might resemble the Executive, but the power relations between the two bodies would be quite different.[4]

The Chambers Report presented the arguments for each of these alternatives. The case for giving LTE a completely independent existence rested on the following four grounds: (1) The British Transport Commission are not responsible for the local public transport services of any other large city, and there is no reason to single out London for different treatment from the rest. (2) The London Transport Executive took over the undertaking formerly entrusted to the London Passenger Transport Board which had been a very efficient public body with a well-developed tradition of service and loyalty and this might be lost if

[1] This is done by the Minister of Transport.
[2] *Report of the Committee of Inquiry into London Transport*, HMSO (1955), paras. 360-1.
[3] *Ib.*, para. 364. [4] *Ib.*, paras. 365-7.

London Transport were merged with a much larger and newer undertaking. (3) The function of London transport is to operate local passenger services while the Commission is mainly concerned with long-distance passenger and goods traffic. The two organizations are fundamentally dissimilar, and policies and practices which are suitable for the one may be quite inappropriate for the other. (4) The London transport undertaking is large enough to stand on its own feet. Complete structural and legal independence need not involve relinquishing the aim of providing a fully co-ordinated system of passenger transport in the metropolis. Close co-operation is frequently brought about in similar circumstances between separately owned road transport undertakings in the provinces. A personal link could be obtained if the organs were separated by appointing a member of the Commission to be a member of the governing board of London Transport.[1]

The alternative remedy of complete subordination of London Transport to the British Transport Commission could be supported on the grounds that (1) it would eliminate the aloofness which at present exists between the LTE and the BTC (2) the handling of matters requiring close co-ordination would be facilitated (3) some economies might result if the Commission had full control over all their passenger road services.[2]

Having carefully analysed the advantages of each of the two possible courses of action, the Chambers Committee lacked the resolution or the courage to recommend which of them the government should take. The decision, they thought, involved factors other than efficiency, such as the relative importance of co-ordinating all forms of passenger transport in the metropolis as compared with the need to give those in charge of the undertaking a more immediate sense of financial responsibility and direct access to the Minister. The Committee clearly entertained a somewhat narrow view of what the concept of efficiency involves in excluding such factors as lying outside its ambit. It is possible that there was a division of opinion among the members on this important question and they decided that evasion was the better part of valour.

There is a strong case in my opinion for separating the London Transport undertaking from the British Transport Commission. This rests partly on the grounds specified in the Chambers Report but also partly on other grounds. London Transport is a much more progressive and well-managed concern than the railways; and to subordinate a first-rate concern to a third-rate undertaking is a step to be taken only for the most compelling reasons, which do not exist here. In the next place,

[1] *Report of the Committee of Inquiry into London Transport,* HMSO (1955), para. 366.
[2] *Ib.*, para. 368.

London Transport is almost the only example we have in the sphere of public enterprise of the integration and co-ordination of services on a regional basis; and since there is much scope for further efforts in this direction, it is a pity to confuse the picture by attaching the LTE to the chariot of the BTC. Lastly, I do not believe it is possible to point to a single advantage which has acrued to London Transport during the past decade by reason of its forming part of the nationalized industry.

BROADCASTING

The question of greater regional independence has been raised on several occasions in connection with broadcasting. The BBC have always claimed that they delegated large discretionary powers to their regional controllers in regard to programme policy and planning; but the Beveridge Committee reported that while the regional controllers have formally almost complete autonomy regarding the contents of Home Service programmes, this is severely limited in practice by central control of staff, accommodation and finance.[1]

Lord Simon of Wythenshawe, who was chairman of the BBC from 1947 to 1952, has lived most of his life in his native city of Manchester. He confesses to a natural disposition to dislike 'Londonization', by which he means the over-centralization of national institutions whose headquarters are in London. In a description of the regional organization of the BBC published in 1953 Lord Simon explained that engineering and building are completely centralized in London, and any building contract above fifty pounds is placed and supervised by headquarters in London. 'This', he wrote, 'is an almost incredible piece of over-centralization, it is most inefficient, and frustrating to the Region.'[2]

It is still necessary today for a region to obtain central approval for any building or engineering work costing more than fifty pounds; and orders are usually issued by headquarters. Responsibility for the execution of the work, if the expenditure does not exceed £2,500, is entrusted to the Regional Controller and the Regional Engineer.

The engineering service is a unified service controlled from the centre. Lord Simon criticized this central control as being excessive and far too rigid, particularly in regard to studio engineering, which he said should be under the Regional Controller.[3] Since Lord Simon published his book the position has in practice been somewhat relaxed. All engineering development work continues to be directed by headquarters in London;

[1] *Report of the Broadcasting Committee 1949*, HMSO, Cmd. 8116/1951, para. 524.

[2] *The BBC from Within* (1953), p. 150.

[3] *Ib.*, p. 148.

and on matters of general engineering policy and practice the Regional Engineers are responsible to the centre. But the central supervision of a Regional Engineer is not too strict; and on day-to-day engineering questions within a region he is answerable to the Regional Controller. Responsibility for transmitters is outside the scope of the Regional Engineering service, and Lord Simon considered that central control on this matter was justified.[1]

Staff policy is determined on a national basis by the BBC in regard to remuneration, conditions of service, grading and training. This is not only right but essential in a public corporation of this kind, for by no other means could justice and consistency of treatment be achieved. The BBC does not differentiate between the salaries paid to staff in comparable grades in London and in the regions. This is advantageous to the latter, since where a distinction is made the London rate is usually higher than the provincial rate. The BBC has a very carefully devised salary and wages structure based on job evaluation, length of service, and personal merit. Continuous efforts are made to maintain relativities within the BBC on the one hand, and between the BBC and relevant outside organizations on the other. In the application of the Corporation's personnel policy a good deal of local discretion has been devolved on the regions and on the various directorates, particularly in regard to recognizing merit by special rewards.

Finance is centrally controlled and this again is essential so far as the allocation of funds to the regions is concerned. Each region is given an annual allowance for its day-to-day administrative and operational needs. It receives also separate allowances to finance its activities in sound and television programmes. Capital expenditure is separately authorized in accordance with the needs and programme capacities of the region. Lord Simon thought the regions have no cause to complain of the share of the BBC's revenue which they receive. Of course they would like to have more money, but the amount allowed to them, in his judgment, has been adequate and reasonable.[2] He thought financial control tended to be too rigid, but found little evidence of red tape or frustration.

The Beveridge Committee on Broadcasting proposed that in each of the three 'national' regions of Scotland, Wales and Northern Ireland, there should be a federal delegation of powers to a Broadcasting Commission appointed by the Government, the chairman being a governor of the BBC. These Commissions should initiate and decide the Home Service sound programme for their respective regions and possess sufficient autonomy in matters of finance, accommodation and staff to

[1] *The BBC from Within* (1953), p. 150.
[2] *Loc cit.*

carry out the decisions. In the English regions, the Regional Controllers should be given a substantially greater measure of freedom, and fuller use made of the Regional Advisory Councils, which should be strengthened. The income and expenditure figures for each region should be published separately. The BBC would continue to provide nationwide services in addition to those of the Commissions and they would retain overall control of finance and capital development; but an extended use of block grants would enable the regions to exercise more initiative than hitherto in regard to capital development schemes.[1]

These recommendations were generally accepted by the Conservative Government in 1952[2], and the new Charter issued to the BBC in that year contained the provisions needed to carry them out. National Broadcasting Councils have been established for Scotland and Wales; and a Regional Advisory Council for Northern Ireland and for each of the three English regions. The chairman of each National Council and of the Advisory Council for Northern Ireland are *ex officio* members of the BBC Board of Governors. The most important function of a National Council is to control the policy and content of the BBC Home Sound Service provided primarily for reception in that country, and in doing so to pay full regard to the distinctive culture, interests, and tastes of the people of that country. The National Councils can also advise the BBC on all matters concerning their television and other broadcasting services; they may select persons for employment by the BBC for work entirely concerned with the Councils' affairs; and each of them is to make an annual report to the BBC and such other reports as either the Council or the Corporation may think necessary.[3]

The Charter also provides for the establishment, functions, tenure, etc. of the Regional Advisory Councils; and it requires that the BBC shall devolve on their Regional Controllers powers which will give them a reasonable measure of independence concerning programmes.[4]

None of the previous inquiries or Charters had gone nearly so far as this in the direction of regional or federal decentralization, nor been so insistent on the devolution of real powers rather than apparent ones to the regional organs and Regional Controllers.

This brings us to the heart of the matter, which is the extent to which devolution in programme-making is permitted and practicable.

The regions have two principal functions to perform in the national system of broadcasting. One is to contribute to the national sound and

[1] *Report of the Broadcasting Committee 1949*, HMSO, Cmd. 8116/1951, paras. 534–6.

[2] *Memorandum on the Report of the Broadcasting Committee*, HMSO, Cmd. 8350/1952, paras. 15 and 21.

[3] BBC Charter, Cmd. 8605/1952, arts. 2 (1), 4, 8, 9, 10 and 12.

[4] *Ib.*, art. 13.

television programmes. The other is to provide programmes to meet the special needs of their own regional audiences. In regard to the first function, this can only be decided on the basis of what each region is able to offer, and the judgment of headquarters as to its acceptability for the national programmes. Sometimes London may suggest to a Regional Controller that he should produce a particular feature for the national network; but the Regional Controller is free to accept or refuse the invitation as he pleases.

So far as the second function is concerned, there is much more regional independence in sound broadcasting than in television. In sound broadcasting, Scotland and Wales enjoy almost complete autonomy within the limits imposed by their resources of money and talent. The regions have a very wide discretion to substitute their own or any other regionally-produced items in place of any national features other than the news bulletins, party political broadcasts, and a few other items of national importance. In 1957-8 the regions originated about one sixth of the content of their Home Services on sound broadcasting. Scotland and Wales originated about one fifth. The proportion seems to be declining, for in 1951 the proportion of the Home Service programmes originating in the regions averaged about one fourth for the whole country.[1]

A further measure of decentralization which has recently begun is the introduction of broadcasting by regions on VHF to smaller areas within their territories.

Much less devolution has taken place in regard to television than sound broadcasting. This is largely due to the very high cost of producing television programmes. Until 1955 the BBC policy was to confine all television to the national network, but since then a relaxation has been permitted. The regions may now opt out of certain parts of the national network, subject to headquarters approval of the times and the kind of subjects they will put on. Within these limits they are free to run their own programmes.

The BBC believe that in sound broadcasting the process of devolution to the regions, Scotland and Wales has now gone far enough to satisfy regional or national sentiment, though it is possible that further efforts could and should be made to meet the needs of area or local communities. In regard to television, the BBC would like to allow the regions—and especially the national regions—much more freedom and scope for originating their own programmes; but this cannot be done without additional revenue and frequencies. If the third television channel were to be given to the BBC, with a corresponding increase of their revenue, progress could be made in this direction.

[1] *Report of the Broadcasting Committee 1949*, HMSO, Cmd. 8116/1951, para. 524.

GAS SUPPLY: THE NEW NEEDS

Gas supply is decentralized to a far greater extent than these other industries. The twelve Area Gas Boards are almost autonomous bodies as regards the manufacture and supply of gas. The Gas Council, which is the central organ, was placed in a far weaker position than that given to the Central Electricity Authority by the Electricity Act, 1947; and in the gas industry there is no body corresponding to the Generating Board which generates electricity for the whole country. The main statutory functions of the Gas Council relate to settling a research programme, co-ordination of training and education programmes, advising on reorganization and development, the manufacture of plant for the area boards, the manufacture, sale, or supply of gas fittings, and raising money for any individual Area Board on the credit of the whole industry. It has also a duty to advise the Minister on questions affecting the gas industry and to assist the Area Boards in the efficient exercise of their functions. The Gas Council are composed entirely of the chairmen of the Area Gas Boards, except for the chairman and vice-chairman; and they have only a small staff of under 200.

In addition to their statutory functions, the Gas Council have been performing a number of other services usually for the gas industry as a whole, but in a few instances on behalf of a number of Area Gas Boards. Among these additional functions performed on behalf of the whole industry are the submission of evidence to departmental committees of inquiry; the division of global allocations of coal and other commodities in short supply between the several Area Gas Boards; entering into contracts with firms engaged in prospecting for natural gas; making large bulk purchasing arrangements for supplies of commodities needed by the Area boards; conducting publicity in such media as films, exhibits, advertising, and press releases; examining all Bills before Parliament with a view to taking action where necessary to protect the interests of the industry or bringing clauses affecting particular boards to their notice; advising Area Gas Boards on legal problems, co-operating with boards involved in litigation, and serving as a clearing house for information about legal advice or judicial decisions. An example of a service afforded to part of the industry is the operation of marketing arrangements for coke on behalf of five Area Boards in Southern England.[1]

When the industry was nationalized in 1948, there was no need, either on technical or economic grounds, for administration on a national scale to manufacture or distribute gas. The Heyworth Committee had,

[1] *Gas Council Annual Report 1953-4*, HMSO, HC 262/1953-4, paras. 66, 67, 70, 74, 80, 85, 86, 90, 107-20, 123, 125 and 126.

indeed, expressly pointed out in 1945 that there were no problems facing the industry which were by their very nature applicable to the whole country. They explained that a national grid was not practicable; it was not economically possible to supply gas in every part of the country; and that selling prices could not usefully be fixed on a national basis. The Committee therefore rejected complete centralization as inappropriate.[1] In these circumstances the Government quite properly adopted a decentralized form of organization for the nationalized industry.

During the past ten years new tendencies have been making themselves felt. In 1953 the Gas Council reported that the integration of gas supplies, calling for the planning and control of production and distribution over far larger areas than was previously necessary, had been a chief factor in modifying the organization since nationalization. There had been a general tendency towards reducing the number of management units and a widening of functional control within the areas. For example, the South Western Gas Board was originally organized in 11 sub-divisions grouped under two divisions. In 1954, control of production, distribution, and accounts was centralized at area headquarters, while commercial services were allocated among six divisions sub-divided into districts.[2] The East Midlands Board reduced the number of divisional and sub-divisional offices in their area from fourteen to eight. The organization which then existed, consisting of divisions, sub-divisions, group and local managers, would be replaced by larger units under Group Managers placed directly under the control of the Divisional General Manager.[3] Such adjustments as these can easily be made within the framework of the gas board areas.

There are, however, signs of an emerging need for gas supplies to be manufactured on a scale which far transcends the areas of the existing Gas Boards. Dr J. Burns, chief engineer of the North Thames Gas Board, in his presidential address to the Institution of Gas Engineers in 1958, said that the future trend should seek to avoid transporting coal long distances up and down the country and then losing a high proportion of its thermal content in inefficient combustion. The trend should lie towards the underground transmission of fuel either in the form of gas or electricity. Gas has been losing ground to coal and electricity for domestic heating, cooking and hot water. It can regain that ground if gas is produced at a competitive price and quality. One of the principal

[1] *Report of the Committee on the Gas Industry*, HMSO, Cmd. 6699/1945, para. 242.

[2] *Gas Council Annual Report 1953-4*, HMSO, HC 262/1953-4 paras. 180, 181, 187, and 481-2.

[3] *East Midlands Gas Board Annual Report 1953-4*, HMSO, HC 254/1953-4, paras. 2-3.

methods for reducing the price of gas is by concentrating its manufacture in large plants, thereby lowering overhead and operating costs.[1]

Dr Burns contended that already there are great advantages to be reaped from transmitting gas underground instead of transporting coal or oil by rail. Hence plants for gasifying coal should be located as close as possible to the coalfields, while plants for making gas from oil should be sited near to the refineries. About seventy per cent of all the gas consumed in Britain is used in a band of territory about 35 miles broad running on either side of a line between Manchester and London. A like proportion of the developed reserves of high grade coal are to be found within this belt. Dr Burns suggests that gas should be produced from coal by very large gas works at the Northern end of this strip, while gas made from oil would be produced on a very large scale at its Southern end. The two giant producing centres would be connected by a 30-inch main transmission pipe. This London-Manchester main could form part of a national gas grid.[2]

The implications of these technical proposals by an eminent gas engineer is that the manufacture and distribution of gas should no longer be conceived on a regional basis but should be envisaged on a national scale. This indicated that the need has already arisen, or is in process of arising, for a central gas producing board comparable to the Central Electricity Generating Board. There may be no legal objection to an existing gas board producing gas in areas other than their own, nor are they precluded from combining in joint schemes for the purpose of large-scale production. But it is far less likely that they will do so than that the system of production and distribution would be transformed by means of a national gas authority. In short, the technical changes now taking place indicate the need for considerable changes in the organization of the nationalized gas industry.

OTHER NATIONALIZED INDUSTRIES

The nationalized air services were originally concentrated in a single corporation—BOAC—which took the whole world for its parish. After a considerable struggle, British air services were reorganized in 1946 on the basis of three separate corporations: BOAC, which was henceforth to operate the North Atlantic and Commonwealth routes; British European Airways, which was given the European services and the domestic services within the United Kingdom; and British South American Airways (later renamed British Latin American Airways) to run services to South America. The Civil Aviation Act, 1946, made it pos-

[1] Published by the Institution of Gas Engineers, p. 18. [2] *Ib.*, p. 27.

sible to create subsidiary airlines and also for the three main corporations to purchase shares in other civil aviation undertakings.

Unfortunately, the Tudor IV aircraft which BLAA were using turned out to be unsatisfactory for the South American services; and for this reason the Labour Government decided to merge BLAA with BOAC. A short-term difficulty concerning the supply of aircraft should never have been allowed to determine a fundamental question of policy of this kind. It is regrettable that a decision of this magnitude, involving statutory changes, should have been made with little consideration being given to the proper organization of British air services. Lord Pakenham, then Minister of Civil Aviation, attempted to justify the change on other grounds, but his arguments were superficial and amounted to little more than debating points.[1]

The most completely decentralized organization was to be found in the iron and steel industry. Here the previous structure of the industry was preserved almost intact in the form of ninety-six commercial companies whose stocks or shares were compulsorily acquired and transferred to the British Iron and Steel Corporation, which thus became a gigantic holding corporation. The result was a two-tier system; but it was entirely different from that which was set up to run the transport industry. It was not only much more decentralized, but also resembled, at both levels, the type of organization found in large-scale capitalist enterprise. The Iron and Steel Act[2] even went so far as to declare that the corporation had a duty to exercise their powers so as to secure the largest degree of decentralization consistent with the proper discharge of their other duties.

Without delving into the details of the other nationalized undertakings, such as the Colonial Development Corporation or the Atomic Energy Authority, we can see the great diversity of organization to be found among the public corporations. The variations are due in part to the differing characteristics of the several industries; they are also due in part to inherent differences in the conceptions applied by different Ministers at different times to the problems confronting the Government in carrying out their nationalization programme. There has been a commendable desire to experiment in this and other aspects of nationalization, or at least to avoid a rigid uniformity.[3] There may also have been a progressive retreat from the extreme legal centralization of the Coal Industry Nationalization Act, 1946.

[1] See his and other speeches on the Second Reading of the Airways Corporations Bill, 164 HL Deb. 5s., cols. 274 ff. (July 20, 1949.)

[2] s. 3 (1) (c).

[3] Cf. Mr Morrison's remarks during the Second Reading of the Gas Bill, February 11, 1948, 447 HC Deb. 5s., col. 480.

PRINCIPLES OF ORGANIZATION

We have now reviewed the organization of the major nationalized industries and considered some of the problems relating to the structure and management of these great undertakings. While it is too early to pronounce final judgment on the several types of organization, two elementary propositions can be advanced. First, the attainment of the correct size and shape of the operating unit is as important in public enterprise as it is in private enterprise. Second, the determination of the optimum unit in a nationalized industry can ultimately be ascertained only with the aid of elaborate statistical yardsticks to supplement and replace the financial criteria used in commercial concerns. Unfortunately, statisticians are lagging behind the public need in evolving the statistical criteria necessary to determine performance. Cost of production is one vital index of efficiency, but this alone will not suffice unless the output of the commodity or service is satisfactory in quantitative and qualitative terms. Meanwhile, we must get along as best we can on the basis of enlightened guesses. Our present forms of organization should be regarded as tentative, except where a single national unit is unmistakably needed, as in the case of the Bank of England.

Most of the problems we have been considering relate to the size of the administrative organization and the degree of centralization which should exist within a nationalized industry, two matters which are closely inter-related.

There is prevalent at the present time in Britain an excessive adulation of decentralization in the field of nationalized industry as though it were an end in itself. This is probably a reaction against the high degree of centralization introduced into the formal structure of some of the public undertakings. There is no doubt that decentralized organization tends to increase the opportunities for technical, administrative, commercial, and financial experimentation, and this should be regarded as a substantial advantage.

But there can also be great advantages in centralization. If we analyse the deplorable plight of the coal industry under private ownership, we shall find that one of the most adverse features of the situation was the existence of about 1,400 separate collieries, each with its independent management, and an absence of any central organization to plan or carry out future development and modernization of the industry. There was no central agency responsible for capital investment, research, the maintenance of the labour force and other matters of fundamental importance to the industry. An equally chaotic position existed in regard to electricity distribution prior to nationalization. Hundreds of municipal or commercial undertakings existed to distribute electricity and there was an immense diversity of voltages, type of current, and charges. Even a great city like London was a veritable jungle of tiny overlapping jurisdictions. Again, the absence of any central organ to control the railways prior to the creation of the BTC failed to give us an up-to-date and well-managed railway system. We should recall these and similar facts to mind when we consider some of the drastic criticism which has been made in some quarters concerning the present organization of the nationalized industries. Quite a number of people write and talk as though the chief defect in the nationalized industries is over-centralization and that a great advance in efficiency would result from decentralization. The Conservative Party manifesto in the 1959 Election stated that the party will do everything possible to ensure less centralization in the nationalized industries. A policy of decentralization for its own sake might, however, reduce efficiency and have many disadvantages.

The Acton Society Trust[1] have attacked the four fundamental assumptions on which the present pattern of organization rests. The first of these is that large-scale organization is advantageous. This, they say, is fallacious, for size may bring disadvantages in terms of slow and cumbersome management, poor human relations, and so forth, and in any case the advantages of large size could have been achieved by smaller organizations than those which were set up. I have already stressed the importance of finding, or at least seeking, the optimum size of the operating unit; and broad generalizations take us no further towards that goal.

A second assumption is that the public corporation is the most efficient instrument of public management. This in my view is unquestionably correct, and its correctness is not weakened by remarking that the pre-war examples of this institution were much smaller than the public corporations set up since 1945. The BBC and the Central Electricity Board, the London Passenger Transport Board, and the Port of London Authority, were sufficiently large, and their functions complex and important enough, to provide a basis for an adequate judgment concerning the efficacy of the public corporation.

The third assumption which the Acton Society Trust criticizes is that final responsibility for each industry should be unified in a single body, designed to facilitate public accountability, central economic planning, and national wage negotiations. It contends that these objectives could probably have been achieved by means of a much looser organization than those which have been set up, which allocates to the central authority not only specified functions which require to be centrally exercised but also overall responsibilities. Again I would say this criticism is mis-

[1] *Patterns of Organization* (1951) (Nationalized Industry Study No. 9), pp. 21-6.

conceived. There should be some focus of responsibility if the need for public accountability is to be satisfied. Unification has not been pursued regardless of all other relevant considerations, as we can see from the examples of the airways corporations and the gas industry, which is highly decentralized. Public enterprise cannot be run on the same lines as private enterprise, without regard to these essential matters. To remove day-to-day management from the political arena was already a very large step; and some substitute for the clearly individualized and concentrated responsibility of Ministers had to be found.

The fourth assumption which is questioned is that each individual can control only a few subordinates, and hence that a multi-tiered organization is needed. The Acton Society Trust claims that experience in private enterprise shows that the span is larger than was formerly believed, and in any event a board should have a wider span than an individual. The implication is that some of the intermediate organs are unnecessary. This was not the view of the Fleck Committee on the coal industry, the organization of which had been the subject of more criticism than that of any other nationalized industry. The Herbert Committee even recommended bringing a further level of responsibility into the electricity supply industry with the creation of a reconstituted central authority in addition to the new Generating Board.

The Acton Society Trust advocates that the nationalized industries should be reorganized on entirely different lines. The basic units should be small enough to preserve personal loyalties and human contacts, both between workpeople and management, and between the industry and the public, for only thus can happiness and efficiency be achieved. Coordination of these units can be assured by much looser arrangements than those which at present prevail. The main object in view would be to eliminate the gulf which now exists between the operating manager and the final authority. Greater responsibility must be conferred on the operational level and the chain of command should be reduced in length. Long chains of command result from the assumption mentioned above that a supervisory organ can control only a limited number of units.[1]

Moreover, the Trust contends, the existence of a multi-tier structure is wasteful of manpower, particularly in regard to the high grade specialists of whom there is a serious shortage. Also, it removes the ablest of them from the day-to-day tasks of direct management and consigns them to a relatively remote position at regional or national headquarters, where they breathe a more rarified air but are able to exercise far less effective influence.[2]

[1] *Management under Nationalization* (1953) (Acton Society Trust), pp. 60-5.
[2] *Ib.*, pp. 58-61.

A similar approach is pushed to far greater lengths in *The Future of Nationalization* by Mr H. A. Clegg and Professor T. E. Chester, who was formerly director of the Acton Society Trust. The authors argue that while it may be necessary to allocate certain specified functions to national, regional, or district organs, there is no justification for giving managerial powers to any of these bodies. Hence, while the grouping of operating units may be desirable in order to secure co-ordinated development, the raising of capital, central purchasing, wage negotiations, and so forth, it is a complete mistake to make each such grouping a unit of management, thereby creating a series of managerial levels. The disadvantages of many tiers of management are in their view overwhelming. They lead to an inflated demand for talent, and call for supermen at the top; they encourage standardization of procedures, regardless of local differences; they discourage the local manager from doing his best because he is unable to take decisions on his own responsibility which would cultivate good relations with the workpeople.[1] These authors accordingly recommend that full and final responsibility should be given to the local managements, subject only to exceptions to be defined by statute in regard to specified matters of the kinds mentioned above which are to be determined by the larger groupings. 'There is no need', they write, 'for over-all managerial bodies at national or divisional headquarters' [in the coal industry], but 'any reorganization must take into account that the areas have become the main centres for the planning of production and development, and for the provision of technical services.' The general outline of their scheme is summarized by saying that regional or area authorities in any of the nationalized industries should be regarded as occupying the position of holding companies to plan and supervise development—to exercise financial control over the operating units. The Minister, advised by an independent commission similar to the now defunct Electricity Commission, would supervise the work of these authorities and see that they satisfy the needs of national planning. The Commission would advise the local or regional boards as well as the Minister, and intervene in disputes. Finally, a federation of regional authorities would conduct negotiations with the trade unions on a national basis and also confer with the Minister as and when required.[2]

This scheme definitely rejects as unnecessary a national board, and especially a national managerial board. Any functions to be exercised at the national level would be performed by the appropriate Minister advised by a commission.[3] The principal object of the proponents of this approach is to concentrate management in the smallest possible units.

[1] *The Future of Nationalization* (1953), p. 170.
[2] *Ib.*, p. 209. [3] *Ib.*, p. 161.

Indeed, the authors state explicitly that they think nationalization is compatible with small-scale operation. They want, not decentralization, but an almost complete absence of centralization. They specifically deny the need for national management.[1]

There is something romantic about this adulation of smallness as a virtue in itself. I have myself been a strong advocate of local government for many years; but when one comes to consider industry one is compelled to recognize the overwhelming advantages of large-scale enterprise in many branches of manufacture and distribution. It is the large joint stock companies which today are the pacemakers in productivity, research, personnel management, capital development and good management generally. The British economy is today dominated by about 500 large companies of this kind. Admittedly none of them is anywhere near as large as the biggest public corporations, but the trend is unmistakable.[2]

I have already expressed disagreement with the assumption of many Socialists that nationalization necessarily means a single giant monopoly; but this does not imply that the correct method of organizing, say, the coal industry is by means of a multitude of independent collieries possessing managerial autonomy. Such a situation existed over a large part of the coal industry under private enterprise, and it produced disastrous results. Similarly, a position of virtual deadlock had come about in electricity distribution and no important advance was possible without a merging of the numerous municipal and commercial undertakings in the large Area Boards.

For these and cognate reasons I regard the nostalgic longing for small and purely local units of management felt by Mr Clegg and Professor Chester as misconceived and unscientific. It certainly does not accord with the view of the Fleck Committee which, while emphasizing that the pit is and must always be the unit of operational management,[3] insisted that there must also be higher forms of management at the area, divisional and national level. 'The character of the division must be managerial' they asserted. It must exist to initiate and stimulate action, and not merely to supervise and co-ordinate.[4] As for the Board itself, we have already noted that the committee recommended it should exert a more decisive and insistent power of control over the divisions than it had previously attempted to do.[5] One could give equally cogent arguments for accepting as necessary a substantial degree of centralized

[1] *The Future of Nationalization* (1953), p. 146.

[2] See P. Sargant Florence: 'Bigness in Business' in *The Problem of Bigness*, LPE Papers, April 1956.

[3] *Op. cit.*, para. 279. [4] *Ib.*, para. 186.

[5] *Ante*, p. 83.

management at national or regional level in the other nationalized industries.[1]

Mr Ernest Davies is undoubtedly correct in stating that some measure of centralization in publicly owned industries is necessary to ensure public accountability; to permit effective planning of the development and management of the industry in the national interest; to carry out such central functions as capital development, marketing, research and training; and to effect economies through unification, integration and standardization. All this seems to be unquestionable. But, he continues, over-centralization encourages bureaucracy, causes frustration and inhibits initiative; and so there should be the maximum amount of decentralization consistent with central control of national policy and planning, and central management of the matters mentioned above. Hence what is needed is not a change in the structure of the industries, nor a shift in the locus of responsibility but rather an increasing devolution of adminstrative functions so as to give the power of decision, where appropriate, to the man on the spot. This must be supplemented by continuous consultation both up and down the line which runs from headquarters to the smallest operating unit.[2]

As for regulatory or advisory commissions, the Electricity Commission was a feeble creature which achieved almost nothing before 1926, when the Central Electricity Board was set up as a constructional, operating and managerial organ on a national scale for electricity generation. The Coal Mines Reorganization Commission was a total failure. It would be helpful if writers[3] who favour the independent commission would understand why the Electricity Commission was so impotent between 1919 and 1926: the reason was that the electricity supply industry refused to be 'encouraged' by the schemes drawn up by the Commission which had no powers of compulsion over the statutory undertakers. And the same applies *mutatis mutandis* to the Coal Mines Reorganization Commission.

Nothing that I have said in any way detracts from the need for decentralization, and especially managerial decentralization. This is, indeed,

[1] See Lord Citrine: 'Problems of Nationalized Industry', XXIX *Public Administration* (1951), pp. 321-3.

[2] Ernest Davies: *Problems of Public Ownership* (1952), p. 7.

[3] E. Goodman: *Forms of Public Control and Ownership* (1951), pp. 91-2 and 97. Mr E. Goodman is among the people who see some special virtue in 'a select body of men with technical or administrative qualifications, who could encourage the industry, prepare plans for its development and satisfy Parliament, through the appropriate government department, that it is being run to the consumers' advantage'. He thinks this would be a more suitable method of public control than a public corporation. It has greater detachment than the latter; it can deal more easily with abuses; and it can look with insight into the major problems of the industry.

essential for efficient operation. It is, however, quite compatible with the exercise of policy control and administrative direction at higher levels. But effective decentralization demands reliable information about consumer needs flowing up to the centre from the responsible staff in charge of the units which are in direct contact with the public.

Finally, in disagreeing with those who reject any form of regional or national overall management, I do not imply that all the centralized types of organization set up by the post-war legislation have been satisfactory. The British Transport Commission in its original form was a top-heavy structure which conferred on the Commission the function of co-ordinating the various transport services, whereas this should certainly have been given to the Minister. Moreover, the interposition of the Executives interposed a considerable barrier between the Commission and the regional or local officers engaged in day-to-day operations and in direct contact with the public. 'It is significant', Lord Hurcomb has remarked, 'that during the whole of the six years I was chairman of the Commission I never saw a report or a recommendation from a regional officer in his own language and in the form in which he originally made it.'[1] That such a thing could occur is not only a reflection on a defective system of communication within the organization, but also an indication of too much top-hamper.

The upshot of the whole matter is that the excessive zeal for national monopolies administered by giant public corporations which enthusiastic socialists assumed must be an indispensible feature of nationalization, must not lead us to swing to the other extreme and become advocates of pettifogging administration by miniscule units whose managers possess complete autonomy except in a few matters laid down by law. This is to go from one extreme to the other, and no amount of cosy talk about the personal touch and human relations in industry will overcome the basic defects and weaknesses of such an approach.

[1] 185 HL Deb. 5s., col. 1137 (November 3, 1954).

CHAPTER V

Competition and Monopoly

WE come now to the question of competition *versus* monopoly in public enterprise. Many British socialists—and also their opponents—have assumed too readily that nationalization must inevitably mean giant monopolies such as the Post Office or the National Coal Board. This assumption deserves consideration.

PUBLIC UTILITIES AS MONOPOLIES

There has always been a monopolistic tendency in the public utility field. This arises inevitably from the nature of the undertaking, no matter whether it is publicly or privately owned, and irrespective of whether a legal monopoly is conferred or not. During the nineteenth century, for example, Parliament tried to foster competition between rival suppliers of gas in London. But the competition was short-lived and was soon replaced by gentlemen's understandings between the companies.[1] Where piped services are concerned, it is clearly impracticable to permit several undertakers to supply the same area. If this were allowed, the suppliers would be forever tearing up the streets, with continual interruption of traffic and inconvenience to the public. It is equally obvious that a big undertaking like a railway requires so much capital outlay that there is not likely to be a great deal of duplication of effort. Where competing lines have been constructed to serve the same areas, there has been a strong tendency to eliminate competition.

But this does not dispose of the matter. It is possible to have many forms of emulation or competition within the socialized sector of the economy. An example is the competition between gas and electricity, and between both of these and solid fuel, for domestic use. There is everything to be said in favour of giving each fuel the fullest opportunity to exploit its competitive advantages. Consumers should be offered a free choice between having gas, electricity, coal or coke for any particular appliance, at the lowest price which reflects the costs of supply and

[1] W. A. Robson: 'Public Utilities' in *A Century of Municipal Progress*, ed. W. I. Jennings, H. J. Laski, and W. A. Robson (1936), pp. 304–5.

[2] The only exception to this seems to be the oil pipes which in US are treated as common carriers for oil producers or distributors.

on the best terms the supplying corporation can offer. Any attempt to 'co-ordinate' the use or prices of gas and electricity should be regarded with great suspicion as a probable plot against the public.

The only circumstances which should be allowed to interfere with free competition of this kind is where there are social reasons of overriding importance. Thus, the injury to public health and amenity caused by the smoke nuisance may justify prohibiting the use of coal for burning in open grates if other types of fuel are available.

This common-sense view of the desirability of competition may sound painfully obvious to anyone of ordinary intelligence, yet it has been abrogated continually in the sphere of transport, under both private and public ownership. The main object of the licensing provisions of the Road Traffic Act, 1930, was to restrict road passenger services so as to reduce their competition with the railways, then in private ownership. The purpose of the Road and Rail Transport Act, 1933, was to curtail the motor haulage industry in the interests of the railways.

CO-ORDINATION AND COMPETITION IN TRANSPORT

The comprehensive structure of the British Transport Commission, in the form in which it was originally created by the Transport Act, 1947, made two consequences exceedingly probable. One was that the Commission would attempt to impose, under the guise of the blessed word 'co-ordination', unnecessarily high rates and charges on road transport which would eliminate most of the economic advantages of motor vehicles over the railways. The other was that a surplus derived from the road transport services would be used to offset an operating deficit on the railways.

Either of these forms of so-called 'co-ordination' is nothing else than an exercise of monopolistic powers to the disadvantage of some consumers and the advantage of others. It should be resisted to the utmost possible extent by the public, whether they are in favour of nationalization or against it. It is a widespread evil alike in private or public enterprise.

The denationalization of the road haulage industry, and the repeal of the scheme-making provisions concerning road passenger services, docks, harbours, and wharves, was a misguided and unnecessary measure; but nevertheless the Transport Act, 1953, contained several good features designed to increase competition between the different forms of transport. Formal legal equality was established between the British Transport Commission and private operators within the sphere of road transport. Changes were introduced into the law relating to the licensing of road hauliers whereby the onus of proof was shifted from the applicant to objectors. The licensing authorities were henceforth to have regard primarily to the interests of transport users, whereas previously the tendency had been to favour existing transport interests as against traders' requirements. Furthermore, the licensing authorities were required to pay attention to specified qualitative criteria in considering the suitability of existing facilities, instead of considering their adequacy wholly or mainly in quantitative terms.

Competition between road and rail was encouraged by freeing the railways from some of the antiquated obligations which had prevented them from competing with road transport on anything like equal terms. A charges scheme for the carriage of goods by rail need no longer prescribe standard and fixed charges, but only maximum charges. The British Transport Commission have full discretion to fix actual charges so long as they do not exceed the maximum. They may agree special charges with individual traders, if this is profitable to the railways; and such charges no longer require the approval of the Transport Tribunal or even publication, and are not open to protest by an aggrieved trader. The prohibition of undue preference, which has been on the statute book for more than a century, has disappeared, and the railways can now exercise their common law right to give preference to one trader against another, and to differentiate in the terms offered, so long as they do not charge unreasonably high rates. The users of transport still possess the right to complain to the Transport Tribunal that rail charges are excessive.[1]

In civil aviation, a competitive element exists in regard to all overseas services, operated under bilateral agreements with foreign governments. These normally provide for reciprocal services: e.g. BEA and Air France have equal rights to run services between Britain and France. Hence, while there is usually a common tariff of fares and frequencies, there is keen competition on everything else. There is, indeed, sufficient competition between the rival airlines of different countries flying the same routes to keep most of them up to the mark. Another great spur to progress in civil aviation is competition between air transport and surface transport.

Some of the dangers of monopoly can be lessened or avoided by the existence of several operating units in the same industry, even where they are not serving the same market. The twelve Area Gas Boards certainly provide opportunities for what Sidney and Beatrice Webb called 'socialist emulation' which, while not the same thing as competition, can be a useful alternative. The same applies to the Area Electricity

[1] C. Grunfeld: 'The Transport Act, 1953', XXV *Political Quarterly* (1954), pp. 49-54.

Boards, and to a lesser extent to the two British airways corporations. Conditions which favour a variety of techniques, flexibility of management, and the opportunity to experiment, should be eagerly sought in nationalized industry. One of the best features of the New Towns Act, 1946, is that it has enabled a separate development corporation to be appointed for each new town which is constructed or developed. This is yielding a much more interesting variety of towns than would probably have resulted if a single giant development corporation had been responsible for all of them.

COMPETITION BETWEEN PUBLIC AND PRIVATE ENTERPRISE

One possibility which has scarcely been tried in Britain except almost by accident, is to have public owned undertakings working alongside privately owned companies in the same field. This occurred, in a limited sense, in gas and electricity supply prior to nationalization, when those industries were divided between municipal and private profit-making enterprise. The commercial and municipal operators in each of these industries were, however, working in separate areas for distinct bodies of consumers. This is quite different from public enterprise working in direct competition with privately-owned companies for the same market. In France, a large number of individual concerns have been acquired by the State; in Britain, by contrast, complete nationalization of an entire industry or a section of it has been the rule in recent years. I should like to see the Government acquire for public ownership and operation a firm manufacturing, let us say, domestic appliances such as mechanical carpet-sweepers or refrigerators, where one can believe that substantial reductions of price could be effected by eliminating the profit motive. I see no reason, again, why the State should not take over or initiate one or two cement works, if there is good ground for intervening in this sphere, without necessarily acquiring the entire industry.

Following an inquiry by the Monopolies and Restrictive Practices Commission into the supply of electric lamps, a member of the Commission recommended that the Government should acquire the share capital of certain companies controlled by firms belonging to the Electric Lamp Manufacturers Association, in order to secure 'a modicum of competition' in the industry.[1] An inquiry by the Commission into monopoly and restrictive practices in the supply and export of matches resulted *inter alia* in three members of the Commission recommending the creation of a wholesale purchasing agency sponsored by the Govern-

[1] See the *Report of the Commission on the Supply of Electric Lamps.* BPP H of C paper 287/1951 HMSO para. 296

ment with statutory powers to act as the exclusive purchaser of all home-produced or imported matches. The aim was to ensure the supply of matches at the lowest possible cost, to eliminate unnecessary costs of distribution, and to stimulate efficient production in Britain.[1]

Competition between private and public enterprise in certain industries might well prove to be beneficial to both sectors of the economy. But the competition must be on equal terms if it is to be genuine. The provision contained in the Civil Aviation Act, 1946, requiring independent operators of civil aviation services to offer their employees not less favourable terms and conditions of employment than those observed by the nationalized airlines was not fair at that time because BEA and BOAC received heavy subsidies from the State, whereas air surveys, charter services, herring-spotting, sky-writing, training schools, aerial photography, and other forms of aerial work open to private enterprise, received no assistance from the Exchequer and had to pay their own way. It was scarcely right that the wage level should be fixed by the subsidized concerns and then be imposed on all undertakers.

COMPETITION IN THE FUEL INDUSTRIES

The Ridley Committee on National Policy for the use of Fuel and Power Resources, which reported in 1952, strongly supported the principle of competition between nationalized industries. The Committee assumed that national policy to promote the best use of fuel and power should aim at the following three objectives. First, to meet in full the demands of the community for the various kinds of fuel and power when they are sold at prices which correspond to the relevant costs of production and distribution. Second, to promote the maximum economic efficiency in the use of each fuel. Third, to encourage the use for particular purposes of the appropriate fuel, which renders the best returns on the resources consumed.[2]

'The right policy,' they declared, 'and indeed the only practicable one, is to leave the pattern of fuel use to be determined by the consumers' own choice between competing services.'[3] This would be far more effective than any form of governmental intervention by means of administrative orders as a means of improving the pattern of fuel uses.[4] But such a policy requires that prices and charges for fuel and power

[1] See *Report on the Supply and Export of Matches and the Supply of Match-making Machinery* BPP H of C paper 161/1953 HMSO para. 228.

[2] *Report of the Committee on National Policy for the use of Fuel and Power Resources*, HMSO, Cmd. 8647/1952, para. 1.

[3] *Ib.*, para. 225. [4] *Ib.*, para. 223.

should correspond closely to the relevant costs; that the fuel industries should not impose any conditions on the supply to consumers of their product which might restrict their freedom of choice and is not justified by supply costs; and that full and objective information about fuel services and fuel appliances be made easily available to the public. 'We look', the Ridley Committee observed, 'upon the nationalized gas and electricity industries as in a sense branches of one undertaking, within which, however, competition is a valuable aid to efficiency.'[1]

A belief in the value of competition in public enterprise is not held by all Socialists. Mr Ernest Davies, a keen advocate and exponent of nationalization, has gone so far as to suggest that the nationalized sector might further be considered as a whole and prices adjusted so as to minimize the effect of changes on the national economy. Profitable industries could subsidize those working at a loss. He proposes that a financial pool be set up for the nationalized industries, though he admits that this would be difficult to operate without 'co-ordination' on wages, working conditions and compensation.[2] Similarly he thinks that co-ordination is desirable among the nationalized industries because they are all basic industries and the charges of one affect substantially the costs of others.

It is difficult to see what the word 'co-ordination' means in this context except charging one lot of consumers more than they should pay for a service in order to give the same or another service to other consumers, at a price below the economic cost. It is easy to see that the latter benefit at the cost of the former; it is less easy to understand in what way the general interest is served by this cross-subsidization. Some members of the Labour Party stated publicly that the financial difficulties of the British Transport Commission were a direct result of the Conservative Government's policy of denationalizing the road haulage industry, since the Road Haulage Executive had been able to make a large surplus which was available for off-setting losses on the railways.[3] If this was the reason for entrusting road and rail transport to a single public corporation, it was a thoroughly bad one; and it is a mistake to attempt to defend it.

The Ridley Committee did not recommend any new central organization to control the fuel and power industries. They considered that the Minister in charge of these industries already had adequate powers of general control and co-ordination. But they did urge the appointment of

[1] *Report of the Committee on National Policy for the use of Fuel and Power Resources*, HMSO, Cmd. 8647/1952, paras. 225 and 287.

[2] Ernest Davies: *Problems of Public Ownership* (1952) (Labour Party), p. 16

[3] See letters in *The Times*, December 30, 1954, January 6, 1955, and January 22, 1955 (Mr Douglas Jay, MP); January 12, 1955 (Mr Ernest Davies, MP).

a Tariffs Advisory Committee to study pricing methods and to advise the Minister on the price and tariff policies of the nationalized industries. The Committee thought that the price structure should not be left entirely to the industries themselves, since their policies may not take full account of the widest national interests in the economic use of fuel.

The Tariffs Advisory Committee was to be a small body comprising five to seven independent persons. It would consider not only principles, but also how far actual prices reflect those principles at any time; and it would draw attention to any apparent conflict between the price policy of a public corporation and the wider national interests. It would report to the Minister of Power, who should seek its advice before approving any major change in tariff policy.[1]

No action has so far been taken to carry out this excellent proposal. The only joint body supposed to exist is a committee of the chairmen of the three national corporations concerned with coal, gas, and electricity, over which the Minister of Power presides. This committee has not met for years.[2] It is not a body of experts, nor has it any special interest in or knowledge of price policy.

The Ridley Committee also recommended that a Joint Fuel and Power Planning Board be set up to facilitate co-operation on production and distribution problems between the fuel and power industries. Its chief tasks would be to determine which projects should be chosen for investigation as possible joint enterprises; to advise the fuel industries and to introduce new projects to them; and to make proposals on such matters as the creation of organizations to operate joint projects. The Board would not be empowered to override the authority of the constituent industries, but the chairman would in the last resort be able to ask the Minister to intervene, where sufficient co-operation was not forthcoming.[3]

It was hoped that by this means adequate co-operation between the public corporations concerned would be achieved in respect of joint planning, the prompt application of the results of research, and routine collaboration in technical matters.[4] It might also secure collaboration in matters where the interests of one industry might not coincide with wider interests. So far this proposal has met with the same fate as the one relating to a Tariffs Advisory Committee.

[1] Report, HMSO, Cmd. 8647/1952, paras. 264-6.

[2] *Reports from the Committee of Public Accounts*, HMSO, HC 48-I, 106-I, and 203-I/1952-3 (one volume), Evidence, Q.2335.

[3] Report, HMSO, Cmd. 8647/1952, Ch. IX.

[4] On the general question of the co-ordination of price policies and measures to promote efficient utilisation see I. M. D. Little: *The Price of Fuel* (1953), pp. 149-54.

THE TUC'S VIEWS

In 1953 the Trades Union Congress discussed an extremely cautious report on public ownership which had been prepared by the General Council in conformity with a resolution carried by the Congress at Margate in 1952.[1] This report contended that the industries to be considered as possibly ripe for public ownership are those falling into four categories, one of which consists of those where monopolistic organization places great economic power in private hands.[2] The report mentioned as a leading example of this, the chemical group, in which forty-eight per cent of the workpeople are employed by the three largest concerns. The report suggested that public control is needed over the chemical industry because of its monopolistic structure and its importance to the entire economy. The nature and extent of that control were not specified owing to the lack of information about the industry. The report did say, however, that if public control were to take the form of public ownership this need not necessarily cover the whole industry but could be confined to one or more of the largest firms.[3] Doubt was expressed whether, in some sections of the engineering industries, existing competition is sufficient to induce the managements to show enough enterprise and initiative to overcome their technical and managerial problems.[4] But neither the report nor the debate touched on the wider question of whether the competitive element can be or has been introduced or maintained in public enterprise.

MR GAITSKELL'S VIEWS ON SIZE

In Mr Gaitskell's view, which is based on his experience as Minister of Fuel and Power as well as on general considerations, genuine difficulties have arisen in the nationalized industries owing to their great size. The real weaknesses, he thinks, are the result not of a change of ownership but of a change in structure. 'They are almost all associated with large-scale management.' One of these weaknesses is that power tends to be concentrated at or near the top and fewer final decisions entrusted to the lower echelons. The other is that it is harder to inculcate a spirit of loyalty and high morale in a large organization.[5] Apathy and indifference among the staff, a feeling among the workpeople of remoteness from the seat of authority, are in his belief characteristic defects of very large organizations. They may be overcome to some extent by good

[1] Report of the Proceedings at the Eighty-fifth Annual Trades Union Congress, App. A (Reprinted separately under the title *Interim Report on Public Ownership*).

[2] *Ib.*, paras. 193-7. [3] *Ib.*, para. 203. [4] *Ib.*, para. 212. [5] *Op. cit.*, p. 25.

local management which seeks to evoke a team spirit and a sense of loyalty among the members of particular groups of workers employed in a unit. Nevertheless, Mr Gaitskell concludes that the major defects of nationalization of entire industries lie in 'the creation of units which are too large to get the best response from those employed in them, and in the weakening of competitive attitudes in the management'. Hence we must be careful to avoid structural changes which produce these results.[1]

We can see that there is now a belief, the truth of which has not been proved or demonstrated, that the great public corporations set up to deal with the nationalized coal, transport, and electricity industries—to mention only the three leading examples—have exceeded the optimum size required for those industries. The denationalization of the road haulage industry, together with the elimination of several of its other activities, involved a substantial diminution in the scope of the British Transport Commission. The separation of generating functions from control over policy and finance, represented an indirect method of reducing the scale and scope of the Central Electricity Authority.

If the need for encouraging emulation within a nationalized industry, or competition between nationalized industry and private enterprise, be kept firmly in view, the problem of organization is likely to be far easier to solve. No longer shall we have to rack our brains to find ways of controlling, managing and operating public corporations of much vaster dimensions than those of any commercial company or of most government departments. More easily manageable units of modest size will inevitably suggest themselves as appropriate rather than the monster corporations created during the years 1945-50.

Despite what I have written above, it would be entirely wrong to assume that small units will always have an advantage over large units in public enterprise. In some industries or services a single national corporation may be the best form of organization. The railway network, for example, should obviously be treated as a single unit. In many spheres of commercial enterprise, the largest undertakings, such as Imperial Chemical Industries, the great joint stock banks, the motor car manufacturers like General Motors or Ford, Woolworth, Unilever, or Shell, are regarded as the most efficient undertakings. Moreover, we must not assume that our knowledge of how to administer successfully very large undertakings will remain static. The scale of operations of armies, government departments, banks, insurance companies, newspapers, industrial and commercial companies, has increased enormously in the past fifty years; and so, too, has the standard of effectiveness with

[1] Report of the Proceedings at the Eighty-fifth Annual Trades Union Congress, App. A. (Reprinted separately under the title *Interim Report on Public Ownership*), p. 36.

which they are run. Any limitations concerning the size of organizations which may exist today are unlikely to continue indefinitely. Man learns by doing.

THE DECLINE OF COMPETITION IN BRITAIN

The desirability of maintaining some degree of competition or emulation in economic activities, so far as it is practicable to do so, is an enduring one. It is, however, unrealistic to assert that the distinction between public and private enterprise corresponds to the difference between monopoly and competition. In most of the important branches of British trade and industry, a belief in competition is no longer found either among the managers or in the trade unions. A vast network of restrictive practices, designed to eliminate many important aspects of competition, permeates not only the important industries but also the lesser ones. The steel industry was probably the most heavily cartellized of any British industry prior to its being nationalized. Neither nationalization nor denationalization has had any serious effect on its character in this respect. Many of our industries are riddled with restrictive practices imposed by trade associations with the object of reducing or eliminating competition. It is uncertain how far the Restrictive Practices Act, 1956, will succeed in reversing the trend which has been flowing so powerfully for several decades. The experience of the Act so far gained shows that the number of restrictive agreements is likely to diminish rapidly; but it remains to be seen how far amalgamations will take the place of restrictive agreements.

I would not deny the greater power of a statutory monopoly possessed by a single public corporation as compared with the monopolistic practices enforced *de facto* by a number of firms through a trade association; but the cumulative effect of the latter in repressing if not suppressing competition is often very great. Mr D. N. Chester does not seem to recognize this latter aspect of the problem when he writes that a large part of the difficulty in determining the proper degree of control over nationalized industries is due to the fact that they are very large-scale monopolies and all our economic thinking and experience is really based on comparatively small-scale competitive industry. We simply do not know how to control national statutory monopolies, he observes, which present a solid front and have a monopoly of the expertize and technical knowledge of the industry. The Minister lacks the technical knowledge necessary to judge the boards, and to stand up to them on any matter except an outstanding popular issue.[1] This is substantially true; but it

[1] D. N. Chester: 'The Nationalized Industries', *Three Banks Review*, December 1952, pp. 38-9.

is equally true that we have not yet shown our ability to control highly cartellized industries and trades, riddled with monopolistic and restrictive practices, which are typical of private enterprise in Britain today.

Mr Aubrey Jones, when Minister of Fuel and Power, pointed out in a parliamentary debate that the Transport Act, 1953, by extending competition with the British Transport Commission, had strengthened the case against political interference in its activities.[1] In his view competition from commercial undertakings eliminates or reduces the need for ministerial control over a public corporation. This conception of competition as the automatic regulator of economic life in the general interest harks back to Adam Smith. Competition in the public sector is desirable for its own sake. Insofar as it can reduce the need for ministerial control over such matters as prices, this is an added advantage.

Mr Chester did not urge the need for competition on the ground that it would make government control unnecessary, but on the much sounder ground that where a giant national monopoly is established there is a danger of a single orthodox view prevailing. People inside the organization with new ideas may not have a chance to put them into practice, or even to advocate their adoption in public.[2]

BROADCASTING AND TELEVISION

The problem of competition in public enterprise was discussed at length by the Beveridge Committee on Broadcasting. The report reviewed the principal arguments against monopoly in this exceptionally important sphere of information, education, and entertainment. These included, first, the danger of excessive power over men's thoughts concentrated in a single organization, resulting in complacency, lack of imagination, and deadly uniformity of public opinion; second, the danger of excessive size and unwieldiness in the organization of the BBC; third, the danger of central control from London over the broadcast programmes, leading to the neglect of the distinctive cultures of other parts of the country; fourth, the danger of the BBC exerting excessive power over the lives of its employees, performers and writers, who might have no alternative opportunities of employment.[3]

Several of the witnesses had proposed remedies which did not involve departing from the principle that broadcasting should remain a public service free from the profit-making motive. The Liberal and Fabian Research Groups had suggested a functional break-up of the monopoly

[1] 536 HC Deb. 5s., col. 1354 (February 3, 1955).
[2] D. N. Chester: *op. cit.*
[3] *Report of the Broadcasting Committee 1949*, HMSO, Cmd. 8116/1951, paras. 175–7.

by creating corporations responsible for different types of broadcasting, such as television, home services, overseas services, and regional services. The Scottish and Welsh organizations had asked for separate corporations to cater for their special interests. Sir Geoffrey Crowther and Sir Robert Watson-Watt had proposed all-round competition between three or more corporations covering the whole country. Lord Simon of Wythenshawe, a former chairman of the BBC, considers that the whole concept of monopoly, indeed even the use of the word, is entirely misleading when applied to a body which is in no way concerned with profits and restrictive practices, and seeks only to promote the public interest.[1] He explains that the BBC takes great pains to give listeners and viewers—including all the majorities and significant minorities—what they want or hopes they will come to desire in due course.

The Beveridge Committee said in their report[2] that if broadcasting is to have a social purpose, competition should not be allowed to become competitors for numbers of listeners. The rejection of competition for mere numbers of listeners does not, however, imply that only a monopoly can have high standards and a social purpose. This is clearly shown by the competition among separate and independent universities to raise the standard of higher education. The difficulty which faced the Beveridge Committee was that they found there was no possibility of having more than three or four broadcasting organs in Britain, and so small a number would rule out anything comparable to the free and open competition among organs of the Press. They therefore considered the choice to lie in practice between creating three or four broadcasting corporations on terms requiring them to co-operate and to accept government vetoes and directions on certain points, and continuing with the BBC subject to the same conditions, while requiring it to make 'steady progress towards greater decentralization, devolution and diversity'.[3] The Committee (with one dissentient) decided without hesitation in favour of a single corporation, despite the fact that they recognized the real dangers which may result from a monopoly, such as remoteness, self-satisfaction, secretiveness, favouritism and unjust dealings with the staff, a sense of divine right, and slowness in exploring new techniques.

The reasons for the Committee's conclusion were that they thought the aims of those who opposed monopoly could be better served by a single broadcasting corporation than by breaking up the BBC into a number of separate bodies. They thought, moreover, that a continuation of the monopoly, if accompanied by a number of reforms which they

[1] Lord Simon of Wythenshawe: *The BBC from Within* (1953), pp. 339-41.

[2] Report, paras. 167-8. [3] *Ib.*, paras. 170-1.

prescribed, would offer the best method of achieving flexible decentralization by means of regional and functional devolution.[1]

The Churchill Government rejected the report of the Beveridge Committee and adopted the policy, so far as television is concerned, advocated by Mr Selwyn Lloyd in his minority report, of competition between a public broadcasting service and commercial stations. The White Paper on the report paid tribute to the 'effective monopoly' of the BBC which the Government recognized had 'done much to establish the excellent and reputable broadcasting service for which this country is renowned and that the BBC have become an important part of the structure of our national life'. They conceded that their services should remain intact and that no other broadcasting body should receive any share in the revenue from licences. But nonetheless the Conservative Government decided that in the expanding field of television an element of competition should be permitted. The reason given for this was that in view of 'the great and increasing power of television in influencing men's minds, the Government believes that its control should not remain in the hands of a single authority, however excellent it may be'.[2] Competition would be in the best interests not only of viewers, writers, artistes and technicians, but also of the nascent export demand for filmed television programmes. No mention was made of the immense pressure exerted on the Government by a small group of Conservative backbench MPs and certain firms of advertising agents who were commercially interested in opening a highly profitable market for their talents.

The Government's policy aimed at three objectives. First, to introduce an element of competition into television and enable private enterprise to participate in its development. Second, to reduce to a minimum the financial commitments of the State. Third, to safeguard the medium from the lowering of standards or the risk of abuse.[3]

The Independent Television Authority were created to implement this policy. The Authority are a public corporation appointed by the Government whose main task is to own and operate the transmitting stations. The facilities thus provided are hired under contract to commercial companies which supply the programmes. The latter draw revenue from advertisements. Sponsoring is forbidden. The ITA also act as the controlling body over the companies to safeguard the character and standard of the programmes they provide in accordance with statutory requirements.[4] These include ensuring the accuracy and impartiality of news telecasts.[5]

[1] Report para. 172. [2] *Memorandum on Television Policy*, HMSO, Cmd. 9005/1953, para. 3.
[3] *Ib.*, para. 17. [4] *Ib.*, paras. 8-11; Television Act, 1954.
[5] See *Independent Television Authority Annual Report 1954-5*, HMSO, HC 123/1955-6, p. 7.

One of the duties imposed on the ITA by the Television Act, 1954, is to do all they can to secure that there is adequate competition to supply programmes between a number of programme contractors independent of each other both as to finance and as to control.[1] The ITA have interpreted this obligation to mean that viewers should be given a choice of two or more programmes. This is not possible at present because each area is provided with only one station. Meanwhile, to secure an element of competition, each station has two contractors, one supplying programmes during weekdays, and the other during the week-end.

This is the system which the Conservative Government considered to be a combination of 'effective control on the one hand and greater freedom on the other' and which they recommended as 'a typically British approach to this new problem'.[2] None of the basic objections to commercial broadcasting was mentioned in the White Paper or even recognized by the Government, though they were understood by a great many persons belonging to all political parties and to none, who strongly criticized the proposals on the platform, in the press, and in Parliament.

I have for long strongly objected to the BBC's monopoly, both in regard to sound broadcasting and television.[3] But I am also opposed to commercial broadcasting.[4] There are in my opinion overwhelming advantages in running broadcasting as a public service. It is, however, quite possible to have an element of competition in public service broadcasting by dividing the service between two, three, or more public corporations. The trouble is that the issue between public service broadcasting and commercial broadcasting has become confused in many people's minds with the quite separate issue of monopoly or competition. The results have been unfortunate. If the BBC spokesmen had not insisted so hard that the monopoly must continue at all costs, the Beveridge Committee might have examined more carefully than they did the case for more than one public corporation, and we might have been spared the intrusion into television of the commercial operators, with all that that implies.

Nevertheless, one must admit that competition between the independent programme companies and the BBC has possibly produced better results than would have occurred if the BBC had been left in possession

[1] s. 5 (2).

[2] *Memorandum on Television Policy*, HMSO, Cmd. 9005/1953, para. 17.

[3] See my chapter 'The British Broadcasting Corporation' in *Public Enterprise*, ed. W. A. Robson (1937), pp. 81-5.

[4] For a discussion of the whole subject see the special issue of the *Political Quarterly* on Commercial Television, October-December 1953.

of their exclusive monopoly.[1] And finally, the method adopted in this country of programme companies who present the programmes is infinitely better than the system of sponsoring which obtains in the United States.

A CHANGE OF OUTLOOK ON COMPETITION

The climate of opinion in the Labour Party on competition and monopoly has changed considerably since 1950. Mr Hugh Gaitskell, MP, has recently emphasized the importance of competition as a stimulus to greater effort in quite general terms. 'I believe', he wrote, 'that it is much easier to get the right atmosphere, and therefore greater efficiency in large-scale undertakings, if the element of competition or rivalry is somehow retained. This is especially true of the staff and management grades. It may be regrettable, but it seems to be a fact that people's enthusiasm about almost any groups to which they belong is enhanced by competition.' He goes on to say that the managers of large firms are not much affected by the profit motive. But what does influence them is pride in their own company, and the desire to see it expand and surpass rival concerns. 'Nationalization', he concludes, 'should try to harness and not to ignore or suppress these natural characteristics.'[2] Many members of the Labour Party today hold views similar to those of Mr Gaitskell.

The most explicit arguments concerning the disadvantages of monopoly and the advantages of competition are those presented by Mr C. A. R. Crosland in his book *The Future of Socialism.*[3] 'We now understand rather better', he writes, 'that monopoly, even when it is public, has definite drawbacks. Not only is there a genuine restriction of freedom involved in forbidding the citizen by law to start producing certain goods, and an even more dangerous restriction, notably in those cases (such as the BBC) which call on highly specialized talent, in having only one employer: but competition is seen to bring greater advantages than pre-war Socialists realized—in preventing sloth and encouraging initiative, and in increasing the sense of consumer welfare . . . by allowing a free choice of goods and suppliers. Naturally this does not mean that monopoly has no advantages and competition no faults, but only that the balance of advantage now looks rather different.'

[1] For a very favourable account of progress to date see Sir Robert Fraser: 'Independent Television in Britain', XXXVI *Public Administration* (1958), p. 115. See also 'Competition on the TV screen', *Manchester Guardian*, September 22, 1958, and a letter by Mr Bernard Levin, *Manchester Guardian*, September 26, 1958.

[2] Hugh Gaitskell: *Socialism and Nationalization* (1956) (Fabian Tract No. 300), pp. 26-7.

[3] 1956. London. Jonathan Cape. p. 469-70.

An even bigger change of view has occurred in regard to the size of undertakings. Before the Second World War the opinion was widely held that the larger the unit of production the greater its efficiency was likely to be. 'Today we are not so sure' remarks Mr Crosland, at least beyond a certain size, mainly on account of the danger of over-centralization.[1] In consequence 'public-monopoly nationalization, despite considerable achievements in certain exceptionally difficult industries, no longer seems the panacea that it used to'.

This does not mean that nationalization will not be extended, but it does imply that it is not likely to take the form of nation-wide monopolies of gigantic size comprising an entire industry in a single unit. Acquisition of a firm or part of an industry is more likely in order to maintain a substantial element of competition. There may be instances where a privately owned monopoly, such as that enjoyed by the British Oxygen Company or the British Match Corporation, can be best dealt with by a transfer of the whole undertaking to the public sector *en bloc*, but such instances are likely to be rare.[2] Socialist Union considers that public enterprise is needed at strategic points in the market in order to curb the bad effects on the market both of monopoly and of excessive competition.[3]

Mr Crosland declares that to impose centralized monopoly control on an efficient competitive industry would be certain to reduce efficiency, and he thinks that this danger is now well understood.[4]

In 'Challenge to Britain' published in 1953, the Labour Party put forward proposals for competitive public enterprises within certain industries. These included the acquisition of a number of key firms in the machine tool industry to act as nodal points for technical rationalization and expansion; the acquisition of a controlling interest in a few firms manufacturing mining machinery; the taking over of any aircraft manufacturing firm which fell down on its job; the entry by the State into the production of essential medical supplies and artificial limbs required for the national health service; the search for and working of minerals; and the taking over of undefined parts of the chemical and engineering industries. There was, however, no indication of the conditions under which the public undertakings would compete with those under private ownership. It was assumed that the nationalized sector would be able, either by the force of its example or through compulsory powers, to counteract sloth, backward technology, a lack of necessary capital, inadequate research, restrictive practices, and lack of initiative.

[1] *Loc cit.* [2] *Op. cit.*, pp. 478–9.
[3] Socialist Union: *Twentieth Century Socialism*, pp. 136-7.
[4] C. A. R. Crosland: *The Future of Socialism*, pp. 480-1.

Mr Crosland considers that for public enterprise to be competitive it must be able to offer to its managerial staff salaries which are comparable to those paid by private enterprise. Nationalized concerns must also have the maximum degree of freedom in day-to-day matters. They should be accountable either through a holding company having on its board MPs and representatives of both sides of industry; or better still, a new public corporation answerable for all public corporations. The object of this is presumably to reduce to the utmost extent political control or influence. Above all, competition should be scrupulously fair.[1]

One of the most recent proposals for competitive public enterprise was contained in the report of a committee[2] appointed by *The Spectator* to inquire into the advantages and disadvantages of the nationalization of the steel industry. The committee were investigating an industry in which the choice is not between nationalization and free enterprise, but between public enterprise and a blend of private ownership with public control.[3]

The committee were impressed by the need of the industry to have more productive capacity over that needed to meet immediate demands than the privately-owned companies are willing or prepared to construct. They were opposed to the renationalization of the entire industry; and recommended instead a division of the industry into a public and a private sector. This would be effected by leaving in State hands some thirteen companies (including Richard Thomas and Baldwins) which have not yet been denationalized as a permanent element of public ownership, amounting to approximately one tenth of an industry otherwise commercially owned and operated. The publicly-owned companies would have the same freedom to develop as those in the private sector. The Iron and Steel Board, an independent body appointed by the Minister of Power to supervise the industry and prescribe maximum prices for its products, should be charged with ensuring that fair competition is maintained between the public and private sectors of the industry.[4]

This 'standstill' solution of a highly controversial question was rejected by spokesmen of the Labour Party soon after it was published. The real objection to it was not fully stated; but it is difficult to see on what grounds the present leaders of the party can reject the principle of dividing the industry between a public and a private sector in view of the opinions expressed by Mr Gaitskell; the advocacy of competitive public

[1] C. A. R. Crosland: *The Future of Socialism*, pp. 487–90.

[2] The committee consisted of Mr D. N. Chester, CBE, Warden of Nuffield College, Oxford (Chairman), Mr Percy Lamb, QC, and Mr H. M. D. Parker. There were two assessors, one Conservative and one Labour, who assisted in preparing the report.

[3] See Steel Inquiry. *Spectator*, March 13, 1959, p. 369.

[4] *Ib.*, p. 370.

enterprise contained in *Challenge to Britain*; and the extensive powers to regulate the industry as a whole in the national interest possessed by the Iron and Steel Board and the Minister of Power. It may well be that a public sector amounting to only ten per cent of the industry is far too small to enable it to hold its own on equal terms with the private sector or to exercise an important influence on the entire industry. The *Spectator* committee seems merely to have grasped at this proportion only because it involves no further movement in the direction either of denationalization or renationalization. If a much larger share of the industry—say forty to fifty per cent—were in the public sector it might greatly facilitate the maintenance of fair competition between the sectors which everyone would agree is desirable. One does not want to see the publicly owned companies in the position of merely owning and operating standby plant used only in time of peak demands or emergencies. Yet this is a danger which cannot be ignored and which might be very difficult to avoid.

There is no reason to believe that if public enterprise is well run it cannot compete effectively with commercial companies. Even in so highly competitive a field as the motor car industry, Renault in France and Volkswagen in Germany have demonstrated the ability of vigorous and up-to-date nationalized concerns to outstrip their privately owned competitors both at home and abroad. Such examples are not in any sense conclusive. Short Bros. is an instance which points in the other direction; but it does not invalidate the views of those who believe that competition between public and private concerns operating in the same industry can be beneficial to both.

The Conservative Party, no less than the Labour Party, have recently come to believe a good deal more than they formerly did in the benefits of competition. From the beginning of the present century the tendency towards restrictive practices and the elimination or reduction of competition have been increasing throughout the British economy. Sometimes the Government, far from opposing the monopolistic trend, have positively encouraged it, as, for example, when the amalgamation of White Star and Cunard was made a condition of government assistance in building the liners *Queen Mary* and *Queen Elizabeth*.

In 1955 the Conservative Party stated in *United for Peace and Progress* that the party reaffirmed their belief in the system of free competitive enterprise. 'The Conservative Party is strongly opposed to any further measure of nationalization. We are equally anxious that private enterprise should be free from any reproach of harmful restrictive practices.'[1] The following year saw the passing of the Restrictive Practices Act, a

[1] *United for Peace and Progress*, p. 17.

measure which has at least begun the task of examining and invalidating the vast network of restrictive agreements, regulations and practices which form a strait-jacket for much of British trade and industry. Hitherto, there has been little difference between the Right and the Left in their attitude towards competition and restraint of trade. For the most part, neither Conservatives nor Labour men believed in competition. Trade union officials and directors, managers and workmen, all shared the same view in opposing competition and seeking to introduce monopoly in one form or another through restrictive practices, amalgamation, price fixing, quotas, tariffs and all the other devices which serve these ends. One may hope that this attitude is now gradually changing.

CHAPTER VI

Government Control

ONE of the most difficult problems in the field of public enterprise is to determine the degree and character of the control which Ministers should exercise over nationalized industries. Too much ministerial control will reduce the public corporation to the status of a government department, with a consequent loss of managerial freedom from parliamentary interpellation. Too little government control will place the nationalized industries outside the democratic regime and be a step towards the corporative state.[1]

We have already noted in an earlier chapter that the most important difference between the earlier generation of public corporations and those established between 1945 and 1950 lies in the much greater degree of ministerial control over the latter.

THE FIRST PHASE

In the first generation of public corporations—that is, those created before 1945—political control was comparatively weak.[2] Ministers possessed extremely few powers over such bodies as the Central Electricity Board or the London Passenger Transport Board, and those which they did possess were limited to specific matters.

There were no general powers of control given to Ministers by the earlier legislation. An exception to the usual position was that the Government possessed an ultimate power of control over the BBC greater than that which existed in the case of any of the other corporations, for in time of emergency the Government have always had the right to take over the transmitting stations and to assume complete control of the undertaking. Ministers can also require particular matter to be broadcast, and the Postmaster-General can prohibit the broadcasting of any matter, whether specific or general. But, 'although the Government possesses enormous contingent power over the BBC, it exercises in practice virtually no control over its day-to-day administration, nor does

[1] Socialist Union: *Twentieth Century Socialism* (1956), p. 95.

[2] Cf. W. A. Robson: 'The Public Service Board: General Conclusions' in *Public Enterprise,* ed. W. A. Robson (1937), pp. 377 and 381-3.

it even have the right to do so'.[1] Even during the Second World War, which was indubitably the greatest national emergency the British people have ever faced, the Government did not exercise their right to take over the BBC. The Minister of Information was content merely to control the programmes relating to the war and to influence the policy of the BBC in many other ways by informal pressure, leaving the constitutional position of the corporation unchanged.

The arrangement in regard to overseas programmes, which are paid for by a Government grant, is that any department specified by the Postmaster-General may prescribe the countries to which the BBC must broadcast, and the languages in which, and the times at which, the programmes are to be sent out. The Postmaster-General and the Treasury must approve the proposed programmes.

The last pre-war Act establishing a public corporation was the British Overseas Airways Act, 1939. This followed the earlier practice of not giving the appropriate Minister (then the Secretary of State for Air) any general power of direction. But in case of war or of great national emergency the Secretary of State could require that the whole undertaking should be placed at his disposal or of such persons as he might designate by order.

Certain activities of BOAC were prohibited except with the authority of a ministerial order. The Secretary of State might direct the corporation during any period in which a subsidy was payable to undertake any air transport service which they had power to undertake; or to discontinue or modify any service they were operating; or to forbid them to undertake any activity in which they were proposing to engage. These provisions were more far reaching than was usual at that time, but they were explained by the subsidy which BOAC was due to receive from public money. During the war, the corporation was financed by a deficiency grant from the Treasury.

THE PATTERN OF LABOUR LEGISLATION

The post-war legislation presents a sharp contrast. The most important controlling powers of Ministers over the industries nationalized by the Labour Government of 1945-51 became quite general. Thus the appropriate Minister may, after consulting the governing board, give a public corporation 'directions of a general character as to the exercise and performance by the corporation of their functions in relation to matters which appear to him to affect the national interest'. The Corporation must give effect to the direction. There are a few slight verbal

[1] W. A. Robson: 'The British Broadcasting Corporation' in *Public Enterprise*, ed. W. A. Robson (1937), p. 75.

variations in the statutes concerning this formulation of ministerial power, but the effect of the enactments is broadly similar.

The statutes expressly declare that the Minister's power to give directions to the corporation shall extend to giving them, with Treasury approval, directions about any matter relating to the establishment and management of a reserve fund, the allocation of sums to reserve, and the application of the reserve fund, notwithstanding that the directions may be of a specific character. The reserve funds must, however, be applied to the purposes of the corporation. A similar provision applies to directions regarding the application of excess revenues.

In addition to these general powers of direction Ministers have specific powers over the nationalized industries in regard to certain matters considered to be of special importance. Thus the National Coal Board, the Electricity Boards, the British Transport Commission and the Gas Boards, in framing programmes of reorganization or development involving substantial capital outlay, are required to act on lines which have been approved by the appropriate Minister. The airways corporations are not required by law to obtain ministerial approval in respect of these matters but in practice they have to do so in order to obtain the necessary funds. A similar obligation to seek and obtain ministerial approval applies to the programmes of training, education and research of these industries.

Other ministerial powers apply only to particular industries. Examples of these are the authority given to the Minister of Power to define and vary the areas of the gas and electricity boards and the power of the Minister of Transport and Civil Aviation to require aircraft used by the airways corporations to be registered in some part of Her Majesty's dominions. The Minister of Transport and Civil Aviation must give his consent before the British Transport Commission can acquire an undertaking wholly or mainly engaged in constructing, owning or operating any railway, harbour, or inland waterway. He may direct the Commission to discontinue or restrict any of their activities or to dispose of any part of their assets. The Transport Acts, 1947 and 1953 give fifty-eight specific responsibilities to the Minister of Transport and Civil Aviation, while the Air Corporations Act confers a further twenty-one specific responsibilities on him. The Minister of Power has fifty-six specific responsibilities under the legislation nationalizing coal, electricity, and gas. The Secretary of State for Scotland carries statutory responsibility for forty-one specified matters connected with the Scottish electricity industry.[1]

[1] *Special Report from the Select Committee on Nationalized Industries*, HMSO, HC 120/1955-6, Memoranda presented by Departments.

The Treasury exercises numerous powers in regard to the nationalized industries concerning matters where action by a Departmental Minister requires Treasury approval. These include the salaries and pensions of the chairmen, deputy chairmen and members of the boards: the establishment and management of the reserve funds and the application of surplus revenue; the payment of the officers of Consultative or Consumers Councils; certain aspects of stock issues and the form of the annual accounts. In some instances Treasury approval is required by statute; in others Treasury influence within the central government has brought about the same result in practice.

The most important responsibilities of the Treasury are those concerned with the borrowing powers of the nationalized industries. The approval of the Treasury is in addition to the consent of the appropriate Minister, which is required for any borrowing by the electricity, gas, transport, airways, and colonial development authorities. In practice the coal industry must also obtain Treasury approval for loans, because the Chancellor of the Exchequer is directly responsible for providing (through the Minister of Power) the capital needed by the National Coal Board. Since 1956 he also provides the sums needed for borrowing by the other public corporations. Prior to that date the Treasury was permitted to guarantee stock issues and temporary borrowings by the nationalized industries.[1]

It is evident that the government possesses very extensive legal powers of control over the public corporations. Their full extent is not altogether clear, for the question of exactly what is meant by the expression 'directions of a general character' is open to doubt; and so too is the question of what the national interest demands. At what point the particular becomes general, and the general becomes particular, is a matter on which differences of opinion can and do exist. The question will have to be decided pragmatically over the years by the practices of Ministers, for it is extremely unlikely that a dispute on the meaning of the term 'directions of a general character' would be brought before a court of law for determination. This may be theoretically possible, since the duty to give effect to ministerial directions is limited to those of a general character, and a corporation could properly demur to carrying out directions they considered to fall outside that category. But it would be quite impracticable for a public corporation to challenge in the courts the legality of a ministerial direction. In such a situation the government would have the means at hand to exert overwhelming pressure in many different ways on the corporation. In a head-on collision between the

[1] See *Report from the Select Committee on Nationalized Industries* (*Reports and Accounts*), HMSO, HC 304/1956-7, Evidence, pp. 1-25 and App. I.

government and a public corporation, the former will always prove to be the victor: and this is not only inevitable, but in accordance with democratic principles.

CONTROL THROUGH INFLUENCE

It has, however, become abundantly clear in recent years that the power to issue directions and the other legal means of control possessed by Ministers are of far less importance in the relations between the government and nationalized industries than the influence exercised informally through discussion, negotiation, and pressure. Occasionally a formal direction will be issued by a Department, but there is usually a special reason for it, as there was when the incoming Minister of Supply, shortly after the Conservative Government had announced their intention to denationalize the iron and steel industry, gave a direction to the Iron and Steel Corporation ordering them not to take any unauthorized action which would alter the financial structure of any company under the Corporation's control; or which would result in the sale or disposal of its undertaking or securities.[1]

The real character of the working relationship between Ministers and public corporations is only gradually becoming known to the public. Until recently Ministers have carefully hidden their activities, doubtless from a desire to avoid having to answer in Parliament for the great variety of matters about which they intervene or are consulted by the public corporations, but for which they do not wish to be responsible either to Parliament or the public.

The nature and extent of ministerial influence is now becoming clearer; but it would be a mistake to assume that its character is necessarily static. There is some reason for believing that Conservative Ministers have in recent years exercised a greater influence over matters of policy and management than their predecessors; but what is more significant are the recent admissions that Ministers have a general right or duty to exercise a comprehensive supervision over nationalized industries. The Minister of Transport's liaison officer told the Select Committee on Nationalized Industries set up by the House of Commons, that 'the Minister has a general oversight in addition to these specific powers [i.e. his statutory powers under the Transport Acts, 1947 and 1953]. He is in constant touch with the chairman of the British Transport Commission. Very many matters are discussed between them which are not enumerated here [i.e. in the statement of statutory powers] but

[1] *Iron and Steel Corporation of Great Britain Annual Report 1951–2*, HMSO, HC 198/1952-3, p. 4.

the responsibility for the decision taken rests with the Commission. The Minister might conceivably feel bound to intervene if he thought things were going wrong, if the Commission were getting into deep water or being mismanaged.'[1] The Minister of Fuel and Power's liaison officer acknowledged in almost similar terms that in addition to his specific statutory powers, the Minister exercises a general supervisory power over the gas, electricity, and coal boards, and that therefore new matters might be arising all the time which came within his sphere of interest. Many of them would be matters for consultation only, and the Minister's responsibility would be indirect.[2] The Minister himself, in a letter to the parliamentary committee, explained that among the important matters of current policy and practice which at that time engaged his responsibility, in addition to his statutory powers of control over the corporations, were an increase in the general level of coal prices, the requisitioning of land for opencast operations, civil defence arrangements, and co-ordination between the various fuels.[3]

The Minister of Transport and Civil Aviation informed the Select Committee that so far as the affairs of BOAC and BEA were concerned, he had either decided or been involved in a responsible capacity in regard to such matters of current policy and practice as the purchases of aircraft; the hiring of foreign aircraft; investment in associated companies overseas; charter policy; routes operated; approval of fares on scheduled services; the advisory councils; the programme of the Helicopter Unit, which is mainly financed from money provided by Parliament; and the transfer of BEA's maintenance base from Renfrew to London.[4] In dealing with some of these matters the Minister could have invoked his statutory powers, but it was not necessary—or politically expedient—for him to do so.

Only two months later, when Mr Boyd-Carpenter (Minister of Transport and Civil Aviation) was asked in the House of Commons to make a statement on his capital allocation for development and modernization of British Railways, he said that he made no such allocation, money being raised on the market with a Treasury guarantee. 'Subject to the approval of the Chancellor and myself, it is the responsibility of the British Transport Commission to carry out the development of its enterprise. *I should very much hesitate to interfere more than the statute compels me to do with its discharge of its responsibilities.*'[5]

[1] *Special Report from the Select Committee on Nationalized Industries*, HMSO, HC 120/1955-6, p. 14, Q. 29.

[2] *Ib.*, p. 22, Qs. 41-2.

[3] *Ib.*, p. 31.

[4] *Ib.*, p. 11.

[5] The italics are mine. 543 HC Deb. 5s., cols. 379-80 (June 29, 1955).

The evidence tends to show that Ministers—including the Minister of Transport and Civil Aviation—are interfering with the public corporations a great deal more than they are compelled to do by statute. Mr George Strauss, MP, who had been Minister of Supply in the Attlee Government, went so far as to say that during his weekly talks with the chairman and deputy chairman of the Iron and Steel Corporation he was accustomed to consider 'every single problem, not only of national interest but on every conceivable detail concerning that Corporation. There was not a subject with which I was not concerned. Therefore, it might be said that I was taking responsibility because if I did not like what the Corporation was doing I could issue a direction.'[1]

There is obviously, Mr Lennox-Boyd remarked in a parliamentary debate, 'a tremendous amount of consultation and correspondence between any government and the boards of the great nationalized industries'; and he went on to say that it would be quite wrong for him to undertake to publish anything relating to such communications.[2] Lord Swinton, speaking on behalf of the government in the House of Lords in 1953, criticized a proposal that Ministers be required to report to Parliament what action they had taken under the statute on the ground that ministerial action, as opposed to the issue of directions, is too extensive and informal to be reported with precision.[3]

THE RELATIONS OF MINISTERS AND THE BOARDS

Lord Swinton then made the remarkable statement that 'the Minister's day-to-day contact with the chairman of a nationalized board is very like one's relationship with one's own officials in one's Department'.[4] In my opinion this is an entirely false analogy. Mr A. H. Hanson has observed that in spite of the clear theoretical distinction that exists between a nationalized industry and a government department, a convention is apparently growing up whereby the relationship between the Minister and a Board is as confidential as that between the Minister and his Permanent Secretary.[5] If that be so, then something has gone seriously wrong with the status of the public corporation, for it was certainly never intended that a chairman should be in a position similar to that of the permanent head of a Department *vis-à-vis* the Minister in charge of that department. In Lord Swinton's eyes the real problem of parliamentary control of the nationalized industries is not to obtain

[1] HC 120/1955-6, p. 36, Q. 14.
[2] 509 HC Deb. 5s., col. 1042 (December 15, 1952).
[3] 180 HL Deb. 5s., cols. 1504-5 (March 12, 1953).
[4] 180 H.L. Deb. 5s., col. 1504 (March 12, 1953).
[5] A. H. Hanson: 'Report on the Reports', XXX *Public Administration* (1952), p. 122.

information about the Minister's actions but to get information about the boards and their activities. This assumes that all that matters is what is done, rather than why it was done, or who was responsible—a proposition which is in my view untenable.

Mr Watkinson, the Minister of Transport and Civil Aviation in Sir Anthony Eden's government, was questioned in the House of Commons in May 1956 about a statement he had made to a newspaper that 'one clear precedent I intend to maintain is that BOAC policy is a matter between me and the chairman'. He admitted that under the Air Corporations Act, 1949, only disposal of any surplus revenue is reserved for settlement between the chairman and the Minister. Everything else is to be decided by the full Board. But, he said, 'the chain of command is that I am responsible to the House and the chairman is responsible to me. But, of course, before coming to me he discusses, clears and brings to me the collective decision of the Board.'[1] It would, he added, be absolutely wrong for a Minister to deal with anyone else except the chairman, who is directly and solely responsible to him.

This statement represents a transformation, if not a travesty, of the relationship which was intended to be established between a Minister and a public corporation under the post-war legislation. To begin with, there should be nothing even remotely resembling a 'chain of command'. This old-fashioned phrase, which is outmoded today even in connection with administration in a government department organized on heirarchical lines, assumes that the superior can give orders to his subordinates about everything, and that the latter will obey the orders without question. The statutes dealing with nationalized industries give the public corporations full authority to determine policy except in respect of those matters where a Minister's approval is required, or in regard to which the Minister has given a direction of a general or a specific character. To say that policy is to be settled between the Minister and the chairman represents a gross infringement of the managerial freedom of the public corporation, and a severe down-grading of the status of the other members of the board. Indeed, the legislation insists that the Minister shall consult with the *Board* before giving a direction[2]—the only exception being the Bank of England, where the Treasury is required to consult only with the Governor of the Bank.[3]

If the chairmen of the public corporations permit Ministers to treat them as though they were departmental officials, then they must be held

[1] 552 HC Deb. 5s., cols. 1212 and 1214-5 (May 9, 1956).

[2] See, e.g. Gas Act, 1948, s. 7; Transport Act, 1947, s. 4; Coal Industry Nationalization Act, 1946, s. 3.

[3] Bank of England Act, 1946, s. 4.

responsible for casting away much of the independence with which Parliament endowed them. If members of the boards allow themselves to be thrust into the background, whence their views are merely conveyed to the Minister by the chairman, and the Minister's decisions conveyed to them by the chairman, then they have only themselves to thank for their diminished status and relative unimportance.

MR MORRISON'S VIEWS

The principal architect of the modern public corporation was Mr Herbert Morrison, who has recently stated the following view of the relationship which should exist between Ministers and the boards.

> 'Clearly it is desirable that the Minister should keep himself familiar with the general work of the Board or Boards with which he is concerned. It is wise for him with his parliamentary secretary and principal officers concerned from time to time to meet the chairman and, indeed, the members of the Board, to discuss matters of mutual interest either formally or informally. On such occasions both the Board and the Minister will be conscious of their legal rights: the legal right of the Minister to give general directions or to withhold approvals, and the legal rights of the Board within the field of day-to-day management; but it is also desirable that such discussion should be free, frank, forthcoming, and co-operative.'[1]

The Minister should take pains not to undermine the board's sense of responsibility, which is not only a legal obligation but a public asset, while the board on their part should understand that the Minister is not bound to defend a nationalized industry from parliamentary criticism unless he agrees with its policy. Frequent informal discussions are useful, but the Minister should not let himself be persuaded to acquiesce in policies which he would find hard to defend in public. On the other hand a board should not be induced or persuaded to take decisions which they consider to be wrong and opposed to the best interests of the industry merely in order to please the Minister. 'The board have a perfect right to say to the Minister, "Give us a general direction in writing which will be published and we will obey, but otherwise we are sorry we cannot act as you would wish". What is wanted is friendly co-operation without prejudice to the rights and responsibilities of either the Minister or board.'[2] There are two dangers to be avoided. One is that the chairmen of the boards should become arbitrary Emperors of Industry,

[1] Herbert Morrison: *Government and Parliament* (1954), p. 264.

[2] *Ib.*, p. 265. See also Mr Morrison's evidence to the Select Committee on Nationalized Industries. HC 332 - I/1951-2, Qs. 854 and 539.

resentful of ministerial or public criticism. The other is that the board should become either officially or unofficially the creature of the Minister and his department.[1]

The wisdom and breadth of Mr Morrison's conception stand out in sharp contrast to the tendencies towards excessive interference and overbearing attitudes which we have noted in the statements of some holders of ministerial office. Everyone agrees that there should be frequent informal discussion between Ministers and the boards. But there is little agreement beyond that. Mr D. N. Chester has put his finger on a very soft spot when he writes that all governments try to get their own way without wanting to be held publicly responsible for the results;[2] and Mr Ernest Davies has on several occasions made the same accusation.[3] In Mr Chester's opinion 'the wide powers given to Ministers in recent nationalization legislation open the way to comfortable back-seat driving, so reducing the responsibility and discretion, and therefore, ultimately, the calibre of the board of management'.[4] He urges that there should be a clearer division of responsibility between the Minister and the board. Lord Reith has made a similar plea that the government's duties and powers of intervention should be specific and formulated in unambiguous terms.[5]

There are two quite distinct points involved in this question. One is the extent and nature of government control over the nationalized industries. The other relates to the method of its exercise: namely, whether Ministers should influence policy through persuasion and inducement exerted in a clandestine manner, and for which they are not held responsible, or exercise control by means of formal directives for which they are answerable to Parliament and the public.

DIVERGENT CONCEPTS

Lord Leathers, speaking as Secretary of State for the Co-ordination of Transport, Fuel and Power in Sir Winston Churchill's last administration, said that in the government's view their task was to appoint the best men they could find to run a nationalized industry, to give them all the practical help, encouragement and advice they could, and then to leave the board so far as possible to run the industry. 'Where the board

[1] *Op. cit.*, pp. 265 and 272.

[2] D. N. Chester: 'The Nationalized Industries', *Three Banks Review*, December 1952, pp. 42-3.

[3] Ernest Davies: 'Ministerial Control and Parliamentary Responsibility of Nationalized Industries' in *Problems of Nationalized Industry*, ed. W. A. Robson (1952), pp. 110-2.

[4] *Ib.*

[5] Lord Reith: 'Public Corporations', *The Times*, July 3, 1956.

have to make decisions which are essentially the board's own responsibility, we are always willing to give them the advice that we can; but we are careful not to interfere.'[1] Lord Leathers was himself a leading industrialist with long experience in the fuel and transport industries, and he undoubtedly believed firmly in the attitude he was enunciating. Moreover, he may have had considerable influence in persuading his ministerial colleagues to accept it. But that was in 1952, and in the subsequent years much has happened to make one feel that the Leathers doctrine has been abandoned or forgotten by Ministers. Certainly their present practices and attitudes are often remote from its spirit.

Some people are in favour of complete government control over the nationalized industries and would like to see them run departmentally, like the Post Office. But this view does not command widespread support and is unlikely to be accepted by any government or Parliament. Mr Austen Albu, MP, has proposed a less old-fashioned method of achieving the same end: he suggests that the Minister should be chairman of the board of the public corporation. This, he contends, would concentrate control of policy in the hands of the Minister, where it properly belongs, while making it easier to decentralize day-to-day management.[2] It would, of course, make the Minister answerable in Parliament for every activity of the industry.

At the other extreme we have the report of the Herbert Committee on the Electricity Supply industry. The Committee laid down the proposition that the sole purpose of the nationalized industry is to generate and distribute electricity as cheaply as possible. All the decisions and activities of the central and regional electricity authorities should be based on strictly economic motives of the narrowest kind. Any consideration of the national interest, in such matters as providing electricity at uneconomic rates in rural areas; or a decision to insure the authorities' plant, premises, and equipment with insurance companies, in order to strengthen their competitive position in the foreign markets; or refraining from inviting tenders for generating plant from abroad, should be regarded as political matters to be decided by the Minister.[3] The boards should not deviate by even a hairsbreadth from their duty to run their undertakings on purely commercial lines. This rigid dichotomy between the economic and the non-economic was intended to draw a clear line between the sphere of ministerial control and the province of corporate autonomy. The committee argued that apart from the selection

[1] 178 H.L. Deb. 5s., cols. 487-8 (July 30, 1952).

[2] Austen Albu: 'The Organization of Industry' in *New Fabian Essays*, ed. R. H. S. Crossman (1952), pp. 128-9.

[3] Report, HMSO, Cmd. 9672/1956, paras. 372-3.

of the board members (to which they rightly attributed the utmost importance) the other tasks falling to the Minister would depend largely on the framework within which the industry would operate. If the industry—and the same would apply to nearly all the nationalized industries—were regarded as 'a strictly commercial undertaking', many questions would answer themselves and the Minister would be involved with few policy questions. 'The further our conception is departed from', they warned, 'the more policy questions will the Minister have to decide.'[1] And, they added, the less the principle of commercial operation is invaded the better it will be for the efficiency of the industry.

The Herbert Committee projected public enterprise in the image of profit-making commercial enterprise as it was assumed to exist in the mid-nineteenth century:[2] this part of their report conjures up a picture of Mr Gladstone walking arm-in-arm with Adam Smith. Whether or not it ever really existed, the conception of private enterprise which they invoked for this purpose is remote from the one which is followed today, especially so far as big business is concerned. Nowadays joint-stock companies frequently act from non-economic motives. They make contributions to charitable appeals; they endow research and teaching in schools and universities, often in branches of knowledge remote from their business interests; they help to found new colleges and universities; they sponsor publications of a scholarly or scientific character, and also those of a popular kind; they sometimes follow policies regarding wages, prices or dividends which are urged on them by the government, regardless of whether it pays them or not to do so; they engage in export drives even when it would be easier and more profitable to sell in the home market; they spent money on Coronation festivities and on victory celebrations after World War II; they are often indifferent to the interests of the stockholder.

The scheme of reform recommended by the Herbert Committee would have denuded the Minister of Power of many of his present powers. The principal duties left to him would have been only the appointment of board members; the authorization of capital borrowing; instructing the industry when it was to act in a way other than that dictated by purely economic considerations; and to satisfy himself through the reports of the central authority and area boards that the industry was being run efficiently as a commercial concern.[3] All other matters of policy concerned with the approval or supervision of the activities and programmes of the operating bodies, would have been reserved to a

[1] Report, HMSO, Cmd. 9672/1956, paras. 495–6.

[2] Especially Chs. XV and XXIV.

[3] *Ib.*, para. 498.

reconstituted Central Electricity Authority, except that the Minister's consent would be required to the issue of directions by that Authority.[1] Thus, the approval of the policies of the area boards and the new Generating Board in relation to development programmes, capital and revenue budgets, depreciation and reserve funds, research and development, and the approval of tariffs for bulk supply and retail distribution, would all have fallen to the proposed central authority.

The government rejected this proposal on the ground that it would confer on the new central authority great power with little corresponding responsibility. They were unwilling to transfer supervisory powers over vital matters from a responsible Minister to an appointed board. Moreover, they thought the proposal would be detrimental to the growth of a sense of initiative and responsibility in the Area Boards which the Herbert Committee said they were anxious to promote, and it was therefore incompatible with the Committee's own major objective.[2] The government decided to set up instead an Electricity Council to advise the Minister on questions affecting the electricity supply industry, and to promote and assist in developing an efficient, co-ordinated and economical system. The Minister retains his statutory powers.[3]

GOVERNMENT CONTROL OVER RAILWAY CHARGES

The greatest amount of government control has in recent years been directed towards the economic aspects of the nationalized undertakings, such as prices, wages, capital development, and so forth. These are precisely the aspects which it might be thought would be most susceptible of being decided on strictly commercial principles in accordance with the doctrines of the Herbert Committee. Yet this has proved not to be the case.

In February 1952 a draft passenger charges scheme for the railways was confirmed with modifications after a public inquiry before the Transport Tribunal lasting thirty-two days, during which ninety-nine objectors appeared. The introduction of the scheme in London aroused much public comment, especially the proposals to raise the so-called substandard charges for monthly and other cheap return fares by a higher percentage than other fares, and to reduce the bus fare stage points. The Minister of Transport thereupon referred to the Central Transport Users' Consultative Committee the question of how the British Transport Commission was fixing fares within the maximum authorized by the scheme. The Consultative Committee reported favourably on the

[1] Report, HMSO, Cmd. 9672/1956, para. 248.

[2] White Paper *Proposals for the Reorganization of the Electricity Supply Industry*, HMSO, Cmd. 27/1956, para. 6.

[3] Electricity Act, 1957, ss. 7, 8, 20, 22 and 27.

fairness of the scheme and did not propose any changes in the fares.

The Minister nevertheless gave a direction to the BTC on April 15, 1952, instructing them not to increase passenger charges for rail travel outside London. The effect of this action was that when the new scheme came into operation on May 1, the reductions in single fares were applied but not the corresponding increases in the level of sub-standard charges. At the end of April, the House of Commons approved the Minister's action and expressed the view that all charges should be increased proportionately, preserving the sub-standard elements; and that so far as practicable this principle should be applied to the fares already introduced in London. After discussion with the Commission, the Minister announced modifications to reduce or eliminate disproportionate increases in sub-standard charges. These were then applied to London and to the railways outside London. The loss of revenue to the Commission was nearly £2 m. a year.[1]

The government defended the intervention simply on the ground that the original charges scheme was unfair to the beneficiaries of sub-standard fares.[2] The Prime Minister (Sir Winston Churchill) made a statement explaining that the decision to intervene was the result of a Cabinet meeting lasting five hours, in the course of which the legal rights of the government were examined and explained by the Law Officers and the Lord Chancellor.[3] The Opposition criticized their action as unjustified in the national interest and said it could be explained only as a political manoeuvre by the government to restore their waning popularity. Mr Herbert Morrison contended that the Executive should deal with any matter which had been before the Transport Tribunal in a judicial spirit; that the Minister of Transport had himself answered earlier questions on the subject by saying it would be improper for him to intervene after a charges scheme had been confirmed by the Tribunal, except by referring it to the Consultative Committee; and finally, that the loss of revenue brought about by the government's action would prevent the British Transport Commission from fulfilling their statutory obligation to cover costs out of revenue.[4]

On at least three occasions since 1951 the Government have intervened in wage disputes on the railways, after the negotiating machinery existing for the purpose had considered the disputes. In 1951 the Labour Government instructed the Transport Commission to grant a 7½ per cent wage increase instead of the 5 per cent advance recom-

[1] *British Transport Commission Annual Report 1952*, HMSO, HC 190/1952-3, paras. 137-40.

[2] 499 HC Deb. 5s., cols. 37-8, 1024, 1029, 1032 and 1162 (April 21 and 28, 1952).

[3] 501 HC Deb. 5s., col. 530 (May 21, 1952)

[4] 499 HC Deb. 5s., cols. 1043-53.

mended by the Court of Inquiry. The 5 per cent had been accepted by the Commission but not by the trade unions.

In 1953 the unions refused to accept an award of the Railway Staff National Tribunal which the Transport Commission were willing to implement. The NUR threated to strike on December 20. Thereupon the Conservative Government instructed the Transport Commission to make further concessions. A subsequent agreement was made under which the NUR accepted the Tribunal's award on condition that a further percentage increase was conceded within two months, and an exhaustive examination of the whole wage and salary structure carried out in the near future.

In 1954–5 further negotiations took place under the 1953 agreement. These were too complicated and prolonged to describe here. In the end the NUR decided to approach the Minister of Transport, recalling the successful use of this method on two previous occasions. This time the Minister refused to intervene, but the Minister of Labour shortly afterwards appointed a Court of Inquiry to investigate the dispute.[1]

In 1958 the negotiations with the railway unions on wages were conducted on a tripartite basis, the Prime Minister and other Ministers participating on several occasions. A settlement granting an increase of 3 per cent without raising charges was made possible only by the Government agreeing to an immediate speeding up of the modernization of the railways. This involved an increase in the authorized rate of capital expenditure.

It is circumstances such as these which have led one Member of Parliament to declare that the position of the railways is such that the Transport Commission must either first obtain the consent of the Government to increases which can only be made with Government assistance, or make agreements with the unions knowing that the Government can compel them to repudiate the agreements because it is financially impossible for the Commission to find the money without increasing their deficit. Hence Mr F. Lee, MP, argues that only the Government are in a position to determine what wage increases can be given to the railway employees.[2]

An even more striking example of Government interference with the price policy of a nationalized industry occurred in 1956; and the British Transport Commission were again concerned. The Commission's deficit for 1955 increased by about £30 m. owing to the railway strike and increased costs. The Commission estimated that their deficit for the year might amount to £55 m., and the cumulative deficit £100 m. In view

[1] B. C. Roberts: 'Wages on the Railways', XXVI *Political Quarterly* (1955), p. 117.
[2] 536 HC Deb. 5s., cols. 1381-2 (February 3, 1955).

of their statutory obligation to pay their way, the BTC felt bound to take steps to increase their revenue, and proposed increases in freight and passenger charges calculated to yield an additional £37 m. a year.

Mr Watkinson, the Minister of Transport and Civil Aviation, declared that the Commission were fully justified in taking this action, and he emphasized that the Government's policy required all the nationalized undertakings to fix charges which truly reflected their costs. But as the Minister believed that he could detect 'signs that renewed and strenuous efforts will improve the financial outlook on the railways through more efficient working arising from better relations in the industry', the Government considered that they would be justified in asking the Commission to defer raising their charges. The Commission had given way on the ground that they desired to co-operate with the Government 'in the national interest'.[1] In consequence, the BTC announced increases in passenger fares designed to yield only about £20m. in a full year, the remaining proposed increases being put into cold storage on the understanding that the situation would be reviewed in six months' time. It was hoped that during this brief period steps could be taken to initiate measures calculated to improve operating efficiency, though vast savings could obviously not be expected in so short a time. The Minister was at pains to reiterate that the Government's request was 'not an interference' and that the decision was reached with the 'willing co-operation' of the Commission.[2] Mr Watkinson did not explain why the Commission should have been willing to accept a rejection of its proposals in the certain knowledge that the result would be to worsen its financial position. We must assume they did so under pressure from the Government.

After making his statement in Parliament, the Minister referred the matter for advice to the Transport Tribunal, sitting as a consultative committee. The Tribunal recommended that the full increases applied for by the Transport Commission should be granted. The Minister nevertheless still held to his course and proposed to make regulations permitting only the lower increases previously announced. Mr Ernest Davies, MP, asked the pertinent question what was the purpose of consulting the Tribunal and then ignoring its advice. Mr Watkinson replied that he was responsible to Parliament and not to the Tribunal; and even here he was answerable only for freight charges. The Transport Commission had no obligation to consult him about passenger charges.[3]

The Transport Tribunal gave their advice to the Minister in a

[1] 550 HC Deb. 5s., cols. 829-30 (March 19, 1956).
[2] *Ib.*, cols. 830-1 and 833-6.
[3] 551 HC Deb. 5s., cols. 183-6 (April 11, 1956).

reasoned memorandum. They pointed out that even if all the increased charges were brought into force at the end of the six months period, the accumulated deficit would have increased by the end of 1956 by about £35 m. to more than £104 m. The BTC estimates already made some allowance for increased efficiency; and even the full advances in charges they had asked for would leave a gap of £18 m. between revenue and expenditure to be bridged. It was impossible to suppose that any conceivable improvement in efficiency could do more than reduce the gap of £18 m. which would still separate the Commission from solvency even if all the measures proposed by them were put into full effect. 'For these reasons', concluded the Tribunal, 'we regret that we are unable to agree with the provisional decisions which you have reached. It may be that there are considerations not expressed in your statement which are thought to make it necessary to disregard, at all events for the time being, the obligations and interests of the Commission.'[1] The Tribunal thus clearly advised the Minister that what he proposed to do in making the Regulations was contrary to the financial interests of the Commission and would prevent them from fulfilling their statutory obligations.[2]

This episode is a particularly flagrant example of ministerial intervention because the Minister overrode the statutory duty of the Transport Commission to pay their way—a matter of doubtful legality—and the government's declared policy regarding nationalized industries. Mr Watkinson set aside the considered judgment of the Transport Commission and the reasoned advice of the Transport Tribunal. His action, Mr Davies contended in the House of Commons, was inconsistent with the policy embodied in the Transport Act, 1953, which authorized the Transport Commission to act with flexibility on a commercial basis; while Mr G. R. Strauss, MP, observed that it provides a precedent for enabling the government to say that any nationalized industry may not increase its charges.[3]

MINISTERIAL CONTROL OVER COAL PRICES

The industry whose prices have been most closely subject to government control is coal, although the control is derived from a so-called gentleman's agreement entered into at the beginning of the Second World War and continued in force after the industry was nationalized in

[1] Transport Tribunal Memorandum to Minister of Transport and Civil Aviation. See *ib.*, cols. 186-90.

[2] See the motion for the adjournment introduced by Mr Ernest Davies, MP, asking for the annulment of the Regulations, 552 HC Deb. 5s., cols. 2338-9 (May 17, 1956).

[3] 550 HC Deb. 5s., cols. 827-32 (March 19, 1956).

1946.[1] Under the agreement the National Coal Board normally have to apply to the Minister of Power for permission to raise prices. The Minister takes into consideration a number of different factors before giving his decision.[2] He tends to stress the short-term view to a greater extent than the NCB, but on the other hand he takes into account much wider considerations than the Board. Out of ten applications which were made between July 1947 and March 1957, in five cases the Minister fixed a later date than that asked for; in four cases he granted a smaller increase than that requested; and in one instance he refused the application entirely.[3]

The NCB in giving evidence before the Select Committee on Nationalized Industries (Reports and Accounts) said that they would prefer to be free of ministerial restrictions of this kind but they did not press strongly for their removal. Mr Latham, the deputy chairman, said that they recognized their public responsibilities as a nationalized industry, and did not seek to evade them. Nonetheless, the effect of the gentleman's agreement has been that from time to time the board have not been able to raise prices in order to cover increased costs and thus achieve a break-even position as required by statute.[4]

Sir John Maud, Permanent Secretary of the Ministry of Power, thought the arrangements could more accurately be described as a sharing of responsibility rather than as control of the board by the Minister;[5] but it is obvious that the last word rests with the Minister.

The Select Committee thought the procedure under the gentleman's agreement to be not unduly hampering the initiative of the board and as a useful way of checking the board's interpretation of the public interest. They therefore approved of the present arrangement but disagreed with the informal and nebulous character of the agreement. The Committee urged that responsibility for coal prices should be clearly defined by law. They recommended a statutory provision requiring the NCB to consult the Minister of Power about the public interest before altering coal prices. Where this had been done, the board would carry full responsibility for price determinations. The Minister should have a statutory power to give the board specific directions in the national interest concerning prices.[6]

[1] *Report from the Select Committee on Nationalized Industries (Reports and Accounts)*, HMSO, HC 187-I/1957-8, paras. 82-6.

[2] *Ib.*, para. 85; Evidence, Qs. 261-3 and 272.

[3] *Ib.*, App. III.

[4] *National Coal Board Annual Report 1956*, HMSO, HC 176 - I/1956-7, Vol. I, para. 67.

[5] *Report from the Select Committee on Nationalized Industries (Reports and Accounts)*, Q. 244. See also HC 304/1956-7, Qs. 1098 ff.; and Memorandum on p. 155.

[6] *Ib.*, Report, paras. 87-9.

It can scarcely be said that the Select Committee's proposals are based on any clear principles or will fix responsibility for prices unambiguously on either the Minister or the National Coal Board. No provision is to be made for informing the public when or whether an application by the board has been refused, nor on what ground. 'The national interest' which is to be the criterion of the Minister's decision is so vague a concept that it can be extended to cover almost every conceivable reason for granting or rejecting or modifying a proposal. Finally, the Select Committee concluded that government control over prices has not hampered the initiative of the National Coal Board. It would obviously be impossible to adduce any evidence to support a negative proposition of this kind.

NON-STATUTORY CONTROL OVER THE AIR CORPORATIONS

The Select Committee on Nationalized Industries have also brought to light the remarkable extent to which Ministers are exercising control over the air corporations without having statutory authority to do so.[1] Thus, there is a gentleman's agreement whereby the fares which the air lines charge for cabotage and domestic services are subject to Ministerial approval.[2] This sometimes imposes policies which the corporations would not have adopted if they had been free to exercise their own discretion. For example, BEA were unable for two years to introduce a cheap night fare on the London-Cyprus route, in order to meet competition from an independent airline. Again, although the airlines can choose the manufacturer, the final decision on the purchase of aircraft can rest with the Minister, who acts without any express statutory power.[3]

After a careful review of the position the Select Committee on Nationalized Industries said they felt bound to ask if the numerous non-statutory powers exercised by the Minister do not amount to 'a degree of control far in excess of that envisaged by the statutes under which BOAC and BEA were created, and so lead to an undesirable diminution in the authority of the chairman and boards of the corporations, and in their feeling of responsibility'.[4] The answer to this question is obviously in the affirmative. The Committee considered it essential to the efficient management of the air corporations that there should be a clearcut division of responsibility between the chairman and his board on the

[1] *Report from the Select Committee on Nationalized Industries* (*Reports and Accounts*). The Air Corporations HC paper 213, 1959, paras. 23, 94.

[2] *Ib.*, paras. 87-90; Evidence Q 171-4.

[3] *Ib.*, para. 36; Q 391.

[4] *Ib.*, para. 23.

one hand and the Minister and his department on the other. When the Minister wishes to override the board on a commercial question for reasons of national interest, he should do so by a published directive.

It is not only Ministers who are to blame for blurring the lines of responsibility and exercising a substantially greater degree of power over the airlines than Parliament has authorized. The chairman and boards of BOAC and BEA must take some share of the blame for accepting so tamely successive ministerial encroachments on their own freedom. Both corporations seem always to have accepted, usually without protest, the Minister's interference with their commercial judgment even when he was acting without legal authority, although they were free in such circumstances to refuse to accept his ruling.[1] The only recorded instance where a strong line was taken was when BEA resisted 'a certain amount of Ministry pressure' before they were allowed to adopt the DH 121 project.[2]

THE NATIONAL INTEREST

These and other examples which could be cited show that Ministers have been taking an increasingly close interest in the finance of the nationalized industries; and Government intervention is likely to be a decisive factor in the more important questions of price and wages policy. What are we to think of this development?

On one view of the situation it can be contended that as the nationalized industries enjoy a high degree of monopoly, their prices are managed prices rather than market prices. In managing prices in a basic industry consideration should be given not only to the solvency of the undertaking but also to the repercussions of prices on the economy as a whole, and to wider issues of public policy. The national interest may play a considerable part in the decision, and Ministers are better judges of the national interest as a whole than the Board of a public corporation.

This view was forcibly expressed by Mr Aneurin Bevan in the House of Commons debate on the resignation of Mr Hardie as chairman of the Iron and Steel Corporation in 1952 owing to disagreement between him and the Minister of Supply (Mr Duncan Sandys) about steel prices and certain other matters which had produced friction between them and disagreement between Mr Hardie and other members of the Board. Labour Opposition speakers severely criticized the Minister for his dealings with Mr Hardie. But Mr Bevan dissociated himself from the position adopted by other Opposition speakers. It is, he said, dangerous

[1] *Report from the Select Committee on Nationalized Industries* (*Reports and Accounts*). The Air Corporations HC paper 213, 1959, para. 92.

[2] *Ib.*, para. 34.

to suggest that the Minister responsible for a Department is a less fit person to judge the national interest than the chairman of a corporation.

'Insofar as Mr Hardie has set himself up—I do not think he has; but insofar as he suggested that he is a better judge of the national interest than is the Minister of Supply, Mr Hardie claims too much. The responsibility of deciding what is in the overriding interests of the nation rests with the Minister, because only by it resting with him can it rest here. Once we deny to the Minister of Supply, or to any other Minister responsible for a great nationalized undertaking, the right to determine what he thinks to be in the national interest, then we are erecting a species of the corporate society more familiar to Italian Fascist principles than to the British democratic constitution. I have always denied the right of these great corporations to decide such issues.'[1]

A contrary view of the position lays stress on the need to give the public corporations the largest possible amount of freedom and responsibility if the nationalized industries are to achieve the best results. Capital expenditure is a matter over which Ministers have been given statutory powers of approval. This is right and inevitable in the present state of the British economy. But the levels of prices and wages are in a different category. If these are subject to government control—whether it is effected by formal direction or through indirect influence—one of the most essential attributes of management is missing. In consequence, many of the advantages claimed for the public corporation will be lost, or at least not fully realized. Those who hold this view would contend that prime responsibility for fixing prices should rest with the nationalized industry concerned rather than with Ministers. They would point out the possibility of ministerial decisions being based on considerations of electoral advantage rather than on the objective needs of the economy or of the industry.

When full allowance has been made for the possibility that Ministers may not always act from politically disinterested motives, there is nevertheless a hard core of truth in the assertion that that most elusive, nebulous, and frequently abused concept 'the national interest' may sometimes point in a different direction from that indicated by the needs of a public corporation considered in isolation. Hence in the last resort the Minister must be able to override the board.

Where he does so, however, there should be a clear and unmistakable allocation of responsibility. Ministerial determination should take the form of a published direction; and in the absence of such a direction one should be able to assume with confidence that the public corporation has

[1] 496 HC Deb. 5s., col. 818 (February 25, 1952). Cf. Mr Bevan's views in his *In Place of Fear* (1952), pp. 98-9.

had an unfettered discretion. When the Minister does intervene, he should state in his direction the reasons underlying his decision.

An example of a proper and authentic regard for the national interest was the Conservative Government's drive to stop inflation, which began with an appeal to the nationalized industries to maintain stable prices.

In June 1956 a meeting took place between the Prime Minister (Sir Anthony Eden) and some six other Ministers with the chairmen of the boards of nationalized industries. The object was to enable the Government to urge the public corporations to refrain from increasing prices as a contribution to the Government's attempt to stop inflation. A statement was issued after the meeting to the effect that Ministers welcomed the action taken by the electricity and coal industries.

Few people would quarrel with this action on the part of the Government or dispute that the national interest was clearly involved. It might have been better for the Government to have issued a direction giving effect to their wishes in the matter; but the communiques published in the press clearly showed the nature, reasons and effect of the Government's intervention. There was, therefore, no doubt about where responsibility lay for the standstill on prices and any results which it might have on the revenue accounts of the nationalized industries.

THE CLEAR ALLOCATION OF RESPONSIBILITY

This is the crux of the matter; and it is on this aspect that there has been most confusion in recent years.

Some of the public statements of Ministers are disingenuous, to say the least, and difficult to reconcile with their actions behind the scenes. It is all very well for Mr Geoffrey Lloyd, for many years Minister of Fuel and Power, to say that he regards the nationalized industries as wholly responsible for the engineering and other details, and that he seeks to leave them the fullest measure of freedom to manage the industries within the framework of general policy agreed with him.[1] It no doubt makes a good impression to declare in public that 'it is in the national interest that these boards should be enterprising and indeed venturesome'.[2] But who can be enterprising and venturesome when he is managing a vast transport undertaking with a rapidly mounting deficit and is restrained from increasing charges? Or is in charge of a fine, up-to-date air line like BEA or BOAC and is persuaded to give an undertaking not to apply for licences for all-freight services on new routes for a year in order to give private operators a better chance? What good

[1] 529 HC Deb. 5s., col. 2504 (July 9, 1954).

[2] 532 HC Deb. 5s., col. 1047 (November 9, 1954).

are verbal tributes to the managerial independence of public corporations if the Government are prepared to compel the boards to pay higher wages than the arbitration tribunal has awarded, or than they think practicable? What is the point of establishing public corporations with a statutory duty to meet expenditure on current account out of their revenues if prices are settled *de facto* by Ministers, even though they are not responsible for them either legally or politically?

Some Ministers have been far from frank in disclosing the true character of their relations with the nationalized industries. Their main preoccupation has been to exercise power while avoiding taking responsibility in public; but this was not the main object, nor indeed one of the aims at all, of the movement which led to the modern public corporation. It may well be that the board members and chairmen should have been more ready to withstand ministerial pressure than they always have been in recent years. The threat of resignation, and especially of collective resignation, is a challenge which few Ministers are prepared to face in their clandestine dealings with the public corporations; and it could be used more often than it has been. When it is used, owing to a disagreement with ministerial policy, the reason for resigning should always be openly stated.

It may be argued that in present-day Britain with its regulated economy and narrow margins it is inevitable that the government of the day will want to control by one method or another the price and wage policies of nationalized industries. If this argument is accepted the case for public corporations would be substantially weakened and there would be much to be said for straightforward departmental administration, or a board with the Minister as chairman: for then the Minister would be answerable in Parliament for his actions.

But I do not accept this contention nor the premises on which it is based. The determination of wages and prices in nationalized industries should not normally be a political matter at all. The Government should intervene only when they are prepared to accept full and formal responsibility to the public and to Parliament for the decision. If this principle were to be accepted, there would be a notable reduction in the 'political' element in most decisions about wages and prices except on comparatively rare occasions. Ministers would be reluctant to intervene on those occasions when electoral considerations, the prestige or popularity of the government, have been the chief motives for their interest in these matters.

Obviously the boards of the public corporations must pay careful attention to the general warnings or advice given by the Government to industrialists and labour leaders about the state of the economy and its needs. But I cannot see that government intervention in prices and wages should go beyond this except where the Government are prepared to issue a formal direction for which they will take full responsibility. Where the Government does assume such responsibility, the statutory duty of the public corporation to pay its way taking one year with another should be suspended or modified if necessary.

Mr Aubrey Jones, when Minister of Fuel and Power, was asked what direction he had given the National Coal Board, the Central Electricity Authority and the Gas Council in prices, wages and capital policy. He replied that none had been given. He said he did not think that general directions on these matters are appropriate, but all in these industries should be aware of the importance of steadiness of prices to the national economy and of the fact that wage increases unaccompanied by increased productivity must inevitably lead to higher prices.[1]

No one could quarrel with this statement, if it truly reflected the attitude of Ministers, but as we have seen, the government had gone far beyond this in inducing the British Transport Commission to withdraw proposed increases of charges even in the face of a rapidly mounting deficit. There is, indeed, much evidence to show that in recent years Ministers have tended to bring greater influence to bear on the boards to ensure that government policy is carried out. Ministers have not, however, in general admitted greater responsibility on their part or shown any more readiness to answer for it in Parliament.

> 'The consequence is that whereas behind the scenes they have exercised a greater influence on the boards, they have not accepted public accountability for their actions. They have exercised their responsibility in private and not answered for it in public. This tendency was noticeable during the previous administration but has been carried considerably further by present Ministers.'[2]

A TWILIGHT ZONE

The reasons for this unsatisfactory state of affairs are by no means simple. It may be due in some instances to a Minister not wishing to make himself liable to accept the blame or public odium for a particular policy which may turn out badly. In others it may be because the corporation have not the courage to tell a Minister point blank that they refuse to adopt a policy he is urging on them unless he gives them a direction to that effect. A background factor is the widespread habit of English

[1] 554 HC Deb. 5s., col. 15 (June 11, 1956).

[2] Ernest Davies: 'Government Policy and the Public Corporation', XXVI *Political Quarterly* (1955), pp. 115-6.

life of preferring an informal understanding or gentlemanly 'persuasion' to a formal instruction or a legal document.

Whatever the reasons may be, this tendency to rely on influence or pressure rather than formal directions is misplaced in the relations between Ministers and the nationalized industries. The formal powers of control which the government possess over this vital sector of the economy are right and proper in principle. They are designed to give Ministers decisive authority in case of need in all major questions of policy, whether relating to operations, finance, development or anything else. To regard them as excessive implies a theory of the state which is inconsistent with the democratic socialism which has resulted in nationalization.

Ministers must be prepared to face up to the responsibilities which they have assumed. They should not be permitted to remain in the twilight zone in which some of them love to dwell, flitting happily from one private meeting to another, talking things over with the chairman at lunch, in the club, in the House of Commons, in the department, without disclosing either to the public or to Parliament the real extent of their intervention. This is not the way to strike the right balance between governmental power and managerial freedom.

To end this chapter on a more satisfactory note, we may observe the contrast presented by the experience of the BBC in its dealings with Ministers. The formal power of the government of the day over the British Broadcasting Corporation is absolute. In practice, as the Beveridge Committee point out, it has become the policy of successive governments, accepted by Parliament, that the Corporation should be independent of the government in the day-to-day conduct of its business, including both the making of programmes for broadcasting and general administration. 'The State has in practice in peacetime made little or no use of the powers formally retained by it in relation to the conduct of broadcasting. . . . No general directions as to television have been issued.' Despite friendly co-operation on informal lines, the Beveridge Committee reported in 1951 that 'In practice, in its current business, the British Broadcasting Corporation is independent of the Government and Parliament . . . '[1]

[1] *Report of the Broadcasting Committee 1949*, HMSO, Cmd. 8116/1951, paras. 28-33

CHAPTER VII

Parliamentary Debates and Questions

A GREAT deal of discussion has taken place on the subject of how far Ministers are or should be answerable in Parliament for the public corporations; and, conversely, the rights of members of Parliament in relation to the nationalized industries. The matter has not yet been finally settled; and in the meantime a good many mistaken ideas are entertained in various quarters.

THE PASSING OF LEGISLATION

To begin with, we may note that all the public corporations have been established by statute, with the exception of the BBC and the Bank of England, which owe their origin to charters. The Bank's charter dates from the seventeenth century and has recently been modified by statute when the Bank was nationalized. The precedent set by the BBC of creating a public corporation by charter is not likely to be repeated. Parliament has an indisputable right to perform the legislative function of nationalizing an industry and of creating the appropriate organ for that purpose.

Parliament is exceedingly effective in this role. The nationalization Acts lay down a clear and coherent framework of policy and structure within which each corporation is required to operate. Much excellent work was done in both Houses in the process of passing these statutes. In enacting legislation of this kind Parliament exerts a permanent influence over the conduct and organization of nationalized industries and services. It is, indeed, in the sphere of legislation that parliamentary debate and discussion are most effective.

Not infrequently new legislation is introduced relating to nationalized undertakings, and this provides members of Parliament with an opportunity for criticism and debate. Among the public statutes passed since the Labour Government's original programme of nationalization was carried out are the Airways Corporation Act, 1949, the Coal Industry Act, 1949, the Coal Mining (Subsidence) Act, 1950, the Iron and Steel Act, 1952, the Transport Act, 1953, the Cotton Act, 1953, the Overseas Resources Development Act, 1954, the Atomic Energy Authority Act,

1954, the Electricity Reorganization (Scotland) Act, 1944, the Transport (Disposal of Road Haulage Property) Act, 1955, and the Electricity Act, 1956. In addition there have been several Acts concerning the borrowing powers of the public corporations.[1]

The British Transport Commission has promoted a private Bill in each of the years 1949, 1950, 1952, 1953, 1954 and 1955; and we may assume that this is likely to be a fairly frequent occurrence. These private Bills are normally debated on second reading. The wide range of debate which is permitted on these Bills was indicated by the Speaker, who ruled in 1951 that according to the previous practice if the Bill is of wide content, the whole administration of the service with which it deals may be debated.[2] Despite this lattitude, members devote much time to discussing the specific powers sought in the Bill under consideration. Nevertheless, members of Parliament have taken the opportunity to raise large questions of policy, such as railway development plans and modernization schemes, branch lines and services run at a loss, the future use and organization of the inland waterways, and the powers of railway police. Some members have also used these opportunities to ventilate matters of interest to their constituencies, such as the elimination of a level crossing, or objections to closure of a canal or a railway branch line. Others have made complaints about dirty rolling stock, inadequate maintenance, or unpunctual trains.

In connection with the legislative functions of Parliament one must include statutory instruments relating to nationalized industries. These are regulations usually made by the relevant Minister under powers delegated by statute. The more important ones require an affirmative resolution by both Houses of Parliament in order to bring them into force; while others come into force automatically after being laid before Parliament unless a negative resolution is prayed against them. Here the debate must be confined closely to the clauses of the statutory instrument.[3] Nonetheless, if the regulation deals with a large subject, such as the transfer of ministerial responsibilities in regard to atomic energy, the debate can cover questions of major policy, including the government's general policy on the organization of atomic energy functions and the proposed establishment of a public corporation.[4]

[1] E.g. Air Corporations Act, 1953, Coal Industry Act, 1956, Finance Act, 1956, s. 42.

[2] 487 HC Deb. 5s., cols. 1760-1 (May 8, 1951). See, however, the limitations mentioned in 497 HC Deb. 5s., col. 106 (March 3, 1952).

[3] For examples of debates on statutory instruments relating to nationalized industries see 515 HC Deb. 5s., cols. 1541-7 (May 14, 1953): Road Haulage Employees (Compensation); 532 HC Deb. 5s., cols. 336-9 (November 2, 1954): National Coal Board (Borrowing Powers); 552 HC Deb. 5s., cols. 2337-68 (May 17, 1956): Transport Charges.

[4] 521 H.C. Deb. 5s., cols. 2284-324 (December 10, 1953): Atomic Energy (Ministerial Responsibility).

THE LIMITS OF PARLIAMENTARY INQUISITION

It has long been recognized that while Parliament has a right to discuss and determine matters of major policy concerning the nationalized industries, the day-to-day conduct of their business by the public corporations should be immune from parliamentary inquisition. The position was first adumbrated in the report of the Broadcasting Committee set up in 1925. 'We assume', said the report, 'that the Postmaster-General would be the parliamentary spokesman on broad questions of policy, though we think it essential that the commission should not be subject to the continuing ministerial guidance and direction which apply to government offices. The progress of science and the harmonies of art will be hampered by too rigid rules and too constant a supervision by the State.'[1] Shortly after the BBC was established in 1927 the Postmaster-General stated in Parliament that he was responsible for questions of general policy, but not for questions of detail and particular points of the service.

The extent to which Ministers should be liable to answer parliamentary questions about the public corporations has been raised again and again in the House of Commons in recent years.

On December 4, 1947, Mr Herbert Morrison, then Lord President of the Council and Leader of the House, stated the principles which would determine the attitude of Ministers to questions about the work of the socialized industries. Under recent legislation, he said, boards have been set up to run socialized industries on business lines on behalf of the community; and Ministers are not responsible for their day-to-day administration.

> 'A large degree of independence for the boards in matters of current administration is vital to their efficiency as commercial undertakings. A Minister is responsible to Parliament for action which he may take in relation to a board, or action coming within his statutory powers which he has not taken. This is the principle that determines generally the matters on which a question may be put down for answer by a Minister in the House of Commons. Thus the Minister would be answerable for any directions he gave in the national interest, and for the action which he took on proposals which a board was required by statute to lay before him.
>
> 'It would be contrary to this principle, and to the clearly expressed intention of Parliament in the governing legislation, if Ministers were to give, in replies in Parliament or in letters, information about day-

[1] *Report of the Broadcasting Committee 1925*, HMSO, Cmd. 2599/1926, p. 13.

to-day matters. Undue intervention by the Minister would tend to impair the board's commercial freedom of action.'[1]

This reply evoked great interest among all parties and an important debate on the statement took place in the House of Commons on March 3, 1948. In this debate, a considerable measure of agreement was shown by private members on both sides of the House that Ministers should be prepared to extend the scope of the matters about which they were willing to answer questions. The discussion showed a substantial difference of opinion between the government and private members, rather than a division on orthodox party lines between Labour and Conservatives.

Captain Crookshank, who opened the debate for the Opposition, remarked that this was not a party question at all. He argued that whatever the exact wording of a statute may be, there is an ultimate responsibility on Ministers for the proper conduct of nationalized industries. There must be a general responsibility, he said, because the reports and accounts come before Parliament through the Ministers, and that indicates general ministerial responsibility. Where a statutory power is given to a Minister he has an obvious duty to answer questions about the way in which he has exercised it or failed to do so. But over and above this, Captain Crookshank urged that a distinction can be drawn between day-to-day management, which should be immune from parliamentary inquisition, and administration, for which Ministers should be prepared to answer in Parliament. He admitted that the difference may be only a matter of degree and gave the example of an unpunctual railway service. If a train were late on one occasion or infrequently, that should be regarded as a matter of management, but if the same train were late every day for a month, that would indicate a defect in the administration of the railway service. He contended that every member should have a right to put down any question about a nationalized industry on the order paper, leaving it to the Minister concerned to use his discretion whether he would answer it.

THE ADMISSIBILITY OF QUESTIONS

The admissibility of questions is a matter for the Speaker, who controls the clerks at the table of the House.[2] On the basis of the rules then prevailing, he disallowed in the ensuing weeks questions about cheap fares on the railways, special trains, directions on notice boards, and the

[1] 445 HC Deb. 5s., col. 566 (December 4, 1947).

[2] The Clerks ask Ministers about their responsibilities in respect of the subject matter of questions but they do not refer to them the actual questions. And, of course, it is for Ministers to decide whether or not they will answer particular questions regardless of their admissibility. Select Committee on Nationalized Industries 1951-2/332 - I, Q. 124.

closing of a railway station. A question was also refused about an electricity breakdown over a wide area because it asked what action the Minister would take to prevent a further recurrence, and under the Electricity Act the matter was not one for the Minister. In the face of steadily increasing pressure from all sides of the House, the Speaker announced on June 3, 1948, that he proposed to extend the area of permissible questioning by modifying the rule which forbade members to repeat questions already answered, or to which an answer had been refused. In future, he would be prepared to allow repetitious questions to be asked if he considered the matters to be of sufficient public importance to justify the concession. Ministers would, of course, retain their right to decide whether or not they would answer such questions. Both the Government and the Opposition readily agreed to this proposal.

One further development related to the responsibility of Ministers in regard to the Overseas Food Corporation[1] and the Colonial Development Corporation. On December 17, 1948, Mr Morrison announced that the appropriate Minister would feel it right to answer questions in connection with these undertakings which fall into one or more of the following categories: (1) question relating to the Minister's specific statutory duties under the Overseas Resources Development Act, 1948; (2) questions arising from the provisions about consulting local interests on safety, health, and welfare of employees; (3) questions relating to the discharge by colonial governments of their general responsibilities which might affect the activities of the corporations; (4) questions asking for statements on matters of public importance allowed by the Speaker under his ruling.

The position described above has been adhered to up to the present time despite the changes of government which have occurred since 1948 and in face of many attempts to extend the possible range of parliamentary questions.

On April 5, 1950 Mr Herbert Morrison, then Lord President, refused to change the policy of not answering questions asking for information on day-to-day administration.[2] On December 7, 1950 he explained that this policy applies regardless of whether the point at issue was mentioned in the corporation's annual report. The Minister's only responsibility concerning the report is to present it to Parliament.[3]

When the Conservative government came into power in October 1951, for the first few days all questions asking for information about the nationalized industries were allowed on the order paper of the

[1] The Overseas Food Corporation no longer exists.
[2] 473 HC Deb. 5s., cols. 1187-90 (April 5, 1950).
[3] 482 HC Deb. 5s., cols. 524-6 (December 7, 1950).

House of Commons, as the Clerks at the Table could not hold the new government to be bound by the statement of their Labour predecessors. But on November 12 Captain Crookshank, who had become Leader of the House, announced that a select committee on nationalized industries would be appointed to report on the position generally, and that meantime the practice of the Labour administration would be continued.[1] This caused the Clerks to revert to the practice of refusing questions on day-to-day management.[2] The temporary change was so brief, and the opportunity it offered so little understood by members of Parliament, that no useful conclusions can be drawn about the results which it might produce. In 1951 Mr W. S. Morrison became Speaker of the House of Commons. On January 27, 1953, he announced that he had accepted the burden of discretion assumed by his predecessor in allowing certain questions on grounds of public importance. He took this to mean that he might allow at his discretion only those questions of administration which are of wide general interest.[3]

At the beginning of June 1954, Sir Winston Churchill, the Prime Minister, said he could see no reason to depart from the prevailing practice whereby Ministers are not expected to concern themselves with the day-to-day administration of the nationalized industries. He was therefore unwilling to alter the policy of not answering questions asking for information on administration.[4] The following session he refused a request for a Minister to answer questions on the finance and administration of the nationalized industries, on the ground that he had no reason to doubt the efficiency of the existing arrangements.[5] In April 1955 his successor, Sir Anthony Eden, refused to consider instructing Ministers to answer questions concerning those nationalized industries which might cause a charge on the taxpayer.[6]

Thus the expanding sphere of ministerial intervention in the work of the nationalized industries was not reflected in a willingness on the part of the Ministers to answer a wider range of questions than hitherto. Nor was Captain Crookshank as Leader of the House of Commons ready to secure a recognition by Conservative Ministers of their general responsibility for the nationalized industries, for which he had pleaded when in opposition.

[1] 493 H.C. Deb. 5s., cols. 648-50 (November 12, 1951).

[2] *Report from the Select Committee on Nationalized Industries*, HMSO, HC 332-I/1951-2, Evidence, Q. 164.

[3] 510 HC Deb. 5s., cols. 843-4 (January 27, 1953).

[4] 528 HC Deb. 5s., col. 1077 (June 1, 1954).

[5] 536 HC Deb. 5s., col. 39 (January 26, 1955).

[6] 540 HC Deb. 5s., col. 65 (April 27, 1955).

HOW THE RULES WORK IN PRACTICE

It may be of interest to look more closely into the manner in which the rules governing parliamentary questions work in practice. Among the matters on which questions were invariably refused by Speaker Clifton-Brown (1943-51) were staff, advertisements, working arrangements, or any question about a single area board.[1] In subsequent sessions some matters on which questions were previously refused have been admitted. Thus in 1954-5 questions were asked and answered about increases in the annual production of the Northern Gas Board since 1948,[2] and about its capital investment programme;[3] about low gas pressure at Gosforth;[4] about the charges of the South Eastern Gas Board;[5] about the retiring age for staff in the nationalized transport industries;[6] and about railway wages and a dispute on the subject.[7] In the same session (1954-5) questions were admitted to the order paper, but Ministers refused to answer them, on such topics as the prices of coal imports and exports,[8] the cost of operating opencast coal sites,[9] and the hold-up of coal shipments because of freezing.[10]

Sometimes Ministers state that a matter on which a question is asked is 'primarily a matter for the board'. An example of this was a question concerning the acquisition of retail coal distribution agencies by the National Coal Board. The Minister of Fuel and Power refused to express an opinion on the desirability of such acquisitions but he did inform the House of the percentage of total retail coal sales being handled by the Board. Another question of this type concerned pension increases for retired railway pensioners. In this instance the Minister stated he had been in communication with the chairman of the British Transport Commission.[11]

Some questions are answered by means of a formula which says that the Minister has information from the board which he makes available to the House. This device has been commonly used to answer questions about particular capital development projects, as Ministers regard them-

[1] *Report from the Select Committee on Nationalized Industries*, HMSO, HC 332-I/1951-2, App. A (IV).
[2] 537 HC Deb. 5s., col. 9 (February 14, 1955).
[3] 536 HC Deb. 5s., col. 694 (January 31, 1955).
[4] 537 HC Deb. 5s., cols. 8-10 (February 14, 1955).
[5] *Ib.*
[6] 536 HC Deb. 5s., col. 1879 (February 9, 1955).
[7] *Ib.*, cols. 4-7 (January 25, 1955) and 154 (January 26, 1955).
[8] 540 HC Deb. 5s., col. 32 (April 25, 1955).
[9] 539 HC Deb. 5s., col. 801 (April 4, 1955).
[10] 536 HC Deb. 5s., col. 225 (February 9, 1955).
[11] 535 HC Deb. 5s., col. 51 (December 8, 1954).

selves as responsible only for approving the general programme, and not for the individual projects of which it is made up.[1]

Ministers use various formulae in order to avoid a direct refusal to answer certain types of questions while at the same time not admitting their responsibility. Among these are 'I am informed by the board . . .', or 'I am satisfied that the board is doing everything in its power . . .' The 'information from the board' formula has been commonly used in answer to questions on particular development projects, such as the progress made in electrifying a railway line, rural electrification projects in South West Scotland, and BTC plans for introducing automatic train control. 'I will make inquiries and write to the Hon. Member' is another formula which is habitually used for answering questions about the adequacy of coal supplies in particular districts. Again, a Minister who is asked a question about something he regards as outside his sphere of responsibility may offer to bring the matter to the attention of the board who will communicate with the Member, or indicate the procedure for obtaining a redress of grievances through another channel.

The form in which a question is asked may determine its admissibility, and the assistance of the clerks and the Speaker is sometimes sought by MPs on how to frame questions in an admissible form. For example, a question referring to the closure of a particular coal mine was changed to a more general question about the closure of pits in Lanarkshire. A request to the Minister asking him to give a general directive on a specified matter in the national interest virtually compels him to answer, and so does any question asking him to take action within his statutory powers.[2]

It is scarcely possible to indicate briefly the subjects on which questions will be answered by Ministers, for the potential scope of the legitimate parliamentary question on nationalized industry is very large. Questions have been answered without demur (in the session 1954–5) on BOAC purchases of Douglas and Britannia aircraft;[3] on the salaries of board members;[4] on the cost of North of Scotland Hydro-Electric Board development schemes;[5] on the possibility of a single meter for gas and electricity;[6] on the lapse of time in making appointments[7] to electricity

[1] 535 HC Deb. 5s., col. 118 (December 14, 1954); 536 HC Deb. 5s., cols. 153 (January 26, 1955), 694 (January 31, 1955), 888 (February 1, 1955), and 1092 (February 2, 1955).

[2] *Report from the Select Committee on Nationalized Industries*, HMSO, HC 332-I/1951-2, para. 4, and Evidence, Q. 141.

[3] 537 HC Deb. 5s., col. 203 (February 25, 1955).

[4] *Ib.*, cols. 1068-9 (February 22, 1955).

[5] *Ib.*, col. 144 (February 22, 1955).

[6] *Ib.*, col. 113 (February 21, 1955).

[7] *Ib.*, col. 8 (February 14, 1955).

boards; on the introduction of diesel trains in Cumberland;[1] on the procedure used by gas and electricity boards at land sales;[2] on the closing of branch railway lines in Wales;[3] on the efforts made by the National Coal Board to improve the quality of domestic coal;[4] and (in session 1955-56) on attempts by the Gas Council to prevent gas poisoning accidents.[5]

There will obviously be general influences at work tending to vary the number of questions asked about the nationalized industries. When an industry or service is giving widespread dissatisfaction or operating at a loss we should expect greater pressure on the Minister from MPs than when it is operating more successfully. When the chairman or members of a board resign or are dismissed, or when differences of opinion are believed to exist between the Minister and the board, parliamentary questioning will be stimulated. A serious accident, a major trade dispute, the dismissal of redundant employees on a large scale, are all likely to increase the number of questions addressed to the relevant Minister. On the other hand, as the principle of excluding matters of day-to-day management from the scope of questions is increasingly understood and accepted by Members of Parliament, this should tend to reduce the number of questions not admitted or not answered; while the increasing acceptance of nationalization as a familiar feature of the national economy is a further factor which should reduce the number of parliamentary questions.

The effect of reorganization and important new legislation in increasing the flow of questions addressed to the relevant Minister is shown by the Table on p. 172. The upward jump in 1953 was due to the passing of the Transport Act, 1953.

Finally we may give some examples of the Speaker's decisions concerning the admission of questions on grounds of their public importance, in accordance with the announcement made on June 3, 1948.

Under this ruling the Speaker admitted a question asking the Minister of Fuel and Power to make a statement concerning the breakdown of electricity services in a large area on a specified date; and a question asking him to state the principles on which the National Coal Board select men for dismissal as redundant, and whether they are protected

[1] 540 HC Deb. 5s., col. 131 (May 4, 1955). (Minister stated progress and referred to BTC forecasts for future plans.)

[2] 535 HC Deb. 5s., col. 99 (December 13, 1954). (Direction refused.)

[3] *Ib.*, col. 152 (December 15, 1954).

[4] 539 HC Deb. 5s., col. 10 (March 28, 1955).

[5] 546 HC Deb. 5s., col. 60 (November 17, 1955); 547 HC Deb. 5s., cols. 4 (December 5, 1955) and 45 (December 6, 1955); 549 HC Deb. 5s., col. 230 (March 9, 1956).

TABLE I

Parliamentary questions asked concerning the British Transport Commission 1950–7[1]

Year	*Total Questions*	*Average questions per week in which Parliament was sitting*	*Cases in which BTC dealt with matters raised by MPs*
1950	77	2·9	not stated
1951	167	5·75	1,743
1952	93	2·9	1,403
1953	200	8·7	1,185
1954	229	6·7	932
1955	258	8·0	1,323
1956	200*	6·9	1,249
1957	235	6·7	1,306

* Report gives figure as 'over 200'.

against discrimination. He allowed a question asking what steps the Minister proposed to take to reduce the price of nutty slack, although previous questions on prices had been refused because prices are not fixed by the Minister. The Speaker justified the admission on the ground that the question referred to the general level of prices over the whole country whereas the previous questions related to particular prices and were therefore matters of day-to-day administration.[2]

The Speaker ruled against questions addressed to the Minister of Transport about the issue of sailing tickets in holiday periods for the short sea routes;[3] about the provision of facilities for mothers and babies travelling long distances;[4] about the sale of an hotel by the Railway Executive and the uncertain position of its staff;[5] about a rule preventing a man dismissed by one branch of the Road Haulage Executive from being employed by another branch?[6] He regarded all these questions as referring to matters of day-to-day management. His decision was sometimes influenced by the degree of generality involved in the question. For example, a question asking if the Minister would instruct an Area Electricity Board not to engage in the retail sale of electrical equipment

[1] Taken from the BTC Annual Reports.

[2] 510 HC Deb. 5s., cols. 1461-2 (January 27, 1953).

[3] *Report from the Select Committee on Nationalized Industries*, HMSO, HC 332-I/1951-2, Evidence, Q. 145.

[4] *Ib.*

[5] 510 HC Deb. 5s., cols. 843-4 (January 27, 1953).

[6] *Report from the Select Committee on Nationalized Industries*, HMSO, HC 332-I/1951-2, Evidence, Qs. 148 and 158.

was admitted after the member had altered it so as to apply to the British Electricity Authority instead of the Area Board.[1]

OBJECTIONS TO UNRESTRICTED QUESTIONING OF MINISTERS

A Select Committee of the House of Commons was appointed by the Conservative government shortly after they came into power towards the end of 1951 to consider 'the present methods by which the House of Commons is informed of the affairs of the nationalized industries' and to report what changes might be desirable within the framework of the existing legislation.[2] The committee received a great deal of evidence from persons who were or had been prominently concerned with the nationalized industries, including former Ministers, the chairmen of public corporations, the Permanent Secretary of the Treasury, and the Leader of the House of Commons.

Very strong objections to parliamentary questions being permitted on matters of administrative detail were put forward by Lord Hurcomb (chairman of the British Transport Commission), Lord Citrine (chairman of the British Electricity Authority), and Sir Hubert Houldsworth (chairman of the National Coal Board). The chairmen of the three giant corporations stated forcibly that unrestricted parliamentary questioning would cause a loss of managerial efficiency and have a bad effect on the initiative of the staffs, who had been trained in industry and were not accustomed to civil service methods.[3] It would involve extra work for which additional staff would be needed. It would encourage caution and centralization. Above all it would make the executive positions in the nationalized industries less attractive to men of outstanding ability with first class business minds. If questions of pay, conditions of service and so forth were liable to be brought into the parliamentary arena, industrial relations might be adversely affected.[4]

Mr Herbert Morrison told the committee bluntly that Parliament cannot have it both ways. If it wants complete freedom in putting questions and in every other respect, then it had better entrust the nationalized industries to a government department. But if it chooses a public corporation 'in which the principle of public ownership is embodied but in which there is business management of a largely independent character, at any rate as regards day-to-day matters', then Parliament must be willing to accept the consequences.[5]

[1] Report, HMSO, HC 332-I/1951-2, Evidence, Q. 141.
[2] *Ib.*, p. iii. [3] *Ib.*, para. 12.
[4] *Ib.*, Evidence, Qs. 922, 926, 998, 1021, 1042, 1045, and 1047.
[5] *Ib.*, Qs. 778 and 792. See also Qs. 780, 786, 794-5, and 809.

Captain Crookshank, now finding himself in a responsible position as Leader of the House, recanted from the view he had advanced four years earlier from the Opposition benches. He explicitly withdrew the proposition that MPs should have the right to put questions of any kind, regardless of whether the Minister would answer them or not. He now argued if Ministers were liable to unlimited questions this would force the boards towards centralization and bureaucracy, and create disincentives to efficient management. He went so far as to say that he thought the present situation to be reasonably satisfactory, though he would have liked the Speaker to adopt a somewhat less rigorous test of urgent public importance and a less strict application of the rule against repetition.[1]

Mr Philip Noel-Baker, a member of the Select Committee and a former Minister of Fuel and Power, testified to the great value of parliamentary questions, even within their existing scope, in promoting the efficiency of the nationalized industries and in getting rid of troubles which had arisen. Mr Morrison strongly endorsed this view.[2] He thought that MPs had not taken full advantage of the possibilities afforded to them by the present rules of procedure: they had not yet shown their customary ingenuity in framing questions that would be in order, but he hoped this would be remedied in due course.[3]

Mr Noel-Baker has emphasized that the parliamentary question is a very powerful instrument of public control which is not only a democratic safeguard but also a factor in the success of the nationalized industries. The questions which he had answered as a responsible Minister did not have the effect of hampering the administration or discouraging initiative on the part of the management of the industry concerned. During his first six months as Minister of Fuel and Power, 250 questions addressed to him out of a total of 343 were on nationalized industries and cognate matters. These questions led to more speedy action being taken about such matters as manpower in the mines, dirty coal, the elimination of competitive advertising between gas and electricity, and power cuts.[4]

Mr A. H. Hanson considers that it has not been proved that the removal of the present restrictions on the scope of parliamentary questions would lead to a loss of efficiency in the nationalized industries, and he considers that the evidence given to the Select Committee of the

[1] Report, HMSO, HC 332-I/1951-2, Evidence, Qs. 715-6, 754, 758-9, 760, 765, and 768.

[2] *Ib.*, Qs. 873-4.

[3] *Ib.*, Qs. 778, 825, and 875. See also Herbert Morrison: *Government and Parliament* (1954), p. 261.

[4] 508 HC Deb. 5s., cols. 2004-6 (December 5, 1952).

House of Commons in 1951-2 supports this belief.[1] It would be not only difficult, but virtually impossible, to 'prove' this contention. How could one trace cause and effect in such a vast and nebulous sphere of activity? How could one 'prove' that a decline in the efficiency of, for example, the station-masters of seaside holiday towns was due to the Minister of Transport being liable to answer questions of any kind about the railways? Moreover, since all the other factors are also continually changing, it would be impossible to conduct a scientifically controlled experiment during a specified period.

The Select Committee of the House of Commons reported broadly in favour of continuing the limitations previously established in regard to parliamentary questions. 'Under their existing constitution', they said, 'the nationalized industries are not subject to any direct control by Ministers in individual matters of detail. Your committee therefore feel that without altering the terms of the statutes under which the public corporations are constituted, which they are not empowered to recommend, questions on matters of detail in the nationalized industries are inappropriate.'[2] The responsibility of the clerks for deciding whether a question be admitted should be confined to the refusal of questions which are obviously matters of detailed administration or repetition. In all other cases the question should be allowed to appear on the order paper and the Minister have to answer or refuse to answer on the floor of the House.[3]

There the matter rests and is likely to remain more or less indefinitely. The range of subjects within which parliamentary questioning is already permitted is surprisingly large when one looks into the matter in some detail, and it is likely to increase as new ways of avoiding the restrictions are discovered. To concede much more would virtually destroy the existing conception of the public corporation and its attribute of managerial freedom, which is already in danger of being undermined by ministerial intervention and backstairs influence. To desire more one must be a whole-hearted believer in full ministerial responsibility of the kind found in government departments. A certain amount of adjustment is still possible and may take place about the interpretation and application of the rules excluding matters of day-to-day management from the Order Paper, in deciding whether and when a matter is of sufficient public importance to admit of a question on a subject on which information has been previously refused, and similar procedural niceties. But the funda-

[1] A. H. Hanson: 'Select Committee on Nationalized Industries: a comment', XXXI *Public Administration* (1953), p. 59.

[2] Report, HMSO, HC 332-I/1951-2, para. 17.

[3] *Ib.*, para. 18.

mental principles may now be regarded as settled on lines which are fundamentally right and sensible.

Although the position is supposed to be settled for the time being, members of Parliament spend a great deal of time and display much ingenuity in seeking ways to avoid the formal rules, trying to cajole unwary Ministers to assume greater responsibilities than they have so far acknowledged, endeavouring to evoke or to reveal inconsistencies of practice between one Minister and another, and attempting to obtain an ever-widening interpretation of the principles which govern the admissibility and answering of questions.

If once the parliamentary question were given free play over the whole field of activity of a nationalized industry, half the advantages of having a public corporation rather than a government department would be lost. Moreover, as Mr Morrison has pointed out in the House of Commons, it is important that we should get the best men in the service of these boards. 'If these men are to live a life which is really a Civil Service life, and are liable to be abused across the floor of the House and subjected to questions attacking them and their commercial ability we shall not get the men to serve on these commercial undertakings, and we shall not get the best out of those who are there.'[1] The importance of this consideration can scarcely be exaggerated.

The demand for subjecting the nationalized industries to almost as much liability to parliamentary questioning as if they were run by government departments rather than by public corporations comes partly from keen Labour back-benchers who equate socialism with the grilling of Ministers over meticulous details every afternoon in the House of Commons. It comes partly from the Conservative opponents of nationalization who seek an opportunity to harrass Ministers with a constant barrage of insinuating questions or to discredit the public corporations no matter what government is in power; although when the nationalizing Bills were before Parliament, some of these members urged the desirability of reducing or eliminating many of the powers of control conferred on Ministers.

So far as questions are concerned, many Members of Parliament on both sides of the House do not appear to have accepted, or have failed to understand, the implications of their own handiwork in creating the public corporations. The institution is a device for running nationalized industries in a way which is divorced from ministerial responsibility to Parliament in the traditional sense. This was one of the two principal reasons which led to the growth of this new form of organization. Yet some MPs seem to want the best of both worlds: to have the freedom,

[1] 448 HC Deb. 5s., col. 456 (March 3, 1948).

independence, and flexibility of the public corporation and yet also to have almost complete answerability to Parliament.

ALTERNATIVE METHODS OF INQUIRY

A further factor is the unfamiliarity of the public with the machinery which has been established to inquire into and consider consumers' grievances. So far very little use has been made of the consumer councils and committees created expressly for this purpose, and in consequence many people are seeking redress through their MPs for complaints which should either be made direct to the public corporation, or, if that fails to produce satisfaction, to the consumers committee or similar organ. Many of the questions which Members of Parliament ask—or try to ask—in Parliament, refer to grievances which have been brought to their notice by individual constituents. We may hope that as the special machinery for voicing consumers' demands becomes better known, most citizens will realize that this is the proper channel for complaints, and will cease to trouble their Member of Parliament save when other methods prove fruitless.

We may hope, too, that Members of Parliament will come to see the wisdom of advising their constituents to take their complaints to the consumer councils unless a question of principle is involved—in which case the floor of the House of Commons is undoubtedly the right place to ventilate the matter.

Another useful channel of complaint for Members of Parliament is by direct communication with the public corporations, whose chairmen normally deal with such correspondence. The British Transport Commission have so far received the largest number of letters from MPs: in 1951-2 they were running at the rate of about 1,700 a year.[1] The former chairman of the National Coal Board (Sir Hubert Houldsworth) told the Select Committee of the House of Commons that he received about 300 letters a year from MPs, all of which he answered himself unless he was away and the matter appeared to be urgent. He added that in his experience Members of Parliament nearly always accepted his replies, and that only two of them had expressed dissatisfaction. The great majority of letters from MPs were on matters of day-to-day management. Sir Hubert considered this method of enabling parliamentarians to obtain information and explanations, and possibly assistance, to be highly satisfactory.[2] The chairman of the British Electricity Authority received only about one hundred letters a year, mostly on minor matters

[1] Report, HMSO, HC 332-I/1951-2, Evidence, Q. 458.
[2] *Ib.*, Qs. 1029-31 and 1069.

urging the authority to use their powers to get an Area Electricity Board to do something. The letters from MPs were 'on the whole helpful and understanding',[1] and enabled the corporation to show their own desire to be helpful to a greater extent than is possible in a parliamentary question.

Sir Thomas Gardiner, a former Director-General of the Post Office, made the interesting disclosure that in that department letters were regarded as efforts to bring about improvements in the service, whereas parliamentary questions were regarded as attempts to embarrass the Mnister. He would like Members to write to the Post Office on matters concerning the day-to-day working, while confining questions to major matters or those of true public interest.[2]

There can be little doubt that Members of Parliament have hitherto spent far too much time and effort in plying Ministers with questions, mainly on matters of detail, to the relative neglect of their other opportunities for discussing nationalized industries. There are several other occasions on which Parliament can review various aspects of the nationalized industries.

OPPORTUNITIES TO DISCUSS NATIONALIZED INDUSTRIES

We may begin with the Queen's Speech on the opening of Parliament. This may include an item announcing the government's policy, such as the development of nuclear power stations, which can be debated; or the Opposition can criticize the omission of a particular aspect of nationalization from the government's programme.

The motion for the adjournment provides another occasion for parliamentary criticism. This offers a frequent opportunity for a somewhat brief debate. Adjournment debates are sometimes quite short. They seldom last more than three hours. The admissibility of the subject is in the hands of the Speaker, and it is usually specific rather than general. There have been adjournment debates on the closure of railway branch lines; on the position of railway pensioners; on the composition of the Road Haulage Disposal Board; on the use of flying boats; on rural electrification; on domestic coal prices; on the service conditions of airline pilots; on the design of buffet cars; on railway passenger fares; on Luga airport, Malta; on charges for electricity, and on many other topics. Some adjournment debates are exceedingly effective. The occasion calls for concise argument, relevant information, and well-considered criticism about a particular aspect, which ought not to be too narrow in its interest.

[1] Report, HMSO, HC 332-I/1951–2 Evidence, Q. 888.

[2] *Ib.*, Qs. 705, 709, and 714.

Many concessions have been wrung from Ministers by the skilful use of this method.

Sometimes the government will put down a motion for the adjournment in order to debate a particular matter; this was the case when a motion was put down to discuss the report of the Select Committee on Nationalized Industries.[1] Another type of debate is where the adjournment of the House of Commons is moved (under Standing Order 9) on a definite matter of urgent public importance. This occurred when the Opposition alleged that the Minister of Supply had forced the chairman of the Iron and Steel Corporation to resign;[2] but the Speaker interprets the Standing Order strictly.

Motions of a more general kind can be debated in the government's time or during the time set aside for private members' business.[3] Debates on motions in government time took place on transport fare increases;[4] on transport policy;[5] on the British Railways wage settlement;[6] and on the railways reorganization scheme.[7]

Supply days can be used to discuss nationalized industry. There are twenty of these each year and the Opposition has the right to choose the subjects for discussion. Supply days have been used to discuss civil aviation, with special attention to the government's new policy favouring commercial operators;[8] to debate the annual reports and accounts of the airways corporations;[9] and to debate an Opposition motion calling on the government to abandon the attempt to dispose of the road haulage assets in order to denationalize the industry.[10] On some occasions the policy and conduct of the nationalized industries have been discussed *inter alia* in the course of Supply Day debates on more general topics.

[1] 523 HC Deb. 5s., cols. 833-962 (February 8, 1954).

[2] 496 HC Deb. 5s., cols. 774-838 (February 25, 1952).

[3] Debates on private members' motions took place on electricity supplies in rural areas: 516 HC Deb. 5s., cols. 1351-442 (June 19, 1953); on trade unions and the airways corporations: 535 HC Deb. 5s., cols. 2809-19 (December 22, 1954); and on parliamentary questions concerning the nationalized industries: 508 HC Deb. 5s., cols. 1989-2009 (December 5, 1952).

[4] 499 HC Deb. 5s., cols. 1022-166 (April 28, 1952). (Government motion approving ministerial direction to suspend increases approved by Transport Tribunal.)

[5] 501 HC Deb. 5s., cols. 475-614 (May 21, 1952). (Government motion approving White Paper on proposed reorganization of BTC and denationalization of road haulage industry.)

[6] 536 HC Deb. 5s., cols. 1280-480 (February 3, 1955). (Government motion approving settlement.)

[7] 532 HC Deb. 5s., cols. 35-153 (November 1, 1954). (Government motion taking note of White Paper.)

[8] 503 HC Deb. 5s., cols. 2155-292 (July 16, 1952); 524 HC Deb. 5s., cols. 1741-870 (March 8, 1954).

[9] 505 HC Deb. 5s., cols. 1935-2060 (October 29, 1952).

[10] 529 HC Deb. 5s., col. 1973-2048 (July 6, 1954).

Thus, a debate on Scottish industry and development included much discussion on transport, the fuel and power industries, and atomic energy in Scotland.[1]

DEBATES ON THE ANNUAL REPORTS

Of greater potential importance than any of these procedures are the debates based on the annual reports of the public corporations. These take place in Government time—an important point—although there have been occasions when a Supply Day was used by the Opposition for this purpose. The current practice is for the Government to allocate three days each year to such debates, which are intended to be general debates on the state of the industry under review. The Opposition are allowed to choose which industries shall be considered. In order to enable as much ground as possible to be covered, the reports of the fuel and power industries, or of gas and electricity, have sometimes formed the subject of a single debate; while the affairs of the two nationalized airways corporations are usually discussed at the same time.[2] A division may take place at the end of the debate, although this is infrequent.

These general debates have on the whole been disappointing. They could and should provide an unrivalled opportunity for searching analy-

[1] 530 HC Deb. 5s., cols. 702-814 (July 15, 1954).

[2] *House of Commons Debates on Annual Reports* 1952-7.

Industry	*Date*	*Volume*	*Columns*
Transport	July 22, 1952	504	285- 413
Fuel and Power Industries	October 28, 1952	505	1749- 864
Air Corporations	October 29, 1952	505	1935-2066
Transport	October 21, 1953	518	1980-2108
Fuel and Power Industries	October 26, 1953	518	2440- 558
Air Corporations	October 27, 1953	518	2623- 748
Coal	October 25, 1954	531	1614- 719
Gas & Electricity	November 9, 1954	532	1044- 155
Air Corporations	November 15, 1954	533	38- 128
Transport	July 11, 1955	543	1579- 706
Coal	July 20, 1955	544	383- 506
Air Corporations	December 20, 1955	547	1876- 981
Air Corporations	November 2, 1956	558	1772- 847
Coal	February 28, 1957	565	1407- 523
Transport	July 10, 1957	573	382- 505
Gas & Electricity	November 26, 1957	578	996-1114
Air Corporations	January 27, 1958	581	35- 103
North Scotland Electricity	January 27, 1958	581	103- 166
Transport	July 17, 1958	591	1447- 505

sis, comparison, contrast, criticism, and constructive proposals. Unfortunately, too many Members have tended to use them as occasions for bringing forward stale arguments in favour of, or against, nationalization; and some of the speeches would have been more appropriate on the second reading debate of a nationalization Bill. Conservatives when in Opposition have usually criticized the public corporations, while Labour Ministers usually defended them, acting, as Mr Ernest Davies, MP, expressed it, 'as counsel for the board'. In the years since 1951, during which Conservative Governments have held office, the responsible Ministers have continued to defend the boards of the nationalized industries. The Labour Opposition, on the other hand, have tended to focus more on government policies regarding the industries rather than on the work of the corporations.

The average level of these general debates has so far not been high. The House of Commons has seldom shown itself at its best in discussing nationalized industries. Nevertheless, there are exceptions to this statement, and the debate on the responsibility to the public of the socialized industries in the House of Commons on October 25, 1950, achieved a notably high level.[1] The House of Lords has also on occasion distinguished itself.[2]

THE ROLE OF PARLIAMENT

Politicians have criticized Ministers for failing to understand the proper relationship which should exist between the government and public corporations. The citizen, and still more the political scientist, may feel disposed to criticize parliamentarians for not comprehending with sufficient insight the proper role which Parliament should fill in this new sphere of activity.

The appointing Minister, observed *The Times* in a pertinent leading article, stands in the position of the shareholders' trustees, with certain defined powers over general policy and the power to dismiss directors

[1] 478 HC Deb. 5s., cols. 2795 ff. (October 25, 1950).

[2] In this review of the opportunities available for parliamentary debate and supervision of the nationalized industries, I have concentrated entirely on the House of Commons. This is due mainly to the overwhelming political importance of the representative assembly but also partly to the fact that the procedure of the Commons is different from that of the Lords. So far as the second chamber is concerned, I will content myself with saying that there are ample opportunities in the House of Lords for debates on Bills concerning nationalized industries (including Bills to abolish public corporations); on government motions to approve draft statutory instruments or on other matters; questions can be addressed to ministers; and there is the so-called motion for papers which provides an opportunity for general debate on the initiative of any peer. All these procedures can be and are used to obtain information and to facilitate debate on the nationalized industries in the House of Lords.

who fail to make their industries pay their way in the long run. Parliament, according to this conception, would be the shareholders' meeting, receiving annual accounts and reports, and holding special general meetings when necessary. Unfortunately, continued *The Times*, 'too many Members of Parliament in all parties seem to believe that a shareholders' meeting should be in permanent session, that extraordinary meetings should be held frequently throughout the year, and that individual members of public boards should be open to personal attack under parliamentary privilege. The tendency has been to expect Ministers to answer a thousand and one questions about the daily doings of the various boards —questions such as would never be asked about comparable private companies.'[1]

The man in the street, whatever his political opinions may be, does not want to hear Conservative Members of Parliament extol the wonderful efficiency of the British coal industry in the good old days before nationalization, or wax sentimental over the cordial relations which existed between management and labour when the collieries were under private enterprise, or the superb, unquestioning discipline attained under capitalism. Nor, on the other hand, does he want to read speeches by Labour members rejoicing in the transformation of our railway system brought about overnight by nationalization, or the inestimable improvement in electricity supply since it was transferred from (largely) municipal ownership to public corporations. Not only is the ordinary citizen too politically mature to be taken in by nonsense of this kind, but the manifest absurdity of such statements can be tested by the experience of his daily life. He remembers the bitter conflicts and prolonged disputes in the coal industry during the inter-war period. He also knows that coal was until recently in such short supply after several years of peace that large amounts had to be imported from America; that it is exceedingly dear; and often extremely dirty. He knows that rail transport is just about what it was before the war, neither better nor worse, but much more expensive. Things could hardly be otherwise, for the results of nationalization will take many years to show themselves; and meantime most of the good and the bad is due to causes which existed prior to 1945, and usually prior to 1939.

The common man, therefore, wants Members of Parliament to stop talking to a non-existent gallery of fanatical pro- or anti-nationalizers and to get down to brass tacks. He wants to hear serious and sober criticism, accompanied by helpful and constructive proposals. He wants both Government and Opposition speakers to be frank and realistic. He wants to know what is being done for him, the consumer, and when he

[1] 'Parliament and Corporations', *The Times*, March 3, 1948.

may expect to receive some of the promised benefits. He wants to know whether the miners or the railwaymen are thinking mainly of feathering their own nests or whether any more socially useful motives are at work.

Whatever other conclusions can be drawn from this examination of the relations between Parliament and the nationalized industries, it is in my opinion quite impossible to contend that adequate opportunities do not exist for enabling MPs to obtain all or nearly all the information they reasonably need, except as to the extent of ministerial influence or intervention on the boards. There is no serious reason to complain of lack of opportunity in Parliament to discuss, commend, or criticize the activities of the public corporations. On the other hand there is some ground for believing that the best use has not been made of these opportunities.[1]

Nevertheless, there has been continuous pressure in recent years from back-bench members of Parliament for a more specialized device for enabling the House of Commons to achieve a closer and more continuous contact with the nationalized industries. This has mainly focused on the proposal for a Standing Committee to be set up with the express purpose of guiding and informing Parliament about the activities of these great undertakings.

[1] This view was shared by Sir Frederic Metcalfe, formerly Clerk of the House of Commons. See his evidence to the Select Committee on Nationalized Industries, HC 332-I/1951-2, Qs. 40-1.

CHAPTER VIII

Public Accountability

THE PROPOSAL FOR A SELECT COMMITTEE

THE idea that the House of Commons should appoint a Select Committee on public corporations originated with Mr Hugh Molson, MP, in 1949 when he was a Conservative back-bencher. He pointed out that a familiar defect of parliamentary debates on large subjects is that the speeches roam over the whole field and there is often no thread of continuity nor even a meeting of minds. A general discussion on a nationalized industry can easily degenerate into 'one of these rambling and discursive debates, with many speeches delivered primarily for constituency consumption'.[1] The House of Commons, he contended, is at its best when it is debating issues which have been sifted and elucidated in a document setting out a limited number of matters for consideration. The Select Committees on Estimates and Public Accounts have proved of great value as devices for enabling the House of Commons to scrutinize expenditure far more effectively than it could otherwise do; and Mr Molson urged that the salient issues relating to each nationalized industry should be elucidated by a Select Committee appointed for the purpose, so that every two or three years an informed and discriminating debate could take place in the House of Commons on the basis of this investigation.[2]

The Labour Government of 1945-51 did not accept the idea of a Select Committee; but shortly after the return to power of the Conservatives under Sir Winston Churchill in October 1951 a Select Committee were appointed 'to consider the present methods by which the House of Commons is informed of the affairs of the nationalized industries and to report what changes, having regard to the provisions laid down by Parliament in the relevant statutes, may be desirable in these methods'.[3]

The evidence given to the Select Committee was both weighty and interesting. The witnesses who testified in favour of a Select Committee included Mr Hugh Molson, MP (then a junior Minister), Lord Hurcomb, Sir Edward Bridges, then Permanent Secretary of the Treasury

[1] Hugh Molson: 'Nationalized Industries', *The Times*, September 8, 1949.
[2] *Ib.*
[3] 494 HC Deb. 5s., cols. 2355-6 (December 4, 1951).

and head of the Civil Service, Captain Crookshank, and Mr Ernest Davies, MP. The Co-operative Party had proposed a series of standing parliamentary committees to scrutinize the nationalized industries in one of its recent publications.[1]

Lord Hurcomb's views must have carried great weight, for he was then chairman of the British Transport Commission. The fact that he has spent most of his career in the civil service may have led him to regard parliamentary committees with less apprehension than the chairmen of other public corporations or the average businessman. But Lord Hurcomb not merely accepted the idea: he actively welcomed it as a means of enabling the board of a nationalized industry to keep more closely in touch with public and parliamentary opinion, and as an opportunity to explain the policies they were following and the aims they were trying to achieve. 'One of the very greatest handicaps under which anyone in my position suffers', he said, 'is that he gets no opportunity of stating his own case or of explaining what are his difficulties direct to Members of Parliament.'[2] MPs on their side would have the opportunity of conveying, not by an attack in the House or on the platform, the points which they thought needed attention. The conception he entertained of a Standing Committee was that of an instrument for achieving better understanding and co-operation. He thought that separate Standing Committees would be needed for different groups of industries.[3] Both he and Captain Crookshank favoured a joint Standing Committee of both Houses of Parliament.[4]

The witnesses who opposed the proposal included Lord Reith, Mr Herbert Morrison, and Sir Geoffrey (now Lord) Heyworth. They argued that the proposal to set up a permanent committee to inquire into nationalized industries was not only contrary to the spirit and intention of the legislation, but contrary to the British constitutional tradition. The nationalization statutes clearly intended Parliament to abstain from interfering in the details of management. If a Select Committee were appointed the lines of responsibility would tend to become blurred; and in any case they thought Parliament is not a suitable body to investigate the managerial efficiency of a complex industrial undertaking. The working of these vast corporations would be impeded and their initiative diminished if a Select Committee were empowered to examine their policies over a wide front; and the consequences would be more serious still if the day-to-day management were liable to investiga-

[1] *The People's Industry* (1951). (Statement on Social Ownership by the National Committee of the Co-operative Party), paras. 48-52.

[2] *Report from the Select Committee on Nationalized Industries*, HMSO, HC 235/1952-3, Evidence, Q. 510.

[3] *Ib.*, Qs. 509 and 532. [4] *Ib.*, Qs. 517 and 939.

tion.[1] Both Mr Morrison and Lord Reith considered that all the arguments against unlimited parliamentary questions on nationalized industries applied with even greater force to the setting up of Select Committees; both of them regarded the prospect as 'terrifying'.[2] All these witnesses emphasized the danger of stifling the spirit of adventurousness and boldness in making decisions.

The Select Committee reported in favour of the proposal for a Standing Committee to serve as a liaison between the nationalized industries and Parliament. They warned, however, that it was essential for the committee to establish a tradition of conduct which will result in its being regarded by the public corporations 'not as an enemy, or a critic, but as a confidant, and a protection against irresponsible pressure, as well as a guardian of the public interest'.[3]

The recommendations of the Select Committee were that a Standing Committee of the House of Commons should be appointed 'to examine the nationalized industries, with power to send for persons, papers and records, power to set up sub-committees, and to report from time to time'. The Committee should direct their attention to the published reports and accounts, and to obtaining further information about the general policy and practice of the undertakings whose boards are wholly nominated by Ministers and whose revenue is not wholly derived from parliamentary money or Exchequer advances. The object of the Committee would be to inform Parliament about the aims, activities and problems of the corporations and not of controlling their work. They should be given as staff an officer of equal status to that of the Comptroller and Auditor-General, who would be an officer of the House of Commons. He would be assisted by one or more professional accountants and whatever subordinate staff was required.

A QUALIFIED ACCEPTANCE

The Government accepted the recommendation to set up a committee on nationalized industries, but proposed substantial modifications in the terms of reference, composition, and other aspects. The committee were to concern themselves with 'current policy' instead of 'general policy'; and in order to preclude them from infringing the position, duties and responsibilities of Ministers, they would be barred from inquiring into matters which have been decided by the relevant Minister

[1] *Report from the Select Committee on Nationalized Industries*, HMSO, HC 235/1952-3, paras. 9-13.

[2] *Ib.*, Evidence, Qs. 593-4, 847, and 850.

[3] Report, para. 15.

or which clearly engage his responsibility and for which he should, therefore, answer on the floor of the House. The terms of reference were also to exclude all matters normally decided by collective bargaining, such as wages and conditions of employment; matters falling to be considered through formal machinery provided by the relevant legislation, such as compensation, consumers' complaints, charges schemes to be submitted to the Transport Tribunal, and many other questions; and finally, matters of day-to-day administration.[1]

The Government also curtailed the recommended size of the committee from twenty-one to fourteen members. They were to have no power to appoint sub-committees in order to remove the temptation to go into excessive detail. Restrictions were introduced on the committee's powers to send for persons, papers, and records, the Government's view being that the normal procedure would be for the chairman of a public corporation to give evidence about its affairs, or a representative nominated by him, accompanied by members of the staff when necessary. The committee should not publish all the evidence they received, but merely report to the House from time to time. 'I am quite sure', declared Captain Crookshank, 'that we must be very careful, as a House, that we do not frighten off the boards, and the people who work under boards. The more chance there is of every detail being published, the more is the risk of their becoming red-tapish, which is one of the things we want to avoid.'[2] The nationalized undertakings within the ambit of the committee would be limited to the corporations in charge of the airlines, coal, transport, gas and electricity.[3] Most important of all, the committee would not have the services of an officer comparable to the Comptroller and Auditor-General. Instead, they would have only the assistance of liaison officers from the Treasury and the departments responsible for the affairs of the nationalized industries.

A debate took place on February 8, 1954, on the report of the Select Committee recommending a Standing Committee of the House of Commons on Nationalized Industries. This opened with an announcement that the Government were considering the appointment of such a body with smaller scope and fewer members than the report recommended.

The discussion showed that opinion in the House was not divided on clear party lines. Seven Labour Members opposed the committee, chiefly because they feared that excessive parliamentary interference would be detrimental to efficient management, especially as the committee would probably be influenced in their judgments to some extent

[1] 530 HC Deb. 5s., cols. 279-81, Captain Crookshank (July 13, 1954). See also 523 HC Deb. 5s., cols. 840-3, Captain Crookshank (February 8, 1954).

[2] *Ib.* [3] 531 HC Deb. 5s., col. 42 (July 27, 1954).

by political considerations rather than by the interests of the nationalized undertakings. Some doubt was expressed as to what, if anything, the committee would be able to do within its narrowly confined terms of reference. The proposal was supported by six Conservative, one Liberal-National, and two Labour Members, in addition to government spokesmen. Five members of the Select Committee (two Conservative and three Labour) also spoke in favour.[1] The supporters varied from staunch advocates to those who were very much aware of the dangers but thought on balance the committee should be tried out as an experiment in making public control more effective. There was great diversity of opinion among the supporters about the functions, composition, procedure and powers of the proposed body. Virtually all the speakers, whether they favoured or opposed the proposal, agreed that public accountability was not wholly adequate or effective in the nationalized industries and that some improvement in methods or machinery was desirable. Various alternative suggestions were made.[2]

Members who had sat on the Select Committee were specially critical of the Government's rejection of an independent officer of high status to give the Standing Committee on nationalized industries the kind of help which the Comptroller and Auditor-General gives the Public Accounts Committee. Mr Ralph Assheton, MP, said he regarded this as the key point in the whole proposal, and that the committee would not be worth much without such an officer. Sir Patrick Spens explained that without a permanent staff, members of the committee would have to set about establishing and maintaining direct personal contacts with the nationalized industries in order to gather information. This would make it difficult to persuade members to serve on the committee and might render the committee inefficient.[3]

Opinion among students of public enterprise outside Parliament has been equally divided. For example, Professor Sargant Florence and Mr Maddick, both of Birmingham University, regard the objections to a parliamentary committee as overwhelming. They consider it is certain to lead to a vast increase of official record-keeping, a time-consuming consultation of every interest whenever the policy of a nationalized industry takes a new turn in a vain search for perfectability, and a cramping of individual initiative.[4] Mr A. H. Hanson of Leeds University, on the

[1] 523 HC Deb. 5s., cols. 833-962 (February 8, 1954).

[2] These concerned the scope of parliamentary questions, improvement of the consumers' councils, septennial external investigations, and the administration of gas and electricity by government departments.

[3] *Ib.*, col. 932.

[4] P. Sargant Florence and H. Maddick: 'Consumers' Councils in the Nationalized Industries', XXIV *Political Quarterly* (1953), p. 267.

other hand, declares that the assessment of efficiency in a public undertaking involves political value judgments which should be made by representatives of the people. The House of Commons ought therefore to have effective powers to supervise, criticize and influence the nationalized industries. Parliamentary supervision has not, in his view, been adequate, and none of the other devices suggested for strengthening public accountability appear wholly satisfactory. He does not think the argument that closer parliamentary investigation will tend to diminish efficiency has been clearly proved, and he even inclines to the opposite view, since the inquiries made by the Estimates Committee into the trading functions of government departments have had beneficial results. While a Select Committee cannot hope to be non-political, they should be able to provide more information, better public relations, and concentrate discussion on those aspects of the nationalized industries most in need of attention.[1]

A FALSE START

Meanwhile, a Select Committee was set up by the House of Commons in 1955 on the lines indicated above.[2] They held a few meetings, heard the evidence submitted on behalf of Ministers, and sought the advice of the Attorney-General (which he confessed he was unable to give) as to interpretation of their terms of reference. They then reported (on November 14, 1955) that the terms of reference as then drafted left 'insufficient scope to make enquiries or to obtain further information regarding the nationalized industries which would be of any real use to the House'. The principal difficulty which made the Committee arrive at this conclusion was that the immense number of matters specified by departments as having been decided by Ministers, or clearly engaging or likely to engage at some time the responsibility of Ministers, left the Committee virtually nothing of any consequence into which they could properly inquire.[3]

After this fiasco the Prime Minister (Sir Anthony Eden) announced that the Government proposed to set up a Select Committee with new and wider terms of reference.[4] Towards the end of 1956 Mr R. A. Butler moved that a committee be appointed 'to examine the reports

[1] A. H. Hanson: 'Parliament and the Nationalized Industries', VI *Yorkshire Bulletin of Economic and Social Research* (1954), pp. 151 ff.

[2] 538 HC Deb. 5s., cols. 1428-30 (March 16, 1955); repeated in 543 HC Deb. 5s., col. 1470 (July 7, 1955).

[3] *Special Report from the Select Committee on Nationalized Industries*, HMSO, HC 120/1955-6, paras. 4 and 5.

[4] 552 HC Deb. 5s., cols. 1423-4 (May 10, 1956).

and accounts of the nationalized industries established by statute'. He explained that, unlike the previous committee, this one would not be debarred from discussing certain questions by a series of specific prohibitions. The scope of their inquiries would be left to the good sense of the committee. To give them unfettered discretion in this way was an act of faith, and the committee must be regarded as an experiment. At the same time, he indicated that the committee should not trespass on matters of day-to-day administration, which are clearly matters for the corporations, or at the other extreme on matters of major government policy, which are the responsibility of Ministers of the Crown. They could properly discuss such topics as the financial results of operations, the devolution of authority within a nationalized industry, the techniques of managerial efficiency, recruitment and training of technical and managerial staff, relations with consumer councils and the public, and with outside industries, and the unremunerative responsibilities of the boards.[1] The Opposition opposed the proposal and divided the House against the Government; but once again the speeches of individual members showed that this question cut across the party alignment in the House of Commons.

The new Select Committee, like their predecessor, do not have an officer of high status analogous to the Comptroller and Auditor-General. They have to rely on the advice of senior Treasury officials in charge of Treasury divisions concerned with the nationalized industries, who are in more or less continuous attendance. In addition, of course, the committee may summon the spokesman of the industries and departments as required.

How much may we expect from the activities of this Select Committee? To answer this question we must consider not merely the competence and resources of the committee, but the much wider question of what accountability on the part of a public corporation really involves.

WHAT DOES ACCOUNTABILITY MEAN?

To account for one's actions means that one gives a report of what one has done in a specified period of time, together with whatever explanations may be necessary to justify the actions performed or the ends pursued. The function of the annual report and accounts of a joint stock company is to *account* to the shareholders in precisely this sense; and the main object of the annual meeting is to enable the owners of the undertaking to decide whether they are satisfied with the manner in which it is being managed and directed, or whether they desire to change the

[1] 561 HC Deb. 5s., cols. 395-603 (November 29, 1956).

board of directors. Shareholders' meetings are notoriously impotent; and the larger and more complex the company, the more futile are the tiny gatherings of shareholders who make it their business to attend the annual meeting. It is manifestly impossible for a large and heterogeneous body of shareholders, most of whom never bother to attend a company's meeting, and many of whom are scarcely able to understand the accounts, to 'control' in any real sense the affairs of a joint stock company. The accountability of the directors—so far as it goes—is nonetheless of fundamental importance. It is imposed by law and safeguarded by the practices and traditions of business executives, professional accountants and solicitors. It is essentially the means by which the directors seek to gain and hold the confidence not only of the shareholders but also of stockbrokers, bankers, issuing houses, and the large institutional investors who can give expert scrutiny to the reports and accounts of companies.

The position is entirely different in the circumstances appertaining to the nationalized industries in Britain. There are no shareholders or equity capital. The undertaking is owned by the nation, and Parliament is supposed to represent the general interest of the public; but it cannot claim an exclusive right to do so, since the appropriate Minister has been given extensive powers to direct the public corporation in the national interest. It is to the Minister that the board submits their annual reports and accounts in the first instance, and it is he who can continue the members of the board in office or replace them by others. The Minister has extensive powers of control and influence over a public corporation which are much greater than those possessed by the shareholders of a commercial company in relation to the board of directors. Parliament has almost no positive powers. In theory it can change the law; but in practice it can only pass, amend, or reject Bills introduced by the Government. On the other hand, Members of Parliament have far more opportunities to express their views and to obtain information than the shareholders of a company; and parliamentary criticism of a nationalized industry may have a considerable influence on the appropriate Minister in his dealings with that industry. Sir Geoffrey Vickers, VC, who was a member of the National Coal Board for some years, observes that it would be wrong to assume that apprehensions, criticism, confidence, satisfaction or other views expressed in Parliament have no influence on a public corporation, 'merely because the sanction behind them is an unwieldy one'.[1] He points out that although so large and heavily burdened a body as Parliament is not well suited to discuss

[1] Sir Geoffrey Vickers: 'The Accountability of a Nationalized Industry', XXX *Public Administration* (1952), p. 78. I am much indebted to this illuminating article.

the elaborate report and accounts of a nationalized industry—this was before the House of Commons had appointed a Select Committee—Parliament is nevertheless 'an infinitely more experienced debating body than the shareholders of any industrial concern'.

Not only are the parties to the account quite different in public enterprise from what they are in private enterprise, but the object of the exercise is fundamentally different. The primary purpose of a joint stock company is to produce as large a return as possible on the capital invested in it. This primary purpose is often modified in practice by a consciousness of obligations to the employees, customers, and even the public interest. It can be convincingly shown that the down-grading of the shareholders in the eyes of the management compared with these other claimants is a striking characteristic of big business today. But the board of a public corporation have no obligation to make a profit. Their principal responsibility is to meet the needs of consumers as fully and as cheaply as possible. They have important obligations in regard to research and development, education and training, and the well-being of the personnel. The activities of a public corporation cannot therefore be assessed in terms of a profit and loss account. Its achievements cannot be recorded in financial terms and their measurement is a task of extreme complexity which is made more difficult by the fact that there are usually no similar undertakings operating in the same field, with which comparisons can be made.[1]

There is no real analogy between the ability of a commercial company to pay a dividend and the fulfilment by a public corporation of its statutory obligation to conduct its operations on current account without loss, taking one year with another, at any rate as a criterion of efficiency. For as Mr Chester points out, a nationalized industry may break even by exploiting its monopolistic position in the market rather than by achieving efficiency. It may fail to do so by giving priority to social or political considerations, as the British Transport Commission were compelled to do when the government refused to allow them to raise substandard fares. Or it could adopt a theoretically valid price policy which would yield large surpluses or deficits. Moreover, whereas the shareholders represent only the proprietary interest in a company, Parliament and the government represent the interests of consumers and of the employees, which tend to be articulate, as well as the diffused and usually unorganized interests of the public in its capacity as owner.[2]

[1] Sir Geoffrey Vickers: 'The Accountability of a Nationalized Industry', XXX *Public Administration* (1952), p. 78.

[2] D. N. Chester: 'Management and Accountability in the Nationalized Industries', XXX *Public Administration* (1952), pp. 44–5.

THE PUBLIC ACCOUNTS COMMITTEE

Some of the difficulties of accountability to Parliament by the nationalized industries are illustrated by the experience of the Public Accounts Committee of the House of Commons. This is a powerful instrument for scrutinizing the expenditure of government departments. In 1948 Mr Osbert Peake, MP, then chairman of the committee, published an article urging that the financial transactions of all the nationalized industries should be liable to scrutiny by the PAC. He explained, however, that if effective inquiries were to be made it would be necessary for the Comptroller and the Auditor-General to have access to information beyond the statutory reports and accounts which have to be presented to Parliament and which contain only such information as the Minister thinks it desirable should be published. The law does not empower the Comptroller and Auditor-General to examine and certify the accounts. Mr Peake conceded that even if all facilities for investigation and certification were granted, the Public Accounts Committee would still not be able to arrive at final judgments about the efficiency of the public corporations, although he hoped it could draw attention to wasteful expenditure and examine the financial results of the year's trading.[1]

Since then the Public Accounts Committee have examined the accounts of a number of public corporations, including the BBC, the National Film Finance Corporation, the Atomic Energy Authority, the Colonial Development Corporation, BOAC, BEA, the British Transport Commission, the Raw Cotton Commission, the Overseas Food Corporation, the New Town Development Corporations, and the National Coal Board.[2] Where a corporation receives a grant of public money from a government department, its affairs are discussed when the department's accounts are under examination. Thus the loans and interest rates of the Colonial Development Corporation were discussed on the Overseas Resources Development Acts Accounts of the Colonial Office; the air line subsidies and the experimental helicopter unit which is financed by a special grant, were discussed on the Ministry of Civil Aviation Account; and the National Coal Board's capital requirements and progress of compensation payments and litigation were taken on the Coal Industry Nationalization Account of the Ministry of Fuel and Power.

In examining the accounts of a public corporation evidence is usually given by one or more members of the board (including the chairman).

[1] Osbert Peake: 'Audit of State Monopolies', *Sunday Times*, February 29, 1948.

[2] Public Accounts Committee Reports for the several sessions of Parliament from 1952-3. See also the Memorandum submitted to the Select Committee on Nationalized Industries, HMSO, HC 235/1952-3, pp. 1-2.

The Accounting Officer of the parent department and the Comptroller and Auditor-General are invariably present, and the former gives evidence when information is desired about public money provided by the department.

The Public Accounts Committee have authority to examine at their discretion any accounts which are laid before Parliament; but in practice a distinction may be drawn between public corporations which are not dependent on public money for their annual revenues and those which receive a grant or subsidy. The essence of the distinction lies in the fact that the Comptroller and Auditor-General is not in a position to report to the Committee on the accounts of the nationalized industries unless he is responsible for examining and certifying the annual accounts of the corporation concerned and he does not have authority to do this in the case of the nationalized industries which are self-supporting. Where a public corporation is wholly or mainly dependent on money voted by Parliament, as in the case of the New Towns Development Corporations or the Atomic Energy Authority, the Comptroller and Auditor-General is usually given power either to audit or to examine and certify the accounts.

The Public Accounts Committee have examined the accounts of some nationalized industries which were not receiving grants or subsidies from money voted by Parliament: for example, the Raw Cotton Commission, the British Transport Commission, and the National Coal Board. The professional auditors appointed by the Minister of Transport were summoned by the Committee when the affairs of the BTC were under consideration; but their work does not extend to anything in the nature of an efficiency audit or even to reporting on extravagant expenditure. The professional auditors' report on one occasion mentioned the internal auditors of the BTC, a large body of professional auditors appointed by the Commission, and the Committee asked to see the reports of these internal auditors. Lord Hurcomb objected to this on grounds of principle but eventually produced an extract from the relevant report.[1]

The reports of the Public Accounts Committee have dealt with a number of points of detail, some of them of importance, concerning the public corporations; but their enquiries are of peripherical interest to any broad conception of the work of the nationalized industries.

Nothing more effective is to be expected from the Public Accounts Committee. The committee rely for their information on the Comptroller and Auditor-General, and this officer has stated that his department could not undertake the audit of the nationalized industries without

[1] Gweneth Gutch: 'Nationalized Industries and the Public Accounts Committee 1951-2', XXXI *Public Administration* (1953), pp. 255-62.

a great increase in its staff of professional auditors. This would cause an immense dislocation in the auditing profession, which is at present substantially occupied with the audit of these industries. Moreover, Sir Frank Tribe did not think it would be possible for his staff to have full access to all the books and accounts of the public corporations.[1]

Sir Frederick Metcalfe, formerly Clerk of the House of Commons, holds the view that an examination of the accounts of the nationalized industries would place an intolerable burden of work on the Public Accounts Committee, which they could not carry unless their membership was increased and they worked through sub-committees.[2]

The late Sir Frank Tribe, the Comptroller and Auditor-General until 1958, made it clear that although it might be possible for his department to undertake an audit of the public corporations, he could not report on their efficiency, since this cannot be judged from the accounts.[3] He thought that the professional auditors might be able, if required to do so, to provide Parliament with information of the kind which he gives to the Public Accounts Committee, though they would not regard it as part of the normal audit.[4] His main suggestion for increasing the effectiveness of parliamentary control was that each nationalized industry should present a brief estimate of annual revenue and expenditure in advance each year. This would enable Parliament to satisfy itself that the corporation was really trying to break even, year by year, in accordance with its statutory duty; and it would enable Members of Parliament to compare the estimate with the achievement at the end of the year.[5] He was also anxious that Parliament should have brought to its notice at regular intervals a full list of loans to the nationalized industries guaranteed by the Treasury, and the accumulated deficits on their annual working accounts.[6]

THE ROLE OF PROFESSIONAL AUDITORS

The Institute of Chartered Accountants has expressed the willingness of the profession to assist Parliament in several ways.[7] They could, if

[1] *Report from the Select Committee on Nationalized Industries*, HMSO, HC 235/1952-3, Evidence, Qs. 88, 89, and 164.

[2] *Report from the Select Committee on Nationalized Industries*, HMSO, HC 332-I/1951-2, Evidence, Q. 20.

[3] HC 235/1952-3, Evidence, Qs. 136 and 179.

[4] *Ib.*, Q. 116.

[5] *Ib.*, Q. 114. The Post Office produced an estimate of this kind for the first time in 1952-3.

[6] *Ib.*, Qs. 76, 92, and 114.

[7] See an interesting talk by Sir Frederick Alban, president of the Society of Incorporated Accountants on *Socialization in Great Britain and its Effect on the Accountancy Profession* (September 1948). Published by the Association.

asked to do so by the Public Accounts Committee or any other committee, carry out *ad hoc* investigations into particular aspects of the nationalized industries. They could, in addition to the normal audit, report on such supplementary matters as the failure of the public corporation to fulfil its statutory obligations and comply with ministerial directions; on a material difference between the advance estimate and the results of the year's working; or on a failure to show clearly in the accounts the results of the undertaking and the effect of any subsidies. And finally they could point out when there was a *prima facie* case for further investigation arising from a lack of proper administrative and financial control, substantial capital expenditure which failed to yield an adequate return, extravagant or wasteful expenditure judged by normal commercial standards, or any other matters of financial administration which called for comment.[1]

Much of this discussion about accountability is in my opinion misdirected. Let us first clear away the belief that the scrutiny of the accounts of the nationalized industries by a parliamentary committee (whether the Public Accounts Committee or the new Select Committee) in order to discover 'wasteful expenditure' will serve any useful purpose. It is impossible to conduct even the most successful business enterprise without a considerable amount of expenditure which turns out to be wasteful. If the management is over-fearful of spending money unless it is absolutely certain to obtain a safe return on the outlay, the result is bound to be a highly conservative, excessively prudent, and technically backward undertaking such as the British railways have been for the past thirty or forty years. The finanical administration must of course be honest and uncorrupt; but we can assume the professional auditors are able to take care of that as they do in the case of joint stock companies.

THE REPORTS OF THE SELECT COMMITTEE

In the light of this discussion we may now consider the work of the Select Committee on Nationalized Industries (Reports and Accounts) set up by the House of Commons—commonly known as the standing committee. Their terms of reference are to examine the Reports and Accounts of the Nationalized Industries established by statute whose controlling boards are appointed by Ministers of the Crown and whose annual receipts are not wholly or mainly derived from moneys provided by Parliament or advanced from the Exchequer. The existence of this committee will doubtless preclude the Public Accounts Committee from

[1] Sir Frederick Alban: *Socialization in Great Britain and its Effect on the Accountancy Profession*, pp. 22-3.

examining in future the accounts of the nationalized industries falling within the definition; though presumably not from investigating any activity financed by a departmental grant or subsidy.

The committee have issued four reports, in 1957, 1958, and 1959. The first one dealt with the North of Scotland Hydro Electric Board and to a minor extent the South of Scotland Electricity Board. The former is an undertaking about which little is known south of the border, though it has some exceptionally interesting features. Its duty is not only to supply electric power but also to assist so far as possible in the social and economic betterment of a sparsely populated area.

The Select Committee declared that they were impressed by the remarkable record of the North of Scotland Board, and the criticism they had made on minor points did not derogate in any material degree from the favourable opinion they had formed of the board's achievements.[1] The report discussed the board's policy of rural electrification in remote areas and its finanical implications; their capital investment programme; the contractors employed by the board on civil engineering and constructional work; depreciation policy; the accuracy of estimates for new development schemes; and the Consultative Council. On all these matters the committee reported briefly but favourably. They ended with a handsome tribute to the Hydro-Electric Board which, they said 'has impressively justified the faith of its progenitors. It has now taken its place in the Scottish scene as a firmly-established concern.'[2]

The second report, issued in 1958, concerned the National Coal Board. This was a much more formidable task and the Standing Committee soon realized the vast scope of the subject and decided to concentrate on a few major topics instead of attempting to cover the whole field. The topics chosen were investment, manpower, prices, and the balance between the production of large and small coal.[3]

The committee received extensive evidence, both written and oral, from the chairman, deputy-chairman, and senior officials of the National Coal Board; from the Permanent Secretary and Deputy Secretary of the Minister of Power; and from a few organizations connected with the coal industry. Their report was based mainly on the evidence of the NCB.

Although members of the committee sometimes revealed their political bias when questioning witnesses, the report represents an honest attempt to be fair and just to the National Coal Board. The committee thought the Ministry of Power and the Treasury should exercise rather

[1] *Report from the Select Committee on Nationalized Industries (Reports and Accounts)*, HMSO, HC 304/1956-7, paras. 22 ff.

[2] *Ib.*, para. 67.

[3] Report, HMSO, HC 187-I/1957-8, para. 2.

more detailed control over the investment programme, particularly in regard to the schemes calculated to give the lowest financial yield.[1] They noted the difficulties the industry has experienced from the shortage of technically trained men capable of initiating and executing major reconstruction or development works. They expressed doubt as to the likelihood of the intermediate targets set in *Investing in Coal* being reached in 1960.[2] They mildly disagreed with the board's policy of depreciating man-made assets on an historical basis, since this means that demands must be made on the general savings of the community to provide sufficient capital investment to maintain even the present level of output.[3] They approved, on the other hand, the board's attitude to coal prices, but recommended changes in the procedure for prices and a clear allocation of responsibility in fixing prices.[4] They thought the board was working on the right lines to increase consumption of small coal but a greater sense of urgency should have informed the research and development effort relating to the use of such coal for gasification and briquette-making.[5]

The minutes of evidence and appendices contain much interesting information. Mr A. T. K. Grant, an Under-Secretary in charge of the Trade and Industry Division of the Treasury, in his evidence to the Select Committee, explained just how and when and why the Treasury becomes concerned with the nationalized industries. Sir James Bowman, the chairman of the NCB, explained some of the grievances of the board: at having to bear the loss on imported American coal bought at very high prices and sold in competition with home-produced coal; at being unable to export British coal at very much higher prices than it sells for in the British market and then being criticized for not making a profit. We find him explaining the technological and manpower problems which confront the industry and the steps the board are taking to solve them. We find him remarking that the nationalized coal industry is not wholly a commercial undertaking nor yet wholly a public service, but has some of the characteristics of both.[6]

On both sides of the table a serious attempt was made to establish harmonious working relations. At the very first meeting of the Select Committee the chairman was asked to write to the chairmen of the boards of the nationalized industries informing them of the terms of reference, and assuring them 'that this committee will be always ready, so far as their terms of reference allow, to help them in their relations with the House of Commons'. The heads of the public corporations con-

[1] Report, HMSO, HC 187-I/1957-58, para. 33.

[2] *Ib.*, para. 48. [3] *Ib.*, paras. 73-5. [4] *Ib.*, paras. 77-89. [5] *Ib.*, paras. 101-5.

[6] *Ib.*, pp. 126-8. See the Report, para. 9.

cerned were obviously anxious to give the committee the fullest information and explanation in their possession. Mr Latham, the deputy chairman of the NCB, said he felt it to be 'desperately important that they should have a chance to express their point of view, particularly on the subject of prices'.[1]

For their part the committee showed a commendable restraint in not scoring easy points based on political prejudices. They tried 'not to become involved as critics with the day-to-day administration of the board on the one hand, and with matters of government policy on the other'.[2] They put on record their diffidence as laymen at forming opinions on technical matters on which they had no expert guidance. Finally, they were aware of the difficulties arising from the absence of a yardstick by which to judge the performance of the board.[3] Any comparison with the era of private ownership in this country, or the performance of coal industries in other countries today, would have taken the committee far beyond their proper function.

The third report, issued in 1959, dealt with the air corporations. It discussed a great many different topics, including the supply of new aircraft, development flying, fares, routes, depreciation policy, aircraft maintenance, the operations of BEA and BOAC, their subsidiary and associated companies, competition between the nationalized and independent air lines, freight, helicopters, relations between the corporations and the Minister,[4] and the general outlook for civil aviation.

The Select Committee inquired into the procedure by which BEA and BOAC obtain new aircraft and the conditions the corporations must fulfil in order to do so. They described the work of the Transport Aircraft Requirements Committee, which plays a vital role in this sphere, and gave an ambiguous evaluation of the Committee.[5] The machinery for ordering new aircraft is complicated and there is a certain diffusion of responsibility; but the air corporations stated that in the end they always got the kind of aircraft they wanted. BEA had, however, encountered difficulty in getting the DH 121 adopted. It took the air corporation several months to persuade the Minister of Transport and Civil Aviation, and BEA were under pressure by the Ministry to accept a different aircraft.[6]

[1] HMSO, HC 304/1956-7, Q. 1007.

[2] Report, HMSO, HC 187/1957-8, para. 5.

[3] *Ib.*, para. 4.

[4] *Report from the Select Committee on Nationalized Industries (Reports and Accounts)*, HC 213, May 14, 1959; HMSO, paras. 32-9, 55-60.

[5] 'Your Committee believe that the operations of the Corporations have on occasion been adversely affected by the past working of the TARC; but they believe that the TARC is now more alive to its important duties.' *Ib.*, para. 60.

[6] Paras. 34 and 54.

The Select Committee praised the air corporations for the way in which they have consistently advocated cheaper travel,[1] and commended their activities in several other respects. The report also contained criticisms of both BEA and BOAC. Thus, the committee urged that a complete review of BOAC's policy towards their subsidiary companies, which are mostly making heavy losses,[2] should take place without delay. They thought the inspectorate employed by BEA for aircraft maintenance was too large and that maintenance costs could be reduced by more mechanization.[3] They also suggested that both the air corporations could and should get higher utilization figures from their aircraft.[4]

The committee reported unfavourably on the slowness with which BOAC had set about reorganizing their methods of overhauling and maintaining aircraft. The methods used by the corporation were twice as costly as those of competing air lines and were capable of being drastically improved. BOAC had moved with extreme slowness towards reorganization and the elimination of redundant staff in their engineering workshops, with the result that defects believed to exist in 1952 and known to exist in 1956 were not remedied by the end of 1959, though a start had been made.[5] The weakness of this part of the report is the Select Committee did not take evidence from the trade unions concerned with these matters; and their report showed little understanding of the labour problems confronting BOAC. The strike at London Airport and the subsequent inquiry ordered by the Government revealed the immense difficulties resulting from the negotiating and consultative machinery in dealing with the maintenance questions. I have described in a previous chapter the remarks of the Select Committee about the exercise by the Minister of many non-statutory powers over the air corporations.[6]

The airlines followed the practice adopted by departments in relation to the reports of the Public Accounts Committee of the House of Commons, by replying to comments made on them by the Select Committee.[7] These replies showed that steps were being taken to carry out some of the Select Committee's recommendations; but that in certain matters it is not easy to see how changes could be made. Consultation would take place at a high level to see whether closer co-operation between the corporations would be beneficial. Detailed information about subsidiary companies would in future be published in the Corporations' reports.

BEA declared that they 'welcomed the inquiries by the Select Committee, and found them useful in directing attention to important aspects

[1] Para. 79. [2] Para. 17. [3] Paras. 19, 177. [4] Paras. 143, 146. [5] Paras. 160-70.

[6] *Ante* page 156.

[7] The comments were presented by the Minister of Aviation as a written reply to a parliamentary question by Sir Toby Low, MP, in the House of Commons on November 16, 1959.

of its business in a way which provides an admirable solution to the problem of public accountability'. This was a considerable tribute, particularly as the airline had not escaped criticism.

The Select Committee repeated a point they had previously made: namely, that their lack of specialized staff added to the difficulty of inquiring into a vast industry such as air transport.[1] Their fourth and final report, issued shortly before the dissolution of Parliament in 1959, was devoted entirely to the question of staff. The point stressed in this special report is that the House of Commons is now attempting to combine politics and economics; and something more than the traditional means is needed to enable it to do so effectively.[2]

The Select Committee asked for two kinds of assistance. One was the services of an accountant experienced in industrial and commercial accounts; the other was the services of an economist to advise the committee on fruitful lines of inquiry and to assist in the actual investigations.[3] The Committee said they should have their own staff, and not have to rely on Treasury officials seconded for the purpose or on outside professional experts engaged in private practice.[4] Mr Butler, the Leader of the House, thought there were objections to hiring outside experts; after reflection he was in favour of an assessor being appointed by the committee and paid a fee for his services. The committee expressed a preference for strengthening the House of Commons staff.[5]

It seems to an outside observer somewhat remarkable that the Select Committee should have had to meet seven times, hear evidence from the highest officers of the House of Commons, the Leader of the House and the Leader of the Opposition, high Treasury officials, and eminent representatives of the Institute of Chartered Accountants, and to issue a report of nine pages and about fifty pages of evidence, in order to obtain the services of an accountant and an economist. The report leads one to hope, however, that future Select Committees on Nationalized Industries will be better equipped with skilled staff than their predecessors. My own conviction is that the assistance asked for by the Select Committee is far too modest if they are to do their job thoroughly.

On the basis of the reports so far issued I would say that the Select Committee have provided some useful information in the evidence they have received; but that they are not and cannot be an authoritative body in their present condition. Without technical, economic, statistical and administrative advice of high calibre, the committee will remain a group

[1] *Third Report*, para. 24.

[2] *Special Report from the Select Committee on Nationalized Industries* (*Reports and Accounts*) House of Commons paper 276, July 28, 1959, para. 4.

[3] Para. 8. [4] Paras. 11, 12, 29, 38. [5] Paras. 17, 26, 27, 39.

of well-intentioned laymen whose opinions are unlikely to carry great weight. The committee are better than nothing for they provide *inter alia* an opportunity to clear up misunderstandings and mistakes; but they would be immeasurably strengthened if they were supplied with the reports of an Efficiency Audit Commission or the advice of a highly qualified staff.

THE CRITERION OF EFFICIENCY

The vital need today is not closer financial accountability or the supply of information on the accounts of nationalized industries to Parliament and the public. It is to discover whether these great undertakings are operated with a reasonable degree of efficiency, and to find out what efficiency connotes in this sphere.[1] Information which can throw light on productivity, on the policies which a board are pursuing and the success with which they are applying them, or the extent to which a public corporation is abusing its monopolistic position, is valuable not only to Members of Parliament, but to the public and to consumers.

I agree with Mr A. H. Hanson that the concept of efficiency relates to means and not ends.[2] Hence the policy aims of a nationalized industry must be considered separately from the efficiency with which they are being realized. The criterion of efficiency does not relieve us of the need to make value judgments about purposes and ends which are often difficult to formulate. Mr Hanson emphasizes that a belief in parliamentary democracy implies that the more important of these value judgments ought to be made by the representatives of the people; and hence that supervision of the nationalized industries by the House of Commons should be as effective as possible. Parliament cannot administer or even decide policy, but it can criticize and influence the decisions of those to whom it has entrusted the power of deciding policy and administration.

A Select Committee of the House of Commons are no more likely than the House itself to be able to agree about the value judgments inherent in the policies of nationalized industries. The premises from which Labour Members approach the subject are very different from those underlying the Conservative attitude; and there is no magic solvent in membership of a committee to dissolve these differences. If it were possible to achieve an agreed view about aims and policies, this would be to the public advantage; but I doubt if it can be accomplished.

[1] See an excellent leading article 'The Management of Public Corporations', CLXXIII *Nature* (1954), p. 479.

[2] 'Parliament and the Nationalized Industries', VI *Yorkshire Bulletin of Economic and Social Research* (1954), pp. 151-2.

Even if that were possible, the question of efficiency of performance still remains; and I do not believe that a committee of overworked MPs burdened with a dozen other interests and innumerable other claims on their time and energy, are competent to assess the efficiency of the nationalized industries even within the framework of agreed policies. This was the view of the original Select Committee which first enquired into the matter and which led them to recommend that the Committee should be assisted by a high officer comparable to the Comptroller and Auditor-General. This has been refused.

AN EFFICIENCY AUDIT

It is becoming increasingly obvious that we cannot expect Parliament and the public to be adequately informed about the condition of the nationalized industries unless we provide some machinery for providing them with expert guidance. The annual report cannot be an entirely impartial statement, though the reports issued by many of the public corporations are admirable documents which provide an immense amount of interesting information about the industries concerned. We know infinitely more about coal and transport, to name only those two industries, than we did when they were under private enterprise. One notes with pleasure, moreover, the statement by British European Airways that their policy is to furnish the fullest possible information concerning their activities to the general public and to their staff. This is indeed the right spirit.[1]

But the magnitude and complexity of the organizations are such that expert guidance is needed to evaluate their performance. I pointed out long ago in a book entitled *Public Enterprise*[2] that if we are to develop effective methods of public criticism, specially devised organs of scrutiny and investigation will have to be created. I suggested that an audit commission should be set up to hold efficiency audits at regular intervals. These efficiency audits would be incomparably wider in scope than the customary audit of accounts. Their object would be to ascertain whether a public corporation is conducting its work well or feebly, to call attention to merits and shortcomings, to make suggestions for improvement, and to act as the eyes and ears of the general public.

The reports of an audit commission would be available to the Select Committee on Nationalized Industries; and their services would be at the disposal of Ministers.

Objections have been made to the efficiency audit on the ground that

[1] *British European Airways Annual Report* 1950–1, HMSO, HC 263/1950–1, pp. 12-4.
[2] Ed. W. A. Robson (1937), p. 380.

the commission would be regarded by the public corporations as hostile to them and would therefore be resisted; that the corporations would tend to withhold information from the commission whenever possible; and that for an outside body to have the right to investigate and criticize would tend to have a paralysing influence on the vigour and enterprise of the public corporations. Hence, it is contended, the governing boards must be left to seek voluntarily any expert advice or criticism of this kind; and any reports or recommendations resulting from such inquiries must remain the confidential property of the public corporation and not be disclosed to the public.

Lord Citrine, when he was chairman of the Central Electricity Authority, declared that while the nationalized industries would undoubtedly avail themselves of the services of industrial consultants, this was an entirely different matter from the creation of an organ which could survey and advise on the organization, administration and operation of the nationalized industries as a whole.[1]

This is undoubtedly true; and it is, indeed, one of the main reasons for the superior advantages of an audit commission. For an important feature of the audit commission would be its ability to accumulate a store of knowledge about all the public corporations working in a variety of industries. It would build up a skilled staff possessing an unrivalled insight into the problems of nationalized industry and an unequalled ability to compare the methods adopted by the several boards for coping with them. There would be great advantages in having somewhere in our governmental system a clearing-house of knowledge and experience about the nationalized industries.

Lord Citrine brought out the usual arguments about undermining the authority and sense of responsibility of the board, and gave the usual warnings about creating a lack of confidence in the members of the board and encouraging a tendency in the staff to play for safety. These arguments have become common form and are continually brought forward by the chairmen as reasons for opposing any reform to which they object. The more conservative the industry, the more its spokesmen talk about 'stifling initiative'.

Mr Morrison, when he was Lord President in the Labour Government, urged the chairmen of the boards to establish a common efficiency unit for their own use. It was to be a product of the corporations themselves which would be used by them collectively as industrial consultants. It was to comprise first-class men who could look constructively at economic, costing and managerial problems on which a nationalized industry might need help. The reports of this common efficiency unit

[1] 'Problems of Nationalized Industries', XXIX *Public Administration* (1951), pp. 325–6.

would usually go privately to the board which asked for its assistance; but the Government might decide that a particular report should be submitted to a Minister and laid before Parliament. Normally it would be better for the reports not to be published, but publication might be desirable if the matter dealt with were of fundamental importance.[1]

This proposal met with a similar resistance by the board chairmen whom Mr Morrison consulted. They considered it implied a reflection on the ability of the boards to administer their undertaking.[2]

MEASUREMENT AND PUBLICITY

This undue sensitiveness on the part of the nationalized industries towards the findings or criticism of such a body as the audit commission should be firmly discouraged and discounted. The Webbs rightly regarded publicity and measurement as the two most potent instruments of efficiency and progress in a socialist commonwealth; and we cannot afford to abandon them merely because the governing boards of public corporations say they cannot bear any demonstration that their handiwork has not attained perfection. This is mere vanity, and we cannot pander to such a human weakness in seeking to attain the highest standards of performance in the nationalized industries. I have argued strongly that the public corporations should be immune from parliamentary inquisition into their day-to-day administration. But this does not mean that they cannot reasonably be asked to submit to periodic inquiries by an expert body concerning the efficiency with which they are conducting the business which Parliament and the nation have entrusted to them.

The views of Sidney and Beatrice Webb on measurement and publicity were so sane and sensible that I venture to remind the reader of what they said. They included in 'measurement' not only quantitative enumeration, but also a determination of kind and a valuation of quality. They understood the term 'publicity' to include not merely the issue of reports and bluebooks, but every means for conveying information to the citizens and to the persons particularly concerned, such as the consumers or the managers, or the employees of a nationalized industry.[3]

In the Webbs' view, public opinion is decisive in a true democracy;

[1] *Evidence to the Select Committee on Nationalized Industries*, HMSO, HC 235/1952-3, Qs. 383, 401, 403, 409, 425, 494, and 485. Mr Ernest Davies, MP (in a Labour Party discussion pamphlet *Problems of Public Ownership* (1952), p. 15) suggested that the common efficiency unit might be placed under a non-departmental Minister, e.g. the Lord President. Further, that Ministers should be able to call on the unit to carry out investigations where the boards failed to do so.

[2] Herbert Morrison: *Government and Parliament* (1954), p. 294.

[3] *A Constitution for the Socialist Commonwealth of Great Britain* (1920), p. 186.

and hence the more effectively public opinion is educated, the greater will be the success of any administration. 'In place of the jealous secrecy in which the 1,400 separate colliery companies at present enshroud their operations, and of the bureaucratic concealment which today marks alike the Post Office and the railways,' they wrote in 1920, 'we visualize the administration of each national industry and service, no longer concerned for magnifying the private gains of particular capitalist groups, or enhancing the net revenue of the Exchequer, but merely for increasing the efficiency of the service to the public, in the glare of a whole series of searchlights, impinging at different angles upon what is essentially the same problem—namely, how to obtain for the community as a whole the greatest possible efficiency in relation to the efforts and sacrifices involved.'[1]

The deliberate intensification of this searchlight of public knowledge they regarded as the cornerstone of successful democracy. The power to decide must continue to be vested in those having responsibility; but they foresaw a gradual elimination of autocratic decisions and the substitution of a process whereby judgments and decisions would be arrived at largely by common consent. 'This common consent would be reached by the cogency of accurately ascertained and authoritatively reported facts, driven home by the silent persuasiveness of the public opinion of those concerned.'[2] They wanted to get rid of the 'stuffiness' of private interests and to usher in a regime in which measurement and publicity would reign supreme.[3]

The new figure required in this improved state of society is, the Webbs declared, 'the disinterested professional expert who invents, discovers, inspects, audits, costs, tests or measures—in supplement of the initiative in all these respects of the administration itself'—but possessing no power to decide or to direct. His function is completed when he has reported. In conducting his investigations, finding facts, drawing conclusions, and making recommendations, he would pay no attention either to the susceptibilities of the management or to the prejudices of the employees. It would then be the task of the directors of a nationalized industry, acting through the appropriate committee, to get each particular part of an expert report explained, discussed, and acted upon by the establishment, district or industry to which it relates.[4]

THE SEPTENNIAL INQUIRY

The Labour Government announced in 1950 that they would adopt as an alternative to the proposals mentioned in the preceding pages and to

[1] *A Constitution for the Socialist Commonwealth of Great Britain* (1920), p. 195.
[2] *Ib.*, pp. 196-7. [3] *Ib.*, pp. 198-9. [4] *Ib.*, p. 356.

the suggestion of a Standing Committee of Parliament, a septennial inquiry on the lines of the Beveridge Committee on Broadcasting which they had appointed in 1949. The chairmen of the public corporations agreed to accept occasional inquiries of this kind into broad questions of policy and organization concerning particular industries.[1] The Labour Party has recently lengthened the periodicity of these inquiries from seven to ten years, on the ground that they occupy the time of the board and their staff, and that more time is needed to see how any changes introduced after one inquiry work out before a further inquiry is begun.[2]

The Conservative view, according to Captain Crookshank's evidence to the Select Committee, is that a full dress inquiry into fundamental questions of policy and organization should not take place periodically at regular intervals but only on rare occasions when there is a clear need for them.[3] His experience as Postmaster-General had convinced him that 'These BBC inquiries from time to time . . . are most terribly upsetting . . . As soon as one is over they begin thinking about the next one . . . If you got these big investigations regularly going on with every industry I am sure it would have a most unsettling effect, and that must be bad'.[4] Lord Reith thought the experience of the BBC shows there is much to be said for periodic inquiries, but it involves great upset and takes up a good deal of time. He sometimes wondered if the result justified the time and trouble.[5]

The Beveridge Committee on Broadcasting, to which Labour politicians frequently refer, was a singularly unsuccessful example of a full-dress investigation. Its members were not agreed on the fundamental question of competition or monopoly; nor whether broadcasting should be a public service or a commercial enterprise. There was disagreement both on the banning of advertising on the BBC services and on sponsoring of programmes on a commercial service. The proposals of the Committee regarding television have not been carried out. The failure of the Beveridge Committee can be ascribed in part to the political nature of some of the problems it dealt with, and the divergence of political views among the members.[6]

[1] 478 HC Deb. 5s., cols. 2814–5 (October 25, 1950); cf. Herbert Morrison: *Government and Parliament* (1954), pp. 275–6.

[2] *Public Enterprise* (1957) (Labour Party), p. 48.

[3] *Evidence to Select Committee on Nationalized Industries*, HMSO, HC 235/1952-3, Q. 941.

[4] *Ib.*, Q. 943. [5] *Ib.*, Q. 658.

[6] For details about the action taken by the BBC on the committee's recommendations, see *British Broadcasting Corporation Annual Report 1951-2*, HMSO, Cmd. 8660/1952, pp. 8 and 83.

Some investigating bodies set up subsequent to the Beveridge Committee have contributed greatly to our knowledge and understanding of the nationalized industries, and have made important proposals for their organization and administration, many of which have been applied in practice. The Chambers Committee was appointed to inquire into the London Transport undertaking by the Minister of Transport in 1953 and its report was published in 1955. The Fleck Committee was invited by the National Coal Board at the end of 1953 to form an advisory committee on organization. The NCB indicated some of the questions they thought needed consideration and the committee reported to the board in 1955.[1] The Herbert Committee of Inquiry into the Electricity Supply Industry was appointed by the Minister of Fuel and Power in 1954 and reported in 1956.

There is undoubtedly a role of great importance which committees such as these can and should play in the sphere of nationalized industry if their personnel are carefully chosen; but they cannot and should not be expected to carry out an efficiency audit. The Herbert Committee explicitly stated that it was 'obviously impossible for us to conduct anything in the nature of an efficiency audit', for which they had neither the time nor the staff.[2] The committee therefore attempted only a broad description of the industry's organization, policy and activities, with a broad appraisal.

My own proposal for an audit commission assumed that an efficiency audit would concern itself only with the work of a nationalized industry operating within a framework of policy already laid down in the statutes, regulations and ministerial directions. It would not normally raise questions involving a change of fundamental policy, such as a different form of organization for the coal industry or the introduction of a subsidy for transport. There need not, therefore, be overlapping or duplication between an audit commission inquiring into the operating efficiency of a nationalized industry and an occasional investigation of a more fundamental character by an *ad hoc* committee. The audit commission would inquire into such matters as the character, quantity, and quality of goods or services provided; price policy; efficiency of administration; personnel questions, including pay, recruitment, and methods of promotion; relations between the board and the consumer; capital expenditure, and the methods of financing it, and so forth.[3] The occasional *ad hoc* committees would be concerned with major policy and organization.

[1] See *National Coal Board Annual Report 1955*, HMSO, HC 263-I/1955-6, Vol. I, Ch. IV for information about the action taken on the Fleck Report.

[2] Report, HMSO, Cmd. 9672/1956, para. 5.

[3] *Public Enterprise* ed. W. A. Robson (1937), p. 380.

One of the disadvantages of the septennial or decennial committee is that owing to the diversity of its membership, which is appointed *ad hoc*, there can be no common approach to those problems which are common to all or several of the nationalized industries, such as labour relations, price policy, the making and use of surpluses, recruitment and training of managerial and technical staff, promotion, insurance, the methods of formulating and carrying out research programmes, and so forth. I am firmly convinced, therefore, that despite the usefulness of occasional committees of inquiry into fundamentals, there remains a need, at present unsatisfied, for a permanent body of experts in regular touch with the administration of the nationalized industries and able to give an informed account of actions which affect consumers and the public generally, with such evaluation as may be possible.[1]

I referred above to the statement that full-dress investigations by committees have an unsettling effect on a nationalized industry, as though this were a strong or conclusive reason against such inquiries. I do not think any such inference can be drawn. Where an industry has got into difficulties, or is obsolete and complacent in its outlook, it is desirable that the management should not be allowed to remain in a 'settled' state; it should be prodded and pricked into a state of acute unsettlement by every possible means. For only by a process of unsettling the minds of the managerial officers and technical specialists can one hope to induce them to depart from their traditional ways and adopt a more progressive outlook. On the other hand, where an industry has been doing as well as the nationalized air lines, there is no need to take up the time and energy of the top management in preparing lengthy evidence and appearing before a departmental committee. I mention this merely to make it clear that the fact that an inquiry produces an unsettling effect on an industry provides no indication of whether such an inquiry is necessary or not.

It does not take much insight into human nature to understand that the board members and chief executives of public corporations desire as much autonomy and freedom from investigation as they can secure. They are busy men burdened with heavy responsibilities. Moreover, most of them are endeavouring in a public spirited way to run the industries as well as they can, often in difficult circumstances. Nevertheless, public

[1] Professor Sargant Florence and Mr Maddick have suggested that a permanent 'efficiency unit' of industrial consultants might be set up in conjunction with a body representing consumers in order to protect their interests and promote efficiency. This is another version of the same idea which I have for long advocated. P. Sargant Florence and H. Maddick: 'Consumers' Councils in the Nationalized Industries', XXIV *Political Quarterly* (1953), pp. 267-8.

accountability must remain an essential feature of the administration of public undertakings. Without it, nationalization is deprived of half its meaning.

THE PURPOSES OF ACCOUNTABILITY

There are three fundamental objectives to be attained. One is to satisfy the Government, Parliament, and the public, that the nationalized industries are being run efficiently and progressively. The second is to prevent consumers from being exploited by an undue use of the monopolistic position enjoyed by the public corporations. The third is to ensure that labour relations and personnel management are sufficiently good to avoid large-scale stoppages of work owing to trade disputes from occurring. This does not mean, however, that the workpeople in the public sector should occupy a privileged position compared with workers in corresponding grades in the private sector.

The function of accountability is to throw light on the activities and policies of the nationalized industries by providing whatever information is necessary to show whether these objectives are being pursued with a reasonable degree of success. There are several channels through which information on these matters may come. There are the annual reports; there are the consumer councils; there are the organs of joint consultation; there is information obtained by government departments in the course of their everyday relations with the nationalized industries, and the information conveyed by Ministers in replies to Parliamentary questions; there is the information which MPs obtain from direct correspondence with the public corporations; that which comes to them from the Select Committee of the House of Commons; and the information which departmental or other committees of inquiry reveal.

If we take into consideration all these potential sources of information, the accountability of the British nationalized industries is in my judgment fully adequate. Nevertheless, I doubt whether it is possible to appraise the efficiency of the nationalized industries without the guidance of an expert body specially constituted for the purpose, such as the audit commission I have proposed. Such a body would apply their own *expertise* to develop criteria of efficiency where these are now lacking.

It will be understood that the attainment of the fundamental objectives set out above is not necessarily assured by even the most perfect system of accountability. Various controls, reforms, expenditures, changes of organization and of personnel, etc., may be required to achieve these ends. But here we are concerned with public accountability and not public control; accountability should be ancillary to public control; it may be a prelude to or even an instrument of public control; but its nature is essentially different.

In the last analysis, however, we should consider public accountability not as a mere giving of information *in vacuo*, but in terms of its effect on the behaviour of those who are called upon to account. The most obvious and important influence which may be traced to accountability is in inducing or enhancing a sense of responsibility in those who are called upon to account. This, indeed, is its most valuable characteristic from an economic or social point of view. No one who is at all acquainted with the nationalized industries can have the slightest doubt about the high sense of responsibility shown by those who direct their administration.

If anything even remotely approaching a similar sense of responsibility had been shown during the inter-war years by the privately owned railway companies or the colliery companies, it is inconceivable that the present state of those industries would be as technologically backward as they are today. But the notion of accountability is only slightly developed today in the sphere of private enterprise, although some of the larger public companies are beginning to tell their shareholders rather more than formerly about the conduct of the business—especially when they can take pride in it. The directors still gloss over adverse features, or dismiss them in a few words.

The public accountability of the British nationalized industries compares very favourably not only with private enterprise but also with publicly owned industries carried on in any other country with which I am acquainted.

CHAPTER IX

The Governing Board

THE governing board occupies a position of crucial importance in the direction and management of a nationalized industry. The success or failure of nationalization is, indeed, likely to depend more on the quality and composition of the boards directing the public corporations than on any other single factor. For from this flow all the decisions on policy and administration which together make up good or bad management.

THE KEY POSITION OF THE BOARD

Let us consider, by way of illustration, the matters which will normally come for approval or decision to the board of a public corporation. The appointment of a chief executive and the principal officers; the programmes of current and future output; plans for development or reorganization; major projects for new equipment; relations with Ministers on matters of policy; the consideration of serious criticism by Parliament, consumers or the public and the action to be taken; the result of negotiations with, or demands by, trade unions on important matters; general policy concerning finance, capital expenditure, prices, surpluses and deficits; the policy of the undertaking in staff matters, including questions of wages, incentives, morale, and consultation with employees; the promotion of further legislation (whether private or public Bills) and the attitude to be taken towards other Bills; the methods by which the corporation is to comply with ministerial directions and the attitude of the corporation to requests or proposals by Ministers; serious conflicts of interest or policy with other public corporations or with private interests; the allocation of sums to reserve, and the management of reserve funds; the action to be taken by the corporation to reduce operating deficits; the adoption of impor tant new inventions, processes or improvements; policy on research and development, training and education.

No self-respecting board could be content with a narrower range of responsibility than this. Some would demand a wider sphere of decision and supervision. I have not mentioned such obvious matters as the board's responsibility for the annual report and statement of accounts.

The governing body of a public corporation occupies a different position from that of any other body. It has far wider responsibilities than the board of a commercial company, for the directors of the latter are essentially the representatives of the shareholders, whereas the board of a public corporation are entrusted with duties to the consumers, to the employees, to the Government, to Parliament, and to the nation. It differs from a local authority (or one of its committees) running a public utility service, for this consists wholly or mainly of councillors answerable to the electors; and all kinds of political and party considerations can and do arise in local government which have no counterpart in a public corporation.

The statutory conditions relating to the boards of the various public corporations are not uniform in regard to the number, tenure and the qualifications of members. All of them are chosen by the appropriate Minister, even where (as in the case of the BBC[1] or the Bank of England) the members are formally appointed by the Crown.

THE NUMBER OF MEMBERS

The first variable concerns the size of the board. The Court of the Bank of England consists of the governor, deputy governor and sixteen directors. The BBC have seven governors in addition to the chairman and vice-chairman. Almost all the other boards have upper and lower limits of numbers within which the Minister has discretion. These minima and maxima follow no fixed rule. Thus, the boards of BOAC and British European Airways must have not less than five or more than eleven members in addition to the chairman; the British Transport Commission have a chairman and between four and fourteen other members; the Colonial Development Corporation have a board of between four and ten members, in addition to the chairman. The board of the Independent Television Authority consists of the chairman, deputy chairman, and from five to eight other members, though the maximum number is required unless the Postmaster-General notifies a lower number in writing to the Authority. The recently created Central Electricity Generating Board is composed of a chairman and between seven and nine other members, one or more of whom may be appointed deputy

[1] A memorandum prepared by Sir Winston Churchill's last Government on the Report of the Beveridge Committee on Broadcasting proposed that, in order to safeguard the BBC from the risk of being subordinated to political purposes, the power of appointing and removing the governors should be entrusted to a committee comprising the Speaker of the House of Commons, who would be the chairman, the Prime Minister, Leader of the Opposition, the Lord Chief Justice and the Lord President of the Court of Session (HMSO, Cmd. 8550/1952, para. 18). The draft Charter originally proposed by the Postmaster-General provided for such a committee, but when the Charter was finally granted it contained no mention of the committee, and under its provisions governors are appointed and removed, as hitherto, by Order in Council.

chairman. Each Electricity and Gas Area Board must consist of between six and eight members (including the chairman and deputy chairman), together with the chairman *ex officio* of the Consultative Council for the area. The Atomic Energy Authority has a board consisting of a chairman and between seven and ten other members.

The National Coal Board was originally defined rigidly as a chairman and eight other members, but an amending Act of 1949 converted the board into a flexible type by permitting the numbers to fluctuate between eight and eleven, in addition to the chairman. This higher maximum number was doubtless introduced to enable the Minister to strengthen the board without infringing the rights of the previously appointed members.

The actual size of the boards of the public corporations seems to be about right for effective discussion by all the members. They are somewhat smaller in most instances than the boards of the French nationalized industries, which were reduced by decree in May 1943, but enlarged again in December 1953. The boards of *Electricité de France*, *Gaz de France*, and *Charbonnages de France* have fifteen members; each of the *Houillères de Bassin* has a board of sixteen members, while the potash mines of Alsace have a board of twenty members.[1] On the other hand, the Tenessee Valley Authority and the Damodar Valley Corporation in India have boards consisting of only three members, which strikes me as too small to obtain sufficient diversity of outlook and experience for a comprehensive view of all the major aspects of policy.

Flexibility of numbers is undoubtedly an advantage in relation to a governing board. It may well be that the board of a public corporation will need more members, in order to include men or women possessing particular qualifications, at one period than another. Nationalized industries are not static in their requirements even at the highest level. There is no magic in a particular number, despite the incantations of certain efficiency experts; and it may often be worth while seizing the opportunity to appoint a man of unusual ability at the moment when he happens to be available. It is an advantage, then, for Ministers to have a certain latitude in determining the size of the board.

The Minister's power in this matter could also be used to overcome a recalcitrant or hostile board by swamping it with additional members; and I have argued elsewhere that the Government of the day should possess such a power.[2] But it is a power which should only be used for

[1] Décréts 1953—416, 417, 418, 419, 420 of May 11, 1953, Décréts 1247, 1248, 1249 and 1250 of December 17, 1953.

[2] W. A. Robson: 'The Public Service Board: General Conclusions' in *Public Enterprise*, ed. W. A. Robson (1937), p. 366.

this purpose in the last resort, for it may easily lead to disagreement, friction and resignations. Discordant elements cannot produce a harmonious and successful board; and it is of the utmost importance that service on these supreme organs of direction should not be discredited in the eyes of men of great ability who are able to pick and choose their work.

QUALIFICATIONS

We may consider now the qualifications of the members. The general policy of our legislation is to require the appropriate Minister to appoint persons whom he considers to have had wide experience and shown capacity in specified fields of activity. The types of experience which are called for vary somewhat between the corporations, but they nearly all include industrial, commercial or financial matters, administration, and the organization of workers. In the cases of the Atomic Energy Authority, the National Coal Board, the Central Electricity Generating Board, the Colonial Development Corporation, the Forestry Commission and some others, scientific attainments are mentioned. The boards of some corporations are to include men of experience and reputation in the industry concerned: this applies to the Transport Commission, the Central Electricity Generating Board, the Area Gas Boards and the Gas Council, and—since 1949—the National Coal Board. On the other hand, no specific qualifications are laid down for the directors of the Bank of England or the members of the airways corporations.

Members of the House of Commons are ineligible for membership of the vast majority of the boards.[1] This is a valuable safeguard.

A new form of geographical qualification has recently appeared which in one or two cases has the effect of ensuring representation on the board of Scotland, Wales, and Northern Ireland. The BBC charter of 1952 requires the appointment to the board of a national governor for each of these three countries.[2] Two members of the British Transport Commission are to be conversant with the circumstances and special require-

[1] See Forestry Act, 1945, s. 1 (3); Bank of England Act, 1946, Sch. II, para. 4 (a) (also excludes employee of Government Department paid out of moneys provided by Parliament); Coal Industry Nationalization Act, 1946, s. 2 (4); Transport Act, 1947, s. 1 (4); Electricity Act, 1947, s. 3 (4); Gas Act, 1948, s. 5 (5); Overseas Resources Development Act, 1948, Sch., para. 2; Air Corporations Act, 1949, Sch. I, para. 4; Sea Fish Industry Act, 1951, Sch. I, para 3; Iron and Steel Act, 1953, s. 2 (5); Atomic Energy Authority Act, 1954, s. 1 (5); Television Act, 1954, s. 1 (6) (also excludes Governor of BBC); Sugar Act, 1956, s. 2 (5). However, the BBC Charter contains no such bar.

[2] Art. 7 (3). A national governor is to be chosen 'in virtue of his knowledge of the culture, characteristics and affairs of Our People in Scotland, Wales or Northern Ireland, and his close touch with Scottish, Welsh or Northern Irish opinion'. Each national governor presides over a Broadcasting Council representing cultural, religious and other interests in the country concerned.

ments of Scotland, and the Secretary of State for Scotland is to be consulted about their appointment. This is a concession to the nationalist feeling in these countries; but it can have a certain administrative value in securing better service in them. It is a British version of the regional representation on many different types of public authority which is commonly found in Canada and the United States.

There can be no doubt that the first aim should be to get the ablest men available to run these great enterprises. This is unquestionably the right policy. The qualities most clearly needed on the governing board are drive, imagination, insight, and the capacity for grasping large questions of policy without becoming confused or absorbed by a mass of detail. Knowledge and experience are valuable, but they are less essential than good judgment and the ability to lead. Moreover, knowledge and experience must be of the right kind; and it does not necessarily follow that a man who has been successful as a civil servant or in business will also be successful in public enterprise.

The second requisite is that the board should embody the greatest possible unity of purpose. There is no magic formula for attaining this, but it is at least possible to avoid manifest errors. The boards of most of the French nationalized industries were originally composed on the tripartite principle, whereby a third of the members represent the State, and consist of high civil servants serving in various ministries or the *Conseil d'Etat*; a third represent the employees engaged in the industry; and a third the consumers, nominated by local authorities, trade associations, family associations, co-operative societies, trade unions, and a great variety of other organizations. The members of the board are not paid for their services in that capacity. All of them are part-time and continue to work as industrialists, trade union officials, civil servants, etc. while serving on the *conseil d'administration*. Their first allegiance is not to the nationalized industry but to the outside organizations they represent.

The tripartite method of composing the boards of the French nationalized industries has undergone several modifications. In some instances the three elements are not equally represented on the board. Thus the board of the Renault undertaking contains seven government representatives, two consumers' representatives, and six representatives of the employees. Sometimes there are not three elements but four or five which are represented on the board, as in the case of the Alsation potash mines, where there are representatives of the local authorities and former French shareholders in addition to the representatives of the government, employees, and consumers. A more important departure from the tripartite principle is the appointment of persons chosen for their special competence in industry, finance, etc. The boards of the nationalized banks and insurance companies, Paris Transport, the shipping lines, and the *Bureau de Recherches de Petrole*, included from the beginning some persons chosen on account of their knowledge or experience. But a modification in the law was introduced in 1953 to require an infusion of persons possessing special competence to be appointed to the boards of *Electricité de France*, *Gaz de France*, *Charbonnages de France*, and the several *Houillères de Bassin*, in place of the consumers' representatives.[1]

This system has tended to make the governing board of a French nationalized industry a meeting place of separate and conflicting interests rather than a coherent, closely-knit team whose members are united by the common desire to achieve the greatest possible efficiency and progress for the undertaking.

The conception of a board as the meeting place for the representatives of divergent interests is wholly mistaken. Similar considerations apply to proposals advanced by persons holding syndicalist or guild socialist views urging workers' control of publicly owned industry. There are a few advocates of direct representation of the employees or their trade unions on the board. They include some Labour MPs and the former Secretary of the National Union of Railwaymen.[2]

A prolonged discussion took place in the Trades Union Congress and within the Labour Party during the 1930s and again in the later stages of the Second World War concerning the direct representation of the workpeople on the board of a publicly owned industry. The Labour movement ultimately decided that it would be detrimental to the interests of the trade unions to have their representatives on the board sharing responsibility for decisions which might not be acceptable to their members and with which they might not themselves be in agreement. In consequence, although almost all of the boards of the nationalized industries contain trade union leaders of high reputation, they invariably resign their trade union posts on appointment, even as part-time members of a board. This serves to avoid conflict of interest.

A number of eminent civil servants have been appointed to the boards of public corporations. They include the late Sir Arthur Street, Sir Henry Self, Sir George Cribbett, Sir Arnold Overton, and Lord Hurcomb, who was chairman of the British Transport Commission. In every instance the individual concerned has retired from the civil service. When Sir George Cribbett was appointed deputy-chairman of BOAC some

[1] Decree of December 17, 1953. This modified an earlier Decree of May 11, 1953.

[2] See Mr Figgins's speech at the annual meeting of the TUC, 1949; Clive Jenkins: *British Airlines* (1953) (Fabian Research Series No. 158), pp. 12-13, and 29.

criticism was expressed in the House of Lords at a senior official going from a department responsible for a nationalized industry to a position on the board of a public corporation in close relationship with that department. Lord Pakenham went so far as to say that he felt it to be 'contrary to constitutional practice for a Minister to appoint to a leading position in one of the nationalized industries a man who has been one of his closest advisers. The practice is open to abuse'.[1] Lord Ogmore also said that in his view 'a senior civil servant should never be appointed to the board of one of the industries which he is controlling or helping to control, as a civil servant'.[2]

These contentions have little force. There is certainly nothing 'contrary to constitutional practice', for it was a Labour Minister of Transport who appointed Lord Hurcomb chairman of the British Transport Commission in 1947. But leaving aside this precendent, is there any merit in the argument that it is inherently undesirable to appoint civil servants of outstanding ability to the boards of public corporations with which they have had a close official relationship? The chief ground of objection is presumably that they will not be sufficiently independent of the Minister whom they have for long been serving, or that they will still be bound by an invisible umbilical cord to the department from which they come. Such a view shows slight understanding of the character and minds of our leading civil servants. Most of them are not only capable of being highly independent, but glad to be free of the day-to-day subjection to ministerial direction and Treasury control to which they have been liable for so long. Their intimate knowledge of departmental administration is more likely to enable them to send their former colleagues packing if they raise some technical objection or procedural difficulty to a course of action, than it is to induce an attitude of deference, simply because they know how easily these obstacles can be swept away in case of need. The value of outstanding civil servants to industrial and commercial undertakings is shown by the number of them who are invited to join the boards of large joint stock companies.

Full-time members of the public corporations are normally required to give up other appointments, though in exceptional cases they may be permitted to hold directorships in outside concerns. The part-time members are allowed to hold outside directorships which the Minister considers would not be likely to prejudice the discharge of their duties in relation to the nationalized industry.

[1] 497 HL Deb. 5s., col. 434 (May 15, 1956).

[2] *Ib.*, col. 410.

POLITICAL TESTS

The question is sometimes raised about the political sympathies of the members of a public corporation. Labour MPs criticized the Attlee Governments from time to time for not manning the boards with Labour supporters, and occasionally pressure was brought to bear on Ministers in this direction. Conservative Ministers, on the other hand, have on at least one occasion been criticized by the Opposition for appointing a chairman of pronounced Conservative views; and also for showing antipathy to the chairman of a board on account of his support for the Labour Party.[1]

The appointments to such important posts have political significance, but that does not imply that they should be made on political grounds. In my view the party politics of a candidate for office should be disregarded unless they are likely to interfere with his whole-hearted devotion to the job, to restrain the energy and enthusiasm which he will put into it, or to undermine the confidence of employees or the public. The major emphasis should be placed on ability, judgment, knowledge and experience. If appointments are made on political grounds, a spoils system is likely to come into existence which will weigh heavily against the national interest. Obviously one should not appoint a man who is known to be opposed to public enterprise to run a nationalized undertaking, but in conceding this we do not admit the case for introducing tests of political party loyalty. There is, however, a strong case against appointing former Members of Parliament to the boards of public corporations. This has happened in the case of both BOAC and BEA. A reasonable safeguard is contained in the Tennessee Valley Act, which requires that members of the corporation shall profess a belief in the feasibility and wisdom of the Act. I should like to see this condition applied to all our board appointments.

MINISTERIAL APPOINTMENT

The power of appointing the boards of public corporations should undoubtedly be in the hands of Ministers. The device of the Appointing Trustees introduced in the London Passenger Transport Act, 1933, was fantastic.[2] I am equally opposed to more recent proposals for an intermediate body of some kind, composed of eminent persons, of all parties

[1] See Mr G. R. Strauss's remarks about Mr Hardie, the chairman of the Iron and Steel Corporation. 496 HC Deb. 5s., cols. 782-3 (February 25, 1952).

[2] W. A. Robson: 'The Public Service Board: General Conclusions' in *Public Enterprise*, ed. W. A. Robson (1937), p. 367.

or of none, to act as an electoral college for the nationalized boards. Suggestions of this type spring from a distrust of democratic government. If Ministers are not fit to make such appointments, for what tasks are they likely to be fitted? If they are not so fitted, we had better change our system of government.

The Fleck Committee[1] recommended that the Minister, before appointing a chairman, deputy-chairman, or full-time member of the National Coal Board should seek the advice of the part-time members (four out of a total of twelve). As regards the part-time members, the Minister should appoint a panel to advise him consisting of the president of the Federation of British Industries, the chairman of the Trades Union Congress, the president of the British Employers' Confederation, and one or two other persons.

The first of these suggestions is very strange. It would give the part-time members a privileged position compared with that of the full-time members, who constitute a majority of the board, in that they would have a special right of access to the Minister on this matter denied to the others. It would tend to divide the board rather than unite it. It implies that the judgment of the part-time members concerning promotion to the highest positions is sounder than that of those members who are giving their whole time to the nationalized coal industry, and who therefore have contact with their colleagues on many other occasions than at board meetings. Moreover one would expect the full-time members to have a much wider and deeper knowledge of the leading executives and technical experts in the industry both at headquarters and in the divisions than the part-time members who may seldom or never come into personal contact with them. This proposal is therefore a most undesirable one.

A less objectionable proposal to the effect that the Minister should seek the advice of the board in selecting a new full-time member was recently made in a Labour Party pamphlet.[2] This pamphlet states that the Minister who appoints the chairman and members should have sufficient confidence in that board to ask their advice before making a new appointment. That may or may not be true: often the Minister in office was not responsible for any or some of the existing members. Again, even if he did appoint them he may not be satisfied with the result and in that event he will not have confidence in their advice. For these reasons it is a mistake to impose on Ministers any requirements about seeking advice, either from the board or any other quarter. Any Minister who has a

[1] *Report of the Advisory Committee on Organization* (1955) (National Coal Board), para. 67 (e).

[2] *Public Enterprise* (1957) (Labour Party), p. 28.

modicum of common sense will take great pains to scan the horizon as widely as possible in order to find the ablest men. It is best to leave him free to consult whoever he considers will give him the best advice.

Although the appointment of boards should be left to the unfettered discretion of Ministers, it does not follow that all the boards which have been appointed are or have been entirely satisfactory. Far from it. Many of the appointments have been conventional and unimaginative. Some Ministers have shown themselves unwilling to back their own judgment, if it means taking a risk, rather than to appoint men almost *ex officio*. They have too often been disposed to play for safety, to select men whose careers lie behind them, to choose reassuring names which would inspire confidence rather than to seek men with the promise of creative ability and dynamic energy.

SOURCES OF RECRUITMENT

Hitherto, with a few exceptions, the boards of most public corporations have included men with a variety of experience and with widely differing backgrounds. They have contained business men, managers and industrialists, former civil servants, ex-trade union officials, an air marshall and a general, engineers, scientists, leading figures from the co-operative movement, former diplomats, journalists and newspaper proprietors, university professors and a vice-chancellor, accountants and financial experts. This catholicity of occupation was inevitable and desirable in a period of transition. During the past decade the field of choice was necessarily limited to men who had achievements to their credit in industry or commerce under private enterprise, or in other walks of life. Only in the case of the early appointments to the British Transport Commission and its several Executives was it assumed that nearly all the key posts should go to the men holding similar posts prior to nationalization. That this was a questionable assumption is shown by the fact that of all the nationalized industries the railways made least progress under these arrangements.

Many of the new men who will direct the public corporations in the future will have been trained and grown up in nationalized industry itself. We must nevertheless take care not to apply this principle too rigidly or too soon.

Several weighty statements have been made recently stressing the desirability of appointing men from inside the industry to the full-time posts on the board. Lord Simon of Wythenshawe writes that all, or very nearly all, board appointments should consist of men who have been trained and gained their experience within the industry. This, he adds, is almost the general practice in successful commercial companies.[1] The Fleck Committee considered that the direction of the coal industry must be largely in the hands of men with experience in the industry; they recommended that most of the full-time members of the board should be drawn from within the industry.[2] The Labour Party's policy pamphlet *Public Enterprise* said that full-time members of the board should be selected so far as possible from within the industries concerned. They want a *carrière ouvert aux talents* to permit every worker to rise to the top; but they expressly leave open the board room door for 'men with outside experience and a fresh approach'.[3]

A major industry ought to be able to produce its own top executives; and most successful industries can do so. I would therefore not question for a moment the desirability of making the nationalized industries self-supporting in this sense. But I think there is something to be said on the other side at any rate so far as coal and railways are concerned. These two industries had been suffering from serious mismanagement under private enterprise for about thirty years. They had been going downhill from almost every point of view. Backward technology and equipment, under-investment, a neglect of research, the extravagant use of manpower, a failure to recruit able young men from the universities, and a decline in the relative earnings of the workers, have been the causes and the consequences of decline. The railway managements were suffering from severe inbreeding; while the coalmining industry in 1945 contained few, if any, leaders of national stature.

In such circumstances I believe the most urgent need has been and still is to attract into these industries as many men of real ability as possible from other occupations. Brains and trained intelligence are wanted above everything else. The practices of highly successful commercial undertakings like ICI and Unilever and Shell are not relevant at this stage, because they have staffs on which to draw for their directors and top executives both more numerous and of higher calibre than the human resources available in coalmining and on the railways. I would therefore look with caution on proposals that all full-time appointments to the board should from now onwards be made from men already in the nationalized industry concerned. We should certainly work towards that goal; but we cannot safely assume that we have already reached it.

I wish to add a further qualification to the view that a lifetime's service in one industry is necessarily the best background for the full-time members of the board. Nationalized industry is still a very new sphere

[1] *The Boards of Nationalized Industries* (1957), p. 29.
[2] Report, para. 68.
[3] *Public Enterprise* (1957) (Labour Party), p. 28.

of activity; it has no traditions and a vast amount of diverse experimentation is taking place in many different directions. There is much to be said for encouraging mobility among the public corporations, so that the managing personnel can obtain some experience of several nationalized industries. The present tendency appears to be rather in the opposite direction. One hears of gentlemen's understandings between the corporations not to take each other's men. Restrictive practices of this kind are against the public interest. They are quite common in private industry and commerce, where they are no less detrimental.

It is essential that ambitious men should be attracted to the nationalized industries by the knowledge that those with sufficient ability can become members of the governing board. It is equally important that no one should assume that the board will be recruited entirely from inside the industry and resentful if it is not. Ministers should never be in a position in which they feel apologetic or on the defensive in seeking members elsewhere. The virtues of cross fertilization between the higher levels of the nationalized industries should receive special attention.

But even if there are opportunities for gaining wide experience in nationalized industry, there will remain a need for having some members who have worked in different fields. Consultants in scientific management, men who have organized great factories, civil engineers who have built great works at home or abroad, outstanding economists or technologists, these are among the men who might make their contribution.

A FUNCTIONAL OR POLICY BOARD?

There has been much discussion in recent years on the respective merits of the functional board, composed entirely of full-time members in charge of particular branches of the work, and the policy board, which contains both part-time and full-time members, none of whom are responsible for specialized functions as executive heads of departments.

The experience of the National Coal Board in this matter is instructive. It was established in 1946 with nine members all serving on a full-time basis. All but one of the members had special knowledge of a particular aspect of the industry, or one which was in future to be developed; and each of them took charge of an executive department, such as production, marketing, finance, manpower and welfare, labour relations, and scientific research.[1] The same principle was applied to the Divisional Boards.

In November 1948 the National Coal Board published the main recommendations of a committee they had set up to review the board's

[1] *National Coal Board Annual Report 1946*, HMSO, HC 174/1947-8, para. 3.

organization, together with a statement of the action they proposed to take on them.[1] This followed the resignation of Sir Charles Reid from the National Coal Board owing to disagreement on how the industry should be organized. The chairman of the committee was Sir Robert Burrows, a prominent coal owner who later became a member of the board; the other members were Sir Charles Renold, chairman of the British Institute of Management, and Sir Mark Hodgson, a trade union leader.

The Burrows Committee advised that the National Board should be enlarged by adding a second deputy-chairman and up to three part-time members. This advice was adopted and is embodied in the Coal Industry Act, 1949. They also recommended that the divisional chairmen should become members of the National Board. Apart from the disadvantage of a board of nineteen members, the National Coal Board saw other objections to this proposal. It would confuse the chain of responsibility, since the Divisional Boards are appointed by, and responsible to, the National Board. It would lead away from the aim of increasing the proportion of members 'free from functional responsibilities and able to concentrate on wide issues of national concern'—a significant remark. It would intensify the difficulty of deciding between the rival claims of the several coalfields in regard to such matters as capital development, wage and price policy, etc. It would weaken the responsibility of the divisions and lead to greater centralization, because the divisional chairmen would tend to become 'headquarters' managing directors with responsibility for particular coalfields and would more and more discuss their local problems round the National Board table'. For these reasons the National Coal Board rejected the proposal.

The third recommendation of the Burrows Committee was that board members in charge of functional departments, while retaining responsibility for their departments, should leave executive action to their chief officials. The Board agreed with this advice and pointed out that only four of the nine members still had departmental responsibilities. In their Annual Report for 1948 the NCB gave a reasoned explanation of their somewhat ambivalent attitude on this matter. The need to associate those at national headquarters who have to carry out the board's decisions with the process of making them, affects the top organization. Under the earlier arrangements described above, the head of each operating department sat on the board and helped to determine policy. This purely functional type of board was necessitated by the fact that until a staff had been assembled there was no one except the members who could get on with the job of organizing the departments.

[1] *Committee on Organization: Statement by the National Coal Board*, November 19, 1948.

Apart from this ground of expediency, reasons of principle were advanced in favour of a functional board. The experience of the Board of Admiralty, the Army Council, the Air Council, the Post Office Board, and Mr Winston Churchill's preference as war-time Premier for dealing with chiefs of organizations rather than counsellors without executive responsibility, were all cited in support of the earlier pattern of the NCB. Nevertheless, the disadvantage was admitted that the members might be so concentrated on their purely departmental duties that they would be unable to take a broad and comprehensive view of general policy concerning the whole industry.

But the policy board, observed the NCB, also has its drawbacks. If its members consist only of non-specialist administrators, there is a danger that technical advice may be rejected by men who do not understand its nature. If they do have specialized knowledge, they must either take 'a day-to-day interest in the doings of specialist departments, in which case the board would be "functional" in fact if not in name, or there would be nothing for them to do except get in each other's way'.[1]

In the end, the board decided to introduce 'a blend of departmental and non-departmental functions such as are found in latter-day Cabinets'.[2] Part-time members were appointed without departmental functions and only four members of the board retained executive responsibilities.

Some confusion seems to have occurred in the early days between the desirability of having on the board men with specialized knowledge of the highly complex and technical coal industry, and the entirely separate issue of placing those men in charge of executive departments of the headquarters organization.

The Fleck Committee, which reported in 1955, considered at length the composition of the board. They advised that it should consist of a full-time chairman and deputy-chairman, six other full-time members and four part-time members.[3] The chairman and deputy-chairman should have no routine duties other than those of presiding at meetings of the board or its executive committees. Their task would be to keep a general watch over the work of headquarters and the more important items of work being carried out in the field. They would maintain high level con-

[1] *National Coal Board Annual Report 1948*, HMSO, HC 187/1948-9, para. 432.

[2] *Ib.*, para. 434.

[3] Dr Fleck himself advised that a larger Board of eighteen members should be appointed. He wanted two deputy chairmen, three additional full-time members with special responsibility for liaison between the NCB and the Divisional Boards, six full-time members with special responsibilities concerning the work of particular departments, and six part-time members instead of four: they might include two with trade union experience, two with wide administrative experience, and two eminent technologists with experience in fields other than mining. See Report: addendum, pp. 80-1.

tacts with Ministers and their departments, and make senior appointments, subject to the approval of the board. They would be responsible for initiating the larger issues of policy.

'It is essential', the Fleck Committee declared, 'that all members of the board should be capable of taking a wide view on all the issues which the board have to decide. This quality must not only be present, it must be exercised all the time. Nevertheless, a full-time board member can and should be given a field of responsibility and interest, of which he should have greater and more detailed knowledge than the board as a whole can have.'[1] But, they said, the full-time member should not be regarded as the head of the department or departments concerned with the matters falling within his field of responsibility. Each department would have an executive head who would be responsible for its day-to-day management. The duty of the board member would be limited to ensuring that a clear policy is laid down to cover the whole work of the departments coming within his sphere of interest, and that this is revised whenever necessary. He would also have to be satisfied with the organization, staffing and progress of such departments.[2]

The model which the Fleck Committee had in mind is the type of board found in many large commercial companies today, in which the chairman, deputy-chairman and most of the other members of the board serve as full-time employees and are often called Executive Directors, although they are not normally the heads of departments. This structure exists even when the board is a policy board. The Fleck Committee considered it to be the proper model for the coal industry, and it is the system they found to exist on the National Coal Board, although they suggested a more comprehensive application of it by giving every full-time member (except the chairman or the deputy-chairman) a defined sphere of responsibility, and allocating each of the board's main functions to one of its full-time members.[3] The board was promptly reorganized on the lines recommended in the Fleck Report.[4]

The Fleck Committee rejected explicitly the alternative model of a board composed mostly of well-known personalities who devote only a small part of their time to the business of the board, leaving the day-to-day decisions to one or more general managers who are not members of the board. This is the system favoured by Lord Reith, who enjoyed a position of unrivalled dominance as Director-General of the BBC from 1927 to 1938.[5]

[1] Report, para. 49.
[2] *Ib.*, paras. 52-60.
[3] *National Coal Board Annual Report 1955*, HMSO, HC 263-I/1955-6, Vol. I, para. 51.
[4] *Ib.*, paras 5 and 117. See also *The Times*, February 17, 1955, p. 8.
[5] Lord Reith: 'Public Corporations', *The Times*, July 3, 1956, p. 11.

THE GOVERNORS OF THE BBC

For some reason which has never been revealed the Director-General of the BBC, who is not a member of the board, has always enjoyed an exceptionally strong position in relation to the chairman and the governors. Neither the chairman or any of the governors has ever had a full-time appointment; and their salaries are far lower than those of comparable public corporations. It had long been the practice to send governors a letter of appointment, known as the Whitley Document, defining their responsibilities as 'general and not particular' and their functions as being 'not executive'.

The Beveridge Committee on Broadcasting thought the governors of the BBC occupied a position different from that of the board of any other nationalized industry. There is not and should not be a Minister authorized to give directions to the British Broadcasting Corporation. In consequence, they recommended that the position of the governors in relation to the staff of the BBC should resemble that of a Minister in relation to his department: in short, the board should have unquestionable authority over the staff in any matter whatsoever, whether of detail or of policy, though in practice the day-to-day work of the staff would proceed without interference. The Beveridge report urged that the Whitley Document should disappear and the tradition against specialization which is derived from it should be abandoned. The position of the governors should be laid down in the BBC's charter. The governors, although remaining part-time, should be expected to devote more time than hitherto to the business of the BBC and should be paid more. The board should be free to invite individual governors to look into particular aspects of the undertaking and advise on specific problems.[1] The chairman should attend meetings of the Board of Management, which is a weekly meeting of the Director-General and directors, and have the power to require any matter under consideration to be referred to the board.[2] The Government accepted the recommendation that the Whitley Document should be withdrawn, and declared that within the framework of the charter the governors collectively would have unrestricted authority and power of decision.[3] The position of the governors is not, however, laid down in the charter as the Beveridge Committee had recommended.

Lord Simon of Wythenshawe, who served as chairman of the BBC for

[1] HMSO, Cmd. 8116/1951, paras. 209, 556, 575, 576, and 577.

[2] *Ib.*, p. 581.

[3] *Memorandum on the Report of the Broadcasting Committee*, HMSO, Cmd. 8550/1952, para. 17.

five years, has declared that the Director-General has been too powerful and the governors not powerful enough. Neither the chairman nor the other members of the board were in his experience sufficiently informed or active enough to give their most efficient service.[1]

This is the system which Lord Reith defends and praises. 'Performance depends in the main on one individual properly institutionalized from above and with an efficient executive system below.'[2] This one individual on whom everything depends should not be a member of the board; nor should there be a full-time chairman, since he becomes 'automatically' chief executive, and if there is anyone else called chief executive they will get in each other's way. 'Of course', he writes, 'the board can be composed of whole-time functional experts—which means no board at all in the ordinary sense: nothing between executives and public; no *custodes*.'[3] He contrasts this with the part-time system, in which all the members are 'men of experience and stature, commanding confidence. Controlling policy, supervising, watching, they stand back from the conduct of affairs, delegating heavily *de facto* to their chief executive and the executive system'.[4] This is a highly idealized version of a system in which the governors can be frequently impotent in face of a strong-willed Director-General.

THE EMERGING PATTERN

The pattern which is emerging in the nationalized industries (other than the BBC) is that of a mixed board composed of full-time and part-time members; in which the full-time members have special responsibilities without being heads of departments; while the part-time members are men of wide experience brought in from outside the industry in order to look at its problems with a more detached view.[5]

The Atomic Energy Authority, for example, has a board of eight members, of whom five (including the chairman) are full-time. Apart from the chairman, the full-time personnel comprises a member for

[1] Lord Simon of Wythenshawe: *The BBC from Within* (1953), pp. 72-4.

[2] Lord Reith: *op. cit.*

[3] *Ib.*

[4] The great sincerity with which Lord Reith holds the views described above is shown by his disinterested action as chairman of the Colonial Development Corporation. When he was appointed the chairman was full-time and acted as chief executive. Lord Reith, with his colleagues' approval, secured the Colonial Secretary's approval to a separation of the two posts. From October 1, 1953 he became part-time chairman at a lower salary, and a general manager was appointed to be chief executive. *Colonial Development Corporation Annual Report 1953*, HMSO, HC 148/1953-4, p. 7.

[5] *Report of the Advisory Committee on Organization* (1955) (National Coal Board), paras. 56-7.

scientific research, a member for engineering and production, a member for weapons research and development, and a member for finance and administration. The chairman and full-time members form a committee known as the Atomic Energy Executive.[1] Here the balance between full-time and part-time members seems to be well adjusted, but on some of the boards the golden mean has been or is lacking.

On the former Central Electricity Authority (now abolished by the Electricity Act, 1957) only the chairman and two deputy-chairmen out of a board of nine members had full-time appointments, and in practice the business of the authority was run mainly by these three men assisted by the chief officers.[2] In consequence the Herbert Committee found they were 'so heavily burdened with important day-to-day tasks and attendance at meetings that they have insufficient time to sit back and consider wider questions of policy and development'.[3] The British Transport Commission seems also since its reconstruction to have too large a proportion of part-time members, since eight out of fourteen fall into this category. Formerly, all its members except one were full-time. Six full-time directors for so large an undertaking as the British Transport Commission operates seems quite inadequate when one considers the huge modernization plan which is now being carried out. The London Transport Executive erred in the opposite direction in having only one part-time member in a board of six. The Chambers Committee recommended that the number of part-time members should not be less than two, since their experience in spheres other than transport enables them to make a valuable contribution to the determination of broad policy.[4]

The emerging pattern is becoming generally accepted as the right method of composing the board of a nationalized industry, subject of course to an intelligent discrimination being exercised in the manner of its application. The modern board is unquestionably intended to be a policy board in the sense that all its members must be able to understand, to discuss, and to share in the determination of policy concerning all matters coming to the boardroom. But the full-time members will also have defined spheres of executive responsibility although they will definitely not be heads of departments or in charge of day-to-day administration. 'I think it right', said Mr Herbert Morrison during a parliamentary debate on the Transport Bill, 1952, 'that there should be an element of full-time and part-time members, the latter bringing in

[1] *Atomic Energy Authority Annual Report 1954-5*, HC 95/1955-6, paras. 12-13.

[2] *Report of the Committee of Inquiry into the Electricity Supply Industry*, HMSO Cmd. 9672/1956, paras. 52-3, and 240.

[3] *Ib.*, para. 239.

[4] *Report of the Committee of Inquiry into London Transport*, HMSO (1955), para. 340.

experience from outside to prevent the Commission becoming too monastic and to bring a breath of fresh air into the Commission's proceedings from outside. I regard it as the duty of the part-time members to be critical of the administration, including the full-time members.'[1]

REMUNERATION

The remuneration paid to members of the boards is obviously a matter of considerable importance. If men of the highest ability are to be attracted to the nationalized industries—and ability should be regarded as the crucial test of eligibility—generous salaries must be paid to members of the governing boards. They should compare favourably with the salary scale for the top civil servants, since the latter enjoy a life tenure followed by a pension, which is not usually offered to board members of a public corporation or similar body.[2] The remuneration should, moreover, be sufficient to make it possible to secure the services of leading industrialists or business men, though this does not necessarily mean that salary scales must be as high as in private enterprise.

Both the Herbert Committee and the Fleck Committee recommended that the salaries of chairmen and members of the board should be substantially increased. The Labour Party has made a similar statement.[3] The then existing salaries were not only inadequate in relation to the responsibilities of the posts and the status which board members should have, but they had the effect of depressing the salary scales which were paid to managerial and technical personnel, since these were fixed by the board with some relation to their own remuneration.[4] The Herbert Committee described the remuneration of £500 a year paid to part-time members of the Central Electricity Authority as 'almost derisory'.

The salaries of the members of public corporations were not in most cases unreasonably low when they were originally fixed. The deplorable feature has been the persistent refusal of successive Ministers to increase these salaries during a period of continuous inflation; or to recognize the adverse effect which these static scales were bound to have on the ability of the nationalized industries to recruit and hold technologists, scientists and other types of highly qualified staff at a time of acute shortage of such personnel. The reluctance of Ministers to raise

[1] 509 HC Deb. 5s., cols. 1707 ff. (December 18, 1952).

[2] But as to the future see *post* p. 240.

[3] *Public Enterprise* (1957) (Labour Party), p. 28.

[4] *Report of the Advisory Committee on Organization* (1955) (National Coal Board), paras. 76 and 78; *Report of the Committee of Inquiry into the Electricity Supply Industry*, HMSO, Cmd. 9672/1956, paras. 312-4.

board salaries has doubtless been due in large part to their fear of the political and economic consequences which might follow, at a time when they have been urging the trade unions to restrain wage demands and companies to keep down dividends and prices. Moreover, it must in justice be added that Ministers' own salaries have not risen since before the War and have even been subject to voluntary reductions. But when due allowance has been made for these factors, the policy of allowing the real remuneration of the members of the public corporations to decline year by year with the progress of inflation was entirely mistaken and should never have occurred. A half-hearted effort has been made recently to rectify the position; but the purchasing power of the augmented salary paid to the chairmen of the largest public corporations is, after deduction of tax, substantially lower than that paid to their predecessors in 1947.[1] Furthermore, the important question is: will it occur again? In my opinion it is almost certain to recur not once but repeatedly, unless some objective method is established of systematically reviewing the remuneration of the top personnel on whom so much depends. The Treasury has recently appointed a Standing Advisory Committee on the pay of the Higher Civil Service. There is a strong case for setting up a similar body to advise the Government on the remuneration of members of the boards of public corporations.

Lord Simon of Wythenshawe[2] has recently urged that the salaries, pensions and expense allowances of members of the great nationalized industries should be at the very least comparable with those paid to the chairmen and directors of the leading commercial firms. We do not know in any detail what the latter receive, as only the total remuneration paid to all the directors is published in the accounts of joint stock companies. But it is clearly very large; and it raises the question whether public opinion would tolerate such salaries being paid to men whom most people regard as being public servants. The difficulty is partly due to the much lower remuneration paid to Ministers, top civil servants, judges and other people of great ability and wide experience. The salaries of judges has never been raised anywhere near the level of the most successful barristers. The nearest equivalent to commercial rates was the £12,500 a year paid to Lord Ashfield as chairman, and £10,000 a year paid to Sir Frank Pick as vice-chairman, of the London Passenger Transport Board when it was first set up in 1934; and this gave rise to considerable criticism.

The high salaries paid by large companies to their chairman and

[1] Lord Simon of Wythenshawe: *The Boards of Nationalized Industries* (1957), p. 32.

[2] *Ib.*, p. 44.

executive directors form part of their insignia of office. They are mainly emblems of status and of authority; and when tax and surtax have been deducted from them, they have a very different look. High salaries would lose some of their political overtones if Ministers were to publish not only the gross figures but also the net sum after deduction of tax on certain specified assumptions.

I do not agree with the view expressed in the Herbert Report and echoed in a recent Labour Party pamphlet[1] that the only criterion to be considered is whether the salary scales are equated with those obtaining in private enterprise. A matter of equal or greater importance is to prevent vast disparities arising between the standards of pay applicable to the boards of public corporations and those prevailing in the highest ranks of the civil service; for this would lead to discontent and jealousy in the civil service leading to an ultimate decline—a disastrous development. After all, the nationalized industries form part of the public service; and the public service can still attract men for non-monetary motives. Prestige, power, the desire to serve the nation, public esteem, status and honours can all play a part in lending a certain lustre to the highest posts in the public service. They play an important part in attracting men of great ability to the civil service, parliamentary life and ministerial office, to the judiciary, to serve on royal commissions and departmental committees, and to other activities. They can play an equally important part in inducing men and women to serve on such bodies as the Atomic Energy Authority or the airways corporations or the National Coal Board.

Details of the salaries paid to members of the boards are given in the table on pages 234–5. They vary according to the size and importance attributed to the undertaking. The items which call for comment are, first, the miserable remuneration paid to the chairman, vice-chairman, and governors of the BBC. The Beveridge Committee recommended that these should be raised[2] but the Government decided to continue the previous levels in the 1952 Charter.[3] The chairman's and vice-chairman's salaries (£3,000 and £1,000 respectively) were fixed in 1926 and have not been raised since then. The governors' salaries were fixed in 1926 at £700; in 1936 they were raised to £1,000; and in 1946 they were lowered to £600. They have remained at this level since 1946. The reason given for this niggardly policy was that the existing salaries were sufficient to secure people of high quality. In the next place, the

[1] *Public Enterprise* (1957) (Labour Party), p. 27.

[2] To £4,000 for the chairman, to £2,000 for each of the national governors, and £1,000 for the others. *Report of the Broadcasting Committee 1949*, HMSO Cmd. 8116/1951, para. 576.

[3] Except that the national governors for Scotland and Wales receive £1,000.

remuneration offered to the chairman and deputy chairman of BEA and BOAC appears unduly low. Why should they receive substantially less than the chairman, deputy-chairman and full-time members of the British Transport Commission? One would like to know if the question of remuneration played any part in the resignation of Sir Miles Thomas from the chairmanship of BOAC, Mr Whitney Straight from his position as a full-time board member and chief executive of BOAC, and Mr Peter Masefield as board member and chief executive of BEA.

TENURE OF OFFICE

I turn lastly to the question of tenure of office. This is one of the most difficult issues concerning the boards of public corporations, no matter from what standpoint it is considered. The boards are clearly intended to be non-political, in the sense that they do not form part of the government of the day, and the members do not resign when there is a change of government. The desire to separate the administration of nationalized industries and services from the Executive was, indeed, one of the principal causes which produced the public corporation.

Members of the board of a public corporation are appointed for a fixed term of years and the tenure of individual members is often staggered in order to preserve an element of continuity. The legislation is not uniform. Some of the statutes provide that members of the board are to hold and vacate their office in accordance with the terms of the instruments of appointment; there is sometimes a proviso that no term shall exceed five years.[1] Other Acts empower the Minister to make regulations with respect to the appointment of, and the tenure and vacation of office by, members of the board. The regulations provide for a term 'not exceeding five years as may be determined by the Minister before the appointment of such member, and upon such conditions as may be determined by the Minister . . .'[2] All members are permitted to resign,

[1] Forestry Act, 1945, s. 1 (1); New Towns Act, 1946, Sch. II, para. 2; Transport Act, 1947, s. 1 (3); Air Corporations Act, 1949, Sch., para. 1; Atomic Energy Authority Act, 1954, s. 1 (4); Sugar Act, 1956, s. 2 (4). (No time limit). Bank of England Act, 1946, Sch. II, paras. 1 and 2; Sea Fish Industry Act, 1951, Sch. I, para. 2; BBC Charter, 1952, art. 7 (1); Iron and Steel Act, 1953, s. 2 (4); Television Act, 1954, s. 1 (4). (Five year limit); four years for directors of Bank of England.

[2] Coal Industry Nationalization (National Coal Board) Regulations, 1946 (SR & O 1946 No. 1094), reg. 1; Electricity (Central Authority and Area Boards) Regulations, 1947 (S. I 1947 No. 1750 as amended by S. I 1957 No. 1382), reg. 1 (1); Gas (Area Boards and Gas Council) Regulations, 1948 (S. I 1948 No. 2233 as amended by S. I 1948 No. 2465), reg. 1 (1); Colonial Development Corporation Regulations, 1948 (S. I 1948 No. 292), reg. 1.

SALARIES AND ALLOWANCES OF MEMBERS OF PUBLIC BOARDS

(as at November 1, 1957)

Board	*Chairman*	*Deputy Chairman*	*Members Full-time*	*Members Part-time*	*Allowances*
	£	£	£	£	
Atomic Energy Authority ...	10,000	—	7,500 (5)	1,000[1] (5)	Expenses reimbursed
Bank of England	2,000[2]	1,500[2]	500[2] (4)	500 (12)	Expenses reimbursed
British Broadcasting Corporation	3,000*	1,000*	—	600[3] (4)	Expenses reimbursed
British European Airways Corpn.	7,500	2,000[4]*	6,000 (1)	1,000–3,500[5] (6)	£1,000 Chairman
British Overseas Airways Corpn.	5,000*	7,500	(1)[6]	1,000[6,7] (6)	£1,000 Chairman; £500 Deputy Chairman
British Transport Commission	10,000	8,000	7,500(5)	1,000(8)	£4,000 for Commission as a whole
London Transport Executive	7,500	5,500	5,000 (3)	1,000 (3)	
Cable and Wireless	3,500*	—	4,000 (2)	Unpaid–(2)[8] 1,000(1)	Up to £350 Chairman; up to £200 one Managing Director (i.e. full-time member); up to £150 the other
Colonial Development Corpn....	5,250*	1,500*	—	1,000[9] (6)	Up to £2,000 for the Board as a whole
Electricity Council	10,000	7,500[10] (2)	7,000 (1)	1,000(1) Unpaid(15)[11]	Expenses reimbursed
Generating Board	10,000	7,500	7,000 (4)	1,000 (4)	
Area Boards	6,500	5,000	—	1,000[12] (70)	

North of Scotland Hydro-Electric Board	Unpaid*	Unpaid*	—	1,000[13] (6)	Up to £1,500 for Board as a whole
South of Scotland Electricity Board	7,500	6,000	—	1,000[14] (6)	
Forestry Commission	3,000*	—	—	Unpaid (9)	Expenses reimbursed
Gas Council	8,500	7,500	—	Unpaid[15]	£1,000 Chairman; £500 Deputy Chairman
Area Boards	6,500	5,000	4,000 (9)	1,000[12] (61)	£500 Chairman; £400 Deputy Chairman; a further allowance not exceeding £600 is available at the discretion of the Chairman of each Gas Board for the use of members
Herring Industry Board ...	3,000*	—	—	1,000 (2)	—
Independent Television Authority	3,000*	1,000*	—	500 (8)	Up to £500 Chairman; up to £250 Vice-Chairman; up to £150 other members
Iron & Steel Holding and Realization Agency	2,000*	—	—	1,000 (4)	Expenses reimbursed
National Coal Board	10,000	8,000	7,500 (6)	1,000 (4)	£1,000 Chairman; £500 Vice-Chairman; £500 each full-time member. A further sum not exceeding £5,000 is available for use at the discretion of the Chairman to meet the Board's entertainment expenses
New Towns Corporations ...	1,700* (11)	750* (11)	—	400* (57)	—
Sugar Board	5,000	3,500	—	Unpaid (2)	Expenses reimbursed
White Fish Authority	3,500	3,000	—	1,000–2,000[16] (3)	£50 for Authority as a whole

Notes overleaf

NOTES TO TABLE SHOWING SALARIES AND ALLOWANCES OF MEMBERS OF PUBLIC BOARDS

Source: Cmd. 332/1957, with the exception of the figures relating to the Bank of England, the BBC, the Forestry Commission, the ITA, and the New Towns Corporations. These figures were obtained from the Financial Secretary to the Treasury.

* Part-time.

[1] One member does not draw his salary.

[2] These members receive in addition remuneration in respect of their exclusive services to the Bank at such rates as the Directors determine. The Bank refuse to disclose this remuneration.

[3] In addition, there are three National Governors who are paid £1,000.

[4] Salary not drawn.

[5] Two £1,000; two £1,500; one £2,000; one £3,500. One salary of £1,500 and one of £1,000 are not drawn. Members paid £1,500 and above are engaged on special duties.

[6] The White Paper (p. 5) does not give the salaries of the full-time members, nor the salary of one part-time member, stating: 'Remuneration for full-time executive appointment has been determined by the Corporation.' The Air Corporations Act, 1949, Sch. I, para. 10, provides: 'If any member of the Corporation, other than the chairman or deputy chairman thereof, is employed about the affairs of the Corporation otherwise than as a member thereof, the Corporation may pay to that member such remuneration (in addition to any remuneration to which he may be entitled in respect of his office as a member) as the Corporation may determine.' The same curious provision is contained in the Civil Aviation Act, 1946, Sch. I, para. 10. Its origin is the British Overseas Airways Act, 1939, s. 1 (6): 'The Corporation may pay to the chief executive member thereof, in respect of his office as such, such remuneration (in addition to any remuneration to which he may be entitled in respect of his office as a member) as the Corporation may determine.' No other nationalization Act contains such a provision; and it is to be noted that BEA's chief executive is paid wholly *qua* board member and not *qua* chief executive, even though BEA are in the same position in this regard as BOAC. BOAC refuse to disclose the salaries paid to these three members.

[7] One member is unpaid.

[8] One £1,000; two unpaid.

[9] £500 only of one salary drawn.

[10] Previously, a part-time Deputy Chairman received £2,000.

[11] Other members are the Chairmen of the Generating and Area Boards, and two members of the Generating Board.

[12] Plus Chairmen of Consultative Councils, who receive £1,500.

[13] Plus Chairman of Consultative Council who receives £1,500. However, only £1,250 is drawn.

[14] Plus Chairman of Consultative Council, who receives £1,500, together with a fee of £500 for special duties.

[15] Members are Chairmen of Area Boards.

[16] One £1,000; two £2,000. The five members (all part-time) of the Committee for Scotland and Northern Ireland each receive £1,000.

and most members are eligible for reappointment.[1] Sometimes Treasury approval is needed for the conditions of appointment.[2] But the important point is that during the fixed period of office the Minister usually has power to terminate the appointment at any time.[3]

The statutes and regulations which thus seem to give a substantial degree of security of tenure to the governing boards nevertheless confer on the appropriate Minister the power to dismiss any member who becomes in his opinion 'unfit to continue in office or incapable of performing his duties'. The exact meaning of these words is open to doubt. They clearly cover not only physical or mental incapacity, but also moral disabilities of the more obvious kind, such as a conviction for a disgraceful crime. Thus, the chairman of the Yorkshire Electricity Board was dismissed by the Minister of Fuel and Power after he had been convicted of serious offences relating to building licences for the headquarters accommodation of the board.

The real question is whether the Minister can dismiss a board member at pleasure owing to disagreement with his policy, dislike of his personality, or disbelief in his ability. We know that Mr Strachey, when he was Minister of Food in the Labour Government, dismissed two members of the Overseas Food Corporation because the groundnuts scheme was turning out badly and proved to be much more costly than was shown by the estimates. One of these (Mr Wakefield) refused to resign on the ground that the board as a whole were responsible for all the decisions which had been taken. The other member, who was responsible for finance, was dismissed because sufficient headway had not been made to overcome the accounting difficulties.[4]

[1] It is strange that the regulations dealing with appointment to the National Coal Board (SR & O 1946 No. 1094) and the Colonial Development Corporation (s. 1 1948 No. 292) contain no reappointment provision. No present member of the NCB has been reappointed (although past members have been), but four members of the CDC—Sir Hugh Beaver, Sir Nutcombe Hume, Lord Macdonald of Gwaenysgor, and Lord Reith—have served on the board for longer than five years. It is therefore possible that a Court might hold the CDC board to be illegally constituted. Both the NCB Regulations (reg. 8) and the Overseas Resources Development Act, 1948 (Sch., para. 4) provide that a defect in appointment shall not affect the validity of an action of the board. But, first, these provisions go to the validity of the board's actions and not to its composition; second, there is a difference between a defect in appointment (usually of a formalistic nature) and no appointment at all: see *Morris* v. *Kanssen* [1946] AC 459.

[2] To the National Coal Board, the Electricity Council and Boards, and the Gas Council and Boards.

[3] There is no provision for termination in the Transport Act, 1947, or in the Atomic Energy Authority Act, 1954. But the instrument of appointment to the BTC makes it clear that the Minister has the power of dismissal. The instrument of appointment to the AEA is presumably the same in effect.

[4] See the exchange of letters printed in *The Times*, November 21, 1949; also 470 HC Deb. 5s., cols. 36 ff. (November 21, 1949).

After the general election of 1950 Mr Maurice Webb succeeded Mr Strachey as Minister of Food. Shortly afterwards Mr Webb announced that he had 'agreed' with Sir Leslie Plummer that he should relinquish the chairmanship of the Overseas Food Corporation. Having regard to the terms of his appointment for a period of seven years, compensation was paid to him for the curtailment of his tenure of office. The sum paid was £8,000 in respect of an unexpired period of four years and eight months at £5,000 a year.[1]

This incident was disquieting because it showed that members of this now defunct corporation, engaged in a particularly difficult enterprise, the results of which were uncertain, were in a precarious position personally, and that the vicissitudes of political life could affect their status and tenure. This would diminish the attractiveness of service on the board and tend to narrow the circle of outstanding men likely to be willing to accept appointment. It also showed that the regulations which seemed to give a fixed tenure for a specific period, subject to good health and conduct, do not really do so.

The line between resignation and dismissal can be a very narrow one if the Minister may dismiss at pleasure. One recalls Mr Gibson's resignation from the chairmanship of one of the Area Electricity Boards after the report of the Lynskey Tribunal. Then there was the resignation of Mr H. O. R. Hindley as chairman of the Raw Cotton Commission after he had been informed by the Commission's auditors that the Board of Trade did not approve of his having on two occasions drawn his salary in advance. After discussing the matter with the Minister, Mr Hindley said he realized he had no alternative but to submit his resignation.[2] There are many situations in which the Minister may give a member an opportunity to resign from the board as an alternative to being dismissed.

The case of Mr Hardie, who resigned as chairman of the Iron and Steel Corporation of Great Britain in February 1952, shortly after the Attlee Government had been replaced by a Conservative administration pledged to denationalize the industry, was an interesting one. There had been differences between the chairman and the Minister both in regard to prices and other matters of importance. Mr Hardie stated that the development programme for the industry had been impeded because he had no control of the industry's raw materials.

An early source of friction between the chairman and the Minister

[1] 475 HC Deb. 5s., cols. 2067-8 (May 24, 1950); 476 HC Deb. 5s., col. 218 (June 14, 1950).

[2] See the exchange of letters between Mr Harold Wilson, President of the Board of Trade, and Mr Hindley, *The Times*, January 6, 1951, p. 6.

was a direction which Mr Sandys gave soon after the Conservative Government came into power prohibiting the corporation from making any changes in the financial structure or management of the industry without first obtaining the Government's permission.[1] This was mentioned by Mr Hardie in his letter of resignation as one of the factors which had prevented him from carrying out his duties and responsibilities as chairman of the corporation.[2] Another cause of difference was that overseas purchasing was carried out by a commercial company and not by the Iron and Steel Corporation. The immediate cause of Mr Hardie's resignation was the Minister's decision that steel prices should be increased forthwith in order to provide a levy to cover losses on imported finished steel. An Exchequer subsidy for this purpose had been abolished by the Labour Government in August 1951. The Iron and Steel Corporation had expressed disagreement with this step at the time and had asked the incoming Conservative Government to re-introduce the subsidy.

In January the chairman wrote to Mr Duncan Sandys, the Minister of Supply, that the board, with one of its members absent, had unanimously disagreed with his policy of immediately raising prices in view of the very large profits being made by the corporation. The Minister then asked the board to see him at the Ministry, and, according to Mr Hardie, he pressed them to withdraw their previous decision. He then left the members alone to consider his memorandum on price increases. On his return, the chairman asked him on behalf of the board if he would substitute the term 'accept the Government's decision' for 'agree'. This the Minister refused, and the chairman then informed him that the board, against his advice and by a majority, was ready to acquiesce with the Minister's wishes. Mr Hardie alleged that it was clear, from views expressed to the Minister on his draft minute, that others besides himself disagreed with the Government's decision. As, however, the other members were prepared to comply with the Minister's requirements, there was no alternative which the chairman could decently take except resignation. In accepting his resignation the Minister remarked that the conflict was not so much between himself and the corporation as between Mr Hardie and the board.[3]

The Labour Opposition in Parliament staged a great outcry at this episode and an acrimonious debate took place in the House of Commons

[1] *Iron and Steel Corporation of Great Britain Report 1951-2*, HMSO, HC 198/1952-3, App. II, p. 98.

[2] See *The Times*, February 23, 1952, p. 6.

[3] *The Times*, February 23, 1952, pp. 6-7; February 29, 1952, p. 4; 496 HC Deb. 5s., cols. 781-831 (February 25, 1952).

on the subject.[1] None of the speakers on either side of the House dealt with the larger question of tenure, but Mr Aneurin Bevan, MP, dissociated himself from the attack on the Government to the extent of saying that if Mr Hardie had set himself up to be a better judge of what the national interest demanded than the Minister, he was claiming too much.

If the chairman or any member of the board of a public corporation finds himself in a minority on an important question of policy, his position is bound to be very weak in any conflict with a Minister. But even apart from this aspect of Mr Hardie's case it is difficult to understand the basis of the Labour Party's attack on the Government when one examines the terms of appointment laid down by Mr G. R. Strauss for members of the Iron and Steel Corporation when he was Minister of Supply in the Labour Government. The letter sent by the Minister to each member when appointing him to the board stated that 'your office may be declared by me to be vacant at any time if, in my opinion, you are for any cause whatsoever unable or unfit to discharge the functions of a member; and upon my giving to you notice in writing of the fact your office shall become vacant and your appointment determined'.[2] This made it possible for the Minister to dismiss without notice, without giving a reason, and without reasonable cause.

Men who serve under such conditions of appointment have no security whatever. Civil servants hold office at Her Majesty's pleasure; but the tradition of security for established civil servants is so strong that it provides an effective guarantee of a permanent tenure subject to good behaviour. There is no similar tradition applying to the boards of the nationalized industries.

It is important that a substantial degree of security of tenure should be given in practice to the full-time members of the board. This is necessary in order to make the appointments sufficiently attractive to secure the services of men of the highest calibre and reputation; and their attractiveness will be greatly diminished if Ministers are free to dismiss members of the board at any time without good cause. Lord Simon of Wythenshawe regards it as essential that any competent person appointed to a board should feel secure up to retiring age, although the Minister should have the right, if things go wrong, to terminate the appointment at any time.[3] He insists that security of tenure is by far the most important step to achieve continuity of policy and efficiency in performance in the nationalized industries. He wishes, in consequence, to

[1] See 496 HC Deb. 5s., cols. 774 ff. (February 25, 1952).

[2] Quoted by D. N. Chester: *The Nationalized Industries*, 2nd edn. (1951), p. 55.

[3] *Op. cit.*, p. 31.

abolish the 'extraordinary custom' of appointing whole-time members to serve on the boards for a period of five years.[1] The Fleck Committee also recommended that the appointment of full-time members should be 'career appointments' normally held until retiring age.

The Herbert Committee took an extremely naive view of this question. They thought that 'top men should receive top salaries and that security should be achieved by results rather than by formal contract'. Relativity with outside industry in the matter of salaries should be accompanied by the acceptance of 'equality of risk as regards tenure and security of employment'.[2] This view overlooks entirely the vicissitudes, the pressures and pulls of political life, which have no counterpart in commercial enterprise. Moreover, it is much harder to judge 'results' in public enterprise than in private undertakings where the profit-motive is dominant. In any event the notion that 'results' are all that will be considered in considering the performance of a public corporation reveals a singular ignorance of recent history and of public life. The attitude of the Churchill Government towards television had nothing to do with the 'results' achieved by the BBC in this sphere; nor had the attitude of Ministers in charge of civil aviation in the Conservative governments towards the scope of activities of the nationalized air lines anything to do with the 'results' achieved by BEA or BOAC.

The Government of the day must be able to direct the undertaking in matters of policy to the extent and in the manner authorized by law: of that there should be no doubt. And if a governing board fails to comply with a direction or with the Minister's declared policy, he must be able to dismiss some or all of its members. Obviously, again, he must be able to replace members who have committed misconduct, who are neglecting their duties, or who are suffering from illness or incapacity. There can be no question about all this. The real issue is whether Ministers should have power to dismiss, or (what amounts to the same thing) to force the resignation of an individual member of the board owing to disagreement with his attitude, dislike of his personality, or disbelief in his ability. My own view is that action of this kind should not be open to Ministers because it lowers the status of the posts. Only by attaching the highest prestige to the posts shall we obtain the best men to serve in them.

The advantage of having appointments for a fixed term of years is that the capacities of members of the board are considered when the term of office expires. In private enterprise the directors are always subject to re-election by the shareholders after a short period of years in office. I can see no reason for dispensing with the principle of five year

[1] D. N. Chester: *The Nationalized Industries*, 2nd edn. (1951), p. 30.

[2] Report, para. 318.

appointments to the boards of nationalized industries on condition—and this is fundamental—that reappointment is regarded as the normal rule except where there is serious cause for dissatisfaction with a member's outlook, conduct, personality, or ability to serve on the board. The Labour Party have recently endorsed this view.[1]

The position as it now exists has been correctly analysed by Mr D. N. Chester when he observes 'the present weakness is not that members are appointed by a Minister. . . . It is that the members appear to be too dependent on the Minister'.[2] Permanency of tenure neither can nor should be guaranteed, but many of the appointments are too brief. Their renewal may depend more than is healthy on the judgment or whim of the Minister and his senior officials. 'Not to please the Minister may lead to not being renewed; to please this Minister may, however, lead to being less pleasing to his successor.' He cites the cases of Sir Charles Reid and Mr Steven Hardie to show that a board member who has a difference with the Minister quickly gets drawn into the arena of party conflict where he has little chance of surviving.

The proper principle to apply is that members of the governing board should enjoy security of tenure for a limited number of years, specified at the time of appointment, and that they should be liable to dismissal at any time for disability, insolvency, neglect of duty, misconduct, *or on other grounds if reasonable cause can be shown*, but not otherwise.

This question of tenure will become of increasing importance if the policy recently urged in several influential quarters, of seeking all or most of the full-time members of the boards from within the nationalized industries themselves, is adopted. For then dismissal from the board will have far more serious consequences than it does for men who have valuable established connections with other industries or companies.

My general conclusion on the whole subject is that it is of profound and fundamental importance that the prestige, status and dignity of these posts should be upheld and enhanced. Only by that means shall we secure at the summit of the public corporations the men of genius and energy whose leadership is essential for the success of these great industries and, therefore, of the economic future of Britain. The more political the posts become, both as regards the qualifications of members and the grounds of their dismissal, the lower will be the public esteem attaching to the appointments. Ministers should reflect on the price they and their colleagues and successors—and indeed the nation—may have to pay for any arbitrary exercise of the power of dismissal which appears to deprive members of the reasonable degree of security they have a right to expect.

[1] *Public Enterprise* (1957) (Labour Party), p. 28.

[2] D. N. Chester: 'The Nationalized Industries', *Three Banks Review*, December 1952, pp. 41-2.

CHAPTER X

Consumers' and Consultative Councils

ONE of the great problems which have to be solved is the relation between a public corporation and the consumers of its product. This gradually merges into the relations between a nationalized industry and the general public. The need to safeguard the interests of the consumer is greatly increased by the monopolistic character of the nationalized industries but it has been a common motive of public utility regulation for more than a century. Public ownership eliminates the shareholder as an adverse interest to that of the consumer, but a conflict of interest can and does frequently occur between consumers and the employees. This affects not only wages, prices, output, redundancy, hours of work, etc., but a wide range of less obvious matters. Restrictions on the amount of recorded music which the BBC is able to broadcast and the number of passengers who are allowed to stand in London buses, are both due to trade union action in the interests of their members.

THE CONSUMER'S NEED OF PROTECTION

It might be thought that Ministers and their departments are sufficiently aware of consumers' interests to provide the necessary safeguards. This is not a correct supposition. One of the most widespread phenomena in modern government is the tendency of Ministers and officials in charge of economic departments to be more favourably disposed towards producers than towards consumers. The Ministry of Agriculture is far more concerned with promoting the interests of farmers and agricultural workers than in keeping down food prices, encouraging competition or increasing output; and a similar attitude is often found in the departments responsible for the fuel, power, and transportation industries. Individual Members of Parliament, who could correct this tendency, are often excessively preoccupied with the local interests of their own constituents. MPs coming from mining constituencies, for example, are usually far more conscious of the needs of coalminers than of coal users either there or anywhere else.

The law courts provide the consumer with a remedy against the public corporation for breach of contract in regard to such matters as price, quality, quantity or delivery; and an action will lie against a public corporation for negligence, nuisance, breach of statutory duty, and other tortious acts. But Courts do not control the level of prices or charges, adequacy of service, output, reasonable facilities, development, and other matters of basic policy. These are decided by the public corporation, subject in certain instances to the approval of a Minister or, in the case of transport, of the Transport Tribunal.

Efforts have been made in the legislation passed since the Second World War to remedy the extremely weak position in which the consumer was placed in relation to the earlier generation of public corporations set up prior to 1939 and the guildlike bodies created to regulate the production and distribution of milk, potatoes, hops and other commodities under the Agricultural Marketing Acts. A series of organs has been set up with the sole duty of safeguarding the consumers' interests in one way or another. These comprise two separate Coal Consumers' Councils, for domestic and industrial users respectively; central and regional Transport Consultative Committees; fourteen Consultative Councils for electricity supply, and twelve for gas; and the Air Transport Advisory Council. The British Broadcasting Corporation has a whole series of Advisory Councils, including a Broadcasting Council for Scotland and a similar body for Wales. About thirty-five such councils are in existence at the present time, and probably nearly 1,000 persons are serving them either as members or officials. Despite this proliferation of organs—perhaps because of it—it cannot be said that the gap between producer and consumer has been completely bridged. Yet there is a general consensus of opinion that the consultative committees are fulfilling a useful function. The consumers' councils are not moulded on a uniform pattern in regard to their composition, functions, and powers.

THE COAL CONSUMERS' COUNCILS

The two Coal Consumers' Councils consist of persons appointed by the Minister to represent various interests. There must be members representing the National Coal Board, and in the case of the Industrial Coal Consumers' Council, members representing industrial consumers of solid fuel and persons engaged in the sale or supply for home use or for export of solid fuel used for these purposes. In the case of the Domestic Coal Consumers' Council, the Minister is required to appoint persons to represent the consumers who use solid fuel for domestic purposes and persons who are engaged in the supply and distribution of fuel for such purposes. In each case the Minister must consult representative bodies of these interests and he has a statutory obligation to pay regard to nominations made to him by these bodies of persons who are recommended by them as having 'both adequate knowledge of the requirements of those interests and also qualifications for exercising a wide and impartial judgment on the matters to be dealt with by the Council generally'.

The personnel of the Councils are not shown in the reports as representatives of interest groups. The one dealing with industrial fuel has members associated with industrial companies, trade unions, the co-operative movement, coal traders, the National Industrial Fuel Efficiency Service, the British Transport Commission, the Gas Council and the Gas Boards, and the electricity authorities. The Council concerned with domestic consumers had as chairman in 1958 Alderman Mrs F. H. Cantwell, of Islington Borough Council, and the members included councillors or officers of local authorities, and persons connected with trade unions, coal merchants, the co-operative movement, the Women's Institutes, the National Council of Women, the Women's Co-operative Guild, gas and electricity Consultative Councils, and the Gas Council. The Director-General of Marketing and a member of the board of the NCB sit on both councils.[1]

The Industrial Coal Consumers' Council is required by statute to consider any matter affecting the sale or supply, whether for home use or for export, of solid fuel on which representations are made to them by the consumers concerned or which appears to them to be a matter which requires consideration. They are to notify their conclusions to the Minister. They are also to consider and report to him on any matter which he may refer to them. The Domestic Coal Consumers' Council is charged with similar duties in regard to the sale or supply of solid fuel for domestic purposes.

If the Minister, after having received from one of the Councils a notification or report on any matter, considers that the National Coal Board's general arrangements for the production, sale or supply of coal or other solid fuel are defective, he may give to the board such directions as he thinks necessary for remedying the defect, and the board is obliged to give effect to any such directions.

The Councils are to make annual reports to the Minister, who is to lay them before each House of Parliament. Their staff is to be provided by the Minister, who is to pay the members of the Consumers' Councils such allowances as he determines, with the approval of the Treasury, and he is also to pay their expenses and the salaries of their officers. Similar Councils may be appointed by the Minister for any region in the country, but no such Councils have been set up.

[1] See the Annual Reports of the Councils for the year ended June 30, 1958.

The Councils normally meet about five or six times a year. The Industrial Council has an informal steering committee which met twice in 1957-8, but the Councils do not possess a developed system of subcommittees or panels. The Domestic Council (with about thirty members) has a slightly larger membership than its industrial counterpart, which usually has twenty to twenty-five members.

What do the Councils discuss? For several years prior to 1958, the Industrial Coal Consumers' Council discussed the subjects of coal supplies, increased productivity, and import policy. Other items on the agenda have included improved labour relations and the need to employ foreign labour; summer stocking by consumers; fuel efficiency; smoke abatement; coke supplies and the gas boards' coke marketing schemes; and the quality of coal. The price structure and complaints about price increases have frequently occupied the time of the Council.

The Domestic Coal Consumers' Council have also shown an interest in supplies and shortages, the need for summer stocking and the problems of consumers who have little storage accommodation, deterioration in the quality of coal, fuel efficiency and smoke abatement. They too have expressed concern at the increased cost of coal and have criticised the price structure. In their report for 1954-5 the Domestic Council gave the case histories of a dozen complaints they had received, relating mainly to the price and quality of particular deliveries of coal or coke. The Council's response consisted mainly of explaining to the consumer the NCB's difficulties or describing their complaints procedure. No matter arising from these complaints was taken up with either the board or the Minister.

In 1957 the Domestic Coal Consumers' Council questioned whether there was any need to continue the control by the Ministry of Power over coal required for domestic purposes. In 1958 they welcomed the Government's decision to end this control, and expressed the hope that the restoration of competition and freedom for the householder to buy supplies from whatever merchant he chose would result in the public obtaining the qualities of coal they wanted at competitive prices.

THE TRANSPORT CONSULTATIVE COMMITTEES

The Transport Acts provide for the establishment of several consultative committees. In the first place there must be a Central Transport Consultative Committee for Great Britain. In the second place there are to be for such areas in Great Britain as the Minister may direct (a) a Transport Users' Consultative Committee for Passenger Traffic, and (b) a Transport Users' Consultative Committee in respect of Goods

Traffic, or (c) a combined Transport Users' Consultative Committee which will deal with both passenger and goods traffic. There is a proviso which stipulates that there shall be at all times a combined Transport Users' Consultative Committee in respect of both passenger and goods traffic for Scotland, and another one for Wales. The intention is that every part of the country shall come within the area of a committee of this kind. These Transport Users' Consultative Committees must be established by the Minister but he may at any time abolish any such committee after consultation with the Central Transport Consultative Committee. There are now eleven Area Transport Users' Consultative Committees, including those established for London, Scotland, and Wales and Monmouthshire.

The committees must consist of an independent chairman; members appointed to represent agriculture, commerce, industry, shipping, labour and local authorities; and members appointed from persons nominated by the British Transport Commission.[1] The Minister makes all the appointments and determines the number of persons who are to be appointed. He must, however, consult with representative bodies before appointing the representative members of the Consultative Committees. Moreover the Central Transport Consultative Committee must include at least one member of the Transport Commission. Members of Parliament are not debarred from membership of a Consultative Committee.

The Central Transport Consultative Committee is a body of twenty persons at the present time. Its present chairman is Lord Coleraine, a former Conservative Minister and MP, and the other members include two representatives of agriculture, five of trade and industry, one of shipping, two of labour, five of local government, together with a member of the British Transport Commission and its principal officer for administration.

The functions of every Consultative Committee set up under the Transport Acts are to consider and where necessary to make recommendations in regard to any matter (including charges) affecting the services and facilities afforded by the Commission which has been the subject of representations made to the committee by users of those services or facilities, or which appears to be a matter to which consideration ought to be given, or which the Minister or Commission may refer to the committee for consideration. The committee can, of course, ignore frivolous complaints.

Under the Transport Act, 1947, the recommendations and conclusions

[1] Transport Act, 1947, s. 6 (4). Members need not be appointed to represent any of the interests mentioned if the Minister considers it unnecessary for that interest to be represented on the Consultative Committee.

of any regional TUCC were to be sent both to the Central Transport Consultative Committee and to the British Transport Commission, while those of the CTCC go to the Minister (who can give directions thereon to the BTC) and to the Commission. But the Transport Act, 1953, changed the position in regard to the committees for Scotland and Wales, and they now report direct to the Minister as well as to the Central Committee and the Commission, and he may issue directions to the BTC on their recommendations. The CTCC makes an annual report to the Minister, who lays it before each House of Parliament. The staff and office accommodation of the Consultative Committees are provided by the Transport Commission on a scale which they consider adequate or such as the Minister may direct. The Commission may pay the members of a Consultative Committee allowances for loss of remunerative time in accordance with a scale approved by the Minister and the Treasury, together with out-of-pocket expenses.

The CTCC do not meet frequently: usually they hold between four and six meetings a year, while the regional committees hold a similar number of meetings. The attendance is not always good, and some members, including those representing the public, seldom attend. The CTCC recommended[1] that bodies asked to nominate members should satisfy themselves of their willingness to attend meetings. The Minister of Transport and Civil Aviation has agreed to bear this in mind when making appointments.

The discussions of the Consultative Committees for Transport have a wider range than those of the Coal Consumers' Councils. For example, the Transport Bill, 1952, was considered by most of the committees, and the CTCC reported to the Minister on some of the specific clauses in the measure. They drew attention to the grave risk of disrupting road haulage services resulting from the disposal of the BTC road haulage undertakings; they urged the desirability of the BTC giving the CTCC an opportunity to comment on their reorganization plans prior to publication; they stressed the need for central organization to control the wagon supply, to promote economies resulting from standardization, and to consider matters of railway policy in consultation with bodies representing trade and industry; and they recommended the preservation of the existing regional boundaries for the railways. The recommendations of the committee were not adopted by the Government.

As already mentioned,[2] the BTC (Passenger) Charges Scheme, 1952, was referred to the CTCC by the Minister, as well as by many users, after it encountered much public criticism. The committee reported that

[1] See their Report for 1953.
[2] *Ante*, p. 150.

the proposed increases were fair and reasonable,[1] but the Government again did not take their advice.

The Central Committee have been asked by the Minister to consider a number of different questions. In 1954 and 1955 these included the reorganization of the railways, standing passengers in motorbuses, road passenger contract carriages, the more extensive staggering of working hours in central London, and the possibility of giving rewards to the finders of lost property in public service vehicles. The British Transport Commission referred to the CTCC their great modernization and re-equipment plan for the railways; their annual report and accounts; and a report of the Board of Survey on Canals and Inland Waterways. Other matters considered were the use of diesel engines and rail buses on branch lines; the transport of motorcars by rail to Scotland; travel facilities in North London; traders' season tickets; railway goods services in East Anglia; the restoration of superior freight services at a differential charge; the BTC's policy in disposing of surplus land; complaints of bad time-keeping by main line trains, etc. Representations were received from numerous bodies, ranging from the Association of British Chambers of Commerce to local farmers' unions.

A very frequent subject on which representations have been received are proposals to close branch lines and little-used stations on main lines, and to withdraw unremunerative passenger services. The regional committees devote much of their time to inquiries into matters of local importance, particularly objections to the closure of branch lines and withdrawal of services. Until 1953 their meetings on these matters were informal, round-table discussions. Since then, however, there has been a tendency for the proceedings to become more formal, with objectors being represented by counsel. For example, when the closure of branch lines in the Isle of Wight was under consideration in 1953, some thirty-eight objectors presented co-ordinated submissions to the South Eastern Area Committee through counsel and the proceedings lasted four days. The closure of the Wivenhoe-Brightlingsea branch line lasted five days, during which counsel were heard, evidence called, and two local Members of Parliament made speeches.

The trend in these cases has been for the proceedings to resemble a typical public inquiry held on behalf of a Minister.[2] A conference of the chairmen of the area Consultative Committees was convened by the CTCC to consider the procedure to be followed in these matters. The

[1] See Report, HMSO, Cmd. 8513/1952.

[2] See W. A. Robson: 'Public Inquiries as an Instrument of Government', I *British Journal of Administrative Law* (1954–5), p. 71, and the *Report of the Committee on Administrative Tribunals and Enquiries*, HMSO, Cmd. 218/1957, Pt. IV.

Central Committee thought that formal and protracted proceedings such as these were not intended by the legislature when the Consultative Committees were set up and were unlikely to lead to the amicable solution of local transport problems. The conference came to the conclusion that the Transport Act, 1947, had contemplated an informal procedure being used by the Consultative Committees, and that lengthy inquiries should be avoided whenever possible. If objectors' cases are presented by counsel or solicitors, the chairman of the committee must use his discretion in deciding what latitude they should have, bearing in mind the need to keep the proceedings as informal as possible. Objectors should always be required to confine themselves strictly to the subject-matter of the proposals before the committee.

In their report for 1957[1] the CTCC state that there are feelings of public distrust, and complaints of injustice, in regard to hearings before local committees. As a general reason, the report attributes this to a lack of understanding of the function of the committees. The committees, the report points out, are not tribunals, but bodies which represent the public: an objector is not participating in an arbitration but in a consultation with his representatives. As particular causes of this distrust, the report stresses, first and foremost, BTC's policy of refusing to supply objectors with relevant facts, on the grounds that by informing the committees they are thereby discharging their duty to the public, and that certain facts 'can only be explained with difficulty to those unfamiliar with them, and can be distorted by facile but unsound reasoning'.[2] Although the CTCC do not condemn this policy, they are examining it with the BTC to see whether a solution can be found. Secondly, the report suggests that a cause of the lack of confidence in the committees is that in nearly every case the objectors have been unsuccessful. The CTCC think that this 'may well be otherwise . . . in the future'.[3]

In 1953 the Central Transport Consultative Committee complained that their advice was being disregarded by the Government. Three important instances were cited in support of this complaint: namely, the rejection of the CTCC's recommendations on the Transport Bill, 1952; on the proposed increase in London Transport passenger fares; and on the Clyde steamship services. The committee also complained of the Minister's refusal to allow them to submit views, on behalf of transport users, to a departmental committee he had appointed to consider the number of passengers who are permitted to travel standing in buses. The Minister tried to soothe the CTCC with an assurance of the value

[1] HMSO, HC 131/1957-8.
[2] *Ib.*, para. 7.
[3] *Ib.*, para. 9.

which the Government attached to their work. He stated that the Ministry of Transport would be encouraged to make more use of the committees' services, and that when questions arose affecting users of public service vehicles, the committee would have an opportunity to make recommendations upon them.

A warm tribute has recently been paid to the Transport Users' Consultative Committees by a senior administrative officer of the British Transport Commission. In an article dealing with the views of the public towards railways services which are run at a loss, Mr M. A. Cameron says that the public attitude towards such services is changing, largely owing to the patient work of these Consultative Committees. When they were established by the Transport Act, 1947, no one knew how these voluntary and unpaid bodies would work. 'In fact, they have built up a reputation for thoroughness and impartiality, and on major and controversial cases, where all the pride of a compact local community was roused, the committees concerned have sat for days to hear evidence. They have established facts and then reached conclusions on the basis not of who is right but what is right in the national interest. In the process thay have done much to educate public opinion on the issues involved in branch line cases.'[1] In conclusion, he expresses gratitude to the committees for their work in helping to make transport users realize that in order to have an up-to-date transport system they must be willing to part with what is out-of-date.[2]

THE AIR TRANSPORT ADVISORY COUNCIL

This body differs in several respects from the consumers' councils, but it shares with them the duty to inquire into complaints about the services provided by the nationalized air lines. The Council are, however, in no sense a body representing consumer interests. The chairman, who must be a barrister, advocate or solicitor of not less than seven years' standing, is appointed by the Lord Chancellor. The other members (between two and four in number) are appointed by the Minister of Transport and Civil Aviation. At least one of them is required to be experienced in the operation of air transport services, and one of them is to have had experience in the operation of other forms of transport. There is no requirement that any of the members should represent the users of air services, whether passenger or freight. No member of the airways corporations nor any of their employees is eligible to sit on the ATAC

[1] M. A. Cameron: 'Non-Paying Services: The Public's View', IV *British Transport Review* (1957), pp. 331-2.

[2] *Ib.*, p. 333.

The Council may, with ministerial approval, appoint expert assessors to assist them in technical or professional matters.

The function of the Air Transport Advisory Council is to consider representations from any person with respect to the adequacy of the facilities provided by the airways corporations or the charges they make for those facilities, except where the matters are governed by international agreements to which HM Government is a party. They can ignore a representation on the ground that it is frivolous or vexatious, or that it concerns a matter which the Council have already sufficiently considered.

The Council will also consider any question which the Minister may refer to them concerning facilities for air transport in any part of the world, or charges for such facilities, or a question concerning the improvement of air transport services.

The Minister provides accommodation and the staff of the Council, and he pays their salaries and expenses. The Minister has an obligation to provide the Council with such information and other assistance as he thinks necessary, and each of the airways corporations must keep the Council informed of all services which they provide or which they intend to provide, and of the charges which they make or propose to make for those services.

The complaint-receiving function of the Air Transport Advisory Council is used to a very slight extent. Only one representation was received in 1952-3, one in 1953-4, five in 1954-5, one in 1955-6, four in 1956-7, and three in 1957-8. The complaints related to such matters as delays in the services between London and Edinburgh, between Birmingham and the Channel Islands, and between London and Luxembourg; booking arrangements; the effect of the closure of Renfrew maintenance base on the Highland air services (this was raised by the Scottish Covenant Association as an item in their nationalist campaign); the inadequacy of various services provided by the air corporations and by independent companies; and the setting down of passengers at intermediate points on the BEA and BOAC bus services between the airports and the terminals. Only in the last mentioned case did the Council make a recommendation to the Minister.

Of much greater importance is the work of the Air Transport Advisory Council in examining all applications for permission to operate scheduled air services and making recommendations on them to the Minister. The work of the Council in regard to licensing resembles that of the Civil Aeronautics Board in the US, although the former have only advisory powers, while the latter actually determine the issue of licences. But in practice the Minister has accepted all the Council's recommendations, except where he has been obliged to vary them for reasons beyond his control, such as the insufficiency of ground services or the impossibility of making arrangements for the proposed services with the foreign governments concerned. In such circumstances the Minister's modifications in the services proposed have been in accordance with qualifications recommended by the Council.

This licensing work has greatly increased since the return to power in 1951 of a Conservative Government anxious to enlarge the sphere of activity open to commercial companies in the operation of air services. A new policy was introduced requiring BOAC and BEA to obtain permission, like other companies, before they can start new services; and the terms of reference of the Council were revised so as to widen substantially the range of services which independent companies may be authorized to operate. The increase in the work of the ATAC is shown by the following table:—

	1952-3 *July-Mar.*	1953-4	1954-5	1955-6	1956-7	1957-8	1958-9
No. of applications[1]	166	130	235	412	428	745	1,006
,, ,, recommendations made	140	118	222	315	363	641	778
,, ,, meetings	65	61	86	80	87	113	114
,, ,, hearings on applications	37	41	108	120	129	n.f.	147
,, ,, discussions with applicant companies	8	13	n.f.	n.f.	n.f.	n.f.	

[1] Includes applications outstanding from previous year. n.f. means no figure given in Reports.

ELECTRICITY AND GAS CONSULTATIVE COUNCILS

The Consultative Councils for electricity and for gas are so similar in many respects that they may be conveniently considered together.

The Minister of Power appoints a Consultative Council for the area of each of the twelve regional Electricity Boards, and Consultative Councils are appointed in like manner for the twelve Gas Board areas. Each Council is to consist of not fewer than twenty nor more than thirty persons.

In the case of electricity, between two-fifths[1] and three-fifths of the

[1] Prior to the Electricity Act, 1957, the minimum proportion was one half. Sch. I, Pt. I, para. 1.

members must be appointed from a panel nominated by the associations which appear to the Minister to represent local authorities in the area—presumably the County Councils Association, the Association of Municipal Corporations, and similar bodies. The remainder represent agriculture, commerce, industry, labour, and the general interests of consumers of the service and other persons or organizations interested in the development of electricity in the area.

In the case of gas, the proportion of local government nominees is to be between a half and three-quarters of the membership. The chairman of a gas Consultative Council must be appointed from the members, but the chairman of an electricity Consultative Council may now be chosen from outside if the Minister wishes. Moreover, the local government nominees on the Consultative Councils for electricity need no longer be members of a local authority; and if they are members when appointed, they need not resign if they subsequently lose their seats on the local authority. All the members are to be selected for their ability to exercise a wide and impartial judgment on the matters to be dealt with by the Council generally.

The chairman of a Consultative Council is *ex officio* a member of the Electricity Board or the Gas Board, as the case may be, for the area concerned. In that capacity he receives a salary and it is doubtless for that reason that Members of the House of Commons are disqualified from being chairman of a Consultative Council, although they may be ordinary members of the Council.

The duties of the Consultative Councils are very wide. They were conceived as having wider functions than merely that of defending the consumers' interest, and it was for this reason that they are designated Consultative Councils instead of being called Consumers' Councils. They are intended to act as two-way channels of communication for the purpose of explaining the board's attitudes and policies to the consumers and of conveying the consumers' needs and point of view to the public corporation. The Consultative Councils therefore have much broader responsibilities than they would have if their principal or sole task was to receive and enquire into complaints or to uphold consumer interests.

The duty of a Consultative Council for electricity is to consider any matter affecting the distribution of electricity in their area, including the variation of tariffs and the provision of new or improved services and facilities. Since the Electricity Act, 1957 was passed they may consider any matter affecting the tariffs regulating the charges for the bulk supply of electricity by the Central Electricity Generating Board for distribution in the area. The Area Electricity Board are to inform the Consultative Council of their general plans and arrangements for exercising and performing their functions, and the Council may make representations to the board. The Area Board are required to consider the reports and recommendations made to them by the Consultative Council for their area. Similar provisions are contained in the enactments relating to the Consultative Councils for gas, except that there is no body in that industry corresponding to the Central Electricity Generating Board. The Councils' functions may be subsumed under three headings: (1) the examination of complaints from individual consumers; (2) the consideration of the factors likely to influence the supply of electricity in a general way; (3) the discussion, criticism or approval of the policies and programmes of the operating bodies concerned with the supply of electricity.

A Consultative Council can act either on receiving a representation by a consumer or by other persons requiring supplies, or on their own initiative. Where action appears to be necessary they notify their conclusions to the Area Board. The board can in turn refer to them any matter on which they desire an investigation and report.

Under the Electricity Act, 1947, a Consultative Council could make representations on any matter falling within their province to the Area Board. If the Area Board returned a dusty answer, they could go to the Central Authority, and in the last resort to the Minister. The Electricity Act, 1957, enables a Consultative Council to send their representations, conclusions or reports either to the Area Board or to the Generating Board. After consultation with either or both of these bodies, the Consultative Council may take the matter to the Electricity Council.[1] If the Electricity Council, on receiving such a representation, think that it discloses a defect in the general plans and arrangements of either the Generating Board or an Area Board, they can give the board concerned 'such advice as they think fit for remedying the defect'. In the last resort, after exhausting all these procedures, a Consultative Council can lay the matter before the Minister, who can give an Area Board or the Generating Board any directions he thinks necessary to remedy the defect.

The procedure for enabling a Consultative Council in the gas industry to make its point of view effectively heard is in principle similar, but it is simpler because the Area Gas Boards are responsible for both the manufacture and distribution of gas.

The Consultative Councils meet on an average seven or eight times a year. Those in the gas industry try to meet at different places in their

[1] This is a new body consisting of a chairman, two deputy chairmen, the chairman and two other members of the Generating Board, and the chairmen of all the Area Boards. The functions of the council are to promote and assist the maintenance and development of an efficient, co-ordinated and economical system of electricity supply and to advise the Minister on matters concerning the industry.

respective areas, and they are sometimes combined with visits to gas board undertakings or to factories using gas. They normally meet in public and their proceedings are reported in the local press.

One has the impression that the Consultative Councils receive a considerable number of complaints and requests from consumers, though few councils give precise figures as to the number, and that the number is increasing. The subjects of complaint in the gas industry include disputes about accounts and charges, low gas pressure, street lighting, gas supply to new houses or additional districts, criticism of a board's policy or services, etc. Among the topics of general interest, that most frequently discussed has been gas tariffs and prices. Other questions of general concern were coal prices, the desirability of both electricity and gas being made available on new housing estates, joint meter readings, hire and hire-purchase terms for gas burning appliances, purchase tax on such appliances and installation charges, the Beaver Report on clean air and smoke abatement, the shortage of shillings for meters, the ban on promotional advertising, etc.

The Consultative Councils for electricity also report a substantial volume of complaints,[1] though here again not all the Councils give detailed figures. As in the case of gas, the number of complaints is tending to increase.

[1] The following table shows the numbers of inquiries and complaints dealt with by the electricity consultative councils:

	London	*South-Eastern*	*Southern*	*South-Western*	*Eastern*	*Midlands*	*South Wales*	*Merseyside & North Wales*	*Yorkshire*	*North-Western*	*South-East Scotland*	*Total*
1948–9	n.f.	n.f.	n.f.	18	n.f.	n.f.	n.f.	n.f.	n.f.	n.f.	n.f.	18
1949–50	n.f.	n.f.	74	106	89	40	n.f.	n.f.	14	n.f	23	346
1950–1	n.f.	n.f.	62	61	78	51	n.f.	155	36	170	25	638
1951–2	n.f.	43	97	87	118	80	n.f.	180	42	243	23	913
1952–3	n.f.	60	98	155	199	84	n.f.	332	n.f.	306	24	1258
1953–4	n.f.	70	165	n.f.	208	97	173	304	50	132	27	1226
1954–5	n.f.	70	84	220	169	n.f.	101	235	55	144	n.f.	1078
1955–6	n.f.	70	74	235	127	226	141	297	27	163	—	1360
1956–7	50	50	69	246	145	205	105	227	30	176	—	1303
1957–8	44	80	54	257	146	267	119	278	36	202	—	1483
1958–9	58	111	56	307	172	287	121	225	21	234	—	1592

n.f. means no figure given in Reports. The East Midlands, North-Eastern, North of Scotland, South-West Scotland, and South of Scotland Consultative Councils have not published any figures.

The figures for the London and South-Eastern Consultative Councils include only important issues.

Only four (North Thames, South-Eastern, East Midlands and Scotland) of the twelve gas consultative councils publish figures of inquiries and complaints.

As regards matters of general interest, tariffs was the subject of predominant concern, followed by rural electrification. Hire and hire-purchase terms, the consumers' contribution to the capital cost of extending supplies, facilities for paying accounts, the Beaver Report on clean air, the use of meter cards, and the use of stamps to spread out electricity account payments, were also under discussion.

The Consultative Councils cover very large areas, and they have a statutory duty to submit to the Minister schemes for the appointment of committees or individuals to represent the Council in different parts of the area. After the Minister has approved the scheme the Consultative Council appoints their local agencies. Their own members are eligible for these appointments either as members of a local committee or as individuals. This devolution serves a double purpose. It enables most of the individual complaints to be dealt with at local level, thereby leaving the Consultative Council free to consider the larger questions affecting consumers as a whole or large categories of them. At the same time the handling of complaints by a local body brings the machinery much nearer to the ordinary householder or small shopkeeper than would be possible if he were dealt with by a remote central office, and helps to break down the sense of aloofness.

A MODEST ACHIEVEMENT

The Ministers responsible for appointing the Consumers' and Consultative Councils have honestly tried to make the machinery work well. Both Labour and Conservative Ministers have avoided packing the councils with political supporters who could be trusted not to make a fuss. The appointees have been either independent persons of repute, non-political representatives of consumers' associations or trade interests of one kind or another; or where they have been political, as in the case of the local authority members of the gas and electricity Consultative Councils, Ministers have scrupulously avoided unduly favouring their own party.

There is general agreement among a considerable number of investigators and competent observers that the Councils have fulfilled their purpose to a limited extent, but that in general the results have so far been less far reaching than might have been expected. 'There is little doubt in our opinion', remarked the Herbert Committee, 'that the vast majority of electricity consumers throughout the country are completely ignorant of the existence or purpose of the Consultative Councils. We are nevertheless satisfied that in a quite modest way the Consultative Councils have done and are doing creditable work in safeguarding the consumers' interests. The volume and quality of their work varies from Area to Area, but . . . the general body of consumers are being well served by their Councils.'[1] This verdict is one which could equally well be applied to the representative bodies dealing with coal and transport.

The limited use made of the machinery may have been due at first to its relative newness, but this should be wearing off by now after more than a decade of existence. Insofar as the public's failure to make fuller use of the system is due to ignorance of the available facilities, this cause may be expected to diminish in course of time. The suggestion has frequently been made that more sustained and vigorous efforts should be made to publicise the existence and work of the Councils.[2] Great scope undoubtedly exists for improvement in this direction. Part of the difficulty arises from the fact that the consumers' councils have no funds of their own to spend on advertising or publicity. In consequence they have had to rely on whatever free publicity they could obtain through the co-operation of the press, the Area Boards, local authorities and other bodies. The Central Electricity Authority and Area Boards agreed in 1954–5 that the latter might pay expenses incurred on publicity by the Consultative Councils. It is now possible, however, to provide the Consultative Councils for electricity with funds of their own for this purpose, subject to Government approval.[3]

The failure of some Councils to make their existence widely known is by no means wholly or perhaps even mainly due to lack of money to spend on this purpose. The admission of the press to meetings of the Councils and their subordinate bodies, the cultivation of good relations with editors and reports, and the display of notices in electricity showrooms and offices, are among the more obvious means by which a closer contact with the public can be fostered; but even these have sometimes been neglected. It has even been alleged that publicity was deliberately avoided by some Councils because they considered that minor disputes should be settled directly between the consumer and the local office of the Area Board without the intervention of an outside body.[4] When coal was in short supply, or load-shedding a common occurrence by the electricity stations, it may well have appeared pointless to some Consultative Councils to go out of their way to invite consumers to make known

[1] Report, HMSO, Cmd. 9672/1956, para. 446.

[2] *Trades Union Congress Report* (1952), pp. 255–7; *Relations with the Public* (1953) (Nationalized Industry Study No. 12 published by Acton Society Trust); Mary Stewart: *Consumers' Councils* (1953) (Fabian Research Series No. 155); *Report of the Committee of Inquiry into London Transport*, HMSO, (1955), para. 334.

[3] Electricity Act, 1957, Sch. I, Pt. I, para. 5. See Report of the Herbert Committee, HMSO, Cmd. 9672/1956, para. 457.

[4] *Relations with the Public* (1953) (Acton Society Trust).

to them the grievances which they would be unable to remedy. This was a most short-sighted and unimaginative point of view; but as the situation in regard to the supply of fuel and power is no longer one of shortages it is in any event no longer relevant.

Publicity is only one method of cultivating relations with the public. More direct methods of communication can sometimes be valuable. Here the difficulty is that some classes of consumers are almost entirely unorganized, including domestic consumers, the occupants of offices, shops, etc. Although there is a distinct consumers' interest in the operation of all the nationalized industries, in most of them it is diffused and not easily identified, organized or expressed.[1] We must, therefore, as the Co-operative Party rightly urges, encourage the growth of consumer consciousness in relation to the commodities and services provided by nationalized industries. This may involve the development of special organizations for the purpose. I do not favour the suggestion that the members of Consultative or Consumers' Councils should be elected by popular vote.[2] The election would not arouse the faintest interest and the poll would be a pathetically low one which would not justiry the effort and expense of an election.

THE STRUCTURE OF THE COUNCILS

A good deal of criticism has been directed at the structure of the consumer councils. Some observers believe that the present machinery is too complex, and that the consumer is confused by the array of separate bodies to which he must take his complaints and which are supposed to represent his needs or interests. They propose that there shall be a single system of Consumers' Councils for all the nationalized industries. The essence of this proposal is that the consumer would be able to go to one local office for all his complaints against any of the nationalized industries.

One version of this proposal envisages the constitution of *ad hoc* bodies in each county and county borough to deal with consumers' interests. They would be composed partly of local councillors and partly of persons representing industries and associations in the area. A central consumers' council would be set up composed of one delegate from each of the local consumers' councils.[3] Another version contemplates a three-tier system consisting of a central consumers' council, regional councils, and district committees. The regional councils would be composed

[1] *The People's Industry* (1951) (Statement on Social Ownership by the National Committee of the Co-operative Party), paras. 39-47.

[2] *Relations with the Public* (1953) (Acton Society Trust).

[3] J. A. G. Griffith: 'The Voice of the Consumer', XXI *Political Quarterly* (1950), p. 179.

of the chairmen of the district committees and representatives of other major interests in the area; while the central council would be composed of the chairmen of the regional councils with up to twenty other persons co-opted to represent particular interests. Several members of the central organ would give their full time to the work and they might even be specialists in such matters as finance or production. Their task would be to carry out investigations into the working of the nationalized industries, and as a result be able to provide the full council with a body of relevant facts and conclusions to enable them to criticize or support intelligently the policies or plans of the public corporations.[1]

Another proposal is that local authorities should be authorized to set up a committee or committees to deal with consumer problems relating to such services as gas, electricity, and local transport.[2] Mr Herbert Morrison, when a Minister in the Attlee Government, stated that local authorities should be encouraged to make representations, complaints, and criticisms to the consumers' committees. The Labour Government's view was that the local government machinery should be used to voice consumer grievances, though it did not embrace the idea of an *ad hoc* local authority, or a separate committee of the local council; nor did the Labour Government consider that local authorities should supplant the special machinery established under the nationalization statutes. Mr Morrison has more recently explained that his aim is to establish local authority organization as 'a channel of public criticism or complaint'.[3] The ordinary man, he says, is not well equipped to argue his case in front of a consumers' council. He should, therefore, be able to obtain the help of the salaried officers of the local authority who know how his grievance should be presented.[4]

I do not think the right course is to abandon the present machinery for dealing with consumers' interests but rather to improve the working and composition of the councils which have been established for that purpose. There is some evidence of an increasing awareness of, and readiness to use, the opportunities which exist to enable consumers to have their grievances considered and their needs expressed. There is no reason to believe that a unified series of consumer councils dealing with all the nationalized industries would make a notably greater impact on the public or be able to deal more effectively with the public corpora-

[1] P. Sargant Florence and H. Maddick: 'Consumers' Councils in the Nationalized Industries', XXIV *Political Quarterly* (1953), pp. 268-70.

[2] L. Freedman and G. Hemingway: *Nationalization and the Consumer* (1950) (Fabian Research Series No. 139).

[3] Herbert Morrison: *Government and Parliament* (1954), p. 268.

[4] *Report from the Select Committee on Nationalized Industries*, HMSO, HC 235/1952-3, Evidence, Q. 506.

tions. We should, however, press local authorities to participate energetically in the working of the existing system. The only specific step which needs taking at the present time is to create an administrative tribunal to deal with certain types of question, but this is a matter to be discussed later.

Meantime, we may note a number of points relating to the existing machinery which call for consideration.

In the first place, all the consumers' organs consist of appointed members. The power of appointment and dismissal is in the hands of the relevant Minister, who must consult bodies representing divers interests. He also appoints the chairman. There would seem to be no reason why consumers' organizations, local authorities, trade interests, and so forth, should not be entitled to appoint their own representatives in accordance with a scheme drawn up by the Minister. The chairman might also be elected by the consumers' committee and not by the Minister, except (as in the case of the gas and electricity Consultative Councils) where he is *ex officio* a member of the corresponding public corporation.

Second, there is much to be said in favour of the chairman of a consumers' committee or consultative council being *ex officio* a member of the board of the public corporation with which they are associated. If the chairman takes full advantage of his dual position, he can see that full weight is given to consumer interests in the vital processes of decision and policy making within the nationalized industry. He can maintain a high degree of liaison between the public corporation and the consumers' committee. There is a possible danger that he may lean over too much in the direction of justifying and defending the board's actions to the committee; but on the whole the chairmen identify themselves more closely with the Consultative Councils than with the public corporation because their membership of the Area Boards is due to their position on the former.[1]

On the other hand, there are obvious drawbacks to the converse arrangement whereby both the Industrial and Domestic Coal Consumers' Councils include members representing the National Coal Board, and the Central Transport Consultative Committee and the Transport Users' Consultative Committees include persons nominated by the Transport Commission. If we regard the consumers' organs as bodies whose duty it is on occasion to criticize the nationalized industries, it is manifestly embarrassing to include in their deliberations leading spokesmen of the corporations. How can we expect a prominent representative of a public corporation to sign a report openly criticizing that body?

[1] *Public Enterprise* (1957) (Labour Party), p. 35.

While a Consumers' Council will usually welcome the presence of a spokesman of the nationalized industry, his usefulness lies in his ability to provide information, to explain difficulties, and to express the views of the corporation, and certainly does not extend to participating in the council's conclusions and recommendations. The Chambers Committee of Inquiry into London Transport expressly recommended that the British Transport Commission and the London Transport Executive should not have representatives on what is intended to be an independent committee representing transport users.[1]

Another point which needs attention is the extremely short period for which at least some members are appointed. It has been quite common for members of the Consultative Councils for electricity to be appointed for only two years, and the chairman for three years. This is too short a period for understanding the complex and technical work of the nationalized industries unless continuity of membership is secured by re-appointing a substantial proportion of the members each time the councils are reconstituted.

RELATIONS WITH THE PUBLIC CORPORATIONS

Some of the Acts dealing with nationalization give the public corporation a statutory right to refer matters to the relevant council for their consideration; while others give no such right. This distinction is reflected in the nomenclature, which uses the term consultative council or committee for bodies which the nationalized industry has the right to consult; while the term consumers' council is used to designate those like the Coal Consumers' Councils to which matters can only be referred from other quarters.[2] There is clearly a broader concept underlying the Consultative Council, for although it has all the powers of the consumers' committee, it also exercises wider functions of deliberation. One can assume, however, that its principal concern should be the safeguarding of the consumers' reasonable interests; but as events have shown, this is not incompatible with recognizing the need to raise prices in a nationalized industry where it is necessary to do so in order to avoid financial loss; or agreeing to the withdrawal of non-paying services on the railways.[3]

[1] Report, para. 335. While the representatives of BTC and LTE are members of the Transport Users Consultative Committee for London and participate in the proceedings, they do not vote.

[2] A. M. de Neuman: *Consumers' Representation in the Public Sector of Industry* (1950), pp. 6-7.

[3] *Central Transport Consultative Committee for Great Britain Annual Report 1951*, HMSO, HC, 79/1951-2, pp. 15, and 16; M. A. Cameron: *op. cit.*, pp. 323 ff.

On the whole, the relations between consumers' or consultative councils and the nationalized industries with which they are associated appear to be good. The public corporations are usually willing to provide whatever information is available, together with explanations of their practices or policies, when they are requested to do so. It does not follow, however, that the supply of information is always adequate.

The public corporations have behaved in a courteous and co-operative manner towards the councils, and I have not heard of any occasion on which an attitude of haughtiness or arrogance has been displayed. The councils themselves have frequently referred in their reports to their good relations and close consultation with the boards.

There have, however, been unfavourable comments about the position of apparent subservience occupied by the councils.[1] This is mainly due to such circumstances as the expenses of the councils being paid by the public corporation; their accommodation being provided by the public corporation in its own premises; the secretary of the council being a member of the staff of the nationalized industry; the reports of the Consultative Councils for gas and electricity being bound up and published with the annual reports of the Area Boards. These are matters which can and should be altered without causing the slightest difficulty either to the nationalized industry or the consumer council.

There are already instances where these objectionable features are not present. Thus the Minister of Power pays the expenses and remuneration of the Industrial and Domestic Coal Consumers' Councils; the Minister of Transport and Civil Aviation pays the remuneration and expenses of the Air Transport Advisory Council and provides accommodation for them. The staff of these councils is also provided by the appropriate Minister. The reports of the Central Transport Consultative Committee, the Coal Consumers' Councils, and the Air Transport Advisory Council are all published separately from the reports of the nationalized industries with which they are associated. The Electricity Council now pay the allowances and remuneration of the members and officers of the Consultative Councils for electricity.[2]

The Herbert Committee on Electricity Supply were of the opinion that these Consultative Councils could obtain a man of higher calibre from the staff of the Area Board to act as secretary than they could hope to get if they went outside the industry, having regard to the salaries and poor prospects attaching to the posts. The Chambers Committee, on the other hand, recommended unequivocably that the secretary of the Transport Users' Consultative Committee for London should be ap-

[1] Mary Stewart: *op. cit.*

[2] Electricity Act, 1957, Sch. I, Pt. I, para. 4.

pointed by the Minister from an outside source and not from the staff of the London Transport Executive, in order to emphasize more clearly the committee's independence.

A recent Labour Party statement has pointed to the embarrassing position in which the secretary of a council may find himself if he is on the staff of the public corporation. He may be faced with a conflict of interest arising from his duty to fight the board on behalf of the consultative council, while at the same time needing to maintain cordial relations with the employer on whom his career ultimately depends.[1] One way of avoiding these difficulties is to appoint able civil servants or local government officers either shortly before or soon after they have retired; and some councils have adopted this expedient.

STAFF

The question of the staff must, however, be looked at from a much broader point of view than the source from which the secretary is recruited and paid. It is, indeed, one of the most important factors which can influence the position of the consumers' councils.

The effectiveness of a consumers' organ will depend largely on the size and qualifications of its staff. At present not one of the councils is in a position to undertake an investigation requiring a knowledge of economics, statistics, accountancy, or any branch of engineering. The staff usually consists only of a secretary, either full-time or part-time, with one or two additional clerks and shorthand typists.

In consequence, we find the Central Transport Consultative Committee for Great Britain referring in their report for 1949 to 'the great strides *claimed* to have been made in the United States, Canada, and elsewhere, in the handling of goods by mechanical means, thereby conserving space, saving time and reducing labour costs',[2] and stating that they have recommended that the British Transport Commission should wherever practicable install modern systems of handling goods. A matter of this importance would certainly have repaid investigation by the Committee. They ought to know what advances have been made abroad —not merely what is 'claimed'. A vast subject is dismissed in nine lines of the report.

It is essential that each consumers' committee should be able, whenever they think fit, to inquire into matters which fall within the scope of their jurisdiction. They cannot do this properly unless they have at their disposal investigators possessing the necessary qualifications. Without

[1] *Public Enterprise* (1957) (Labour Party), p. 34.

[2] Para. 13. The italics are mine.

such personnel they will always have to accept whatever factual or other information the public corporation chooses to give them. The consumers' committees and consultative councils are not intended to be primarily research organs; but neither are they intended to be merely representative bodies. They should be in a position to bring a critical and discriminating viewpoint to bear on the questions with which they are concerned. It is difficult to see how they can do this if they are denied the possibility of independent sources of information and disinterested expert advice. For this reason the staffs of the consumers' committees should be strengthened both in quantity and quality. This need not be done on an extravagant scale. Two or three of the Consultative Councils for electricity in the less populous regions could perhaps share the services of a specialized investigating staff among them; and the same applies to the Consultative Councils for gas. Some of the investigations which the consumers' organs may want to make could probably best be carried out under contract by university faculties, research institutes, or technical colleges. It would be worth while giving a few of the consumers' committees such facilities as these to see what difference it would make to the effectiveness of their work.

Some critics of the consumers' councils have advocated an independent central research organization which would carry out investigations on behalf of the councils.[1] Professor Sargant Florence and Mr Maddick contemplate setting up a research unit of their proposed central council which would have a permanent staff of efficiency experts, statisticians, and specialists in various fields who would work under the direction of the full-time chairman and other members of the central consumers' council and brief them with material, criticism, and arguments to promote the interests of consumers. These proposals seem too elaborate and generalized. The need is for more specialized inquiries in particular matters affecting individual industries or undertakings.

The consultative councils are not the right bodies to carry out widespread investigations into the general efficiency of the administration and organization of the nationalized industries. They have a most useful function to perform but their role should not be inflated into that of supervisor of the public corporations. Professor Gilbert Walker and Mr Maddick are proposing something very like this when they urge that the Central Transport Consultative Committee should be made responsible for the overall examination of the services of the British Transport Commission and for assessing their efficiency.[2] They would even give

[1] Mary Stewart: *op. cit.*; P. Sargant Florence and H. Maddick: *op. cit.*, pp. 268-70.

[2] G. Walker and H. Maddick: 'Responsibility for Transport', XXIII *Political Quarterly* (1952), pp. 229-32.

the committee the task of dealing with parliamentary questions which are refused admission to the order paper of the House of Commons. This is going much too far; for it would place on the consumers' organs tasks and duties far in excess of their capacities, judging by the qualities they have so far displayed.

It is, however, true that the consideration which the consultative councils can give to the plans or policies of the nationalized industries, and their ability to criticize particular services, is largely ineffective owing to the absence of a staff capable of carrying out investigations, or indeed of any research facilities whatever. The aim should be to provide them with such staff or facilities without seeking to transform the character of the councils.

The limited capacity of the councils at the present time was by implication recognized by the Minister of Fuel and Power when he decided in 1956 to appoint a Departmental Committee to inquire into the costs of distribution of coal supplied to inland consumers and to investigate the merchants' profit margins in respect of these supplies. This inquiry was set on foot owing to criticism by consumers, yet it was not considered a matter which could be referred to the Coal Consumers' Councils. In principle one would have thought that distribution costs was a very suitable subject for the Coal Consumers' Councils to inquire into; but they were deliberately passed over in favour of an *ad hoc* committee. Was this due to their lack of an investigating staff? Or to the presence among the members of persons prominently connected with the coal trade? Whatever the reason may have been, it is evident that the effectiveness of the councils is at present seriously reduced by the absence of any facilities for carrying out their own investigations.

THE FUNCTIONS OF THE COUNCILS

Lastly, insufficient thought has been given to the functions which consultative councils are suited to perform and those for which they are clearly unsuitable.

A fairly large committee composed of representatives of commercial or industrial undertakings, co-operative societies, trade associations, voluntary organizations, trade unions, agricultural and similar interests, local councillors and independent persons, should be able to work effectively in considering and reporting on general matters affecting consumers as a whole or a particular category or section of consumers. They should collectively possess sufficient knowledge and wisdom to be able to exercise a discriminating judgment on broad questions of policy, supply, service, facilities and price—assuming always that adequate information and technical advice are available to them. In consequence, they should be reasonably well fitted to express an intelligent opinion on representations which reach them on such matters, or to formulate views of their own.

They should also be fairly well adapted to comment, from the consumer's standpoint, on the plans of the public corporations and to make valuable suggestions for their improvement. The extent to which the consumers' councils are intended to perform this function varies; and this diversity seems to arise from an uncertainty in the mind of the legislature about the proper role of the councils. The Minister of Transport and Civil Aviation or the British Transport Commission may refer policy or plans to the Central Transport Consultative Committee for their consideration; but there is no obligation to do so. On the other hand, the gas and electricity Area Boards are required by law to notify their general plans and arrangements to the respective Consultative Council and to consider their observations thereon. There is no statutory provision requiring or even authorizing the National Coal Board to consult the Coal Consumers' Councils about their future plans or policy, though the Minister can refer any matter to them for consideration. The great plan for the coal industry issued in October 1950, which sets out the National Coal Board's proposals, was apparently not considered by the Domestic Coal Consumers' Council, though this is by far the most important scheme ever drawn up for the industry. It was, however, shown to the Industrial Coal Consumers' Council and briefly considered by them.[1]

The consumers' committees and councils are also expected to receive, inquire into and report on the grievances of consumers who have failed to obtain satisfaction after taking complaints to the public corporation through other channels. While, as we have already indicated, the councils are suited for dealing with questions of general import, such as the absence of electricity supply in a particular rural area, or the closing down of intermediate railway stations or branch lines, they are not well adapted to deal with complaints by individual consumers. How can a council of between twenty and thirty members, most of whom are heavily occupied with their other work, investigate an individual complaint? The councils meet only at long intervals; and this is probably one of the reasons why the business of dealing with complaints is usually left in the hands of the secretary and chairman of the council. These individual officers should certainly not possess an apparently unlimited discretion in dealing with consumers' grievances.

The main objection to the councils from this standpoint is that they

[1] Report of the ICC Council, 1951, paras. 11-15.

are advisory or representative organs whose chief purpose is related to the administrative operations of the nationalized industries. The task of inquiring into individual complaints requires a tribunal of some kind to ensure a painstaking and detailed investigation of the facts, a concentration on the particular circumstances of the grievance, consideration of the situation in terms of the consumers' reasonable expectations and the corporations' responsibilities towards him. The weakness of the machinery for safeguarding the interests of individual consumers is that it attempts to use advisory committees for performing a function which requires an administrative tribunal. This fact serves to emphasize the error of leaving a consumers' committee or consultative council which includes representatives of a public corporation among the members to investigate a charge or consider a criticism against that corporation by a person who is usually one of their customers. There could scarcely be a more blatant example of an interested party participating in what should be an impartial inquiry.

THE ROLE OF ADMINISTRATIVE TRIBUNALS

Parliament set up administrative tribunals to decide claims by present or former employees whose position was injured by nationalization;[1] and also a number of specially constituted arbitration tribunals to determine various types of dispute in matters where nationalization may have affected private interests of different kinds. The public corporations are subject to the general law of the land so far as their rights and liabilities in contract and tort are concerned. They and their officers can be prosecuted for offences which they commit against the criminal law.

In only one instance has an administrative tribunal been established with power to hear and determine complaints by consumers or to adjudicate on questions of prices or charges. The exception is the Transport Tribunal, which owes its existence to historical reasons. The Railway and Canal Commission, set up in 1888, had for long been obsolete, and it was abolished when the railways were nationalized in 1947. Its jurisdiction in such matters as the provision of reasonable facilities and undue preference was transferred to the Transport Tribunal, which also superseded the Railway Rates Tribunal and the Road and Rail Appeal Tribunal.

The Transport Act, 1947 required the British Transport Commission to make and submit to the Transport Tribunal their proposed charges schemes. This involved notice and hearing of objections, a lengthy public inquiry, after which the scheme could be confirmed, altered, or rejected.

[1] See W. A. Robson: *Justice and Administrative Law*, 3rd edn. (1951), pp. 297-309.

The Tribunal could also sit in an advisory capacity to the Minister. In none of the other nationalized industries were tribunals set up to deal with similar matters.

The circumstances which had led to the creation in turn of the Railway and Canal Commission, the Railway Rates Tribunal, and the Transport Tribunal, had all changed entirely by 1947. The railways, far from being in a position to exploit their monopoly in an unfair manner, were on the defensive and were losing ground heavily to competing forms of transport. The obligations towards traders, passengers and the public imposed on them in the nineteenth century hung round their neck like a millstone. The whole method of control over charges embodied in the Transport Tribunal was obsolete.

In 1952, the Conservative Government announced as part of their plan to denationalize the road haulage industry, the proposal to give the British Transport Commission a much greater degree of commercial freedom than the railways had previously enjoyed in Britain. Under the new system introduced by the Transport Act, 1953, the British Transport Commission are required to prepare and submit one or more charges schemes to the Transport Tribunal in respect of railway freight charges and passenger fares, railway tolls, canal charges, charges for port facilities owned by them, London omnibus fares, and charges ancillary to these.

A scheme need no longer provide fixed or standard charges. Its purpose is to fix maximum charges; and the BTC are entirely free to charge traders whatever they think fit, provided it does not exceed these maxima. The old statutory obligation to afford equality of treatment to all persons in like circumstances, which originated in the Regulation of Railways Act, 1868, has disappeared; and so too has the prohibition of 'undue preference' which has also a long history. The BTC may arrange with traders to make whatever charges they are able to agree, and they can differentiate between one trader and another, so long as the rate charged does not exceed a maximum approved by the Transport Tribunal. Nor need the Commission publish agreed charges, or obtain the approval of the Transport Tribunal or any other body—this enables them to avoid giving valuable information to competing forms of transport, which have in the past used this information to undercut the railways.[1]

There is a safeguard to protect persons sending merchandise by railway which cannot reasonably be sent by any other means of transport: they can complain to the Transport Tribunal against any charge made by the BTC which they think unreasonable or unfair. By means of a special

[1] Transport Act, 1953, ss. 20-2.

procedure the Commission can by their own declaration effect an immediate increase of maximum charges not exceeding ten per cent to meet rising costs which would otherwise seriously impair their financial position and where increased charges are the only 'reasonable' way of obtaining the additional revenue needed.[1] But if passenger fares are involved in such emergency action, an application must be made to the Transport Tribunal *ex parte* and in private, without publication of the application, and the Tribunal must authorize the scheme or amend it as they think fit. In any event the BTC must apply to the Tribunal for an alteration of the relative charges scheme within a month after any temporary increase of charges. These provisions were intended to enable the railways 'to assume a more aggressive, commercial posture'.[2] Unfortunately, the railways have for so long been lying almost dormant that they have developed severe muscular cramp which has so far precluded them from adopting a posture of this kind. However, the freedom now given to them is far greater than any they have enjoyed since the mid-nineteenth century; and the opportunity to compete with road transport on more equal terms is now open to them.[3]

It is impossible to justify the Transport Tribunal as it exists at present. Why should the railways be selected as the only nationalized industry for this type of procedure? The prices of gas, electricity, coal, or air transport can be altered without objectors being given a chance to state their case, without a public hearing, or the approval of a tribunal. Professor Arthur Lewis has urged that the prices of every public corporation should be subject by law to the scrutiny of an independent tribunal.[4] I agree with him subject to two important conditions.

The first condition is that the Tribunal should be less legalistic in its approach than the Transport Tribunal or the Railway and Canal Commission. Railway tribunals and regulatory commissions in this country have usually had a lawyer as chairman and observed a highly legalistic code of procedure. The Transport Tribunal in its short existence has scarcely looked beyond the question of whether an application for increased charges is supported by evidence of increased costs of operation. It has neglected the deeper and more difficult question whether by improved organization, better equipment, and methods of operation it would be possible to reduce costs and thereby make ends meet without increasing charges. But inquiries on this plane would re-

[1] Transport Act, 1953, ss. 23–4.

[2] C. Grunfield: 'The Transport Act, 1953', XXV *Political Quarterly* (1954), p. 52.

[3] Gilbert Walker: 'Transport Policy before and after 1953', V *Oxford Economic Papers* new series (1953), p. 109.

[4] W. Arthur Lewis: 'The Price Policy of Public Corporations' in *Problems of Nationalized Industry*, ed. W. A. Robson (1952), pp. 193–4.

quire a knowledge of such matters as economics, work study, scientific management and market research, rather than of law.[1] The Transport Tribunal has no expert staff of its own and no independent organization on which it could call for expert evidence. It would therefore be unable to pronounce on matters of this kind even if it wanted to do so.

The second condition is that the Tribunal should really possess power to hear and determine applications regarding prices made by the public corporations running the nationalized industries. For some time past Ministers have been having the final word on prices, particularly in respect of transport and coal. Even when the Transport Tribunal has advised the Minister to agree to increased rail passengers charges and the Central Transport Consultative Committee recognized the need for the increases, the Minister of Transport has refused to permit the British Transport Commission to put them into force. And the Government has from time to time exerted strong pressure on all the nationalized industries to refrain from increasing prices. In such circumstances it is nonsensical to go through the elaborate procedure of submitting applications to a tribunal, producing evidence and lengthy arguments, when the real centre of authority lies elsewhere.

Since 1953 the competence of the Transport Tribunal has been greatly reduced, as it now determines only maximum charges for the carriage of freight by rail. Subject to these maxima, actual charges will be settled between the railways and their customers on commercial lines. Professor Walker and Mr Maddick regard any intervention by a body of this kind as an anachronism because it is incompatible with modern ideas about management motives and the spirit of service which imbues the responsible members of a public corporation. They consider that the governing board should have the right to determine prices without let or hindrance, subject to the undertaking being subjected to modern methods of testing efficiency and an expert evaluation of the services provided.[2]

There is much to be said in favour of a forum where the arguments for and against proposals to alter the prices of goods and services produced by the nationalized industries can be ventilated in public before an objective and expert tribunal: provided that the evidence and arguments are not confined to the formal or legal aspects but are directed to the basic questions concerning the management of the industry. There is certainly no reason to distinguish public transport in this matter from the other nationalized industries.

Quite apart from this function, there is a need for administrative

[1] P. Sargant Florence and H. Maddick: *op. cit.*, pp. 264-5, and 270.

[2] G. Walker and H. Maddick: *op. cit.*, pp. 227-9.

tribunals to take over from the consumer and consultative councils a task they are unable to perform effectively: namely, inquiring into complaints by individual consumers or members of the public against the public corporations in matters other than those which can properly form the subject-matter of a legal action or criminal proceedings in the ordinary courts. There would of course have to be a provision against frivolous or unfounded allegations and a *prima facie* case would have to be made out before the tribunal would take cognizance of the matter.

PUBLIC RELATIONS

I said at the beginning of this chapter that the relations between the public corporations and consumers gradually merge into the relations between a nationalized industry and the general public. It will therefore be appropriate to say something in this chapter about public relations.

It is sometimes suggested that although our fuel, power and transport industries have been nationalized they have not been socialized. At worst, a nationalized industry may be little more than one in which the proprietary interest has been transferred from private ownership to the state. The profit-making motive has disappeared; but nothing else may have taken its place. Much more is possible, but it may not have been realized in practice.

A socialized industry, by contrast, is one in which the social implications of public ownership and operation have been substantially realized. There will be, throughout the undertaking, full recognition of the consumer's right to the most ample service or supplies at the lowest possible price; and, so far as practicable, the consumer will be offered the widest possible choice and his preferences will be respected. This means, of course, that individual prices would be closely related to the costs of each item.

Under socialization the consumers' and consultative councils would be working as genuine channels of communication between the consumer and the public corporation. The apathy, the timidity, the ignorance, and the ineffectiveness which these bodies sometimes display would have disappeared. There would be tribunals to which aggrieved consumers could bring their complaints by cheap and easy methods of procedure; and others before which the public corporations would be required to justify price increases. There is much else that would be needed, particularly in regard to joint consultation and labour relations, and the attitude of Parliament towards the nationalized industries; but these matters fall outside the scope of this chapter.

Public relations has a part of immense importance to play in this transformation from nationalization to socialization. Nationalization is only the beginning of a process. Its continuation demands a re-orientation of attitude and a new spirit both in those who work for the industry and in those who are served by it. It is essential, Mr Herbert Morrison remarked, that there should be a new consciousness of their responsibilities to the citizen on the part of management, technicians and labour. 'This new spirit should in particular operate where workers or members of the staff have personal contacts with the public—a readiness to be helpful, to explain difficulties and to be patient, all these are essential elements in public relations.'[1]

A public relations service can further many different purposes in a nationalized industry. It can provide two-way lines of communication to convey the views and feelings of the public to the corporation, and the policy of the corporation to the public. It can mediate between the great corporation and the individual citizen. It can enable the management to be flexible and to be in a position to adapt its policies to the needs of the public by keeping the executives informed of the state of public opinion. It can counteract ill-informed or malicious criticism and dispose of unfounded rumours. It can help to build up a relationship of trust and confidence with the public. Mr Leslie Hardern, public relations officer of the North Thames Gas Board, remarks that if these purposes are well carried out, they will ensure that instead of having nationalized industries which are unpopular, incoherent, and unresponsive, there will be mutual respect, mutual helpfulness, and mutual co-operation between the public corporation and the public for continuous improvement in efficiency and morale. He stresses the need for collaboration between the consumers' council and the public relations department.[2]

The scope and effectiveness of the public relations work of the nationalized industries varies enormously. The National Coal Board have sometimes appeared to make no effort whatever to rebut ill-informed statements about such harmful charges as their alleged extravagance in acquiring country houses for administrative purposes, or over-staffing the headquarters and divisional offices.[3]

The Chambers Committee which inquired into London Transport reported that the functions and problems of the London Transport sys-

[1] Herbert Morrison: Foreword to Sir Hubert Houldsworth and others: *Efficiency in Nationalized Industries* (1952), p.i. See also the same author's *Government and Parliament* (1954), pp. 268-72.

[2] Leslie Hardern: 'Public Relations in the Nationalized Industries' in *Problems of Nationalized Industry*, ed. W. A. Robson (1952), pp. 171-81.

[3] D. W. Kelly: 'The Administration of the National Coal Board', XXXI *Public Administration* (1953), pp. 10-1.

tem are insufficiently understood by members of the public and by many public bodies. Much misguided criticism and undeserved unpopularity might be avoided if the British Transport Commission and the London Transport Executive were to devise more effective ways of explaining their task and its problems to the public. The Committee wanted to see more done to explain the necessity for certain unpopular features of the service; and more attention given to complaints about such vexatious occurrences as the crawling and bunching of buses.[1] Improvements have been made in regard to some of these matters since the Report was published in 1955 but further progress is needed.

Successful public relations depends partly on the degree of importance attached to it by the board and the higher executives of nationalized industry; partly on the calibre of the staff recruited for the work; and partly on the scope of the opportunities which are accorded to them by the management.

So far as the first factor is concerned, it was clear that Sir Miles Thomas, when he was chairman and chief executive of BOAC, considered public relations to be of great value to the corporation; and he himself was an extremely successful exponent of the art at a high level. A more explicit statement is to be found in the evidence given by the South Western Electricity Board to the Herbert Committee to the effect that they attached considerable importance to public relations in the fullest sense of the term. 'The chairman has regarded . . . public relations as an important part of his personal responsibilities, and had made it his duty to give Members of Parliament the fullest information on any aspect of the board's work.'[2]

The board had made substantial efforts in their dealings with the Consultative Council for the area to ensure that the council were fully informed. Thus, the board had encouraged the Council to appoint a small committee with which they had kept in close touch concerning tariffs, finance and policy. The committee had access to the chairman and were given confidential papers and advance information on proposed changes of policy. 'The board's Information Officer ensures that the Press and the BBC are kept fully informed on our policy, plans and progress. As a result, news and comments about South Western Electricity are regularly featured in the West Country papers and on the West Region programmes of the BBC.' The board's work and the benefits of electricity are brought continuously before the public by means of speeches at public functions, talks to organizations, exhibitions, films and other media.

[1] Report of the Committee, paras. 331-3.

[2] *South Western Electricity Board Annual Report 1954-5*, HMSO, HC 61/1955-6, para. 37.

This is the kind of activity which sounds obvious and even commonplace once it is accepted and established as the normal practice; but it is very far from being generally recognized and adopted in so thorough a manner throughout the nationalized industries. The status of public relations officers is often relatively low, and although they usually report directly to the chairman or chief executive, their duties are not generally considered to be of equal importance to those of the heads of the administrative, technical or commercial departments. One must add that the qualifications and the calibre of the public relations staff are not always as high as they should be.[1]

There has been a tendency in some of the public corporations to concentrate wholly or mainly on the outward-flowing aspect of public relations and to ignore the inward-flowing aspect. Where this occurs, its function is conceived to be the supply of information, explanation, and exposition of the corporation's policy. The task of conveying the grievances, desires, and feelings of members of the public to the management is of least equal importance; and where this is neglected public relations is deprived of at least half of its potential utility.

The inward-flowing aspect of public relations is closely related to consumer research and to the wide-ranging types of inquiry carried out by the Social Survey Unit of the Central Office of Information. The Audience Research organization of the BBC has been for many years an instrument of great value for enabling the corporation to assess the responses and desires of the public to broadcast programmes. Some of the other public corporations, such as the North Thames Gas Board, have their own market research sections, while others employ outside bodies to carry out market surveys from time to time. On the whole, however, consumer research and the probing of public opinion by sampling methods is much less well-developed in nationalized industry than the outward-flowing aspect of public relations. Some executives would fail even to recognize that public relations is concerned with these matters at all.

The Beveridge Committee on Broadcasting recommended that the outward and inward functions of public relations are best dealt with by separate organs. They advised that the inward-flowing aspect requires a public representation service, with a director in charge, to act as 'an organ for full-time self-criticism'. Its responsibilities would include the management and extension of the Audience Research service; receiving and reporting on outside criticisms and suggestions; arranging for outside experts to make critical reviews of all home programmes; the systematic review of overseas programmes; putting forward suggestions

[1] *Relations with the Public* (1953) (Acton Society Trust), pp. 3, 10-2, and 28-9.

for setting up advisory committees and providing their secretariat; and studying broadcasting methods and programmes in other countries. It could also help in dealing with charges of injustice or favouritism in the choice of performers or of partiality in the selection of topics for discussion or presentation.[1]

Whether the inward-flowing aspect of public relations is separately organized from the outward-flowing aspect is a matter on which it is difficult to lay down a hard and fast rule. Much will depend on the range and scale of activities involved in the two aspects; and the volume of work arising. The decisive factor may sometimes be whether one aspect alone would be sufficiently important to attract and justify the services of a director of high calibre. Where the inward functions have been grossly ignored, the best way of seeing that they receive adequate attention may be to set up a separate organization on the lines proposed by the Beveridge Committee. Later, perhaps, the situation may change, and co-ordination of the inward and outward functions become the chief need. In such circumstances it will be necessary to bring them together in a single department under one head.

In conclusion, I should like to express a few words of appreciation of the annual reports by the nationalized industries, and the statements of accounts which accompany them. I know that the reports vary in length, style, arrangement, type of information provided, and coverage; and that there are variations not only between different industries but often within the same industry from year to year. I am aware of the quite acute criticisms which have been made of the reports[2] and I do not seek to discourage the careful scrutiny and thought which such criticism implies.

My present object is, however, to pay a tribute to the remarkable interest, fullness, frankness, and standard of presentation of the annual reports issued by the National Coal Board, the Electricity Authorities, the British Transport Commission, the Gas Council and area boards, BEA and BOAC and the area electricity and gas boards.[3] That they are capable of improvement no-one would deny. But surely the important point is that the British nation is now in a position to acquire almost for the first time a vast mass of accurate and systematic knowledge about its basic industries. Our nationalized industries compare very favourably in this respect not only with the reports issued by commercial companies

[1] Report, HMSO, Cmd. 8116/1951, paras. 558-64.

[2] A. H. Hanson: 'Report on the Reports', XXX *Public Administration* (1952), p. 111; Raymond Nottage: 'Reporting to Parliament on the Nationalized Industries', XXXV *Public Administration* (1957), p. 143.

[3] The Beveridge Committee severely criticized the BBC annual reports and accounts. See Report, paras. 405, 407-8, and 593. There has been some improvement since then.

in the private sector, but also with nationalized undertakings in other countries.

These reports are an instrument of public relations. They are also an element in the process of public accountability.

CHAPTER XI

Finance

THERE are many aspects of nationalized industry which affect or are affected by finance. Those which we propose to discuss in this chapter are compensation, price policy, the raising of capital, redemption and depreciation. They are all of great importance and some complexity.

The question of compensation inevitably arises whenever an established industry is taken into public ownership. The case for paying compensation rests on moral, political, and economic grounds and is accepted by all three political parties. Although there is agreement about the need to pay compensation to the former owners who have been expropriated, there is often wide disagreement about the methods to be adopted.

THE BASIS OF COMPENSATION

The principles used in calculating the compensation payable to the owners of an undertaking compulsorily acquired for public ownership are of considerable interest. Their importance is well expressed by the remark that the success of the public corporation from the community's point of view turns on the extent of the capital burden it inherits from the companies it supplants. This observation was made by Mr Ernest Davies, MP, when he examined the terms offered[1] to the stockholders of the London Traffic Combine on the acquisition of their undertaking by the London Passenger Transport Board. His detailed analysis showed that the compensation terms were generous beyond the dreams of avarice.[2]

There was, however, nothing unusual about this extravagantly tenderhearted attitude towards proprietors. Compensation on an excessive scale has been the rule rather than the exception during the past hundred years. Public authorities were nearly always obliged to pay unduly large sums by way of compensation when they expropriated water, gas, electricity, dock or street transport undertakings, or acquired land compulsorily.

[1] *Public Enterprise*, ed. W. A. Robson (1937), p. 189.

[2] *Ib.*, p. 385. These words were my own comment on his analysis.

One of the mistakes usually made in determining compensation is to leave out of account the financial value of a monopoly. Thus, in the case of London Transport, the shareholders of companies which had been facing severe competition were given almost equivalent rights in a public corporation possessing a statutory monopoly, regardless of the enhanced security given to their holdings.[1]

It is against this background that the compensation polices of 1945–50 must be set. The Labour Government was determined to avoid the mistakes of the past.

The Bank of England presented no difficulty. The Old Lady of Threadneedle Street could be, and was, regarded as a gilt-edged security. The stockholders were given Government securities to yield the same gross dividend as that which they had received during the preceding twenty years.

Coal was dealt with on the basis of 'the net maintainable income' which the colliery undertakings might have expected to be able to earn in the future if they had continued under private ownership, multiplied by a certain number of years' purchase. This is probably the fairest of all methods, but it is often extremely difficult to apply, since it involves a prophetic element. So far as the coal industry was concerned, agreement was reached between the Government and the Mining Association as to the terms of reference of an arbitration tribunal which fixed the global sum to be paid for all the assets transferred to the National Coal Board. The ultimate settlement is believed to have been generally acceptable. It gave rise to very little criticism. Wherever practicable this method should be adopted in future.

It was not adopted in the case of any of the other nationalized industries. Stock Exchange prices on specified dates were taken as the basis for calculating the compensation payable to railway stockholders, electricity and gas companies, iron and steel shareholders. An immense barrage of criticism was directed at this method of valuation by the Conservative Opposition in Parliament, by the press, by the City of London, by the Stock Exchange, and by other representatives of financial interests. My own view is that Stock Exchange prices are often not a reliable guide to true values, in the sense of earning capacity, because they are based on estimates of future trends made by speculators or investors, who seldom possess the necessary knowledge of either the industry as a whole or the particular undertaking on which to base a wise forecast. For this reason they are unsatisfactory guides to valuation for compensation purposes: though as much for the reason that they may be too high as that they may be too low.

[1] *Public Enterprise*, ed. W. A. Robson (1937), p. 386.

The great advantage of Stock Exchange quotations is that they are exceedingly simple to apply. Wherever possible, however, we should prefer the 'net maintainable income' basis; where this is considered impracticable, and the Stock Exchange price adopted, a right of appeal should lie to an arbitration tribunal either by the stockholders or the Government or the public corporation concerned, on the ground that the Stock Exchange quotations are too low or too high, as the case may be.

Despite this theoretical objection, there is little reason to believe that substantial injustice to legitimate expectations occurred in any of these industries in which Stock Exchange quotations were used to calculate compensation. Most of the fuss has been political. Professor Walker and Mr Condie take the view that, so far as the railways are concerned, compensation was inflated by the high degree of protection afforded to railway revenues—and hence to railway stocks—by the State. It is indisputable that the Road Traffic Act, 1930, and the Road and Rail Traffic Act, 1933, severely restricted the competition of road transport services with the railways. Professor Walker and Mr Condie contend that since railway shareholders had no legitimate right to expect the continuance of these statutory aids, Parliament should first have driven the railways to the verge of bankruptcy by exposing them to unrestricted competition from road services, and then bought them up at knock-down prices.[1]

This may be a tenable view in theory. In practice it has grave objections. First, governments must time their programmes with an eye mainly on political considerations. In 1947 the Labour Government was on the crest of the wave. If they had delayed nationalizing transport until the railways had been ruined by the repeal of the protective statutes, they might no longer have been in power or the opportunity for getting the Bill through Parliament might have passed. Second, physical rehabilitation of the railways was badly needed after the tremendous strain and neglect of the Second World War, and this would have been ruled out completely if the railway companies had been faced with bankruptcy. Third, the railway services would have deteriorated severely at a time when the public was expecting and needing improved facilities; and the Labour Government would have been rightly blamed for this. Lastly, to repeal legislation with the express purpose of reducing compensation might be legally tenable, but it would almost certainly be regarded as a malevolent and unjust act. Deeds of this kind usually turn out to be unwise in the long run; and they often have unforeseen consequences.

[1] See 'Compensation in Nationalized Industries' in *Problems of Nationalized Industry* ed., W. A. Robson (1952), pp. 64 and 71.

Various other methods of assessing compensation were used to deal with securities not quoted on the Stock Exchange, the half a million privately-owned railway wagons taken over by the British Transport Commission, and the road haulage concerns. Local authorities which lost municipal gas or electricity undertakings received almost no compensation at all: they were merely relieved of their obligations in respect of any outstanding debt and given a small *douceur* to make up for the additional expense arising from the loss of contributions by the utility undertakings to the municipality's central establishment charges and the loss of net surpluses transferred in aid of the rates.

The mistake made in 1933 of giving the shareholders of the London Transport Combine almost equivalent rights in perpetuity in the stock of a public corporation enjoying a statutory monopoly has not been repeated.[1] All the compensation stocks are guaranteed by the Treasury; but while their capital values were equal to the quoted values of the stocks or shares in the nationalized industries, their yield is substantially lower, as befits their gilt-edged status.

A criticism which is often made is that the interest payable on these Treasury-guaranteed stocks becomes part of the cost of production. Unlike dividends, which are payable only if profits are adequate and made available, interest on these stocks must be paid whether or not it is earned. The only alternative would be either to make the payment of interest dependent on the public corporation making a surplus, which would involve the abolition of the Treasury guarantee and a return to something like a fixed interest preference share. This would be a quite unacceptable policy in the context of nationalized industry.

We must, therefore, regard the obligation to pay interest on compensation stocks as a necessary concomitant of nationalization, despite its manifest disadvantages.

No really satisfactory solution of the compensation problem has yet been found. There are clear disadvantages in the present arrangements, but they are at any rate a great improvement on former practices. They have at least avoided the grossly excessive over-compensation of private owners which has been so persistent a feature of the public acquisition of property in British experience. In most cases, nationalization has resulted in assets being acquired by the State of a value roughly corresponding to the compensation paid in respect of them, though the railways were described at the time by Mr Dalton, then Chancellor of the Exchequer, as a poor bag of physical assets. Nevertheless, publicly

[1] Moreover, no further attempt has been made to reproduce the provisions of the London Passenger Transport Act whereby the holders of 'C' stock were entitled to a rate of interest which varied according to the earnings of the undertaking.

owned undertakings which have been initiated by the State, such as the BBC, or British European Airways, and which in consequence carry no burden of compensatiom, are in a much more favourable position than the public corporations which must get along as best they can with a heavy burden of indebtedness towards the former owners.

THE GENERAL FINANCIAL AIM

What financial purpose should a nationalized industry pursue, and how much freedom of choice does it possess in determining its financial policy?

It is sometimes assumed that the nationalized industries are obliged to follow the break-even principle, which means operating the undertaking in such a manner that so far as possible it will make neither a deficit nor a surplus.

The legal obligation imposed on most of the public corporations[1] requires them to conduct their undertaking in such a way as to ensure that its revenues are not less than sufficient to meet its outgoings properly chargeable to revenue account, taking one year with another. These outgoings include repayment of and interest on loans and the establishment of a reserve fund. Thus, a nationalized industry is required to avoid making a continuing loss extending over a period of years, though no one knows the precise meaning of the phrase 'taking one year with another'. There is, however, no legal prohibition of a surplus nor any limit to its amount.

A good many people take the view, however, that, irrespective of any legal duty, publicly-owned industries should serve the public without making either a deficit or a surplus. This is their *raison d'être*, and they should sail along on an even keel, neither receiving subventions from the State nor contributing revenue to the Exchequer (apart from the repayment of any advances which may have been made, and the ordinary liability to taxation). Thus, their finances should be not only self-contained, in the sense of being separated from the Exchequer and the Budget, but also self-supporting.

This principle was originally evolved by the Webbs and other leading Fabians as the proper basis for municipal trading. Their idea was that local authorities should administer their public utility undertakings without profit or loss for the benefit of the whole local community. The views of these 'gas and water socialists' contrasted sharply with those of men

[1] BOAC and BEA were not subjected to this obligation because they needed subsidies for several years after 1945. The power to subsidize them lapsed in 1956, and BOAC has not received a subsidy since 1951-2.

like Joseph Chamberlain, who, as Lord Mayor of Birmingham, induced the city corporation to embark on municipal trading and the large-scale ownership of land in order to make profits which could be used to reduce the local rates.[1]

At the national level a protracted struggle took place to secure self-contained finance for the Post Office, which for long was regarded by the Treasury as a source of revenue for the Exchequer to be used in relief of general taxation.[2] The Bridgeman Committee recommended in 1932 that the Post Office should contribute a fixed sum annually to the Treasury and be entitled to retain any surplus over and above that figure. This arrangement was rescinded on the outbreak of the Second World War and was not revived until 1956, when an annual contribution to the Exchequer of £5 million was agreed for a trial period of five years, any remaining surplus going to the Post Office's revenue reserve. The figure of £5 million compares with commercial surpluses averaging £6 million a year which had accrued to the Exchequer during the four years preceding 1956. It is also an approximate estimate of what the Post Office would have to pay in taxation if it were not exempt from tax liability.[3]

While we may agree wholeheartedly with the proposition that publicly-owned industries should not be run in order to provide a source of revenue for either the national government or for local authorities, this by no means concludes the question. There are other purposes for which a surplus may be required.

If a public corporation makes a surplus in the course of its business, it must by law be applied for the purposes of the corporation as defined by Parliament in the relative statute. This means in practice that any excess revenue would ultimately be ploughed back into the undertaking, or be spent on improving the service or quality of the goods, in pursuing research or development, reducing prices, increasing wages, or bettering conditions of employment. The normal method of disposing of a new surplus is to place it to reserve. Indeed, the main reason for making a net surplus is to build up the reserve fund.

THE PROBLEM OF THE RAILWAYS

It has proved increasingly difficult to apply the break-even principle, or any other test of solvency, to the railways during the past ten years.

[1] J. L. Garvin: *The Life of Joseph Chamberlain*, Vol. I, pp. 188-200.

[2] See *Report of the Bridgeman Committee on the Post Office*, HMSO, Cmd. 4149/1932; John Dugdale: 'The Post Office' in *Public Enterprise*, ed. W. A. Robson, pp. 304-9.

[3] *Report on Post Office Development and Finance*, HMSO, Cmd. 9576/1955, paras. 22-5.

The annual surplus or deficit made by the British Transport Commission since nationalization was introduced is shown in the following table:

BTC—Annual Surpluses and Deficits
Source: BTC Annual Reports

	Deficit *£ million*	*Surplus* *£ million*
1948	4·7	
1949	20·8	
1950	14·1	
1951		0·1
1952		4·5
1953		4·2
1954	11·9	
1955	30·6	
1956		3·1[1]
1957		4·6[1]

Until the passing of the Transport Act, 1953, the BTC undertaking included a very large number of road haulage vehicles; thereafter the process of denationalization rapidly reduced the size of this element. The net surplus or deficit for the different services were not given separately in the BTC accounts. One can, however, safely assume that the railways have been running at a heavy loss since 1948 and that the road haulage business contributed a substantial surplus to the funds of the Commission. The table shows that a deficit is not just the result of the Transport Act, 1953, as there were heavy deficits in 1949 and 1950 and a substantial one in 1948. According to a statement published by the Bureau of Railway Economics, seventy per cent of the unassigned charges of BTC could properly be allocated to the railways, since in 1949 the railways accounted for seventy per cent of the total book value of the assets, seventy per cent of the total staff, and a like proportion of gross receipts and operating expenses. On this basis the railways would have shown a deficit of £12·7 million in 1948, £26 million in 1949, and £12·8 million in 1950.[2]

A memorandum submitted by the Transport Tribunal to the Minister of Transport and Civil Aviation in April 1956 stated that in only one year (1952) of the preceding eight years had British Railways paid their way: that is, earned their working expenses and an appropriate share of

[1] In respect of activities other than British Railways. In 1956 £57·5 million, in 1957 £68·1 million, and in 1958 £90·1 million were transferred to the statutory Special Account in respect of revenue deficit of British Railways.

[2] *Nationalized Transport Operations in Great Britain* (1948) (Bureau of Railway Economics), p. 33; (1949), p. 19; (1950), p. 14.

central charges. In 1955, when the overall deficiency was £30·6 million, the deficit on the railways was about £38 million. In the absence of any further remedial measures and at the then current rates and charges, the overall deficit would increase to about £55½ million.[1]

The central charges comprise mainly interest payable on compensation stock and capital redemption. These charges, which amounted to £57·2 million in 1954 and £60·1 million in 1955, transformed aggregate working surpluses on the year's operations of £45·5 million in 1954 and £29·5 million in 1955 to the deficits of £11·9 million and £30·6 million shown in the previous Table.

The plight of the railways was made much worse by the findings of a Court of Inquiry appointed by the Minister of Labour to report on the dispute between the BTC and the National Union of Railwaymen in 1955. The Commission argued that they could not grant the wage increases demanded by the union because of their statutory obligation to cover expenses from revenue. The Commission stated that the earnings from railways in past years had been insufficient to meet their statutory obligations, and that the wage increases ahead fixed by agreement and award in 1954 would in any event cause an even greater deficit in 1955.

The Court of Inquiry refused to accept this argument. They declared in a notable passage:

> 'The nation has provided by statute that there shall be a nationalized system of railway transport, which must therefore be regarded as a public utility of the first importance. Having willed the end, the Nation must will the means. This implies that employees of such a national service should receive a fair and adequate wage, and that in broad terms, the railwaymen should be in no worse case than his colleague in a comparable industry. The argument which has been repeatedly used by the British Transport Commission, that they found themselves unable to pay rates of wages which they might otherwise deem proper and desirable, is, of course, wholly inconsistent with such a view. In these circumstances it is plain that there is no substance in the argument that there is an absolute statutory bar which prevents the Commission from paying such rates of wages as may involve them in any particular year in a deficit.'[2]

The Court also commented on the vagueness of the phrase 'taking one year with another' in the enactment defining the financial duty of the BTC and several of the other public corporations. They thought it was sufficiently elastic to permit the Commission to incur a deficit in any one year, or even in successive years, so long as they could see their way to an overall financial balance in a long-term estimate of their prospects. The statutory obligation would operate as a bar to the payment of

[1] 551 HC Deb. 5s., cols. 186-90 (April 11, 1956).

[2] *Court of Inquiry: Interim Report*, HMSO, Cmd. 9352/1955, para. 10.

adequate and proper wages for efficient service only if the BTC reached a position where the imposition of further burdens would render it impossible for the Commission to fulfil its legal duty over such a period of years as they had chosen.[1]

This view of the situation involved more than a defeat for the Commission. It meant also a defeat for Parliament, the Government, and the nation in their attempt to impose solvency by law on an antiquated railway system, worked by a highly organized labour force whose unions were not prepared to allow wages and conditions to be kept down in order to comply with the statutory obligation to avoid a continuing deficit. The true position of the railways had been partly concealed by the Labour Government's Transport Act of 1947, which enabled the railway deficit to be offset by a surplus from road transport; but now it was revealed in all its nakedness. No one had faced up to the problem of how to make the railways pay their way while maintaining a permanent labour force of adequate size and skill. The problem is admittedly a very difficult one. It involves great technological advances; better management; many changes in services and facilities, rolling stock and equipment; and large adjustments in the employment of labour.

Meanwhile, the situation could not be allowed to continue unchanged. Some way had to be found to check the rising tide of annual deficits or to modify the statutory obligation. The long-term remedy for the plight of the railways is to be found neither in legislative amendments nor in the mysteries of accountancy: it lies in modernization of equipment, management, services, facilities, and labour practices. A long overdue plan entitled the 'Modernization and Re-equipment of British Railways', estimated to cost £1,200 million, was issued by the British Transport Commission in 1955. This document stated that greater financial self-sufficiency of the separate services was one of the major benefits expected to result from the plan.[2]

FINANCING THE TRANSITION

In 1956 the BTC announced their proposals for the future financial administration of the railways.[3] Annual deficits would be likely to continue during the early years of the modernization plan. This was partly because the economic benefits will lag some considerable time behind

[1] *Court of Inquiry: Final Report*, HMSO, Cmd. 9372/1955, para. 55.

[2] *Modernization and Re-equipment of British Railways* (1955) (British Transport Commission), para. 35.

[3] *British Transport Commission Proposals for the Railways*, HMSO, Cmd. 9880/1956, p. 29.

increased interest charges on the capital expenditure incurred on the new works, and partly because other measures already in hand would not effect economies on a substantial scale until two or three years had elapsed. The over-all estimate of future prospects is shown in the following Table:

	£ *million*		
	Dec. 1956	1961 *or* 1962	1970
Annual rate of deficit at starting point, disregarding Modernization Plan	−40	−40	−40
Improved contributions from activities other than railways	0	+ 5	+ 5
Improved contribution from railways:			
(*a*) Modernization		+35	+85
(*b*) Pruning Services		+ 3	+ 3
(*c*) Productivity		+ 5	+10
(*d*) Greater Freedom		+20	+25
TOTAL		+63	+123
Less: Interest on Modernization borrowings	− 2	−25	−40
Net surplus or deficit	−42	+ 3	+48
Interest on accumulated deficits (at 5%) ...	− 6	−20	−10

Thus, the BTC estimate that the yield from modernization of the railways together with other savings will enable them to balance their accounts by 1961 or 1962, and to have an annual surplus of about £50 million by 1970.

Government proposals to capitalize the interest on deficits from 1956 for a limited period, altered the estimated net results set out in the above Table.

The Government plan involved a series of special advances to the Commission to meet their revenue deficits until expenditure and income on current account can be made to balance. The total sum to be advanced will be limited to £250 million. This is repayable; and the first three years' interest on it will also be advanced and capitalized.

The estimated result of this special aid on the future financial position of the British Transport Commission is to increase the annual rate of deficit at December 1956 to £45 million; to produce a larger surplus in 1961 or 1962; and to reduce the annual surplus expected to be available in 1970 to £35 million.[1]

[1] *British Transport Commission Proposals for the Railways*, HMSO, Cmd. 9880/1956, paras. 25–7, p. 7.

The policy of attempting to increase the revenue of the railways in the near future was not considered to be expedient. The Commission thought that charges could not be raised sufficiently to cover costs because higher rates would be offset by a falling off in traffic. Additional charges would have to be concentrated on heavy bulk traffic and even if this did not drive such traffic off the railways it would substantially increase manufacturing costs. The Government, said the Commission, considers this to be opposed to the national interest, and accepts the view of the BTC that in the long run by destroying public goodwill it would be unsound from a commercial standpoint. It would therefore be wiser to pursue a policy of price restraint for the next few years.[1]

Meanwhile, if the annual deficits were allowed to continue, the vast and increasing accumulation would have a demoralizing effect on the railways. Financial discipline would be undermined, and reliance on permanent subsidization would be disastrous to the self-respect of the undertaking and would certainly be a disincentive to efficiency. Ultimately the accumulated deficit would reach unmanageable proportions and default in some form would become inevitable.[2]

In view of the fact that BTC are financed entirely by capital bearing a fixed rate of interest, there was no possibility of asking the stockholders to forego their interest during the period of reconstruction.[3] The Commission were therefore compelled to look to the Government for aid for a strictly limited period. The Government also considered it reasonable that the Commission should not have to pay out of their revenues the interest payable on the capital sums borrowed to finance the railway modernization plan during the time when the expenditure is taking place and has not yet begun to yield benefits. The policy of not charging to revenue the full burden of servicing capital costs during the years in which the expenditure occurs but prior to the assets thereby acquired becoming productive, is a correct one from an accountancy point of view.[4] The Government therefore proposed that for a specified number of years advances should be made to the Commission out of the Consolidated Fund to enable them to cover their revenue deficits in those years. These advances would be limited to a total of £250 million and would be ultimately repayable. The payment of interest on these advances would also be covered by additional special advances to the Commission.[5] The carrying out of these proposals for government help from public money was authorized by the Transport (Railway Finances) Act, 1956.

[1] *British Transport Commission Proposals for the Railways*, HMSO, Cmd. 9880/1956, paras. 25 and 26.

[2] *Ib.*, p. 13. [3] *Ib.*, p. 28. [4] *Ib.*, para. 26, p. 7. [5] *Ib.*, p. 25.

In addition to this first aid by way of financial assistance and the blood transfusion involved in the modernization plan, the Commission's proposals for putting their house in order included a series of operating reforms and commercial improvements in railway administration designed to effect financial economies. These included, first, the pruning of unremunerative services, by such means as the substitution of road for rail services; and the introduction of diesel or electric traction or light railway equipment; second, increased productivity through the development of work study, incentive bonus schemes, and the wider use of office machinery and electronic equipment in operating departments; and third, the promotion of more efficient freight transport services and practices by offering to traders financial inducements now permitted under the Transport Act, 1953.[1]

The estimated savings from all these sources are included in the table on page 287. This shows that, leaving aside interest on accumulated deficits, the BTC hope to earn a small net surplus of £3 millions by 1961 or 1962, and £48 million by 1970. One hopes the forecast will be realized but it is difficult to believe it is anything more than an optimistic guess.

The crisis in the financial position of the railways had some interesting repercussions in Parliament. Mr Ernest Davies, MP, stated as far back as February 1955, that the accumulated deficits were likely to mount to a greater height than the Government had envisaged, if no subsidies were given. He suggested that the Government should contribute to the capital charges on BTC compensation stock as a temporary measure.[2] There was thus no disagreement about the need for Government assistance. But Mr Davies argued for the Labour Opposition that the BTC should not in future be asked to break even, since it no longer had a duty to provide an integrated system of public transport. This meant, in effect, that unless the British Transport Commission could subsidize the railways from a surplus on road transport, and control both road and rail services, it was not right or reasonable to expect the Commission to pay their way.

This was equivalent to asserting that nationalized industries should support each other: for example, that electricity supply should provide a surplus to cover a deficit on coal. This was not accepted by the Government, and in my opinion it is an untenable proposition. Mr R. A. Butler, speaking as Chancellor of the Exchequer in February 1955, said unequivocably that the Government expected all nationalized indus-

[1] *British Transport Commission Proposals for the Railways*, HMSO, Cmd. 9880/195, pp. 20, 22-3, and 24-5.

[2] 536 HC Deb. 5s., cols. 1757-66 (February 8, 1955).

tries to carry out their statutory duties in regard to covering their costs. 'We certainly expect the Commission to balance its current accounts, taking one year with another.'[1] He also seemed to wave aside the prospect of an Exchequer subsidy as something the Commission had neither asked for nor expected.[2] Mr Watkinson, the Minister of Transport and Civil Aviation, had to explain to the House of Commons more than a year later (in May 1956) the Government's policy in refusing to allow the Commission to raise their charges in a desperate attempt to bridge the gap between revenue and expenditure. 'If something cannot be done in the next year or so to gain improvements in operating efficiency,' he said, 'the Commission may well find itself crushed between the upper and lower millstones of an increased deficit and an inability to recoup the deficit by increased charges, because the economic limit of increasing charges has been reached.'[3] This fact alone made it essential that the whole position of the railways should be reviewed during the coming months. It was during this breathing space that the Commission produced their proposals for achieving solvency.

This excursion into the financial affairs of the British Transport Commission should suffice to show that there is no magic in the statutory obligation imposed on the public corporations to pay their way out of revenue. A nationalized industry may not be able to fulfil its duty in this respect if it is technologically obsolete or obsolescent, or if it has to meet demands put forward by powerful trade unions for increased wages which are beyond its capacity to pay, or if it has to face actual or potential competition from alternative commodities or services, and if the demand is not highly inelastic. The railways and the coal industry are confronted with all these conditions; and while they prevail the statutory obligation requiring them to pay their way out of revenue is likely to be of no greater effect than the enactment in the Railways Act, 1921, which provided that rates and charges were to be fixed so as to yield a 'standard net revenue' equal to that earned in 1913, which was a bumper year.

PRICE POLICY

So far we have been considering the general financial aim of nationalized industries in terms of their total revenue and expenditure arising from current operations. We may now turn to the question of price policy.

Many economists advocate that a public corporation should break

[1] 536 HC Deb. 5s., col. 1362 (February 3, 1955).
[2] *Ib.*, col. 1310.
[3] *Ib.*, cols. 2353-7 (May 17, 1956).

even not only on the undertaking as a whole, but also on its various parts, unless there is a clear instruction to the contrary. If this principle is pushed to its logical conclusion, the prices charged for each unit or category of goods or services should always correspond to their relative costs.

The advantage of keeping prices as close as possible to costs is that it gives the consumer an opportunity to assert his preferences. This is as true in the public sector as in the private sector of the economy. The consumer gets what he is willing to pay for at its proper cost—assuming that the undertaking is able and willing to provide it.

The main controversy is whether prices should be based on marginal costs or on average costs. Marginal cost is the cost of producing additional supplies; and marginal cost pricing aims at ensuring that the price of a service or commodity corresponds with the cost of producing additional supplies.

The average cost system is to fix prices so that they cover the average costs of providing the service or commodity. The Post Office system of postal charges appears to be mainly based on average costs. Letters are carried at the same rate from one street to the next or halfway round the world, regardless of the enormous differences in cost. The difference between the overseas postal rates for foreign countries and the Commonwealth has obviously nothing to do with relative costs.

Most economists favour marginal cost pricing on theoretical grounds, but it is usually quite incompatible with the break-even principle. If coal had been priced in accordance with the marginal cost of production since the war, the National Coal Board would have made an annual surplus of many millions of pounds. The arguments for and against the two methods as applied to coal were set out at length in the report of the Ridley Committee on National Fuel Policy. The committee were evenly divided on the merits of the two methods.[1]

In 1953 Mr I. M. D. Little argued strongly in favour of raising the price of exportable coal sold to consumers in this country to the level of its export price; and of lifting the prices of non-exportable coal until demand was equal to supply instead of being far ahead of it. He wanted to effect a large expansion in the export of coal and thought that the export prices then prevailing were low enough to make this possible. He contended that coal was sold in the domestic market at too low a price.

Mr Little's policy would have involved a rise of 10*s.* to 15*s.* a ton in the price of coal sold in the home market, yielding a surplus of about £150 million a year. He proposed to distribute a third of this large

[1] HMSO, Cmd. 8647/1952, Ch. IV.

sum on increasing miners' wages, improved training and education programmes for mine managers and technicians, and subsidizing more economical coal-burning appliances to replace inefficient domestic grates and ovens; while £100 million would go to the Treasury to be spent on higher pensions, family allowances, and other social benefits.[1] This scheme did not involve making the price of coal equal to its marginal cost, for the author thought there was no point in doing so while demand exceeded supply.[2]

The same economist criticized even more severely the price policy of the electricity supply industry, on the ground that it has completely failed to produce the correct amount of electricity which should be produced in the national interest. He alleged that the Electricity Boards were concerned only to sell as much electricity as possible and not in selling the right amount.[3] More specifically, they had used the virtual monopoly which they enjoy in supplying electricity for light and power in order to make up the losses they incurred 'in inducing customers away from the gas industry, which could provide many of the services it has lost to electricity at lower cost to the community'.[4]

The late Sir Arthur Street, when deputy chairman of the National Coal Board, declared that consumers should be free to choose between the various kinds of goods and services which are available, and the only way to prevent a waste of national resources is to use the price mechanism so as to guide their choice in accordance with the costs of production.[5]

How far one can go in this respect depends on circumstances and common sense. There frequently comes a point when the economies of uniform charges outweigh their disadvantages. There are many instances when the business of working out the detailed costs of particular items of service is itself too costly a process to be acceptable. Moreover, we need not believe that in private enterprise prices always correspond with costs. It is quite a common practice for some goods to be sold below cost or with a very small profit in many different types of shop, in which other goods are sold at an extremely high rate of profit. Again, there may be large economies of administration resulting from a uniform charge for services of unequal cost. This is the justification for a standard telephone charge in a large metropolitan area or provincial region, regardless of whether the service is provided by private or public enter-

[1] I. M. D. Little: *The Price of Fuel* (1953), pp. 28-31.
[2] *Ib.*, p. 7.
[3] *Ib.*, p. 151.
[4] *Ib.*, p. 97. See Ch. XV post.
[5] 'Quasi-Government Bodies since 1918' in *British Government since 1918* (1950), p. 189.

prise. The averaging of costs and prices is quite common in private enterprise.

The important point is that we must reject the notion that there is something 'democratic' about charging uniform prices for goods or services which are provided at differential costs. There is nothing 'democratic' about the uniform 15-cent fare on the New York subway. Nor is it 'democratic' to charge excessively high bus fares in inner London in order to subsidize cheap fares to the outer suburbs.

The Chambers Committee stated that London Transport's interpretation of their statutory obligation did not mean that every service must cover its own costs. So long as the aggregate revenue from fares is sufficient to meet total expenditure and interest charges, the question of whether a particular route or service or journey pays or runs at a loss is not the dominant consideration in deciding whether it shall be operated. 'The profitable services must subsidize the unprofitable, the latter being as important as the former.'[1] The Committee reported that elimination of the most unprofitable services would cause intense hardship to certain sections of the community, which would conflict with the obligation imposed on the London Transport Executive to provide an adequate service over their whole area. Public need is the ultimate criterion applicable to unremunerative services; and the fact that a service loses money is not regarded by the LTE as evidence that it is unnecessary, or less necessary in fulfilling public needs than services which are highly remunerative. The meaning of public need cannot be precisely defined. The number of persons involved and the existence or absence of alternative means of transport, will usually influence the decision. In establishing new services the economic aspects are carefully considered, and the LTE seldom departed far from ordinary commercial principles. The committee did not criticize this aspect of the Executive's administration; but they were not sure that the Executive adopt an equally firm attitude about cutting down unremunerative services.[2]

The averaging of costs by a transport undertaking is severely condemned by Professor Gilbert Walker on the ground that a common carrier cannot operate on a competitive basis if it is burdened with unremunerative services or obligations. If a railway averages its costs for different traffics and carries them at a uniform rate calculated to cover overall average costs, it runs the risk of losing all or some of the traffic carried at a cost below the average, since competing carriers, such as road haulage contractors, may be able to undercut rail charges for this particular traffic without incurring a loss. To avoid this type of situation,

[1] *Report of the Committee of Inquiry into London Transport*, HMSO (1955), para. 72.
[2] *Ib.*, paras. 75 and 76.

rail charges must be highly differential not only between traffics but also, for example, between main line or branch line services, and between express and slow trains.[1]

The principle of averaging costs has hitherto prevented the British Transport Commission from lowering their charges for services which the railways can carry out at lower cost than any other form of transport; while at the same time public opinion, the pressure of interest groups, and the habitual pattern of the past conspire to induce the Commission to continue to provide rail services which cannot effectively compete with motorbuses or lorries on grounds either of cost or convenience.[2]

Mr Gilbert Ponsonby has urged the railways to divest themselves of all traffic carried at a loss and which could be more economically transported by road. If this were done they would be able to reduce their charges for many other traffics without rendering them unprofitable. By this means the railways could expand the remunerative traffics which they are best qualified to carry, while diverting the remainder to more appropriate forms of transport. This and other benefits may be expected to flow from a resolute attempt to relate charges closely to costs. Mr Ponsonby indicates some of the principal factors which would justify differential charges, but he nevertheless believes that a much larger proportion of charges can be safely and properly based on average costs than it has hitherto been customary to assume.[3]

THE RELATION OF COSTS TO CHARGES

In electricity supply, the Herbert Committee declared that the first principle in tariff-making should be to ensure that charges reflect costs.[4] They advised that further progress could be made in this direction by relieving the Boards of their statutory obligation to simplify charges;[5] by varying the charges for bulk supplies by the generating authority as between day and night, and winter and summer;[6] by trying to relate the charges to commercial, agricultural, and domestic consumers more

[1] Gilbert Walker: 'Transport Policy before and after 1953', V *Oxford Economic Papers* new series (1953), pp. 111 ff.

[2] Gilbert Walker and Henry Maddick: 'Responsibility for Transport', XXIII *Political Quarterly* (1952), pp. 224–5.

[3] Gilbert J. Ponsonby: 'Towards a New Railway Charges Policy', XXV *Journal of the Institute of Transport* (1954), p. 2.

[4] *Report of the Committee of Inquiry into the Electricity Supply Industry*, HMSO, Cmd. 9672/1956, para. 398; see also I. M. D. Little: *The Price of Fuel* (1953) pp. 127, 136, 148, and 153–6.

[5] Report, para. 397.

[6] *Ib.*, paras. 382 and 408.

closely to the costs of supplying them;[1] by investigating the problems of spreading the load and pursuing a more vigorous policy in promoting off-peak consumption by the offer of tariff incentives;[2] by more research into the problems of utilization with a view to discovering the characteristics of different classes of consumers in order to improve the tariff-making process.[3]

The Beveridge Committee on Broadcasting had to deal with a different type of situation since all listeners or viewers pay a uniform licence fee. They recommended that the BBC should publish separate accounts giving details of revenue and expenditure for different regions, services and programmes, but should not generally try to make each service pay for itself. There is, they held, good reason for using the surplus contributed by densely populated areas containing many licences to facilitate the extension of broadcasting in sparsely populated areas where the advantages to listeners are especially great. It is also reasonable that the BBC should allocate money to school broadcasting or the Third Programme in excess of any specific income which can be attributed to those activities.[4]

The committee considered, however, that television should be made to stand on its own feet financially, instead of receiving subsidies from the income paid by listeners for sound broadcasting. This is necessary for two reasons. One is that it is inequitable to require those listeners to sound broadcasting, who do not or cannot acquire television sets, to contribute towards the cost of providing television.[5] The other is that separate financial resources for television are essential if the corporation are to have a full sense of financial responsibility and if the greatest possible amount of freedom is to be given to them.[6]

The committee therefore recommended that the corporation should abandon its policy of regarding twenty per cent of sound revenue as freely available for television. Any surplus from one service spent on the other should be treated as a repayable advance.[7]

British European Airways operates some internal air services at a loss. Where the areas concerned are very sparsely populated and the income level of the inhabitants is very low, as in the case of the Highlands and Islands of Scotland, there is no prospect of the air services ever being able to earn their costs. Nevertheless, these services are considered desirable in the public interest and there would be a great outcry if they were discontinued. All the Scottish members of Parliament would combine in a strong and persistent protest.

[1] Report para. 396. [2] *Ib.*, paras. 403-8. [3] *Ib.*, paras, 409-10.
[4] *Report of the Broadcasting Committee, 1949*, HMSO, Cmd. 8116/1951, paras. 413-4.
[5] *Ib.*, para. 416. [6] *Ib.*, para. 415. [7] *Ib.*, para. 407.

Members of all political parties have repeatedly urged in Parliament that these unremunerative routes should be treated as social services and the losses on them covered by a special Exchequer subsidy to be clearly shown in BEA's accounts. The present position is that these losses reduce substantially the surplus made on other services and give a misleading and unduly unfavourable picture of BEA's financial position.[1]

The Select Committee on Nationalized Industries (Reports and Accounts) in their report on the air corporations discussed this matter at length. They were told by BEA that the main reason they fly to the Highlands and Islands is because the Government wishes them to do so. The deficit on this service is substantial, but has not so far been revealed in the published accounts.[2] It brings no commercial advantages to BEA and is a form of social service.

The Minister of Transport and Civil Aviation has no statutory power to pay a subsidy to reimburse BEA for the loss on this service. The question of whether he should seek the necessary statutory power has been considered from time to time and a negative conclusion reached. The Government's view is that BEA receive a certain amount of protection, and in return are expected to operate some uneconomic services for the public good. The position is regarded as analogous to that affecting motorbus services, which are also protected by a licensing system. This enables them to provide many unremunerative services which are paid for out of the profits on the more popular services.[3]

The Select Committee expressed disagreement with this view. They saw no good reason why the users of remunerative air services should subsidize the uneconomic routes. They recommended that BEA should insist on a formal direction from the Minister in order to show that the responsibility is his. They urged that losses should be made good by a subvention paid by the Department out of money voted by Parliament. Lastly, they said that the position should be accurately explained in the corporation's annual accounts.[4]

This proposal accords with the view that the nationalized industries should be administered on strictly 'commercial' principles. Every activity should be required to pay for itself, so far as it is possible to ascertain its cost and attribute the amount to the appropriate service. Any con-

[1] 518 HC Deb. 5s., col. 2725, Mr Pargiter; col. 2679, Mr Grimond; col. 2707, Sir W. Wakefield (October 27, 1953). 533 HC Deb. 5s., col. 44, Mr Beswick (November, 15, 1954).

[2] *Report from the Select Committee on Nationalized Industries* (*Report and Accounts*). The Air Corporations. HC Paper 213. May 1959. Para. 107. The deficit was £264,000 in 1956–7 and £365,000 in 1957–8.

[3] *Ib.*, paras. 107, 110-11; Appendix 19; Q 1978, 1991-2, 1998-9, 2011.

[4] *Ib.*, paras. 108, 115-17.

sideration of the national interest, of social need or public convenience, of Commonwealth solidarity or the comity of nations, should be ruled out as irrelevant and inappropriate to the purposes of the public corporation and undertaken only by direction of a Minister. If compliance with such a direction costs the corporation money, it should be paid out of the Exchequer.

'POLITICAL' AND 'ECONOMIC' DECISIONS

A conception of this kind led Professor Walker and Mr Maddick to contend that policies on such matters as standard fares on the railways, unremunerative services to isolated parts of the country, services provided on strategic grounds, and even the duty—imposed by the Transport Act, 1947, but repealed in 1953—to provide an efficient, adequate, economical and properly integrated system of public transport, could not be safely entrusted to the British Transport Commission because political and social matters were involved in the decisions. They should therefore be left to the Minister and defended by him in Parliament.[1] The Act was at fault in 'blurring the possible conflicts between the social criteria of "an adequate and convenient service" and the orthodox accountancy view of balancing its books'.

A similar but more extreme position was taken up by the Herbert Committee, which recommended that 'If it is thought in the national interest that some course other than a purely economic course should be followed, it is in our opinion the responsibility of the Minister acting on behalf of the Government to require that course to be adopted. . . . It is not for the persons running the industry to undertake uneconomic schemes of expansion, whether in rural or urban areas, in the supposed national interest, if the effect is to subsidize one particular body of consumers out of the pockets of others'.[2] The report criticized the Central Electricity Authority for having decided to insure its undertaking with the insurance companies rather than to carry their own risks, in order to maintain the strength of the British insurance industry in foreign markets.[3] Matters of 'supposed national interest' should be regarded as political questions to be decided by the Government.

We can see here the disinterment of something resembling the mythical Economic Man of the classical economists and its projection on to the plane of public enterprise. There is something faintly comic in this attempt to embody in the public corporations the ghostlike figure

[1] Gilbert Walker and Henry Maddick: 'Responsibility for Transport', XXIII *Political Quarterly* (1952), p. 232.

[2] *Report*, para. 373. [3] *Ib.*, paras. 220 and 373.

L

of a creature motivated solely by crude economic motives which were once supposed to inspire every action of the successful capitalist. For after all, the nationalization movement represents a repudiation of the whole concept of Economic Man and his ceaseless search for profit and the avoidance of loss.

Furthermore, the standard of conduct which bodies like the Herbert Committee—manned often by people who are either hostile to or at least unsympathetic towards public enterprise—are seeking to impose on nationalized industries is one which is not followed in either public or private enterprise today. Neither the BBC, nor London Transport, nor the Port of London Authority, nor the Post Office, nor the Bank of England, nor any other type of public authority invariably or even habitually behave as though they were blind and deaf to all considerations other than purely economic ones. Furthermore, large commercial undertakings no longer behave in that manner, whether or not they ever did so. Great joint-stock companies like ICI and Unilever and Courtaulds and Vickers are continually taking into consideration non-economic considerations in determining their business policies. A board of directors which was not influenced by social and political questions, and which failed to take account of public sentiment and the national interest, would undoubtedly be a very bad board. The philosophy of hedonism is no longer regarded as a suitable guide for the modern business executive.

To expect a board composed of men of outstanding ability and long experience to draw a sharp line between the commercial aspects and the wider considerations which have a bearing on many important questions of policy, and to deny themselves the right to take the latter into account in their deliberations, is little short of absurd. The idea that they should do so is quite unrealistic.

An imaginary case will test the soundness of the hypothesis. Is the amount of money and effort which an airline devotes to air safety[1] to be determined exclusively by economic considerations? Suppose, for example, an airline were to find that by reducing the standard of maintenance of its aircraft it could run the airline more profitably but at the cost of doubling its accident rates, and that this had almost no effect on its volume of traffic, would this be a decision which the board would be justified in taking? Or should they solemnly submit this matter to the Minister on the ground that it involved a 'political' question: namely, the expenditure of money on the saving of human life? If they were to do so, the Minister would probably think the members of the board were suffering from mental aberration and should be replaced as soon as possible.

[1] Over and above the legally defined standard.

THE RAISING OF LOANS

We may now consider the position of the nationalized industries in regard to capital expenditure and borrowing of money. The statutes require—the Bank of England Act is an exception in this respect—that the public corporations, in framing their programmes of re-organization or development involving substantial capital outlay, shall act on lines settled from time to time with the approval of the appropriate Minister.

The Board of a nationalized industry must therefore obtain ministerial agreement to the purposes and content of a development or investment scheme of any magnitude. The big plans which have been published for the rehabilitation of the coal industry and the modernization of the railways, the programme of nuclear energy electricity stations, are outstanding examples of development schemes which required Government approval.

A public corporation must also obtain Government approval when it wishes to borrow money. There are several methods of raising loans, but they all involve ministerial approval. In the case of the coal industry, the Minister of Power is authorized to make advances to the NCB for the purpose of defraying capital expenditure, including the provision of working capital; and under this procedure the advance of money involves the Minister's approval.[1]

The Gas Council may, with the consent of the Minister and Treasury approval, borrow money by the issue of British Gas Stock in order to provide working capital required by any Area Gas Board or by the Council itself or to meet any expenditure incurred by a board or the Council in connection with capital works.[2] BOAC and BEA may, with Treasury consent, borrow temporarily by way of overdraft, or for long term borrowing by the issue of stock. The stock is to be issued, transferred, dealt with and redeemed upon such terms in accordance with such regulations as the Minister of Transport and Civil Aviation, with Treasury approval, may prescribe.[3] The Treasury may guarantee both stock and temporary loans issued by the airways corporations, in such manner and on such conditions as they think fit.[4] Similar provisions apply to the British Transport Commission.[5]

The Electricity Act, 1957,[6] enables the Electricity Council, with the consent of the Minister of Power and the approval of the Treasury, to

[1] Coal Industry Nationalization Act, 1946, s. 26. The NCB may borrow temporarily by way of overdraft or otherwise for meeting their obligations and discharging their functions up to a limit of £10 million at any one time, with the consent of the Minister or in accordance with any general authority given by him. *Ib.*, s. 27.

[2] Gas Act, 1948, s. 42. [3] Civil Aviation Act, 1946, s. 8. [4] *Ib.*, s. 9.

[5] Transport Act, 1947, ss. 88-9. [6] Electricity Act, 1957, ss. 15-6.

borrow money by the issue of British Electricity Stock for such purposes as the redemption of any existing British Electricity Stock, the repayment of Exchequer advances to the former central authority or the Electricity Council, or capital expenditure by the Council, the Generating Board, or any Area Board. The Treasury may guarantee such stock. These constitute the main borrowing powers of the industry; but additional powers are conferred on the Central Electricity Generating Board and the Area Boards which authorize them, with the agreement of the Government and after consulting the Council, to borrow money for similar purposes relating to their respective undertakings, but without a Treasury guarantee.

THE STATUTORY CEILING

Some degree of parliamentary control is always exercised in connection with the borrowing powers of the public corporations. This usually takes the form of a statutory limitation on the total amount which can be advanced to, or borrowed by, each nationalized industry. The maximum thus fixed will normally be sufficient to cover the estimated capital expenditure of the undertaking for several years, after which Parliament will be asked to sanction further borrowing by the corporation.

The advances of the Minister to the National Coal Board were originally limited to £150 million for a period of five years from the commencement of the Coal Industry Nationalization Act, 1946. The borrowing powers of the Board were subsequently increased in 1951 to £300 million, with a limit of £40 million in any year or such higher sum as a ministerial order might specify.[1] Ministerial orders were made authorizing advances up to £75 million in 1954–5, and £95 million in 1955–6. In 1956 a further statute raised the maximum aggregate amount of advances outstanding to £650, with an annual permitted increase of £75 million. These borrowing powers are to apply for a period of five years.[2] Similar provisions have been made for the other public corporations, although the maximum sums authorized have of course varied according to the capital requirements of the industries.[3]

The largest borrowing powers given to any public corporation are those conferred on the Electricity Boards. The British Electricity Auth-

[1] Coal Industry Act, 1951, s. 1; Coal Industry Nationalization (Borrowing Powers) Orders SI 1954 No. 1456 and SI 1955 No. 1083.

[2] Coal Industry Act, 1956, s. 1. *National Coal Board Annual Report 1956*, HMSO, HC 176-I/1956-7, Vol. I, para. 89. The total advances outstanding at the end of 1955 to the National Coal Board were £247·2 million and £261·7 million at the end of 1956.

[3] See Transport Act, 1953, s. 26, and Transport (Borrowing Powers) Act, 1955, s. 1; Air Corporations Act, 1953, s. 1; Colonial Development and Welfare Act, 1955, s. 1; New Towns Act, 1955, s. 1; Transport (Borrowing Powers) Bill, 1958.

ority was initially authorized to raise loans amounting in the aggregate to £700 million for purposes other than the payment of compensation for the acquisition of electricity undertakings.[1] The Gas and Electricity (Borrowing Powers) Act, 1954, authorized a maximum amount outstanding on stock or loan of £1,400 million for electricity and £450 million for gas. Borrowing in excess of the statutory limit is permitted for the purpose of redeeming stock or repaying a temporary loan.[2]

The purpose of parliamentary control over borrowing is a twofold one. It enables the House of Commons to keep a check on the extent to which the Government is pledging the national credit by means of stock guaranteed by the Treasury; and it gives the House an opportunity to review the plans and progress of the nationalized industries in respect of their crucially important capital development programmes.[3]

Treasury minutes embodying the guarantees are laid before Parliament when they are granted, and a list of the total loans which have been guaranteed appears in the annual Finance Accounts. Guarantees are of very frequent occurrence—there were thirty-eight given between 1948 and 1953 for the British Transport Commission alone; and already in 1952 the total sum guaranteed by the Treasury approached in magnitude the Funded Debt of the realm. Yet all this, the then Comptroller General remarked, goes on very quietly and attracts very little notice.[4]

EXCHEQUER ADVANCES

Mr Macmillan, when making his Budget statement as Chancellor of the Exchequer in April 1956, stated that the capital requirements of the nationalized industries which had hitherto been met by the issue of stock carrying a Treasury guarantee would in future be met out of the Exchequer. He explained that the new system was to be regarded as a temporary measure intended to avoid the embarrassing consequences which flow from borrowing by guaranteed stock. If these stocks are not fully subscribed by private investors they have to be supported by the Exchequer. Substantial and prolonged support by the Exchequer had recently been necessary and appeared likely to be needed in the future. Very large sums were involved as the industries concerned had had to raise by this method about £1,600 million, equivalent to about 60 per cent of their total capital requirements since nationalization.

[1] Electricity Act, 1947, s. 39. [2] s. 15 (5).

[3] The Coal Industry Act, 1956, provides opportunities for parliamentary scrutiny when the annual level of advances exceeds £75 million, as the Minister of Power has then to obtain the approval of the House of Commons.

[4] Sir Frank Tribe in Evidence to *Select Committee on Nationalized Industries*, HC 235/1952-3, Q. 76.

The embarrassing results to which Mr Macmillan referred were, first, that Exchequer support can only be given by borrowing on Treasury Bills, which impedes the whole operation of monetary control; and second, that the national programme of borrowing, refinancing and funding is prejudiced by the necessity of making frequent issues of Government credit, often at inconvenient times, for particular industries which have reached their borrowing limits with the banks.

Mr Macmillan said that the nationalized industries would be quite unable to borrow money in the market without a guarantee from the Exchequer, because the various Acts of Parliament do not allow them to pledge their undertakings as security for the loan. Nor are the public corporations entirely free to determine their own prices, since Ministers can and do intervene on this matter. Moreover, the sheer magnitude of the capital needs of the public sector of the economy adds a further difficulty to the nationalized industries floating loans on the strength of their credit. The electricity supply industry alone has to raise about £150 millions a year at the present time.

In these circumstances he announced that the Government had decided it would be far better and more realistic for the Exchequer to control the whole operation by accepting responsibility for meeting the external capital requirements of the nationalized industries. It would give the Treasury much more control of the situation and simplify the problem of dealing with the National Debt. The method of approving the development programmes of the various boards by the Departments and the Treasury would continue unchanged, except that 'if one actually pressed the fee oneself into the piper's hand, one has a better chance of influencing the tune'.[1]

To implement this decision, the Finance Act, 1956,[2] provided that sums which the public corporations concerned with electricity supply, gas, transport and air services are empowered to borrow by stock issues may instead be raised by advances made to them by the appropriate Minister, to whom the Treasury may issue the necessary sums from the Consolidated Fund. A sum of £700 million was specified as the total sum which could be advanced in this way during the period ending in March 1958. The total sum fixed by the 1956 Act was increased by the Finance Act, 1958,[3] to £1,070 million and time extended to the end of August 1959. The Finance Act, 1959, increased the total amount to £1,620 million and extended the time to the end of August 1960. The money thus advanced is to be repaid at such times and by such methods as the Minister may, with Treasury approval, direct. The rate of interest is similarly determined.

[1] 551 HC Deb. 5s., cols. 862-5 (April 17, 1956). [2] s. 42. [3] s. 36.

An interesting innovation was contained in the Air Corporations Act, 1956. This authorizes BOAC to borrow from the International Bank for Reconstruction and Development or the Export-Import Bank of Washington to cover expenditure on the purchase of aircraft manufactured in USA, and any spare parts or equipment required in connection with such aircraft. This was intended to prevent dollar purchases of Douglas and Boeing aircraft from affecting the balance of trade position of Great Britain and the sterling area with the United States.

GOVERNMENT CONTROL OF INVESTMENT

In a debate on the Coal Industry Bill, 1956, Mr Nabarro, one of the more troublesome of the Conservative Government's backbench supporters, criticized the system whereby Parliament enacts a statutory ceiling to a board's borrowing in terms of a sum which is large enough to meet their needs for several years. He urged that the statutory limits should be designed to cover shorter periods and should be increased by smaller steps. Within these statutory limits, he considered that annual allocations should be prescribed in advance by statutory instruments laid before Parliament.[1]

Mr Aubrey Jones, the then Minister of Fuel and Power, said in reply that long-term statutory limits to borrowing powers are essential for planning the investment programmes demanded by great development schemes. The Government retains annual control by fixing the sum available each year for capital development, and Ministers are responsible for this to Parliament.[2] Sir Edward Boyle, speaking for the Treasury, said that annual investment forecasts for the nationalized industries (and also for the private sector) may be included in future Economic Surveys. These forecasts could then be debated in Parliament.[3]

Shortly after this debate the Minister of Fuel and Power announced his intention of publishing an annual White Paper at the beginning of each financial year setting out the capital expenditure position in the fuel and power industries. This White Paper would describe what investment has taken place in the year just elapsed and deal with the programme proposed for the coming twelve months. It will contain an estimate of the advances which are expected to be required during the year. It will thus be both retrospective and prospective. This was clearly an attempt—and a very reasonable attempt—to conciliate some of the opposition to the Coal Industry Bill which the Government had encountered from

[1] 552 HC Deb. 5s., cols. 1453-8 (May 10, 1956).

[2] *Ib.*, cols. 1456-7. [3] *Ib.*, cols. 1533-4.

its own backbench supporters. It was accompanied by a promise that the Government would if possible provide ample time to debate the new White Paper except when investment in the coal industry would come before the House for review automatically under the terms of the Bill.[1] Some of the critics still pressed for closer parliamentary control over borrowing, but the edge had been taken off the opposition within the Conservative Party.

The first issue of the new White Paper entitled *Capital Investment in the Coal, Gas and Electricity Industries* was presented to Parliament in April 1957.[2] It was a short statement devoted mainly to the financial aspects of approved expenditure in the preceding year and to the estimated programme for the impending year. It deals entirely with aggregate heads of capital expenditure and makes no attempt to describe the many individual projects of which these are composed. It does not embody an analysis of the present state of the economy nor does it contain any indication of the total amount of industrial investment which is forecast for the coming year, or what proportion of that total is to be devoted to the fuel and power industries.

Government control over the capital investment programmes of the nationalized industries will usually consist of either approving proposals submitted by a public corporation, or reducing the expenditure which is requested. The initiative in preparing and recommending schemes of development must come from the industry itself. A Government department does not have the technical knowledge or commercial experience to be able to formulate proposals.

A good deal of information about the methods adopted by the National Coal Board and the Government departments in determining the annual investment programme was made available to the Select Committee on Nationalized Industries (Reports and Accounts). The Committee remarked that the National Coal Board 'instead of having to undergo the discipline of the market to obtain their money, [they] have to convince the Ministry and the Treasury that the money will be well spent'.[3] There is no attempt by either the Ministry of Power or the Treasury to reconsider the board's proposals from a technical point of view, and the Select Committee agreed this would be undesirable and impracticable. The discussions are based instead on a scrutiny of the average figure of the yields calculated to result from the investments planned for the coming year. The Ministry assume that the board would not submit any proposal which is uneconomic; and details of the estimated return on individual schemes have not been provided.

[1] 555 HC Deb. 5s., col. 1552 (July 5, 1956).
[2] HMSO, Cmd. 132/1957. [3] Report, BPP. 187/1958, para. 25.

The Select Committee thought that this was rather too general a check, and that a more detailed financial check on the anticipated return would be an improvement. They therefore recommended that the board should give the two departments concerned information about the major schemes estimated to give the lowest yield, and the reasons justifying the proposed schemes.[1] The committee questioned whether any private borrower without a firm record of profitable investment could expect to raise money at regular intervals without giving more details than the National Coal Board have hitherto given the Ministry; but they gave no information of any kind on the current practice. The parallel is in any event not a true one since the nationalized coal industry could have made enormous profits in the postwar years if the NCB had pursued the purely commercial considerations open to a profit-making company. The estimated yield on investment in the coal industry is presumably based on assumptions concerning the peculiar restrictions on price policy which have so far applied to the National Coal Board.

In view of the shortage of capital for industrial investment which has prevailed since 1945 and the immense needs of the nationalized industries for re-equipment, rehabilitation or expansion on a vast scale, the negative type of control exercised by the Government has been on the whole suited to contemporary circumstances, since the nationalized industries have usually demanded more than could easily be spared. But there are exceptions to this: and the most obvious one is the railways. Government control of a positive kind might have expedited the formulation and submission of a scheme for re-equipping and modernizing the railways; but neither the Ministry of Transport nor the Treasury possessed the technical or commercial competence needed to do more in a positive sense than to invite the BTC to 'look into' the possibilities of electrification or dieselization.

On the negative side there has been no secret of the impact of Government control. Several times in the past ten years cuts in the investment programme of the public sector have been officially announced.[2]

[1] *Report*, BPP. 187/1958, paras. 31 and 32.

[2] The Central Electricity Authority stated in their Annual Report for 1955–6 that the industry had been asked to reduce its capital investment for the rest of 1955–6: cuts were made in the programmes of the Area Boards and the CEA but the construction of power stations was not curtailed. In response to further requests from the Government to cut programmes for 1956–7, the electricity authorities reduced their proposed expenditure from £213 million to £204 million; but they were later told that further reductions amounting to another £9 million would be necessary. Thus the planned expenditure of the industry for 1956–7 was reduced by £18 million, or nearly 9 per cent. This meant postponing work on power stations, and in consequence the amount of generating plant which could be brought into operation in 1958 was substantially reduced. *Central Electricity Authority Annual Report 1955–6*, HMSO, HC 367/1955–6, paras. 53–6.

Generally speaking, the CEA have not been permitted to decide for themselves how much plant should be installed each year to meet the ever-increasing load.[1] The Government have limited the new generating capacity to be installed each year, in order to allocate investment resources among the various national requirements and to secure a balance between home and export demands. In 1955 the Government settled the level of plant to be installed in power stations for each year up to 1959, although this was subsequently reduced.

Another example of Government control was the statement made by the Chancellor of the Exchequer in September 1957, following the rise in the Bank rate to 7 per cent, that the capital expenditures of the nationalized industries would have to be cut.

SELF-FINANCING OF DEVELOPMENT

Part of the capital funds required by the nationalized industries are provided out of their income or surpluses. The NCB development scheme entitled *Investing in Coal*[2] showed that out of £1,000 million to be spent during the period 1955–65, about two-thirds would come from internal sources chiefly through provision for depreciation, leaving only £350–400 million to be raised by external borrowing.[3]

The modernization and re-equipment of the railways, estimated to cost £1,240 million during the period 1955–70, will be financed as to £400 million from internal sources, the remainder being borrowed from external sources.[4]

The capital requirements of the electricity supply industry (excluding Scotland) were estimated by BEA in 1954 at £1,442 million for the seven years 1953–60. Of this £435 million was to be financed from internal sources, leaving a little over £1,000 million to come from external loans.[5] The capital needs of the gas industry for the same period were given as £366 million, of which £92 million was to come from inside the industry and the remainder borrowed.[6]

[1] *Report of the Committee of Inquiry into the Electricity Supply Industry*, HMSO, Cmd. 9672/1956, para. 80.

[2] This was *Plan for Coal* (published in 1950) brought up to date in 1956.

[3] *Investing in Coal* (NCB 1956) Ch. II; NCB Annual Report 1956. para. 80. Indeed, arrangements have been in force between the Minister and the Board since its inception to ensure that there is no recourse to borrowing until full use has been made of the Board's internal resources. Actually, the advances made by the Minister are not earmarked for specific capital purposes but are merely sums paid into the Board's central banking account to maintain a credit there at a minimum figure of £100,000. *Capital Investment in the Coal, Gas and Electricity Industries*, HMSO, Cmd. 132/1957, para. 27.

[4] *BTC Annual Report* (1954), p. 32.

[5] BEA *Power and Prosperity* (1954), p. 100; Memorandum on the Gas and Electricity (Borrowing Powers) Bill. Cmd. 9175/1954, para. 6.

[6] *Ib., Fuel for the Nation* (1954), pp. 48–50.

British European Airways, with a programme of aircraft replacements in hand costing about £85 million, expect to finance their purchases during the five year period from 1956–60 by drawing on internal resources to the extent of £26 million and by external borrowing up to a maximum of £60 million. The corresponding figures for BOAC aircraft purchases during the same period, calculated to cost £200 million, are £47 million to come from internal resources and the balance from outside.[1]

Aggregating these figures for the separate undertakings it will be found that slightly over 30 per cent of the capital investment programmes of the major national industries (leaving aside nuclear energy, the BBC and a few marginal cases) will be financed from internal sources.[2]

This follows a long way behind the pattern normally adopted in private enterprise. For many years past retained profits ploughed back into the business have afforded by far the largest source of finance for company investment programmes. During the quinquennium 1949–53 the public companies whose stocks or shares are quoted on the London Stock Exchange paid for no less than 75 per cent of their investments out of retained profits and sums allocated to depreciation, leaving only 25 per cent to be raised from outside sources. During the same period in the US, 64 per cent of the $150 thousand million invested in company extensions and improvement of plants was financed from internal sources.[3] The sterling oil companies have spent since 1945 £1,000 million on capital investment, of which only £70 million consists of new borrowing, the remainder coming from the companies' earnings.[4]

The Herbert Committee on the electric supply industry frowned on this practice so far as public enterprise is concerned. In capitalist enterprise, they remark, the customer has no cause to complain if profits are ploughed back into the business, since these profits are 'the prize of success' won 'in active competition or against potential competition'.[5] The directors decide on behalf of the shareholders what is to be done with the profits; and if the latter are dissatisfied they can protest. In practice the shareholders are virtually impotent to influence the directors on such matters. Presumably they could hold a mass meeting in Trafalgar

[1] 560 HC Deb. 5s., col. 1391, Mr Profumo (November 19, 1956); col. 2086, Mr Watkinson (November 23, 1956).

[2] The Paymaster General said that from April 1949 to March 1957 the Gas Council provided about two-fifths of the industry's capital requirements from its own resources. A similar proportion of the new capital required by the electricity supply industry from April 1948 to March 1957 came from its own resources. 582 HC Deb. 5s., cols. 105-6 (February 17, 1958).

[3] *Industry and Society* (1957) (Labour Party), p. 21.

[4] *Ib.*, p. 22. [5] Report, para. 344.

Square or Hyde Park, if the company is a large one, and demand the chairman's head on a charger.

But in public enterprise the situation is alleged to be quite different. The electricity supply industry is not operating in 'a fully competitive market'—a statement which is applicable to the major part of British industry. Price determination is 'an act of policy' instead of being, as so often in private business, the decision of a restrictive trade association or a gentleman's understanding between the biggest producers. It would therefore be possible to raise prices so as to yield a considerable part of the capital requirement for development. 'These prices would not, however, have been fixed in open competition and the surpluses accruing would not have been won as the price of efficient rivalry. Further, the policies adopted by the management of the electricity supply industry are not subject to the ultimate sanction which can be exercised by shareholders of a private undertaking.'[1] Hence, any yield from prices available for capital purposes can be regarded as a tax imposed on consumers in proportion to their electricity consumption, in order to develop the industry for the benefit of future consumers. And this is said to be both inequitable and conducive to inefficiency. The electricity supply industry ought to have to face 'the same kind of problems that other industries face, and in particular it ought to have to fight for its capital by going to the market'.[2]

The contrast presented here is a travesty of the position. Far from public corporations being protected in regard to their price policies, they are much less free to fix prices than commercial companies. They have a statutory duty to supply their products as cheaply as possible.[3] They are exposed to all the winds of hostile criticism which blow from the press, from Parliament, and from the public platform. They have to run the gauntlet of ministerial scrutiny, which is conducted with one eye on the political repercussions likely to result from any increase of charges and the other on the needs of the economy as a whole. They are subject to the detailed examination and potential opposition of Consumers Councils. In the case of the railways there is the severe hurdle of the Transport Tribunal to be overcome; in the case of coal the Gentleman's Agreement; and in the case of the airlines the bilateral agreements between HM Government and foreign governments granting mutual traffic rights. None of these deterrents exist in the private sector, and to suggest that nationalized industries are in a favourable situation to charge what they like, and to exploit gaily and irresponsibly their monopolistic position, is the very reverse of the truth. By comparison with

[1] *Report*, para. 344. [2] *Ib.*, para. 345.
[3] Electricity Act, 1947, s. 1 (6); Gas Act, 1948, s. 1 (8); Civil Aviation Act, 1946, s. 2 (1).

private enterprise they are in a position of conspicuous disadvantage in this respect. It is only very recently that the monopolistic practices of price fixing agreements and trade associations which exist in almost every trade or industry in Britain have even been liable to public investigation and exposure by the Monopolies Commission or to invalidation by the Restrictive Practices Court.

One has only to observe the complete absence of criticism in the press of price increases by commercial firms—especially those which advertise—compared with the strong and often malevolent criticism which greets similar movements on the part of the nationalized industries, to see how unrealistic is the contrast drawn by the Herbert Committee on this matter.

Equally remote from reality is the desire to make nationalized industry 'fight for its capital by going to the market'. In the first place, the market is not there—or at least not in sufficient strength to produce the large sums needed annually. It was for this reason that the Government decided to introduce legislation to enable Ministers to advance money on loan as an alternative to the issue of stock guaranteed by the Treasury.[1] Secondly, the picture of a kind of all-out wrestling match or scrimmage among the dignified gentlemen who direct the affairs of our great joint-stock companies in a strenuous attempt to secure for their companies the hard won savings of the investor is a purely imaginary one. What happens in practice, as we have already seen, is that in this country on an average three-quarters of the money needed for capital expansion and re-equipment comes from internal sources, leaving only about 25 per cent to come from external sources.

The most widespread method used by commercial companies to find new money from 'external' sources is to offer shares on very favourable terms to the existing stockholders, who thereupon gladly accept the allocation and either subscribe the money required or sell their rights to the new shares on the Stock Exchange at a premium. If this is fighting for capital in the market it is difficult to see who are the combatants, and who wins or loses. The company gets its money, and the existing shareholders get new shares at a price substantially lower than their market value. The market value is of course determined by investors' estimates of the future earning capacity of the company, and its ability to maintain or improve its position. But the elimination of most of the risk from the equity of the larger public joint stock companies is one of the most significant features of modern business; and it has deprived the investor of much of his historic function. There has undoubtedly been a permanent decline in the rôle of the private investor.

[1] *Ante* p. 301.

The real distinction between private and public enterprise is that in the nationalized industries there are no equity shareholders. The equity is owned by the nation. Where a public corporation issues stock to the public, the holder of such stock is merely in the position of a creditor for the amount of his interest. He has no voting rights, no power of control, no voice in the appointment of the board, no right to participate in a surplus, and no right to share in the break-up value of the undertaking. He cannot, as was provided in the case of the former London Passenger Transport Board, even apply to the Court for a receiver to be appointed in the event of non-payment of interest. In consequence the only practical method of borrowing from private or institutional investors is by the issue of fixed interest bonds. These have hitherto been guaranteed by the Treasury, partly no doubt in order to keep the interest as low as possible, and also (according to Mr Macmillan) because the public corporation cannot pledge the undertaking as security for the loan.

One doubts how far this is necessary, although I believe it to be highly desirable to use the credit of the State to keep interest rates low on the loans of nationalized industries. The Central Electricity Board, established in 1926 to construct and operate the grid, were authorized to borrow money with a Treasury guarantee if the Board wished and the Treasury agreed; but in fact the CEB floated many issues of stock without a Treasury guarantee.[1] Yet the CEB were not able to pledge the undertaking to the holders of their stock.

Lastly there is the point that it is inequitable to charge the present body of consumers higher prices in order to expand or improve the industry for the benefit of future consumers. The answer to this is that the nation is in fact being taxed to a considerable extent in order to provide many different kinds of improvements of a capital nature which will be enjoyed by future citizens. These include roads, bridges, schools, hospitals, sewage systems, universities, etc. No one appears to regard this as inequitable; and even if we concede for the sake of argument the highly disputable proposition that electricity charges are a form of taxation, it is difficult to see why it is any more inequitable to raise money by this means to expand the electricity industry than it is to raise money from taxes on drink or tobacco in order to build new secondary schools.

The nationalized industries are now as much part of the estate of the realm as any of its other more traditional assets. It is the proper task of each generation to do what it can to improve and develop that estate. Inevitably the burden of doing so must fall on the present generation and some—but not all—of the benefit will be enjoyed by future genera-

[1] See Graeme Haldane: 'The Central Electricity Board and other Electricity Authorities in *Public Enterprise*, ed. W. A. Robson (1937), pp. 124–6.

tions of citizens. Where, as in the case of the nationalized industries, the services and commodities provided are of almost universal consumption, the body of consumers corresponds fairly closely to the mass of the nation; and the only remaining grounds of objection are that some form of general taxation would be preferable as a means of raising money for capital purposes, or that only voluntary subscriptions should be used for this purpose. Both these grounds seem to me quite untenable, and I see no reason why nationalized industries should not be as free as profit-making companies to find as much money for capital development from internal resources as they think fit.

DEBT REDEMPTION

Heavy obligations in regard to depreciation and capital redemption are imposed on the nationalized industries by the relevant legislation.

The National Coal Board are required to pay to the Exchequer such amounts as the Minister of Power may direct with the approval of the Treasury by way of recouping the Crown for expenses and liabilities incurred in respect of compensation paid to the previous owners of the industry and of subsidiary assets, or to interests injuriously affected by severance, etc., and the payment of interest and capital redemption on advances made to the board by the Government.[1] The Electricity Boards are required to charge to their revenue accounts, *inter alia*, 'proper provision' for redemption of capital, 'proper provision' for the depreciation or renewal of assets, and for compensation payments made to local authorities.[2] Similar obligations are imposed on the British Transport Commission[3] and on the gas industry.[4]

Thus, the public corporations have in effect to repay their capital indebtedness over a period of years. This follows the practice which has for long existed in local government, where local authorities have to repay municipal loans over periods which vary according to the estimated life of the assets they represent. It contrasts sharply with the practice in the private sector, since commercial companies are not permitted by law to repay their equity capital save with the special permission of the High Court.

The period fixed for the redemption of British Transport stock was 90 years from vesting date; and the same period applies to the redemption of British Gas stock and British Electricity stock. The repayment of

[1] Coal Industry Nationalization Act, 1946, ss. 10, 17, 18, 22, 26, 32 and 44.
[2] Electricity Act, 1947, s. 45.
[3] Transport Act, 1947, s. 93.
[4] Gas Act, 1948, s. 49. See also the Coal Industry Nationalization Act, 1946, ss. 29-30.

long-term debts by the National Coal Board has been fixed at fifty years by the Minister, no doubt in view of the shorter life considered to be appropriate in coal mining.[1] A period of fifty-two years is fixed for the repayment of advances made by the Minister of Power to the fuel and power industries and by the Minister of Transport to the British Transport Commission.[2]

Prior to nationalization the municipally-owned gas and electricity undertakings were required to redeem their loans over periods of years intended to correspond with the estimated life of the capital assets acquired by them. They generally established sinking funds so as to be able to produce at a specified date the money required to repay the loan or replace an asset. Provision for depreciation was not necessary since the loan redemption periods were often shorter than the life of the asset.[3] It was thus possible to pay off the loan out of the proceeds of the sinking fund investments, and subsequently to raise a new loan when it became necessary to replace the asset.

The nationalized industries, however, in addition to providing for debt redemption, must also each year provide out of revenue for the depreciation of their fixed assets, plant, etc. This means that in theory they are required to carry a double burden, since the purpose of debt redemption is essentially similar to that of depreciation: namely, to spread the cost of capital assets over their estimated working life. In practice, however, the effect of this double burden is eased by the fact that the period of ninety years is much longer than the estimated life of most fixed assets. Furthermore, the annual sums set aside for the stock redemption fund are with Treasury consent not invested externally but left in the industry 'temporarily' to finance further capital expenditure.[4]

The method of meeting the statutory obligations regarding redemption varies considerably among the several industries. The British Electricity Authority decided that contributions to their Redemption Fund Account in respect of British Electricity stock issued for compensation should consist of equal annual sums computed by the 'straight line' method. The Gas Boards adopted the same principle. The British Transport Commission, on the other hand, set aside annual sums which, in-

[1] *National Coal Board, Annual Report* 1947, para. 402.

[2] *Central Electricity Authority Report and Accounts* 1956-7, p. 154; *British Transport Commission Annual Report*, 1956, Vol. II, p. 14.

[3] Idris Hicks: 'The Finance of the Gas Industry,' XXXVI *Public Administration* (summer, 1958), p. 159.

[4] See *Central Electricity Report and Accounts 1957-8*, HMSO, 288, para. 383. The total amount of the contributions to the Redemption Fund on March 31, 1958 was £81·4 m. of which £1·1 m. had been applied in redemption of stock, £43·7 m. invested in subsidiary securities outside the industry, and £36·6 m. used in the electricity undertaking. *Ib.* statement B21, page 213.

vested at 3 per cent compound interest, will after ninety years produce the sum of £1,150 million which was paid to the former owners as compensation. The National Coal Board have a system of terminable annuities, each of which is of fifty years duration, for funding their liability to the Minister in respect of compensation and advances.

The sums involved in stock redemption payments over a period of ninety years are not large in relation to the revenues of these great undertakings. The British Transport Commission began with a payment of under £2½ million in 1948, which had risen to slightly over £3¼ million in 1956. Electricity began with £3·8 million in 1947–9; it had risen to about £13 million by 1957–8, but this included instalments for stock other than compensation stock. The NCB set aside about £1 million in 1947 to redeem compensation on assets vested in them; it rose to £3·3 million by 1955.

Interest on and amortization of capital advances or loans incurred since nationalization is a much heavier item. The interest charged to revenue account of Central Electricity Authority rose from £15·8 million in 1947–9 to £46·9 million in 1956–7. As a percentage of revenue this item has been increasing at a somewhat alarming rate from about 8 per cent to 10 or 11 per cent and is likely to go on increasing in view of the much heavier capital cost of nuclear power stations. The annual charges for depreciation and interest in the gas industry were £16·7 million in 1949–50 and had risen to £42·1 million in 1956–7. This was an increase from about 7 per cent of gross revenue to 11·4 per cent.[1] The British Transport Commission have been charging interest to capital account at a figure which began in 1948 at £42 million and was running at £72·4 million in 1958.

DEPRECIATION POLICY

Depreciation is quite distinct from stock redemption though it often serves a similar purpose. Here, again, we find several different methods and standards being used. The British Electricity Authority and its successors make annual provision for 'the discharge of capital expenditure (including depreciation of fixed assets)' on scales based on their estimated lives. The sum so provided is allocated to (*a*) stock redemption instalments, (*b*) the payments due to local authorities in respect of electricity undertakings transferred from them, and (*c*) meeting new expenditure on capital account. As already explained, the stock redemption instalments can be, and are, used 'temporarily' in financing capital development from internal resources. In depreciating their fixed assets

[1] Report, HMSO, 288, p. 164. Table II.

the electricity authorities have once again used the straight-line method, whereby the cost of each asset is written off by equal annual instalments over its estimated life. This historical basis of depreciation has the great disadvantage that it takes no account of replacement cost.

The British Transport Commission proceed on similar principles, except that they divide their assets into two categories: one consisting of those with a wasting character, such as rolling stock, which are eventually scrapped; and the other, such as tunnels, roads and docks, which are not usually scrapped but renewed piecemeal or often modernized or reconstructed. The former are depreciated in the manner already described; while repairs and renewals on those in the second category are charged to revenue account, and only the cost of additional assets or the improvement of existing assets are charged to capital account.

The gas industry after nationalization had to find a satisfactory basis for valuing its fixed assets. There were no common principles generally observed by the gas undertakings in the treatment of their fixed assets for accounting purposes. After considering several possible alternative methods the Gas Council recommended that the net values shown in the books of the former undertakers should be taken as the point of departure for valuing the nationalized assets; and that the straight line depreciation basis of accounting should be everywhere applied.[1] This was unanimously adopted by all the Area Boards.[2]

The nationalized airlines have recently introduced a useful distinction between the concept of obsolescence, which is applied to aircraft, and the concept of depreciation, which is used in relation to other plant or equipment. BOAC and BEA have agreed, after consulting their auditors and with the Minister's approval, to provide for obsolescence in future on the basis that aircraft and major spare parts will be written down to their estimated realizable value by equal annual amounts spread over the working life of the aircraft. As a first approximation to applying these principles, BOAC announced that they would apply to new aircraft, as a minimum, a seven year life with a residual value of 25 per cent of the cost. Thus, for every £100 spent on a new airliner, £10·7 would be written off during each of the first seven years of its service. But both the life of the aircraft and its estimated realizeable value will be subject to review from time to time.[3]

[1] Report, HMSO, 288, para. 272.

[2] The remaining period of useful life was calculated for the assets taken over by the Area Gas Boards, and the book value of the assets written off during the appropriate period on the straight line method of equal instalments. Rates of depreciation thus varied according to the condition of the plant and equipment acquired. The average for the whole country is slightly less than 5 per cent a year. Hicks, *op. cit.*, p. 160.

[3] *BOAC Report and Accounts* 1956-7, p. 3.

The distinction between obsolescence and depreciation based on mere physical durability is essentially sound, and other industries—whether nationalized or not—should be encouraged to observe it. Assets such as machinery and plant, transport vehicles and even buildings, have very often a much longer physical life than the span of years in which they can truly be said to maintain their earning capacity. A high rate of obsolescence is usually one of the signs of a progressive industry; and the former British railway companies, for example, made far too little provision for obsolescence even in their days of prosperity.

Looking broadly at the nationalized industries, we can conclude that the policies they have been obliged to follow, and the methods they have chosen to adopt, have resulted in a combination of commercial principles and municipal trading techniques in regard to depreciation and capital redemption. The former is to be seen in the spreading of the original capital cost over the estimated life of the assets. The latter is found in the obligation to redeem after prescribed periods the compensation stock and loans subsequently raised or advanced by the Minister. The sinking fund usually associated with local authority public utility practice has, however, become much attenuated and has now only a shadowy existence; while the period of redemption has been extended far beyond the remunerative life of most of the assets concerned.

One serious criticism of the present practice is that the public corporations, in depreciating their assets on the basis of their historical cost, are not providing for their replacement at current prices. In a period of inflation, such as we have experienced since 1945, the depreciation of capital assets at their original cost, or in accordance with the transfer price, will provide only a small fraction of the cost of renewing those assets. The extent of the short-fall is stated to be in excess of £1,100 million during the ten years 1948–57[1] in respect of assets whose total replacement cost is estimated at £2,592 million. The actual amount set aside was £1,467 million, which was only 56 per cent of the sum required for replacement.

The soundest view seems to be that each generation of consumers should contribute fully to making good the real resources which are used up in satisfying their needs. This means that depreciation should be related to the replacement of plant and equipment at current prices and not on the basis of their historical cost. 'It is not the same thing', observed Professor Edwards and Mr Townsend, 'to calculate depreciation on historical cost and then so set aside out of profit or surplus a special replacement reserve. To do this, in periods of inflation, is to present a

[1] Report on Nationalization by the Federation of British Industries, p. 16. The figures are taken from the National Income Blue Books.

false picture to both customers and employees and to invite unjustified pressure for lower prices and higher wages.'[1] The Post Office has adopted the replacement cost basis and nationalized industries should also do so.

Another serious criticism of the present practice is that the public corporations are charging annual interest on loans or advances and depreciation of capital assets before the assets have come into use. In consequence, current revenue is made to bear part of the cost of producing future income. Mr Idris Hicks has shown the impact of this in the fuel and power industries. Depreciation and interest and interim income per ton of coal produced rose from 3·07*s*. in 1947 to 5·86*s*. in 1956; depreciation and interest per therm of gas sold rose from 1·86*d*. in 1949–50 to 3·47*d*. in 1955–6; and depreciation and interest per unit of electricity sold rose from ·29*d*. in 1948–9 to ·36*d*. in 1955–6. His comment is that 'The time lag between incurring this capital expenditure and the realization of its fruits means that present output is being asked to absorb the costs of producing future output'.[2] This practice is having a most adverse effect on the finances of the industries concerned, particularly gas.[3] Ultimately, of course, nationalized industries should meet their loan costs out of earnings; but to require them to do so during a period of development is to create an inflationary tendency.

Mr Hicks urges that price increases are justified when the nationalized industries cannot cover their current costs out of revenue, but not when they cannot meet future costs. A distinction should be drawn between costs incurred in maintaining or increasing output from existing plant and equipment, and costs incurred in respect of capital expenditure undertaken with the object of increasing productive capacity in the future. The latter type of expenditure should be treated on the same principles as those applied by the British Transport Commission in their accounts for 1956. The method adopted is to transfer to a special suspense account[4] the additional costs and losses incurred during the period of modernization and development, for amortization at a later date. A similar method should be applied to the capital costs of nuclear generating stations, and of major reconstructions and the sinking of new mines in the coal industry.

RESERVE FUNDS

More important than either of these criticisms is the confusion which

[1] Ronald S. Edwards and Harry Townsend: *Business Enterprise: Its growth and organization*, p. 515.

[2] Idris Hicks: Capital Costs and Fuel Prices, *The Accountant* (August 31, 1957), p. 237.

[3] *Ib.*, p. 240. [4] Authorized by the Transport (Railway Finance) Act, 1957.

now exists regarding reserve funds. The nationalization statutes require 'proper allocations' to the reserve fund to be charged against the revenues of nationalized industries. These allocations are regarded as legitimate expenses to be taken into account before the net surplus for the year is determined. The principle followed by professional accountants and adopted in private business is to treat allocations to reserves as appropriations of profits. The nationalized industries appear to be following the latter practice despite the statutory requirements.[1]

There is thus a difference of method in transferring sums to the reserve fund; but there is a much more fundamental distinction at present existing between the functions and size of reserve funds in private enterprise and those in nationalized industry.

The great industries which have been nationalized obviously need reserve funds; and such funds are required by law to be established. The responsible Minister may, with Treasury approval, give directions on any matter concerning the establishment or management of a reserve fund, irrespective whether such directions are general or particular in character.

A reserve fund can be used to absorb a net surplus or to offset a deficit in any year. It can be used to prevent frequent fluctuations in prices by absorbing temporary changes in trading conditions. It is available to meet unexpected emergencies of various kinds. The existing legislation in all instances precludes the reserve fund from being applied 'otherwise than for the purposes of the board'[2]—that is, it must be used to assist in fulfilling the aims for which the respective public corporation was established.

In private enterprise the normal function of a reserve fund is to provide a source of finance for the development or expansion of the business. Depreciation funds and reserves together constitute the main sources of 'internal financing' of capital investment. To make this possible, prices are fixed so as to build up reserves in order to finance growth; and by this means much expansion is self-financed out of profits.

In the sphere of nationalized industry, for reasons which have never been adequately discussed or explained, the reserve fund is not regarded as performing this function in any important sense. Accordingly, little or no consideration is given to building up the reserve fund in determining price policy. The reserves of the public corporations therefore amount to only a tiny fraction of their annual capital expenditure. In

[1] Idris Hicks: 'Reserves in Nationalized Fuel Industries', *Accountancy*, May 1958, pp. 226-7.

[2] Coal Industry Nationalization Act, 1946, s. 29 (2) (e); Civil Aviation Act, 1946, s. 17 (2) (a); Transport Act, 1947, s. 92 (2); Electricity Act, 1957, s. 20 (4); Gas Act, 1948, s. 47 (2) (a).

1957 the capital reserves of the fuel industries were in the aggregate only £50·2 million, most of which were supplementary reserves for the depreciation of fixed assets. The revenue reserves of the same industries amount to a similar sum, of which £8·8 million was allocated for taxation, £1·5 million for insurance, leaving only £40 million for central and area reserve funds—against capital liabilities of £2,514·3 millions.[1]

In my opinion, much larger allocations to reserve should be made, whenever possible, in the nationalized industries, in order to enable them to finance a much higher proportion of their capital investment from internal resources. These allocations should be charged against revenue, as required by the statutes, in order to preclude unfounded demands for higher wages or lower prices. The allocation of such reserves is in no way incompatible with the obligations of the public corporations about breaking even, but in order to do so they would have to increase prices.

[1] Idris Hicks: *op. cit.*, p. 228.

CHAPTER XII

Labour Relations

THE labour problem in a nationalized industry is a complex one. It consists partly of inculcating all who work in the organization with a spirit of public service; partly of permeating the lower ranks of the industry with the radical change of outlook which has taken place at the top; partly of integrating and personifying the authority of the corporation at the lower levels of management.

The interests of the employees of a nationalized industry are no longer in conflict with those of the shareholders or the proprietor, whether or not actively engaged in the business. But they are very often in conflict with the interests of the consumers and of the general public. The proper ordering of labour relations is for this and other reasons the most important problem in the entire field of nationalization. It is also the most difficult.

Labour is bound to occupy a strong position in the huge key industries of fuel, power, and transport no matter under what form of ownership and management they may be conducted. When the workpeople are completely organized on a national basis in powerful trade unions, the position of labour can become dominant, oppressive, and sometimes menacing. The change from private to public ownership has in some respects profoundly altered the situation. In other respects it has made little difference.

NATIONALIZATION AS A CAUSE OF CHANGE

It is not, however, true to say that 'so far as labour relations are concerned, nationalization is essentially irrelevant'. These are the words of an able American investigator, who qualifies his statement by saying that labour relations in a nationalized industry are no different from labour relations in any other industry.[1]

There are indeed several very important differences, although not all of them are susceptible of objective proof. To begin with, nationalized industries are publicly accountable in a way which does not apply to even the largest commercial companies. The directors of a profit-making com-

[1] George B. Baldwin: 'Nationalization in Britain: a Sobering Decade', CCCX *Annals of the American Academy of Political and Social Science* (1957), p. 41.

pany may have a high sense of responsibility, but their position is quite different from that of the members of a public board who are accountable to the Government, to Parliament, and to the public. The board of a nationalized industry is liable to ministerial influence or control; to parliamentary scrutiny; and to a much more critical attitude on the part of the press than is given to private enterprise. This in turn affects the attitude of the public. Secondly, nationalized industries are not usually as free financially in negotiating wage agreements as joint stock companies because they are not generally permitted to pursue a purely commercial price policy. Since their charges are often much less easily raised than the prices of commercial companies, they enjoy less freedom and elbow room in wage negotiations than they would have if they possessed unrestricted freedom to increase their revenues to the fullest extent allowed by the market. Thirdly, labour disputes in nationalized industries often have political overtones of a kind seldom found in the private sector. This is partly due to the political influence which the trade unions can exercise in persuading Ministers or Members of Parliament to bring pressure to bear on the boards. It is also partly due to the fact that public money is often involved in an important wage dispute, if the increased costs resulting from higher wages cannot be met by internal economies or increased prices.[1] Lastly, the threat of insolvency does not possess the same force as an ultimate sanction in the sphere of nationalized industry as it does in the private sector.

As regards the changes brought about by nationalization, we may note that industrial relations are an important aspect of the public accountability of nationalized industry. This is a new factor. Second, monopoly may cause more serious consequences to flow from a trade dispute than might otherwise result. Public utility services such as gas and electricity were already monopolistic undertakings prior to nationalization, but the new dispensation has greatly intensified the tendency towards monopoly and centralization in all the industries concerned.

[1] In a debate in the House of Commons on the railway strike in July 1956, an Opposition speaker asserted that the Government had responsibility for handling the ASLEF dispute and could not make the British Transport Commission wholly responsible. Mr J. Enoch Powell, MP, formerly Financial Secretary to the Treasury, said the Government were inevitably involved in wage disputes in any nationalized industry. 'The profitability of the industry is guaranteed by the State. In these circumstances . . . we cannot prevent the immediate transmission to the Government of the responsibility for dealing with any industrial dispute in wage matters. . . . I take it that we are all agreed in waiting a decent wage structure to be met out of the proceeds of the industry concerned. Under private enterprise that is what has to happen, because there is nowhere else from which it can be met; but wherever these issues are raised about a nationalized industry, they immediately become political because of the ultimate responsibility of the Treasury, the State and the taxpayer for guaranteeing profitability—by which I mean guaranteeing the payment of interest upon stock.' 543 HC Deb. 5s., cols. 1654 and 1660 (July 11, 1956).

Third, the demand for nationalization has come in large part from the trade unions; and although there is no trace of guild socialism in the public corporations, the transfer of these great industries to public ownership raised high hopes in the employees.

These hopes were both ideological and material. Ideologically, public ownership was regarded as the gateway to a new society, in which there would be greater plenty and less hardship for the toiling masses, and in which co-operation would supplant competition. Materially, the unions and their members expected better treatment in every respect from nationalized industries than they received under private enterprise. They hoped that the elimination of profits would bring them higher wages and better working conditions; that State control would ensure full employment; and that industrial democracy would be brought appreciably nearer.[1]

These expectations have a political and psychological significance which no public corporation can afford to ignore. In fact none of the public corporations has attempted to ignore them. Substantial advances have been made in many different directions, especially safety and welfare.[2] Personnel management has greatly improved in the nationalized industries in many respects, such as training and education, methods of promotion, work study, job analysis, methods of payment, personnel records and personnel research. The nationalized industries, some of which were formerly very backward in these matters, are now in the forefront of the British economy.[3]

'Yet nationalization', Mr Baldwin remarks, 'has not provided the workers with a horn of plenty into which they could dip their hands whenever they felt pressed by the struggle for life.'[4] The attitude of management has generally been firm, and the Government have not intervened to an abnormal extent. While nationalization has by no means failed in the sphere of labour relations, he thinks it might have succeeded to a greater extent than it has were it not for the extravagant hopes which were pinned on the transfer of industries to the public sector.

The experience of the past decade has shown these hopes to have been largely illusory insofar as they were based on the idea that the mere transfer of an industry from one sector to another could effect a radical change in the position of labour, and, be it added, in the outlook and morale of the workers.[5] I have myself always stressed the fact that mere nationalization by itself does little more than eliminate the shareholder: it leaves nearly all of the problems of management, organization, productivity, technology, research and development still to be solved.

[1] B. C. Roberts: 'Trade Unions and Nationalization', XLIV *Progress*, (1954-5), p. 114

[2] George B. Baldwin: *op. cit.*, p. 43. [3] *Ib.*, p. 45. [4] *Ib.*, p. 42. [5] *Ib.*, p. 50.

This does not mean that socialists were wrong in claiming that nationalization could make a unique contribution to the labour problems of modern industry; it means only that nationalization is a point of departure and not the end of the journey. Unfortunately, many advocates of public ownership speak and write as though the political aspirations of the socialist movement could be relied upon to change the incentives and transform the motivation of the workers. It may well be that nationalization can pave the way for fundamental change in labour relations: but it will require prolonged effort, much creative thought, and a transformation in the values which now prevail in industry, whether public or private.

The success of public enterprise will ultimately depend in large measure on the degree to which nationalized industries can induce their employees to work better than they would under capitalist enterprise. In emphasizing the importance of labour relations we must not, however, overlook the other factors in increased productivity, such as better planning, more intensive investment, superior management, more research and better equipment. This is especially true in the coal industry, where the productivity of labour depends in considerable part on further mechanization (particularly in respect of power-loading and underground transport), the better layout of mines, and other environmental factors.

THE HERITAGE OF THE PAST

The aspects of the situation which are not perceptibly changed are the traditional attitudes of the employees in the older nationalized industries towards such matters as management, productivity, redundancy, manpower, trade unions, and earnings. These attitudes are, of course, the result of historical influences over a long period in conditions which were entirely different from those prevailing today.

The coalmining industry underwent a terrible and prolonged period of unemployment and decline between the two world wars. This was largely due to bad management, technological backwardness, inadequate investment of the capital required for modernization and mechanization, and misguided legislation which facilitated restrictive policies while doing nothing effective to rationalize or improve the organization of the industry. The world depression was a major factor which contributed substantially to the plight of coalmining in Britain. All that has passed into the limbo of the unhappy past. But the memory of it has left a deep imprint on the minds not only of those who experienced the suffering it brought but of a younger generation of miners who were in their infancy at the time. The profound bitterness and mistrust which grew out of the events of the inter-war period have by no means dispersed. They hang like a stormcloud threatening the fairer prospect and immeasurably improved conditions which now obtain in the nationalized coal industry and hold back the energies and co-operation of men who could do more if they were determined to give their best.

Something of all this is to be found in a letter to *The Times*[1] by Mr G. A. Sparrow, Secretary of the Leicestershire Colliery Overmen, Deputies, and Shotfirers Association, on the subject of absenteeism in the mines and the great public concern which had been expressed at it. 'I am sure the miner will take little notice of this, for he knows how not to listen when he chooses that course.' After reciting the well-known hardships and difficulties of coal mining, Mr Sparrow concludes: 'Having worked underground for over fifty years, I know the conditions and the problems the industry is having to face, but I regard the human strata, the miners, as doing a job of work and doing it splendidly. But it is only eighteen to twenty years ago that they were the forgotten men—their fathers have eaten sour grapes and it has set the children's teeth on edge.' He ends on a note of confidence that the miners will respond to the challenge now made to them.

The objective conditions have immensely improved in the miners' favour. Already by the end of 1951 the earnings per shift of adult workers had trebled whereas the cost of living had only doubled since 1938, and mining wages had risen from about the eightieth place to the top of the list of wage rates. A very favourable pensions scheme was introduced in 1952, and the National Insurance Industrial Injuries scheme has been heavily augmented by the NCB. But it will take a long time before the miner's traditional attitude towards his work, towards the management of the industry, towards proposals to relieve the manpower shortage by recruiting Italian or Hungarian workers, and similar matters, is radically altered. He will have to be convinced that full employment has come to stay; and that he can look forward to steadily improving conditions. It will require a sustained effort on the part of both the NCB and the general public to make the miner identify himself more closely with the larger community of the nation and less exclusively with the smaller community of the pit, the colliery, and the members of his union.

The point I am making is that it is absurd to blame public ownership for the fact that nationalization has not been able to wipe out in a decade the evil results of a century of mismanagement by the former colliery companies. It was quite unrealistic and naïve to expect that there would

[1] September 24, 1957.

be a change of heart the moment the NCB's pennant fluttered from the pithead masts in 1947. It is equally unrealistic to deny that the progress so far made in inducing a more receptive, co-operative and flexible frame of mind among the miners has been disappointing to say the least, despite the assiduous and unremitting efforts of the NCB. The same is true of the railwaymen, although earnings and conditions of work in their industry have been and still are much less favourable than in coalmining.

Industrial relations in the industries which were more progressive, well-managed, and technologically advanced before nationalization, such as electricity supply, steel, gas, and civil aviation have been far better than in coal. But even in these one still finds the persistence of antiquated practices which are both anti-social and ludicrous in an era of over-employment when labour is in short supply in almost every occupation. In the electricity supply industry, opposition by the trade unions to discharging surplus employees is so great that the Central Authority has made little or no effort to discover redundancy or to procure the more effective use of manpower by work study and similar means. They were rightly criticized for this by the Herbert Committee, who drew attention to the demoralizing effect of under-employment both on the men concerned and on their fully-occupied fellow workers.[1]

Nationalization of an industry, then, does not automatically result in the employees abandoning forthwith their traditional antagonisms and inhibitions, and endeavouring wholeheartedly to increase productivity. On the other hand, where good work-habits and attitudes were in existence prior to nationalization, they are likely to be carried forward into the new regime. Such attitudes and practices, whether good or bad, are normally subject to only slow modification.[2]

THE FACTOR OF SIZE

The management of enterprises employing large numbers of workers presents problems which do not exist in the management of smaller units. In consequence a new element has been introduced into the problem of human relations in nationalized industry by the immense size and complexity of their organization. In every case the structure is much larger than that which existed prior to nationalization. This does not mean that the problem of securing good human relations among the workpeople is insoluble, but only that it is different and more difficult in

[1] Report, HMSO, 9672/1956, paras. 272-4.

[2] R. W. Revans: 'Industrial Morale and Size of Unit', XXVII *Political Quarterly* (1956), p. 303.

a very large organization. It is not a matter of simple decentralization, for as Mr Austen Albu, MP, has wisely remarked, decentralization cannot succeed without harmonious relations founded on integrity at the top of the organization and mutual confidence between its members at all levels. These conditions cannot be created overnight. They needed to be carefully fostered over a long period of growth.[1]

The factor of size is not one which is peculiar to the public sector. It applies equally to large coal mines, large factories, large chemical works, large railway stations and large hospitals. As Professor Revans writes: 'When statistics measuring the response of men at a number of comparable units can be found, the chances are that larger units will display a loyalty among their employees less firmly held than the smaller.' There tends to be, in groups susceptible to comparison, 'a significant and positive correlation between the size of the unit and, say, sickness absenteeism'.[2]

In coalmining, the differences in the rate of absenteeism from all causes between large and small mines were very great before nationalization. In 1942, to quote Professor Revans again:[3]

> 'There were 450 coalmines in Britain employing between ten and 100 persons; the average total absenteeism among all the men employed in these mines was 7·15 per cent. In the same year there were 218 mines employing over 1,000 men; in these the corresponding figure was 11·66 per cent. The difference of 4·51 per cent was very highly significant; an analysis of these national figures by the major regional coal-fields showed in every case similar significant differences between the small and the large pits. Hence, to talk of absenteeism among "the miners" is meaningless. When we remember that in 1942, the middle of the war, the average national absenteeism was about 6 per cent, we see that the extra absenteeism due to being a miner in a small pit was just over 1 per cent, whereas in a large pit it was about 5½ per cent. In other words, it is not being a miner alone that makes one's absenteeism the subject of comment; one needs also to be a miner in a large pit. There is something about the size of the unit that the men do not like. We have already noticed the same effect among the two sets of factories. (It can incidentally also be seen among girls who work in a chain of stores of wide size range.) To censure miners for bad attendance, therefore, without understanding the association of absenteeism with size of mine, is to ignore one of the fundamental principles of social psychology.'

[1] Austen Albu: 'The Organization of Industry' in *New Fabian Essays*, ed. R. H. S. Crossman (1952), pp. 128–30.

[2] *Op. cit.*, p. 305. [3] *Ib.*, p. 306.

Professor Revans explains that the effect of size in coal mining disputes is particularly strong. Taking the South Wales and Yorkshire mines and dividing them according to numbers employed, there is a regular procession in the amount of coal lost per man owing to stoppages caused by trade disputes as we move up the scale from the smaller to the larger mines. In the Yorkshire collieries employing fewer than 500 men, each miner loses about one ton a year from this cause. In the big mines employing more than 2,500 men, the loss per man is five times as high. In the South Wales bitumenous coalfield the loss per man in the mines employing fewer than 500 men is below two tons a year. In the collieries employing 1,500–2,000 men the loss rises to six tons a year.[1]

The causes of these differences in human response to the size of the undertaking are not known. But the importance of the phenomena is unquestionable. It should not be assumed that the obstacles to good industrial relations arising from size are insuperable; for this is obviously not the case, since some of the largest firms have the best record of industrial relations. But the existence of these obstacles and the need to take special steps to overcome them should be recognized.

Professor Revans's investigations show that the size of the actual working cell within the colliery is a contributory factor to morale; so that even within a particular size group, mines which have smaller cells enjoy a higher morale than those with larger cells. It is possible that the size of the actual working unit is more important than the size of the undertaking as a whole.

Supervision is also a matter of great importance. Mines with a high supervision ratio enjoy a higher morale than those with a lower ratio in the same size group. Their higher morale is reflected in a more regular attendance of face workers, a lower underground accident rate, higher average earnings per man shift, and a lower record of stoppages due to trade disputes.[2] The effect of increased supervision is not confined to coal mining but extends to other industries. 'Supervision' can have many different meanings; its effects will no doubt vary according to the interpretation which is given to it in any particular circumstance. The best interpretation would seem to be that it is an 'organ of management which gives the men the opportunity to get on with their tasks'.[3]

CENTRALIZED LABOUR NEGOTIATIONS

Nationalization has brought its own problems, and centralization is one of them. Lord Citrine, for many years General Secretary of the Trades Union Congress before becoming chairman of the CEA, remarked that

[1] *Op. cit.*, p. 307. [2] *Ib.*, p. 309. [3] *Ib.*, p. 310.

the statutory insistence on national agreements in nationalized industry presents a special difficulty in the way of establishing close and cordial relations with the employers. This requires centralization of negotiations and the transfer of power from local members to national representatives authorized to negotiate on their behalf. He tells us that the question of consultation between unions and their members during the progress of negotiations became so intractable that in a number of industries the negotiating bodies were given power to settle collective agreements without referring the final outcome of the negotiations to their members. While Lord Citrine believes that few trade unionists would tolerate a return to the system of purely local negotiations, he admits that the centralization resulting from national agreements has undoubtedly led to a sense of frustration on the part of the individual member. The submission of reports to delegate conferences by a handful of trade union officials who conduct national negotiations does not completely overcome the psychological troubles of the individual workman or secretary of a local branch who realizes that he no longer has any real power over the processes of collective bargaining which determine the terms and conditions of his work.[1]

The Herbert Committee commented on the rigidity and comprehensiveness of the national agreements governing labour conditions in the electricity supply industry which attempt to impose uniformity throughout the country rather than to lay down principles and minimum standards which could be applied with more flexibility in the districts. In consequence, minor questions concerning individual applications of an agreement or deviations from it are referred up to the national level instead of being settled lower down, and 'the machine has tended to clog with the mass of minor problems which continually demand the attention of the national bodies. The consequent frustrations and delays in obtaining settlement have inevitably had their effect on the working of the industry'. And perhaps worst of all, the national agreements leave the Area Boards no opportunity of rewarding exceptional effort or ability. No one in the industry really likes this highly centralized system. It arose largely through an excessive regard either on the part of the electricity authorities or of the trade unions concerned for a meticulous uniformity, and through fear that district or local bodies might exercise any discretionary powers given to them in a way which would lead to what the Treasury calls 'repercussions'.[2] The Committee thought that if

[1] Lord Citrine: 'Problems of Nationalized Industry', XXIX *Public Administration* (1951), pp. 327-8; see also W. W. Haynes: *Nationalization in Practice* (1953), pp. 176-8.

[2] *Report of the Committee of Inquiry into the Electricity Supply Industry*, HMSO, Cmd. 9672/1956, paras. 433-4.

efforts were made on both sides it should be possible to arrive at an understanding by which much greater decentralization in regard to the detailed local application of national agreements would be accepted.

A similar analysis leading to similar conclusions has been made of the results of national negotiations in the coal industry. The tendency towards centralized bargaining has diminished the miner's understanding of the collective agreements made on his behalf; it has encouraged demands for uniformity in an industry in which local traditions and conditions are highly diverse; it has led to delay in settling the claims of certain categories of workers because the national conciliation machinery is inevitably slow; and the claims and grievances of small groups are often lost sight of in national negotiations.[1]

In a study of the British Railways under nationalization published in 1950, Mr Pickstock remarked that from the standpoint of human relations, some form of decentralization of management into smaller regions, each under a manager having overall responsibility for all departments, would be preferable to the existing system.[2] The then existing arrangements provided for very large regions, corresponding approximately to the four great amalgamated groups of railway companies. The departmental heads in these regions were responsible to their functional superiors at headquarters, though a Chief Regional Officer was supposed to exercise the co-ordinating powers of a general manager. Greater delegation of authority to local departmental officers, said Mr Pickstock, will help, but it is not enough. 'What is required is a person, or group of persons, known and accessible to all workers as *the* local railway management, and who are, as far as possible, responsible within defined limits for all aspects of railway working in a defined area.'[3]

Several very recent studies of personnel management show the immense value of group or team loyalties in upholding or enhancing industrial morale. This is particularly important in an industry such as transport or mining, where much of the work is done by men working on their own or in small groups, and is thus directly related to the team spirit or individual initiative. It was probably inevitable that the reorganization involved by nationalization would disrupt many long-standing groups of workers imbued with a sense of loyalty; but it is essential that efforts be made to re-create and foster this team spirit by every device known to industrial psychologists.

The reorganization scheme drawn up in 1954 by the British Transport

[1] W. W. Haynes: *Nationalization in Practice* (1953), pp. 176-8.
[2] Frank Pickstock: *British Railways—the Human Problem* (Fabian Society), pp. 8 and 12-3.
[3] *Ib.*, p. 13.

Commission divided Britain into six areas of management for the railways in the manner described in a previous chapter.[1] These regions are very similar to the territories of the four amalgamated railway companies prior to nationalization, with the addition of Scotland and the North Eastern Area of the former London North Eastern Railway as separate regions. The BTC stated in their scheme that these are very large areas for management purposes. They considered therefore that they should either be broken up into smaller areas, or that a substantial measure of management decentralization should be introduced within the regions—functional decentralization not being sufficient. The Commission cautiously decided in favour of the latter course for the time being, in order to avoid the major upheaval which would result from carving up the regions.

Under the new system the Commission remain responsible for 'labour relations of a major character'[2] which obviously include the conduct of national negotiations with the trade unions. The establishment of subordinate organs of management within subdivisions of the regions was intended *inter alia* to 'assist the staff by removing their feeling of remoteness from the management', to introduce more effective local supervision and co-ordination, and to encourage initiative from below, thus increasing efficiency and raising morale.[3] The regional authorities have been specially charged with the task of fostering a sense of loyalty and *esprit de corps* among the staff and ensuring attention to their welfare.[4]

These measures, if fully carried out, would go part of the way towards meeting the requirements formulated by Mr Pickstock. It will be interesting, when a sufficient period of time has elapsed to enable a judgment to be formed, to compare the labour relations now beginning to emerge on the railways with the state of affairs which existed during the earlier stage of nationalization (1947–54). The difficulty in making an evaluation of this kind is, however, to distinguish between the effect of 'objective' conditions such as wages, hours of work, conditions, promotion, etc., and that of the more subjective aspects which we have been considering.

Parliament has placed on the corporations explicit duties regarding labour. In most of the statutes there is an express requirement that the policy of the board shall be directed to promoting or securing, consistently with the proper discharge of their other duties, the safety, health, and welfare of their employees; and, also, the benefit of their

[1] *Ante* Ch. IV, pp. 98-101.
[2] *Railways Reorganization Scheme*, HMSO, Cmd. 9191/1954, para. 13.
[3] *Ib.*, para. 22. [4] *Ib.*, para. 27.

practical knowledge and experience in the organization and conduct of the operations in which they are employed.

There is, moreover, a statutory duty on each corporation to take the necessary steps to conclude agreements with the trade unions for the establishment and maintenance of joint negotiating machinery for two purposes. One of these is the settlement by negotiation of the terms and conditions of employment, with provision for arbitration in default of agreement in cases to be specified. The other purpose is to provide for consultation on questions relating to the safety, health, or welfare of the employees; the organization and conduct of the operations in which they are employed, and other matters of mutual interest.[1] In several statutes this last sentence has been expressed in language which makes it clear that the scope of joint discussion is not confined to the terms and conditions of employment, but includes anything which is directly connected with the efficient conduct of the industry.[2]

The governing boards of the public corporations have taken their obligations towards organized labour with the utmost seriousness. Indeed, one of the most promising features of the situation is the fact that the boards and the chief executives have shown every sign of understanding the immense importance of the labour problem and the need to adopt a new and creative attitude towards it.

But the trade unions concerned must be no less ready on their part to adapt their policies and outlook to the new situation which confronts them; and so far they have not found this easy to do.

STRIKES, OFFICIAL AND UNOFFICIAL

The general tendency of miners to strike is not primarily related to the form of ownership of the coal industry. The propensity to strike is greater in coalmining than in any other industry. The cause of this phenomenon is not known, but is probably due to the conditions in which miners work. The large number of unofficial strikes since nationalization is mainly due to the persistence among the miners of traditional attitudes in dealing with the management.

There has been no official strike in the coal industry since nationalization. But as the following table shows, there have been between 1,500 and 3,400 unofficial stoppages or 'go-slow' campaigns each year during the past ten years, and the number has been increasing. Most of the output lost in consequence of these disputes is accounted for by a

[1] Coal Industry Nationalization Act, 1946, s. 46.

[2] Air Corporations Act, 1949, s. 20: Electricity Act, 1947, s. 53; Gas Act, 1948, s. 57; Transport Act, 1947, s. 95.

very small proportion of the stoppages. Thus, in 1951 two per cent of the stoppages were responsible for forty per cent of the lost output, while the following year three major disputes accounted for nearly a third of the lost output.[1] The incidence of these unofficial disputes varies widely between the different coalfields; but three divisions, namely, Scotland, Yorkshire, and South Wales, have consistently been responsible for over eighty per cent of the loss of output each year.[2]

Disputes causing unofficial stoppages and 'go-slow' working in the coal industry

	Number of Disputes	*Tonnage Lost*	
		thousand tons	*% of total output*
1947	1,635	1,654	0·9
1948	1,528	1,062	0·5
1949	1,634	1,543	0·8
1950	1,613	1,040	0·5
1951	1,637	1,113	0·5
1952	2,365	1,900	0·8
1953	2,324	1,150	
1954	2,614	1,505	0·7
1955	3,587	3,180	1·5
1956	3,771	2,146	1·0
1957	3,771	1,829	0·9
1958	3,114	1,451	0·7

The officials of the National Union of Mineworkers have consistently opposed strikes, whether official or unofficial, in the nationalized coal industry.[3] The causes of these unauthorized stoppages have usually been purely local disputes about wages, methods of working, and so forth. There is, however, little that the NUM can do to impose discipline, since almost the only sanction at its command is expulsion from the union, which would mean exclusion from the industry. This sanction

[1] The information is taken from the Annual Reports of the NCB 1951-5.

[2] Within these three divisions most of the stoppages have occurred in ten areas. These areas contain about a quarter of the Board's total labour force, but have repeatedly accounted for over half the total output lost (56 per cent in 1951, 66 per cent in 1952, and 58 per cent in 1953).

[3] George B. Baldwin: *Beyond Nationalization* (1955), pp. 92-4. This writer observes that since nationalization there has been some reduction in the incidence of strikes; but the expectation of any great reduction was founded on an incorrect analysis of their causes and character. Since the industry was nationalized, collective bargaining has become 'more complete, more standardized, and more centralized'. More attention is given to voluntary arbitration, p. 63.

is far too extreme and damaging to both the union and the industry to be of any practical use except on very rare occasions.

The union officials at the higher levels often endeavour to persuade the branch leaders to adopt a conciliatory attitude. The constitutional right to authorize a strike resides in the National Executive Committee and hence any strike which is not so authorized is unofficial. When permission to strike is refused, a subsequent stoppage of work may be directed at the union rather than at the management. A lodge secretary is reported to have said, at the end of a strike lasting thirteen days at Haston, Durham, in 1954: 'We have not been fighting the Coal Board; we have been fighting the union.'[1]

Much careful study has been given to the conflicting currents of thought and feeling which are at work below the surface in the nationalized coal industry; and it is possible to diagnose the present maladies. Nationalization has involved the NUM in a reorientation of its outlook from what Mr Baldwin calls 'protest unionism' to one of 'administrative unionism'.[2] The union officials now have to serve on joint committees and to devote much time and energy to discussing problems which are causing concern to the management. They appear before administrative tribunals on behalf of their members to support industrial injury claims; they help to administer pension and welfare schemes; they participate in production drives; they spend time mediating with Government departments and briefing MPs. They often act as a buffer between the National Coal Board (or its subordinate organs) and the criticism or resentment of their own members, and defend the Board against unfounded charges or unfair criticism. In such circumstances there is an ever-present risk that the union leaders will appear as mere apologists of the management and thereby forfeit the confidence of the rank and file. This danger is enhanced by the tendency to give union officials some of the lighter and better paid jobs in the pits[3]—a tendency which originated long before nationalization took place.

COMMUNICATION AND MORALE

The remedy for this unsatisfactory state of affairs must be sought partly in vocational education and partly in improved communication. The problem of communication between management and employees cannot be solved merely by providing more and better factual information about the industry. A more fundamental need is to break down misconceptions, to allay suspicions, and to dispel cynicism which induces the men to give

[1] N. Dennis, F. Henriques, and C. Slaughter: *Coal is our Life* (1956), pp. 103-4.
[2] George B. Baldwin: *op. cit.*, p. 51. [3] *Ib.*, pp. 51-3.

a wrong interpretation to the actions of the management or a false meaning to the information which reaches them.[1]

A survey carried out by the Acton Society Trust in 1951 found that misinformation among the miners was clearly prejudicial to a willingness on their part to co-operate with the management. Miners in general are dominated by the fear of unemployment; by a deep suspicion of everyone in authority; and by a belief that they are regarded by the public as inferior human beings. These deep-seated fears and prejudices are found among those who read official publications no less than among those who take no interest in what is going on within the industry. In short, the provision of information by itself does not disperse distrust; it is simply fitted into the pattern of existing prejudices.[2]

Almost everyone who has studied the question of labour relations in nationalized industries has come to the conclusion that the attainment of a higher morale, a greater respect for management, and improved incentives depend in large measure on facilitating and promoting communication within these great organizations.

The problem of communication has many facets. One of them relates to the creation of a higher degree of confidence between management and men than exists at present in some of the nationalized industries. Where lack of confidence is the result of long years of distrust and mismanagement under private enterprise, as in the coal industry, the first aim should be to make the workpeople understand that the direction and management of the nationalized industry is not just the old management in a slightly different guise, but is fundamentally different and with a new purpose and outlook. An understanding, and still more the acceptance, of this important truth requires a highly developed and continuously used system of communication linking all branches and levels of the management with the whole working force. Again, the highly damaging suspicion that every workman who has been promoted to a staff post has 'gone over to the other side' and has sold his loyalty to his former comrades, can be dispelled only by an immense effort in communication between the managers and the workpeople. These are mainly negative tasks, involving the clearing away of misconceptions. The positive aims of communication are both more difficult and more important.

In the first place there is a need to instill among the employees a sense of pride in the undertaking and a feeling of responsibility for its well-being and efficiency. Second, there is a need to inculcate a sense of common purpose among all the employees of the industry. Third, there

[1] *The Worker's Point of View* (1952) (Nationalized Industry Study No. 11 published by the Acton Society Trust).

[2] *Ib.*, pp. 5-14, 19-20, and 21.

is a need to spread among the workpeople an understanding of the major problems facing the industry, such as those relating to improved technology, capital investment, productivity, manpower, redundancy, and so forth. This is not just a matter of circulating information but of trying to spread understanding.

Information is nevertheless important, provided it is relevant. Thus, in an industry like coalmining, which has been notoriously short of qualified staff in such spheres as personnel management, planning and execution of underground work, the design of mining machinery, it becomes necessary to distribute information explaining the functions of administrative and technical officers fulfilling 'new' duties. In an economic situation of over-employment, it will certainly be desirable to bring home to everyone in the nationalized industries that there is a shortage of manpower and that labour must be treated as a scarce commodity. The attitudes, qualifications and experience of those in authority should so far as possible be widely communicated to the employees.[1] The oppportunities for promotion open to those who are willing and able to take advantage of the facilities for vocational education and training should be the subject of frequent communication.

The Chambers Committee reported that the general standard of efficiency and conduct of motorbus drivers and conductors employed by London Transport is high and compares favourably with that found in any other city in Britain. A limited number of complaints did, however, emanate from the public about the bus services, mainly in regard to the crawling and bunching of buses, or their departure from a stopping place before passengers had time to enter or alight. These complaints, the Committee remarked, may indicate an unsatisfactory attitude of mind on the part of the bus crews towards the undertaking. It is possible that some drivers and conductors, 'whilst regarding the London Transport Executive as good employers, may not be sufficiently aware of the important part which they can and should play individually in providing an efficient public service, attracting passengers and improving the financial position of the undertaking'.[2] If this is the case it clearly indicates the need for more and better communication within the London Transport organization.

EDUCATION AND TRAINING

The nationalized industries are required or authorized by statute to provide training and education facilities for the purpose of advancing

[1] *The Worker's Point of View* (1952) (Acton Society Trust), pp. 20-3.
[2] Report, paras. 311-5.

the skill of their employees. They must submit programmes of such facilities to the Minister for his approval, and carry out the schemes thus approved. But however good the training programmes provided under these auspices may be, there will remain a strong need for the trade unions themselves to carry out educational work among their members concerning the new world of publicly owned and publicly administered industry in which they now find themselves. There is need also for the unions to give their rising generation of younger officials some training in the opportunities and responsibilities of leadership in a nationalized industry.[1] The unions themselves have a great need for a competent research staff; and also for the services of management consultants and engineering specialists who can advise them of the measures required to improve organization and management which they can press on the public corporations concerned. Some educational work has been done by a few unions; but there is a very slight understanding in this country of the contribution which larger and more highly specialized staffs could make to effective trade union work, especially in the public sector of the economy. The NUM in particular relies mainly on the judgments and impressions of line officials who may not always be well-informed and who in any case are likely to be pre-occupied with immediate problems rather than with long-term policies.[2]

In discussing the wages of railway workers, Mr B. C. Roberts drives home the same point when he writes that the unions must sink their mutual differences, educate their members about the problems which confront the industry, and be constantly spurring on the British Transport Commission to make the railways more efficient by improved management.[3] This is especially necessary in connection with the great new plan of modernization and re-equipment on which the BTC have embarked. Mr Roberts says that so far the unions have contributed little or nothing towards the achievement of substantial operating economies, although great advances are needed in this direction if the railways are to be rescued from their present plight and the position of the railway workers materially improved. The union leaders have at no time publicly denounced the BTC for failing to produce a new charges scheme which would have greatly increased their revenue; nor did they criticize the Commission for delaying until 1954 the publication of a modernization plan, although this has been a crying need for the past twenty or thirty years. The NUR and the other unions must bear part of the blame for the deplorable state of the British Railways.

[1] George B. Baldwin: *Beyond Nationalization* (1955), pp. 51-3.
[2] *Ib.*
[3] B. C. Roberts: 'Wages on the Railways', XXVI *Political Quarterly* (1955), p. 125.

If training within the unions is to make a significant impact not only on operating efficiency but, as a consequence, on the continuous improvement of wages and conditions in the industry, one of its main purposes should be to enable both officials and the rank and file to appreciate the problems of their industry, its relation to the national economy, the rôle of the unions, and the major aspects of organization.

BEA and BOAC

The air corporations themselves seem to be making impressive efforts in the sphere of training and education. British European Airways has a Technical Training Unit which provides courses for flying staff and engineers. Before 1953 much of this work was carried out by outside organizations, but since then BEA have taken it over in order to promote economy and enable a more practical type of training to be given. In recent years the Technical Training Unit has provided ground courses for about 2,000 members of the flying and engineering staff each year, and training courses for cabin and traffic staff. Training flights amounting to a total of about 2,000 hours a year have also been provided. In addition BEA operate apprenticeship schemes for engineering and craft apprentices; special courses for flying staff, organized in collaboration with Ealing Technical College; management development courses lasting three weeks for the higher grades and a fortnight for the middle management grades, with subsequent shorter refresher courses; and training-within-industry courses for supervisors arranged in collaboration with the Ministry of Labour. The management development courses are residential; and so, too, is a course in training methods and techniques introduced in 1955. The management courses are well designed and carried out with the help of both internal and outside lecturers. BEA also send selected members of their senior staff to the Administrative Staff College. BOAC have a much more extensive engineering apprenticeship scheme than BEA, which one would expect in view of its much larger body of employees; their other courses are more or less similar in type to those offered by BEA.

Gas

The Gas Council are responsible for co-ordinating the training and education programmes of the Gas Boards and for settling a general programme in consultation with the Minister. For this purpose the Council rely on an Advisory Committee on Education and Training, composed of representatives of the Council and each Gas Board, the Ministry of Education, the Institution of Gas Engineers, and of the employees. The Area Boards draw up their own training programmes in the light of the general scheme approved by the Minister, taking into account special local requirements and the existing training facilities. They work in close collaboration with local education authorities and with the district education committees of the Institution of Gas Engineers. Courses are given at local technical colleges, or at a university within the Board's area; or at residential colleges which happen to be available. Many of the Boards have their own training centres. The one owned by the North Thames Gas Board is the largest and best equipped and is claimed to be one of the finest in any industry. Some of the Boards have residential staff colleges; others have educational advisory services to keep employees informed about the educational and training facilities which are available to them. The Boards employ more than 400 full-time and part-time tutors.[1] These part-time tutors, in the South Western Area for example, are members of the staff who are appointed to assist and supervise employees taking courses in their districts.

Most of the employees who undergo training courses are seeking technical or scientific qualifications; but a substantial number—nearly 1,000 in 1955–6—are studying to improve their qualifications in administrative, secretarial, accountancy or commercial subjects. The number of those who attend courses in management or business administration is growing rapidly. The Gas Council also organize courses in management and general subjects at Brooklands County Technical College, Weybridge, and about fifteen students attend each course, of which several are held in a year. The Area Boards also organize management development courses. Thus, the West Midland Board run a course on higher management; the Northern Board offer a residential course for middle management and supervisors; the North Eastern Board encourage junior technicians to attend courses on management at a residential county college in the West Riding; while the East Midlands Board run information courses for managers on the Board's policies, practices, and procedures. There are many other special courses for various grades of foreman and supervisors. The training of supervisory staff has been an outstanding feature of the Boards' training programmes. The Eastern Board, for example, have established a full-time course of training for foremen at the Hendon Technical College. This lasts two weeks and all foremen will eventually be asked to attend it.[2]

Technical and professional training in the gas industry comprises apprenticeship schemes for gas fitters and other craftsmen; facilities for evening, day-release, and correspondence courses, the cost of which is

[1] In 1954–5 the figures were 101 full-time and 307 part-time.

[2] *Gas Council Annual Report 1955–6*, HMSO, HC 393/1955–6, pp. 26-7.

borne by the Boards; student apprenticeship and pupilage schemes for gas engineers for recruits possessing the necessary educational background; short courses lasting from a few days to eight weeks for particular categories; and research scholarships to enable specially able men to undertake research for a period of three years in the departments of chemistry or chemical engineering at a university.

Electricity

The electricity supply industry has also been extremely active in providing training and education for its employees. On the technical side there are apprenticeship schemes for training youths to become craftsmen. There are also about 1,500 student apprentices under training. There is a two-year graduate training scheme for training graduates and men who hold the National Certificate. This consists of eighteen months on practical work in electricity supply and six months spent in the workshops of a firm manufacturing electrical equipment. This scheme is the principal source of recruitment for the technical engineering staff; but the industry has encountered increasing difficulty in recent years in attracting a sufficient number of engineering graduates, largely owing to the low starting salaries and slow promotion prospects offered in comparison with competing industries.[1] It is not surprising that there has been a considerable wastage through resignations after the training is completed.

There are many other training courses provided for technical personnel. There are courses for school leavers preparing to become power station chemists; and for engineering apprentices who wish to qualify as draughtsmen. There is a training centre in London for welders, and numerous short courses for semi-skilled workers such as boilerhouse and turbine-house operatives.

On the management side there are training courses for middle management grades drawn from different branches of the industry and lasting about three weeks. They are held in residential centres for groups of about 16–18 members. The participants are divided into syndicates which investigate selected problems and report orally on their conclusions to panels of visiting experts. At a lower level are the courses for foremen, also held at residential centres. These usually last about ten days and consist of lectures, discussions and case-study examination in such subjects as organization, industrial relations, safety, health and welfare, costs and efficiency. There are also supervisory classes pro-

[1] The Herbert Committee stated that until recently graduates were paid only £400 on recruitment and that the starting salary had been raised to only £475, a figure, they considered insufficient. Report, HMSO, Cmd. 9672/1956, para. 324.

vided for the technical staff in many subjects such as communication, human relations, etc.

The Central Electricity Authority organized a great many courses of great value. Among these were the schools held at Oxford and Cambridge colleges or at the CEA's own residential training centres at Buxton and at Horsley Towers in Surrey. Four of these spring and summer schools were arranged each year, and some 450 members of the staff participated annually. These courses have been taken over by the Electricity Council, who are adding some new ones.

Residential training has been a major feature of the electricity supply industry since nationalization. More than 5,000 employees attended 181 courses and conferences at the CEA's above-mentioned training centres during the year 1955–6. The courses and conferences held at the centres cover a very wide variety of subjects concerning technical matters, industrial relations, background knowledge and management; and new topics are being introduced into the field of training every year. Quite recently new courses have been developed in communications, the supergrid, supervisory problems, and methods of instruction.

A considerable number of courses are organized by the Area Boards, especially the North Western Board; and also by the divisions of the generating authority. Some training is carried out jointly by an Area Board and the appropriate generating division. Thus the South Wales Board have established a school for apprentices and other courses at their Education and Training Centre in Cardiff; while both the North Eastern Board and the Eastern Board have instituted training courses for senior management staff. In the latter's area discussion groups for supervisors are held at regular intervals.

The nationalized electricity supply industry has also made extensive use of external facilities for education and training. A dozen electricity supply scholarships have been offered every year since 1953 to enable selected employees to take courses at a university or college. These are open to manual workers as well as to other employees; but the number of applicants who are engaged in manual work has been declining from 248 in 1953 to 141 in 1956. These scholarship awards cover not only first degree courses in engineering, law, and economics, but also postgraduate study and research. Senior staff attend courses at the Administrative Staff College, the British Institute of Management, the Business Summer School at Oxford, and elsewhere. Members of the staff who are intended to work in or on the nuclear power stations are seconded to the Atomic Energy Authority for special training at Harwell and at one of their stations. A special course on operational research was organized in conjunction with Birmingham University in 1955–6; and educational exchanges with foreign countries have now become a regular and interesting feature of the industry. Members of the staff go not only to France, Italy, Western Germany, and Sweden, but they may have a chance to go as far afield as the United States.

Coal

The National Coal Board's training and education schemes can be divided into training for mining, training for promotion, and training for management. As regards the first of these heads, compulsory preliminary training is given to all underground workers; and further training is given before starting work at the coal face.

In 1952 the NCB issued their comprehensive 'Policy for Youth' which emphasized the need for progressive employment and planned experience after preliminary training. The Board have a Mines Mechanization Training Centre at Sheffield at which special training is given, such as intensive refresher courses for electricians and ropemen. The Board introduced a national scheme for training colliery boilerhouse staff in 1952; a national system of apprenticeship for engineering craftsmen in 1953; and a standardized system of training for apprentice mining surveyors in 1955.

The so-called Ladder Plan which the NCB have introduced offers a ladder of promotion to the higher ranks for all new recruits to the industry who undergo preliminary training. As a man progresses upwards, the ladders which are available to him increase in number as they diminish in width.[1] The training and education which young men receive in their early years in the industry will enable them to qualify either as a certified tradesman or as a deputy possessing a statutory certificate. Those who obtain the Ordinary National Certificate and the Higher National Certificate become eligible to become under-manager, surveyor, mechanical or electrical technician. One important object of the scheme is to ensure that men who are potentially capable of filling responsible positions shall not be held back in later life through having failed to pursue their general and technical education to a sufficiently advanced point in their early years in the industry shortly after leaving school.

The Ladder Plan involves the provision of extensive day-release technical courses for many thousands of employees who are preparing to take either the National Certificates or the General Certificate. A substantial group are released to undergo a full-time course lasting nine months leading to the National Diploma in Mining.

[1] R. W. Bell: 'The Relation of Promotion and Training to Management in British Nationalized Industries', XXIX *Public Administration* (1951), pp. 201-2.

A National Advisory Committee on Mining Education has been set up to advise on these and other matters of a similar nature. This committee includes representatives of all the interested bodies.

Most important of all, in the special circumstances of the nationalized coal industry, is the training for management organized by the NCB. This includes university scholarships of similar value to State scholarships but without a means test attached to them. A hundred of these have been offered each year since 1948. The greater part of them are awarded to men who intend to take degrees in mining engineering, but the recipients include those who are studying mechanical, electrical, or chemical engineering or fuel technology. A few awards outside the technological sphere have enabled men in the industry to read for degrees in the social sciences or in pure science. The university scholarships in social science are offered to those who have worked underground for at least five years, under a scheme inaugurated in 1955, when five awards were given. It is hoped that men who take these courses will later join the staff of the Board's Industrial Relations Department.

Another type of preparation for management is directed practical training. This consists of post-entry courses lasting three years designed for graduates in technical subjects and others in the industry who have qualified by part-time study. This training course involves experience in another coalfield at home or abroad during the final year. Engineers are seconded for training to outside firms.

A more restricted scheme for training administrative assistants was introduced in 1950. This provides special training over a period of two or three years to candidates chosen by group-selection tests from among university graduates and men in the industry. The trainees are intended to be qualified for high managerial positions of a non-technical character. The selected men may be attached either to a division or to headquarters; the object is to ensure a wide variety of experience.

There is also a Junior Training Scheme to fit clerical workers and other employees of the Board for junior administrative posts, with the possibility of promotion to higher positions if their abilities merit advancement. This scheme was launched in 1954 to attract youths leaving school at 18 years of age. They would be employed as junior clerks prior to entering on the training course. Employees already in the service of the NCB are selected between the ages of 20 to 25 and are given 18 months' training in one department. They are encouraged to study for professional qualifications or to embark on a serious course of further education.

For the older men there are residential courses for senior officials organized both in the divisions and at headquarters. These are shorter and more intensive courses in management problems and techniques designed for area and sub-area production managers, area cost accountants, area mechanical engineers, senior stores and purchasing officers and similar categories. The NCB regard these courses for senior management officers as exceptionally important, and intend to develop this type of training at their new staff college. This college, situated at Chalfont St Giles, was opened in 1956 to provide training courses which can best be organized on a national scale. It will accommodate about forty-five students. Initially it will provide the courses previously held elsewhere for colliery managers and senior management officers. For some time it will be necessary to organize monthly management courses, but eventually, when the pressure on these courses is reduced, the aim will be to work out less specialized training courses in management lasting three months.

Summer schools have been held at Oxford every year. The participants are drawn from every section of the nationalized coal industry. The programme is divided between study groups and talks on general and specialized subjects.

These constitute the principal features of the training and education programme which the NCB have themselves organized. In addition the Divisional Boards also arrange courses; selected members of the senior staff are sent to the Administrative Staff College; and the clerical staff is encouraged to attend day and evening classes provided by local education authorities and other outside bodies.

Transport

The training and education programme of the British Transport Commission appears to be much less comprehensive and ambitious than those of the other nationalized industries whose activities we have examined.

On the technical side there are apprenticeship schemes for engineering and other technical apprentices at the big engineering workshops operated by the Commission. In 1955 a new Works Training School to take 300 apprentices was opened at Crewe and others are planned at Eastleigh and elsewhere. Shorter vocational courses are provided at a number of training centres at Derby, Darlington, and Woking. The BTC have taken over a Staff College established originally by the former Road Haulage Executive at Watford. There is a Central Training School for refreshment room staff at Marylebone; six Primary Clerical Training Schools for booking office, parcels and goods depot staff; two schools for freight traffic staff; and three schools for civil engineering staff. Most of these have been established since the railways were nationalized.

A good deal of training is arranged in collaboration with outside bodies. An example is the sandwich courses for aspiring engineers initiated in 1955 in collaboration with Southampton University. Four technical colleges are associated with a scheme for training signals engineers. In general the employees are encouraged to use outside training facilities. They are helped to do so by the payment of tuition and examination fees; and examination successes receive recognition by salary increments or lump sum payments.

Most of the purely vocational training is, however, given on the job. With this in view much attention has been given to the training of supervisors, using for that purpose the Training-within-Industry scheme of the Ministry of Labour and National Service.

Background education and training for management is offered in the form of general courses intended to give railwaymen belonging to all grades and regions a better understanding of their job in relation to the organization as a whole. These are residential courses which were initiated at the end of 1955. There are also courses in human relations and personnel management held at the Woking Staff Training College. There are induction courses, lasting a fortnight and also residential, for graduate recruits entering the traffic apprenticeship, accountancy, and civil engineers training schemes. There appears to be no general programme for the development of senior managerial staff in non-technical grades, other than the very small numbers who are sent to the Administrative Staff College at Henley.

The Commission are rightly concerned with the need for expanding the technical training facilities required for the new railway modernization and re-equipment plan on which they have embarked. The shortage of engineering staff is one of the chief obstacles to be overcome in the fulfilment of the plan. Mention has already been made of new training schools for technical personnel recently opened and of the new sandwich courses. The training period for civil engineers has been reduced by a year—from three years to two years for graduates and from five to four years for student trainees.

No one would question the indispensable need of the nationalized transport industry to raise the standard of competence and skill of its technical and engineering personnel at all levels. By no other means can the railways move forward from their present deplorable condition. It is not too much to say that the backward state of the British railways is largely explained by the old-fashioned outlook and muscle-bound traditionalism of the senior engineering, operational and commercial executives. But the need for a high standard of management at all levels is an urgent need also; and it is satisfactory to learn that the BTC have recognized the need for the improvement of knowledge and skill at the higher managerial levels.

The efforts made by the nationalized industries in regard to education and training are on the whole impressive. It is clear that the obligations imposed by legislation and the duty to submit general schemes to the Minister for his approval have induced the public corporations to attach great importance and a high priority to the training function. But it would be unfair to the Boards to attribute their interest and zeal in this respect wholly or even mainly to a desire to discharge their statutory duties. The governing boards have undoubtedly recognized the immense need for thorough and extensive training programmes as a vital necessity if the public sector of the economy is to be efficient, progressive, and contented. These programmes have an essential part to play in the future of nationalized industries in several ways. Training can fit the employees to desire, to accept, and to assist in technological progress, and to understand the causes which make industries decline or advance from a technological standpoint. The need for active acceptance of technological progress by the managers and chief executives no less than by the rank and file is a matter of primary importance in the basic industries. Training can raise to an incalculable extent the standard of management, particularly in those nationalized industries (such as coal and railways) where it has been backward, and thereby raise productivity and improve the material position of the employees. And finally, training can make the workpeople grasp much more fully than they do at present the transformation wrought by nationalization in their relations with the management and the public.

THE MACHINERY OF JOINT CONSULTATION

The method of joint consultation between management and the workpeople has been established in each of the nationalized industries in accordance with their statutory obligations and also, no doubt, as an elementary requirement of good management.

Joint consultation is taken very seriously by the governing boards of the public corporations and is not regarded as a mere gesture to be made in a perfunctory manner. Elaborate machinery has been set up at various levels. In coalmining, for example, there is a Consultative Committee at almost every colliery and also in each area and division; and there is a National Consultative Council presided over by the chairman of the National Coal Board.[1]

An important question is whether separate organs should be set up

[1] H. Townshend-Rose: *The British Coal Industry* (1951), pp. 119-20.

to negotiate wages and conditions of employment, distinct from the bodies concerned with joint conciliation. Separate machinery exists in the coal and electricity supply industries; while the machinery for joint consultation and collective bargaining is combined in transport and civil aviation. In the gas industry, the functions are combined at the national and regional levels but separate committees exist locally.

The duplication of machinery for these purposes is usually justified on the ground that negotiation consists of bargaining over matters of divergent interest whereas consultation is concerned with matters of common interest.[1] Some who are familiar with the processes of joint consultation favour separate machinery for this purpose because the function demands a partnership of minds seeking a right decision and this does not exist in wage negotiations. The converse view is that combined machinery possesses superior advantages in that the organs of collective bargaining possess the confidence of the union members; that joint consultation is a logical extension of collective bargaining; that separate machinery may arouse the apprehensions of the unions that their status will be undermined; and lastly that there are marginal questions such as welfare facilities which impinge both on collective bargaining and on joint consultation.[2] An experienced personnel manager in a nationalized industry has expressed the view that to be effective, joint consultative committees must cover all questions relating to production, organization, health, and safety, as well as wages and conditions of service. Separate committees to consider wages and conditions on the one hand, and efficiency and welfare on the other, are in his opinion likely to lead to friction, rivalry, and misunderstanding, as well as demarcation disputes. If separate committees deal with these matters, then they should have the same membership. The important point is that the same people should deal with all questions at each level.[3]

It is obvious that no decisive conclusion can be reached on the respective merits of the two types of organization; otherwise one may assume there would not be the divergence of practice which now exists. Moreover, there are sometimes considerable differences in jurisdiction. Thus, in electricity supply the consultative machinery covers all grades of staff at each level, whereas the negotiating machinery is not comprehensive but deals with specified categories.[4]

The method of representation is of great importance in connection

[1] Frank Pickstock: *British Railways—the Human Problem* (1950) (Fabian Society), p. 29.

[2] *The Framework of Joint Consultation* (1952) (Nationalized Industry Study No. 10 published by the Acton Society Trust), pp. 2-3.

[3] 'Personnel Policy in a Public Corporation', XXXI *Journal of the Institute of Personnel Management* (1949), p. 74.

[4] Sir Henry Self and E. M. Watson: *Electricity Supply in Great Britain* (1952), p. 136.

with joint consultation. Those who advocate combining this function with collective bargaining assume that the employees' representatives for consultative purposes will be chosen by the trade unions rather than elected directly by the employees in the various sections of the undertaking, or by the different grades of labour employed in it. There is, however, a great deal to be said against trade union nomination, although, unfortunately, it has been widely conceded by the publicly owned corporations in order to secure the co-operation of the trade unions in joint consultation.[1]

In the coal industry, the consultative organs at the area, divisional, and national levels are drawn from representatives of the NCB and of the three mining unions. At the colliery level the Consultative Committee consists of six representatives elected by the several grades of workers on a secret ballot, the colliery lodge secretary of the National Union of Mineworkers, the NUM area agent, the Board's mining agent, and three members appointed by the manager from among the underground and surface officials. The manager is *ex officio* chairman. The method of direct election here introduced is potentially capable of bringing the rank and file of the undertaking, and also its supervisory staff, into a much closer and more vital relationship with the management; but the advantages of this method are curtailed by the right that the NUM has acquired to nominate, through its local branches, the candidates for election to the colliery Consultative Committee. It names two candidates for each vacancy, and the voting is confined to those candidates.[2]

In 1954 the National Coal Board introduced on an experimental basis a more elaborate organization of the colliery committees. Hitherto the committees represented the employees according to their occupations or trades but not according to the shift or district of the pit in which they work. Many problems concern the co-ordination of work among men engaged on successive shifts in a particular district or between adjacent districts, so the new system extends consultation to representatives of the three shifts in the same districts. The Consultative Committee for the entire colliery remains in existence and considers the results of these more concentrated deliberations.[3]

[1] For a strong statement of the arguments in favour of having full-time trade union officials on the organs of joint consultation see R. D. V. Roberts and H. Sallis, 'Joint Consultation in the Electricity Supply Industry 1949-59. XXXVII *Public Administration* (1959), p. 121.

[2] The only exception is the representative of the deputies, who is usually a member of the National Association of Colliery Overmen, Deputies and Shotfirers. For details of the reasons which led the NUM to demand the power to nominate, and the motives for granting it to them, see Baldwin: *op. cit.*, p. 102.

[3] *National Coal Board Annual Report 1954*, HMSO, HC 1/1955-6, para. 250.

According to the authors of *Coal is Our Life* joint consultation at the pit level has had some success in persuading the miners' representatives of the value of co-operation, but has tended to alienate these representatives from the men without reconciling the men to the management. The conciliation machinery has had a similar effect in increasing the mutual influence on one another of management and union officials.[1] This sometimes introduces an element of ambivalence into the attitude of branch leaders: as union officials they are expected to display qualities of militant leadership in their dealings with the National Coal Board when endeavouring to secure improved conditions of employment for their members, while as representatives on the colliery Consultative Committees they are expected to co-operate with the management to the best of their ability.[2] This is not an easy position to occupy; but the awkward dilemma can be solved only if the unions are willing to forgo the dominating rôle they have insisted on playing in the system of joint consultation.

For several years now complaints have been made that the machinery of joint consultation is insufficiently representative owing to the insistence of the principal unions that control should remain in their hands. Employees who do not belong to a union, or who are members of unions too small to be represented, are automatically excluded from the Consultative Councils, regardless of the positive contribution they might make. The representatives on the national and divisional or regional bodies sometimes have no organic relation to the local committees; and in consequence the union officials at the higher levels are frequently unaware of the views of the rank and file and therefore unwilling for that reason to support a constructive policy for fear it may be unpopular.[3] Moreover, consultation requires an intimate knowledge of the subjects with which it is concerned; and trade union officers are often unfamiliar with the details of industrial processes and factory conditions. The men in the workshop or in the mine who know the issues are not permitted to sit on the national or divisional consultative committees, except in electricity supply.

On the railways consultation between labour and management has been developed continuously since 1921. Very elaborate machinery has been evolved, organized largely according to departments on the railways. Thus, local departmental committees were set up for the employees in each department at the larger stations or depots (a 'department' usually signifying goods, passenger, traffic operating, and locomotive) subject to a minimum number of employees being engaged

[1] N. Dennis, F. Henriques, and C. Slaughter: *op. cit.*, pp. 99-100. [2] *Ib.*, pp. 105-6.
[3] *The Framework of Joint Consultation* (1952) (Acton Society Trust), pp. 16-26.

therein. Then there are sectional councils covering certain defined categories of labour or particular departments in each railway region; and a number of national organs. The machinery has been criticized on the ground that it is too compartmentalized and watertight, with the result that matters affecting several departments of railway work fail to get adequately discussed; and that the smaller depots and stations have been left without any consultative organs.[1]

Other grounds of criticism are that only union members are in practice elected to serve on the departmental committees and sectional councils, although the unions are not formally represented thereon; that these bodies are highly inefficient and bureaucratic, and fail to awaken the interest of the ordinary railwayman; that there is excessive centralization within the NUR, so that many matters which could and should be dealt with at local level are referred to headquarters, with consequent delay.[2]

A similar complaint of excessive centralization has been made about joint consultation in the electricity supply industry. The time of the National Council has been taken up with minor questions which should be dealt with at either the district or local level. An example of this was the design of a long-service certificate.[3] A disposition on the part of the higher organs to concern themselves with minor questions is bound to have detrimental effects on their prestige, and to lower the authority and status of joint consultation at all levels.

Nevertheless, substantial improvements in the machinery of joint consultation have recently been made in the electricity industry as a result of an examination of the advisory system carried out by an *ad hoc* committee of the National Joint Advisory Council. The original scheme introduced in 1949 provided for the organs of joint consultation at the national and district level to be composed of the chief executives of the Electricity Boards and trade union officials. At the local level, the employees' representatives were not trade union officials but persons elected by the workpeople of all grades employed in the locality. Such persons had to be members of the appropriate trade union.

In 1957 an effort was made to integrate the three tiers of the structure, and also to ensure a direct link between the higher management and the men working in the power stations and on the distribution network. Ten elected members of the Local Advisory Committees were thenceforth added to each District Joint Advisory Council, and one of the

[1] Frank Pickstock: *op. cit.*, pp. 19-25.

[2] B. C. Roberts: 'Wages on the Railways', XXVI *Political Quarterly* (1955), pp. 124-5.

[3] *Report of the Committee of Inquiry into the Electricity Supply Industry*, HMSO, Cmd. 9672/1956, paras. 442-3.

elected members from each District Joint Advisory Council sits on the National Joint Advisory Council.

The Local Advisory Committees, of which there are now about 500, are generally related to a single unit of local management, such as a power station or a distribution district. A local committee usually includes five or six representatives of the management and nine or ten persons elected by the manual, clerical, administrative, and technical staff. The manager acts as chairman.[1] Local committees are to arrange at least one meeting of the employees in their area each year and are to render an annual report of their activities. The chairman of each local committee will present a progress report to each meeting of his committee; and every year a conference will be held in each district of the members and secretaries of the local committees in that district. Training courses in the techniques of joint consultation have been given on an extensive scale at the CEA residential training centres.[2]

The most fundamental objection to the system of representation on the organs of joint consultation stems from the vast divergence between the organization of the trade unions and the organization of the nationalized industries. There are forty or fifty unions, some of whose members are employed in the nationalized industries, and each one of these industries has to deal with at least fifteen unions. Only four of the larger unions have most of their membership in either transport or coal mining; the others have a majority of their members in other industries under private enterprise. The largest British union, the Transport and General Workers' Union, has members in all the nationalized industries; but they account for a very small proportion of its membership. Moreover, the geographical organization of the unions does not coincide with that of the public corporations; and while the unions organize their members according to their place of residence, joint consultation is related to the workplace. The discordances could scarcely be greater; and nothing has been done or is being done to bring the unions into closer conformity with the organization of the nationalized industries.

THE SCOPE OF JOINT CONSULTATION

In theory and in law the scope of joint consultation is virtually as wide and comprehensive as the scope of the nationalized industries themselves. There are no reservations such as one often finds in private

[1] R. D. V. Roberts and H. Sallis: 'Joint Consultation in the Electricity Supply Industry 1949-1959', XXXVII *Public Administration*, pp. 117, 118, 120, 122.

[2] *Central Electricity Authority Annual Report 1955-6*, HMSO, HC 367/1955-6, paras 319-20.

enterprise, where financial matters are excluded from joint consultation.[1]

It is difficult to give a generalized view of the subjects brought before the Consultative Committees for consideration without grossly over-simplifying the position. It would, however, be true to say that questions of welfare, safety, amenities, education and training have loomed very large on the agenda of most committees and that questions of efficiency and productivity have occupied a much less prominent place. Yet in studying the annual reports of the public corporations one gets the impression that increasing attention is being paid by the advisory councils to matters of technical or administrative efficiency. Among the types of questions discussed by Colliery Consultative Committees we can find the alteration of conveyor belt machinery to prevent spilling, inquiries into the high cost of workmen's gloves, procedures for interviewing, warning or fining absentees, the distribution of the NCB magazine *Coal*, the allotment of houses, underground lighting, and Saturday working.[2] A survey of about 120 Yorkshire collieries carried out in 1951 showed that the great bulk of the questions discussed by the Colliery Consultative Committees were of local concern.[3] This is not only to be expected but is, indeed, entirely desirable at the colliery level. It would be quite inappropriate for a colliery committee to discuss national or divisional questions, and could only lead to a sense of impotence and frustration. It is important, however, that the local matters discussed by the colliery committees should embrace productivity and improved techniques, and not concentrate only on welfare, safety and amenities.

The National Coal Board in the 'Guide to Consultation' which they issued on behalf of the National Consultative Council, have indicated a very wide range of subjects for discussion. Beginning with an analysis of recent accidents and the possible means by which they might have been prevented, the Consultative Committee would consider other aspects of health and safety. Then would come a review of colliery production figures for the weeks since the last meeting of the committee, with an analysis of the causes of lost output covering mechanical breakdowns, disputes, absenteeism, shortages of supplies and defects in organization. Improvements in underground working is suggested as the next topic, with special attention to roof control. After that the committee's attention should be directed to loading points and the possibility of better use of manpower and improved equipment; the

[1] Eldon L. Johnson: 'Joint Consultation in Britain's Nationalized Industries', XII *Public Administration Review* (1952), p. 183.

[2] George B. Baldwin: *Beyond Nationalization* (1955), p. 105.

[3] *The Worker's Point of View* (1952) (Acton Society Trust), pp. 16-17.

transport system; coalface organization and equipment; the consideration of future plans and development projects for the colliery; welfare; and finally such questions as recruitment, training and education, the employment of foreign labour, and so forth. The terms of reference suggested here for the colliery committee are extremely wide; to carry them out demands a high degree of intelligence, a persistent interest in the affairs of the pit and its well-being, and a large amount of accurate information on the many topics to be discussed. The NCB clearly intend that joint consultation shall play an important and effective part in the practical running of the collieries.

In the electricity supply industry the National Joint Advisory Council for some years devoted their meetings mainly to questions of safety, education and training, and welfare; and little change of emphasis can be observed in the report of their activities for 1955–6.[1] The same was broadly true of the district and local committees.

A new stage appears to have been reached in the work of the advisory bodies at all levels in the electricity supply industry, for they now often take an interest in matters of general importance affecting the well-being of the industry. Thus, we find the National Joint Advisory Council discussing the current problems of area boards, planning and research, the present and future financing of the industry, and safety precautions in the construction of power stations; while at the local level an interest has been evinced in such topics as the effective use of transport, the siting and efficient reading of meters, measures to promote the sale of electrical appliances to consumers, improved methods of handling equipment, ways in which waste can be prevented, and rural electrification. Senior officials of the Industrial Relations Department of the Electricity Council say there has been a swift and remarkable shift of emphasis on the part of the advisory committees from 'fringe interests and activities to the main problems affecting the industry's efficiency and well-being of the employees'.[2] Such a movement would not only indicate a remarkable success for joint consultation, but it would place the electricity supply industry well ahead of any other nationalized industry in this respect.

On the railways a British Railways Productivity Council was set up by agreement between BTC and the trade unions in May 1955. The object of this was to obtain the fullest co-operation of the unions and staff in increasing productivity. The Council are composed of nine members representing the British Transport Commission and an equal number representing the unions. The creation of this body implies a recognition that the pre-existing organs of joint consultation—in particular, the

[1] *Central Electricity Authority Annual Report 1955–6*, HMSO, HC 367/1955–6, App., XXVII.
[2] R. D. V. Roberts and H. Sallis: *op. cit.*, p. 131.

British Transport Joint Consultative Council—were either unwilling or unable to grapple with the vital question of increasing productivity on the railways. During the first six months of their existence, the Council held four meetings, at which such large questions as the utilization of rolling stock, the productive time of locomotive drivers, and general proposals for increasing efficiency were under consideration. A plan was drawn up to enable teams from each region representing management and staff representatives to visit transport undertakings in foreign countries and various industries at home in order to become acquainted with methods of work study.[1]

The National Joint Council for Civil Air Transport, which was intended to serve as a consultative organ for the entire industry, have not succeeded in fulfilling that aim. Private operators do not engage in joint consultation; the two nationalized air lines, which do consult fully and freely with their employees, have separate consultation.

British European Airways established a Joint Consultative Working Party in 1952, consisting of twelve representatives of the trade unions and eighteen members of the management. The Chief Executive acted as chairman, and the director and deputy-director of every department sat on the working party, which thus brought together virtually the whole top management of the airline. BEA supplied the working party with a vast mass of information about their operations; and the working party (or the sub-committees) met from time to time at overseas stations so that it could study relevant problems on the spot. Thus, the Overseas Manpower sub-committee examined manpower problems at overseas stations in the light of local conditions. The deliberations of the working party led *inter alia* to the re-arrangement of duties and working hours; to the introduction of a new grade of 'flight clerks', to the expansion of temporary staff to cope with seasonal peak loads. A 'Flying Staff Forum' was established to provide an opportunity for the informal discussion of matters of mutual interest to the flying staff and the management. About sixty local panel committees have been set up in the United Kingdom and these meet regularly for the discussion of problems of interest to the local management and staff. An annual conference of the chairmen and secretaries of these local panel committees is also held for the purpose of reviewing the progress of the corporation and its future plans. The chairman and senior executives of BEA usually meet officials of the national trade unions concerned with their employees at an all-day conference. A productivity campaign was launched among local BEA Consultative Committees in 1952–3, and discussions were

[1] *British Transport Commission Annual Report 1955*, HMSO, HC 290-I/1955-6, Vol. I paras. 13 and 40-6. 543 HC Deb. 5s., col. 1583, Mr Molson (July 11, 1955).

initiated on local financial budgets in order to give these committees a definite task and provide a measuring rod to evaluate their work.[1]

All these activities give an impression of vigour and worthwhile effort on the part of the nationalized airlines. The weakness which exists here, as in other nationalized industries, is the gulf which separates the union officials who sit as members of the working party from the employees whom they are supposed to represent.[2]

An evaluation of joint consultation in the gas industry published in 1954 admitted that the right atmosphere and climate of opinion for this movement was at that time only beginning to be created. Among the criticisms listed were preconceived attitudes on the part of the management, such as a belief that the problems facing the industry were too technical to be usefully discussed with representatives of the employees, or that any criticism of Board officers which might be made across the table would undermine the authority of the management. Analogous prejudices were found among the employees, such as a fear that joint consultation might be used to by-pass the negotiating machinery charged with the settlement of wages and conditions; or conversely, that it should be used to promote the interests of the union's own members. Other criticisms were that there was too much feeling that management and labour were on opposite and separate 'sides' for successful joint consultation; that most of the items on the agenda were raised by the workpeople, whereas the management conceived the committees more as platforms for announcing decisions already made; that the employees' representatives suffered from a lack of knowledge of industrial problems; and that there was insufficient communication between committees and the rank and file of the employees in each undertaking and throughout each area.

A number of recommendations were made as a result of this evaluation. They included better co-ordination between the Divisional Consultative Committees and the district or local committees; the holding of area conferences by representatives of all Consultative Committees; an annual review of the whole industry by the National Joint Industrial Council; better publicity for committee decisions; regular meetings and more attention to drafting and circulating the minutes; a readiness on the part of the management to raise matters for discussion before decisions have been made, and not afterwards; and a sustained effort to give employees a greater knowledge of industrial problems.[3]

[1] *BEA and BOAC Annual Reports* 1952-3 and 1953-4.

[2] Clive Jenkins: *British Airlines* (1953) (Fabian Research Series No. 158), pp. 24-5.

[3] *Gas Times*, April-June 1954. These articles include evaluations by the Industrial Relations Officer of the Gas Council, and by manual workers and staff representatives on their respective National Councils.

AN EVALUATION

What are the objectives of joint consultation? Its main purpose is to achieve a substantial measure of industrial democracy, an aim which has for decades formed part of the ideology of socialism. When all traces of workers' control were rejected in the constitution of the public boards it became all the more important to ensure that the employees were represented on bodies which the management was obliged to consult on a wide range of questions affecting the industry. Another important aim was to evoke the interest of the rank and file in the industry and thus enable them to contribute from their personal experience to its successful running. A third objective was to create new, regular channels of communication between the management and the workpeople, and thereby reduce the chance of misunderstanding and friction, and increase goodwill. During the Second World War the Regional Councils for Industry had achieved great success in a wider sphere of activities; and their example doubtless influenced the Attlee Governments of 1945-51. But quite apart from these special circumstances, there has been an increasing tendency both in private industry and in the public services to regard regular consultation with representatives of the employees as necessary for good personnel management.

It is easy to criticize the shortcomings of joint consultation in the nationalized industries and to identify the various factors which have prevented it from attaining the ideal results expected of it by those whose enthusiasm outran their judgment. It was inevitable that there should be disappointment at the results so far achieved by those who either expected too much too soon or who failed to appreciate the tremendous changes of attitude demanded by its introduction. It is unquestionable that the machinery of joint consultation has made a substantial contribution to improved labour relations in most of the nationalized industries, although on the railways it was impossible for joint consultation to overcome adverse factors in the industry which were detrimental to the interests of railway workers. In considering the potentialities of joint consultation, far too little attention has been paid to the record of labour relations prior to nationalization. Where the record was good, as in the case of electricity supply or civil aviation, it was possible to plant joint consultation in a soil favourable to its growth and flowering. Where relations between labour and management had been full of conflict under private enterprise and the nationalized industry entered into a heritage of bitterness and suspicion, joint consultation was severely handicapped from the outset.

This is so obvious that it should scarcely need saying. But so many people have rushed into print on the subject of the shortcomings of joint consultation, whereas little or nothing is said about the state of labour relations prior to nationalization, that one feels it to be necessary to see the matter in perspective. It would, indeed, be miraculous if consultative committees had transformed the situation overnight. It would be equally surprising if they had not encountered in some instances apathy on the part of the workpeople and hostility on the part of the management. Over a great part of the field there is need for improved communication between the organs of consultation and the mass of the employees; for workers' representatives who are better informed and better equipped to understand industrial problems; for more zeal, interest and enthusiasm. But when all this has been admitted, there is no shadow of a doubt that joint consultation is making a substantial contribution to good and improving labour relations in the nationalized industries. This contribution can be immensely increased if the necessary effort is made on both sides.

Whether joint consultation is likely to become a decisively important factor in the operation of the nationalized industries is a question which it is not easy to answer. The experience of Whitleyism in central and local government, and experiments carried out by the Glacier Metal Company suggest that the answer may well be in the negative. This firm has pushed joint consultation to an extremely advanced point, but the general conclusion reached is that 'consultation by itself makes little impact on the basic attitudes of the ordinary worker'.[1] Most of the workpeople are not interested in anything outside their own immediate sphere of work;[2] and even when the firm established a works council whose unanimous agreement was required for all policy decisions, representatives of the works committee (directly elected by the hourly-paid workers and lower grade staff) were relatively uninterested in these discussions on top level policy.[3]

This pioneering firm abandoned the use of the expression joint consultation as its limitations have become better understood. 'The main reason why Glacier Metal no longer uses the language of joint consultation', writes Mr John Mack, 'is not that the institutions in question were over-valued. It is because the practice of consultation was extended in such a way as to interfere with the effective management of the factory. The later developments in experimental management stem from this discovery by trial and error of the dangers of consultative or democratic management.'[4]

[1] John A. Mack: 'The Glacier Metal Experiments', XXVII *Political Quarterly* (1956), p. 318.

[2] *Ib.*, p. 316. [3] *Ib.*, p. 317. [4] *Ib.*, p. 315.

A reaction has set in against the assumption that authoritarian behaviour can be identified with instructing anyone to do anything, and is necessarily reprehensible both morally and from the practical point of view of encountering opposition. The fallacy of believing that acceptance of a decision is more important than the merits of the decision has gradually become clear. The organs of joint consultation continue to exist and to function; but it is no longer assumed that they can constitute the management or replace executive leadership; that they will make a deep and widespread impact on the employees about matters outside their immediate work and experience; or that they will necessarily dissolve the conflicts and opposition between labour and management.[1]

Joint consultation undoubtedly can be and is of substantial use, especially as a means of engendering confidence among the employees in the management; but to suppose that it will become in the foreseeable future an instrument for harnessing the enthusiastic interest of the mass of the workpeople to the task of solving the problems facing a great industrial undertaking is to invite disillusion. We need both better managerial practices and the development of industrial democracy; and the two aims are not incompatible with one another.

There is an obvious parallel between joint consultation and Whitleyism in the civil service. Whitleyism may not have realized 'the full grandeur of its original objects and functions',[2] but it has been instrumental in making the civil service more contented, which is no mean achievement, and one which both sides greatly value. The National Whitley Council machinery is invariably used for discussing and reaching agreement on many matters relating to conditions of service applicable to all or several sections of the civil service, such as hours of work, vacations, pensions, the principles of promotion, recruitment, and so forth. But in general, as Mr Douglas Houghton, MP, remarks from his long practical experience as General Secretary of the Inland Revenue Staff Federation:

> 'It is not the job of the Whitley Councils to try to run departments or to usurp the functions of those responsible for administration. They can do a great deal to help with suggestions and ideas, and staff sides may come near sometimes to grafting themselves on the structure of management. It must not be forgotten, however, that they are all the time representative of the staff: they are the spokesmen of trade unions. They have no other right to be there. All the complex and controversial questions of what are the functions of trade unions in

[1] John A. Mack : *Political Quarterly* (1956), p. 319.

[2] Douglas Houghton: 'Whitley Councils in the Civil Service' in *The Civil Service in Britain and France*, ed. W. A. Robson (1956), p. 148.

a changing society trouble them just as much as they do the National Union of Railwaymen and others.'[1]

In recent years, the formal joint meetings and similar occasions, which the heads of Government departments found so onerous and time-consuming, have been largely abandoned. The full National Whitley Council have met only twice since 1939; and most of the members have never been summoned to attend a meeting. The departmental Whitley Councils also seldom meet. In place of these formal meetings new and more flexible procedures have grown up for discussion and negotiation between the staff side representing the civil service trade unions, or its full-time chairman, or the general purposes committee, and senior Treasury or departmental officials in charge of establishment or similar matters. Sometimes a small *ad hoc* committee will be set up to discuss a particular problem.

The new methods and machinery work smoothly and successfully, and a vast mass of detailed questions, many of them potentially capable of giving rise to friction or discontent, are settled in a way which usually gives satisfaction to both sides. No longer do permanent secretaries of great departments find Whitleyism a heavy drain on their time and energies. In short, Whitleyism has come to fill a most valuable rôle in maintaining a reasonably contented civil service; it is strongly supported by both sides and by Ministers; but its aims are limited, and no one expects it to perform great flights of fancy.

Those who expect much more from joint consultation in nationalized industries should ask themselves realistically how many of the men and women they know are really prepared to devote a considerable part of their leisure time to reading indigestible documents dealing with productivity, financial statistics, investment, manpower, sales and commercial policy, wages and hours of work, and all the other matters which demand the attention of management. The notion that the great majority of employees are straining at the leash in order to participate actively in a system of industrial democracy is not borne out by the figures for attendance of trade unionists at branch meetings; or by the percentage of members who vote at the election of trade union officers at any level. Moreover, as the standard of living rises, the rival attractions of television and broadcasting, of gardening and motoring, of enjoying a more comfortable home life and sharing in the cultural heritage of the nation, become more insistent.

None of these considerations invalidates the observations of an

[1] Douglas Houghton: 'Whitley Councils in the Civil Service' in *The Civil Service in Britain and France*, ed. W. A. Robson (1956), p. 149.

American observer of our nationalized industries when he wrote: 'In stating the purpose of joint consultation in this new environment it becomes apparent that attention must be fixed not only on the end sought—the production of goods and services—but also on the means to that end: the human factors and values found in the workplace conceived as a community. *Accepted* authority is based on understanding, and understanding is made possible by the establishment of special channels of communication, with an agreement to use the channels freely. That is the essence of joint consultation. Authority also has an infinitely better chance of being accepted if it is exercised in a working environment which is persistently and consciously aware of the worker's dignity, his possibilities for creativeness, and his right to a share in the determination of policies in which his co-operation is needed.'[1]

This perception of the ideals underlying the system of joint consultation need not blind us to the practical difficulties and obstructions which lie in its path. President Eldon Johnson, whose words I have quoted above, rightly draws attention to the need for constantly combating the tendency towards apathy on the part of the employees and self-sufficiency on the part of management, if joint consultation is to make real headway.[2] And above all we are confronted with the perpetual problem of creating, improving and maintaining an adequate system of communication. It is not only the lines of communication *between* management and labour which are defective. The channels of communication—and what passes through them—within the ranks of management on the one hand, and between the trade unions and their members on the other, usually need improving if joint consultation is to yield the favourable results of which it is potentially capable.

When all is said and done, it is no small thing that as a result of the legislation passed by the Labour Government in 1945-51 'the world is now witnessing in the nationalized industries the greatest application of the principle of democracy in industry'.[3]

It is obvious that joint consultation can succeed only if all those who participate in the process are convinced of its essential value. There must be no mental reservations; no sense among the management representatives that the whole business is a waste of time, or a concession to the employees' demand for a higher status. There must be a full realization that there is, or should be, a community of interest among those who serve the public in publicly owned undertakings; and that the

[1] Eldon L. Johnson: 'Joint Consultation in Britain's Nationalized Industries,' XII *Public Administration Review* (1952), p. 182. The author is now President of the University of New Hampshire.

[2] *Ib.*, p. 189. [3] *Ib.*, p. 183.

object of joint consultation is to enable this common interest to find creative expression. One of the essential aims of consultation for many years to come will be to cultivate a sense of community of purpose throughout the organization.

A PUBLIC SERVICE IN THE MAKING?

Those who emphasize the need to imbue the employees of the public corporations with the spirit of public service are right from every point of view.[1] Without it nationalization cannot succeed; nor democratic socialism prove to be a superior conception of social or economic life. If the vast industrial forces which work in the public corporations merely seek to exploit their position to the full, the future of Britain will be grim and joyless indeed.

We must not, however, expect that nationalization by itself will transform the outlook or influence the motives of those who work in an industry. Nor should we expect a miracle of unselfishness on their part. What we must seek is to awaken in the workpeople a strong desire to serve the public as well as they possibly can together with the desire to improve their own standard of living. This is a reasonable and practicable objective; for while the unions will remain zealous to safeguard and advance the interests of their members, they are, or can be made to become, deeply interested in ensuring that nationalization succeeds. The railway unions, for example, have centred their wider aims on nationalization in the threefold hope that it would enable the railways to provide the most efficient service to the community; that it would give the railway workers a better and more secure standard of life; and that it would enable them to exert a greater influence on the administration of the industry.[2]

These aims are all to be commended, and they are all capable of realization—but only if the unions are willing to abandon some of their most cherished prejudices and to change some of their obsolete practices. For one thing, they must recognize the weakness of clinging to the principle of promotion according to seniority. The administration of British Railways is weakened at every level by the pernicious, all-pervading influence of seniority as a guide to promotion. I know a number of able men with a university education who entered the railways prior to nationalization. Nearly all of them left in disgust at the insurmountable

[1] The late Sir Arthur Street emphasized this in his pamphlet *The Public Corporation in British Experience* (1947); see also his essay 'Quasi-Government Bodies since 1918' in *British Government since 1918* (1950), pp. 188-90.

[2] Frank Pickstock: *op. cit.*, p. 18.

barriers which blocked the prospect of a reasonably early rise to positions of responsibility.

The trade unions are largely conditioned in their outlook and practices by the capitalism which produced them. With the elimination of private ownership and the profit motive from the nationalized industries, radical changes are needed in the unions. They evolved historically as organs for defending or improving the workers' standard of living. Today they are called upon to co-operate in the administration of vast industries operated for the benefit of the community. They need to abandon their defensive, negative, demanding attitude, and to display qualities of constructive leadership, understanding and co-operation with the management. The unions, it has been wisely said, must be in the management but not of it.

Above all, the trade unions must improve the quality of their own officers. At present, even the largest and wealthiest unions are handicapped by a lack of skilled staff in their own offices. They lack economists, statisticians, and research workers. They are reluctant to appoint men who have had a university education, even when they are their own members who have won scholarships paid for by the union. The time has come when the unions must consider the part they have to play in the sphere of nationalized industries, and recognize the need to revise their own organization, attitudes and practices so as to enable them to play it effectively.

CHAPTER XIII

Research

PUBLIC opinion in Britain has at last begun to recognize the overwhelming importance to our economic future, and indeed to our whole position in the world, of research and development.

THE CLIMATE OF OPINION

This belated recognition of the value of research is due to a number of different causes. An important influence was the massive contribution made by men of science to the national effort in the Second World War, a contribution so immense and all-pervading that it made a deep impression on those who had formerly been contemptuous or indifferent. Another influence is the realization that, despite the outstanding achievements of British men of science, research is accorded far greater prestige and a more generous share of available resources in other countries, such as Germany, the Soviet Union, the USA, not to mention Sweden and Switzerland.

The status of the scientist in industry and business has hitherto been relatively low in England. A scientific training is seldom found among members of the Establishment. The vast majority of Ministers, senior civil servants, top executives in business, industry and finance, in accountancy and insurance, who have attended a university have graduated in arts subjects or in law and not in science, technology or mathematics. Nowhere in the world does the cleavage between the study of science subjects and the study of arts subjects begin at so early a stage of education and result in so complete a separation of knowledge and outlook as in England. The cumulative effect of these influences over the years has been to produce a great undervaluation of science in many walks of life.

A change of opinion has for long been greatly needed in Britain. This is gradually coming about, partly as a result of a dawning appreciation of the fact that the serious rivalry which our goods encounter in export markets cannot be attributed to 'unfair competition' by our trade rivals, or a lower standard of living by their employees, or the unreasonable demands and slackness of British workers, but it is quite often due to a greater use of research and its applications by manufacturers abroad and their willingness to spend more money on it.

There are a number of general factors which also point unmistakably in the same direction. The rapid development of electronics, the gas turbine, jet aircraft, plastics, synthetic textiles, chemical engineering, nuclear energy, etc., have not only revealed a serious shortage of scientists and technologists in this country, but also emphasized the crucial importance of research in these and other branches of technology. The recent demonstration of Soviet advances in rockets and ballistic missiles has added an element of fear to the consequences of being left behind in the technological race.

Efforts are being made to improve the situation in several directions, though no one who is qualified to express an opinion on the subject considers them to be adequate. Scientific manpower has been more than doubled since the war, but is today probably in shorter supply relatively to our present needs than at any previous time. More generous grants of money have been allocated to the science and engineering departments of the leading universities and colleges of technology; considerable sums of public money are being devoted to research through such bodies as the Medical Research Council, the Agricultural Research Council and the Aeronautical Research Council; Government research institutions have increased in number, size and scope, and some departments are devoting a high proportion of their resources to research and development.

INTERACTING FORCES

It is against this background of deepseated neglect and indifference in the past that we must see the question of research in the nationalized industries. It is, however, important not to conceive research as an isolated function divorced from the surrounding circumstances which give it life and significance.

It is easy, for example, to see that there was a gross neglect of research in the British coal industry under private ownership. Many collieries were technologically backward, none of them was equipped with power-loading machinery and there was a widespread lack of mechanical traction underground. Coal was handled at railhead depots by antiquated methods of manual bagging and shovelling; it was delivered to the domestic consumer by methods which had scarcely changed for a hundred years; and it was used by him in highly inefficient open-hearth grates.

Facts like these can be attributed only partly to the failure of the British coal industry to make adequate use of research in the mining, distribution and consumption of coal. They show also that the industry was starved of capital and of brains. It is even difficult to distinguish cause from consequence. If an industry lacks the necessary capital there will be little incentive for those in control of it to initiate and support research and development projects, since these usually demand a substantial investment of resources and the scrapping of old equipment. An industry which is stagnant or declining will have difficulty in attracting young men with brains from the universities; and the abler executives and technicians will tend to leave it if they can find better opportunities for their abilities elsewhere.

The result is to create a vicious circle which lowers productivity or prevents it from rising. Hence, the low standard of living of the British miner and the severe decline in his relative earnings before 1947, compared with other categories of labour, were the end result of a series of inter-related causes of which backward technology, under-investment, a lack of research and development and a shortage of able executives and technologists were the most important. This declining standard of living in turn provoked a further reaction in terms of conflict, discontentment, bitterness and low morale among the workers.

I have attempted to trace the interactions between research and some of the other functions of management in order to avoid the error of supposing that an industry which has become technically backward can bring itself up to date merely by spending a few thousand pounds on hiring scientists and equipping laboratories. The problem of replacing a momentum of decline by a momentum of progress is a highly complex one.

ORGANIZING FOR PROGRESS

Mr A. H. A. Wynn, the scientific member of the National Coal Board, pointed out in a brilliant lecture that progress must be organized by means of specialized institutions deliberately created for that purpose. In a declining industry, the incentives to establish organizations specializing in research, development and capital investment are very weak. An advancing industry, on the other hand, will have an elaborate research organization, costly laboratories and testing facilities for development, and a strong organization for planning and carrying out capital investment. It is impossible to organize progress and to arrest decline without a series of organizations specially devised for the purpose. But even after they have been set up, it may take some years before new engineering methods can be introduced, the staff and employees trained to understand and accept technical changes, and new capital effectively invested.[1]

In the nationalized coal industry, the special organizations designed to

[1] *Science in the Nationalized Industries*, a lecture given to the Royal Institute of Public Administration on November 28, 1955.

promote progress include the Coal Survey, which, together with the Planning Branch and the Geological Survey,[1] have greatly increased knowledge about British coal resources. This is an essential condition precedent to the opening up of new mines or the development of existing collieries. The Planning Branch is an engineering organization responsible for the major reconstruction of old mines and the opening up of new ones. Little or nothing of this kind existed throughout most of the industry prior to 1947. The task of organizing the Planning Branch has been extremely difficult owing to the shortage of qualified engineers, technicians, and skilled manual workers. A Mechanization Branch, supported by an Engineering Branch, was established to advise on mechanical and electrical engineering problems—both organs being essential to progress. A Central Engineering Establishment to work on the development of new machinery and to guide manufacturers supplying the Board also forms part of the organization for progress; and so, too, does the Mining Research Establishment. One could mention in this context several other institutions designed to serve the same purpose, such as the Scientific Control Organization, the Field Investigation Group, and the research branches concerned with the study of medical problems, staff and management problems, and the problems of labour relations.

Mr Wynn was concerned to show not only the need to create special organizations to ensure progress, but also the importance of their interrelations. Enterprise is essential to progress; but one cannot isolate one element of enterprise, such as research, without considering it in relation to the other elements with which it must be associated in order to achieve fruitful results.

Thus, research carried out by an industrial undertaking should form part of a continuum which links research with development and production on the one side, and with sales, finance, investment, consumer needs and general policy on the other. I am not suggesting that research must necessarily be *ad hoc*. There will always be a need for fundamental and long-term research which does not bear directly on present plans or even future hopes. What I am emphasizing is the importance of seeing industrial research as a vital part of a complex process involving many branches of the undertaking, rather than as something operating on its own in an isolated compartment. As a consequence of this, it is essential that research activities shall be properly located within the organization so that they can have an effective impact on policy and administration.

Another object of integrating research with other parts of the organization is to ensure that research projects are wisely chosen from the standpoint of the needs of the industry and especially its capital invest-

[1] *Post* p. 370.

ment plans. Projects should be selected for investigation not only because they offer a reasonable prospect of success, but also because there is a good chance of successful results being developed and applied in the productive and commercial operations of the undertaking, even if this involves great expense and the abandonment of existing plant.

The British Transport Commission seem to be fully alive to the importance of bringing research and development into the closest possible relationship. Their annual report for 1957 discusses both functions in a single chapter entitled 'Research and Development'.[1] Here we find an account not only of the research activities in which the Commission's scientific staff are engaged but also of the Locomotive Performance and Efficiency Development Unit set up at Derby in 1956, and the still more recently authorized Carriage and Wagon Engineering Development Unit at Darlington. 'This concentration of development work', the Commission point out, 'will enable new ideas to be worked out, tested, and applied more quickly and widely than is now possible. . . . As well as initiating new development projects, the Development Unit will also be responsible for co-ordinating ideas which emanate from the Regions, and for guiding development work on carriages and wagons carried out by private firms for the Commission.'[2]

THE NEED FOR RESEARCH

There can be no two opinions about the need for research in the nationalized industries. The dire consequences which the absence of it, together with other causes, produced in the coal industry have already been mentioned. If further evidence is needed, one has only to note the heavy pollution of air in Britain, particularly in the towns, which is highly detrimental to health, wealth and happiness; for this is also a reflection of the unscientific use of our most precious mineral. The railways, again, have, hitherto, made little use of research on the fundamental problems of traction. British railways are almost the last system in the world to burn raw coal in its locomotives, though the days of steam are at last coming to an end. The gas industry has also suffered from not having done enough research and development to keep itself in the van of progress. So far as the air lines are concerned, the major need is for a continuing effort in the aircraft manufacturing industry. There is considerable doubt whether this will be forthcoming on an adequate scale in view of the greatly reduced programme of military aviation which has been announced.

[1] *British Transport Commission Annual Report*, 1957, HMSO, HC 215-I/1957-8, Vol. I, Ch. 4.

[2] *Ib.*, para. 97.

Progress in research is thus crucial to the future of the nationalized industries; and this is part of a larger picture which demands a more intensive, comprehensive and sustained effort in research in many branches of our national life. But to champion research by itself is to fight on too restricted a front. Research and development must go hand in hand; and even that combination will not suffice. The need is for industry to be infused with an urge to create opportunities for technical innovation and to organize itself so as to be able to seize those opportunities when they occur.

Despite the commendable efforts which the National Coal Board are making to organize for progress, including many which are linked with research, it is disappointing to find in their *Plan for Coal*, first published in 1950, an outlook which certainly does not reflect the conviction that enterprise is essential for progress and that research is essential for enterprise.[1] There the Board explained that, in drawing up their capital investment plans for the succeeding fifteen years, 'no credit was taken for discoveries or technical advances likely to be made in the future'.[2] Yet the Board 'expected' discoveries and technical advances in the future; and admitted that they are essential.

In 1956, when a revised edition of this great plan was issued, the Board reiterated that, 'In arriving at these new estimates the Board have made no allowance for new mining techniques as yet unproved'.[3] The Board hoped that a contribution would result from this source but thought it would not be prudent to make any allowance for it. To announce in the capital development plans for a whole industry, covering the next fifteen years, that no provision is made for the large-scale exploitation of the successful results of research is scarcely likely to stimulate or encourage scientists engaged in research or to attract scientists to the industry.

Scientists like other men, will often do their best work in response to an urgent and explicit demand or a situation which challenges their abilities and ingenuity to the utmost. This happened again and again during the Second World War and in the years preceding it. There seems to be a complete lack of such a challenge in Lord Hyndley's statemen as chairman of the National Coal Board when the 1950 plan was published. 'It is not a plan to settle the future of the industry for all time, or indeed for the next fifteen years. We are not prophets. All we can do is to study the evidence we have from our present knowledge and our past experience and make the best assumptions we can about facts still

[1] A. H. A. Wynn: *op. cit.*

[2] *Plan for Coal* (1950), (National Coal Board), para. 170.

[3] *Investing in Coal* (1956) (National Coal Board), p. 11-12.

unknown and about events still to occur.' This was reproduced in 1956 in *Investing in Coal.*[1]

The assumptions made in the plan were, as we have noted, that no allowance should be made for the fruits of research in shaping the future of the industry. How can men of science feel that their investigations are significant when so little reliance and so little expectation is placed on them? Lord Hyndley's statement derives from the natural history approach, based on observing and recording events, rather than that summed up by Bergson in his remark, 'We create the future'. One feels that the young physicists and engineers working on the exciting new developments in nuclear energy are more likely to be stimulated by the Bergsonian philosophy of Creative Evolution than by the 'wait and see' attitude of the natural history approach.

The British Transport Commission, in presenting their plan for the Modernization and Re-equipment of British Railways, struck a more encouraging note. We are convinced, they said, that an efficient and modernized railway system is essential to the economy of the country. 'This plan aims to produce a thoroughly modern system, able fully to meet both current traffic requirements and those of the forseeable future.'[2]

With these broad considerations in mind, we can now take a somewhat closer look at the nationalized industries.

The public corporations are displaying varying degrees of interest in scientific research. All of them show some interest: they could scarcely do otherwise in view of their obligation to frame programmes of research for submission to the relevant Minister for his approval. But there is a very wide margin between carrying out the minimum amount of research which would satisfy a Minister and embarking on an ambitious and imaginative programme covering a wide field. In approaching this subject, there are questions both of scope and of method to be considered. There is also the question of the status of science in a nationalized industry.

THE STATUS OF RESEARCH

One indication of the importance attributed to science in a nationalized industry is the presence or absence of scientists on the governing board. This, however, is not conclusive for obvious reasons. The members of the board are appointed by the Minister, and their qualifications and experience will depend on his judgment rather than that of those who

[1] *Investing in Coal* (1956) (National Coal Board), p. 3.

[2] Introduction.

are running the industry. But one can assume that, if the members of a board feel that they need a scientific colleague at board level, they would have little difficulty in persuading the Minister to appoint a suitable person. On the other hand, the mere presence of a scientific member on the governing board affords no assurance that a vigorous and adequate programme of research is being carried out. But even when we have made allowance for these modifying factors, it does seem strange that as late as the end of 1955 there were still no full-time members of the boards of the British Transport Commission, the Central Electricity Authority, the Gas Council, or the air corporations who could be regarded as scientists. Sir Charles Ellis was no longer a member of the National Coal Board; and had become scientific adviser to the Gas Council. Mr A. H. A. Wynn, formerly Director of the Safety in Mines Research Establishment of the Ministry of Fuel and Power, and a man of outstanding ability, had become a member of the NCB. At this time three scientists were giving their full-time services as members of the Atomic Energy Authority while a fourth, in the person of the late Lord Cherwell, was a part-time member.

The need for the representation of science at the highest level of management was one of the soundest points made by the Herbert Committee which inquired into the electricity supply industry. They therefore recommended that the new Central Generating Board should have a full-time member responsible for the whole range of scientific research and development on the generation side of the industry; and that he should be supported by a research staff of high quality.[1] This has now been carried out.

The status of science in an industrial organization is indicated with some degree of accuracy by the proportion of total expenditure devoted to research and development.

In 1952, the expenditure on research of the NCB was £488,000, of which £316,000 was incurred in the board's own research establishments.[2] By 1955, the total was in excess of £1 million, of which more than half was spent on research conducted in the Board's establishments.[3] This was 0·1 per cent of their annual turnover. The expenditure of the Central Electricity Authority on research in 1956-7 was £890,000,[4] equal to 0·23 per cent of the annual revenue of the industry. The Herbert Committee urged that the electricity supply industry should under-

[1] *Report*, HMSO, Cmd. 9672/1956, para. 472.

[2] *National Coal Board Annual Report 1952*, HMSO, HC 197/1952-3, para. 172.

[3] *National Coal Board Annual Report 1955*, HMSO, HC 263-5/1955-6, Vol. I, para. 72.

[4] *Central Electricity Authority Annual Report 1956-7*, HMSO, HC 257/1956-7, paras. 338 and 354. The total research expenditure of the supply industry in 1958-9 was £1,300,000. *The Electricity Council First Report* 1958-9, para. 178.

take a greater research and development effort by the Area Boards individually, in combination, and in association with the Central Electricity Generation Board. Only by so doing could the nationalized industry become less dependent than it had hitherto been on the manufacturers of electrical plant and equipment for technical progress and innovation.[1]

In 1956-7 the gas industry spent £1,150,256 on research,[2] equal to about 0·3 per cent of the gross revenue of the industry.[3] Of this sum £621,000 was spent by the Area Boards,[4] £316,000 of this being by way of capital expenditure for research instituted by them on behalf of the Council.[5] The amounts spent on research have increased from year to year (£845,114 was spent in 1954-5, and £998,022 in 1955-6); there has also been a very slight increase in the amounts considered as percentages of the gross revenue of the industry.[6]

The sums devoted to research by the British Transport Commission are not ascertainable. Hitherto they have not been calculated or published.

We may compare these figures for the three great industries of coal, electricity and gas supply with the expenditure of £8½ million by Imperial Chemical Industries on research in 1957, equivalent to 1·8 per cent of the revenue from sales.[7]

Our object in seeking to show the inadequate position so far occupied by research in the total activities of the three major industries concerned with fuel and power is not to criticize those who are at present directing and managing the public corporations, but rather to show the great leeway which must be made up if these industries are to present a satisfactory record of achievement in this vital sphere. It is scarcely necessary to state that the mere expenditure of money does not suffice to guarantee that research will take place on the most worthwhile projects or that good results will be obtained therefrom. But the magnitude of the resources devoted to research and development are likely in the long run to bear a discernible relation to the results which are achieved.

It can be contended that the research efforts of these and other nationalized industries are conditioned mainly by the skilled scientists and ancillary staff available and not by other factors such as finance. There is an element of truth in this, for the overall shortage of scientists of all kinds is unquestionable; but it cannot be accepted as a sufficient explana-

[1] *Report of the Committee of Inquiry into the Electricity Supply Industry*, HMSO, Cmd. 9672/1956, para. 473.

[2] *Gas Council Annual Report 1956-7*, HMSO, HC 285/1956-7, para. 127.

[3] About £370·6 m. *Ib.*, para. 269. [4] *Ib.*, para. 127. [5] *Ib.*

[6] From 0·25 in 1954-5 to 0·29 in 1955-6 and 0·31 in 1956-7.

[7] *ICI Annual Report 1957*, p. 11.

tion. In the first place, much more research is needed in the social science aspects of public enterprise; and there would be no serious difficulty in recruiting economists, sociologists, psychologists, and men trained in public administration to work on serious research projects. Secondly, the vast size and resources of the nationalized industries should give them an advantage in attracting research staff, at any rate compared with any but the largest firms in the private sector.

Of much greater importance than these factors is the influence of prestige, and the sense of participating in a large and important programme of research. Here again, as so often, we touch upon the historical background of an industry. It is extremely difficult for an industry which has become technologically backward to attract the ablest young men from the universities and research institutes. At the present time there is possibly a greater need for able scientific research in coalmining and the railways than in electronics or atomic energy; but the latter have prestige while the former do not. The former are backward industries; the latter are the *avant-garde* of Britain's post-war efforts.

I am not suggesting that little or nothing can be done to improve the present position; I am trying to indicate some of the points which are easily overlooked in large organizations. The public corporations, if they want to increase the supply of research scientists available to them, must make deliberate efforts to give an enhanced status and prestige to research within their organizations and in the eyes of the world. This is partly a question of remuneration, conditions of employment and promotion. It is much more a question of atmosphere, of leadership, of public relations both internal and external. At present, for example, there is a tendency towards secrecy in regard to research carried out in the research centres belonging to the corporations; and this may be due mainly to a desire to avoid the staff work involved in making the work more widely known. This is certainly a false economy.

THE SCOPE OF RESEARCH

When the NCB came into existence there was almost no research taking place in the mining industry. The entire research organization had to be created by the Board. Much has already been done although it is only a small part of what is needed.

The Coal Survey, which is engaged in the exploration and survey of natural resources, was transferred to the NCB from the Department of Scientific and Industrial Research in 1947. It is now more than three times as large as it was at the time of transfer. It works in close collaboration with the DSIR Geological Survey and the planning branch of the Board's production department. The combined efforts of these organs have doubled the available knowledge of British coal resources, thus providing more adequate data on which mining development plans can be based. The staff has risen from eighty-eight to 213; it includes forty-five scientists and 100 scientific technical officers.[1]

The NCB have two central research establishments. The Coal Research Establishment near Cheltenham is concerned with the processing of coal, such as the development of smokeless fuels, treatment of by-products, the preparation and briquetting of coal. The Mining Research Establishment at Isleworth investigates all aspects of underground operations, including coal-getting, tunnelling, transport, and the improvement of working conditions. Another establishment which may be mentioned here, although it is primarily concerned more with development than research, is the Central Engineering Establishment set up at Bretby, in Derbyshire, in 1955. Its task is to develop, in conjunction with the manufacturers, types of equipment required by the industry, and to test new equipment and materials. The NCB do not intend to manufacture machinery, but they do not wish, on the other hand, to take only what the manufacturers are prepared to offer them. The Board will therefore undertake development to the prototype stage, leaving further development to the production stage to be a joint effort carried out in association with the manufacturers. The Engineering Establishment is primarily concerned with applying the results of research, encouraging manufacturing firms to introduce new machines and techniques, and generally assisting the movement towards increased and improved mechanization. The Establishment comes under the Board member for production and not under the member for science.

The Safety in Mines Research Establishment is directly under the Ministry of Power. It owes its origin, however, to trade union initiative rather than to Government foresight. As its name indicates, the scope of its activities is limited to investigations into mining safety. Until a few years ago, it was the only important research centre in the British coal industry. It is still the largest. The National Coal Board are also engaged in research into ventilation, the control of dust and firedamp, explosives and equipment for fire-fighting and mine rescue work.[2]

The NCB have a Field Investigation Group for conducting operational research. This is a mixed team composed of scientists, engineers, mathematicians, social scientists and scientific technical officers, together with administrative and clerical staff. The group is engaged in making

[1] NCB Annual Reports: 1954, para. 82; 1955, paras. 72-82; 1956, para. 221.

[2] *National Coal Board Annual Report 1956*, HMSO, HC 176-I/1956-7, paras. 233-4.

detailed studies of mining or processing operations in order to discover methods by which costs can be lowered or efficiency raised. Their work brings them into touch with scientific and engineering problems and they work in close co-operation with the specialized engineers employed by the board. Some of their recent tasks have included tunnelling methods, shaft-sinking, power-loading, labour turnover and strata control.[1]

Considering the difficulties of creating a research organization in a backward industry during a period of acute shortage of scientists and technicians, the NCB have made a praiseworthy effort. The scope of the investigations is comprehensive, even though the number of projects which can be undertaken in different subjects must necessarily be very restricted at present. The organization needs both expanding and strengthening, but at least a promising beginning has been made. In addition to the research carried out within the industry, the National Coal Board make good use of extra-mural research facilities.

In the nationalized electricity industry, the major emphasis in research has so far been placed on the engineering side, rather than on questions relating to the consumption of electricity. The Herbert Committee pointed out that only five per cent of the money allocated to research by the electricity authorities was earmarked for utilization projects, and they considered this to be insufficient.[2]

On the engineering side, problems relating to the design and operation of power stations must necessarily occupy a major place, in view of the very large capital investment which they involve. These include combustion, steam raising and cooling, and the maximum rates of starting and loading boilers and turbo-alternators consistent with safety.[3]

Laboratory investigations are carried out at the Central Electricity Research Laboratories at Leatherhead, and at the specialized testing stations located elsewhere. A laboratory at Grove Road Power Station in London has been specially equipped to undertake research into the causes of corrosion in high-pressure boilers, about which little is known at present.[4] Other work being done in the laboratories includes the examination of materials and equipment, vibration and noise measurements. The characteristics of cooling towers are being studied in co-operation with the National Physical Laboratory.[5] So, too, are the heat transfer

[1] *National Coal Board Annual Report 1956*, HMSO, HC 176-1/1956-7, paras. 236-43.

[2] *Report*, para. 409.

[3] *Central Electricity Authority Annual Report 1956-7*, HMSO, HC 257/1956-7, pp. 25-6, 34 and 35.

[4] *Ib.*, para. 196. [5] *Ib.*, para. 201.

characteristics of condenser tubes and the behaviour of water in estuaries. Special equipment has been installed at the Grove Road Laboratory to test the effect on fish of water of varying temperatures. The dispersal of flue gases and the deposit of dust in varying meteorological conditions have been the subject of enquiry.[1] The testing of electrical equipment in connection with the cross-Channel scheme which is to link up the British and French electricity supply systems; and of equipment for use with a possible high voltage transmission system operating at 380,000 v, is also being carried out.[2] A small unit has been set up, in connection with the nuclear power station programme, to study the heat transfer characteristics of fuel elements.[3]

Operational research has been in existence for some years in the electricity supply industry and research teams for this purpose have been appointed in all divisions of the country. These teams have been enquiring into such questions as the operation of coal handling plant, ash handling, the carrying out of maintenance work, the optimum flow of coal from colliery to power station,[4] and divers other problems. But operational research is on an unduly small scale and only £12,500 was allocated for this important work in 1955-6.

On the distribution side, attention has been given to the load characteristics of domestic consumers, hospitals, churches, public buildings, greenhouses and other types of premises.[5] The electricity authorities assisted other bodies in the standardization of electrical appliances and accessories, and in preparing new or revised British Standard specifications for many different types of domestic appliances.[6] An extensive enquiry into methods of off-peak heating is being conducted in a number of office buildings owned by the Electricity Boards.[7]

In addition to research carried out directly by the Electricity Boards' own staff, a substantial number of research projects are sponsored by the industry at universities and university colleges. In 1956-7 there were twenty-two of these projects in hand, most of them estimated to take three years to complete. All of them appear to be in the spheres of physical science and technology.[8]

The electricity supply industry has an undeniably large programme of research on hand; but the criticism made by the Herbert Committee of the strong tendency to neglect the utilization side in comparison with the generation and engineering aspects was clearly justified.

The Herbert Committee also criticized the Central Electricity Auth-

[1] *Central Electricity Authority Annual Report 1956-7*, HMSO, HC 257/1956-7, para. 202.
[2] *Ib.*, para. 203. [3] *Ib.*, para. 199. [4] *Ib.*, paras. 125-6. [5] *Ib.*, para. 273.
[6] *Ib.*, para. 264. [7] *Ib.*, para. 274. [8] *Ib.*, para. 193.

ority for relying on the work done by the Atomic Energy Authority in the field of research and development for knowledge about nuclear generation stations. The Committee recognized that the AEA must be the principal centre of knowledge about the application of nuclear energy to industrial purposes. They claimed to understand the difficulties which the CEA would encounter if they sought to obtain scientific personnel capable of carrying out research in this field, and they also mentioned the security problems involved. But they emphasized as the overriding factor the dangers which a user industry would incur 'in being committed for a long period to rely completely on outside organizations for advances in those fields which are of particular and vital concern to that industry'. The Committee felt it was outside their term of reference to pursue this matter to its ultimate conclusion because it involved the functions of the Atomic Energy Authority; but they did express the view that the CEA should set up an organization dealing with nuclear engineering which would be capable of ensuring not only that the nuclear power station programme is carried out economically and promptly, but also that the Authority (now the Central Electricity Generating Board) are able 'to exert effective pressures at the scientific and technological levels on the AEA and the manufacturing consortiums'.[1]

Obviously the electricity supply industry must have at its disposal men who know what they are talking about in the field of nuclear energy—this is elementary. The Herbert Committee went beyond this and implied that the CEA should embark on their own research and development programme in order to test whatever proposals may come to them from AEA or the manufacturing firms. This objective may be difficult to achieve in view of the extreme shortage of qualified scientists and technologists at present existing in this field, though in principle there are great advantages in the users of machinery or equipment conducting research relating to its performance independently of the research carried out by or on behalf of the producer organization.

There is therefore an incontestible case in favour of the Central Electricity Generating Board having their own research staff able to deal with problems relating to nuclear generating stations. Hitherto the extreme shortage of highly qualified scientists and technologists has prevented this from being done; but the shortage is decreasing and the Board are beginning to form a research staff.

In the nationalized gas industry, the rôle of the Gas Council in the sphere of research covers the search for fundamental knowledge of existing processes and the search for knowledge likely to lead to new ideas,

[1] *Central Electricity Authority Annual Report 1956-7*, HMSO, HC 257/1956-7, para. 134.

new methods, and their development up to and including the pilot stage. The task of the Area Boards and the commercial manufacturers is to be responsible for the normal development of existing processes and appliances.[1]

The Gas Council have established two research stations, one in London and the other in Solihull. The efforts of the Council are mainly aimed at improving the efficiency of the methods used for carbonizing coal and manufacturing water gas; at developing processes for the complete gasification of coal; at the utilization for gasmaking of qualities of coal other than gas coal; and at finding more efficient ways of using gas and coke. The London station is engaged on the first of these aims which concerns the chemistry of gasmaking; while the Birmingham station concentrates on the problem of complete gasification. The London station is also occupied with research directed towards the improved purification of gas and the recovery of valuable by-products. The Birmingham centre is engaged on research into fundamental problems affecting the industrial uses of gas.[2]

In view of the heavy increase in the price of coal and the declining supplies of gas coal, the gas authorities are seeking alternative sources of gas. Heavy oil is one source which is under investigation at experimental plants. A research and development project has recently been launched by the South Western Gas Board for producing gas by the hydrogenization of light oil distillates. A costly—and so far unsuccessful—search for natural gas has taken place through a subsidiary of the British Petroleum Company. A much more promising development is the importation from overseas in refrigerator tanks of liquid methane for gasmaking. This methane has hitherto been running to waste in some of the oilfields in the United States and elsewhere.

The Watson House laboratories established by the former Gas Light and Coke Company are the leading centre of research concerning the use and efficiency of gas for domestic, industrial and commercial purposes. These laboratories became part of the North Thames Gas Board's undertaking when the industry was nationalized, but they have subsequently

[1] The Area Boards, at the request of the Council or after consultation with it, from time to time undertake special items of research for which they have the necessary facilities: *Gas Council Annual Report 1954–5*, HMSO, HC 86/1955–6, para. 89.

[2] For some excellent articles on research and development in the gas industry see *The Modern Gas Industry: Balanced Research the Basis of Future Development* by Professor Sir Cyril N. Hinshelwood, President of the Royal Society; *Methods of Transforming Carbon Compounds into Energy* by Sir Roy Robinson, OM, FRS; *New Techniques based on Chemical Engineering* by Sir Harold Hartley, FRS; *Scope and Organization of Research* by Sir Charles Ellis, FRS. All these were published as a supplement to *The Financial Times* newspaper, December 3, 1958.

been made available for use by all the other Area Boards. The Gas Council have now become responsible for the Centre in view of its importance to the whole gas supply industry; but its administration remains in the hands of the North Thames Gas Board.[1]

Great improvements have been made in the efficiency of cooking and heating apparatus as a result of research carried out both by the supply industry and the manufacturers. A modern gas cooker consumes only three therms to perform work done by five therms in a cooker designed thirty years ago. An almost equal economy has been achieved in gas stoves; and the introduction of partial convection has introduced an important improvement in the comfort and effectiveness of open-fire gas stoves.

The gas industry does not, however, appear to have embarked on any operational research, although one would assume that there is a considerable opportunity for fruitful investigation of this kind, not only in the manufacture of gas, but also on the distribution and service side of the industry.

Neither of the nationalized air lines has a research programme, except as regards medical research. The Ministry of Supply and the Ministry of Transport and Civil Aviation both carry out research programmes relating to civil air transport.[2] A body called the Transport Aircraft Requirements Committee, which include among their members senior representatives of the airways corporations, the fighting services and the two Government departments (with the Minister of Supply in the chair), act as a centre of information about what is going on in the aircraft industry. The Committee also formulate the requirements of the civil and military users for the next generation of aircraft. There is a separate technical committee dealing with air traffic control, ground services, and telecommunications. This should be brought into closer touch with the Transport Aircraft Requirements Committee.

It is difficult to understand why, alone among the nationalized industries, the air lines should not engage in systematic research. The notion that all the research which is necessary can be left to the aircraft manufacturers on the one hand and the Government departments on the other, is singularly unconvincing.

The British Transport Commission have stated that the modernization of the railways has caused large demands to be made on the Research Department of British Railways; and that the research facilities are being enlarged to meet these demands.

All the scientific resources of the railways have been gathered together

[1] *Fuel for the Nation* (1954) (Gas Council), pp. 14-16.

[2] These will presumably be transferred to the new Ministry of Aviation.

in a Research Department, which serves all the regions and all departments of British Railways. Prior to nationalization, only the LMS railway had concentrated its scientific personnel and facilities in a single department; and this formed the basis of the present organization.

The work of the Research Department comprises technical activities, chemical and allied services and operational services. Each of the main technical divisions carries on research and gives technical advice when needed. The engineering division deals with seven main groups of problems relating to instrumentation, construction of the permanent way, structures, materials, mechanical and electrical engineering, dynamics and fluid flow. Much of the engineering research takes place in the field on special test sites, such as the one at Totton for testing wagon buffers and that at Ilkeston Junction for testing vacuum brakes. Soil mechanics under the permanent way are being investigated at a number of centres and provide an essential service to the civil engineering department.

The chemical and allied services carry out research in a number of specialized central laboratories, such as the Cavendish House Laboratories in Derby, where work is done on corrosion and protective coatings and the characteristics of textiles. There are also seven area chemical laboratories at Ashford, Crewe, Darlington, Doncaster, Glasgow, Harwich and Swindon. The operational research division is located in London. It is concerned with the analysis and measurement of operations.

Among the subjects of research for the railways are a number of problems relating to main line electrification; the construction and maintenance of the permanent way;[1] vacuum brakes; hydraulic buffers; refrigeration; lubrication; bogies; train heating; wagon design; automatic couplers; the durability of painted surfaces on outdoor structures; and a great variety of other questions.[2] British Railways are using electronic computers in connection with research, operational and statistical purposes to a greater extent than any other railway system.

'Railway engineering research is generally of a long-term nature,' we are told; 'but in every case the solution to a problem is regarded as incomplete unless it is suitable for handing over to the practising engineers for direct application or engineering development.'[3] There is thus a close and desirable relationship between research and development.

[1] See K. D. Rhodes and M. R. Dart: a paper on long welded rail track, VII *Proceedings of the Institution of Civil Engineers* (1957), p. 344.

[2] *British Transport Commission Annual Report* 1957, HMSO, HC 215-1/1957-8, Vol. I, Ch. 4.

[3] J. M. Beskine, 'Scientific Research Makes Big Contribution to Railway Modernization', I *Transport Age* (1958), pp. 10-1. I have drawn freely on Mr Beskine's article in describing the work of the Research Department.

The Docks and Waterways Divisions of the Commission are also interested in research and so, too, is London Transport.

London Transport has carried out research into the fuel consumption of buses and coaches; the design of accumulators; the efficiency of various methods of painting motorbuses; the internal lighting of buses; methods of preventing corrosion; improved maintenance procedures; the atmospheric conditions in London Transport garages; axle and rail stresses on the underground railway. Tests are being carried out about the behaviour of outdoor clocks and ticket machines in cold weather conditions; the use of de-icing fluids on conductor rails; the door-opening and closing equipment on underground rolling stock; and the components used in air-brakes on motorbuses.

London Transport is also engaged in operational research into such matters as the design of escalators, the capacity of subways and of railway lines, and the causes of traffic delays to buses in the Central London area.

In addition to investigations carried out directly, the British Transport Commission have sponsored a number of research projects undertaken by universities and other outside bodies.[1]

RESEARCH ASSOCIATIONS

The main nationalized industries support several research associations to which they make substantial financial contributions. Thus, the NCB contribute annually to the British Coal Utilization Research Association (CURA), the British Coke Research Association, the Coal Tar Research Association, and the British Hydro-Mechanics Research Association. The CEA in 1955-6 listed nine specific research associations to which they were contributing as members £270,000 a year. These included the British Electrical and Allied Industries Research Association, the British Welding Research Association, the British Non-Ferrous Metals Research Association, the Boiler Availability Committee, and the Flame Research Foundation. The BTC belong to about twenty-nine research associations and the Gas Council are members of several. Many of the public corporations belong to bodies in which they have a common interest, such as CURA.

The nationalized industries also collaborate with organizations other than research associations in the ordinary sense of the term. Most of them belong to the Royal Institute of Public Administration, which carries out research but also engages in numerous other activities intended to improve the standard of efficiency in all branches of public ad-

[1] *British Transport Commission Annual Report 1956*, HMSO, HC 187-I/1956-7, Vol. I, pp. 53-4.

ministration. The NCB, the Electricity Council and the Gas Council all support the National Industrial Fuel Efficiency Service, to which they contribute large annual subventions. The National Coal Board support the Medical Research Council and their Pneumoconiosis Research Unit, while the electricity supply industry collaborates with the Forest Products Research Laboratory run by DSIR and the International Joint Committee on Flame Radiation. There are many other organizations which one or more of the public corporations support and with which they co-operate.

An American student of the British nationalized industries, Mr Edmund Dews,[1] argues strongly in favour of using research associations as a principal instrument, although the original *raison d'être* for these bodies was the existence of many small firms which could not afford individually to undertake research activities on a serious scale. An association often possesses the advantage of drawing its members from several industries and of serving several industries; it can engage in inter-industry research; and it can draw its funds from several sources, both public and private. For these reasons it is more likely to be able to provide its scientific staffs with the atmosphere of freedom and independence which is essential for the most creative work than a research institution linked too closely with a public corporation, and entirely dependent upon it for finance.

The usefulness of research associations to the nationalized industries is substantial; and much of the scientific research which they undertake could not and would not be carried out if they did not exist. But it is equally clear that the public corporations should be able to engage directly in research when they see fit to do so. One reason is that many of the problems which require investigation are peculiar to a particular nationalized industry and do not properly come within the scope of a research association. A second and more compelling reason is that if the public corporations are to attract and retain a certain number of outstanding men of science, as they must if the identification and investigation of problems requiring research is to play a prominent part in the nationalized industries, and the results of new knowledge be promptly understood and applied as it becomes available, these men must be given the essential interest of directing or engaging in research on at least some of the fundamental problems which they have formulated. A research department cannot hope to operate successfully as a mere distribution centre; nor will a scientist of creative ability be willing to serve for long merely as an itermediary.

[1] 'Scientific Research and Nationalized Industry' in *Problems of Nationalized Industry*, ed. W. A. Robson (1952), pp. 208 ff.

The direct research activities of the nationalized industries may be fruitful and meritorious, but it would be unwise to rely on them exclusively as sources of new knowledge and improved technology. It is generally true that technological progress in any industry requires a knowledge of research and development in fields extending beyond that occupied by the particular industry. An industry which is eager to advance must, therefore, take steps to enable its managers, scientists and technologists to be aware of useful contributions arising from sources beyond its frontiers; and be able to adapt them to their own activities. Membership of research associations is one of several possible ways of pursuing this objective.

We must not, moreover, expect the public corporations to look very far ahead in the scientific sense. Great industrial organizations, whether public or private, tend to be pre-occupied with their current production, economic, or commercial problems or with those which lie a little way ahead. It is unreasonable to expect them to embark on far-flung flights of the scientific imagination.

It would be unwise to rely overmuch on a great public corporation to foster or initiate those great pioneering researches which transform the life of man and reshape whole industries. Opportunities must therefore be provided for the free flight of the scientific imagination in laboratories and research institutions separated from the public corporations and not under their control.

Operational research, on the other hand, must take place inside nationalized industry itself. It must, in consequence, be conducted from within the public corporation. This type of research has great possibilities in economic life. It made its first appearance during the Second World War, when it was used in the armed forces with remarkable results.

It is important that operational research should be conceived in the widest possible terms. Its scope should not be confined to the physical, natural, and medical sciences, but should extend to the social sciences. There are many aspects of economics, statistics, public administration, sociology, industrial and social psychology, in which research—particularly operational research—might yield results as valuable as any to be expected from the customary fields of engineering, physics, chemistry, geology, and physiology. In addition to operational research carried on by qualified members of the staff, the fullest use should be made of independent bodies, such as the Royal Institute of Public Administration, the British Institute of Management, the Institute of Human Relations, and the National Institute of Industrial Psychology, to carry out specialized investigations on behalf of the public corporations.

THE ORGANIZATION OF RESEARCH

There are two main questions about the organization of research in the nationalized industries which may appropriately be considered here. One concerns the organization of research within the industry; the other its organization within the Government. We will consider these in turn.

In each of the largest nationalized industries we find a research advisory council appointed by the relative public corporation, the members of which include both the principal scientists within the industry and also some leading scientific experts chosen from outside.

The British Transport Commission have a Research Advisory Council of this kind. A series of small specialist panels are being formed which will include some younger men occupying more junior posts in outside organizations who will be able to assist the research department and technical officers of the Commission in investigating special problems of a scientific nature. These panels will report from time to time to the Research Advisory Council.

The British Transport Commission have also a Technical Development and Research Committee. This consists of three members of the Commission, together with an outside expert. Its principal function is to stimulate, organize, and finance research and development. One of its first tasks was to establish development centres to deal with such matters as signalling and rolling stock which would be separate from the ordinary engineering installations engaged in routine maintenance and overhaul operations.

A recent innovation is to arrange for joint meetings of the Research Advisory Council and the Technical Development and Research Committee. The chairman of the Commission will preside.

There is also a Research Co-ordination Committee whose function is to survey and correlate research activities in all branches of the undertaking. Finally, a Research Information Division keeps the Commission in touch with new knowledge or practices (mainly relating to operational and commercial matters) in other countries.[1] One of the most commendable features of the recent renaissance of British railways is the readiness of the British Transport Commission to learn from foreign experience. The Commission have not hesitated to draw on the knowledge available in the Netherlands, France, Germany, Switzerland and other countries concerning many of the aspects of the modernization plan.

[1] *British Transport Commission Annual Report 1956*, HMSO, HC 187-I/1956-7, Vol. I, paras. 196-7.

In the gas industry it is the duty of the Gas Council to settle from time to time in consultation with the Minister a general programme of research into matters affecting gas supply and carbonization and other matters affecting the functions of the Area Gas Boards or the Gas Council.[1] For this purpose the Gas Council have set up a Research Committee to advise them on the broad lines of policy, to see that the policy decided by the Council is carried out, and to report annually to the Council on the progress achieved. The members of this Research Committee include six members of the Gas Council, the directors of their two research stations, the president of the Institution of Gas Engineers, the Livesey Professor at Leeds University, the scientific adviser to the Gas Council, and three distinguished independent men of science.

A Research Liaison Committee keeps the Area Boards informed of progress in research and of research in progress; it also keeps the directors of research stations informed of problems arising in the industry. The Committee are composed of a senior scientific or technical officer from each board, the directors of the Council's research stations, a professor from Leeds University—where research for the gas industry has been long established—and a member of the Gas Council as chairman. A Joint Consultative Committee on Research has as its object to ensure liaison and collaboration with the Society of British Gas Industries, which represents the manufacturers of appliances.

I have already explained the broad division of responsibility for research between the Gas Council and the Area Boards. The Gas Council settle the general programme of research relating to matters of importance to both the Council and the Boards. This programme, when approved by the Minister, may be carried out either by the Council themselves, or by any of the Area Boards, or by an outside body or person. Thus the North Thames Gas Board administers not only the Watson House Centre and laboratories but also the London research station; while the West Midlands Gas Board administers the new Birmingham research station. The advantages of such arrangements are substantial. The chemical engineers and chemists at the North Thames Board's gasworks, who come under the station engineers for operational purposes, are also responsible to the Controller of Research for their technical work; and they can refer any problems arising at the gas works to the laboratory. The research station can in its turn ask for the collaboration of the Chief Engineer's department in carrying out full-scale experiments under working conditions. Thus the research workers and the operating staff are kept in close touch and are able to co-operate freely.

[1] Gas Act, 1948, s. 3.

The Controller of Research mentioned above is a high official of the North Thames Gas Board. Similarly, the Manager of Watson House has close relations with the Commercial Department of the Board. Since the Gas Council are not an operating body, such close links with the industry would be much more difficult to attain if the research stations were not run by the Area Boards.

The Area Boards are not, however, limited to carrying out research functions delegated to them by the Gas Council. The Gas Act, 1948, expressly authorizes them to conduct research into matters affecting their undertaking even though they are not included in the general programme drawn up by the Gas Council, provided they consult the Council before doing so.

When the electricity supply industry was nationalized, a duty was laid on the CEA to conduct research into matters affecting the supply of electricity,[1] and the Area Boards could engage in research only at the request of the central authority.

In 1949 CEA appointed the Electricity Supply Research Council to advise them on research and the Council have remained in existence since then. They comprise a dozen members sitting under the chairmanship of Sir David Brunt, FRS. About half the members are high-ranking engineers drawn from the central authority or the Area Boards while the others come from outside. Working in close consultation with the Research Council are a Committee on Research in Universities, which control the numerous investigations which the industry has arranged to be carried out by universities under research contracts.[2] Research work relating to the design and operation of power stations is co-ordinated by a Research Liaison Committee, which bring together members of the headquarters staff and that of the generating divisions.

The Herbert Committee reported that in their opinion responsibilities for research and development were too diffused. The Electricity Supply Research Council, who were supposed to keep under review the planning of research over the whole field covered by the industry, have not lived up to their terms of reference and have been mainly occupied with advising on particular problems. The Herbert Committee regarded with disfavour the fragmentation of responsibility represented by the existence of a separate Committee for Research in Universities and the Research Liaison Committee for power station problems. Moreover, utilization research was separately directed by a Utilization Research Committee reporting to the Deputy Chairman (Administration). Expendi-

[1] Electricity Act, 1947, s. 2 (1).

[2] *Central Electricity Authority Annual Report 1956-7*, HMSO, HC 257/1956-7, paras. 190-3 and App. XXX.

ture on all these different activities was brought together for consideration by a standing committee of the CEA before being adopted by them for submission to the Minister; but the Herbert Committee were troubled by the lack of a comprehensive view of the programme from a scientific standpoint. The organization appeared to them inadequate[1] if the potential contribution of science to the industry were to be fully realized.

The Electricity Council have now appointed a Research and Technical Planning Committee to make a detailed examination of research projects of all kinds submitted by various specialized bodies. This Committee is also charged with the general supervision of the carrying out of approved programmes. The Electricity Supply Research Council remains in existence with wider functions over the whole field of research, particularly that which takes place in universities.[2]

We can see, then, that two things are needed for the satisfactory organization of research in a nationalized industry. One is a Research Advisory Council which will not only advise on particular problems and projects, but also review the whole field of actual and potential investigation with a view to formulating a well-balanced programme of research over a period of years. The other is the appointment to the governing board of a full-time member responsible for research at the highest level of management.

THE GOVERNMENT ORGANIZATION OF SCIENCE

An important aspect of scientific research is the organization and resources of the relevant government departments. The old Mines Department of the Board of Trade, its successor the Ministry of Fuel and Power, and the Ministry of Transport had before and during the Second World War almost no scientists on their staffs. None of these departments considered that they had any part to play in regard to research and development—or any responsibility for the lack of it—in the industries with which they were concerned. They were not interested in, and probably not even aware of, the technological backwardness of the railways and the coalmines: they no doubt regarded this as a matter entirely within the competence of the commercial companies which at that time owned them.

The position today is entirely changed. The legislation nationalizing coal, transport, gas and electricity requires the public corporations to

[1] *Report*, para. 128.
[2] *The Electricity Council. First Report*, 1958-9, paras. 169-182.

settle programmes of research in consultation with the relevant Minister. But quite apart from this statutory function, the Ministers who are ultimately responsible to Parliament and the public for our fuel, power and transport industries have an overwhelming need to understand the scientific problems which the industries confront, and the efforts which should be made to solve them through research and development. We may now look at the organization and resources at the disposal of Ministers to enable them to achieve these aims.

A notable event in recent years has been the building up in the Ministry of Power of a small staff of able scientific civil servants under a Chief Scientist, who ranks as deputy secretary. The Minister of Power, to whom the coal, electricity and gas industries must submit their research programmes, has therefore the means at hand for obtaining first-hand and knowledgeable advice. Beyond this lies a Scientific Advisory Council which the Minister has appointed to assist his department to initiate, co-ordinate, and stimulate research in fuel and power problems. This is composed partly of representatives of the three nationalized industries and partly of independent men of science. The Council's scrutiny ensures that duplication of effort is avoided and that the three programmes of research are looked at as a whole by the Minister and his department.

Nothing comparable to this excellent organization appears to exist in the Ministry of Transport and Civil Aviation for advising the Minister about the programmes of research undertaken by the British Transport Commission. There appear to be no scientific officers of high rank in the department, nor a scientific advisory council to bring in a wider point of view.

This may explain the remarkable fact that up to the end of 1958 the British Transport Commission had not at any time submitted to the Minister of Transport and Civil Aviation a programme of research for his approval, despite the explicit requirement to this effect in the Transport Act, 1947.[1] Both the Ministry of Transport and the Commission appear to have neglected their statutory duty in this respect.

A strengthening of the scientific staffs of departments dealing with nationalized industries along these lines is desirable if Ministers are to exercise their statutory functions with knowledge and discrimination. Without scientific advisers of high calibre, a Minister can easily become a mere cypher when he is asked to approve a programme of research. An absence of expert knowledge in the department concerned is a public danger which should not be tolerated. It should be axiomatic that, if a Minister is required to pronounce on or take responsibility for any matter of importance respecting a nationalized industry, he should have

[1] s. 4.

at his disposal independent sources of advice and knowledge at least as good as those on which the public corporations rely.

Another important fact concerning ministerial responsibility is that the public corporations are not required to discuss their development programmes with the department concerned or to obtain ministerial approval of them unless expenditure thereon involves substantial outlay on capital account. This is a weakness which should be remedied. As I have already explained, research and development must go hand in hand in any producing organization which is to achieve progress: one without the other can be of little use.

The Ministry of Power is responsible for the Safety in Mines Research Establishment. This is the proper location of the establishment for several reasons. The department includes the Mines Inspectorate, which is mainly conerned with the health and safety requirements of the Mines Acts; and research and inspection are closely linked in this sphere. Second, the Ministry of Power is sufficiently detached from the NCB to take an independent view of health problems and safety practices, but sufficiently close to the industry to avoid aloofness and indifference to the human and political issues involved in the yearly toll of death, disablement and disease in the mines. Third, the scientific staff in the Ministry must have some research problems of their own to work on or at least to supervise if they are to keep alert and interested.

The Coal Survey organization was originally set up in 1918 in the Department of Industrial and Scientific Research. It remained there until it was transferred to the NCB in 1947.

This movement was well founded. The DSIR originated in 1916 at a time when scientific research was regarded as a separate activity requiring special treatment in a separate department. In those days very few departments had any interest in research or any scientists on their staffs. Since then the position has been transformed, and in several departments scientific work has become integrated in the general administration—a highly desirable result.

The Fuel Research Station started work in 1919 as part of DSIR, when there was almost no systematic investigation into fuel problems taking place in the United Kingdom. The initial aims of the station were to produce oil from coal, mainly with a view to the needs of the Navy; the surveying of the coal resources of the country; and the production of smokeless solid fuel for domestic purposes. The subsequent work of the station has related to questions of combustion, carbonization, gasification, atmospheric pollution, domestic heating and the constitution of coal. The emphasis has been on the treatment and utilization of fuel. Recently, the station has engaged on work relating to the synthesis of oil and chemicals from coal, radiation chemistry and the effect of storage on fuel oil carried in tankers.[1]

The situation has entirely changed since the Fuel Research Station was founded forty years ago. Industrial research associations such as the British Coal Utilization Research Association (CURA), the British Coke Research Association, the Coal Tar Research Association and the others mentioned above have come into existence and are actively engaged in conducting substantial programmes. The nationalized fuel and power industries, as we have seen, have their own research establishments, and they have both a statutory responsibility to undertake and promote research and an inherent desire to do so for the sake of the possible gains which it offers. Above all, in 1919 there was no central department responsible for fuel and power. The old Mines Department, responsible to the President of the Board of Trade, was not set up until 1920. It was superseded in 1942 by the Ministry of Fuel and Power (now renamed the Ministry of Power) as a separate and more comprehensive department; but it was not until about 1948 that that department built up the nucleus of a scientific staff. The Ministry of Power is now responsible for 'the co-ordinated development of all sources of fuel and power and for promoting their economical and efficient use'. The Minister, advised by the Chief Scientist and a Scientific Advisory Council, has to approve and co-ordinate the scientific work carried out by Government establishments, the nationalized industries, and industrial research associations.[2]

These developments inevitably detracted from the status and importance of the Fuel Research Station, which gradually receded into a twilight zone in which it has exercised little or no influence on policy.

In these circumstances there is little to be said in favour of continuing a station of this kind separated from the department responsible for the fuel and power industries. Because the station has been so remote from questions concerning Government policy in these industries, its scientific staff were bound to live in an ivory tower; and this had an adverse effect on the reputation of the establishment. These disadvantages were inherent in the position of the station and could only have been remedied by transferring it to the Ministry of Power.

A change of this kind would threaten a large part of the structure of DSIR, since it might lead to similar transfers of several of its other fifteen research establishments. Thus the Building Research Station might go to the Ministry of Works, the Fire Research Station to the Home Office, the Forest Products Research Laboratory to the Board of Trade,

[1] *DSIR Report 1955-6*, HMSO, Cmd. 213/1957, pp. 50-4.

[2] *Government Scientific Organization in the Civilian Field*, HMSO, (1951), p. 30.

the Water Pollution Research Laboratory to the Ministry of Housing and Local Government, and so forth.[1]

In view of the probable repercussions of such a change it is not surprising that a prolonged struggle took place over the future of the Fuel Research Station. As recently as 1954–5 the Advisory Council for Scientific and Industrial Research of DSIR recommended the construction of a new DSIR Fuel Research Station on condition that it should remain a 'national centre for the study of fuel problems', free from political considerations and the pressure of sectional interests; that the station should aim at becoming the central organization in Britain for long-term basic research on fuel; but that it should not undertake applied research beyond the stage at which this could properly be transferred to other organizations engaged on fuel research. The then Minister of Fuel and Power expressed broad agreement with this misguided policy and the recommendations of the Advisory Council were accepted by the Privy Council Committee which deals with scientific and industrial research.[2]

Fortunately, however, the matter was not allowed to rest there. The report of the Research Council of DSIR for the year 1956–7 gives further information about the Fuel Research Station. For several years the department had intended to move the staff and equipment from the inadequate building at Greenwich, which was badly damaged during the war, to new premises outside London. A new laboratory at Stevenage has become the home of any fuel research carried out by the department. The Council state that this is an appropriate occasion for considering how much of the existing programme should be retained and what new work may usefully be started.

After reviewing the growth and development of other fuel research organizations in the years which have elapsed since the Fuel Research Station was set up, the Council said that in these circumstances there is much to be said for concentrating the work of DSIR in this field on projects of national importance not being carried on elsewhere. Thus, work on air pollution would be transferred to Stevenage, in order to provide a full scientific service for the several departments administering the clean air legislation.[3] The Council had also agreed, at the request of the

[1] The Select Committee on Estimates in their Fifth Report for the session 1957-8 discussed at length the question of which departments should control certain of the DSIR Research Stations, particularly the Pest Infestation Laboratory, the Radio Research Station, the Road Research Laboratory, and the Water Pollution Research Laboratory. They recommended that this should be the subject of a review by the Government. HC 245/1957-8, paras. 17 and 34 (1).

[2] *DSIR Advisory Council Report 1954–5*. HMSO, Cmd. 9690/1956.

[3] The Ministry of Housing and Local Government is the department chiefly concerned.

Ministry of Power, that research on the synthesis of oil and chemicals from carbon monoxide and hydrogen should also go to Stevenage. The remainder of the work being done at the Fuel Research Station would be either discontinued or completed at Greenwich.

The Council made it clear that the new establishment at Stevenage is in no sense merely a continuation or a new version of the Fuel Research Station. It is intended to be 'a versatile station, not confined to one field of technology but free to do work on any subject which becomes important to the nation and which cannot be fitted into the programme of another research body. Such a station could give the department greater flexibility of operation by providing facilities for specific short-term projects, for pioneering research in new fields, and for work which, though established, is not yet far enough advanced to justify the creation of a new laboratory. The new station will, therefore, be free to take up any research requiring staff and facilities of the type that will be provided for the fuel and mineral processing research we have in mind. We envisage that each new project will entail some expansion of facilities and that gradually the scope of the station will be extended so that it can take on a wider range of projects.'[1]

The Fuel Research Station will thus fade out of the picture within a few years, leaving the new multi-purpose station at Stevenage free to pursue such projects as may be entrusted to it. It will not be an establishment confined to problems relating to fuel and power, although its activities may include research carried out at the request of the Minister of Power.[2]

I have not attempted to deal with all the nationalized industries in this chapter. The aim has been to examine the problems arising in connection with research in the four main industries dealing with coal, electricity, gas, and the railways, and thus to indicate the aspects of the matter which call for consideration in the public sector of the economy.

ATOMIC ENERGY

In particular, I have not said anything in this chapter about atomic energy, on which our hopes are so largely pinned for the future. This sphere of activity has from the beginning been in the domain of public enterprise. It is nationalized in all important respects except for the consortia of engineering firms which have been formed to construct nuclear electricity generating stations.

[1] *DSIR Report of the Research Council 1956-7*, HMSO, Cmd. 428/1958, pp. 9-10.

[2] The work on oil synthesis now being carried out covers only about fifteen per cent of the total effort of the new station.

The Atomic Energy Authority have hitherto comprised three groups enjoying a substantial degree of autonomy, but four groups have recently been formed. The Industrial Group, which has been replaced by two new groups, formed part of the atomic energy organization set up under the Ministry of Supply in 1946. Its specific task was to design, construct and operate the factories needed to produce fissile material for military purposes. This complex task fully occupied the Industrial Group for about five years. By the beginning of 1952 the possibilities of using atomic energy for the generation of electricity had become visible, and this led to consideration being given to the design and construction of a large prototype reactor to produce power. The effect of this was to extend the Industrial Group's activities to include a large amount of work for civil purposes.

The Research Group has its main centre at the Atomic Energy Research Establishment which was set up at Harwell in 1946. It has now become the largest specialized research establishment in Europe and one of the largest in the world. There are more than 1,500 scientists and technologists working at Harwell; and with the supporting staff of technicians, industrial employees, administrative, executive and clerical officers, the total manpower is about 6,000.

Harwell is dedicated to research and development in a wide and rapidly expanding field which includes many branches of physics, chemistry, reactors, and engineering. It is also concerned with specialized applications of certain kinds, such as the use of isotopes for medical, industrial, and agricultural purposes. The original research for the Calder Hall nuclear power station was done at Harwell up to the stage when its feasibility had been determined. When a prototype was authorized, the design and building of the first large-scale atomic power station was entrusted to the Industrial Group, and some of the research and development work was transferred with it.

Harwell is the principal centre of fundamental research; and research is carried on there on a vast scale. But research is also undertaken in other parts of the Atomic Energy Authority. The Industrial Group found it necessary to create their own Research and Development Branch, not in order to duplicate the basic work of the Research Group but rather to apply the knowledge obtained from work done at Harwell to the solution of problems arising from the design and construction work carried out at Windscale, Calder Hall, Dounreay and elsewhere.[1] The Weapons Group is, to a larger extent than the Industrial Group, engaged in research and development. The Atomic Weapons Research

[1] *Report of the Committee appointed by the Prime Minister to examine the Organization of certain parts of the UK Atomic Energy Authority*, Cmd. 338/1957, HMSO, para. 40.

Establishment at Aldermaston conducts both fundamental and applied research for the weapons programme.[1]

In addition to the research carried out by the Authority's own staff there are numerous investigations assigned to universities and to industry under agreements; and the Authority are participating prominently in the National Institute for Research in Nuclear Science, whose new High Energy Laboratory, named after Rutherford, is being constructed by the Authority on land adjoining their establishment at Harwell. The Rutherford Laboratory will provide facilities for advanced nuclear research required by the universities or other institutions which are so costly as to be beyond the resources of a single university or other body. The money required for the construction of the Rutherford Laboratory is provided through the Atomic Energy Authority; and the Authority are responsible for the design and construction of the great particle separator which will be a very important part of the equipment. The governing board of the Institute contains members representing the universities, the Atomic Energy Authority, and the Department of Industrial and Scientific Research. The objects for which it was established include co-operation with the Authority in the solution of specific problems in nuclear or related research, and the dissemination of scientific and technical knowledge in this field.

From this brief sketch it can be seen that research and development are key activities which permeate the whole range of the Atomic Energy Authority's work; and it is this fact which offers the best hope that this country will play a prominent part in the application of atomic energy to peaceful purposes not only at home but throughout the world. It is no doubt true that because of its novelty, fascination, and glamour, and the vast opportunities it offers, nuclear energy is able to attract the most creative scientists and technologists much more easily than many older industries, especially those which are technologically and economically backward; and the Authority have been able to obtain money and resources for research on a scale unknown in other industries except aeronautics and aircraft manufacture. But that is far from being the whole explanation of Harwell and Risley and Calder Hall. A large share of the credit must go to the magnificent leadership of Sir John Cockcroft, Sir Christopher Hinton, Sir William Penney and some of the other men who have guided the destinies of the Authority and imbued the groups with an atmosphere of intellectual excitement and a sense of adventure.

Despite its great achievements, Harwell has its problems, not all of which have been solved completely. There is the problem of size, which can be summed up by asking at what point a research establishment

[1] Atomic Energy Authority Annual Report 1954–5, paras. 99, 100-121.

loses the advantages of scale and multiplicity of resources by reason of the difficulties of management becoming too great. By what methods or devices can genuine communication among so vast a concourse of men of science be most effectively facilitated? What opportunities for meeting and for exchanging ideas are provided and how adequate are they? How far and by what means should research be co-ordinated in a rapidly advancing sphere of knowledge such as atomic energy? How best can the organization be kept flexible and responsive to changing needs without becoming financially irresponsible and extravagant? How can the administration be reasonably efficient without becoming a straitjacket of restrictive and frustrating procedures? What are the proper relationships between the administrator and the scientist or technologist? How far can Group autonomy be permitted to go without endangering the coherence and unity of the Authority? How often should research programmes be reviewed and by what criteria can they be appraised in an establishment whose horizon is as boundless as that of Harwell? These are but a few of the questions which have inevitably arisen in one form or another to those in charge of the general direction of the Research Group. They would arise in some form in any large research organization.

Some of the questions can be answered in part at least by reference to more or less formal machinery. Thus, research within the Authority as a whole is co-ordinated by a Committee for the Co-ordination of Research Policy, consisting of the Member for Research in the chair, the Directors of Research Establishments, and the Technical Secretary from Harwell. Large projects are considered by the Reactor Programme Committee, an advisory body to the Atomic Energy Authority. Within the Research Group there are a number of informal Research Review Committees surveying particular fields, over which the Director presides. There is a formal Research Group Management Board which brings together senior members of the scientific and administrative staff at Harwell, representatives of the Industrial Group, the Weapons Group, and the London office. There is also the Harwell Council, which is a small committee presided over by the Director and comprising half-a-dozen senior officers as permanent members and four heads of research divisions serving in rotation for a year. Finally, there is a much larger Division Heads Committee which, meeting less frequently, provides a forum in which the direction and administration can be discussed and challenged. But while all this formal machinery is useful, it is perhaps less valuable in practice than the informal contacts and negotiations which make up the daily working life of this great centre.

The Industrial Group is much larger than the Research Group, for its staff numbered 15,000 (in December 1957)[1] of which about 1,200 possess professional qualifications. As already explained, it is mainly engaged in designing, constructing and operating factories producing fissile material and designing nuclear power generating stations. The Committee appointed by the Prime Minister, and presided over by Sir Alexander Fleck, to consider the organization of the Atomic Energy Authority after the Windscale accident in 1957 went out of its way to pay a tribute to 'the extraordinarily rapid and successful development, in an entirely new field of technology, of what is now the Industrial Group'.[2] The Committee drew attention to 'the extraordinary degree of vitality and efficiency with which the staff of the Industrial Group have carried out the responsibilities that have been laid upon them'.[3] It cannot be open to doubt that without the work in the field of fundamental research carried out at Harwell the practical results of the Industrial Group could not have been achieved.

[1] *Report of the Committee appointed by the Prime Minister to examine the Organization of certain parts of the UK Atomic Energy Authority*, HMSO, Cmd. 338/1957, para. 57.

[2] *Ib.*, para. 38. In 1959 the Industrial Group was divided into the (*i*) Production Group and (*ii*) the Development and Engineering Group. This was contrary to the recommendations of the Fleck Committee. Fifth Report from the Select Committee on Estimates of the House of Commons, Session 1958-9. UK Atomic Energy Authority (Production Group and Development and Engineering Group). HMSO 1959.

[3] *Ib.*, para. 39.

CHAPTER XIV

Development

BY far the most important factor affecting the future prospects of the nationalized industries are the large and ambitious development plans which have been adopted for coal, electricity, railways and gas. The basic industries concerned with fuel, power and transport inevitably require very large capital expenditure for their successful development and efficient operation. Under private enterprise or municipal administration their capital investment programmes were often seriously inadequate.

COAL

The NCB published in 1950 their proposals for the reconstruction and development of the mining industry under the title *Plan for Coal*. This involved a survey of the coal reserves of the country, and of the possibilities of exploiting them, on a scale that had never been attempted before in this country. The Plan was intended to be a broad programme which would be subject to whatever modifications experience might show to be necessary.

The Plan was designed to cover the period 1950 to 1965. It aimed at an annual output which would rise to 240 m. tons from 1961 to 1965, an increase of 37 m. tons over the 1949 output. It called for the reconstruction of 259 collieries, the opening of about twenty large new collieries and fifty smaller surface mines. About 250 of the remaining collieries would stay in their present condition, and the rest be closed or amalgamated with others in the course of reconstruction.

The capital cost was originally estimated to be £635 m. at prices prevailing in 1949. In 1955, the board reconsidered the plan in the light of experience gained during the previous five years. They concluded that the plan would take longer to carry out and cost much more than *Plan for Coal* had assumed. A revised plan was issued early in 1956 called *Investing in Coal*. This raised the ultimate output to 250 m. tons by 1970, which includes 10 m. tons a year from opencast working. The estimated cost was set at £1,350 m.—more than double the previous figure. This large increase was attributed partly to the rise in prices, partly to underestimates of the cost of particular projects, and partly to an increase in the number of schemes needed to achieve the output aimed at and to offset the constant loss of productive capacity.

The plan envisaged a reduction in the labour force in the industry accompanied by a substantial rise in productivity. Thus in 1949 the labour force was 720,000 and productivity 280 tons per man year; in 1955 704 m. men and 299 tons per man year. The targets for 1960 were 682,000 men and 319 tons, and for 1965 672,000 men and 342 tons.[1]

A further revision of the plan was carried out in 1959, mainly in view of the difficulty which the NCB had encountered, in common with other European coal producers, in disposing of their output, and the accumulation of excessively large stocks.

The *Revised Plan for Coal* stated that while it was no longer necessary to plan for a continuous increase in the demand for coal, the Board did not contemplate a serious contraction of the industry. They envisaged a more or less stable demand. The revised plan therefore aimed at a production of 200–215 million tons in 1965. The industry would by 1965 employ a labour force of between 587,000 and 626,000 men work-in 550 collieries, compared with about 750 collieries in 1959. Productivity is set at 30–31 cwts. a shift, which on the basis of five shifts a week for 50 weeks would yield 375 tons per man year. This compares with 25·3 cwts. a shift in 1958.

The cost of the revised plan in terms of capital expenditure for the period 1960–65 is estimated at £511 m. at 1959 prices. Capital expenditure for the decade 1956–65 will be £175 m. less than the estimate given in *Investing in Coal.* Despite this, the industry will be reconstructed on the lines indicated in the original *Plan for Coal.* By 1965, no less than 80 per cent of the output is expected to come from new or reconstructed collieries.[2] Most of the capital expenditure will be financed from internal resources; and, if wages and prices remain steady, surpluses can be earned by means of reduced costs.

Among the improvements which are expected to increase both output and productivity are the introduction of power loading in all coalfields where the conditions permit; the development of a fully-mechanized system of roof support; the installation of locomotive haulage wherever the roads are or can be made suitable; improved lighting of roads and coal

[1] *Investing in Coal* (1956), p. 21. *Plan for Coal* set the manpower requirements for 1965 at 618,000. The figure was raised in *Investing in Coal* to 672,000. The reasons given were that the proportion of unsaleable coal in total output was rising at the rate of 1 m. tons a year; and the 2½ per cent improvement in attendance rates allowed for had not so far been realized. The forecast in the revised plan assumes that working time will remain unchanged. *Ib.*, Ch. III.

[2] *Revised Plan for Coal.* NCB Ch. VI.

faces; dust suppression, better ventilation and other means of improved working conditions underground.[1]

To draw up an ambitious plan for the reconstruction of an entire industry is one thing. To carry it out is another. By the end of 1952 it was evident that the total real expenditure (at 1949 prices) on development work in the first three years had failed to reach the planned level of about £108 m. by nearly £36 m. and that the rate of investment would continue to lag for the following year at least. This calculation was based on the estimated expenditure in the *Plan for Coal* and the actual expenditure reduced to 1949 prices.

The causes for the lag in performance were accurately analysed in a knowledgeable article in *The Times*. They included the general slowness which had characterized much constructional engineering and contract work in Britain since the end of the Second World War. Of greater importance was the scarcity of mining engineers possessing the training and experience needed for planning. Many mines lacked staffs capable of preparing detailed estimates of the cost of development and reconstruction work which must be available before decisions can be made. In consequence, most of the preliminary calculation had to be left to outside contractors who could not always spare staff for the work. The inability of the collieries to make detailed designs and estimates meant that only contractors with special experience of this type of work could be employed. 'No single cause would alone account for the lag in investment,' said *The Times* Industrial Correspondent, 'but the insufficiently specialized overhead organization in the mines is almost certainly a more serious factor than alleged delays due to over-centralization.'[2]

This situation was one which the NCB had inherited from the past. Under private enterprise, capital investment in the mines was seriously and continuously inadequate from at least 1925 if not earlier; and this, indeed, was the basic cause of all the many difficulties which have subsequently confronted the industry. The British coal industry was comparatively efficient until 1925; by 1939 it was more technically obsolescent, compared with continental coalfields, than it had ever been. In 1925, the output per man-shift in Britain had fallen slightly behind that in the Ruhr; it was ahead of the Dutch and not far behind the figure for Poland. By 1936, output per man-shift in Germany was 1,710 kg., in the Dutch mines 1,781 kg., and in the Polish mines in Upper Silesia 2,073 kg. In Britain the figure was 1,195. The productivity of our mines had risen between 1913 and 1936 by only ten per cent. This compared with a rise during the period of twenty-two to twenty-five per cent in France and the

[1] *Revised Plan for Coal.* NCB Ch. IV.

[2] 'Capital Investment in Collieries', *The Times* newspaper, November 19, 1952.

US bituminous industry, fifty per cent in Belgium and Czechoslovakia, seventy-three per cent in Poland, eighty-one per cent in the Ruhr, and not less than 117 per cent in Holland.[1]

With very little new development or reconstruction work going on during the twenty years preceding nationalization, it is not surprising that the collieries have since then lacked the highly qualified personnel required for planning, designing, and estimating capital works on a large scale. The shortage is being gradually overcome but men with the necessary qualifications and experience cannot be obtained quickly in a period of full employment.

The annual rate of capital expenditure since vesting date is shown by the following table:

TABLE I

Annual Capital Expenditure by the National Coal Board 1947-58 (£ million)

	1947	1948	1949	1950	1951	1952	1953	1954	1955	1956	1957	1958	*Total*
Expenditure on collieries—													
Major schemes	2	3	4	7	9	15	21	32	39	42	44	51	269
Other ...	13	18	23	18	18	23	31	36	35	34	40	39	328
Expenditure on ancillaries	4	4	4	4	5	10	13	16	19	19	19	14	131
Expenditure on house building ...	—	—	—	—	—	2	17	15	2	1	—	—	37
TOTAL ...	19	25	31	29	32	50	82	99	95	96	103	104	765

(Source: Report of the NCB 1958, Vol. I, p. 19)

The Table shows that the rate of expenditure has been increasing rather rapidly since 1953 even if allowance is made for the decline in the value of money. In 1957 the capital expenditure was £103 m. Moreover, an increasing proportion of the expenditure is going into major colliery schemes, which yield the largest increases of output and productivity. The other schemes for the most part are undertaken only in order to maintain existing capacity. During the ten year period, 1947-56, only £171 m. out of a total of £558 m., or thirty per cent, was devoted to major schemes. In 1956, £42 m. or forty three per cent, of the total capital expenditure was allocated to major colliery schemes; and work

[1] W. H. B. Court: *Coal* (Official History of the Second World War), pp. 25-6.

began on twenty-seven large schemes. The proportion of capital expenditure allocated to major colliery schemes is expected to rise from thirty per cent in 1947-55 to fifty-five per cent in 1956–65.[1] The large schemes take many years to complete; and very few of those begun in 1947–56 had come to fruition in 1956.

By the end of 1956, the NCB could report that work was in progress on 162 major colliery schemes, including thirty-one large new mines. About two-thirds of these should be completed by the end of 1960.[2]

One step which the NCB took in order to speed up the fulfilment of the plan was to set up a Reconstruction Department at headquarters. This is charged with keeping the plan under continuous review, and ensuring that work on the major colliery projects and the opening up of new mines proceeds with the utmost speed and efficiency.[3]

Very great progress has been made in regard to mechanization, improved transport and winding, and the preparation of coal. In 1947, about eighty locomotives were in use underground. By the end of 1956 there were over 900. The amount of coal loaded by power went up from 8·3 m. tons (3·8 per cent of total output) in 1950 to 36·4 m. tons (15·5 per cent of total output) in 1956. More than 200 new cleaning plants have been constructed and by the end of 1956 nearly sixty per cent of coal was being mechanically cleaned.[4] Many other examples of technological progress could be given.

Much of the investment contained in *Plan for Coal* is required to maintain existing output. Over three-quarters of the deep-mined coal comes from shafts which were sunk more than fifty years ago. The mere age of the industry is making it harder to win coal, for with the passage of time the best seams become worked out, the underground roadways grow longer, and the ash content becomes higher. Hence increasing capital expenditure is necessary to prevent loss of output.[5]

The National Coal Board's current development plan was based on two assumptions: one is that the total working time in the industry would remain what it was when *Investing in Coal* was drawn up; and the other is that the Board will be able to obtain the working force they need. In 1958, the Board still adhered to a belief in the availability of manpower, but were apprehensive at the attendance figures and 'labour attitudes' in the industry.[6] The easing in the terms for earning the bonus shift had resulted in a substantial increase of absenteeism, and this has

[1] *Investing in Coal*, p. 21.

[2] *Ib.*, Ch. II. See also the *Revised Plan for Coal*, p. 5, for the position in 1959.

[3] NCB Annual Report for 1956, para. 77. [4] *Ib.*, para. 55.

[5] Report from the Select Committee on Nationalized Industries (Reports and Accounts), HC 1956-7, 187-I, paras. 10-14.

[6] *Ib.*, para. 46-7; Evidence, Q. 497.

cast doubts on the probable fulfilment of the plan. The Board's previous assumptions about the output of saleable coal and the attendance rate had on a previous occasion required a substantial revision of the original *Plan for Coal.* The Select Committee on Nationalized Industries took a somewhat pessimistic view of the prospect of fulfilling the development plan, but the Board were not prepared early in 1958 to agree that revision would be necessary, despite certain discouraging features such as the slow pace of reconstruction and unsatisfactory attendance figures.

The recession in the demand for coal which occurred in the latter part of 1958 produced a surplus of supplies for the first time since 1940. The effect of this might be to provide a stimulus to pushing forward more rapidly with the reconstruction and new construction work in hand; or it could encourage a go-slow attitude on the part of the men, in order to eke out employment. The Board's decision to close down uneconomic pits was clearly a right one. The modernization of the industry is made more and not less necessary by the increased competition with other fuels which coal now has to face seriously for the first time for many years. The trade union demands that the working week should be reduced and the import of fuel oil restricted would benefit the miners, but no one else. They would merely create conditions of shortage and monopoly which no sensible person wishes to see established.

Both mineworkers and consumers should pin their hopes in the great development plan the NCB are carrying out. For this aims at increasing productivity which, if rightly applied, can benefit both producers and users of coal.

ELECTRICITY

The British Electricity Authority's development plan was published in 1955 under the title *Power and Prosperity.* This contemplates an increase of total demand from 52,264 m. units in 1952-3 to 80,500 m. units in 1959-60—an increase of fifty-four per cent. Generating capacity was to show a net increase of sixty per cent by the end of 1959 compared with 1953. This plan has now been replaced by a later plan which envisages an increase in the consumption of electricity by nearly eighty per cent in the nine years 1957-8 to 1965-6. An increase in the amount of generating plant by about seventy-five per cent will be required to meet this demand.[1] The limiting factors in the capital development programme of the industry since nationalization have been the capacity of the electrical manufacturing industry and the restrictions imposed by the Government in view of the country's economic condition.

[1] Report, HC 1956-7, 187-I, para. 67.

I have already referred to the nuclear energy power station developments which are now in process of being carried out. In addition to Calder Hall, construction on two further generating stations at Bradwell in Essex and at Berkeley in Gloucestershire began in January 1957. A third station is now under construction at Hinkley Point, Somerset. A fourth station is likely to be situated in North Wales. The Minister of Power announced in March 1957 that the nuclear power programme would be trebled. This would aim at bringing into operation nuclear plant producing five-six m. kilowatts by the end of 1965. The total estimated development of conventional and nuclear generating stations for the six years 1960–1 to 1965–6 is shown in Table II, opposite.

The nuclear stations in this programme are expected to come into operation at an increasingly rapid rate between 1960 and 1965.

Electricity supply has been responsible for by far the largest share of capital investment in the nationalized industries since vesting date. This is partly due to the very high cost of electricity generating stations and partly to the big expansion programme which BEA and the Area Electricity Boards drew up and began to implement soon after nationalization.

The capital investment estimated to carry out the developments planned in *Power and Prosperity* was £1,421 m. The total cost was later raised to £1,520 m.[1] The nuclear power programme has substantially increased the estimated capital expenditure for the years 1960 to 1965. The capital costs for the first nuclear stations are about £145 per kilowatt of output capacity, to which the cost of the initial nuclear fuel charge adds another £30. The total of £175 compares with a capital cost of under £50 per kilowatt for the most up-to-date conventional steam power stations.[2] Thus a nuclear station is likely to require approximately three times as much capital investment as a conventional station of similar size, without including the cost of the nuclear fuel charge. This disparity will probably be reduced in course of time.

The programme of expansion of electricity supply for the years 1956-7 to 1965-6 by means of nuclear stations is calculated to cost £750 m. more than the cost (estimated at £2,600 m.) which would have been incurred if a similar expansion were carried out by means of conventional stations. The prospective capital budget is thus £3,350 m. made up as follows on page 402.[3]

[1] *Capital Investment in the Coal, Gas and Electricity Industries*, HMSO, Cmd. 132/1957, para. 10-11.

[2] *BEA Report for* 1956-7, paras. 69-70.

[3] Cmd. 132/1957, Appendix. See also *Power for the Future*, issued by the Electricity Council, 1958, p. 31.

TABLE II

Classes of Generating Plant	Central Electricity Authority Generating Plant at End of Year				Unit Output (as supplied from the power stations)			
	Output Capacity, 1960–1		Output Capacity, 1965–6		1960–1		1965–6	
	thousand kilowatts	*per cent*	*thousand kilowatts*	*per cent*	*million units*	*per cent*	*million units*	*per cent*
Conventional steam (coal and oil fired)	25,850	99	30,000	84	99,000	99	102,000	77
Nuclear	—*	—*	5,500	15	—*	—*	30,000	22
Other plant[1]					—	—	—	—
Units purchased[2]	150	1	500	1	1,000[1]	1	1,000[2]	1
Totals	26,000	100	36,000	100	100,000	100	133,000	100

(*Source*: CEA Annual Report, 1956–7, p. 12)

* It is hoped, however, that at each of the Authority's first two nuclear stations, the first reactor with its associated plant will be brought into operation in 1960.

[1] This plant includes hydro-electric, diesel, etc.

[2] Including estimated purchases from the Atomic Energy Authority.

		£ *million*
I. Generation and Transmission		
1. Expenditure on stations commissioning before 1961—		
(*a*) Conventional stations	460	630
(*b*) Transmission	170	
2. Expenditure on stations commissioning between 1961 and 1965—		
(*a*) Conventional stations	316	
(*b*) Nuclear stations		
(i) construction	742	1,460
(ii) initial fuel charge	177	
(*c*) Transmission	225	
3. Expenditure on stations commissioning after 1965—		
(*a*) Conventional stations	60	
(*b*) Nuclear stations		220
(i) construction	145	
(ii) initial fuel charge	15	
II. Distribution		1,000
III. Increase in working capital requirements		40
		£3,350

The annual capital expenditure of the English and Scottish Electricity Boards under this scheme will average £280 m. a year from 1957–8 to 1960–1, thereafter rising to an average of £400 m. a year from 1961–2 to 1965–6. This compares with about £150 m. a year in recent years.

An important feature of the development plan is the construction of the supergrid for bulk transmission of electricity at 275,000 volts. This will supplement the national grid, which transmits power at 132,000 volts, and will facilitate bulk transmission of power from the midland coalfields to the great consuming areas in the south and north-west. When complete it should be capable of meeting all bulk transmission requirements for the next twenty years. The cost is considerable but it will be much more than offset by savings in generating capacity and transmission plant.

Another important project is the cross-Channel cable to connect the British supply system with that of Electricité de France. This will permit the transmission of electricity between the two countries, whose peak loads do not occur at identical periods.[1] This interconnection may effect a saving to the UK electricity supply industry of £5-6 m. in capital costs and £0·6 m. a year in operating expenditure.

[1] *Central Electricity Authority Report for 1956-7*, paras. 257-9.

Rural electrification forms another type of capital investment which continues apace. On April 1, 1948, only 31·1 per cent of farms had electricity laid on. By March 31, 1958, the proportion had increased to 72·8 per cent. The connection of eighty-five per cent is believed to be practicable, and this figure should be reached by 1963 at a total cost of £130 m. Many other kinds of rural premises have been provided with electricity supply since nationalization—40,000 rural consumers other than farmers were added in 1957-8,[1] bringing the total proportion to 89 per cent.

GAS

The development plan for the gas industry was published by the Gas Council in 1954 under the title *Fuel for the Nation.* The objects of the programme are as follows: First, to meet the constantly rising demand for gas both by increasing the industry's own productive capacity and by taking from outside sources all supplies of gas which are available on economic terms. Second, to secure greater efficiency, co-ordination and economy by the integration of undertakings, by replacing obsolete plant, and by improved methods of production and utilization. Third, to seek for sources of gas which do not require gas coal, the supply of which is diminishing. Among the possible sources are the carbonization of low grade coals, the total gasification of coal and oil, and natural gas.[2]

The plan does not appear to look beyond the year 1959-60. The demand for gas was expected to reach 2,924 m. therms by that date, compared with 2,524 m. in 1952-3—a rise of sixteen per cent. This modest growth shows that the demand for gas is growing much more slowly than the demand for electricity or for oil.

The development plan of the gas industry is consequently a much smaller and less ambitious affair. The Gas Boards will buy additional quantities of gas, mainly from coke ovens, of about 144 m. therms a year, and will install the new plant required to expand their own gas-making by about 261 m. therms a year. A substantial programme for replacing obsolescent plant is also being carried out.[3] Plant capacity will be provided with a daily capacity of 2,750,000 therms compared with 1,934,000 therms in 1953.

The integration of undertakings is being effected by the construction of gas grids and the elimination of small and uneconomic gasworks. Expenditure on mains, services, and gas transmission will absorb more

[1] *Central Electricity Report and Accounts, April 1–December 31, 1957*, etc., HMSO, 288/1958, paras. 266-271.

[2] *Fuel for the Nation*, p. 9. [3] *Ib.*, pp. 27-8.

than twenty-eight per cent of the total capital expenditure included in the programme. This capital cost should be more than offset by a reduction in the total capacity required to meet peak loads, an improved load factor, co-ordinated repair programmes, and economies of administration. Consumers will benefit by a more constant quality of gas and fewer reductions in pressure.[1] Two of the Area Gas Boards have calculated that interconnecting mains will give them a net capital saving of £1,650,000 and £2,848,000 respectively by rendering unnecessary the provision of additional gasmaking plant which they would otherwise have needed.[2] Many of the Gas Boards are carrying out or have carried out integration schemes either within their own areas or among their respective undertakings. The reduction in the number of small gasworks is striking. There were, for example, at the time of nationalization, 105 gasworks in the South-Western area. The South Western Gas Board aims at reducing the number to only sixteen, of which all but two will be interconnected.

The capital expenditure to be laid out between 1953 and 1960 is estimated at about £345 m., most of which is divided in equal proportions between manufacturing plant and distribution of consumer equipment.

RAILWAYS

The British Transport Commission published in 1955 their Modernization and Re-equipment Plan for the railways. This plan is expected to require a period of fifteen years for its complete fulfilment. In 1958 the Minister of Transport and Civil Aviation stated that the British Transport Commission were reviewing the plan in the light of the prevailing conditions. The phasing has been altered from time to time in accordance with the general economic position of the country, and the resources available for capital investment in the public sector.

The modernization plan is part of a four-pronged attack by the BTC on the problem of placing their undertaking on a sound economic basis and raising the low standard of efficiency which has resulted from thirty years mismanagement and neglect. The other 'prongs' of the attack comprise the elimination of services for which there is insufficient demand or which other forms of transport can perform more efficiently; increased productivity; and the freeing of the railways from antiquated statutory obligations regarding such matters as the maintenance of road

[1] *Fuel for the Nation*, p. 33.

[2] *Ib.*, p. 36. The figure of net capital savings takes into account the cost of the interconnecting mains.

bridges over the permanent way, the manning of level crossings, etc. and, above all, the charges they may make. Much greater freedom in fixing fares and freight rates, and the elimination of unremunerative services, are essential to the restoration of the economic health of the railways.[1]

Our concern here is with the Modernization and Re-equipment Plan, since this alone involves large-scale investment.

As regards passenger services, the plan aims at achieving greater speed, safety, comfort, cleanliness and punctuality for the long distance services, thereby making them more competitive and profitable. Improvements in heating, ventilation, lighting, decoration, and quietness will be provided on passenger trains. Stations and facilities for the issue of tickets will also be improved. The suburban lines round the major centres of population and the very intense inter-urban services will be served by diesel trains. The feeder and secondary line services will be entirely remodelled; trains with diesel or electric traction will replace steam trains now operating at a heavy loss on these services.

The plan relies chiefly on the long overdue elimination of steam locomotives and the substitution of modern types of diesel and electric traction as a means of attaining the objectives set out above. This will facilitate higher average speeds, greater punctuality and cleanliness, more frequent services, and lower operating costs.[2]

The plan includes the electrification of the major trunk routes from London (King's Cross) to Leeds and York, and from London (Euston) to Liverpool and Manchester. These electrified routes will ultimately be continued to Scotland. Another main line scheme will complete the electrification of the route from London (Liverpool Street) to Harwich and Ipswich. Suburban electrification schemes will cover the services in and around London and Glasgow, as well as the services between London, Tilbury and Southend. The progress of electrification has been more rapid than was expected, and the BTC therefore hope to carry out a greater amount of it than was included in their plan; but it will be long after 1970 before the whole electrification programme can be carried out.[3]

The plan calls for the acquisition of 4,600 multiple-unit diesel vehicles of several types for a great variety of services. Some are required for

[1] See The British Transport Commission: *Proposals for the Railways.* White Paper, HMSO, 9880/1956, p. 15.

[2] *Ib.*, p. 16, para. 26. Sir Reginald Wilson: *Technical Modernization and new freight charges on British Railways.* A paper prepared for the British Institute of Management National Conference (Sectional Meeting, November 28, 1958).

[3] Sir Brian Robertson: *The British Railways Modernization Plan,* in 'Progress'. Winter 1957-8 (Published by Associated Enterprises).

inter-city services between, for example, Glasgow and Edinburgh or Birmingham and Swansea. Others are needed for suburban services; while others again are earmarked for cross-country or branch lines. Many of them are already in use; the remainder are expected to be in operation by the end of 1961.

As regards freight traffic, the plan aims at greater speed and reliability combined with economic operation. One of the methods employed to achieve these ends is the fitting of all goods wagons with continuous brakes to enable them to run safely at speeds up to sixty miles an hour. Another is the construction of larger marshalling yards equipped with mechanized braking equipment and up-to-date systems of communication, to replace many small and old-fashioned yards. A further step is the construction of goods wagons of much greater size and capacity. A fourth item is the concentration of freight business at a smaller number of modern goods terminals equipped with mechanical handling equipment; these will be operated in conjunction with radial road services. The use of containers to facilitate the quick transfer of goods between road and rail will be developed on a large scale; and mechanized handling equipment will be introduced wherever practicable.

The total cost of the Modernization Plan was estimated at £1,200 m. This has now been increased to £1,600 m.[1] Of this about £800 m. must be borrowed, the remainder being provided from internal sources. The aim of the British Transport Commission was to raise the annual rate of investment for the railways to about £120 m. in 1957, with further increases in later years.[2] The annual investment was £140 m. in 1958. It is expected to rise from £178 m. in 1959 to £210 m. in 1963.

To get these figures into perspective we may note that the present written-down book value of the capital assets of British Railways is about £1,500 m., while their replacement value at 1956 prices was estimated in that year at £4,000 m.[3] 'For thirty years', declared the White Paper presented to Parliament by the Minister of Transport in 1956, 'the railways have been unable to undertake any large schemes of modernization or, indeed, to keep up an adequate programme of replacement.'[4]

In 1959 the British Transport Commission's re-appraisal of their Modernization and Re-equipment Plan was presented to Parliament. This was made mainly, though not entirely, because of the sharp decline in freight traffic in 1958, and a consequential increase in the Commission's deficit for the year to £90 m. A deficit had been expected,

[1] *Proposals for the Railways*, p. 20.

[2] *Ib.*, p. 5. *BTC Re-appraisal of the Plan for the Modernization and Re-equipment of British Railways*, HMSO, Cmd. 813, 1959, paras. 9 and 49.

[3] *Ib.*, p. 28. [4] *Ib.*, p. 4.

but the forecast was £55 m. The worsening of the position of the railways was due to a general decline in industrial activity, especially in such industries as coal and steel, which provide a high proportion of the heavy traffics.

The review reaffirmed the Commission's belief in the essential soundness of their plan, and the complementary reforms associated with it. The Commission adhered to the fundamental principles of their scheme, but introduced certain changes in emphasis, priorities and timing.[1] The essential aim remains that of creating a more compact, efficient, and economic railway system;[2] but the process of accomplishing this is to be speeded up. The reduction in route mileage, the number of stations, depots, marshalling yards, the fleet of rolling stock and locomotives, will proceed at a faster rate and on a larger scale than was previously envisaged;[3] while the rate of procuring new equipment, and of changing over from steam to electric and diesel traction will be speeded up.[4] 'The result', say the Commission, 'will be a more rapid streamlining of British Railways than was originally conceived.'[5]

Some economists, although not opposed to the principle of nationalization, have expressed the view that British Railways cannot be placed on a self-supporting finanical basis by the Modernization plan. Mr J. R. Sargent, for example, said in a broadcast talk that 'beautiful as the prospect may be of getting the railways into the twentieth century before the beginning of the twenty-first, we shall be deluding ourselves if we think that to modernize the railways will be enough to make them pay'.[6] Mr Sargent's unfavourable forecast is based partly on the public pressure on the railways to maintain uneconomic services; partly on the lack of realism in the public's ideas about how railway charges and rates should be fixed; and partly on the improved competitive position which road haulage will derive from the main road improvements which are now under construction or projected.

It is of course true that if the public comes to regard the railways—or any other nationalized industry—as a social service which can and should be subsidized year after year from the taxpayer's money, then there will not be the slightest prospect of achieving financial solvency. But I see no good reason why public opinion should be allowed to solidify in so unfortunate a mould. It is against the express legislative enactments contained in the nationalizing statutes. It is against the example set by the Post Office, public utility undertakings run by local authorities, and the

[1] British Transport Commission. *Re-appraisal of the Plan for the Modernization and Re-equipment of British Railways*, HMSO, Cmd. 813, 1959, para. 55.

[2] *Ib.*, para. 18. [3] *Ib.*, paras. 24–7. [4] *Ib.*, para. 47. [5] *Ib.*, para. 57.

[6] J. R. Sargent: *Will the Railways Ever Pay?* in 'The Listener', June 12, 1958, Vol. LIX, No. 1524, p. 963, see also his book *Transport Policy*.

general tradition in this country, which dislikes the subsidization of industry save in exceptional circumstances. It is contrary to the wishes of the governing boards of the nationalized industries. It is in conflict with the position taken up both by the Conservative Party and the Labour Party. It is against the views of the Treasury and every Chancellor of the Exchequer on the canons of sound public finance. It is incompatible with the policies of successive Governments and of every Minister of Transport since 1945. A concerted attempt to scotch this pernicious idea should undoubtedly be made and I see no reason why it should not succeed.

The chief doubt which arises in my own mind is whether the Modernization Plan is sufficiently ambitious to overtake in the shortest practicable time the 'decades of under-investment'[1] from which the railways are suffering and to achieve 'the planned revolution of the railway system'[2] which is admitted to be necessary. The sum of even £200 m. a year seems a modest one; and so does the total cost of the plan. The limiting factors are, however, probably not financial but those arising from the productive capacity of the manufacturing and constructional resources available for electrification and dieselization, etc. and the capacity of the railway staff to use modern equipment and adapt themselves to new practices. The fulfilment of the plan will obviously not accomplish the complete modernization of British Railways. It can form only the first stage of a process which will require a much longer period and much more investment to complete. But it is an important beginning which represents, one hopes, a complete break with the shocking mismanagement of the railways during the past forty years and the foolish policies of restriction imposed both on the railways and on competing road services by the State.

Sir Brian Robertson, chairman of BTC, has stated that a very important and difficult part of the plan is the recruitment and training of staff. The railways, he admits, have not only been short of equipment 'but they have failed for some years to attract a sufficient number of men of the right calibre and attainments to fill the higher positions of management, or to staff the technical branches'. The plan has made the need for such men more urgent and the Commission are making strenuous efforts to recruit them.[3]

CONCLUSION

These great plans for the modernization and development of the nationalized industries are essential for their progress, and while they do not guarantee their successful operation they are an indispensable

[1] Robertson: *op. cit.*, p. 6. [2] *Loc. cit.*
[3] *Op. cit.* 'Progress', Winter 1957-8, p. 108.

prerequisite of it. They involve a total capital investment in excess of about £700 m. a year; and the figure is likely to rise sharply in the near future as the construction of nuclear power stations expands and the railway programme gets into its stride. In 1956 public corporations were responsible for 18·8 per cent of the total gross fixed capital formation of the British economy.[1]

Prior to nationalization few, if any, economists or publicists appeared to take any interest in the virtual starvation of the coal industry and the railways of the capital investment which was and is indispensable to their efficiency. If they felt any concern at the serious consequences to the whole economy which would inevitably follow the running down of these industries, no expression of it reached the outside world. Now, however, that as a direct result of nationalization these and the industries in the public sector are able to embark on capital development programmes which are more adequate to their needs, some economists are busily engaged in criticizing the 'distortion' of the impeccable norm which the market is supposed to ensure in the distribution of capital resources. Professor A. K. Cairncross considers that there is 'no justification for making the simple fact of public ownership lead to a change in the pattern of investment in favour of electric power'.[2] Would he say the same in regard to coal and the railways?

In the same article Professor Cairncross states that the nationalized industries were taken over partly because of their large capital demands; but that as they were only required to break even, they are not able to finance a substantial part of their investment programmes out of profits. This is in fact not true, for as we have already seen, a considerable part of these programmes is financed from internal resources, although the word 'profit' is not strictly applicable to the earnings of public corporations.[3] Having made this initial error, Professor Cairncross proceeds to make the consequential mistake of blaming the Government and Paraliament for throwing the whole burden of power development on to the capital market. He is also annoyed because public corporations are able to borrow money at gilt-edged rates of interest instead of having to pay the much higher rates which they would have to pay if they were commercial companies. He is vexed because these low rates of interest enable the nuclear power programme to look more attractive than it would if the interest rates were twice as high.

One gets the impression from this and similar utterances that for some protagonists of private enterprise any stick is good enough to beat

[1] A. K. Cairncross: *The Pattern of Fixed Capital Investment in Britain*, in Westminster Bank Review, February 1958, p. 4.

[2] *Ib.*, p. 7. [3] *Ante* p. 306.

a nationalized industry with. A privately-owned industry can be as inefficient or as backward as it pleases, with disastrous results to the national economy, and no notice will be taken of its performance, no criticism made of its shortcomings. The moment it is nationalized, its development is likely to be immediately discounted and its progress denigrated by a certain school of economists on the ground that public ownership and control confer certain special advantages which it would not otherwise possess. What Professor Cairncross and others who share his attitude do not appear to see is that the case for public ownership rests in part on just these advantages. He thinks that 'the distribution of investment has been biased in favour of the public sector' because he does not recognize the primacy of political decisions concerning the allocation of the nation's investment resources among the basic industries. He is entitled to his opinion—but it is no more than a point of view.

Equally biased views are being put forward on the subject of restrictive trade practices and monopoly. During the past fifty years there has been a tremendous drive in most British industries towards the growth of monopolies, and the formation of trade associations imposing all kinds of restrictions on the free activities of member firms in regard to price, quality, output, etc. Few writers appear to have drawn attention to this movement or to have denounced its baneful effects on the interests of the consumer and the economy as a whole. But now that the nationalized industries have been established, unfavourable comparisons are continually being drawn between the privileged conditions under which they are supposed to operate and the competitive conditions which are alleged to prevail in the private sector. I have yet to see any protest against the obligations placed on some nationalized industries to repay capital and also to provide for depreciation—a double burden for which there is no parallel in private industry.

It is as well to be aware of these prejudices and symptoms of professional or political bias lest the pronouncements of publicists and organizations on these matters should be assumed to possess a degree of validity and objectivity which they cannot always claim.

It is unquestionably true that the development plans of the nationalized industries are far more ambitious and involve a much greater volume of investment than would have occurred if these industries had remained in private ownership. This undoubtedly applies to coal, electricity, gas, the railways and the air lines. Yet no more is to be spent on these industries than they need or are likely to be able to absorb on a break-even or more remunerative basis.[1] This in my view is the greatest single advantage which has resulted from nationalization.

[1] The break-even basis is inadequate as a yield on capital investment. See *post* p. 412.

Mr R. Kelf-Cohen, a former civil servant, in his recent book admits that large scale capital programmes have been essential. He goes so far as to say that the run-down condition of these basic industries, and the need to modernize them by embarking on heavy capital expenditure, was the only 'reasonable justification' for the nationalization measures of 1946-9.[1] Yet he then goes on to complain that owing to lack of adequate machinery for supervising these industries, the nation has had to provide vast sums for development without being certain that they are all really required.[2]

The Federation of British Industries, in a report aimed at demonstrating the disadvantages of public ownership and the advantages of private enterprise, drew attention to the allegation which has been made from time to time that the nationalized industries as a whole have been unduly favoured compared with private industry in regard to the provision of capital, and the further assertion that electricity has been unduly favoured in comparison with the other industries in the public sector. On this matter the FBI are careful to state that 'there is, clearly, no positive criterion to which such assertions could be submitted'.[3] The FBI therefore confine themselves to stating that the development plans of the nationalized industries are not subject to the same tests as those of commercial companies because their capital is either advanced by the Exchequer or borrowed with a Treasury guarantee. Political considerations may have played a part in the decisions affecting the public sector but it is not possible to say whether the capital could have been employed more productively in other industries.[4]

It must be frankly admitted that the capital investment programmes of the nationalized industries cannot be based on a yardstick of financial profitability, or on any other simple quantitative criterion, unless the public corporations are to be required or allowed to operate with profit-making as the main purpose in view: a policy which is so unlikely to be accepted that it need not be seriously considered. But to argue from this that there is no sound basis for allocating capital resources is quite a different matter. The Government are continually allocating capital resources to the building of roads, highways, hospitals, houses, and many other public works; and it is not a self-evident truth that these decisions are less 'correct' than those made by commercial companies. If one assumes that the boards of public corporations are composed of lazy, incompetent, irresponsible people whose main object is to extract an excessively large share of the nation's savings for investment in their respective industries, then some kind of supervision more effective than that

[1] R. Kelf-Cohen: *Nationalization in Britain. The End of a Dogma*, p. 183.
[2] *Ib.*, p. 186. [3] *Nationalization*, FBI (1958), para. 59. [4] *Ib.*, p. 60.

exercised by the Ministry of Power or the Ministry of Transport and Civil Aviation and the Treasury, will obviously be required. But I do not believe there is any ground for making this assumption.

The critics are on far sounder ground in arguing that the public corporations should endeavour to create much larger surpluses, depreciation funds, and reserves with which to finance a much higher proportion of their investment programmes. The break-even concept is wholly inadequate for this purpose, and much larger surpluses could and should have been made by the fuel and power industries at least. But this would involve much greater freedom for the boards to fix prices on commercial principles. On this point the Federation of British Industries show no liking for the conditions of the market which elsewhere in their report are held up to the highest praise. They admit that prices should fully cover costs, and they deplore the frequent inability of the public corporations to break even, and their failure to make provision for depreciation on a replacement cost basis. But this does not mean, the FBI tell us, that the increases of prices made in the past by nationalized industries were justified, and 'still less that a further increase is now to be advocated'.[1] Great play is made with the suggestion that costs have been too high; but no word is said about prices being too low—which they certainly have been in all the nationalized industries.

[1] *Nationalization*, FBI (1958), paras. 47 and 52.

CHAPTER XV

Performance

I SHALL examine in this chapter some of the most important questions relating to the operation of the nationalized industries and their development. Although I do not expect to be able to dispose of these questions finally or in a way which will satisfy everyone, I hope to be able to throw some light on them.

One frequently hears statements made about the efficiency or inefficiency of nationalized industries or of a particular industry. How far do such statements have serious meaning? On what criteria are they based?

In the sphere of private enterprise the yardstick normally used to judge the efficiency of business undertakings is their profitability, present and future. Other considerations, such as productivity and labour relations, management and research, may from time to time influence, directly or indirectly, judgments about the performance of commercial companies. It is also true that the interests of the employees, the customers, and even the public, are sometimes placed before those of the shareholders by the directors and executives of leading companies. Nevertheless, the fact remains that the making of profit is the fundamental purpose of private enterprise; and it is by its actual or potential success in achieving this purpose that a commercial undertaking will be judged by those whose opinions carry most weight in the business world. Everything else is ancillary to that overriding aim.

THE PURSUIT OF GAIN

The position is quite different in the public sector of the economy. The legal obligation of the nationalized industries is only to conduct their undertakings in such a way as to avoid making a loss, taking one year with another. There is no prohibition against making a surplus, and most of the public corporations have shown a surplus from time to time.[1] There is no inherent objection to public enterprise being conducted on a profitable basis, but this should not be the main purpose or the *raison d'être* of any form of public enterprise. The concept of profit is extraneous to public enterprise because there are no equity shareholders to whom

[1] See tables pp. 455-9.

dividends can be distributed, nor anyone to whom it can properly be paid as a bonus or commission. The term surplus is therefore more appropriate than the word profit.

There is no difficulty, however, in disposing of a net surplus. It can be placed to reserve as a cushion against bad times; or be ploughed back into the undertaking to finance capital development; or be used in reducing prices; or applied to repaying advances from public money made by a government department. These are all legally permissible purposes, and they are all desirable in appropriate circumstances. Public corporations should certainly be able to build up substantial reserves; and they should be encouraged to finance a much larger proportion of their capital development from internal resources than they have so far been able to do.

The existing legislation precludes in all instances the reserve fund from being applied 'otherwise than for the purposes of the board'[1]—that is, for the fulfilment of the aims for which the public corporation was established. Some of the statutes impose a like stipulation on the application of the board's surplus revenues, while in other cases a similar condition appears to be implied. In the case of the airways corporations the Minister has power to require them to pay to the Exchequer sums not exceeding the total amount of the grants they have received from public money in the past.[2] The statutes prevent public corporations from subsidizing other industries or services operating at a loss;[3] or from extending their operations into an entirely different field of activity; or from acquiring companies or firms in other industries. Nor can they lawfully be required to hand over to the Exchequer their surplus revenues to be used for general expenditure, though they are of course subject to taxation in the ordinary way. These provisions are all based on sound principles. Subsidization of one nationalized industry by another is not economically or socially desirable. Any extension or contraction of the sphere of public enterprise is a matter of major policy which should be decided by the Government and approved by Parliament, rather than by the board of a public corporation. And above all, nationalized industries should not be run in order to provide revenue for the Exchequer.

We may conclude, then, that there is a great deal to be said in favour of public enterprise making a substantial surplus in favourable conditions,

[1] Coal Industry Nationalization Act, 1946, s. 39 (2) (a); Civil Aviation Act, 1946, s. 17 (2) (a); Transport Act, 1947, s. 92 (2); Electricity Act, 1957, s. 20 (4); Gas Act, 1948, s. 47 (2) (a).

[2] Civil Aviation Act, 1946, s. 18; Coal Industry Nationalization Act, 1946, s. 30; Electricity Act, 1957, s. 22.

[3] This does not include subsidiary air lines in which BEA or BOAC have an interest.

but nevertheless the pursuit of gain should not occupy the central position in the public sector which the search for profit occupies in private enterprise. There are several reasons for this. The most important is that the industries so far nationalized possess a high degree of monopoly; and by exploiting their monopolistic position for services or commodities for which the demand is relatively inelastic they could make very large surpluses. It has been estimated that the National Coal Board could have made a surplus of £300 m. in the first decade of its existence; and some economists have contended that they should have followed this policy.[1]

In order to prevent the nationalized industries from exploiting their statutory monopolies, the public corporations have been subject to restraints of one sort or another from the time when they first came into existence. The clearest case is the NCB which have been required to observe a 'gentleman's agreement' entered into by the former coal owners in 1939, whereby they undertook not to raise the general level of coal prices except with the consent of the Government. This agreement was subsequently extended to cover the individual prices of different qualities of coal. The agreement was presumably adhered to by the board under pressure from the Government. The effect of it has been that at times the NCB have not been able to raise prices in order to meet rising costs as promptly or by as large a percentage as they would otherwise have done.[2] Doubtless the Board would in any case have exercised great moderation in fixing their prices, but they would scarcely have been prepared to show a deficit on the year's working in consequence of inability to adjust prices if any other course had been open to them.[3]

Prior to the Transport Act, 1953, the railways were subject to the decisions of the Transport Tribunal in regard to freight charges and to those of the Minister of Transport respecting passenger rates. The Act of 1953 removed the obligation to treat everyone in a strictly equal manner. It permitted the BTC to submit to the Transport Tribunal a new Merchandise Charges Scheme which would fix maximum charges except in cases where it was impracticable or undesirable to do so, and then left the railways free to charge traders or passengers what they thought fit so long as they did not exceed the maximum.

Despite the intentions of the Act to give the Commission a much larger measure of commercial freedom than hitherto, the Tribunal have continued to set limits to their discretion concerning charges. Thus, the

[1] I. M. D. Little: *The Price of Fuel.*

[2] National Coal Board Annual Report 1956, para. 67; Report from the Select Committee on Nationalized Industries (Report and Accounts). House of Commons Sessional Papers 187–1, April 1958, HMSO, paras. 81–9.

[3] Net deficits were shown in 1947, 1951, 1952, 1954, 1955, 1957, and 1958.

Tribunal excluded from the maximum charge provisions all consignments weighing one hundred tons or more, and any goods carried in the owner's railway trucks. This meant that the charges in these cases must be 'reasonable'; the reasonableness being determined by the Tribunal in case of disagreement. Furthermore, the Transport Tribunal rejected the BTC's application for a single scale of charges; they lowered the maximum charges proposed; fixed a separate list of charges for specified commodities conveyed in bulk; and introduced in each series of charges lower maximum charges as an alternative for goods consigned to or from a private siding.[1] In addition to these restrictions, the Government have intervened from time to time, as we have seen, to prevent the British Transport Commission from raising fares and charges even when approval had been given to the proposed increases by the Transport Tribunal and the Central Transport Consultative Committee.[2]

The air lines are subject to decisions of the International Air Transport Association respecting charges and rates; and these decisions must be approved by the Governments concerned. The Area Gas Boards and the Area Electricity Boards are under strong and continuous pressure by the Consultative Councils in their respective areas to keep down prices. These councils are mainly representative of consumer interests.

One obvious reason why the pursuit of gain is not a major aim in British nationalized industries is that there are no incentives tending in that direction. No individual, no group of persons, no sectional interest has any real motive in inducing the public corporations to run their industries primarily in order to create a surplus. Even the Treasury, apart from wishing to see the repayment of capital advances, interest charges, or grants by way of subsidy, would not be able to appropriate for the Exchequer any surplus in the way which applied for many years to the Post Office surplus. There has been, moreover, apprehension expressed that a substantial surplus would immediately cause the trade unions to put forward claims for higher wages.

PROFITABILITY AS A TEST

Since profitability is not a primary aim of nationalized industry, it cannot be regarded as a valid test to measure the efficiency of public enterprise. Even if the public corporations were to run their undertakings in order to maximize profit, the annual surpluses would still tell us little about their efficiency, in view of their monopolistic position.

[1] *The British Transport Commission. Proposal for the Railways.* Cmd. 9880/1956, HMSO, p. 24.

[2] *Ante* p. 150.

Lord Latham, a former chairman of London Transport Executive, has insisted that profitability is not a reliable test of efficiency in a nationalized industry. If circumstances are favourable, satisfactory profits can mask inefficiency, while in unfavourable circumstances a proper degree of efficiency may be achieved despite an absence of profits.[1] He insists that in a public service there are other criteria which must also be considered.[2] The test of efficiency must, in his view, be whether the service provides facilities which are reasonably adequate to meet the public needs at prices which are also reasonable and which will enable the undertaking to pay its way. The pursuit of maximum efficiency becomes, in this wider context, the most economical use of resources for a given return in goods and services.

Economy and efficiency, Lord Latham observes, are not synonymous. In a public transport undertaking, for example, there must be unremunerative services to outlying areas or in off-peak hours, and these can only be supported by heavy traffics in peak hours. It may be impossible from a practical point of view to employ the staff and equipment in the most economical manner theoretically possible, because it would result in a quite inadequate standard of service. Hence, the claims of economy must be balanced constructively against the demands of efficiency.[3]

Professors Sargant Florence and Gilbert Walker have contended that breaking even or making a surplus is the best primary test of efficiency in the public sector provided that certain conditions are fulfilled. These conditions are: first, that the surplus must not have been made by exploitation. The employees, for example, should be organized in trade unions which are able to negotiate with the management on equal terms. Second, money costs should reflect real costs, and must not leave social costs out of account. Third, the surplus should result from a small margin on a large output rather than a large margin on a small output. In short, the prime measure of efficiency is the ability to break even, or slightly more than even, at the greatest level of production. Ancillary tests of vigorous management would be lower prices, higher quality, or an extended range of goods and services.[4] These authors urge that the public corporations should strenuously avoid meeting increased costs

[1] Lord Latham: *London Transport*, in 'Efficiency in the Nationalized Industries', by Sir W. Houldsworth and others (1952), p. 29.

[2] Professor Herbert A. Simon remarks that the concept of efficiency must be given a much broader meaning than that accorded to it in profit-making concerns if it is to be applied to undertakings in which factors are involved which cannot be measured in monetary terms. See his *Administrative Behaviour* (2nd edition), p. 173. The whole of Ch. IX of this book, entitled 'The Criterion of Efficiency' is worth reading.

[3] *Ib.*, p. 30.

[4] P. Sargant Florence and Gilbert Walker: 'Efficiency under Nationalization and its measurement', in *Problems of Nationalized Industry*, ed. W. A. Robson, pp. 195-7.

by raising prices and relying on their monopoly to provide the surplus. Indeed, the proper test of the efficiency of a nationalized industry, in their view, lies in the degree of success shown by the management in lowering the cost of production. They urge that no price increase should be allowed in a nationalized industry except after a most stringent inquiry by an independent tribunal concerning the efficiency of the undertaking.[1]

The Florence-Walker hypothesis is useful as a preliminary test but it cannot be accepted as a satisfactory criterion. As Mr D. N. Chester has pointed out, the absence of loss in the trading operations of a public corporation is not truly comparable as an index of efficiency to the size of the dividend made by a joint stock company. Among the criticisms which can be levelled at the validity of the analogy are that balanced accounts may reflect high prices made possible by monopolistic exploitation rather than efficiency; that a nationalized industry should fix their prices to cover marginal costs and not average costs in order to ensure a proper distribution of resources, and that this may produce a large deficit or a large surplus; and that social needs, rather than economic consideration, should determine the policies of public corporations.[2]

In 1952 BOAC stated that one phase in the reconstruction of the airways corporation during the preceding five years was 'the imprinting on the mind of staff at all levels the idea that the corporation was essentially a commercial undertaking; that the financial aspect of every single activity mattered, and that the ultimate tests of the corporation's success was not only the standard of public service it provided but also the normal business criterion of whether it could be made to pay its way'.[3] This was unquestionably a desirable objective, especially in view of the fact that BOAC had been receiving substantial subsidies from the Exchequer for some years. But a better formulation would be to say that the ultimate test of the corporation's success is not only the profitability of its operations but also the volume, standard and extent of the services which it provides.

The Herbert Committee on the Electricity Supply Industry devoted an early chapter in their report[4] to the meaning of efficiency in a nationalized industry. In it they explained that the task is complicated by the absence of 'the major benchmarks' that exist in competitive industry.[5] They considered that the aims of the electricity supply industry could be

[1] P. Sargant Florence and Gilbert Walker: *Problems of Nationalized Industry*, p. 203.

[2] D. N. Chester: *Management and Accountability in the Nationalized Industries*, 30, Public Administration (Spring, 1952), pp. 44-45.

[3] *BOAC Annual Report*, 1951-2, para. 14.

[4] *Report*, Cmd. 9672/1958, Pt. II, Ch. 2.

[5] *Ib.*, para. 23.

stated in the following terms. It should be run as a business concern, be financially self-supporting, and be able to raise new capital without requiring a Treasury guarantee. Furthermore, the industry should compare favourably with leading commercial firms in the service it provides to its customers and the welfare of its staff. Finally, the industry should seek to supply electricity at the lowest possible price. They recognized that the clear intention of Parliament was that the primary aim is not to make profit.[1]

Having formulated these complex factors as criteria, the committee did not hesitate to express a broad general judgment on the efficiency of the industry. Electricity supply, they concluded, is not an inefficient industry. 'It is an efficient industry that could be improved but is in danger of losing efficiency partly for reasons beyond its control.'[2] The committee advised that the efficiency of the industry could be improved in several respects. Its formal organization was not the best that could be devised; a more extensive delegation of responsibility was required within the formal structure; greater use should be made of modern management techniques, such as those relating to budgeting, work study, operational research, and incentive wage systems; more resolute efforts were wanted to deal with redundancy and to recruit and retain men of outstanding technical and managerial ability.[3]

The Herbert Committee were right in conceiving the overall efficiency of a nationalized industry in terms of its ability to satisfy certain complex conditions. This appears to me the only practicable and reasonable course to adopt.

I do not, however, entirely agree with the conditions formulated by the committee as criteria of efficiency. Why, for example, should private industry even at its best be taken as the model for a nationalized industry to follow in regard to the service given to customers or in respect of staff welfare? Prior to nationalization, the large municipal electricity undertakings were, with one or two exceptions, the leaders in the field. The BBC can give lessons to private enterprise in regard to service to consumers despite the mass appeal of commercial television. It should be noted that the Herbert report does not anywhere appear to apply tests to the electricity supply industry designed to ascertain how efficiently it is fulfilling the postulated aims. There is no examination of the wages and conditions of employment of the labour force to see how they compare with those obtaining in private enterprise; nor any comparison of the service afforded by the Area Boards with that provided by commercial firms. So far as the postulated duty to supply electricity at

[1] *Report*, Cmd. 9672/1956, paras. 28-9.
[2] *Ib.*, para. 508. [3] *Ib.*, Ch. 25.

the lowest cost possible is concerned, the committee thought the prices charged to consumers had been, if anything, too low.[1]

The Chambers Committee on London Transport were also prepared to express a broad judgment on the efficiency of London's transport system. Their main conclusion was that 'the undertaking carried on by the London Transport Executive is conducted efficiently and with due regard to economy'.[2] They went on to say that 'London has one of the best passenger transport systems in the world and it is served by a body of workers of all grades who have a fine tradition of loyalty and public service'.[3] The report recommended a number of measures which would result in a marked improvement in efficiency and substantial economies.

We can see that while there are no simple yardsticks or hard-and-fast criteria of efficiency in nationalized industries, it is possible for committees of inquiry to form broad judgments about individual industries, based on factors which they consider to be relevant. These criteria are at present mainly qualitative, but we may hope and expect that in course of time statistical indices will be devised to cover at least some of them. To determine which parts of the production function are susceptible to scientific measurement will require extensive and prolonged research.[4]

The Federation of British Industries, in a recent report, state that in the absence of the tests of a free market, it is a complex and difficult matter to determine whether maximum efficiency and minimum costs have been achieved. A correct judgment cannot be formed on the basis of changes in operational efficiency, such as increases in the output of coal a man shift, or ton miles for each railway engine-hour, etc., because these do not by themselves reveal costs. It is therefore necessary in each case to examine the factors governing costs, 'even though it may be impossible in any given case to say what the optimum should be'.[5]

This argument does not throw much light on the problem. Certainly it is desirable that costs should be brought into the picture in assessing efficiency, but if we do not know what the optimum should be how are we to judge the degree of efficiency reflected by the costs? Even in a free market, it is impossible to determine whether maximum efficiency and minimum costs have been attained by the firm. No one can say whether the best possible organization or management have been achieved by a successful company which is making a large profit.

The line taken by the Federation of British Industries is to deny any suggestion that the nationalized industries have gained in efficiency as

[1] *Report* Cmd. 9672/1956, paras. 339–46.
[2] *Report of the Committee of Inquiry into London Transport*, 1955, para. 391.
[3] *Ib.*, para. 392.
[4] Herbert A. Simon: *op. cit.*, pp. 188–9.
[5] *Nationalization*. Federation of British Industries (1958), para. 50.

measured by the indices of technical performance; and this is undoubtedly one of the main objects of their heavily biased report.

Without attempting to examine costs and prices in the nationalized industries, or to compare them with those prevailing in private enterprise, the FBI declare *ex cathedra* that there are four reasons for believing that costs are too high in the public sector. These are: first, the national scale of operations has produced remote and ineffective control and a lower sense of responsibility; second, political influences have weakened the restraints on labour costs; third, there has been a tendency to base prices on average costs without sufficient regard to differential variations, thereby distorting the pattern of consumption and of investment, which leads to higher costs; fourth, the obligation to break even over a period of years permits public corporations to show a deficit in any particular year, which removes the necessity for the strict control of costs when trading conditions are difficult.

This statement is based on *a priori* reasoning, and is not supported by any evidence. No allowance whatever is made for the cost-reducing developments which have been introduced into the nationalized industries during the past ten years, such as the concentration of gas making at larger plants and the closing down of the small and inefficient ones.

The Federation of British Industry refer to 'the constant pressure to increase efficiency, reduce costs, produce better products or service, and meet changes in customers' requirements' in private enterprise.[1] But they make no attempt to explain why these forces failed to produce desirable results in, for example, the coal industry or the railways when they were run by private enterprise. The efficiency of these industries had been declining for many years prior to nationalization.

THE PHILOSOPHY OF PUBLIC ENTERPRISE

In any discussion about efficiency it is essential to remember that 'efficiency' does not determine the ends which an industry or service seeks to attain, but only the effectiveness and economy with which given ends are pursued.[2] The determination of ends will inevitably involve value judgments of a political, social, or economic character. In defining the ends it will be difficult to find a basis of agreement between those who believe that the sole purpose of public enterprise is to provide goods or services to consumers at the lowest possible prices and those who have other considerations in view. Mr A. H. Hanson has pointed

[1] *Nationalization.* Federation of British Industries (1958), para. 75.

[2] Stephen Wheatcroft: *The Economics of European Air Transport*, p. 67; Herbert A. Simon: *Administrative Behaviour* (2nd ed.), pp. 176 *et seq.*

out that there are several different ways of running a nationalized industry, and a preference between them cannot be decided by scientific means.[1] The question whether an industry has achieved the best possible balance between different objectives will always involve a value judgment. The more important of these value judgments should, he contends, be made by the representatives of the people. Hence, supervision of the nationalized industries by the House of Commons ought to be as effective as possible; for although Parliament cannot administer or decide policy, it can criticize and influence those to whom administration and policy have been entrusted.

Lord Simon of Wythenshawe urges MPs to confine their attention to debates on policy, and to recognize that Parliament is utterly unfitted to deal with questions of efficiency in the nationalized industries. The board should have the maximum freedom and responsibility subject to the necessary minimum of control by the Minister.[2] Much would turn on the precise meaning given to maximum and minimum; but the general intention is to reduce political direction as far as possible.

The Herbert Committee, while insisting that the electricity supply industry should have 'one duty and one duty alone: to supply electricity to those who will meet the cost of it and to do so at the lowest possible expenditure of resources consistent with the maintenance of employment standards at the level of the best private firms',[3] also recognized that other aims might be pursued on instructions from the responsible Minister.[4] In short, the electricity boards should take into account only purely economic considerations when acting on their own authority; but the Government should be free to take into account social, political or international matters and be able to give instructions to the Electricity Boards to shape their policies so as to promote non-economic ends.

Mr H. A. Clegg has criticized the Fleck Report on the ground that its recommendations assume that the coal industry can and should be managed in accordance with the best commercial practices. In commenting on the recommendation by the Fleck Committee urging permanent appointments for the full-time members of the board, he agreed that this might be desirable from the standpoint of securing continuity of top management; but 'the emphasis on the responsibility of boards through the Minister to Parliament was one of Labour's contributions to the public corporation'.[5] To abolish fixed terms of office for members of the

[1] A. H. Hanson: Parliament and the Nationalized Industries, *Yorkshire Bulletin*, VI, September 2, 1954, pp. 151-2. See also *The Management of Public Corporations*, an editorial article in *Nature*, Vol. 173, (March 13, 1954), p. 479.

[2] Lord Simon of Wythenshawe: *The Boards of Nationalized Industries*, p. 45.

[3] *Report*, para. 507. [4] *Ib.*, para. 125.

[5] H. A. Clegg: The Fleck Report, *in 33 Public Administration* (Autumn 1955), p. 271.

board is likely to reduce both ministerial control and parliamentary influence over the public corporation. There is thus a question of balancing one desirable aim—continuity of top management—against another desirable aim—that of government and parliamentary responsibility. A decision of this kind cannot be arrived at by merely considering 'efficiency' without regard to other considerations.

Another criticism which the same writer makes is that the Fleck report exalts authority in seeking to increase the effectiveness of the NCB in getting their policies adopted throughout the industry.[1] He cites a passage in which the committee declared that anyone who is unable or unwilling to fit properly into the Board's organization and accept the methods and discipline necessary in a large organization should be removed. Such an attitude, he argues, does not accord with the philosophy which imbued the Labour Party when it embarked on nationalization. Socialists may no longer believe that public ownership will by itself bring about a free and happy co-operative commonwealth; but they 'have not entirely abandoned the view that public ownership should enable advances towards the "good society" beyond what is possible in private enterprise. In this society men would be more free; discipline, if required, would be self-discipline; and some kind of "industrial democracy" would flourish. Admittedly socialists have not found it easy to demonstrate the exact steps necessary to attain those ends. But, if the Fleck Report is right, the ends are unattainable. Private enterprise is to set the standard for public undertakings and, according to the report, the lesson private enterprise has to teach is: more discipline. This, of course, does not prove the Fleck Report wrong; it only shows what must be abandoned if the report is accepted.'[2] It is possible, moreover, that stricter discipline will not solve the maladies which afflict the industry. Mr Clegg also criticized the report on the ground that it affords little guidance on how to improve bad labour relations in the coalfields, one of the most vexed and important problems which faces the industry. In conclusion, he asks whether the philosophy underlying the Fleck Report correctly represents the experience of large-scale private enterprise; and whether the lessons gained from that experience can be applied without qualifications to public enterprise.[3]

A similar point of view is pushed to greater lengths in a recent book entitled *Twentieth Century Socialism*, produced by Socialist Union.[4] The authors state that productivity is becoming the principal measure of good management both in private enterprise (where it is gradually replacing the notion that profit is the sole measure of success) and in public

[1] H. A. Clegg : The Fleck Report, *in* 33 *Public Administration* (Autumn 1955), p. 273.
[2] *Ib.*, p. 274 [3] *Ib.*, p. 275. [4] A Penguin Special published in 1956, p. 140.

enterprise. Hence the case for nationalization is based mainly on the need to secure greater efficiency, control of monopolies, better co-ordination and improved labour relations, all of which are regarded as means for increasing productivity. 'To suggest that public enterprise might provide the great opportunity for applying socialist ideals, with their respect for the individual, to the actual running of industry, is to invite dismissal as a hopelessly impractical idealist. A business enterprise, we are told, exists to produce goods and services and must therefore justify its existence only by its success in the market. What effect it has on the lives of people who work in it is irrelevant.' The authors urge that socialist ideals should be applied to the conduct of industry, both as regards man as consumer and man as producer. They concede that efficiency is desirable, but insist that the rights of man as producer deserve at least equal consideration. The human rights of the work-people should be a criterion by which society judges the exercise of managerial power.

In answer to this, one can say that labour relations are already one of the criteria usually taken into account in judging the administration of the nationalized industries. It would be easier to give greater weight to the interests of the workers if they and their unions would give greater weight to the interests of the consumers. On the whole, the human rights of labour have been fully recognized by the National Coal Board and the other public corporations, including the railways, where sluggish management in the past, antiquated equipment, and conservative attitudes on the part of the workers, reacted adversely on the terms and conditions of employment.[1] Whether the human rights of labour have been sufficiently recognized in the nationalized industries is a matter on which opinions are likely to vary, for this is a matter of values. I believe that most people in this country wish to see the nationalized industries run with high efficiency in terms of productivity, costs, service, and prices, while at the same time ensuring a reasonably contented and well-treated labour force. These objectives are not incompatible: indeed, they are complementary. Oh the other hand, except among trade unionists as such, there is no preference for the interests of men as producers over those of men as consumers.

It is desirable that fundamental questions concerning the aims of nationalized industries should be asked from time to time; and that we should understand the philosophy not only of the managers and employ-

[1] Sir Brian Robertson, Chairman of the British Transport Commission, has publicly stated that 'The conditions under which our men have to work at present are in many places quite disgraceful'. *The British Transport System*, a lecture delivered to the Royal United Service Institution on February 1, 1956 and published by the Commission.

ees in the industries, but also of those who criticize and report on them. There is a strong tide at present running in the direction of regarding public enterprise as indistinguishable in its purposes from private enterprise except for the elimination of the profit motive. Few of those who make this assumption stop to enquire why certain industries were nationalized; what was hoped or expected of them under public ownership; and what is implied by public accountability and control.

The fact that the public corporation has been used as a device for administering the nationalized industries is of only secondary importance in considering their status. The nationalized industries are as much part of the *res publica* as the Post Office, the British Museum, or the highway system. Mr D. N. Chester warns us to avoid the danger of confusing the management of nationalized industries with the State. But is there not a greater danger in failing to see the connection between public enterprise and the State? Where are we to draw the line? There are those who would like to see at least some nationalized industries administered by government departments headed by Ministers. Would such industries then become identified with 'the power and glory of the State'?[1]

Mr Chester does not consider that a nationalized industry is necessarily more important than any other industry. This scarcely seems the right way to look at the matter. Of course there are many industries in the private sector which are of very great importance; but it is nevertheless true that the industries chosen for nationalization were selected because of their exceptional importance to the whole economy. This made it desirable to bring the industries concerned under public control and disinterested management. There were other contributing factors which influenced the decisions, such as the unsatisfactory condition of the industry under private ownership or municipal administration, the monopolistic nature of the industry, *et cetera*, but these do not detract from the main motive.

Mr Chester also questions the assumption that the employees of a nationalized industry are to be considered as performing a public service to a greater extent than those in private enterprise; and that in consequence they should be expected to refrain from striking on the ground that it would be unpatriotic to do so or a blow against the State.[2]

This conception of employment in the nationalized industries as being more or less the same as any other job is possibly held by large numbers of workers in those industries. Indeed, the very lack of a sense of public spirit comparable to that which we find in the civil service, in the better run local authorities, in the fighting services at their best, in hospitals

[1] *Ante* p. 148.

[2] D. N. Chester: *The Nationalized Industries*, in *Three Banks Review*, December 1952, p. 24.

and schools and universities, has been the most disappointing feature of the coal industry since nationalization. There are well-known reasons for this phenomenon in the embittered history of the coal industry under private enterprise; but that does not make the result less unfortunate or less of an impediment to success. The high sense of public spirit which prevails among civil servants is one of the greatest assets of the nation, and unless we can evoke a measure of that same spirit among the miners, the railwaymen, the gas and electricity workers, and the other employees in nationalized industries, those industries are unlikely to attain a high degree of success. The hardboiled view of public enterprise will in the end yield poor results.

THE AIMS OF NATIONALIZED INDUSTRIES

The aims of public enterprise cannot be embodied in a single formula applicable to all the nationalized industries at all times. We must consider each industry in the light of the prevailing needs and circumstances of the time. The Fleck Committee may well have been right in believing that the principal need of the coal industry was to increase the authority of the Board and the headquarters staff over the subordinate formations, and to introduce stronger sanctions for disobedience or failure to co-operate. It does not follow that enhanced discipline is the right prescription for all public corporations, or even for the National Coal Board for ever. We must preserve a sense of relativity in considering both ends and means. The BBC, for example, were for many years too authoritarian and paternalistic towards their staff; and it became necessary to require the corporation to relax their excessively strict code of discipline and morality concerning the private affairs of the staff, and to strengthen the organs of association and negotiation available to the employees.[1]

To return to the main theme. It is essential that the nationalized industries should be administered so as to promote productive efficiency on the one hand and such social or political purposes as may from time to time be regarded as in the national interest on the other. Most people would probably agree with this proposition. The main point of disagreement is whether the public corporations themselves should be free to take non-economic considerations into account in deciding policy or whether such decisions should rest with Parliament or the Government.

Here again one should avoid sweeping generalizations. It would be fantastic to require the BBC to follow 'economic' considerations in making their programmes, or even to try to compete with the commercial television programmes for mass audiences. Educational, aesthetic, en-

[1] For a full account see Parliamentary Debates, Commons, 1935–6, Vol. 311 (April 29, 1936), cols. 958 *et seq.*

tertainment, social and political factors enter into decisions about the sound and television services all the time, and decisions of policy about them must be left to the corporation so far as the internal services are concerned. The major questions about broadcasting for overseas audiences are properly decided in consultation with the departments concerned, since the decisions depend on political, strategic, and trade considerations which concern the British Government and Commonwealth Governments. Several departments have an interest in the decisions and the BBC does not have sufficient knowledge of government policy to be able to decide what the national interest demands. Moreover, the overseas services are paid for out of parliamentary money voted for the purpose and not out of the licence fee.

Another example can be taken from the nationalized air services. The aims of BOAC and BEA are to provide the best and safest air services at the lowest operating costs in the most suitable aircraft which they can obtain. This is a perfectly reasonable and legitimate interpretation of the national interest from the standpoint of the airways corporations. But if BOAC wishes to buy American aircraft, as they have on more than one occasion, two other aspects of the national interest will immediately arise. One will be the effect of such a purchase on the British aircraft industry. The other will be its effect on the balance of payments between the UK and the US. A conflict of views may in these circumstances easily arise as to what the national interest demands, and this must be resolved at ministerial or Cabinet level.

I believe that the views of the air corporations should prevail in matters of this kind. Moreover, as our aircraft manufacturers are selling —or trying to sell—aircraft abroad on their merits, it is not a good sales policy for them to adopt a highly nationalistic attitude of protest and resentment if British air lines wish to buy from abroad. But whatever one's views on this may be, it is not politically realistic to say that such matters must be left entirely to the corporations and that the Government shall not intervene. Equally impractical is the proposal that any decision by the Government which overrides the economic interests of the corporation should carry with it a subsidy payable out of general taxation as a form of compensation to the board.

One must not go to the opposite extreme of insisting that the economic calculus shall dominate the minds and thoughts of the board of a nationalized industry to the exclusion of everything else. This would mean demanding of them an outlook far narrower and more rigid than that which is found in commercial companies, in central or local government, in the professions, or in any other walk of life. We shall not find men of high ability willing to lead lives cribbed, cabined, and confined by the laws of supply and demand. The proper resolution of the difficulty is to say that the most important questions of policy, whether involving non-economic considerations or not, should be decided or approved by Ministers, while all other matters should be determined by the board, regardless of whether they involve economic or non-economic considerations, or both.

Whatever may be desirable in theory, it is extremely probable that in practice the nationalized industries will be run so as to take account of political or social purposes—not necessarily on a large scale or continuously, but from time to time on particular matters. Anyone who thinks otherwise has failed to estimate the strength of the forces which underlay the nationalization movement in its origin and the forces which it has generated.

The provisions for parliamentary discussion and government control on major questions provide ample opportunity for ensuring that dominant conceptions of the national interest prevailing at any time shall influence the policies and conduct of the public corporations, as well as the scope of their activities. This is a necessary and inevitable condition of democratic government, which rightly limits the autonomy of public corporations.

An illustration may be taken from the sphere of civil air transport. Soon after a Conservative government took office in 1951, Mr Lennox Boyd, then Minister of Civil Aviation, announced the Government's policy on civil air transport. This was intended to give 'more scope and security' to independent companies operating for profit. The private companies were to have special opportunities in regard to all-freight services, seasonal inclusive tours, and 'colonial coach services' at cheap fares not directly competitive with the services provided by the corporations. They were also to have the bulk of charter operations, for the airways corporations were not to be allowed to maintain aircraft specially for charter work although they might charter standby aircraft required for scheduled services during busy periods. The private operators were to be authorized to operate internal services on a long-term basis in addition to those provided by BEA.[1] The Minister proposed to implement the Government's policy of encouraging private operators by an extension of the arrangements under which the airways corporations appoint independent companies as associates.[2]

Here the policy of the Government was designed to confine the activi-

[1] All applications for the operation of new overseas or internal services, whether by the airways corporations or private operators, are considered by the Air Transport Advisory Council, whose recommendations go to the Minister for his decision. Parliamentary Debates, Commons, May 27, 1952, Vol. 501, cols. 1152-3. See the Reports of the Air Transport Advisory Council 1952-3, para. 19; 1956-7, para. 1 and App. C.

[2] Terms of Reference of the Air Transport Advisory Council, (July 30, 1952), para. 1-2.

ties of the nationalized air lines so far as possible to their existing routes and services. Private operators were made eligible to apply on equal terms with the airways corporations for the right to develop new routes and all new types of scheduled services. In addition only the private operators were to be allowed to undertake various types of air work (other than scheduled services) in which large developments were expected. This policy stemmed from the political philosophy of the Conservative Government, which sought to promote private enterprise and to restrict the sphere of the public sector although no attempt was made to denationalize the airways corporations.

We are not concerned with whether this policy was wise or unwise. I am only pointing out that the Conservative Government were able to inject their policy into the air transport industry, just as a Labour Government would be able to expand the sphere of activity of BEA and BOAC and to discourage or curtail private operators. Whether justified or not, this kind of thing is almost certain to happen because there must be a substantial amount of political control over the public corporations in a democratic regime.

As a result of the Government's change of policy, the share of the airways corporations in the traffic carried by UK airlines dropped by nearly nine per cent as regards passengers, and nearly five per cent as regards load, between 1953 and 1957. As the following Table shows, the corporations nevertheless greatly increased their business under both heads.

It is obvious that the fall in the share of the nationalized undertakings and the rise in the share of the independent companies has nothing to do with their efficiency. It is not due to private enterprise competing successfully with public enterprise but is the result of a political decision.

General Sir Brian Robertson, chairman of the British Transport Commission, has urged the public to make up their mind about the purposes for which the nationalized transport system should be run. At present, he says, British railways are expected to do more than they should undertake under the prevailing conditions. They are expected, for example, to provide a ubiquitous parcels service, for any kind of goods at any time, with collection and delivery, at quite unremunerative charges. It is essential that the country should decide whether public transport should be run as a commercial enterprise, financially self-supporting and with the same amount of freedom to run its affairs as a commercial company; or alternatively as a service obliged to minister to every want of the community, however uneconomic it may be. This would inevitably mean subsidizing the public transport system from taxation.[1]

[1] General Sir Brian Robertson: *The British Transport System.* A lecture delivered to the Royal United Service Institution February 1, 1956. Published by the BTC pp. 12 and 18.

TABLE I

Air Corporations' share in traffic of UK airlines, 1953–7

	BOAC		*BEA*		*Independent Companies operating Scheduled Services as Associates of BOAC or BEA*		*Percentage carried by BOAC and BEA*	
Year	*Passengers carried*	*Load Short Ton Miles*	*Passengers carried*	*Load Short Ton Miles*	*Passengers carried*	*Load Short Ton Miles*	*Passengers*	*Load*
1953–4	290,156	136,068,000	1,656,779	53,119,000	252,550	8,100,000	88·6	95·9
1954–5	281,373	133,343,000	1,874,316	63,039,000	360,686	12,235,000	85·7	94·1
1955–6	371,215	155,758,000	2,224,747	77,903,000	552,326	23,453,000	82·5	90·9
1956–7	410,992	174,822,000	2,461,065	88,828,000	733,069	25,277,000	79·7	91·3

Note. The figures for 1956–7 are subject to final adjustment.

Source: Report of the Air Transport Advisory Council 1956–7, par. 7.
(The figures in the last two columns do not appear in the Report; they have been calculated from the information in the other columns)

THE SEARCH FOR EFFICIENCY

I have tried to show that there are no simple criteria of efficiency in nationalized industries, and also that 'efficiency' cannot be considered as an abstract entity but must be related to the ends which a nationalized undertaking pursues.[1]

This does not mean that the search for efficiency should not go on continuously within every nationalized industry. Indeed, the high degree of monopoly they enjoy makes this all the more necessary. Sometimes particular improvements can be measured statistically in terms of labour costs, cost of maintenance, fuel efficiency, the amount of capital investment required, productivity, reduced accident rates, and so forth. All these measurements may be perfectly valid in their own context and may demonstrate that a particular innovation does or does not increase efficiency in a particular respect. Yet these indices, although very valuable as guides to management, will not provide a single over-all measurement of the efficiency of a nationalized industry.

Thus we arrive at the conclusion that while it is desirable to seek continually for increased efficiency in nationalized industry and although it is possible to achieve it in many different ways, the over-all efficiency cannot be reduced to a simple quantitative measurement. Nevertheless, many particular aspects of a nationalized industry can be measured statistically and the efficiency of the undertaking can in part be assessed by assembling a large number of these relevant measurements. In the last resort, however, we must in the present state of knowledge rely on a broad and informed judgment for our estimate of the degree of success which a public undertaking has achieved.

This conclusion is consistent with the inquiry into the British electricity industry carried out by a team of experts from the United States which visited this country in 1952. The team included representatives from both privately owned and publicly owned electric power agencies in America, and also two trade unionists. The visit followed those of two electricity supply teams from the UK to the US in 1949. The report,

[1] Mr S. Wheatcroft distinguishes entrepreneurial management from executive management. The functions of the former involve estimating the market and consumer preferences, and the exercise of judgment about risk-bearing. The assessment of efficiency in entrepreneurial management is largely a matter of intuition and deductive reasoning, owing to the difficulties of applying methods of measurement.

Executive management involves producing the desired output of goods and services after relevant entrepreneurial decisions have been made. This requires choosing the best equipment and the best combination of factors to produce the output. Efficiency here is supposed to mean achieving the maximum output with the minimum input; but it should be widened to include such 'non-material outputs' as the welfare of the employees, Stephen Wheatcroft: *The Economics of European Air Transport*, pp. 67 and 69.

issued by the Anglo-American Council on Productivity, compared the electricity supply industries in the two countries and made recommendations to the British industry on fourteen major matters. These included technical aspects of generation and distribution, the speeding up of approval for the use of sites for new power stations, the installation of meters on the outside of new houses, greater wage differentiation for skilled workers, increased work on safety precautions, greater opportunities for the less highly trained technical personnel, and extended rural electrification.[1] It was implied that all these recommendations would, if carried out, increase the efficiency of the British electricity supply industry; and their desirability was not assumed to depend on the possibility of measuring quantitatively the existing overall efficiency of the industry.

THE PERFORMANCE OF THE NATIONALIZED INDUSTRIES

What can be said about the performance of the nationalized industries during the period which has elapsed since they were brought into the public sector in the years 1946 to 1948? What measure of success have they achieved?

After what has been said in the preceding pages, the reader will not expect either a precise quantitative statement of their efficiency nor a single statement applicable to all the industries. The record of each industry must be looked at in turn. In doing so, we should recall the extremely difficult economic conditions which existed in this country in the immediate post-war years, some of which have persisted up to the present time. These included a shortage of staff, particularly of engineers, technicians and scientists, a shortage of capital, the balance of payments problem, the need to give priority to rebuilding the export trade, the heavy accumulation of arrears in construction and replacement of worn-out or obsolete equipment, the physical devastation caused by the war, the shortage of raw materials and the need to restrict imports. The transference to public ownership of the basic industries concerned with fuel, power and transport would in any event have been a difficult and complex process; the circumstances in which it took place added greatly to the difficulties of the operation.

The Airlines

The nationalized airlines have made good progress, despite their initial handicap of being unable to procure up-to-date aircraft designed for civil transport purposes.

[1] United States Productivity Team Report *The British Electricity System* (British Productivity Council, 1953) paras. 2, 92, 246, 260-2, 283, 335, and 350.

The following Table gives comparable figures for 1947-8 and for 1958-9 for BOAC and BEA respectively:

TABLE II

British Overseas Airways Corporation

Year ended March 31	1948	1959	% *Change*
Capacity ton miles offered for sale	89,551,080	376,733,000	320
Average aircraft capacity (tons)	3·02	9·09	201
Average speed (mph)	182	271	49
Number of Employees... ...	24,101	19,010	–21·0
Capacity ton miles per employee	3,716	19,583	427
Operating revenue ,, ,,	£607	£3,009	395
Passengers carried	115,675	495,170	328
Freight ,, (tons) ...	2,447	8,778	258
Break-even load factor... ...	115%	60%	—47
Load factor carried	64·9%	57·0%	—12

British European Airways

Year ended March 31	1948	1959	% *Change*
Capacity ton miles offered ...	19,739,000	181,054,643	817·2
Revenue hours flown	96,442	194,058	101·2
Number of line aircraft (*average*)	105	115·8	11·0
Number of employees (*average*)	7,500	11,606	54·7
Capacity ton miles per employee	2,632	15,600	492·1
Revenue per employee... ...	£550	£2,737	397·6
Passengers carried	511,522	2,828,715	456·9
Freight ,, (tons) ...	2,284	28,020	1126·8
Break-even load factor ...		60%	
Load factor carried*	62·3%	60·4%	— 3·0

This Table shows that both productivity and efficiency have increased in several directions. The capacity ton miles offered by BOAC was more than quadrupled in 1958–9 compared with 1947–8, and the capacity ton miles per employee was also quadrupled. The load factor required to break even was reduced by nearly one half; and the load factor carried had reached the break-even standard. Well over four times as many passengers and over three times as much freight was carried in 1958–9 as in 1947-8.

We know, however, that owing to intransigence on the part of the trade unions, BOAC have not yet been able to deal with a heavy burden of redundancy among the maintenance staff. In the dispute which came

* BEA Report calls this: 'Revenue load factor'.

to a head in the strike at London Airport in 1958, it was disclosed that there were 3,000 redundant engineering employees on the staff of BOAC. This is a matter which is of critical importance to the future conduct of the nationalized industries. To allow employment in the nationalized industry to be regarded as a right, irrespective of the needs of the industry, would be to court disaster.

BEA increased the capacity ton miles offered by sevenfold. The capacity ton miles per employee likewise increased fivefold. A slightly larger fleet of aircraft flew eighty-eight per cent more revenue hours. The load factor carried exceeded by about one per cent the break-even load factor. The traffic in passengers rose by about 380 per cent and the freight traffic by about 886 per cent. In the five years 1951-6 BEA increased their traffic in passenger miles by 144 per cent. This compared with an average increase of only eighty per cent in the world's air traffic.

The Select Committee on Nationalized Industries examined in 1959 the statistics relating to the performance of nine airlines engaged in international services, and attempted a comparison between the British air corporations and their competitors.[1] The committee recognized that in making comparisons, allowances must be made for many important differences in the circumstances applicable to the airlines concerned. There are differences of size, which may enable the very large American airlines to obtain economies of scale which smaller undertakings cannot achieve. There are differences in the character of the services provided; BEA, for example, is the only major airline in the world which is confined entirely to short-haul services. There are differences in the efficiency of the aircraft available. One cause of BOAC's higher costs has been the troubles they have had with the Britannia, and at an earlier date with the original version of the Comet, which had to be withdrawn from service. The enormous orders given by the US Air Force for large transport aircraft have put the American aircraft manufacturers and also the American airlines in a position of great advantage compared with that of the British manufacturers and airlines, who have had little or no military support of this kind. In consequence, most of the development flying has fallen on the shoulders of the airlines, often with very serious consequences both financial and non-financial.

The Committee considered in relation to each of the British air corporations four separate factors. First, the passenger load factor, defined as the percentage relationship of passenger miles to available seat miles. Second, aircraft utilization, which is the average number of hours of revenue earning flight performed by each aircraft on the days when it is

[1] *Report from the Select Committee on Nationalized Industries* (Reports and Accounts), HC paper 213/1959, HMSO.

available for such flying, or held up only by routine maintenance. The third factor was capacity ton miles per employee. Fourth, operating cost as measured by the amount spent in carrying one ton of payload for one mile.[1]

Some of the assumptions made by the Committee are open to question. They stated that 'the unoccupied seats in an aircraft can be used as a measure of failure'.[2] But few people would regard as successful an inadequate service which resulted in every seat being filled, and with long queues of passengers waiting to be carried at each stage of the route. Yet such a service could achieve a passenger load factor of 100 per cent.

The aircraft utilization factor must also be approached warily as an index of efficiency. An airline can easily increase its aircraft utilization by operating more services or by increasing the density of its services. But this may reduce the passenger load factor, with adverse financial results. There is obviously no point in flying aircraft which are half empty in order to raise the utilization factor.[3] Good management will aim at achieving the best balance between these two factors from an economic standpoint.

The Committee refers to the quotient of an airline's capacity and the number of its employees as 'a rough gauge of the output being achieved by the airline's staff'[4] subject to considerable reservations as a basis of comparison. But the chairman of BEA challenged vigorously the validity of any inferences about productivity which can be drawn from this factor. BEA, for example, handles the aircraft of 26 other airlines at London Airport, and this necessitates a much larger staff than would be needed for their own services. Again, in countries where wage rates are low, it will pay to employ a larger number of employees rather than to save labour by introducing mechanized methods involving expensive equipment. The differences of productivity in terms of c.t.m. per employee have little significance as an index of efficiency in such circumstances. Long distance routes and routes of high traffic density tend to produce the highest returns per employee. Routes with big seasonal fluctuations tend to show low returns of productivity, because a larger staff must be employed to deal with peak loads than can be fully employed at other times. Airlines differ, also, in the amount and kind of work they carry out themselves. An airline which undertakes all its own aircraft maintenance and repairs, and perhaps similar work for other lines, will employ a much larger staff than one which contracts for such work to be carried out by outside firms. A further cause of variations in this factor

[1] *Report*, HC 213/1959, HMSO, paras. 130–40.
[2] *Ib.*, para. 130. [3] *Ib.*, Q. 2430-1. [4] *Ib.*, para. 137.

is the introduction of new aircraft, for this demands much development, testing and training flying, all of which is excluded from the 'capacity ton miles' figure.

The operating cost normally comprises wages, fuel, landing fees, aircrew utilization and aircraft utilization.[1] Landing fees are outside an airline's control, and so is the cost of fuel, although this will vary largely with the type of aircraft used. Aircrew utilization will be influenced to some extent by the causes which affect aircraft utilization, though there are additional ones such as the human needs of the aircrews and the statutory or international safety requirements. It is obvious that the shorter the journey, the greater the proportion of time which both aircraft and aircrew will spend on the ground in relation to flying time.

With these considerations in mind we may turn to the Select Committee's observations about the performance of BEA and BOAC respectively.

They found BOAC's passenger load factor to be well above average in 1956–7; in 1957–8 it was slightly above the average of the airlines for which figures were available. BOAC lost ground in this respect on their Eastern route partly owing to the difficulties they experienced in maintaining punctuality with the Britannia aircraft. They hope to increase their passenger load factor, but may find it more profitable to achieve a higher aircraft utilization with a lower load factor.[2]

BOAC's aircraft utilization for 1956–7 was slightly lower than SAS and TWA, a good deal lower than PAA, but higher than Swissair, KLM or Air France. The Britannia was introduced in 1957 and for the next two years this was a substantial cause of low utilization.[3] Utilization depends in large measure on the amount of time an aircraft is out of service for repair or maintenance, since this bears directly on the number of hours it is available for flying. We have already seen that the inability to deal promptly and effectively with the problem of redundancy among their maintenance staff was the Achilles heel of BOAC. This was reflected both in their low aircraft utilization factor and also in their high operating cost. BOAC's costs under this head were 39·1 pence per c.t.m. in 1957, compared with 30·9 pence for all services of Pan American Airways, or 33·4 pence for the Atlantic services of PAA. The position appears now to be in process of rectification and better results may be looked for from BOAC in the near future.

In general, the Select Committee held that BOAC have in recent years been operating with less efficiency than most of the other international airlines with which they were compared. I do not regard this conclusion as well-founded except in regard to the inflated costs of

[1] *Report*, HC 213/1959, HMSO, para. 142. [2] *Ib.*, paras. 144–6. [3] *Ib.*, para. 148.

maintenance and its repercussions. It is certainly not fair or reasonable to hold BOAC responsible for the withdrawal of the original Comet or for the defects of the Britannia. Moreover, the Committee made virtually no attempt to inquire how far the circumstances of the various airlines are really comparable beyond indicating in a quite general way the matters for which allowances should be made.

As regards BEA, the Select Committee stated that the corporation have achieved a satisfactory load factor on international routes.[1] They agreed that BEA's relatively low figure of aircraft utilization is due to the short-haul character of their business. The Committee was, however, disturbed by the fact that BEA's utilization figure had been declining. The corporation explained this as due to the fact that they were flying faster aircraft, which meant that a higher proportion of time was spent on the ground. The Committee were not convinced that this was an adequate explanation and were glad to be told that better results were in sight.

BEA's operating costs are high compared with those of the other airlines; but this again is due to the fact that they run only short-haul services. The Committee agreed with the air corporation that their performance under this heading is 'quite creditable'.[2] The Committee did think, however, that there was room for improvement both in regard to aircraft utilization and maintenance costs, and they thought that with better aircraft the corporation would achieve better results under both headings.

The Select Committee was a body of serious politicians striving to be fair in appraising the activities of the air corporations. Only three out of the thirteen members are believed to have shown a special interest in nationalized industries prior to their appointment to the Committee. By their own admission the Committee were seriously handicapped by a lack of expert knowledge of economics and accounting in interpreting the reports and accounts, and the large volume of evidence submitted to them. Therefore, while in no way belittling the value of their report, it cannot be regarded as an authoritative document.

An indication of the weakness of the report is the tact that it makes no reference whatever to the rate of growth and present size of the British air corporations, either absolutely or in comparison with foreign airlines. Yet this is surely fundamental to an appraisal of their performance.

Coal

The results of the first twelve years of nationalization in the coal industry are shown in Table III overleaf.

[1] *Report*, HC 213/1959, HMSO, para. 131. [2] *Ib.*, 141.

TABLE III[1]

The Coal Industry, 1947-58

	1947	1948	1949	1950	1951	1952	1953*	1954	1955	1956	1957	1958
COAL OUTPUT (million tons)												
Deep-mined	186·5	196·7	202·7	204·1	211·3	212·7	211·8	213·6	210·2	209·9	210·1	201·5
Opencast	10·2	11·7	12·4	12·2	11·0	12·1	11·7	10·1	11·4	12·1	13·6	14·3
Total	196·8	208·5	215·1	216·3	222·3	224·8	223·5	223·6	221·6	222·0	223·6	215·8
AVERAGE MANPOWER (thousands)												
Faceworkers	288	293	296	288	287	294	293	290	289	286	278	274
Other workers	423	431	423	409	411	422	420	417	415	417	432	425
All workers	711	724	720	697	699	716	713	707	704	703	710	699
Recruitment	93	74	52	55	73	75	52	61	61	66	71	39
Wastage	66	66	69	76	63	54	62	61	67	62	65	62
Net change	+27	+ 8	−16	−21	+ 9	+22	−11	—	− 6	+3	+ 6	−23
ATTENDANCE (all workers) Shifts worked per man												
per week	4·69	4·71	4·67	4·72	4·81	4·79	4·67	4·71	4·68	4·65	4·61	4·38
per year	244	245	243	245	250	249	243	245	243	242	240	228

PRODUCTIVITY												
(tons per manshift)												
Faceworkers	2·856	2·922	3·020	3·110	3·175	3·147	3·216	3·257	3·275	3·333	3·447	3·519
All workers	1·074	1·108	1·160	1·194	1·210	1·193	1·224	1·231	1·225	1·232	1·231	1·265
Tons per man year	262	272	282	293	302	297	297	302	299	298	296	288
EARNINGS												
(per manshift)[2]	s. d.	s. d.	s. d.	s. d.	s. d.	s. d.	s. d.	s. d.	s. d.	s. d.	s. d.	s. d.
Faceworkers	36 10	41 1	43 1	44 10	48 6	54 0	56 10	59 7	63 7	69 4	75 1	78 6
All workers	28 10	33 1	34 4	35 6	38 10	43 2	45 5	47 9	50 11	55 8	60 0	62 5
COLLIERY FINANCIAL RESULTS (per ton of saleable coal)	s. d.	s. d.	s. d.	s. d.	s. d.	s. d.	s. d.	s. d.	s. d.	s. d.	s. d.	s. d.
Costs	41 3	45 7	45 0	45 5	49 2	56 9	59 2	61 11	67 3	74 5	81 6	83 11
Proceeds	40 3	47 3	47 11	47 10	51 2	57 3	61 2	63 6	68 0	77 0	82 0	85 1
Profit (+) or loss (−)[3]	−1 0	+1 8	+2 11	+2 5	+2 0	+0 6	+1 11	+1 7	+0 9	+2 7	+0 7	+1 2

[1] NCB Report, 1958, Vol. 1, p. 1.

* New definitions of manpower and attendance were introduced in 1954 and of face manpower in 1958. The relevant figures for 1953 and 1957 have been adjusted to the new basis.

[2] Including the value of allowances in kind.

[3] Operating profit or loss, i.e., before paying interest.

So far as productivity is concerned, output per manshift for faceworkers rose from $2\frac{3}{4}$ tons in 1946[1] to $3\frac{1}{2}$ tons in 1958, the highest figure ever reached in Britain and the highest in Europe. The total output per man increased from 262 tons to 288 tons in 1958. This was a recession from the highest figure of 302 tons in 1951 and 1954. The general picture shown by the Table is one of increasing output up to 1952 with a very slight falling-off until 1957. Manpower has fallen substantially since 1948, and declined continuously from 1952 until 1957, when it rose again. In 1958, the widespread fall in the demand for coal led the NBC to reduce their labour force by suspending recruitment of all adult workers other than craftsmen, except at a limited number of mines known to be short of men. The average earnings of faceworkers have more than doubled during the decade and the same is true of all workers in the industry. Despite large increases of prices and wages, British coal is still the cheapest in Western Europe for comparable qualities.[2]

Conditions of employment in the mines have improved notably. The standard of safety has risen, and in 1958 there were fewer fatal accidents than ever before in the recorded history of the industry.[3] In 1958, however, there was a substantial increase in the number of persons injured. There are now over 350 medical centres compared with eight in the whole industry in 1946. Pithead baths have increased from 366 in 1946 to 718 in 1958, with a capacity sufficient for ninety-five per cent of the men.[4]

No one with any knowledge of the coal industry could expect nationalization to produce a spectacular or sudden improvement in the deplorable condition of the industry. A much longer period than twelve years will be required before the backward technological state of the mines can be overcome and the embittered industrial relations be replaced by a more constructive and co-operative relationship. Both these changes are bound to need sustained efforts over a prolonged period. It cannot be claimed that either of these two objectives has been attained during the first ten years of nationalization, but it is undoubtedly true that a good start has been made and that substantial progress has taken place in both directions.

ELECTRICITY

Three major problems confronted the nationalized electricity supply industry from 1947 onwards, apart from the need to reorganize the in-

[1] This was well below the pre-war level of 2·97 tons in 1939. See W. H. B. Court: *Coal*, p. 114.

[2] *Public Enterprise* (Labour Party), pp. 10–11. [3] NCB Report for 1958, Vol. I, p. 42.

[4] *NCB Report* for 1958, Vol. I, p. 40.

dustry, merge the 560 authorized undertakings in twelve Area Electricity Boards and integrate the generating stations under a single authority. First, it had to overcome the serious shortage of generating plant—estimated at fifteen to twenty per cent—which had arisen during the Second World War. Second, it had to meet a vast increase in the industrial demand for electrical power during the post-war years. Demand leapt up by more than a third between 1946 and 1950. Third, it had to cope with an electrical manufacturing industry which was unable to deliver quickly enough the generating plant needed by the supply authorities. The success of the Central Electricity Authority in overcoming these difficulties is one of the brightest features of Britain's post-war effort.

The progress of the industry can be judged by the following figures[1] which relate only to England and Wales:

Annual Sales of Electricity increased from 32,669 million units in 1948, (the year preceding nationalization) to 84,497 million units in 1959, a rise of 160 per cent.

New plant brought into service from 1948 to 1957 amounted to an aggregate capacity of 11,878,000 kW sent out (114·6 per cent). The annual amount of plant brought into commission in 1947 was 340,000 kW s.o. and in 1957 1,788,000 kW s.o. This was two-and-a-half times as great as the highest figure for any pre-war year, and five times as great as in 1947.

Generating capacity. Installed capacity more than doubled from 11,680,000 kW in 1948 to 25,409,000 in 1959. A similar rise took place in maximum output capacity, which increased from 11,271,000 kW sent out in 1948 to 23,400,000 in 1959.

The average thermal efficiency of the steam generating stations was 20·91 per cent in 1948 and 26·10 per cent in 1959. The thermal efficiency was hampered for several years after the war by a government regulation limiting the size of turbo-generators for use in this country to relatively small sets. These are less efficient than the larger sets which the Central Electricity Generating Board is now free to order; but most of the generating sets installed during the years 1955–60 are of the smaller size required by the regulations. A large saving of cost has been effected by the improved average thermal efficiency. If average thermal efficiency had remained at the 1948 figure, the additional coal consumed would have cost nearly £200 million in 1958–9. We are still below the US standard, but this is partly due to the causes already mentioned. In

[1] All the figures are taken from the Annual Reports of BEA, CEA, and CEGB.

1959 the Central Electricity Authority's twenty stations with the highest thermal efficiencies ranged from 28·59 per cent to 33·04 per cent, with an average of 30·30 per cent.

Loss of generating capacity due to breakdowns, overhaul of plant and other causes dropped from 13·5 per cent of total capacity in 1948-9 to 7·8 per cent in 1959. There has been continuous improvement during the past decade.

The load factor (i.e. the amount sent out expressed as a percentage of what would have been sent out if maximum demand had continued throughout the year) rose from 42·7 per cent in 1948 to 46·5 per cent in 1959.[1]

Productivity. The number of employees per 1,000 kW sold has dropped from 4·1 in 1948 to 2·6 in 1957, a reduction of thirty-seven per cent. The average number of 'generation employees' per 1,000 kW of output capacity has declined from 2·74 in 1948 to 1·63 in 1959, a reduction of greater magnitude.

Prices rose from 1·144 pence per unit in 1948 to 1·554 pence in 1959, an increase of thirty-four per cent. The average price of the greatly increased output of electricity supplied to consumers in 1957 was only forty-four per cent higher than that prevailing in 1938, despite an increase in the price of coal of over 300 per cent.

The performance of the nationalized electricity industry since 1947 is a remarkable achievement which compares favourably with that of any other industry operating under like conditions.

The development of nuclear generation of electricity is one of the most exciting chapters in contemporary history. An ambitious programme, of which Calder Hall was the first decisive step, aims at ensuring that some ten per cent of the total units of electricity sent out in 1965-6 will come from power stations based on nuclear energy. This great scheme involves the Atomic Energy Authority, the Ministry of Power, the Treasury, the Central Electricity Generating Board (formerly the Central Electricity Authority), and the consortia of firms which are constructing the stations.

The rôle of the Central Electricity Generating Board as the planning and operating body is crucial. It is impossible to believe that the programme now under way, which has put Great Britain in the forefront in the peaceful use of atomic energy, would have been carried out on

[1] These figures are adjusted so as to base the calculation on certain assumptions about the weather and the availability of adequate generating plant. See Report 1958-9, CEGB, paras. 277-9.

anything like the present scale or speed if the electricity supply industry had not been nationalized, and if primary responsibility for developing atomic energy had not been recognized as requiring public enterprise and public finance.

GAS

The progress of the gas industry since nationalization has been much less striking than that of electricity and is in some respects unsatisfactory.

On the manufacturing side the most important development has been the closing of small, inefficient gasworks and the concentration of production in larger and more modern works. This was one of the major aims of nationalization and it has been accomplished rapidly and extensively. When the industry was taken over there were 1,050 separate works in which gas was manufactured: by 1958 the number was 536—a reduction of almost one half.[1]

In consequence, production is on the whole more efficient. The average yield of gas per ton of coal carbonized rose from 71·6 therms in 1950-1[2] to 76·7 therms in 1959. The thermal output of gas, coke, breeze and tar to the thermal input of coal and oil rose from seventy-one in 1948 to 77·4 in 1958. There was a substantial economy in the consumption of coal effected since vesting day. In 1957 this was equivalent to 2½ million tons for the year and the cumulative figure was nearly 12 million tons.

The figures for the trading activities of the industry are given in Table IV. These show that the number of domestic and commercial consumers has been rising slightly, while the number of industrial consumers and public authorities using gas has been declining. But the total amount of gas used by domestic consumers has fallen, despite the increased number of them. This may be due partly to more efficient apparatus and partly to the greater use of electricity in the home. Whatever the cause, it is a disturbing feature of the position, having regard to the fact that one half of all the gas sold goes to domestic consumers. The industrial trend is moving the other way: a smaller number of industrial users are consuming more. Only among commercial consumers—mostly shops and offices—is there a fairly steady increase in both the number of consumers and the amount of gas taken by them.

It is unsatisfactory that, after carrying out a large programme of modernization and concentration of production in more efficient gas works, and greatly improving the distribution system, the industry should show disappointing results on the sales side. More than £500 million have been spent in capital developments during the past decade,

[1] *Gas Council Annual Report*, 1957-8, para. 327.

[2] *Gas Council Report*, 1952-3, para. 19. This is the earliest figure available.

TABLE IV[1]

The Gas Industry 1950–9

Year ending March 31	1950	1951	1952	1953	1954	1955	1956	1957	1958	1959
Numbers of Consumers (thousands)										
Domestic	11,151·0	11,223·3	11,366·8	11,517·2	11,725·9	11,915·3	12,035·5	12,125·7	12,180·4	12,177 6
Industrial	119·8	114·1	111·8	107·0	105·7	101·9	98·3	95·4	93·2	92·4
Commercial	550·8	583·9	592·2	601·9	596·2	603·0	616·2	615·7	617·0	615·6
Public Administration	53·2	52·1	50·0	47·2	47·0	44·8	42·2	39·1	38·8	38·3
Total	11,874·8	11,979·4	12,120·8	12,273·3	12,474·8	12,665·0	12,792·2	12,875·9	12·929·4	12,923·9
Gas sold (million therms)										
Domestic	—	1,391·7	1,383·2	1,366·0	1,347·5	1,378·5	1,350·3	1,328·6	1,326·3	1,308·3
Industrial	571·2	589·6	634·1	639·1	659·0	720·0	751·2	749·6	788·7	769·6
Commercial	—	310·2	330·5	353·5	346·3	375·7	394·6	387·0	398·6	400·1
Public Administration	—	56·6	52·8	51·2	50·0	52·1	45·3	42·4	42·5	42·0
Public Lighting ...	48·8	53·3	51·6	50·6	48·4	46·6	42·8	38·5	34·6	31·5
Total ...	2,130·9	2,401·4	2,452·2	2,460·4	2,451·2	2,572·9	2,584·2	2,546·1	2,590·7	2,551·5
Revenue from Gas sold (£m.)										
Domestic	—	85·8	92·9	101·6	104·6	109·2	115·7	123·5	131·2	133·6
Industrial	22·06	23·4	27·6	31·1	33·5	36·8	41·7	44·5	49·3	49·4
Commercial	—	17·1	19·6	23·1	23·6	25·8	29·4	30·8	33·6	34·3
Public Administration	—	2·8	2·9	3·1	3·2	3·4	3·2	3·2	3·4	3·4
Public Lighting ...	1·63	2·0	2·1	2·4	2·5	2·5	2·5	2·4	2·3	2·2
Total ...	111·4	131·1	145·1	161·3	167·4	177·7	192·5	204·4	219·8	222·9
Average Revenue from Gas sold (Pence per therm)	12·55	13·00	14·20	15·73	16·39	16·58	17·87	19·27	20·35	20·97
Total Employees ...	140,611	143,506	147,937	147,461	145,031	143,378	141,918	138,742	136,379	132,576

[1] The figures are taken from the Annual Reports of the Gas Council.

and consumers in many parts of the country are getting a much better gas supply than prior to nationalization, both as regards pressure and quality.

The relative disparity in the prices of gas and electricity may go some way towards explaining the difficulties the gas industry has encountered in selling gas in the home. The average price of gas sold for domestic consumption rose between 1950 and 1957 from 14·8d. to 22·34d. a therm, an increase of fifty-one per cent. During the same period the average price of electricity supplied to the domestic consumer increased from 1·346d. to 1·581d. a unit, a rise of only seventeen per cent. Thus, the price of gas increased three times as much as that of electricity.[1]

Mr I. M. D. Little contends that the Electricity Boards have been selling electricity to domestic consumers far below its economic price; in consequence, electric heating appliances are extensively used although gas is far more efficient for the purpose of space heating. Writing in 1953, he asserted that for continuous heating the use of gas and coke was twelve per cent cheaper in *real resources* than electricity and coal, but 12½ per cent dearer to the householder owing to the distorted price policy of the Electricity Boards. For intermittent heating gas and coke was seventeen per cent cheaper in real resources but thirty-six per cent more costly to the householder. 'The householder', he averred, 'is firmly persuaded by present prices to adopt forms of heating which are not in the national interest.'[2] For cooking and water-heating the divergencies were much less marked.

These divergencies were, in Mr Little's view, mainly caused by the Electricity Boards selling electricity to domestic consumers below its true cost. The figures given in support of this showed that for heating purposes electricity was sold at a figure of twenty-two per cent below cost for continuous heating, eight per cent for semi-continuous heating, and fifty-five per cent for intermittent heating.

This situation was not brought about by nationalization; it existed long before the Second World War. It arose because the electricity supply industry has a virtual monopoly of the domestic consumers' demand for lighting and small power units. The Electricity Boards use their monopolistic position to supply electricity at uneconomic rates for other uses in which they compete with gas, such as cooking and space heating. The gas industry does not enjoy a monopolistic position regarding any of the domestic uses of gas, for cooking, refrigeration, water heating, and room heating can all be provided by other means.[3]

[1] *Gas Council Reports*, 1948-50, paras. 304-6; 1955, para. 329; 1957-8, para. 169; R. Kelf-Cohen: *Nationalization in Britain*, p. 119.

[2] I. M. D. Little: *The Price of Fuel*, p. 88. [3] *Ib.*, p. 96.

Mr Little published his book at a time when Britain was suffering from what seemed likely to be a chronic shortage of coal. That state of affairs no longer prevails and there is now (1959) a surplus of coal at current prices. But his argument was not mainly based on the need to save coal but rather on avoiding unnecessary expenditure of capital in order to provide domestic consumers with supplies of electricity at heavily subsidized rates for needs which could be more economically met by gas or coke.[1] This objective remains of fundamental importance; and to it we can add the aim of enabling the gas industry to secure its proper share of the domestic users' market to which it is entitled on economic and technical grounds. To make this possible, the prices of electricity would have to be adjusted so as to reflect true costs. 'Nationalization', remarked Mr Little, 'undoubtedly provides the ideal framework within which a proper integration of costs and prices could easily be arranged. . . . But the framework has not been used in this way.'[2] This is a matter which could and should be put right without delay. Until it is remedied, the gas industry is likely to remain in an unfavourable competitive position and to suffer accordingly.

THE VERDICT ABOUT EFFICIENCY

The truest answer that can be given to the question about the performance of the nationalized industries since they were taken over, is that each one of them is undoubtedly in a better condition than it would have been under private enterprise or, as was the case with gas and electricity, divided between private and municipal ownership. By this I mean that its operating efficiency is higher, its equipment more up-to-date, and its future prospects brighter than they would have been if the industry had not been nationalized.

I do not assert that the nationalized industries have been or are being conducted at the highest possible level of efficiency. Such a claim cannot be made in respect of any industrial or commercial undertaking, or indeed of any institution whatever. I have drawn attention again and again in the course of this book to the shortcomings and defects, largely inherited from the past, from which the railways and the coal industry are suffering. But they would suffer from the maladies which afflict them much more acutely if they had remained in private ownership. This is certainly true of the technological backwardness of the mines, which was partly due to insufficient capital investment over a prolonged period, and partly due to lack of research; and the same can be said of the obsolete state of British railways. The embittered industrial relations engendered

[1] I. M. D. Little: *The Price of Fuel*, p. 78. [2] *Ib.*, p. 97.

during the inter-war years among the miners were largely due to these causes combined with severe and prolonged unemployment; and they would have reached a state of chronic distrust and ever-deepening suspicion between employer and worker if the mismanagement of the mines under private enterprise had continued.

British railways have suffered to a specially severe extent from the capital starvation and hardening of the managerial arteries which occurred during the inter-war period. But they also face difficulties which are confronted by almost every railway system in the world, and which are neither peculiar to Britain nor the result of public ownership. As Sir Brian Robertson has observed: 'On railways everywhere there is a malaise brought about largely by road and air competition and often disguised by subsidies in one form or another.' In this country there is neither subsidy nor camouflage.[1]

In asserting that the nationalized industries are more efficient under public ownership than they were under private enterprise, or would be if they had remained in the private sector, or divided between private and municipal undertakers, I do not wish to imply that all is going well with them and that we need not concern ourselves seriously about their future. That is far from being the case. Substantial improvements could and should be made in the running of the undertakings, both by management and by labour.

ADVERSE FACTORS

One cause for concern is the atmosphere of latent or open hostility towards the public corporations to be observed in much discussion in the press and on the platform. The late Sir Hubert Houldsworth, a former chairman of the NCB had this in mind when he declared that 'the real danger to efficiency in a nationalized industry . . . arises far more from the limelight of public criticism under which the work has to be carried out—criticisms in the press and in speeches of mistakes or of actions which in many cases would pass unnoticed under private enterprise'—than from the absence of the profit motive.[2] Criticism which is well-intentioned and constructive is usually welcome and helpful; but malevolent criticism which seizes on every weakness and shortcoming in order to discredit the institution, while overlooking or taking for granted any favourable achievement, is intensely discouraging. Professor Edwards and Mr Townsend have protested that a State undertaking

[1] Sir Brian Robertson: *The British Transport System*. A lecture delivered to the Royal United Service Institution, February 1, 1956 (published by the BTC), p. 17.

[2] Houldsworth and others: *Efficiency in the Nationalized Industries* (1952), p. 1.

should not be required 'to operate in a glasshouse, subject to detailed day-to-day criticisms to which no private firm would be subject', because this conflicts with the pursuit of efficiency and economy.[1]

Mr Harold Watkinson, Minister of Transport and Civil Aviation in the last Conservative Government, was presumably thinking of this when he remarked in a public speech that the nation has a split mind about the nationalized industries: it wants them to succeed and yet is always running them down. He urged the people to take an interest in their business prospects and their chances of development rather than in their political past.[2]

To ask for less malevolence and disparagement in public discussion does not mean, however, that the public corporations should not be prepared to accept all the informed criticism and constructive proposals which can be brought to bear on the nationalized industries. Hitherto they have not always been willing to do so. Mr Herbert Morrison has revealed that when he was Lord President in the Labour Government he urged the chairmen of the boards to establish a common efficiency unit which would have been a collective organ of the corporations themselves. It would have acted as a body of industrial consultants to look into problems of management, costing, finance, organization, and so forth. It would have been called in whenever required by the board of a public corporation and would have reported to them. The chairmen rejected the idea on the ground that it was a reflection on the ability and efficiency of the boards.[3] Mr Morrison has explained that he did not wish to impose on the boards an external commission of industrial investigation, but he considered that 'some efficiency organization is necessary'.[4]

Lord Citrine, when chairman of BEA, thought there were strong objections to what he called 'a super body which could survey and advise upon the organization, administration and operation of the nationalized industries as a whole'. The most important of these was that it would undermine the authority and sense of responsibility of the board, and create a lack of confidence in the board and their staff. He was not

[1] R. S. Edwards and H. Townsend: *Business Enterprise. Its Growth and Organization*, p. 515.

[2] *The Times*, June 1, 1956, p. 7. The speech was made at a luncheon of the Executives Association of Great Britain.

[3] *Evidence to Select Committee on Nationalized Industries*. HC 1952-3/235, Q. 383, 401, 403, 409, 425, 485, 494.

[4] Herbert Morrison: *Government and Parliament*, pp. 274-5. A more far-reaching proposal was made by Mr Ernest Davies, MP. (*Problems of Public Ownership*, 1952, p. 15) that the common efficiency unit should be placed under a non-departmental Minister such as the Lord President who would have power to set it in motion.

averse, however, to a nationalized industry calling on the services of industrial consultants if they wished to do so.[1]

This touchiness about independent investigation by experts is a sign of weakness which seems to stem from a defensive attitude. Far from undermining confidence in the board it could positively increase it. The main argument in favour of a common efficiency organ is not that it would need or have larger powers than an outside firm of consultants but that the nationalized industries have certain common problems which do not exist in private enterprise; that the scale of their operations is much larger; that a body of specialized advisers might evolve acceptable criteria for determining the efficiency of these industries; and that they might be better able to assist the public corporations than consultants accustomed to the smaller undertakings with different objectives in the private sector.

The notion that if a public corporation were to avail themselves of the services of a common efficiency unit this would reflect on the abilities of the governing board and their staff is a curious one. Whenever a public corporation or a joint stock company call in a firm of industrial consultants they are saying in effect: 'Give us the benefit of your advice. Your outlook is fresher and more detached than ours. You have expert knowledge of a special kind drawn from a wide experience, and you may be able to detect errors and to suggest improvements which have not occurred to our board and the management.' No more and no less than this would be implied if the nationalized industries agreed to use the services of a common efficiency unit, or if they were subject to the investigations of an efficiency audit commission, which I proposed many years ago.

Indeed, the NCB were going much further than this when they appointed the Fleck Committee to review the organization of the coal industry. The Fleck Committee, as we have seen, made some severe criticisms of the National Coal Board and their methods of managing the industry, which presumably led members of the board to offer their resignations to the Minister. If a public corporation are prepared to go so far, it is difficult to see what reasonable objection they can have to a common efficiency unit.

A third cause for concern arises from the conservative attitude both of management and labour which still persists in some of the nationalized industries. Electricity supply is a forward-looking industry in every sense of the term; the airways corporations are among the world's leading air lines and have pioneered many innovations. Gas supply can scarcely be described as in an expanding phase of its development, al-

[1] Lord Citrine: *Problems of Nationalized Industry*, in 29, Public Administration (Winter, 1951), pp. 325–6.

though it is undergoing fundamental technical changes. Coalmining and the railways are facing much more difficult problems than these newer industries; and the most serious of them is how to overcome the dead-weight of tradition which obstructs or slows down the prompt acceptance of necessary changes in regard to technology, labour practices, redundancy, price policy, productivity, etc.

There are able and vigorous men at work in these industries, with new ideas and new techniques to offer. But the acceptance of innovation depends in large measure on the outlook and adaptability of large numbers of people occupying positions at all levels. A sympathetic American observer has remarked that if the National Union of Mineworkers and its membership do not accept the changes which the engineers recommend, the outlook for modernization is dim indeed. The attitude of the mineworkers is by no means the only factor in setting the pace of technological change; but a co-operative attitude on their part towards change is a necessary condition of a successful investment programme. On the record to date, Mr Baldwin remarks, the slow rate of introducing new methods and machinery and of disseminating them widely throughout the industry has been due at least as much to the cautiousness and conservatism of managerial personnel as to opposition from the labour force. He recognizes that since nationalization there has been a significant change in the pace of technical improvement in the coal industry; but he is not convinced that technological change is taking place with all the energy that might reasonably be expected.[1]

The same thing applies *mutatis mutandis* to the railways. The British Railways Productivity Council was set up in May 1955. The BTC reported in 1956 that much progress had been made in studying the problems involved in achieving greater productive efficiency; and also in applying work study methods to particular fields of work. The Productivity Council aims at applying work study techniques to all spheres of railway work in order to ensure the most efficient use of manpower, equipment and materials. About forty work study schemes had been implemented on the railway system by the end of 1956; many more schemes have been authorized since then.

Unfortunately, reported the BTC in 1956, 'for reasons that go back into railway history' the application of work study principles on the railways themselves has not made the progress which it has received in such ancillary fields as civil engineering, signal engineering, depots concerned with motive power, wagon repair, outdoor machinery, carriage cleaning, marine work and stores.[2] In their report for 1957, however,

[1] George B. Baldwin: *Beyond Nationalization* (Harvard UP 1955), p. 275.
[2] *British Transport Commission Report for 1956*, Vol. I, paras. 53-5.

the commission were able to report an increasing awareness of the benefits to be derived from the application of work study throughout their undertaking.[1]

INCENTIVES

Any discussion of adaptability and readiness to accept change eventually leads to the question of incentives.

Professors Sargant Florence and Gilbert Walker allege that the administrators of nationalized industries are particularly prone to the diseases of security, conservatism, and procrastination.[2] To combat these diseases they should be required to show that their undertakings satisfy appropriate tests of efficiency applied to such criteria as productivity, economy in staff, industrial morale and goodwill, public satisfaction. In particular, these writers criticize the tendency of nationalized industries to meet every increase of costs with a rise in price and a reliance on their monopoly to yield the necessary increase of revenue. They would require a public corporation to submit to the most stringent inquiry by an independent tribunal able to assess the efficiency of the undertaking before it is permitted to raise its prices. They cite one example in support of this statement. It relates to an increase of railway freight rates which the BTC were permitted to make in 1949-50 without any inquiry to see whether the efficiency of the railways could be improved as an alternative way of meeting higher costs. They also stated that only the British Transport Commission need apply for consent; 'the Coal Board, for example, can raise its prices without the unpleasant necessity of asking anybody's permission.'[3]

These sweeping generalizations will not withstand close examination. The facts do not show that those in charge of nationalized industries are specially liable to the maladies mentioned. No one can seriously accuse BOAC, BEA, the Electricity Boards, the AEA, or the BBC of conservatism, procrastination, or an excessive desire to play for safety. Even the Post Office, that very old nationalized industry, is a most progressive institution. On the contrary, it was under private ownership and management that the coal mining industry and the railways became obsolescent, conservative and restrictive. It is only under nationalization that they have begun to shed these characteristics.

Again, it is not true that nationalized industries invariably try to pass on increased costs in the form of higher prices. It has not occurred in the case of electricity, and in the gas industry not all the increased costs have

[1] *Report for 1957*, vol. I, paras. 35-8.

[2] Sargant Florence and Gilbert Walker: 'Efficiency under Nationalization and its Measurement', in *Problems of Nationalized Industry*, ed. W. A. Robson, p. 198.

[3] *Ib.*, p. 204. See also Sargant Florence: *Industry and the State*, pp. 140-44.

been met by higher charges. Nor is it true that the National Coal Board is free to fix their prices as they wish. They have always been subject to ministerial consent; and the level of prices in all the nationalized industries has been strongly restrained by the Government on several occasions. It is virtually certain that if the nationalized industries had been under unregulated private ownership, prices would have risen much more steeply than they have done since 1946.

Nevertheless, while rejecting the allegation that the public corporations are slow, sluggish and unenterprising in their outlook one cannot deny the possibility that these diseases could infect them. The same is true of the dangers of which Lord Salter warns us: undue centralization of management, resulting in inelasticity and inflexibility, excessive staffs, an inability to resist unreasonable demands from trade unions when the possibility of bankruptcy no longer threatens the undertaking. He also stresses the need to replace adequately the powerful incentives of commercial gain and loss.[1] These are dangers of which we must be aware if we are to avoid them, as I believe we can.

One of the least recognized changes resulting from nationalization is that the industries affected have been brought into the limelight of public opinion. The British press was formerly not in the least interested in the economic condition of the railways or the coalmines except on rare occasions when a strike occurred or a stoppage of work was threatened. In general the newspapers confined their interest to accidents involving loss of life, holiday train services, and similar matters. The general well-being of the basic industries; their technological condition; prices and profits; their ability to meet consumer needs; their competitive position; labour relations; capital development—all these vital matters were ignored by the national daily and evening press. Today, these matters are regarded by the press as questions of public concern, and as opportunities for criticizing the public corporations. The same thing is to some extent true of Parliament. The House of Commons takes an infinitely greater interest in the nationalized industries than it took in those same industries prior to nationalization.

This enhanced interest by the organs of public opinion is the first safeguard against the maladies which may afflict large-scale, publicly owned, monopolistic undertakings. An alert and informed public opinion is the best guarantee against sloth, inertia, complacency, or lack of initiative.

In appraising nationalized industries it is pertinent to inquire how intensely what Lord Salter calls 'the pervasive, intimate and powerful

[1] Rt. Hon. Sir Arthur Salter: The Crux of Nationalization, in *Problems of Nationalized Industry*, ed. W. A. Robson, pp. 228-37.

compulsions of the profit and loss system'[1] operated in these and similar industries under private ownership.

The coalmining industry was our worst-managed major industry during the twentieth century. How else can we explain the technological backwardness of so large a proportion of the collieries; the lack of adequate capital development; the absence of planning and of research; the catastrophic fall in the relative wage position of the miner; the almost static average output per man shift; the suspicion and mistrust which poisoned relations between owners and organized labour; the disastrous coal strike and general strike of 1926, with its heritage of bitterness; the loss of overseas markets; the recourse to legal restriction introduced by the Coal Mines Act of 1930, with its 'quotas' which could be bought and sold.

The railways also did not display the qualities which are alleged to characterize private enterprise. Their principal efforts during the period between the two world wars were directed towards restricting competition on the roads by opposing the licensing of road haulage and road passenger services: and to acquiring interests in competing motor-bus companies and domestic airlines. The 'powerful compulsions of the profit and loss system' failed to induce the railway companies to provide us with decent railway terminals, up-to-date stations, modern rolling stock, or faster services on most of the lines.

These examples illustrate the phenomenon that in modern industry the divorce between the functions of ownership and management is often so complete that the profit motive has been reduced sometimes to negligible proportions.

The creation or encouragement of effective incentives in nationalized industries is a problem of supreme importance. But it cannot be claimed that a satisfactory solution to the problem had been found, in the industries which have now been nationalized, during the time they were operating under private enterprise. Whether under public ownership or private enterprise, the great bulk of the managers consist of salaried officers. There is no reason why the substantial salaries paid in nationalized industries to the chief executives and members of governing boards should prove insufficient to evoke the energetic and intense efforts which are required from men in those positions, assuming that they are capable of making such efforts.

Financial remuneration will seldom by itself be the spur to the highest achievements. I do not claim to know the answer to the problem of incentives in large scale industry. Much research and experimentation will be required before we really know how to unleash the secret springs

[1] Rt. Hon. Sir Arthur Salter: *Problems of Nationalized Industry*, p. 231.

of action on which so much depends. The public service motive will undoubtedly count for much—if we can awaken it. And so, too, will the stimulus of social esteem, if we can attach it to work in the nationalized industries. All one can say at this stage is that the question of incentives at all levels must be given a foremost place on the agenda for a very long time to come.

CONCLUSION

In conclusion, we may recall that the Trades Union Congress in a report on the public control of industry mentioned six objectives as constituting the purpose of public ownership: These were:—First, providing the best possible service at the least real cost to the community. This would be brought about by making additional capital available for development, obtaining the advantages of large scale without the evils of monopoly, and changing the attitudes of the workpeople. Second, improving the wages and conditions of employment for the workpeople. Third, attaining a higher degree of equality, because the interest on compensation stock is less than the dividends payable under private enterprise, and capital on public undertakings can be raised at a lower rate of interest. Fourth, ensuring increased public control over the economic system. Fifth, maintaining full and stable employment. This can be achieved by extending the sphere of public investment so as to counteract the instability of private investment, which is a principal cause of fluctuations in employment. And lastly, increasing industrial democracy by means of greater opportunities for joint consultation.[1]

If we ask how far these objectives have been realized, the answer is somewhat as follows. Nationalization has made much larger amounts of capital available for investment than would otherwise have been forthcoming and the rates of interest are considerably lower. It cannot be said, however, that the best possible service at the least real cost to the community is being provided by the coal industry or by the railways, partly because the process of modernization and re-equipment is not sufficiently advanced, and partly because of the attitudes of the workpeople. A much closer approximation to this goal has been achieved by the electricity and gas industries, by the BBC, by the Atomic Energy Authority and by the airways corporations, although the performance of BOAC is gravely handicapped by the attitude of the maintenance staff at London Airport towards redundancy.

Wages and conditions of employment, while not uniformly satisfactory throughout the nationalized industries, are almost certainly better than they would otherwise have been. Much higher profits would have

[1] TUC Report, 1950, App. D, para. 4.

been made by commercial companies than has been paid by way of interest on the stock of the public corporations, except in the case of the railways. But this has had a negligible effect in promoting a greater degree of equality, since the sums involved are comparatively small.

The existence of a substantial public sector covering the basic industries providing fuel, power and transport ensures a higher degree of public control over the whole economy. This control has been used in the recent past to counteract inflation; it could be used to assist in maintaining a high and stable level of employment. The attitudes of the workpeople have not, I believe, been changed in any fundamental sense by nationalization, though a good deal of the bitterness which had accumulated among the miners for several decades before 1946 has at least softened. Industrial democracy has been fostered in many ways; but there are no clear signs of the growth of a spirit of public service among the rank and file of the employees in any one of the nationalized industries. Yet among the staff, higher executives and members of the boards of the public corporations one finds plenty of evidence of enthusiasm for the work, a genuine solicitude for the public interest, and the kind of dedicated attitude which distinguishes the true public servant in every walk of life from the man who merely earns his living in a job.

APPENDIX TO CHAPTER XV

The following Tables give the annual deficits and surpluses for each of the major public corporations running nationalized industries:

TABLE V

National Coal Board: Annual Surpluses and Deficits 1947–58
Source: Annual Reports

	£1 *m.*	
	Deficit	*Surplus*
1947	23·3	
1948		1·7
1949		9·5
1950		8·3
1951	1·8	
1952	8·2	
1953		0·4
1954	3·6	
1955	19·6	
1956		12·8
1957	5·3	
1958	3·5	
Accumulated deficit	32·6	

TABLE VI

British Transport Commission: Annual Surpluses and Deficits 1948–58

	£1 m.	
	Deficit	*Surplus*
1948	4·7	
1949	20·8	
1950	14·1	
1951		0·1
1952		8·0[1]
1953		4·2
1954	11·9	
1955	30·6	
1956		3·1
1957		4·6[2]
1958		28·1
Accumulated deficit		90·2

Notes:

[1] After bringing to account £3·5 m. in respect of road haulage sundry stores and acquisition expenses previously charged to revenue.

[2] In respect of activities other than British Railways.

London Transport: Annual Financial Results[1] 1948–57

		£m.	
	Net Deficit	*Net Receipts*	*Surplus on Deficit after contribution to two Central Charges*
1948		7·4	+1·9
1949		5·2	—0·3
1950		3·1	—2·4
1951	0·1		—5·6
1952		2·3	—3·2
1953		2·0	—3·5
1954		3·8	—1·7
1955		5·0	—0·5
1956		4·5	—1·0
1957		5·7	+0·2
Accumulated deficit			£16·1 m.

Notes:

[1] The receipts for the years 1948–55 have been corrected to allow for income derived from advertising.

[2] Estimated at £5·5 m.: BTC Annual Report 1956, Vol. I, para. 287.

Q

TABLE VII

CEA & Electricity Boards: Annual Surpluses and Deficits 1948–58 (before Transfers to Reserves)

£1,000

Area Boards	1948–9	1949–50	1950–1	1951–2	1952–3	1953–4	1954–5	1955–6	1956–7	1957–8	1958–9	*Total*
London	1,145	1,901	1,137	499	1,465	1,160	857	1,059	827	1,456	3,629	15,135
South Eastern	172	423	216	− 97	175	−106	709	428	438	−807	753	2,304
Southern	382	920	826	67	106	604	873	775	780	−117	1,660	6,876
South Western	−106	1	− 76	−142	−149	98	437	506	337	228	612	1,746
Eastern	−355	434	96	128	−412	−195	58	1,056	152	806	3,273	5,041
East Midlands	748	873	407	−826	−311	241	526	308	26	− 63	1,860	3,789
Midlands	628	697	− 6	−661	−642	381	1,434	668	−282	−643	119	1,693
South Wales	318	451	255	324	356	193	−179	−160	134	520	487	2,699
Merseyside & North Wales	141	359	312	105	197	539	625	141	− 97	−146	129	2,402
Yorkshire	487	1,331	671	−196	−113	269	194	− 78	−442	925	1,166	4,214
North Eastern	401	672	110	−162	33	419	493	366	791	324	872	4,319
North Western	393	618	−138	224	671	1,022	902	219	206	447	2,012	6,476
South East Scotland	409	467	239	−114	179	236	133	Transferred to South of Scotland Electricity Board				1,549
South West Scotland	379	154	−106	−482	−101	315	156					315
Total Area Boards	5,142	9,300	3,942	−1,333	1,456	5,177	7,218	5,288	2,869	2,930	16,572	58,561
Central Elect. Generating Board	−749	−2,137	2,635	4,252	5,824	8,012	11,576	6,924	8,849	13,132	10,763	69,081
Total	4,393	7,163	6,577	2,919	7,280	13,189	18,794	12,212	11,719	16,062	27,335	127,642

TABLE VIII

Gas Boards: Annual Surpluses and Deficits 1949–59 (After Transfers to and from Taxation Reserves)

£1,000

Area Boards	1949–50*	1950–1	1951–2	1952–3	1953–4	1954–5	1955–6	1956–7	1957–8	1958–9	*Total*
Scottish ...	−284	154	35	−270	−168	389	−321	370	51	−1,000	−1,044
Northern ...	40	11	32	261	24	0	−344	550	428	383	1,385
North Western	1	−351	−511	159	992	1,028	100	787	532	283	3,020
North Eastern	7	− 53	− 31	101	166	190	160	311	14	322	1,187
East Midlands	143	281	274	279	148	78	87	367	539	646	2,842
West Midlands	168	151	313	310	532	−104	171	450	651	280	2,922
Wales ...	60	182	106	124	94	127	25	68	134	269	1,209
Eastern ...	−247	−169	290	184	− 17	160	56	118	47	289	711
North Thames	556	314	186	567	466	−156	−309	260	290	317	2,491
South Eastern	213	589	330	298	−146	701	929	235	29	1336	4,514
Southern ...	− 98	125	131	132	7	21	23	140	−205	199	475
South Western	−570	272	287	128	12	38	− 47	13	−209	−120	−196
Total Area Boards ...	− 11	1,506	1,441	2,273	2,112	2,473	532	3,668	2,321	3,203	19,518

* Eleven months

TABLE IX

BOAC: Annual Surpluses and Deficits 1947-59 (After paying interest on capital)

£1,000

	Deficit	*Surplus*	*Exchequer Grant*
1947–8*	7,581		6,560
1948–9*	7,805		5,750
1949–50	7,791		6,350
1950–1	4,565		6,000
1951–2		274	1,500
1952–3	838		—
1953–4		1,065	—
1954–5		261	—
1955–6		117	
1956–7		303	
1957–8	2,839		
1958–9	5,174		
Accumulated deficit	14,681		

* Includes British South American Airways Corporation

TABLE X

British European Airways: Annual Surpluses and Deficits 1946-59 (After paying interest on capital)

£1,000

	Deficit	*Surplus*	*Exchequer Grant*
1946–7*	2,157		
1947–8	3,573		3,400
1948–9	2,763		2,150
1949–50	1,363		1,535
1950–1	976		1,000
1951–2	1,423		1,400
1952–3	1,459		1,250
1953–4	1,773		1,500
1954–5		63	1,000
1955–6		603	
1956–7		216	
1957–8		1,054	
1958–9		223	
Accumulated deficit	13,321		

* Eight months only

In all cases the figures have been obtained from the annual reports of the public corporations.

CHAPTER XVI

Public Ownership

IN the last chapter an attempt was made to assess the performance of the nationalized industries. The general result of that assessment was that the industries are in a substantially better condition from most points of view than they would have been if they had remained in private hands. At the same time it is clear that the performance of the nationalized industries is defective in certain respects which have received detailed consideration in the preceding pages. Moreover, it would be foolish to claim that the deplorably backward condition of the coal industry and the railways when they were taken over by the State has been overcome, though progress has been made in modernizing the equipment, the management and the outlook of these industries.

Yet despite these considerable achievements the nationalization movement appears to have lost its impetus. Profound changes have taken place on the subject in the Labour movement. Some of the most influential thinkers no longer regard public enterprise as a basic aim of socialism; and one powerful section of opinion doubts whether nationalization is the most effective way of increasing efficiency or productivity. In this chapter I shall outline these trends of thought and examine alternative policies which have been proposed.

MR GAITSKELL'S VIEWS

Mr Hugh Gaitskell, as long ago as 1953, writing in *The Political Quarterly*, explained that the Labour Party's major economic aims are full employment, high productivity and social justice, and that 'the nationalization of the means of production, distribution and exchange' should not be considered as something good in itself but only as a means of realizing these ends. Its relationship to socialism, he pointed out, is by no means the same as it was,[1] but it remains important as a means. The extension of public ownership will continue to play an essential part in the strategy of the Labour Party, although nationalization is no longer regarded as the be all and end all of socialism.[2]

[1] Hugh Gaitskell: *The Economic Aims of the Labour Party*. Political Quarterly, XXIV (1953), pp. 6-8.

[2] *Ib.*, p. 8.

Mr Gaitskell did not reject nationalization as a means to the achievement of the socialist aims he had mentioned. On the contrary, he pointed out that it had assisted in their realization in various ways; and the article contained a vague reference to pushing out the frontier of the public sector beyond its present line. But taken as a whole the article sought to disengage the Labour Party from its long established commitment to nationalization.

The older, traditional doctrine that further nationalization must be pursued as the only possible road to socialism was being vigorously advocated in the same year by Mr John Strachey, MP, on the Marxist ground that 'no decisive advance to socialism can be made without breaking the class monopoly in the ownership of the means of production by changing society's relations of production'.[1] The British people must and will assume the ownership of the means of production which they operate; and in the conditions of large-scale modern industry this can only be achieved through collective ownership.[2]

In 1955 the Labour Party was still officially supporting not only the renationalization of steel and road haulage but also the nationalization of sections of the chemical and machine tool industries. Where necessary, the party declared, 'we shall start new public enterprises'.[3]

In 1956 the leader of the Labour Party carried out a much more explicit and far-reaching act of disengagement. 'The most vital question', wrote Mr Gaitskell in Fabian Tract No. 300, 'is how far greater social and economic equality can be achieved without more nationalization and public ownership. A distinction can be drawn between nationalization, which is generally understood to mean the taking over by the State of a complete industry so that it is owned, managed and controlled for the community, and public ownership, which signifies the ownership by the community of any property, whether individual or not, whether embracing a whole industry or only part of it. The State may become the owner of industrial, commercial or agricultural property without necessarily exercising detailed control even over an individual firm—much less over a whole industry.'[4] This can be done by various means, such as taking equity shares in settlement of death duties, using a budget surplus to purchase equity shares, or imposing a capital levy which could be used for the same purpose.[5] He considered an extension of public ownership to be a necessary condition for a further advance towards a

[1] John Strachey: *The Object of Further Socialization*, XXIV Political Quarterly, January-March 1953, p. 74.

[2] *Ib.*, p. 73.

[3] *Forward with Labour*. Labour Party, 1955.

[4] *Socialization and Nationalization*, pp. 6 and 34.

[5] *Ib.*, p. 34.

more equal distribution of wealth; but thought the case for further nationalization on this ground has not been made out.

In this Fabian tract Mr Gaitskell severely criticized certain aspects of the nationalized industries: in particular, the desire of some groups of workers to get more for themselves at the expense of the rest of the community;[1] the low standard of staff loyalty or *esprit de corps*; the difficulty of attracting men of the highest ability to accept the top posts at salaries which compare unfavourably with those in private industry; and the failure to devolve sufficient discretion to the lower echelons.[2]

THE NEW FABIAN ESSAYISTS

A year earlier Mr Roy Jenkins, MP, in *New Fabian Essays* had argued that if the public sector were much larger it could set the standard of remuneration for the managerial class throughout the economy, whereas with a public sector of only twenty per cent its influence is negligible. For this and other reasons he urged a substantial extension of public ownership as 'an essential prerequisite of greater equality of earned incomes and an inevitable concomitant of greater equality in the ownership of property'.[3]

The Labour governments of 1945–51 had carried out nationalization in order to ensure planning of the industries concerned and adequate government control over the whole economy. Future transfers to public ownership would, Mr Jenkins believed, aim primarily at securing greater equality, though possibly in part be intended also as anti-monopoly and efficiency measures. It would therefore no longer be necessary to associate public ownership with highly centralized organization, and more intimate forms of ownership and control could be attempted. The essential aims would be to achieve a pattern of public ownership compatible with the abolition of great fortunes, and to ensure that the rewards and privileges of managers are confined to those strictly necessary to the success of the economy.[4]

Mr Austin Albu, MP, another contributor to *New Fabian Essays*, explained that the reason nationalization and public ownership had been given less emphasis in Labour programmes was not because the nationalized industries were unsuccessful or unpopular, but because the most urgent objects of public ownership had been achieved by other means, such as taxation, price control, and the increased power of trade unions.[5]

[1] *Socialization and Nationalization*, p. 12.
[2] *Ib.*, p. 25.
[3] Roy Jenkins: *Equality*, in 'New Fabian Essays,' ed. R. H. S. Crossman, p. 83.
[4] *Ib.*, p. 84.
[5] Austin Albu: *The Organization of Industry*, *op cit.*, p. 124–7.

MR CROSLAND AND THE FUTURE OF SOCIALISM

The most elaborate exposition of the changed attitude towards nationalization was made by Mr C. A. R. Crosland in *The Future of Socialism*. He begins by analysing the pre-war case for nationalization which led to the programme carried out by the Attlee governments of 1945-51. All the arguments pointed to the industries which were selected for transfer to the public sector;[1] and Mr Crosland does not question the correctness of the action which was taken in regard to them. He does emphasize, however, that the present position is entirely different. Except for water there are no more public utilities worth considering; and except for steel there are no more industries which are basic in the sense that coal or railways are basic. If size is used as the criterion of selection, it would point to the industries producing ships, motor cars, chemicals, aircraft, radio apparatus, and electrical equipment. But these industries have very different characteristics from those already nationalized. They are not, for the most part, monopolies, nor are they inefficient. They do not need to be planned or organized on a national scale.[2] Nationalization may make it possible to improve the structure of an industry—this was certainly true in regard to electricity distribution and coalmining;[3] but the shortcomings of the motor car industry are not to be found in its organization. They lie in such spheres as design, sales and marketing, and these are weaknesses which nationalization would be unlikely to cure.[4] In general, Mr Crosland does not believe that industries working for highly competitive markets at home and overseas, and often manufacturing branded goods, are likely to prosper under a centralized public corporation. The mere delimitation of these industries would be extremely difficult.

Unlike Mr Strachey, Mr Crosland believes that socialism, whether conceived in social, ethical or economic terms, would not be brought much nearer by nationalizing the aircraft industry or cement or sugar.[5] In his view, the purpose of socialism is to eradicate the sense of class and to replace it by a consciousness of common interest and equal status;[6] and this aim would not be advanced by the establishment of more public corporations. A substantial change of ownership, in Mr Crosland's opinion, is not necessary in order to raise the standard of living of the working class, to improve labour relations, to secure the proper use of economic resources, to promote social and economic equality, or to

[1] C. A. R. Crosland: *The Future of Socialism*, p. 462-3.
[2] *Ib.*, p. 470-1. [3] *Ib.*, p. 481. [4] *Ib.*, p. 473-4. [5] *Ib.*, p. 475.
[6] C. A. R. Crosland: *The Transition from Capitalism*, in 'New Fabian Essays', ed. by R. H. S. Crossman, p. 62.

spread power more evenly through society;[1] nor would a change of ownership ensure the realization of these aims.

Mr Strachey takes up his stand on an older socialist position which derives from Marx. It postulates that unless you change the relations of production, nothing is changed. If they are changed, everything is changed.

Mr Crosland is essentially liberal and non-Marxist in his approach; but he is not always as realistic or empirical as he appears to be. He makes a number of unfavourable statements about the nationalized industries which will not stand up to close examination. It is not true, for example, to say that ministerial control has been slack in the fuel and power industries;[2] or that the boards of public corporations have been less accountable, or less amenable to public control, than commercial companies.[3] It is not true that the level of salaries has been restricted by financial stringency due to the nationalized industries not making a substantial surplus; nor that the research programmes have been curtailed for financial reasons.[4] I could give other examples.

So far as economic planning is concerned, he thinks the Government can, without difficulty, impose their will on the private sector: they have all the power they need for that purpose. This is quite inconsistent with his statement that there is an overwhelming case for the renationalization of steel because no Government can induce the steel companies to expand their production capacity sufficiently while they are in private hands.[5]

Most of the disillusion which Mr Crosland feels for nationalization appears to arise from his belief that the large corporation, whether publicly or privately owned, confronts problems which are essentially similar, and that it acts in essentially the same way in dealing with them.[6] Unquestionably the management, technology, organization, research, production and distribution of basic industries must have certain features in common in a given society at a given time, irrespective of who owns or administers them. But to recognize these similarities and to overlook the differences between public and private undertakings is to miss some factors of great importance.

We can see that there has been a widespread rejection within the Labour movement of any further nationalization of whole industries on the model which characterized the legislation of 1945–51. This excludes, of course, the renationalization of steel and road haulage, for these are existing commitments which it is difficult for the Labour Party to disavow without making a confession of past error. By no means all Labour

[1] *The Future of Socialism*, p. 475.
[2] *Ib.*, p. 466. [3] *Ib.*, p. 30. [4] *Ib.*, p. 405. [5] *Ib.*, p. 477. [6] *Ib.*, p. 480.

politicians or their supporters hold this view; but there are enough of them who do to make the Labour Party disunited and uncertain in its attitude. 'For the first time for a century,' observes Mr Crosland, 'there is equivocation on the Left about the future of nationalization.'[1] This uncertainty is shared by the Labour Party, the Co-operative movement, and the Trades Union Congress.

SOCIALIST UNION

The conflicting trends of thought are reflected in Socialist Union, founded in 1951 by members of the Labour Party to think out afresh the meaning of socialism in the modern world.

This group insists that we should not identify the public sector too closely with the nationalized industries—to do so is 'an error deriving from the days when all economic power was identified with the ownership of the means of production'. Today economic power is seen to assume many forms; and all those which are under the direct control of the State should be included in the public sector. The public sector thus comprises many different kinds of property, such as land and buildings, the national museums and art galleries, municipal libraries and swimming pools. It also includes many different types of public enterprise, ranging from new towns to the municipal savings bank at Birmingham. Even the budget is an important part of the public sector because it enables the Government to exert control over the expenditure of State revenue.[2]

But however much we may extend the scope of the public sector, the advantages are not all to be found inside it. Public accountability, formerly regarded as one of the most beneficial aims of public ownership, is now considered by Socialist Union to have both advantages and disadvantages. Experience of the nationalized industries, they remark, shows how hard it is to create an active and informed public opinion, and thereby to make public accountability truly effective. But even if it were effective, 'public opinion is by its nature a two-edged sword. It may discourage waste; it may insist on a fair deal for the worker; it may demand a high quality product. But it may also be fearful of risk; it may frown on experiments involving public money; it may hesitate too long before sanctioning a plunge. Public accountability encourages rectitude, but it may inhibit flexibility and experiment.'[3]

This statement is not based on any investigation of the effects of public opinion on public undertakings. There is, indeed, no evidence to show

[1] *The Future of Socialism*, p. 406.
[2] Socialist Union: *Twentieth Century Socialism*, (1956) Penguin Special, pp. 148-9.
[3] *Ib.*, p. 93.

that nationalized industries are over-cautious or inflexible, as compared with the private sector. The groundnut scheme was an example of the State taking risks of the most reckless kind and of plunging into large-scale operations at far too early a stage and without taking the most elementary precautions. The development of the gas turbine, radar, nuclear generating stations, and broadcasting are examples of highly important innovations pioneered by the State with great enterprise and foresight.

The main conclusion at which Socialist Union arrives is the desirability of a mixed economy in which all economic power, whatever its nature and by whomsoever exercised, is subject to political, economic or social control.[1] The antithesis of private versus public enterprise based on the notion that one leads to damnation and the other to salvation is dismissed as 'too crude to be fruitful'.[2] Another misconception which is rejected is the belief that ownership is only dangerous in private hands. Experience has shown that even when entrusted to public authorities the power of ownership can be dangerous. 'It is still open to abuse and the individual has still to struggle to assert his rights in face of it. Ways have to be found to control the powers of ownership, whether they are privately or publicly held.'[3] The theories which regard complete common ownership as the gateway to the promised land must now be abandoned, for the experience of communist regimes has shown us that 'if capitalism is individualism run riot, then communism is collectivism run riot; the remedy is no better than the disease'. The reason is that complete collectivization of property leads to a monopoly of power in the hands of the State; and every economic activity, every decision affecting industry, trade, agriculture or the professions, is subject to the will of the Government. Hence, the abolition of private property leads towards totalitarianism. Socialists must therefore revise their traditional beliefs that the private ownership of property is necessarily bad; and that the ownership of property is dangerous only in private hands.[4]

The authors then proceed to argue that the needs of a socialist society can best be attained by a system of checks and balances operating in the economic sphere. By this means the power of sellers will be balanced by the power of purchasers; the power of employers by that of trade unions; the power of borrowers by that of lenders, and so on. The deliberate aims of a socialist government should be, first, to see that countervailing

[1] *Twentieth Century Socialism*, p. 141.
[2] *Ib.*, p. 96. [3] *Ib.*, pp. 125–6.
[4] W. A. Robson: *Freedom, Equality and Socialism*, in 27, The Political Quarterly. October-December 1956, p. 378.

forces exist to offset the power of each major section or element in the market; and second, to occupy, when necessary, strategic positions at key points of the economy in order to exercise internal pressure on particular market situations. The concept of countervailing power occupies a central place in the position taken up by Socialist Union. It has replaced competition as the principal regulatory principle in the distribution of economic goods and services; but no attempt is made to show why or how struggles between conflicting forces—which may be huge employers associations and trade unions—will work out to the general advantage.[1]

In this theory the centre of gravity has shifted from the ownership of the means of production, distribution and exchange to the control of power in the market. Market power, in the authors' analysis, forms one of the two principal forms of concentrated economic power. Those who wield it do not usually own the resources they control. They are the higher executives of banks, insurance companies, building societies, trade associations, marketing boards, trade unions, co-operative societies and public authorities, who can dispose of land, labour, capital, goods, services and technical knowledge owned by others.[2]

The other principal form of economic power is the large industrial or commercial concern. In this the expert manager has supplanted the proprietor as the effective wielder of power. The exercise of power by this managerial class may well be unaffected by a transfer of the undertaking from private to public ownership. This is Burnham's thesis restated. Its acceptance by Socialist Union has led the authors to reject nationalization as a certain path to socialism—a highly significant change of outlook. This does not mean, however, that they are opposed to any extension of public enterprise. They suggest, indeed, that it could with advantage be extended to wholesale trade, since wholesaling is a strategic point from which countervailing power can be brought to bear on producers who are not subject to strong competitive pressure.

In summarizing their conclusions the authors declare that economic power can and should be controlled by the balance of contending forces; and by imposing social accountability on all enterprises. The public sector will include many different forms of public enterprise and various types of property and undertakings. They assert there is no virtue in public enterprise in itself. The question is not how much but for what purposes it is needed. The merit of public enterprise lies in the contribution it can make to an expanding economy and to social security.[3]

[1] *Twentieth Century Socialism*, p. 131.
[2] *Ib.*, p. 127-9.
[3] *Ib.*, p. 149.

THE CONSERVATIVE PARTY'S ATTITUDE

Strange as it may seem, the views advanced by Socialist Union are not far removed in one important respect from those put out by the Conservative and Union Central Office. 'Conservatives', says the latter, 'believe that nationalization is founded on a fallacy—namely, that a public corporation can always be relied upon to act in the public interest. . . . The Socialists flew to the State to protect the worker against the capitalist, but nationalization simply takes power from a multiplicity of shareholders and concentrates it in the hands of a single State. Conservatives believe that . . . industrial ills are not cured by a transfer of ownership.'[1] The point of similarity between the views of Socialist Union and those of the Conservative Central office lies in the scepticism about the extent to which a public corporation can be relied on to act in the public interest.

Nationalization has, of course, done much more than merely transfer power from private shareholders to the State. Indeed, the powers of shareholders are today so reduced that if that were the only aim it could well be regarded as trivial. Nationalization has drastically reorganized and unified whole industries. It has enabled the Government to intervene in many important matters. It has eliminated the profit motive. It has introduced a large measure of industrial democracy and required consultation with consumers' representatives. It has made available vast sums for capital development which would not otherwise have been forthcoming.

A number of other views have been expressed in recent years about alternative forms of public enterprise and the criteria of selection which should be applied for the transfer of undertakings to the public sector.

THE CO-OPERATIVE PARTY'S APPROACH

The Co-operative Party have stressed the importance of employing diverse forms of social ownership not only in different industries but also in different sectors of the same industry. Nationalization is recommended for certain types of industry, such as the extraction of minerals, the common services of water, power and transport, and certain others.[2] But with these exceptions the administration of the public utility type of nationalized industry is, the party find, too remote from consumers. Centralization is necessary for large-scale planning but it has removed the advantages of municipal enterprise, where the councillor felt himself

[1] *The Campaign Guide* (1955), pp. 82-3.

[2] *The People's Industry.* Statement on Social Ownership by the National Committee of the Co-operative Party (1952), paras. 61-4.

to be directly responsible to the electors and the citizen felt he could get his complaint remedied by appealing to his elected representative. It would be a retrograde step to restore to local authorities all the functions they formerly exercised, but much greater use should be made of locally-elected councillors in running the nationalized industries. Boards for distributing gas and electricity should be composed of representatives of local authorities. The boards for producing these products should be constituted on their present lines except that a third of their members might be elected by and from the distributive bodies. In suitable cases the larger local authorities might be entrusted with distribution. Elsewhere, smaller local authorities could combine by means of joint boards or federations for this purpose.[1]

Municipal enterprise could also be extended to enable local authorities to provide, either individually or jointly, for their own needs. This would apply to printing, the manufacture of school furniture, and other goods and services for which there is a substantial and stable demand which could be met economically by means of municipal enterprise.

Not unnaturally the Co-operative Party demands recognition of consumer co-operation as a form of public enterprise. They say that form is appropriate whenever the consumer is closely concerned with the range, quality and design of the product or service; and they cite the distributive trades and the manufacture of consumer goods as examples. Retail co-operatives should control their own supplies by setting up federal productive organs and wholesale societies. They even propose producers' co-operation in industries catering for consumer needs where monopoly control is not desirable, and in the organization of professional and artisan services, despite the widespread failure of 'co-operative co-partnership' throughout the western world.

Above all, the Co-operative Party wish to encourage diverse forms of social ownership. Thus, even within a single industry, such as building, there could be a combination of government departments, local authorities, public corporations, co-operatives, and federal associations of local and co-operative organizations. A government department might be given general powers of supervision, planning, information, research, and encouragement of mutual assistance between the units in the industry. A development of this kind would result in diversity without fragmentation, the preservation of initiative without anarchy, social ownership without an undue concentration of social power, and planning without bureaucracy.[2] It is difficult to believe that the deliberate encourage-

[1] *The People's Industry*. Statement on Social Ownership by the National Committee of the Co-operative Party (1952), paras. 35-8.

[2] *Ib.*, paras. 15-24.

ment of a medley of public authorities and collectivist bodies of different types and sizes, will possess all the virtues and avoid all the vices in the manner claimed for it; one can think of plenty of instances where diversity has had overwhelming disadvantages: an example was the friendly societies, which played a major part in the administration of the national health insurance scheme from 1911 until 1948, when it was superseded by the national health service.

The Co-operative Congress is strongly opposed to any suggestion that nationalization should take place in any trade or industry in which the co-operative sector is providing efficient service to the consumer. The Executive have said they would never agree to nationalization in those circumstances; and they would oppose even an extension of municipal trading if that meant less public control than obtains in co-operative enterprise. The Congress are anxious not only to preserve their territory from incursions by the State, but to obtain government support for an extension of the co-operative sector. Why should they not claim the right to distribute milk or bread on a national basis, asked Mr F. Leeman, a delegate from the Midland Sectional Board. A delegate from Barnsley (Mr T. Clayton) complained that the National Coal Board had entered into direct competition with co-operative trading not only in regard to the retail distribution of coal, but in the sale of such sidelines as books, soap, towels, and even furniture and gramophones. Mr P. M. Williams, who introduced a special report entitled *Co-operation and Socialism* on behalf of the Executive, said that delegates were anxious to obtain from the Labour Party a promise to encourage public authorities to use their goods and services, and to give special consideration to co-operative societies wishing to open shops on municipal housing estates.[1]

Nationalization, according to Mr A. S. Shelton of Nottingham, has simply replaced private capitalism by State capitalism with little advance in public control or public accountability.[2] Mr N. Blakey of North Shields remarked that the co-operative movement does not care what the Labour Party does with any other activity so long as they regard co-operative undertakings as sacrosanct from State interference.[3] Statements of this kind reveal a narrow concern with co-operation as a vested interest; but they also show a hostility towards nationalization not far removed from that found among private traders.

THE ATTITUDE OF THE TRADES UNION CONGRESS

In 1953 the General Council of the TUC presented an extremely cautious report on public ownership to the Congress held that year in Doug-

[1] Report of the 89th Annual Co-operative Congress, pp. 91, 321-2, and 325-6.
[2] *Ib.*, p. 329. [3] *Ib.*, p. 324.

las. After reviewing the experience so far gained of nationalization and the economic needs of the nation, the report stated that public ownership in the major industries had been a success; but nevertheless there were certain disadvantages in the present structures, particularly the tendency to centralization. No mention was made of the fact that the trade unions insist on national negotiation of collective agreements, and that this inevitably causes centralization so far as labour relations are concerned. This tendency, the TUC report observed, is not a reflection on public ownership but only on the forms it had hitherto assumed. Attention should therefore be given to other possible forms, such as the acquisition of key firms in an industry, or the purchase of a financial interest in exceptionally important companies.[1]

The TUC then examined industries falling into four separate categories. First, those providing basic commodities and services; second, highly monopolistic industries in which great economic power is concentrated in private hands; third, industries in need of rapid development to expand output and raise technical efficiency; fourth, industries requiring improved organization and techniques.

Industries in the first group are often best organized as monopolies, because competition may mean duplication of costly facilities and waste of resources. Public ownership is essential to secure co-ordination and to avoid the exploitation of basic services and commodities for private advantage. One of the few basic services remaining to a small extent in private hands is water supply, the greater part of which is owned and operated by local authorities. The report states there is a clear case for the complete public ownership of this industry in order to provide a universal service and to eliminate waste.[2]

Investing institutions, such as insurance companies, investment trusts and joint stock banks, were regarded as belonging to this first group, but as the record of their activities since the end of World War II is considered to have been good, no proposals relating to them were made. They were put into cold storage for further 'detailed study' by the General Council of the TUC.

Discussion about the second group centred almost wholly on the chemical industry. This is said to be dominated in most sections by ICI; while a number of other large firms occupy dominant positions in certain sections. The TUC General Council contended there is need for public control over the industry because of its monopolistic structure and its significance to the economy as a whole; but they declined to make any specific recommendations except to say that the next Labour govern-

[1] *Public Ownership*. An Interim Report. TUC, paras. 171-2.

[2] *Ib.*, para. 185.

ment should institute an inquiry into the facts of the industry. The idea of supervising an industry of this kind by a public board of control seemed to the TUC to have 'obvious disadvantages when what is required is to ensure that essential investment is undertaken . . . it would be difficult for a board of this sort to promote development, especially when one firm has such a predominant position in the industry'.[1] The report stated that there was no ground whatever for suggesting that investment in the chemical industry has been, or is likely to be, inadequate.

In considering industries requiring rapid development, the TUC discussed the important branches of engineering—such as the manufacture of machine tools, agricultural and civil engineering equipment, mining machinery, railway equipment, aircraft, motor cars, textile machinery, and shipbuilding. Only in the case of mining machinery was public ownership of a few firms (by the National Coal Board) definitely advocated. It was considered but not recommended in several others, such as aircraft manufacture, shipbuilding, and ship repairing. In some of the industries the TUC proposed that development councils should be set up.

So far as industries in serious need of improved organization were concerned, the TUC touched lightly on wholesale and retail distribution, especially that part of it dealing with agricultural products. They referred to a previous report suggesting that commodity commissions should be established to provide a framework into which public ownership of the distributive trades concerned could be fitted[2] by progressive stages in the light of further knowledge and experience.

The dominant theme of the TUC report was that the case for public ownership and control should be constantly related to Britain's need to improve her economic position in the world.[3] This led the General Council to recommend measures of public ownership only where it appeared likely that no other method of improving the present position would succeed. The general trend and temper of the report was strongly conservative and disclosed no predilection in favour of nationalization or any other form of public ownership for its own sake.

On several important issues the TUC, in rejecting nationalization, differed from leading trade unions. The Confederation of Shipbuilding and Engineering Unions, for example, favoured public ownership of the aircraft industry on the ground that an industry largely dependent on public money should be subject to close public control and this is best achieved by public ownership.[4] The Co-operative Party had also favoured the

[1] *Public Ownership*, para. 206.

[2] *Ib.*, paras. 259-60. [3] *Ib.*, para. 256. [4] *Ib.*, para. 226.

nationalization of industries vital for defence. But the TUC thought that the existing combination of public and private finance and research had worked very well in the aircraft industry and should not be disturbed except for compelling reasons. They thought the profits had been earned and were a price worth paying for the continued smooth running of the industry. They took into account the psychology of the leading figures in the industry, mostly eminent designers, who would be strongly opposed to public ownership.[1]

The interim report of the TUC also differed both from the Confederation of Shipbuilding and Engineering Unions and the Labour Party about State intervention in the machine tool industry. The Confederation, while not advocating nationalization at this stage, believe that public ownership of the entire industry is required to make it fully efficient. The Labour Party concluded that the State should acquire a number of key firms, and make them centres for technical rationalization and development. The TUC proposed only to consult the Confederation about the possibility of setting up a development council, and of promoting an industrial research association and a co-operative sales organization with government support.[2] At the 1957 Congress, however, a resolution was passed that 'the greater part of the machine tool industry should be brought under public ownership'. Nothing was said during the debate about the form which public ownership should take.[3]

The 1953 report of the TUC also rejected the Confederation's suggestion for public ownership of the maritime industries of shipping, shipbuilding, ship repairing, and marine engineering. The report recommended a development council for the shipbuilding and marine engineering industries, and this was accompanied by a warning that the probable attitude of employers towards such a body would require further consideration. Even the mild step represented by a development council was further than the TUC were prepared to go in regard to some industries, such as motor car manufacture. Much more investigation and consultation with interested bodies would be required in almost every case before definite action could be taken.

At their 1958 meeting held in Bournemouth the TUC rejected a proposal for state ownership of the tobacco industry contained in a resolution moved by the Tobacco Workers' Union. Mr Belcher, the secretary of the Union, contended that nationalization was necessary in view of the fact that the industry was fast becoming a monopoly.[4] Mr Alan

[1] *Public Ownership*, para. 228.
[2] *Ib.*, paras. 214-6.
[3] *Report of the Proceedings at the 89th Annual Trades Union Congress*, pp. 461-2.
[4] *Trades Union Congress Report*, 1958, p. 454-5.

Birch, chairman of the TUC Economic Committee, insisted that monopoly is only one of the criteria for nationalizing an industry. The tobacco industry could not satisfy the other criteria such as the national importance of the product or service provided by the industry, its need for improved organization or rapid development in order to raise living standards, etc.[1] It is true that a little earlier the Congress had carried a resolution moved by the general secretary of the left-wing Electrical Trades Union declaring the urgent need for nationalizing Britain's basic industries, with priority for the key sections of the engineering industry, and the renationalization of steel and road transport.[2] But a general resolution of this kind is far from being a specific commitment; and the attitude of the TUC appears to be unfavourable to any considerable extension of public ownership.

THE LABOUR PARTY'S CHANGING POLICY

In *Challenge in Britain*, issued in 1953, the Labour Party declared that its policy on public ownership consisted partly of straightforward nationalization and partly of establishing competitive public enterprises in a number of industries. As regards the former, steel and road haulage would be renationalized; water supply nationalized; and the British Sugar Corporation brought into complete public ownership. As regards the latter, the next Labour government would take over a number of key firms engaged in the manufacture of machine tools to act as centres of technical rationalization and expansion. They would acquire a controlling interest in a few firms making mining machinery whose products are of vital concern to the National Coal Board, or to the export market. They would acquire any aircraft construction firm which falls down on its job, and particularly if it neglects valuable opportunities to expand. In the chemical industry, Labour would establish positive control over the investment programme, and introduce a sufficient degree of public ownership to offset the dangers inherent in private monopoly. The State would be given power to acquire the ownership of mineral deposits and to search for minerals. The possibility of the State producing some of the essential supplies needed for the national health service was also envisaged.[3]

Labour's programme in 1953 also included a National Housing Corporation to build houses either directly or through existing contractors in areas where local authorities have difficulty in providing houses for workers in new industries.[4] Finally, industrial insurance would become a public service.

[1] *Trades Union Congress Report*, 1958, p. 455. [2] *Ib.*, p. 451.
[3] *Challenge to Britain*. Labour Party Report (1953), pp. 67-71. [4] *Ib.*, p. 79.

In *Challenge to Britain* the Labour Party explained that competitive public enterprise would consist either of new units created and operated by the State, or existing firms in which the State acquired a controlling interest. Mention was also made of mixed enterprise, in which the Government would join with private enterprise in providing the capital needed to finance projects of national importance. Other forms of co-operation between public and private enterprise would be State-sponsored research organizations, factories provided by the Government for the use of private industry; and the installation by the State of capital equipment which would be leased to private firms.[1]

Among the general public there had for some years been a feeling of indifference towards the question of public ownership, despite the efforts of the Labour Party to present nationalization in a favourable light and of the Conservative Party to denigrate it.

In the General Election of 1951 nationalization is said to have played little part in the campaign.[2] The subject no longer aroused much originality in the contending forces.[3] Nationalization was mentioned by only twenty per cent of Labour candidates in their election addresses. Among the Conservative candidates sixty-eight per cent—roughly two out of three—referred to it in their election addresses.

In the General Election of 1955 fifty-two per cent of the Conservative election addresses mentioned nationalization while thirty-six per cent of the Labour candidates mentioned the subject in their addresses, chiefly in connection with steel and road transport, and to a lesser degree chemicals and machine tools.[4] There was little publicity for nationalization in the campaign, and Mr David Butler's verdict was that it no longer evoked genuine enthusiasm.[5]

In July 1957, a decisive point was reached in the Labour movement with the issue of two policy pamphlets on public ownership. These formed part of the 'new thinking' which the Labour Party had undertaken following their electoral defeat in the two previous general elections.

One of the pamphlets, entitled *Public Enterprise*, is a review of the nationalized industries. It is a sober, carefully documented, balanced statement which does not attempt to gloss over difficulties or to evade awkward questions. The general conclusion of the pamphlet is that the nationalized industries have a fine record of achievement, especially on

[1] *Challenge to Britian* (1953), pp. 67-71, and 74. For Mr Hugh Gaitskell's views on mixed enterprise see *Socialism and Nationalization*. Fabian Tract No. 300, pp. 35-6.

[2] D. E. Butler: *The British General Election of 1951*, p. 104.

[3] *Ib.*, p. 246.

[4] D. E. Butler: *The British General Election of 1955*, pp. 32-3.

[5] *Ib.*, p. 163. The principal issue which secured substantial publicity was Labour's promise to nationalize the chemical industry and this took place mainly near the ICI factories, p. 86.

the technical side, and that the foundations laid during the previous decade are sound. This did not mean, however, that everything was perfect or that there was no room for improvement. The pamphlet recommended a number of changes in regard to the governing boards, the consumer councils and complaints by consumers, joint consultation, finance, relations with Ministers, and several other matters. The gist of *Public Enterprise* was a reasoned justification of the policy which the Attlee governments had carried out in 1945-51.

INDUSTRY AND SOCIETY

The other pamphlet, entitled *Industry and Society*, was an enquiry into the wider question of the place, character and purpose of public ownership in the kind of society the Labour Party wishes to bring about in Britain.

The pamphlet begins by referring to a clause in the constitution of the Labour Party calling for the common ownership of the means of production, distribution and exchange and the best obtainable system of popular administration and control of each industry or service 'as a method of securing for the workers the full fruits of their industry and the most equitable distribution that is possible'. It then sets out the five main reasons why socialists have attached so much importance to public ownership. First, it would lessen class divisions, diminish unjustifiable inequalities of wealth, and reduce unearned income; second, it would create a new spirit of co-operation and fellowship in industry in place of the competitive struggle for gain; third, it would make the exercise of economic power more responsible; fourth, it would facilitate central economic planning and prevent slumps and severe unemployment; fifth, it would lead to higher productivity through improved organization. Socialists expected that these aims would be furthered by the extension of public ownership generally. The furtherance of these aims did not imply any particular form of organization which public ownership should take, or any particular order of priorities. The pamphlet then briefly explains the reasons which led to the nationalization policy of 1945-51 and claims that the programme then carried out has made a real contribution to the broader aims of socialism.[1]

The main concern of *Industry and Society* is, however, to consider the mixed economy which now exists. The pamphlet contains a remarkable analysis of the changes which have taken place in recent decades in the private sector of the economy. It argues that it is unrealistic to lump together all the privately owned firms regardless of their size and

[1] D. E. Butler: *The British General Election of 1955*, pp. 7-8.

irrespective of whether they are public or private companies. The vital element on which attention should be concentrated is the relatively small number of large firms (about 500) who earn nearly half of the total profits earned by private industry. They are directly responsible for about half of the total investment in the private sector and indirectly for a good deal more. These great undertakings constitute a new sector which dominates the economy. Moreover, they are of growing importance, for they alone can command (either singly or in co-operation) the vast capital resources and the elaborate research facilities which modern developments in industry require.

These large concerns differ vastly from the classic model of capitalist enterprise which socialism has traditionally rejected and fought. Ownership has become separated from control and management. The shareholders are virtually impotent because their holdings are so widely dispersed; and they are functionless because they bear an almost negligible risk and provide only a small proportion of the capital required for investment, by far the greater part coming from retained profits ploughed back into the business, from insurance companies, and other corporate institutions.

The control of the great industrial concerns is now in the hands of a managerial elite possessing special abilities and qualifications. 'The world of the managers is not the world of the shareholders. Their concern is with production as much as with profits and with expansion far more than with dividends. Salaries, pensions, status, power and promotion—these rather than wealth are their operating incentives.'[1] The interests of the managers diverge from those of the owners in regard to the allocation of profits. Yet despite this divergence of interest and the disappearing rôle of the proprietor, the rewards going to the individual shareholder have tended to increase. In consequence, the ownership of stocks and shares as a continuing cause of economic inequality has in no way diminished. The heavy taxation of incomes has been largely offset by the capital gains enjoyed by those who own stocks or shares in the large firms. Private ownership of the equity is thus a potent influence in supporting and increasing inequality.

The pamphlet recommends that the path to greater equality lies through acquisition by the State of stocks and shares in the large companies. This would enable the community to participate in the heavy capital gains which accrue almost automatically to the owners. It could acquire these holdings by various means, such as acceptance in payment of death duties, by purchase, or through the national superannuation fund proposed by the Labour Party.

[1] D. E. Butler: *The British General Election of 1955*, pp. 16-17.

Socialism has hitherto always involved both public ownership and public administration in one form or another of industries or services. Municipal trading, government operation on the Post Office model, management by means of the public corporation or the joint stock company, and consumers' co-operation (in which the emphasis is on social ownership and non-governmental administration)—all these different forms can easily be fitted into the traditional concept of socialism. *Industry and Society* departs from the concept by advocating State participation in the ownership of commercial companies which will remain in the hands of their present directors and managers. The State will not acquire the entire capital stock or even a majority holding. It will be one shareholder among many.

The aim of the Labour Party in wanting the State to become an equity holder in the large joint stock companies is to secure a fairer distribution of income and of wealth. The policy is advocated as a means whereby the community can secure to itself some of the substantial earnings which will otherwise enrich the functionless private shareholder. The object is not to obtain control over the direction of the great commercial companies. This is made fairly clear in *Industry and Society*, and it has been asserted publicly on several subsequent occasions by Labour spokesmen who have denied the allegation that they intend to 'take over' the leading industrial and commercial concerns. *Industry and Society* does contain explicit proposals for government control over the level and composition of investment, major building construction,[1] and the allocation of goods for export and for home consumption. There might also be a legally enforceable code of conduct drawn up by the Government to regulate company policies in such matters as joint consultation, notice and compensation for redundancy, equal pay for women, recruitment, training and promotion, and the employment of older workers.[2] But intervention of this kind would be an expression of governmental authority unrelated to the proprietary interest of the State as shareholder. The pamphlet states that where regulation is insufficient, public ownership may be desirable—meaning, presumably, complete acquisition by the State. But this would seem to be regarded as an exceptional step to be taken only when all else had failed.[3]

THE ABANDONMENT OF PUBLIC ENTERPRISE

The reasons for the rejection of public administration as a concomitant of public ownership are complex. The most important one is the belief

[1] D. E. Butler: *The British General Election of 1955*, pp. 43–4.
[2] *Ib.*, Chs. V and VI (pp. 51-9). [3] *Ib.*, p. 47.

that the large concerns are well-managed, and that to nationalize them would be detrimental to their well-being and hence injurious to the nation's standard of living. The pamphlet states that 'The Labour Party recognizes that under increasingly professional managements, large firms are as a whole serving the nation well. Moreover, we recognize that no organization, public or private, can operate effectively if it is subjected to persistent and detailed interventions from above. We have, therefore, no intention of intervening in the management of any firm which is doing a good job.'[1] This leaves out of account, however, State regulation of the general matters mentioned above.

A highly important factor which has influenced the Labour Party's change of outlook is a feeling of disillusion with the results of nationalization. The disillusion is partly due to the fact that socialists expected too much from the mere fact of nationalization and showed insufficient understanding of the problems concerning development, organization, management, technology, and labour in the industries taken over. The successful operation of State-owned industries was regarded as mainly a political and legal problem to be solved in Westminster and Whitehall; whereas the real problems are to be found in the collieries, the railway workshops and marshalling yards, the research and development establishments, the divisional headquarters, the board room, and other places where work is done, ideas evolved, and management carried on.

The disillusion has been mainly induced by the persistent denigration of the nationalized industries by the Press, by Conservative politicians both inside and outside Parliament, by leading business men, and by organs like the Federation of British Industries and the Institute of Directors. For more than ten years a ceaseless campaign has been waged by the great majority of the daily newspapers to present a continuously unfavourable picture of the nationalized industries. Anything which might show in their favour is usually suppressed or discounted or given a minor place, whereas every fact which could arouse resentment or prejudice or dissatisfaction is magnified and given prominence. Every price increase made by a public corporation is highlighted and criticized as due to inefficiency and the absence of competition, while far greater price increases in the private sector are not even mentioned. All the shortcomings of the railways and the coal industry are ascribed to nationalization, although most of them are due to prolonged mismanagement under private ownership.

In its policy pamphlet entitled *Public Enterprise*, published in 1957, the Labour Party stoutly defended the nationalized industries, and presented a favourable though not exaggerated picture of the success which they

[1] D. E. Butler: *The British General Election of 1955*, pp. 48–9.

have achieved.[1] It reasserted the party's determination to renationalize the road haulage industry and iron and steel. But apart from these old commitments the future policy of the Labour Party towards public enterprise will not be based on the performance of the nationalized industries, but rather on the new conception of the State in its relations to industry set out in *Industry and Society*. It can be contended that there are solid reasons for this change of attitude, since the industries providing power, fuel, and transport constitute the infrastructure of the economy, and they differ in several essential respects from the constructional, manufacturing and processing undertakings which form the bulk of the remaining large-scale industries. But there can be little doubt that the continual disparagement of the nationalized industries has had a significant though imponderable and perhaps unconscious effect in inducing the Labour Party to abandon public enterprise as an important part of its programme.

The abandonment of public enterprise has not been an easy operation for the Labour Party to undertake. The publication of *Industry and Society* led almost immediately to a strong protest by thirty-two Labour MPs who published a joint letter expressing their disappointment and dismay at the policy of retreat from a long-established socialist tradition.[2] They called for a reversal of this policy. There are many more members of the party who hold views which cannot be reconciled with the new doctrine. This was made clear in the Conference held at Blackpool in 1959 to discuss the causes of Labour's defeat in the recent general Election.

THE STATE AS RENTIER

In considering the policy laid down in *Industry and Society* the first question to be asked is whether it is consonant with a socialist philosophy, or even with a sound Welfare State policy, for the State to acquire an interest in the large private firms solely in order to share in their profitability. In my opinion it is not, for several reasons. First, the policy leads to the functionless private shareholder being replaced by the functionless State and I can see few advantages in the change. Second, if the State comes to have a substantial interest in the profitability of particular companies, many invidious situations could occur which might embarass the Government in its other capacities. Already there are conflicts of

[1] On one point the pamphlet gives a distorted account. It suggests that a great programme of integration and co-ordination between road and rail was rudely shattered by the Transport Act, 1953. Virtually no progress had in fact been made in that direction during the preceding six years.

[2] *Reynold's News*, July 28, 1957; *The Times*, July 29, 1957.

interest arising out of fiscal policy. For example, is the Government seriously concerned to discourage cigarette smoking on health grounds in view of the enormous revenue which the Exchequer receives from tobacco tax? Did successive Governments do all that could have been done to make the activities of the former Anglo-Iranian Petroleum Company acceptable to the rising tide of Iranian nationalism, or were they inhibited by their desire to obtain from their very large shareholding in that company the highest possible profit?

Third, since an equity holder does not realize a capital gain unless and until he sells the stock to which it attaches, if the State is to participate in the capital gains of equity stocks it will have to buy and sell shares on the Stock Exchange for that purpose, in precisely the same way as any private speculator or investor. The spectacle of the Government operating on the Stock Exchange solely with a view to realizing the maximum capital gains on their stocks is not an attractive one. One would have thought it would be particularly unattractive to those members of the Labour Party who already regard with disfavour such activities by private persons as containing an anti-social element. Here again there is a potential danger of the State being influenced in its Stock Exchange operations by foreknowledge of Government decisions which could influence the market prices of the stocks it holds. If, for example, the Government had prepared a plan of road construction involving a very large expenditure over a period of years, the mere announcement of this might increase the prices of stocks of companies supplying roadmaking materials and equipment. What could be easier than a purchase by the Government of those stocks prior to the announcement and a subsequent sale? Some may applaud this kind of manipulation, but it has within it the seeds of corruption.

It is not clear to whom the State will sell its publicly owned equity stocks. The Exchequer already takes a large share of the profits of public companies by direct taxation, in addition to the income tax which is deducted from dividends before they are distributed to shareholders and any surtax subsequently payable in respect of them. *Industry and Society* contains a proposal to introduce a capital gains tax. The main attractiveness today of equity holdings in the larger companies is often their potential capital appreciation. If this were to be substantially reduced by a severe tax on capital gains, the Government might find that the market for realizing capital gains on State holdings of equity shares had been greatly curtailed.

At present, it is estimated that a typical efficient expanding company pays a third of its profits to the Exchequer in taxation. Another third is distributed as dividends, on which income tax is deducted and paid to the Inland Revenue. The remaining third is placed to reserve. This is invested in the business and in due course it will be capitalized, and a bonus issue may be made to the stockholders. The reserve fund increases the earnings of the companies which are reflected eventually in higher dividends.[1]

If this estimate is correct, the Exchequer is already taking about forty-six per cent of the profits of such a company, excluding any surtax payable by stockholders. Mr Douglas Jay, MP, who held office in the Labour governments of 1945-51, first as Economic Secretary and later as Financial Secretary to the Treasury, wants the State to get a still larger share of the growing increment of private enterprise in order to increase the revenue available for expenditure on the social services. He considers this to be the only way by which better education, housing and pensions can be achieved without higher taxation.[2]

There is nothing novel in obtaining State revenue from the profits of industrial and commercial concerns. The taxation of profits earned by companies has for many years been the practice in this and other countries. What is new is the Labour Party's proposal to obtain revenue from the ownership of stocks instead of by means of a direct fiscal levy. This, however, is the method adopted in the Soviet Union, where the greater part of State revenue is obtained from trading and manufacturing trusts wholly owned by the State. In such a system prices are fixed so as to yield whatever sums the State decides it requires to spend. The result in effect is a system of concealed indirect taxation.

Something of the same kind would be almost certain to happen if the situation envisaged by Mr Jay were to come about. The Government as equity holder would bring pressure to bear on the big joint stock companies to fix prices so as to maximize earnings, and hence dividends; and in course of time ways would be found to give these companies a monopolistic or privileged position to prevent them from being undersold by competitors. There would be far less parliamentary control and public understanding of such a system of concealed indirect taxation than exists now in the case of our present direct and indirect taxes.

The case in favour of State holdings of equity stocks is argued in *Industry and Society* mainly in terms of its effect in promoting greater equality. But if a substantial share of the profits and capital gains earned by large companies were to be channelled into the Exchequer, would this promote greater equality? The correct answer is that we cannot assume this would necessarily occur. If the revenue thus obtained were used to pay for social services of an egalitarian character, then obviously

[1] Herbert Jay: *Public Capital and Private Enterprise.* 28 Fabian Journal, July 1959, p. 13.
[2] *Ib.*, p. 14.

the final result would be to promote equality; but this would be achieved by the application of the revenue rather than by the nature of its origin. *Industry and Society* advocates the public ownership of commercial stocks as a measure designed in itself to promote equality. This is by no means the same thing as advocating it as a method of financing the Welfare State.

The acquisition of shares by the State in commercial companies has taken place on a large scale in Italy. To the best of my knowledge, the results which according to *Industry and Society* are expected to flow from such a policy, and in particular the attainment of greater economic and social equality, have not occurred in Italy. A brief description of the Italian situation is contained in the Appendix.

THE ACQUISITIVE STATE

The policy outlined in *Industry and Society* means that the State should acquire wealth for the sake of acquiring wealth; or, to put it another way, in order to prevent it from falling into private hands. The policy accepts profit-making as a legitimate and desirable function of industry, and quarrels only with the destination of the profits. If members of the Labour Party attack the whole notion of profit as inherently wrong, they are likely to find themselves in a position of some difficulty. None of the nationalized industries is debarred from making a surplus; and it requires a good deal of hardihood to argue that British Petroleum, BOAC, and BEA should not be allowed to make a profit on doctrinal grounds. Surely a stronger argument is to urge that the State should not behave like an avaricious private individual. It should not give way to a mere desire to acquire wealth regardless of the purpose for which it is needed and the source from which it comes. There may on occasion be a genuine public interest to justify a State investment in a particular industry or firm; but where that occurs the State should have some share in its policy. This may lead towards mixed enterprise, of which we have little experience in Britain, though there is a great deal of it in France and other continental countries. This is quite different from the mere acquisition by the State of stocks or shares.

The policy set out in *Industry and Society* has been strongly criticized both by the Right and by the Left.

The critics of the Right object to any further incursion of the State into the economy. They believe that if the State were to acquire the equity stocks of commercial companies, it would lead inevitably to government interference in the policy and the management of the companies in question. This, they are convinced, would lessen efficiency and introduce political considerations into business decisions. They hold strongly that profit-making business can best be run by business men and industrialists, and that politicians and civil servants should keep away both in the interests of the economy and of the State.

The most pungent comment from the Left appeared in *Universities and Left Review*. It declares that the Labour Party's new policy accepts the corporate economy and the institution of private property on which it is based. The State could not hope to appropriate the great commercial companies merely by acquiring equity shares in them. 'Nevertheless, as shareholder, it would of necessity be involved with the whole complex process by which wealth is maximized. The State would appropriate for itself—as the managerial elite has done in another way—the motives and behaviour patterns of a propertied class. It seems now almost unnecessary to say that this pattern can only serve to ramify and stabilize the forms of wealth and power in our society. There is no hint anywhere . . . of an attack—direct or indirect—upon this structure of power.'[1]

The article remarks that as a large shareholder, the State could not propose the restriction of dividends because this would diminish its own share of the profits it is so eager to obtain. Nor could the Government be expected to object to a high level of retained profits, for this would lead to an appreciation in the value of the State's holding. As regards price policy, the State would share with other investors a desire to see prices fixed in the most profitable way possible. 'In sum, as a private shareholder, the State would legitimize the most anti-social behaviour of the modern oligopolies. It would help to maximize the wealth of the private shareholder. It would underwrite the present hierarchical structure of British society—it would swell the power and increase the status of the propertied rich. It would have, by default, a vested interest in maintaining the disproportionate distribution of wealth and power which, even at present, makes Britain one of the most class-bound and stratified of modern states.'[2] It would enable a system of State capitalism to be established on an unprecedented scale.

Socialist Union takes a similar view of the proposal that the Government should buy up a proportion of shares in prosperous concerns rather than nationalize them entirely. The public, they say, would thereby be able to reap the benefits of high revenue yields and participation in capital gains, without incurring the heavy responsibilities of administration. This is a dangerous course because, in acquiring a vested interest in high profits, the Government would be induced to assent—or

[1] 'The Insiders'. *Universities and Left Review*, Winter, 1958, p. 32.

[2] *Loc cit.*

at least not to disapprove—of high profits, with all the inequalities which flow from them, not only in the companies partly owned by the State, but throughout the whole of industry.[1] So when the State participates in industry, it should have in mind, not merely increasing its revenue, but the Government's whole economic policy.

NATIONALIZATION AS AN END IN ITSELF

Within the Labour movement there is a considerable body of members who favour nationalization for its own sake. They believe that every Labour government should as a matter of principle carry out a substantial programme of nationalization, so that ultimately the private sector of the economy will dwindle away and vanish almost completely.

Mr Herbert Morrison, at a meeting held in his honour on the eve of his retirement from Parliament, urged the parliamentary Labour Party to retain nationalization as an integral part of their policy. He said it was fundamental to the party's future that they should strive for nationalization, which he saw as a means of enabling the British people to become masters of their own house and not just tenants. But nationalization should never be imposed on the country. The case for nationalizing an industry must always be proved before the measure was introduced.[2]

Different and more urgent reasons for pursuing a policy of nationalization were given by Mr John Dugdale, MP, in an article published in 1957 in *The Political Quarterly*. He pointed out that even at the level of taxation then prevailing, and without a capital gains tax, some large firms are already transferring their headquarters abroad. If taxation were to be tightened up and all forms of tax avoidance eliminated, 'the move to leave England may become a stampede. Many business men reckon that it is worth while working hard in order to earn business expenses and capital gains. Would they work so hard if both these sources of income were removed from them? They might well consider that if there were no chance of earning money through either of these methods, they would transfer their business headquarters abroad.'[3] To make this illegal would present serious difficulties, but even if that were done it would be impossible to prevent the business men themselves from leaving the country.

Mr Dugdale believes that private enterprise cannot be relied upon to develop production without the rewards normally expected by business

[1] *Twentieth Century Socialism* (1956), p. 85.

[2] *The Times*, July 30, 1959, p. 4.

[3] John Dugdale: *The Labour Party and Nationalization*, in 28, *The Political Quarterly* (July-September 1957), p. 256.

executives; and he thinks that an attempt to combine a high degree of government control, high taxation, and public abuse will lead to disaster. In his view it is a fallacy to think that private enterprise can be 'milked' indefinitely in order that it may pay for the Welfare State, while at the same time it is continually denigrated. 'There comes a time when the cow refuses to give any more milk, and if Labour comes into power, brings about a drastic increase in taxation, and stops all loopholes, this time may well arise.'[1] In consequence, nationalization must be adopted as the only practicable method by which industry can be run for the benefit of the community.

The weakness of Mr Dugdale's approach is that he seizes on nationalization as a way of avoiding certain difficulties which are likely to arise in the private sector of the economy under a Labour government without enquiring whether similar or comparable difficulties may not occur in the public sector also. Can we assume that the directors, managers and technical experts of high ability who are needed in public corporations no less than in private enterprise are indifferent to financial incentives and oppressive taxation? This is certainly not the view expressed in *Public Enterprise*. This pamphlet cited with approval the criticism voiced by the Herbert Committee on the relatively low salaries paid in the electricity supply industry to board members and management generally, and declared that the salaries of such men should not fall below those paid for corresponding positions in private business.[2] It would be rash to assume that men possessing the administrative abilities and technical knowledge which are in worldwide demand at the present time, will be willing to work in British nationalized industries if the fiscal conditions are such as to drive business men abroad. In its policy statement on *Equality* the Labour Party has already expressed concern at the emigration of scientific and technical personnel. The Labour Party will have to face up to these disagreeable questions sooner or later; and the sooner the better.

Nationalization should not be regarded by any means as a policy which has served its purpose and is no longer useful. On the other hand it is difficult to believe that there is any inherent virtue today in a policy of further nationalization as an end in itself, regardless of the industries concerned or the ends in view. It is still more difficult to believe that there would be any large amount of electoral support for such a policy. Mr Morrison's understanding of British public opinion is surely not in error on this point.[3]

[1] *The Political Quarterly* (July-September 1957), p. 257.
[2] *Public Enterprise* (Published by the Labour Party), p. 27.
[3] *Ante* p. 485.

THE CRITERIA OF NATIONALIZATION

The fundamental questions on which clearer thinking is needed are the criteria which should be applied in deciding whether an industry or a firm should be nationalized. The following considerations may throw some light on the subject without claiming to be the last word on the question:

First, where an industry or a firm is working with obvious success and efficiency, there is no point in urging nationalization merely because of its large size. If it is shown after official inquiry that a firm which dominates an industry is in fact using its monopolistic position to the public disadvantage, that would be a good reason for taking it over. An example of this was the British Oxygen Company.

Second, industries or firms engaged in operations abroad or in export trade, might well meet with considerable sales resistance on political grounds in several countries (notably the United States) if they were nationalized. Neither the Volkswagen or Renault Companies appear to suffer from this handicap, but the evidence from these two examples cannot be regarded as conclusive.

Third, if the State takes over an industry which is suffering from bad management, technological backwardness, a shortage of able executives and technical experts, or capital starvation (e.g. coal mining and railways), it is extremely difficult to arrest the momentum of decline and replace it with a momentum of progress. In short, the conditions are highly unfavourable to public enterprise.

Fourth, the best results have so far been achieved in industries or services which came under public ownership and administration at an early stage of their existence, such as broadcasting, the airlines, and atomic energy. Public enterprise can do much better in new and expanding industries than in old and contracting ones.

Fifth, it is a mistake to identify nationalization with giant undertakings running an entire industry on monopolistic lines. An effort should be made to discover the optimum size of the operating unit in each instance and to encourage as much emulation or competition as possible between separate undertakings within a nationalized industry, or between public and private enterprise within the same industry or service.

Sixth, although the decisions to nationalize in their entirety coal, gas, electricity, railways, road haulage and the air services were correct in view of the technical, organizational and financial circumstances of those industries, in future it might be better in most instances to take over individual firms or establish a new undertaking rather than acquire a whole industry.

The importance of establishing the right criteria for nationalization can be seen if we consider the policy of the Labour Party to nationalize the whole or part of any industry which is found to be 'failing the nation'. Mr Harold Wilson, MP, explained on behalf of the National Executive Committee to the Annual Party Conference in 1957, that this expression was not limited to pure operational efficiency. 'When we say failing the nation,' he said, 'we mean failing the nation, and not necessarily just being inefficient. Of course, efficiency would be one test, and an important one, but there are others, such as failing to play an adequate part in the national export effort, abuse of monopoly power, unwillingness to expand sufficiently in the national interest, lack of drive in investment, bad industrial relations, failure to co-operate in government planning measures, and other tests.'[1]

Whatever may be the precise meaning of operational efficiency, most of the other shortcomings mentioned by Mr Wilson are aspects of inefficiency. That is certainly true of inability to export, inadequate capital investment, bad labour relations, and unwillingness to expand sufficiently. An industry or firm would be expected to expand 'in the national interest' only where it would be financially profitable to do so. This leaves only an abuse of a monopoly and failure to co-operate in government planning measures as matters not directly connected with efficiency.

It would seem, therefore, that in undertaking to nationalize industries which are 'failing the nation', the Labour Party is likely to saddle the State with all the most inefficient, backward, contracting or stagnant industries. This might be disastrous, for these are the industries where the conditions for successful operation and development by public enterprise are most unfavourable. We know from our experience of coal and the railways how hard it is to overcome a momentum of decline in an old industry. To add to the number of such backward, declining, or stagnant industries in the public sector would almost certainly discredit the principle of nationalization beyond hope of recovery. I would not rule out absolutely the acquisition of a firm or even an industry which was 'failing the nation' in the sense described by Mr Wilson, but it should be regarded as generally undesirable, as presenting the most unfavourable conditions to public enterprise, and to be used only in the last resort when all else has failed.

It is highly probable that the proprietors and directors of industries which are 'failing the nation', together with the organs representing business and financial interests, and even Conservative politicians, will not really object (whatever their ostensible attitude may be) to the

[1] *Labour Party Annual Report*, 1957, p. 128.

nationalization of contracting or unprofitable industries. There is, indeed, no reason why they should. The Conservative Party and business associations made no demand for the denationalization of coal or the railways; but the profitable and expanding industries of steel and road haulage were promptly denationalized when a Conservative government came to power. Why does the Federation of British Industries distinguish between the nationalized industries or services which 'it is now impracticable to restore to private hands even if it is in principle desirable' and civil air transport, which it regards as 'both practicable and desirable to set free'?[1] Obviously the answer lies in the simple test of profitability. The Lancashire cotton industry would no doubt be extremely glad to be nationalized on the ground that it was 'failing the nation', and there would be little genuine political or business opposition.

STATE AID FOR PRIVATE ENTERPRISE

A very important phenomenon in Britain today is the demand by industrialists for government assistance to enable them to undertake capital projects or for subsidies to help them to cover the current costs of production. The Government recently agreed to advance £50 million to the Scottish steel firm of Colvilles to build a new strip mill at Motherwell.[2] The Cunard Steamship Company are seeking financial aid from the State to enable them to replace the *Queen Elizabeth* and *Queen Mary* by two new liners which are expected to cost £50 million each. The aircraft industry is openly declaring its need for financial support by the Government in one form or another, now that the demands of the Royal Air Force for military aircraft are greatly reduced. The makers of civil aircraft are also asking for financial help from the Exchequer to enable a new generation of supersonic civil transport aircraft to be designed and developed. The film producing industry has been in receipt of a State subsidy for many years. British agriculture has been heavily subsidized for so long that the farmers' dependence on State aid is almost taken for granted.

[1] *Nationalization.* A report by the FBI, para. 9.

[2] A like sum is being advanced for a similar project in South Wales to Richard Thomas and Baldwin, which is still nationalized. The reasons given by the British Iron and Steel Federation were, first, that the threat of renationalization made it impossible for steel companies to borrow money in the market; and second, that the Government wished to locate the strip mill in Scotland to conform with their general policy for the location of industry. But this may not be the full explanation. The steel firms have been accused frequently of reluctance to construct capacity in advance of demand; and doubt has been cast on the ability of the individual steel companies to raise the finance needed for their development. Both these allegations would provide additional reasons for the Government to provide capital out of public funds. See *Steel: Fact and Fiction.* (BISF) pages 13-15; *The 'Spectator' Steel Inquiry.*

There are sometimes good reasons why, in the national interest, financial assistance should be given by the Exchequer to assist the capital development projects or production programmes of commercial companies. On the other hand, there is little to be said in favour of the State paying £30 million to facilitate the contraction of the Lancashire cotton industry.[1]

Assuming that a good case is made out in the national interest to help an industry or a firm, the important question is what form the necessary State finance should take. I agree entirely with Mr Douglas Jay, MP, that the Government should not normally give away the taxpayer's money to private shareholders in the form of a subsidy, but should insist on the State receiving ordinary shares in respect of its investment. If the new venture succeeds, it will bring increased profits in which the taxpayers who have contributed part of the capital are fully entitled to share. If it fails, the equity shareholders will get nothing; but in that event the taxpayer, as shareholder, will not be in a worse position than if the money had been given outright as a subsidy.[2]

There are two advantages in the State acquiring equity shares in exchange for its financial aid. One is that they are free from the rigidity of fixed interest holdings. The obligation to pay a fixed rate of interest regardless of the yield actually produced, may force an undertaking to show annual losses, and even be unable to meet its obligations, if the economic position happens to be unfavourable.[3] We have already seen that this sometimes occurs in the nationalized industries in regard to their obligations arising from compensation stock. It is far better to avoid the possibility of such a demoralizing situation from occurring; and this can easily be done within the normal framework of private enterprise by requiring that the State shall receive equity shares.

The other advantage of equity shares is that they carry voting rights and therefore a certain measure of control, whereas debentures and other forms of loan capital have a non-voting status. If the State is to find large sums of money to assist private enterprise, it should have rights and powers not less than those normally accorded to private investors. What those rights are has recently been explained by Sir Frank Morgan, chairman of the Prudential Assurance Company, which holds about £200 million in ordinary shares out of a total investment portfolio of nearly £1,000 million. In the chairman's annual speech in May, 1959, Sir Frank remarked:

'We are long-term investors and normally expect to continue to hold

[1] Cotton Industry Act, 1959.

[2] Douglas Jay: *Public Capital and Private Enterprise*. 28, Fabian Journal (July, 1959), p. 13.

[3] *Ib.*, p. 11.

our investments, looking for a steady and, we hope, expanding income . . . We do not regard it as proper to us as shareholders to interfere in the day-to-day management of the companies in which we have taken an interest. There are, however, certain broad issues of policy on which we feel shareholders have a right to be consulted.'[1]

The relationship described in this passage might be a quite satisfactory one in many instances for the Government to have in relation to commercial companies in which the State had invested money.

Where the investment by the State is substantial, or where there are any other special circumstances to justify it, the Government should have the right to nominate a proportion of the directors. There is nothing new in this idea. The Government possess this right in regard to the British Petroleum Co Ltd. The Treasury has often obtained the right to appoint directors in order to safeguard loans made to companies out of public money. This applies both to public and private companies to which loans have been made under the Distribution of Industry Act, 1945; to companies whose loans were guaranteed by the Treasury under the Trade Facilities Act, 1921 and subsequent Acts; and to companies which have had money advanced on loan from the Building Materials and Housing Fund. There are many other companies in receipt of public funds which are in a like position.[2]

MIXED ENTERPRISE

For the State to acquire ordinary shares in a commercial company in which the Government have invested money in order to further ends they consider to be of national importance, is entirely different from the policy advocated in *Industry and Society* of acquiring equity stocks of large companies solely in order that the State may participate in the high earnings and capital gains accruing to such stocks. The distinction lies in the fact that in the former case public money is invested because the Government are convinced that the nation's interests are served by enabling new ships, or new aircraft, or a Channel tunnel, or whatever it may be, to be built, and that financial aid from the Exchequer is necessary to bring this about. The investment in this case is an instrument of national policy; and the rôle of the State is an active one. In the latter case the motives of the State are purely acquisitive, and its rôle resembles that of a functionless property owner.

[1] Quoted by Douglas Jay: *op. cit.*, p. 14.

[2] A list of Treasury-nominated Directors of certain firms was given in Parl. Deb. Commons 1951-2, Vol. 496 (February 27, 1952), col. 162. The information has been supplemented by the Treasury, to whom the author's thanks are due.

The participation by the State in private enterprise here envisaged, can be of potential benefit to all the interests concerned. It points the way to types of mixed enterprise of which we have had little experience hitherto in Britain, but which may prove to be particularly suitable for the mixed and regulated economy which has evolved in these islands and which is likely to persist for as long as one can foresee the future.

Mixed enterprise is very widespread in many countries all over the world. Mixed undertakings have already been proposed by the Labour Party as a means of encouraging private enterprise to venture capital on risky projects in the national interest. State participation in the private sector would take the form in some cases of joint companies in which private enterprise and the Government would co-operate, the latter providing part of the capital.[1]

If mixed enterprise is to stand any chance of success, it will demand a change of attitude towards public enterprise and public ownership on the part of many leading industrialists and business men, of bodies like the Federation of British Industries and the Institute of Directors, and of Conservative politicians. It is among these that some of the most rabid doctrinaires are to be found today. One recalls ill-considered onslaughts against bureaucracy and officials, the denunciation of political interference, the denigration of the nationalized industries, the indiscriminate adulation of private enterprise and competition. Yet when times become difficult, and the profits disappear from the aircraft industry, or when enormously profitable Atlantic liners are to be replaced, or when the cotton industry cannot face foreign competition, the tune is quickly changed and government support is immediately invoked. We hear no more about bureaucratic incompetence and the importance of avoiding State intervention. The emphasis is now placed on the need to uphold the national interest, to maintain British prestige, and to consider the matter from a standpoint which disregards the oft-proclaimed ability of private enterprise to manage its business in its own way. This kind of double talk cannot continue if any serious development of mixed enterprise is expected.

The opportunities for mixed enterprise are not confined to those which may arise when an industry is in need of financial help from the Government. There are many other occasions when collaboration between public and private enterprise could be fruitful and successful. For example, in some of the new developments resulting from the application of nuclear energy, joint undertakings by the Atomic Energy Authority and private firms may be useful. The hotels which need to be built in the National Parks might well be provided and operated by mixed under-

[1] *Challenge to Britain*. Labour Party Report, 1953, p. 74.

takings. In such cases public authority and private interests would participate in the management as well as in investing money.

CONCLUSION

Although mixed enterprise may sometimes offer the best solution, this does not rule out the possibility that straightforward nationalization may be required in certain industries and services. We should, however, always bear in mind that the most favourable conditions for public enterprise are likely to exist in new or expanding industries or services; and the least favourable conditions in old, declining, or stagnant branches of the economy.

In industries which are divided between public and private enterprise, care will be required to ensure that fair competition is maintained. Some publicists have stressed the need to ensure that government departments and other public authorities do not give preferential treatment to nationalized undertakings in regard to the amount of interest on, and conditions attaching to loans, to priorities when goods or services are in short supply, government contracts, etc. A danger from the other side could be a boycott by private firms either in the industry concerned, or in other industries on which a nationalized undertaking might depend for orders, raw materials, etc. Complaints about such matters could possibly be entrusted to the Monopolies and Restrictive Practices Commission for investigation and report.

The most neglected form of public enterprise is municipal trading. This applies both to individual enterprises owned and controlled by a particular local authority, and to collective enterprises owned and controlled by local authorities in association, for the purpose of providing for their common needs such things as stationery and printing, uniforms, and public supplies generally.

The public corporation is in my judgment by far the best organ so far devised in this or any other country for administering nationalized industries or undertakings. Allowing for some teething troubles which are still not entirely cured, the public corporation which we have evolved is an outstanding contribution to public administration in a new and vitally important sphere. It is far better than the joint-stock company owned and controlled by the State; or than government departments engaged in business activity; or than State administrations set up to manage commercial or industrial undertakings, such as those existing in the Netherlands, Scandinavia, France and other countries. Government departments have on the whole not shown up particularly well as bodies administering nationalized industries, and I can see no good reason for moving in that direction.[1]

I will quote in conclusion the remarks of a Swedish authority on public enterprise, the late Mr Elis Hastad, Governor of Uppsala, formerly professor of political science in the University of Stockholm and for long a Conservative member of the Riksdag. 'The United Kingdom with its public corporations achieved most of what it set out to do, and has brought to State enterprise flexibility, initiative, enterprise, adventurousness and the desire to experiment, which private enterprise shows at its best.'[2] Mr Hastad was aware that there are still some problems to be solved, such as the right balance for the corporation's relations with the Government and Parliament. But this should not detract from the tribute which he paid, and which I have tried to pay, to the remarkable achievements of the public corporations in dealing with some of the most difficult economic, political, and social problems of our time.

[1] Mr Herbert Morrison does not rule out the direct management of publicly owned industries by Government Departments. He has suggested gas or electricity as a suitable industry for this purpose. *Government and Industry*, p. 283-4; see also evidence to Select Committee on Nationalized Industries. House of Commons 1951-2/332 I, Q. 778, Q. 830.

[2] In a paper presented to the Fourth Congress of the International Political Service Association held in Rome in September, 1958.

APPENDIX

Public Ownership in Italy

IN ITALY, a large proportion of the shares in a wide variety of industries are owned by the State. They include shipbuilding (72 per cent), passenger shipping lines (66 per cent), cargo lines (8 per cent), methane gas (93 per cent), mining for iron-ore (100 per cent), antimony (100 per cent), tin (70 per cent) and other metals, crude oil (21 per cent), and the basic industries providing transport, power and communications.[1]

The acquisition of these holdings by the State took place in Italy mostly during the depression of the 1930's. Some of it was due to the accidental consequences resulting from the action of the Fascist government acting through the Institute for Industrial Reconstruction, in coming to the rescue of three of the largest banks[2] which had got into difficulties, rather than to a deliberate policy of public ownership. The banks in question had extensive investments in Italian industry, and when they were taken over by the State their portfolios went with them. In other cases, however, there were specific motives for nationalization. Among them was the policy of autarchy followed under Fascism after 1935, which led to the establishment of the Mineral Metals Corporation (AMMI) and the Coal Corporation (ACI); the desire to secure at least partial freedom from foreign trusts, particularly in respect of the exploitation of natural gas in North Italy; the need to search for oil, develop Italian oilfields, and control the import and distribution of oil products; the urge to meet the country's defence needs, which led to the development of the steel and armaments industries under State auspices; the desire to promote undertakings which were neglected by private enterprise either on account of a lack of capital or the high risk involved, which led to public enterprise in civil aviation, the industrial development of backward areas, and electricity supply.

These extensive holdings are now administered by two bodies created for the purpose. One is the Instituto per la Ricostruzioni Industriale (IRI) found in 1933, which covers banks, mines, electricity supply, shipbuilding, merchant shipping, chemicals, telephone services, air-

[1] All the percentages given above relate to production.

[2] The Bank of Rome, Credito Italiano, and the Banca Commerciale Italiana.

lines, and various types of manufacture or construction. The other is the Ente Nazionale Idrocarburi (ENI) established in 1953 to handle fuel oil and natural gas products. Both these bodies are public corporations. Below IRI is a series of subholding companies carrying out technical and financial co-ordination of enterprises in particular sectors. There is Finmare for merchant shipping, Finsider for iron and steel, Finmeccanica for engineering, Finelettrica for electricity, and STET for the telephone service. Below the sub-holding companies are a great number of subsidiary operating companies. ENI has a slightly different structure, as the sub-holding companies which it controls (AGIP Mineraria, AGIP, AGIP Nucleare, ANIC, and SNAM) not only have holdings in 48 other companies but are also themselves engaged in production operations. The organization of public ownership in Italy is very complex, and there is an elaborate system of interlocking directorates. While IRI and ENI are public corporations, the sub-holding and subsidiary companies are ordinary joint stock companies. The latter are not subject to any form of administrative regulation other than that applicable to all commercial companies.

The Governing Board of IRI is composed of a full-time chairman and deputy chairman, who with three financial and industrial experts form the Executive Committee. The other eight members of the Board consist of the Accountant-General, and the Directors-General of the interested Departments. Any increase in the capital of IRI must be voted by Parliament as part of the national budget, and this is the only respect in which Parliament has real power in regard to IRI. It is important because many of the subsidiary companies were originally rescued from bankruptcy and a number of them are still showing losses. The Cabinet is responsible for deciding the general policies which IRI is to follow in the national interest. In practice a committee of Ministers decides all political questions concerning IRI and ENI.[1]

The statutory provisions relating to the distribution of surpluses made by IRI and ENI are that 20 per cent will go to the ordinary reserve fund, 15 per cent to a special fund to promote training and social welfare of the employees, and the remaining 65 per cent to the Treasury. In the case of IRI the sums payable to the Treasury are in repayment of capital sums and contributions advanced by the State. When all the outstanding advances have been refunded, the 65 per cent will go to an extraordinary reserve fund. In the case of ENI this provision does not limit the obligation, and ENI will therefore always have to pay 65 per

[1] The Ministerial Committee is the Comitato Interministeriale for State shareholdings provided for in Article 4 of Law No. 1589 of December 22, 1956, which created the Ministry of State Shareholdings.

cent of its annual net surplus to the State. So far, the annual working results of IRI have usually shown a loss since 1945, although a small surplus has occasionally been made.

IRI is a vast undertaking which owns and controls a large proportion of the engineering and chemical industries in Italy. It owns the three most important commercial banks, the Italian airlines, the well-known Siemens company, and a great variety of other enterprises. IRI acquired many minority shareholdings, but its policy has been to dispose of interests in concerns over which it did not exercise effective control, and to concentrate its investments in certain sectors. It nevertheless retains a minority holding (8 per cent) of the stock of Montecatini, the great chemical firm.

ENI is a similar body working in a narrower field. Its governing board is composed on similar principles, except that it contains two elected representatives of the employees, and no *ex officio* officials, as all five civil servants are nominated by their respective Ministers. It engages in searching for oil and developing oil fields both in Italy and in other countries, such as Egypt. Through AGIP, its largest subsidiary, it carries on a big business in refining and selling petroleum products. It is also interested in natural gas, and constructs and operates gas pipe lines. The use of methane is now becoming very widespread in Italy, largely replacing imported coal, and this is one result of ENI's work in exploiting methane and constructing thousands of miles of metanoduct. The financial results have been good, and large surpluses have been earned by ENI.[1]

In addition to the holdings which it possesses through IRI and ENI, the State directly owns shares in a few companies. An example is the Società Nazionale Cogne, a large company engaged in iron ore mining, the manufacture of iron and steel, and engineering. The State owns all the shares, the holding being managed by the Minister of State Shareholdings. There are also some important public enterprises administered as semi-independent units of government departments. A leading example is the railways. There are also some other public corporations, such as the Banca Nationale del Lavoro.

Both IRI and ENI have valuable achievements to their credit. IRI has effected the reform and modernization of the banking and industrial credit systems; the reconstruction of shipbuilding and engineering after the second World War; the development of industries and basic services in sectors of the economy or in parts of Italy where private enterprise

[1] ENI annual net surpluses from the year of its formation, were as follows: 1954 L2,340 m.; 1955 L4,117 m.; 1956 L4,157 m.; 1957 L4,585 m.; 1958 L4,812 m ; 1959 L4,615 m.

was lagging or lacking; and the co-ordination of activities and of investment policies in particular sectors of industry. ENI has made Italy much less dependent on the great international oil companies than she would otherwise be; and has enabled Italy to participate actively in oil producing, refining and distribution, both at home and abroad.

So far as I am aware, however, this form of public ownership appears to have done little or nothing to promote economic or social equality in Italy. The undertakings which IRI owns are in every field in competition with privately owned undertakings. The companies raise as much of their capital in the market as possible, and IRI finds the balance. The present practice of IRI is to issue fixed interest bonds with a right to convert them into equity shares. Sometimes IRI is guaranteed a minimum rate of interest on its bonds with a possible increase depending on the profits. The price policy is to avoid subsidization and to seek to make a profit.

Until recently the policy of IRI was to get rid of its minority holdings in order not to be a shareholder in concerns which it cannot control. Early in 1959, however, Mr Fascetti, the chairman of IRI, announced a new policy of minority shareholding finance to promote the development of Southern Italy. He emphasized the need for additional finance from a source willing to participate in the actual running of the enterprise, sharing in the risks incurred, even without having a majority control.[1]

Italian experience does not conform in all respects with the policies advocated in *Industry and the State*, but it bears a sufficiently close resemblance to be relevant. The conclusions which emerge from that experience do not appear to support the assumptions on which the Labour Party is basing its new policy. They indicate at the very least a need for a first hand and objective investigation of the Italian situation before the policy of State acquisition of equity shares in commercial companies is allowed to remain in the Labour Party's programme as a means of achieving economic and social equality.

[1] *Lo Stato e l'iniziativa nell'esperienza italiana* in 'Notizie IRI' No. 10. Feb.-March 1959, p. 9.

Select Bibliography

The following select bibliography begins with the material dealing with the subject generally. This is divided into (*a*) Statutes, (*b*) House of Commons papers, (*c*) Government Reports or White Papers, (*d*) Books, articles, and pamphlets. Thereafter the bibliography is divided into chapters corresponding with those of the book.

General

(a) Statutes

Forestry Act, 1945, 8 and 9 Geo. VI, C.35
Bank of England Act, 1946, 9 and 10 Geo. VI, C.27
Coal Industry Nationalization Act, 1946, 9 and 10 Geo. VI, C.59
New Towns Act, 1946, 9 and 10 Geo. VI, C.68
Civil Aviation Act, 1946, 9 and 10 Geo. VI, C.70
Cable and Wireless Act, 1946, 9 and 10 Geo. VI, C.82
Forestry Act, 1947, 10 and 11 Geo. VI, C.21
Cotton (Centralized Buying) Act, 1947, 10 and 11 Geo. VI, C.26
Transport Act, 1947, 10 and 11 Geo. VI, C.49
Electricity Act, 1947, 10 and 11 Geo. VI, C.54
Overseas Resources Development Act, 1946, 11 and 12 Geo. VI, C.15
Gas Act, 1948, 11 and 12 Geo. VI, C.67
Coal Industry Act, 1949, 12, 13 and 14 Geo. VI, C.53
Airways Corporations Act, 1949, 12, 13 and 14 Geo. VI, C.57
Overseas Resources Development Act, 1949, 12, 13 and 14 Geo. VI, C.65
Civil Aviation Act, 1949, 12, 13 and 14 Geo. VI, C.67
Iron and Steel Act, 1949, 12, 13 and 14 Geo. VI, C.72
Coal Industry (No. 2) Act, 1949, 12, 13 and 14 Geo. VI, C.79
Air Corporations Act, 1949, 12, 13 and 14 Geo. VI, C.91
Overseas Resources Development Act, 1951, 14 and 15 Geo. VI, C.20
Sea Fish Industry Act, 1951, 14 and 15 Geo. VI, C.30
Coal Industry Act, 1951, 14 and 15 Geo. VI, C.41
Forestry Act, 1951, 14 and 15 Geo. VI, C.61
Hydro-Electric Development (Scotland) Act, 1952, 15 and 16 Geo. VI and Eliz. II, C.22
New Towns Act, 1952, 15 and 16 Geo. VI and Eliz. II, C.27
Transport Act, 1953, 1 and 2 Eliz. II, C.13
Iron and Steel Act, 1953, 1 and 2 Eliz. II, C.15
White Fish and Herring Industries Act, 1953, 1 and 2 Eliz. II, C.17
New Towns Act, 1953, 1 and 2 Eliz. II, C.38
Cotton Act, 1954, 2 and 3 Eliz. II, C.24
Atomic Energy Authority Act, 1954, 2 and 3 Eliz. II, C.32

Gas and Electricity (Borrowing Powers) Act, 1954, 2 and 3 Eliz. II, C.52.
Television Act, 1954, 2 and 3 Eliz. II, C.54
Transport Charges, etc. (Miscellaneous Provisions) Act, 1954, 2 and 3 Eliz. II, C.64
Electricity Reorganization (Scotland) Act, 1954, 2 and 3 Eliz. II, C.60
Overseas Resources Development Act, 1954, 2 and 3 Eliz. II, C.71
New Towns Act, 1955, 3 and 4 Eliz. II, C.4
Transport (Borrowing Powers) Act, 1955, 3 and 4 Eliz. II, C.10
Sugar Act, 1956, 4 and 5 Eliz. II, C.48
Finance Act, 1956, 4 and 5 Eliz. II, C.54, S.42
Transport (Disposal of Road Haulage Property) Act, 1956, 4 and 5 Eliz. II, C.56
Air Corporation Act, 1956, 5 Eliz. II, C.3
Coal Industry Act, 1956, 4 and 5 Eliz. II, C.61
British Transport Commission Act, 1956, 4 and 5 Eliz. II, C.74
Transport (Railway Finances) Act, 1957, 5 and 6 Eliz. II, C.9
White Fish and Herring Industries Act, 1957, 5 and 6 Eliz. II, C.22
British Transport Commission Act, 1957, 5 and 6 Eliz. II, C.33
Electricity Act, 1957, 5 and 6 Eliz. II, C.48
New Towns Act, 1958, 6 and 7 Eliz. II, C.12
Overseas Resources Development Act, 1958, 6 and 7 Eliz. II, C.15
Nationalized Industries Loans Act, 1958, 6 and 7 Eliz. II, C.19

(b) HOUSE OF COMMONS PAPERS

Select Committee on Nationalized Industries: Report, with evidence, 1951-2/125
Select Committee on Nationalized Industries: Report, with evidence, 1952-3/235
Select Committee on Nationalized Industries: Special Report, with evidence, 1955-6/120
Report from the Select Committee on Broadcasting (Anticipation of Debates), with evidence, etc., 1955-6/288
Select Committee on Nationalized Industries (Reports and Accounts): *Report with evidence*, 1956-7/304
Select Committee on Nationalized Industries (Reports and Accounts): *Report with evidence*, 1957-8/187-I
Select Committee on Nationalized Industries (Reports and Accounts): *Report with evidence*, 1958-9/213
Select Committee on Nationalized Industries (Reports and Accounts): *Special Report with evidence*, 1958-9/276
Annual Reports or Reports and Accounts of the following:
National Coal Board
British Transport Commission
British European Airways Corporation
British Overseas Airways Corporation
Cable and Wireless Limited

Central (formerly British) Electricity Authority and Area Electricity Boards
Electricity Council and the Central Electricity Generating Board
Gas Council and Area Gas Boards
Colonial Development Corporation
Iron and Steel Corporation of Great Britain
Overseas Food Corporation
Raw Cotton Commission
Atomic Energy Authority
Independent Television Authority
British Broadcasting Corporation
Iron and Steel Holding and Realization Agency
Road Haulage Disposal Board (bi-annual reports)
Industrial Coal Consumers' Council
Domestic Coal Consumers' Council
Central Transport Consultative Committee
Air Transport Advisory Council
Consultative Councils for Electricity
Consultative Councils for Gas

(c) GOVERNMENT REPORTS OR WHITE PAPERS

Broadcasting
Report of the Broadcasting Committee, (Crawford Committee) Cmd. 2599/1926
Report of the Broadcasting Committee, Cmd. 5091/1936 (Ullswater Committee)
Report of the Broadcasting Committee, 1949, Cmd. 8116/1951
Memorandum on the Report of the Broadcasting Committee, 1949, Cmd. 8291/1951
Memorandum on the Report of the Broadcasting Committee, 1949, Cmd. 8550/1952
BBC Charter, Cmd. 8605/1952
Memorandum on Television Policy, Cmd. 9005/1953

Transport
British Air Transport, Cmd. 6605/1945
Report of the Royal Commission on Transport, Cmd. 3751/1930
Transport Policy, Cmd. 8538/1952
London Transport, Report of Committee of Inquiry, Ministry of Transport and Civil Aviation, January 1955
British Transport Commission: Proposals for the Railways, Cmd. 9880/1956
Railways Reorganization Scheme, Cmd. 9191/1954

Fuel, Power and Atomic Energy
Report of the Committee on Electricity Distribution, (McGowan Committee) 1936
Report of the Technical Advisory Committee on Coal Mining, Cmd. 6610/1945 (Reid Committee)
Report of the Committee of Enquiry into the Gas Industry, Cmd. 6699/1945
Coal Industry Nationalization, Cmd. 6716/1945

Report of Committee on a National Policy for the Use of Fuel and Power Resources, Cmd. 8647/1952
The Future Organization of the U.K. Atomic Energy Project, Cmd. 8986/1954
Memorandum on the Gas and Electricity (Borrowing Powers) Bill, 1954, Cmd. 9175/1954
A Programme of Nuclear Power, Cmd. 9389/1955
Report of Committee of Inquiry into the Electricity Supply Industry, Cmd. 9672/1956
Memorandum on the Coal Industry Bill, 1956, Cmd. 9745/1956
Proposals for the Reorganization of the Electricity Supply Industry, Cmd. 27/1956

Other Topics

Report of the Committee of Inquiry on the Post Office, Cmd. 4149/1932 (Bridgeman Committee)
Iron and Steel Industry, Cmd. 8617/1952
Report on Post Office Development and Finance, Cmd. 9576/1955
Inquiry into Certain Allegations made by the Civil Service Union relating to the Carlisle and District State Management Scheme, Cmnd. 168/1957

(d) BOOKS, ARTICLES, PAMPHLETS AND NON-GOVERNMENTAL REPORTS

ACTON SOCIETY TRUST. A series of 12 research booklets on *Nationalized Industry*. Claygate and London (1950–2)
BEST, R. D'ARCY. 'The United Kingdom Atomic Energy Authority', XXXIV *Public Administration* (1956), p. 1
BRAND, LORD. 'Nationalization', *Lloyds Bank Review*, April 1949, p. 1
BUREAU OF RAILWAY ECONOMICS. *Nationalized Transport Operations in Great Britain*, series of 5 booklets. Washington, 1948–53
CHESTER, D. N. 'The Nationalized Industries', *Three Banks Review*, December 1952, p. 23
The Nationalized Industries: an Analysis of the Statutory Provision, revised edn. London, 1951
CITRINE, LORD. *Nationalized Industries Face the Test*, address to the Trades Union Congress, September 1950. London, Trades Union Congress, 1950
'Problems of Nationalized Industries', XXIX *Public Administration* (1951), p. 317
CLEGG, H. A. 'Nationalized Industry' in *The British Economy* 1945-1950, ed. G. D. N. Worswick and P. H. Ady. Oxford, (1952), p. 424
and CHESTER, T. E. *The Future of Nationalization*, Oxford, 1953
'The North of Scotland Hydro-Electric Board', XXXI Public Administration (1953), p. 213
CO-OPERATIVE PARTY. *The People's Industry*. London, 1951
DAVIES, E. A. J. *National Enterprise*. London, 1946
Problems of Public Ownership. London, Labour Party, 1952
NEUMAN, A. M. DE. *The Economic Aspects of Nationalization in Great Britain*. 1952

DUMPLETON, C. W. *Colonial Development Corporation*, Fabian Research Series No. 186. London, 1957

FLORENCE, P. SARGANT. *Industry and the State*. London, 1957. Ch. VI

FRIEDMANN, W. (ed.) *The Public Corporation: a Comparative Symposium*. Toronto and London, 1954

GAITSKELL, H. T. N. *Socialism and Nationalization*, Fabian Tract No. 300. London, 1956

GOODMAN, E. *Forms of Public Control and Ownership*. London, 1951

GORDON, L. *The Public Corporation in Great Britain*. London, 1938

GRIFFITH, J. A. G. 'The Forestry Commission,' XXII *Political Quarterly*. (1951), p. 154

GROVE, J. W. 'British Public Corporations: some Recent Developments', XVIII *Journal of Politics*. (1956), p. 651

HANSON, A. H. (ed.) *Public Enterprise*. Brussels, International Institute of Administrative Sciences, 1955

Public Enterprise and Economic Development. London, (1959)

HART, W. O. 'New Town Development Corporations', XXVI *Public Administration*. (1948), p. 147

HAYNES, W. W. *Nationalization in Practice: the British Coal Industry*. Boston, Mass., 1953

JENKINS, C. *British Airlines*, Fabian Research Series No. 158. London, 1953

JENKINS, SIR GILMOUR. *The Ministry of Transport and Civil Aviation*. London, 1959

KELF-COHEN, R. *Nationalization in Britain*. London, 1958

Public Enterprise. London, 1957

XVI. *Law and Contemporary Problems*. Autumn 1951. Issue on the nationalization of British Industries

LEWIS, B. W. *British Planning and Nationalization*. New York, (1952)

LEWIS, W. A. *Overhead Costs*. London, (1945). Ch. VII

The Principles of Economic Planning. London, (1950). Ch. VIII

LONGHURST, J. *Nationalization in Practice: the Civil Aviation Experiment*. London, 1950.

MACKENZIE, N. *The New Towns: the Success of Social Planning*, Fabian Research Series No. 172. London, 1955

MORRISON OF LAMBETH, LORD. *Socialization and Transport*. London, 1933

NEUMAN, A. M. DE. *The Economic Aspects of Nationalization in Great Britain*. 1952

O'BRIEN, T. H. *British Experiments in Public Ownership and Control*. London, 1937

OSTERGAARD, G. N. *Labour and the Development of the Public Corporation*, XXII Manchester School, May 1954

XXI. *Political Quarterly*, April-June 1950. Special issue on the nationalized industries

REID, SIR C. 'The Problem of Coal', *The Times*, November 22-4, 1948

REITH, LORD. *Into the Wind*. London, (1949)

ROBSON, W. A. (ed.) *Problems of Nationalized Industry*. London, 1952

(ed.) *Public Enterprise*. London, 1937

SCAMMELL, E. H. 'Nationalization in Legal Perspective', V *Current Legal Problems.* (1952), p. 30

SELF, SIR H., and WATSON, E. M. *Electricity Supply in Great Britain.* London, 1952

SIMON OF WYTHENSHAWE, LORD. *The BBC from Within.* London, 1953

TOWNSHEND-ROSE, H. *The British Coal Industry.* London, 1951

TRADES UNION CONGRESS. *Interim Report on Post-war Reconstruction.* London, 1945

The Public Control of Industry. Report, London

Public Ownership: an Interim Report. London, 1953

WOOD, A. *The Ground-nut Affair.* London, 1950

CHAPTER I: PUBLIC ENTERPRISE TODAY

ALBAN, FREDERICK J. *Socialization in Great Britain and its effect on the Accountancy Profession,* The American Institute of Accountants. Chicago, 1948

BOPP, K. R. 'Nationalization of the Bank of England and the Bank of France', VIII *Journal of Politics.* (1946), p. 308

CHARLES, ROGER. 'Port Development in the United Kingdom: review of a century of enterprise and achievement', *Dock and Harbour Authority.* London, June, July, August 1951

CHESTER, T. E. 'Public Enterprise in South East Asia', XXVI *Political Quarterly.* (1955), p. 43

CLAPP, GORDON R. *The Tennessee Valley Authority.* Chicago, 1955

DERYCK, ABEL. 'British Conservatives and State Ownership', XIX *The Journal of Politics.* Florida, (1957), p. 227

DIMOCK, M. E. 'Government Corporations—a focus of Policy and Administration', XLIII *American Political Science Review.* October and December 1949

DURISCH, L. L. 'The TVA Programme and the War Effort', VIII *Journal of Politics,* (1946), p. 531

EINAUDI, M. 'Nationalization of Industry in Western Europe: Recent Literature and Debates', XLIV *American Political Science Review.* (1950), p. 177

BYE, M. and ROSSI, E. *Nationalization in France and Italy.* New York, 1955

FLETCHER, H. A. 'The Regie Renault: a nationalized Enterprise in the French Automobile Industry', VIII *Public Policy,* ed. C. J. Friedrich and S. E. Harris. Cambridge, Mass., (1958), p. 173

FOLDES, LUCIEN. 'Control of Nationalized Industries', *Public Law.* Summer 1957, p. 122

GENDARME, R. *L'Experience Francaise de la Nationalization Industrielle et ses Enseignements economiques.* Paris, 1950

HODGETTS, J. E. 'Administration and Politics: the case of the Canadian Broadcasting Corporation', XII *Canadian Journal of Economics and Political Science.* (1946), p. 454

'The Public Corporation in Canada', XXVIII *Public Administration.* (1950), p. 283

JULLIOT DE LA MORANDIERE, L., and BYE, M. (eds.) *Les Nationalizations en France et à l'Etranger: les Nationalizations en France.* Paris, 1948

KEWLEY, T. H. 'Australia Commonwealth Government Corporations', XXVIII *Public Administration.* (1950), p. 195

LAUFENBERGER, H. 'Entreprise Privee et Entreprise Publique', *L'Acualite Economique.* Montreal, January-March 1952, pp. 603-34

LAVERGNE, B. *Le Probleme des Nationalizations.* Paris, 1946

LEUCHTENBURG, W. E. 'Roosevelt, Norris and the "Seven Little TVAS" ', XIV *Journal of Politics.* (1952), p. 418

LILIENTHAL, DAVID. TVA—*Democracy on the March.* New York, 1944

MYERS, M. G. 'The Nationalization of Banks in France', LXIV *Political Science Quarterly.* (1949), p. 189

'Les Nationalizations en France et en Grande-Bretagne', *Le Documentation Francaise,* August 27, 1948, *Notes Documentaires et Etudes,* No. 983

'Nationalization in France', II *World Today.* (1946), p. 365

PINKEY, D. H. 'Nationalization of Key Industries and Credit in France after the Liberation', LXII *Political Science Quarterly.* (1947), p. 368

PRITCHETT, C. H. *The Tennessee Valley Authority.* Chapel Hill, 1944

PUGET, H. (ed.) *Les Nationalizations en France et à l'Etranger: les Nationalizations à l'Etranger.* Paris, 1958

RAY, J. M. 'The influence of the Tennessee Valley Authority on Government in the South', XLIII *American Political Science Review.* (1949), p. 922

ROBSON, W. A. 'Nationalized Industries in Britain and France' in *Problems of Nationalized Industry.* Ed. W. A. Robson, London, 1952, p. 238; also published in XLIV *American Political Science Review.* (1950), p. 299

STURMTHAL, A. 'The Structure of Nationalized Enterprises in France', LXVII *Political Science Quarterly.* (1952), p. 357

'Le Tripartisme et l'Administration des Enterprises Nationalisees', *Economie Contemporaire.* April 1948, p. 13

UNITED NATIONS. *Some Problems in the Organization and Administration of Public Enterprises in the Industrial Field.* New York, 1954

VENTENAT, M. *L'Experience des Nationalisations.* Paris, 1948

WILMET, B. and FABER, M. 'De la Societe Anonyme à la Regie Nationale des Usines Renault', VI *Economie et Humanisme.* (1947), p. 496

CHAPTER II: MOTIVES AND BACKGROUND

BRITISH IRON & STEEL FEDERATION. *Steel: Fact and Fiction.* London, 1959

CENTRAL ELECTRICITY BOARD. *The Grid.* London, 1947

CLEGG, H. A., and CHESTER, T. E. *The Future of Nationalization.* Oxford, 1953. Ch. I.

COLE, G. D. H. *Why Nationalize Steel?* New Statesman pamphlet. London, 1948

CONSERVATIVE CENTRAL OFFICE. *The Campaign Guide* 1951. London, 1951. Ch. IV

The Campaign Guide 1955. London, 1955. Ch. V

The Right Road for Britain. London, 1949

CONSERVATIVE PARTY. *Notes on Current Politics: Nationalization Arguments Examined,* London, 1958

CONSERVATIVE POLITICAL CENTRE. *Power: a Report on the Retail Distribution of Electricity*. London, 1946

Steel. London, 1948

CONSERVATIVE RESEARCH DEPARTMENT. *Six Years of Socialist Government*. London, 1951. Ch. XV

COURT, W. H. B. *Coal*. London, 1951

CROSLAND, C. A. R. *The Future of Socialism*. London, 1956. Chs. I, III, IV, V and XXII

DAVIES, A. EMIL. *The Case for Nationalization*. London, 1920

The Case for Railway Nationalization. London, 1912

Nationalization: Some Facts for Mr Baldwin and Others. London, 1928

Nationalization of Railways, 2nd edn. London, 1911

Public Ownership: Points from Prospectuses, Fabian Tract No. 224. London, 1928

The State in Business; or, the Collectivist State in the Making, new edn. London, 1920

State Purchase of Railways, Fabian Tract No. 150. London, 1910

DAVIES, E. A. J. *British Transport*, Fabian Research Series No. 95. London, 1945

National Enterprise. London, 1946. Chs. I and X

Nationalization of Transport. London, Labour Party, 1947

The State and the Railways, Fabian Research Series No. 51. London, 1940

'Denationalization of Iron and Steel', XXI *Public Administration*. (1953), p. 277

FIENBURGH, W., and EVELY, R. *Steel is Power: The Case for Nationalization*. London, 1948

FRASER, H. *The Nationalization of Steel*. Conservative Political Centre. London, 1949

GAS COUNCIL. *Nationalization of the Gas Industry*. London, 1949

HALL, J. E. D. *Labour's First Year*. Harmondsworth, 1947

HARROD, R. F. 'Consequences of Nationalizing the Bank of England', XVII *Political Quarterly*. (1946), p. 214

HAYNES, W. W. *Nationalization in Practice: the British Coal Industry*. Boston, 1953. Chs. II-IV

HEINEMANN, M. *Britain's Coal*. London, 1944

Coal Must Come First. London, 1948

HELDMAN, H. 'The Economic Problems of Denationalization,' LXVI *Political Science Quarterly*. (1951), p. 576

HOGG, Q. *The Case for Conservatism*. Harmondsworth, 1947. Chs. XIX, XX, XXVII and XLIV

'Ingot', *The Socialization of Iron and Steel*. London, 1936

LABOUR PARTY. *The Bank of England and the Nation*. London, 1946

British Steel at Britain's Service. London, 1948

Coal and Power, National Executive Committee Report. London, 1944

Electricity Transformed. London, 1947

Fuel Crisis: the Facts. London, 1947

The National Planning of Transport. London, 1932

Nationalization of Coal. London, 1946

Post-war Organization of British Transport, National Executive Committee Report. London, 1943

Public Enterprise. London, 1957. Ch. I

The Reorganization of the Electricity Supply Industry. London, 1932

Socialism in Action: the Reorganization of the Electricity Supply Industry. London, 1932

Steel and the Nation—Labour's Plan. London, 1959

LABOUR RESEARCH DEPARTMENT. *The Case for Nationalization and Control*. London, 1945

Electricity: Public versus Private. London, 1944

MITCHELL, J. *The British Gas Industry, Present and Future*, Fabian Research Series No. 103. London, 1945

MORRISON, H. S. *British Transport at Britain's Service*. London, Labour Party, 1938

NEUMAN, A. M. DE. *Economic Organization of the British Coal Industry*. London, 1934

PALMER, A. M. F. *The Future of Electricity Supply*, Fabian Society Research Series No. 69. London, 1943

PARKER, J. *Labour Marches On*. Harmondsworth, 1947. Ch. VI

RIDLEY, G. *Labour's Policy for Coal and Power*. London, Labour Party, 1937

ROBSON, W. A. (ed.) *Public Enterprise*. London, 1937

TAWNEY, R. H. *The Nationalization of the Coal Industry*. London, Labour Party, 1919

TRADES UNION CONGRESS. *Coal: the Labour Plan*. London, 1936

Cotton: the T.U.C. Plan of Socialization. London, 1935

Interim Report on Post-war Reconstruction. London, 1945

WEBB, S., and B. *A Constitution for the Socialist Commonwealth of Great Britain*. London, 1920

WHITE, A. B. *The Nationalization of Banking*. London, 1934

CHAPTER III: THE PUBLIC CORPORATION

BLAND, F. A. 'Some implications of the Statutory Corporation', XV *Public Administration*. (1937), pp. 393-405

CHESTER, D. N. *The Nationalized Industries: an Analysis of the Statutory Provisions*, revised edn. London, 1951

'Public Corporations and the Classification of Administrative Bodies', I *Political Studies*. (1953), p. 34

CLEGG, H. A., and CHESTER, T. E. *The Future of Nationalization*. Oxford, 1953. pp. 40 ff.

COATMAN, J. 'The Constitutional Position of the BBC', XXIX *Public Administration*. (1951)

DAVIES, E. A. J. *National Enterprise*. London, 1946. Chs. II and III

'FABIAN.' 'The Nationalization of the Railways', XVIII *Political Quarterly*. (1947), p. 21

FRIEDMANN, W. 'The Legal Status and Organization of the Public Corporation', XVI *Law and Contemporary Problems.* (1951), p. 576
'The New Public Corporations and the Law', X *Modern Law Review.* (1947), pp. 233 and 377
As for *General*
GOODMAN, E. *Forms of Public Control and Ownership.* London, 1951. Chs. III and IV
GORDON, L. See *General*
GOWER, L. C. B. *The Principles of Modern Company Law,* 2nd edn. London, 1957, pp. 224–32
GREAVES, H. R. G. 'Public Boards and Corporations', XVI *Political Quarterly.* (1945), p. 67
GRIFFITH, J. A. G., and STREET, H. *Principles of Administrative Law,* 2nd edn. London, 1957. Ch. VII
HANSON, A. H. 'Labour and the Public Corporation', XXXII *Public Administration.* (1954), p. 203
HAZARD, J. N. 'Soviet Government Corporations', 41 *Michigan Law Review.* April 1943, pp. 850–71
KEYES, L. S. 'Some Controversial Aspects of the Public Corporation', LXX *Political Science Quarterly.* (1955)
LAW REPORTS. *Tamlin* v. *Hannaford* [1950] 1 K.B. 18
Smith v. *London Transport Executive* [1951] A.C. 555
MORRISON OF LAMBETH, LORD. *Socialization and Transport.* London, 1933
NEUMAN, A. M. DE. 'Some Economic Aspects of Nationalization', XVI *Law and Contemporary Problems.* (1951), p. 702
O'BRIEN, T. H. As for *General*
OSTERGAARD, G. N. 'Labour and the Development of the Public Corporation', *The Manchester School* 1954
'The Public Corporation', *The Times,* 20–22 January 1947
ROBSON, W. A. 'General Conclusions' in *Problems of Nationalized Industry,* ed. W. A. Robson. London, 1952, pp. 276 ff.
'The Public Corporation in Britain' in *Problems of Nationalized Industry,* ed. W. A. Robson. London, 1952, p. 15; also published in abbreviated form in LXII *Harvard Law Review.* (1950), p. 1321
(ed.) *Public Enterprise.* London, 1937
SEIDMAN, H. 'The Theory of the Autonomous Government Corporation: A Critical Appraisal', XII *Public Administration Review.* Chicago, 1952, p. 89
STREET, SIR A. M. 'Quasi-Government Bodies since 1918' in Sir G. Campion and others, *British Government since* 1918. London, 1950, p. 171
The Public Corporation in British Experience, address to the Institute of Public Administration. London, Institute of Public Administration, 1947. Published with slight alterations in the *Transactions of the Royal Institution of Chartered Surveyors.* March 1948
SYLVESTER, E. *The Management and Control of Public Corporations.* Institute of Municipal Treasurers and Accountants. London, 1951

THURSTON, J. *Government Proprietary Corporations in the English-Speaking Countries*. Cambridge, Mass., 1937

Governmental Reports

Report of the Committee of Inquiry on the Post Office, Cmd. 4149/1932
Report of the Committee on the Machinery of Government, Cmd. 9230/1918

CHAPTER IV: ORGANIZATION AND MANAGEMENT

ACTON SOCIETY TRUST. *The Extent of Centralization*, Nationalized Industry Series Nos. 6 and 7. Claygate, 1951
Patterns of Organization, Nationalized Industry Series No. 9. Claygate, 1951
Management under Nationalization. Claygate, 1953
ALBAN, SIR F. J. 'Socialization in Great Britain and its Effects on the Accounting Profession' in *Studies in Accounting*, ed. W. T. Baxter. London, 1950, p. 429
ALBU, A. H. 'The Organization of Nationalized Industries and Services' in *Problems of Nationalized Industry*, ed. W. A. Robson. London, 1952, p. 73
BEACHAM, A. 'Efficiency and Organization of the British Coal Industry', LV *Economic Journal*. (1945), p. 206
BEEVOR, M. 'The British Transport Commission' in *Large-scale Organization*, ed. G. E. Milward. London, 1950, p. 69
BRITISH ELECTRICITY AUTHORITY. *British Electricity: its Organization under Public Ownership*. London, 1949
BRITISH INSTITUTE OF MANAGEMENT. *Management Efficiency in Nationalized Undertakings*. London, 1950
CHESTER, D. N. 'Organization of the Nationalized Industries', XXI *Political Quarterly*. (1950), p. 122
CLEGG, H. A. 'The Fleck Report', XXXIII *Public Administration*. (1955), p. 269
and CHESTER, T. E. *The Future of Nationalization*. Oxford, 1953. Chs. II, III and IV
DAVIES, E. A. J. 'The London Passenger Transport Board' in *Public Enterprise*, ed. W. A. Robson. London, 1937, p. 155
Problems of Public Ownership. London, Labour Party, 1952, pp. 5 ff
DIAMOND, G. LE B. 'Organizational and Other Problems of the Nationalized Industries' in *The Accounting Field*, ed. Cousins. 1954
EDWARDS, R. S., and TOWNSEND, H. *Business Enterprise: its Growth and Organization*. London, 1958
FLORENCE, P. SARGANT. 'Bigness in Business' in *The Problem of Bigness*, L.P.E. Papers No. 3. April 1956
GENERAL POST OFFICE. Report on the Present System of Regionalization in the Post Office. London, 1951
GOODMAN, E. Forms of Public Control and Ownership. London, 1951. Chs. VI and VII, and App. II
HANSON, A. H. 'Electricity Reviewed: the Herbert Report', XXXIV *Public Administration*. (1956), p. 211

HAYNES, W. W. *Nationalization in Practice: the British Coal Industry*. Boston, 1953. Chs. XIII-XV

HURCOMB, LORD. 'The Development of the Organization of the British Transport Commission', XXVII *Public Administration*. (1950), p. 163

KELLY, D. W. 'The Administration of the National Coal Board', XXXI *Public Administration*. (1953), p. 1

LABOUR PARTY. *Public Enterprise*. London, 1957. Chs. II and III

LANCASTER, C. G. *The Organization of the Coal Board*. London, Conservative Political Centre, 1948

and others. *Structure and Control of the Coal Industry*. London, Conservative Political Centre, 1951

LATHAM, J. 'Common Services in a Public Corporation', XXXII *Public Administration*. (1954), p. 274

LAVERACK, F. W. R. 'The Bank of England' in *Large-scale Organization*, ed. G. E. Milward. London, 1950, p. 103

'The Management of Public Corporations', CLXXIII *Nature*. (1954), p. 479

MASEFIELD, P. G. 'Some Economic Factors in Air Transport Operations', XXIV *Journal of the Institute of Transport*. (1951), p. 79

NATIONAL COAL BOARD. *Committee on Organization: Statement by the National Coal Board*. London, 1948

Reorganizing the Coal Mining Industry. London, 1949

Report of the Advisory Committee on Organization. London, 1955

NOTTAGE, R. 'O & M in the Nationalized Industries', XXXIII *Public Administration*. (1955), p. 395

RENOLD, SIR C. *The Organizational Structure of Large Undertakings*. British Institute of Management. London, 1949

ROBERTS, C. A. 'The National Coal Board and the Fleck Report', XXXV *Public Administration*. (1957), p. 1

ROBERTSON, SIR B. 'The Organization of Transport', V *British Transport Review*. London, (1958), p. 75

ROBSON, W. A. 'The British Broadcasting Corporation' in *Public Enterprise*, ed. W. A. Robson. London, 1937, p. 83

'General Conclusions' in *Problems of Nationalized Industry*, ed. W. A. Robson. London, 1952, pp. 291 ff.

ROSS, N. S. 'Management and the Size of the Firm', XIX *Review of Economic Studies*. (1951-2), p. 148

SELF, SIR H. *The National and Area Organization of Electricity Supply* The Institute of Municipal Treasurers and Accountants. London, 1948

'Organization of the British Electricity Authority', XXVII *Public Administration*. (1949), p. 10

Problems of Decentralization in a Large Scale Undertaking: the Organization of the . . . Electricity Supply Industry British Institute of Management. London, 1951

and WATSON, E. M. *Electricity Supply in Great Britain*. London, 1952. Ch. VIII and pp. 202-9

SIMON OF WYTHENSHAWE, LORD. *The BBC from Within.* London, 1953. Pts. I and II.
SIMPSON, J. R. 'Organizing the Larger Units: Government Departments and Nationalized Industries,' VIII *British Management Review.* (1949), No. 2, p. 38
'Ten Years of Nationalized Transport,' *Railway Gazette.* October 2, 1957, p. 391
THORNTON, R. H. 'Nationalization—Administrative Problems Inherent in a State-owned Enterprise', XXV *Public Administration.* (1947), p. 10
TOWNSHEND-ROSE, H. *The British Coal Industry.* London, 1951. Ch. III
'The Transport Act, 1953', XXXI *Public Administration.* (1953), p. 399
WALKER, G. and MADDICK, H. 'Responsibility for Transport', XXIII *Political Quarterly.* (1952), p. 22

Governmental Reports

British Electricity Authority Annual Report 1948-9, H.C. 336/1948-9. Chs. II and III and App. XXXVI
British Transport Commission Annual Report 1948, H.C. 235/1958-9. Chs. I and VI
British Transport Commission Annual Report 1949, H.C. 135/1950. Chs. I and V
British Transport Commission Annual Report 1955, H.C. 290-1/1955-6. Vol. I, Ch. I
The Future Organization of the U.K. Atomic Energy Project, Cmd. 8986/1955
Gas Council Annual Report 1948-50, H.C. 69/1950-1, Chs. I and II
The Gas Industry: Report of the Committee of Enquiry, Cmd. 6699/1945
National Coal Board Annual Report 1948, H.C. 187/1948-9. Chs. X and App. V
National Coal Board Annual Report 1955, H.C. 263-I/1955-6. Vol. I, Ch. IV
Proposals for the Reorganization of the Electricity Supply Industry, Cmnd. 27/1956
Railways Reorganization Scheme, Cmd. 9191/1954
Report of the Broadcasting Committee 1949, Cmd. 8116/1951
Report of the Committee of Inquiry into the Electricity Supply Industry, Cmd. 9672/1956
Report of the Committee of Inquiry into London Transport. 1955. Chs. I-X and XVII-XIX

CHAPTER V: COMPETITION AND MONOPOLY

BRONOWSKI, J. 'Atomic Energy and the Future of Coal', IV *British Transport Review.* p. 135
COASE, R. H. *British Broadcasting—a Study in Monopoly.* London, (1950)
COATMAN, J. 'The Future of the BBC', XXI *Political Quarterly.* (1950), p. 271
CROPPER, R. 'Road Freight Transport and the Act of 1947', XVIII *Manchester School.* (1950), p. 244
CROZIER, M. *Broadcasting: Sound Radio and Television.* London, 1958
DAWS, H. 'Competition and Rivalry,' XXIX *Public Administration.* (1951)

FABIAN SOCIETY. *The Future of Broadcasting*, Fabian Research Series No. 138. London, 1950

FRASER, SIR R. 'Independent Television in Britain', XXXVI *Public Administration*. (1958), p. 115

GRUNFELD, C. 'The Transport Act, 1953', XXV *Political Quarterly*. (1954), p. 43

HARRIS, J. S. 'Television as a Political Issue in Britain', XXI *Canadian Journal of Economics and Political Science*. (1955), p. 328

HURCOMB, LORD. *The Organization of the London Transport Commission*. London, 1948

INCORPORATED SOCIETY OF BRITISH ADVERTISERS AND INSTITUTE OF INCORPORATED PRACTITIONERS IN ADVERTISING. *Television: the Viewer and the Advertiser*. London, 1953

Competitive Television: Open Letter to the Postmaster-General. London, 1953

INSTITUTE OF INCORPORATED PRACTITIONERS IN ADVERTISING. *Commercial Broadcasting: Note on the Report of the Broadcasting Committee*. London, 1951

MILNE, A. M. 'Passenger Road Transport and the Transport Act, 1947, with Particular Reference to the North-East of England', LXI *Economic Journal*. (1951), p. 310

PLOWMAN, E. G. 'An Appraisal of Nationalized Transport in Great Britain—Part II', XL *American Economic Review*. (May 1950), p. 248

XXIV *Political Quarterly*. (October-December 1953). Special issue on Commercial Television

ROBSON, W. A. 'General Conclusions' in *Problems of Nationalized Industry*, ed. W. A. Robson. London, 1952, pp. 298 ff.

'Public Utilities' in *A Century of Municipal Progress*, ed. W. I. Jennings, H. J. Laski and W. A. Robson. London, 1936, p. 304

SARGENT, J. R. As for *General*

SIMON OF WYTHENSHAWE, LORD. *The BBC from Within*. London, 1953. Pts. III and IV

SPANN, R. N. 'Reith and the BBC', XXVIII *Public Administration*. (1950), p. 211

'The Transport Act, 1953,' XXI *Public Administration*. (1953), p. 355

VALENTINE, A. B. B. 'Monopoly and Competition in Rail and Road Transport', II *British Transport Review*. London, (1952), p. 171

WALKER, G. As for Ch. III

'Competition in Transport as an Instrument of Policy', LXVI *Economic Journal*. (1956), p. 405

'Transport Policy Before and After 1953', V *Oxford Economic Papers*. N.S. (1953), p. 90

WILSON, SIR R. 'Competition in Public Passenger Transport', II *British Transport Review*. London, 1952, p. 363

Governmental Reports

Broadcasting Policy, Cmd. 6582/1946

Memorandum on the Report of the Broadcasting Committee, Cmd. 8350/1952

Memorandum on Television Policy, Cmd. 9005/1953

Report of the Broadcasting Committee 1949, Cmd. 8116/1951. Chs. IV, XIV, XXI and App. H.

Co-operation between Electricity and Gas Boards, Cmnd. 695/1959

Parliamentary Debates

501 H.C. Deb. 5s, cols. 475-614, May 21, 1952. (Debate on Government transport policy)

CHAPTER VI: GOVERNMENT CONTROL

ACTON SOCIETY TRUST. *The Powers of the Minister*. Nationalized Industry Series No. 2. Claygate, 1951

BALLS, H. R. 'The Financial Control and Accountability of Canadian Crown Corporations', XXXI *Public Administration*. (1953), p. 127

DAVIES, E. A. J. 'Government Policy and the Public Corporation', XXVI *Political Quarterly*. (1955), p. 104

'Ministerial Control and Parliamentary Responsibility of Nationalized Industries' in *Problems of Nationalized Industry*, ed. W. A. Robson. London, 1952, p. 109

National Enterprise. London, 1946. Ch. V

Problems of Public Ownership. London, Labour Party, 1952, pp. 16 ff.

FINNEGAN, M. 'Ministerial Control of Electricité de France', XXXII *Public Administration*. (1954), p. 441

JOHNSON, E. L. 'The Accountability of the British Nationalized Industries', XLVIII *American Political Science Review*. (1954), p. 366

KEETON, G. W. *The Passing of Parliament*, 2nd edn. London, 1954. Ch. XI

MILLIGAN, F. 'Ministerial Control of the British Nationalized Industries', XVII *Canadian Journal of Economics and Political Science*. (1951), p. 164

MILNE, R. S. 'Control of Government Corporations in the United States', XXXIV *Public Administration*. (1956), p. 355

PLEASE, S. 'Government Control of the Capital Expenditure of the Nationalized Industries', XXIII *Public Administration*. (1955), p. 31

REITH, LORD. 'Public Corporations: Need to Examine Control and Structure', XXXIV *Public Administration*. (1956), p. 351. See also *The Times*, July 3, 1956

ROBSON, W. A. 'General Conclusions' in *Problems of Nationalized Industry*, ed. W. A. Robson. London, 1952, pp. 302 ff.

Parliamentary Debates

168 H.L. Deb. 5s, cols. 41-126, July 5, 1950

478 H.C. Deb. 5s, cols. 2795-919, October 25, 1950

496 H.C. Deb. 5s, cols. 774-834, February 25, 1952. (Debate on resignation of chairman of Iron & Steel Corporation)

499 H.C. Deb. 5s, cols. 1022-166, April 28, 1952. (Debate on transport fare increases)

551 H.C. Deb. 5s, cols. 183-91, April 11, 1956. (Oral answer on increase in freight charges, setting out memorandum by Transport Tribunal)

552 H.C. Deb. 5s, cols. 2337-68, May 17, 1956. (Opposition motion on transport charges)

H.C. Deb., Standing Committees, 1946-7, vol. II, Standing Committee B, cols. 1500-28, February 25, 1947 (Transport Bill)

1946-7, vol. IV, Standing Committee E, cols. 633-51, March 13, 1947 (Electricity Bill)

1947-8, vol. II, Standing Committee D, cols. 334-45, March 23, 1948 (Gas Bill)

CHAPTERS VII and VIII: PARLIAMENTARY DEBATES AND QUESTIONS PUBLIC ACCOUNTABILITY

ACTON SOCIETY TRUST. *Accountability to Parliament,* Nationalized Industry Series No. 1. Claygate, 1950

ADMINISTRATIVE STAFF COLLEGE. *The Accountability of Public Corporations.* Henley-on-Thames, 1955

BAILEY, S. D. *British Parliamentary Democracy.* London, 1959. Ch. XI

BEEVOR, M. 'The Public Accountability of the Commission', I *British Transport Review.* London, (1950), p. 146

BIRD, R. 'Public Bodies and Public Accountability', *Lloyds Bank Review.* January, 1950, p. 12

BRADSHAW, K. A. 'Parliament and the Public Corporation', III *Cambridge Journal.* (1950), p. 707

CHESTER, D. N. 'Management and Accountability in the Nationalized Industries', XXX *Public Administration.* (1952), p. 27

'Select Committee on Nationalized Industries: Second Report', XXXI *Public Administration.* (1953), p. 269

'The Select Committee on the Nationalized Industries', XXXIV *Public Administration.* (1956), p. 93

DAVIES, E. A. J. 'Ministerial Control and Parliamentary Responsibility of Nationalized Industries' in *Problems of Nationalized Industry,* ed. W. A. Robson. London, 1952, p. 109

National Enterprise. London, 1946. Ch. V

Problems of Public Ownership. London, Labour Party, 1952, pp. 19 ff.

'The Select Committee on the Nationalized Industries', XXIX *Political Quarterly.* (1958), p. 378

GOODHART, A. L. 'Parliamentary Control over the Nationalized Undertakings' in Lord Campion and others, *Parliament: a Survey.* London, 1952, p. 252

GUTCH, G. 'Nationalized Industries and the Public Accounts Committee, 1951-2', XXXI *Public Administration.* (1953), p. 255

'The Select Committee on Nationalized Industries', *ib.* (Spring, 1953)

HANSON, A. H. 'Parliament and the Nationalized Industries', VI *Yorkshire Bulletin.* (1954), p. 145

'Parliamentary Control of Nationalized Industries', XI *Parliamentary Affairs.* (1958), p. 328

'The Select Committee on Nationalized Industries', XXXI *Public Administration.* (Spring, 1953)

'Parliamentary Questions on the Nationalized Industries', XXIX *Public Administration.* (1951), p. 51

HEALD, SIR L. 'Nationalized Industries and the Legislature', II *British Transport Review.* London, (1953), p. 472

JENNINGS, SIR W. I. *Parliament,* 2nd edn. Cambridge, 1957. Ch. X

JOHNSON, E. L. As for Ch. VI

KEETON, G. W. As for Ch. VI

MAY, SIR T. E. *Parliamentary Practice,* 16th edn. ed. Sir E. A. Fellowes and T. G. B. Cocks. London, 1957, pp. 361 and 858–66

MILNE, R. S. As for Ch. VI

MOLSON, H. 'Nationalized Industries: Select Committee to Secure Parliamentary Control', *The Times,* September 8, 1949

MORRISON OF LAMBETH, LORD. *Government and Parliament,* London, 1954. Ch. XII

'Public Control of the Socialized Industries', XXVIII *Public Administration.* (1950), p. 3

'Mr Morrison's Views on Public Accountability', XXVIII *Public Administration.* (1950), p. 176

'Parliament and the Corporations', *The Times,* March 3, 1948

PEAKE, O. 'Audit of State Monopolies', *Sunday Times,* February 29, 1946

REITH, LORD. As for Ch. VI

ROBSON, W. A. 'General Conclusions' in *Problems of Nationalized Industry,* ed. W. A. Robson. London, 1952, pp. 310 ff.

'The Public Service Board: General Conclusions' in *Public Enterprise.* London, 1937, pp. 376 ff.

SCULLY, M. 'Parliamentary Control of Public Corporations in Eire', XXXII *Public Administration.* (1954), p. 459

'Select Committee on Nationalized Industries', XXXI *Public Administration.* (1953), p. 55

SELF, SIR H. 'The Public Accountability of the Corporation', XXV *Public Administration.* (1947), p. 131

SMITH, J. H., and CHESTER, T. E. 'The Distribution of Power in Nationalized Industries', II *British Journal of Sociology.* (1951), p. 275

VICKERS, SIR G. 'The Accountability of a Nationalized Industry', XXX *Public Administration.* (1952), p. 71

WALKER, G., and MADDICK, H. 'Responsibility for Transport', XXIII *Political Quarterly.* (1952)

CHAPTER IX: THE GOVERNING BOARD

ACTON SOCIETY TRUST. *The Men on the Boards,* Nationalized Industry Series No. 4. Claygate, 1951

BRANTON, N. 'The Directing Authority in Private and Public Enterprise', I *Journal of the Glasgow and West of Scotland Commercial College.* (1951), p. 73

COLE, G. D. H. *The National Coal Board*, Fabian Research Series No. 129. London, 1948

DAVIES, E. A. J. *National Enterprise.* London, 1946. Ch. IV

JENKINS, C. *Power at the Top.* London, 1959

'Retreat: the Labour Party and the Public Corporations'. *Universities and Left Review*, Winter, 1958, p. 42

KAHN, H. R. 'Payment for Political and Public Service', XXXII *Public Administration.* (1954), pp. 189 ff.

LABOUR PARTY. *Public Enterprise.* London, 1957. Ch. III

LEWIS, R., and MAUDE, A. *The English Middle Classes.* Pelican edn. Harmondsworth, 1953, pp. 91-2, 103-4

MORRISON OF LAMBETH, LORD. *Socialization and Transport.* London, 1933. Chs. IX, X and XI

REITH, LORD. As for Ch. VI

ROBSON, W. A. 'General Conclusions' in *Problems of Nationalized Industry*, ed. W. A. Robson. London, 1952, pp. 325-6

'The Governing Board of the Public Corporation' in *Problems of Nationalized Industry*, ed. W. A. Robson. London, 1952, p. 91

SIMON OF WYTHENSHAWE, LORD. *The Boards of Nationalized Industries.* London, 1957

SMITH, J. H., and CHESTER, T. E. As for Chs. VII and VIII

VICKERS, G. 'Personal Incentive and Public Service,' XVII *Political Quarterly.* (1946), p. 152

Parliamentary Papers

Public Boards (List of members of public boards of a commercial character as at various dates, with salaries and allowances)

Parliamentary Debates

425 H.C. Deb. 5s, cols. 532-64, July 11, 1946. (Civil Aviation Bill)

496 H.C. Deb. 5s, cols. 774-834, February 25, 1952. (Debate on resignation of chairman of Iron & Steel Corporation)

H.C. Deb., Standing Committees, January-April 1946, Standing Committee C, cols. 1206-24, February 26, 1946. (Coal Bill)

1946-7, vol. IV, Standing Committee E, cols. 600-24, March 11, 1947. (Electricity Bill)

1947-8, vol. II, Standing Committee D, cols. 245-64, March 16, 1948. (Gas Bill: workers' representatives on boards)

1948-9, vol. I, Standing Committee A, cols. 1789-1882, December 14 and 16, 1948. (Coal Industry Bill)

CHAPTER X: CONSUMERS' AND CONSULTATIVE COUNCILS

BRITISH INSTITUTE OF MANAGEMENT. *Efficiency and Consumers' Choice* Conference Series No. 1. London, 1949

CAMERON, M. A. 'Non-Paying Services: the Public's View', IV *British Transport Review*. (1957), p. 323

DAVIES, E. A. J. *National Enterprise*. London, 1946. Ch. VI

Problems of Public Ownership. London, Labour Party, 1952, pp. 26 ff.

FLORENCE, P. SARGANT, and MADDICK, H. 'Consumers' Councils in the Nationalized Industries', XXIV *Political Quarterly*. (1953), p. 259

FREEDMAN, L. and HEMINGWAY, G. *Nationalization and the Consumer* Fabian Research Series No. 139. London, 1950

GRIFFITH, J. A. G. 'The Voice of the Consumer', XXI *Political Quarterly*. (1950), p. 171

GROVE, J. W. 'The Consumer Councils for Gas and Electricity', XXVIII *Public Administration*. (1950), p. 221

HANSON, A. H. 'Report on the Reports', XXX *Public Administration*. (1952), p. 111

JOHNSON, E. L. 'Consumer "Control" in British Nationalized Industries', XVI *Journal of Politics*. (1953), p. 88

LABOUR PARTY. *Public Enterprise*. London, 1957. Ch. IV

MILLIGAN, F. 'The Consumer's Interest' in *Problems of Nationalized Industry*, ed. W. A. Robson. London, 1952, p. 144

MORRISON, H. S. *Government and Parliament*. London, 1954, pp. 265-72

NEUMAN, A. M. DE. *Consumers' Representation in the Public Sector of Industry*. Cambridge, 1950; also published in XVIII *Manchester School*. (1950), p. 143

NOTTAGE, R. 'Reporting to Parliament on the Nationalized Industries', XXXV *Public Administration*. (1957), p. 143

ROBSON, W. A. 'General Conclusions' in *Problems of Nationalized Industry*, ed. W. A. Robson. London, 1952, pp. 326 ff.

Justice and Administrative Law, 3rd edn. London, 1951, pp. 297-309

RUSHOLME, BARON. 'Consumer Councils in Transport', I *British Transport Review*. London, December 1951, p. 355

SELF, SIR H., and WATSON, E. M. *Electricity Supply in Great Britain*. London, 1952. Ch. XI

STEWART, M. *Consumers' Councils*, Fabian Research Series No. 155. London, 1953

Public Relations

ACTON SOCIETY TRUST. *Relations with the Public*. Nationalized Industry Series No. 12. Claygate, 1953

BREBNER, J. H. *Public Relations and Publicity*. London, 1949

HARDERN, L. 'Public Relations in the Nationalized Industries' in *Problems of Nationalized Industry*, ed. W. A. Robson. London, 1952, p. 171

INSTITUTE OF PUBLIC RELATIONS. *A Guide to the Practice of Public Relations*. London, 1958

WILLIAMS-THOMPSON, R. *Was I Really Necessary?* London, 1951

WILSON, P. A. 'Public Relations Departments' in *Some Modern Business Problems*, ed. Arnold Plant. London, 1937, p. 123

Governmental Reports

Annual Reports of the Councils. (The Gas and Electricity Consultative Councils' Reports are published as parts of the Area Boards' Reports)

Report of the Committee of Inquiry into London Transport. London, 1955. Chs. XVI and XX

Increase in Passenger Fares: Report of the Central Transport Consultative Committee for Great Britain, Cmd. 8513/1952

Report of the Broadcasting Committee 1949, Cmd. 8116/1951. Chs. VII, XX and XXI

Report of the Committee of Inquiry into the Electricity Supply Industry, Cmd. 9672/1956, pp. 17, 119-24 and 149-50

Report of the Committee on Administrative Tribunals and Enquiries, Cmnd. 218/1957. Pt. IV

Parliamentary Debates

422 H.C. Deb. 5s, cols. 1559-98, May 13, 1946

426 H.C. Deb. 5s, cols. 709-38, July 29, 1946

H.C. Deb., Standing Committees, January-April 1946, Standing Committee C, 1290-306, March 5, 1946. (Coal Bill)

1946-7, vol. IV, Standing Committee E, cols. 660-712, March 13 and 18, 1947 (Electricity Bill); also cols. 1277-92 and 1305-10, May 6, 1947 (Discussion of review of charges by Electricity Commissioners)

1948-9, vol. I, Standing Committee C, cols. 1677-1708, March 16, 1949. (Proposal of Iron and Steel Prices Board)

CHAPTER XI: FINANCE

BALLS, H. R. As for Ch. VI

BEACHAM, A. 'Planned Investment in the Coal Industry', III *Oxford Economic Papers,* N.S. (1951), p. 125

BEESLEY, M. and WALTERS, A. A. 'Investment in British Railways', *Westminster Bank Review,* May 1955, p. 4

BRITISH TRANSPORT COMMISSION. *Draft Outline of Principles Proposed to be Embodied in a Charges Scheme for Merchandise Traffic.* London, 1949

Modernization and Re-equipment of British Railways. London, 1955

CAIRNS, M. B. 'Some Legal Aspects of Compensation for Nationalized Assets', XVI *Law and Contemporary Problems.* (1951), p. 594

CASSELL, F. 'The Pricing Policies of the Nationalized Industries', *Lloyds Bank Review.* October, 1956, p. 1

CHESTER, D. N. 'Notes on the Price Policy Indicated by the Nationalization Acts', II *Oxford Economic Papers,* N.S. (1950), p. 69

CROPPER, R. 'Compensation for State Acquisitions', CXVI *Accountant,* N.S. (1947), p. 223

CROSLAND, C. A. R. 'Prices and Costs in Nationalized Undertakings', II *Oxford Economic Papers,* N.S. (1950), p. 51

DAVIES, E. A. J. *How Much Compensation?* New Fabian Research Bureau Series No. 33. London, 1937

National Enterprise. London, 1946. Chs. VII-IX

Problems of Public Ownership. London, Labour Party, 1952, pp. 11 ff.

DENNISON, S. R. 'The Price Policy of the National Coal Board', *Lloyds Bank Review*. October 1952, p. 17

DENTON, G. R. 'Investment and Location in the Steel Industry—Corby', VII *Oxford Economic Papers*, N.S. (1955), p. 272

EASTHAM, J. K. 'Compensation Terms for Nationalized Industry', XVI *Manchester School*. (1948), p. 29

ELLIOT, SIR JOHN. 'Should Public Transport be Self-supporting', *National Provincial Bank Review*. November 1955

FLEMING, M. 'Production and Price Policy in Public Enterprise', XVII *Economica*, N.S. (1950), p. 1

GRIBBIN, T. K. 'Production Costs in the Gas Industry', V *Oxford Economic Papers*, N.S. (1953), p. 190

HARTSHORN, J. E. 'Financing the Public Industries', CVIII *Banker*. London, (1958)

HENDERSON, A. M. 'The Pricing of Public Utility Undertakings', XV *Manchester School*. (1947), p. 223

HOUTHAKKER, H. S. 'Electricity Tariffs in Theory and Practice', LXI *Economic Journal*. (1951), p. 1

JOHNSTON, J. 'Statistical Cost Functions in Electricity Supply', IV *Oxford Economic Papers*, N.S. (1952), p. 68

JOY, N. V. 'Fair Compensation under the British Labour Government', LXV *Political Science Quarterly*. (1950), p. 538

LABOUR PARTY. *Labour Party Conference Report* 1934. App. II. 'Public Enterprise and Compensation Terms'

Public Enterprise.London, 1957. Ch. VII

LATHAM, J. 'The Accounts of Nationalized Industries', CXX *Accountant*, N.S. (1949), p. 487

LEWIS, W. A. *Overhead Costs*. London, 1949. Chs. I and II, and pp. 185-90

'The Price Policy of Public Corporations' in *Problems of Nationalized Industry*, ed. W. A. Robson. London, 1952, p. 181

LITTLE, I. M. D. *The Price of Fuel*. Oxford, 1953

LOMAX, K. S. 'The Demand for Coal in Great Britain', IV *Oxford Economic Papers*, N.S. (1952), p. 50

MASEFIELD, P. G. As for Ch. IV

MORRISON OF LAMBETH, LORD. *Socialization and Transport*. London, 1933. Ch. XIV

MUNBY, D. L. 'The Price of Fuel', VI *Oxford Economic Papers*, N.S. (1954), p. 226

NORRIS, H. 'Accounting and Public Enterprise', CXIV *Accountant*, N.S. (1946), pp. 191 and 203

'State Enterprise Price and Output Policy and the Problem of Cost Imputation,' XIV *Economica*, N.S. (1947), p. 54

PLEASE, S. As for Ch. VI

PONSONBY, G. J. 'Depreciation with Special Reference to Transport , LXVI *Economic Journal.* (1956), p. 84

PRESTHUS, R. V. 'Financial Aspects of Britain's National Coal Board', XII *Journal of Politics.* (1950), p. 348

PRICE, F. E. *Some Aspects of Public Board Finance,* a paper presented to the Institute of Municipal Treasurers and Accountants, June 1950

'The Provision of "Public Sector" Capital', *Midland Bank Review.* August 1955, p. 1

ROBERTS, B. C. 'Wages on the Railways', XXVI *Political Quarterly.* (1955), p. 117

ROBSON, W. A. 'General Conclusions' in *Problems of Nationalized Industry,* ed. W. A. Robson. London, 1952, pp. 286 ff. and 334 ff.

SARGENT, J. R. See *General*

SCOTT, M. F. 'Investment Policy in a Nationalized Industry', XVII *Review of Economic Studies.* (1949-50), p. 179

SHANKLEMAN, E. 'The Growth of the Electricity Supply Industry', *Westminster Bank Review.* February 1957, p. 7

SLEEMAN, J. F. 'Municipal Gas Costs and Revenue', XVIII *Manchester School.* (1950), p. 31

WALKER, G., and CONDIE, R. H. B. 'Compensation in Nationalized Industries' in *Problems of Nationalized Industry,* ed. W. A. Robson. London, 1952, p. 54

WALKER, G. 'The Economics of British Transport: First Principles for 1950', *Westminster Bank Review.* August 1950, p. 1

WHELDON, G. F. 'Financing the Nationalized Industries', XVI *Law and Contemporary Problems.* (1951), p. 620

Governmental Reports

Coal Industry Nationalization, Cmd. 6716/1945. (See on compensation terms)

Report of the Committee of Inquiry into London Transport. London, 1955. Chs. VIII-XIV

TRANSPORT TRIBUNAL. The reports of hearings before the tribunal are published by H.M.S.O.

Capital Investment in the Coal, Gas and Electricity Industries—Cmnd. 132/1957, Cmnd. 415/1958, Cmnd. 713/1959

Parliamentary Debates

521 H.C. Deb. 5s, cols. 2333-431, December 11, 1953. (Debate on sale of denationalized steel shares)

H.C. Deb., Standing Committees, 1946-7, vol. II, Standing Committee B, cols. 1438-82, 1731-72 and 2248-84, February-March 1947. (Transport Bill)

1946-7, vol. IV, Standing Committee E, cols. 1027-68 and 1261-78, April-May 1947. (Electricity Bill)

1948-9, vol. I, Standing Committee C, cols. 643-830 and 1163-1206, February 1949. (Iron and Steel Bill)

CHAPTER XII: LABOUR RELATIONS

ACTON SOCIETY TRUST. *Problems of Promotion Policy,* Nationalized Industry Series No. 3. Claygate, 1951

The Miner's Pension, Nationalized Industry Series No. 5. Claygate, 1951

The Future of the Unions, Nationalized Industry Series No. 8. Claygate, 1951

The Framework of Joint Consultation, Nationalized Industry Series No. 10. London, 1952

The Worker's Point of View, Nationalized Industry Series No. 11. London, 1952

BALDWIN, G. B. *Beyond Nationalization.* Cambridge, Mass., 1955

'Nationalization in Britain: a Sobering Decade', CCCX *Annals of the American Academy of Political and Social Science.* (1957), p. 39

BELL, R. W. 'The Relation of Promotion and Training to Higher Management in British Nationalized Industries', XXIX *Public Administration.* (1951), p. 201

'Selection and Training for Management in British Nationalized Industries', XVI *Law and Contemporary Problems.* (1951), p. 633

BRITISH ELECTRICITY AUTHORITY. *You and Electricity Service—a Handbook for Employees.* London, 1953

BRITISH INSTITUTE OF MANAGEMENT. *The Recruitment and Training of Men Intended for Management Positions.* London, 1955

CHALMERS, J. M., MIKARDO, I. and COLE, G. D. H. *Consultation or Joint Management?* Fabian Tract No. 277: really No. 278. London, 1949

CLEGG, H. A. *Industrial Democracy and Nationalization.* Oxford, 1951

Labour in Nationalized Industry, Fabian Research Series No. 141. London, 1950

Labour Relations in London Transport. Oxford, 1950

COLE, G. D. H. *The Case for Industrial Partnership.* London, 1957

'Labour and Staff Problems under Nationalization' in *Problems of Nationalized Industry,* ed. W. A. Robson. London, 1952, p. 120

Labour in the Coalmining Industry 1914-1921. Oxford, 1923

COLE, M. *Miners and the Board,* Fabian Research Series No. 134. London, 1945

CROSLAND, C. A. R. *The Future of Socialism.* London, 1956. Ch. XVI

DAHL, R. A. 'Workers' Control of Industry and the British Labour Party', XLI *American Political Science Review.* (1947), p. 875

DAVIES, E. A. J. *National Enterprise.* London, 1946. Ch. VI

Problems of Public Ownership. London, Labour Party, 1952, pp. 21 ff.

DENNIS, N., HENRIQUES, F., and SLAUGHTER, C. *Coal is our Life.* London, 1956

FLANDERS, A. and CLEGG, H. A. (eds.) *Industrial Relations in Great Britain.* Oxford, 1954

GAS COUNCIL. *A Career in Gas Industry.* London, 1954

GAS TIMES. April-June 1954. (Series of articles on labour relations)

GRATWICK, W. K. 'Labour Relations in Nationalized Industries with Particular Reference to the Coal Mining Industry', XVI *Law and Contemporary Problems.* (1951), p. 670

HAIME, J. W. 'Nationalization and Employer/Employee Relations', VIII *British Management Review.* (1949), p. 36

HAYNES, W. W. *Nationalization in Practice: the British Coal Industry.* Boston, 1953. Chs. II, III, V and VII-XI

HEILBRONNER, R. L. 'Labour Unrest in the British Nationalized Sector', XIX *Social Research.* March 1952, p. 61

HOOPER, F. C. 'Management in the Public Services', XXVI *Public Administration.* (1948), p. 217

HOUGHTON, D. 'Whitley Councils in the Civil Service' in *The Civil Service in Britain and France*, ed. W. A. Robson. London, 1956, p. 139

HUTCHISON, J. R. H. *The Great Betrayal.* Conservative Political Centre. London, 1950

JOHNSON, E. L. 'Joint Consultation in Britain's Nationalized Industries', XII *Public Administration Review.* (1952), p. 181

XXXI *Journal of the Institute of Personnel Management.* 1949, 'Personnel Policy in a Public Corporation', p. 74

LABOUR PARTY. *Public Enterprise.* London, 1957. Ch. V

LINDGREN, G. S. 'The Role of Joint Consultation in Nationalized Industries', XXXI *Journal of the Institute of Personnel Management.* 1949, p. 133

MEYERS, FREDERIC. 'Nationalization, Union Structures, and Wage Policy in the British Coal-Mining Industry', XXIV *Southern Economic Journal.* Chapel Hill, 1958, p. 421

MOOS, S. 'The Statistics of Absenteeism in Coal Mining', XIX *Manchester School.* (1951), p. 89

MORRISON, H. S. *Socialization and Transport.* London, 1933. Ch. XIII

NATIONAL COAL BOARD and NATIONAL CONSULTATIVE COUNCIL. *Guide to Consultation.* London, 1948

NATIONAL COAL BOARD. *Handbook on the Wage Structure of the Coalmining Industry.* London, 1955: in progress

NATIONAL COAL BOARD and others. *The Ladder Plan.* London, 1950

NATIONAL COAL BOARD AND NATIONAL UNION OF MINEWORKERS. *Mineworkers' Pensions: Outline of Proposed Scheme.* London 1951

PALMER, A. M. F. 'Joint Consultation in Nationalized Industry' in *Problems of Nationalized Industry*, ed. W. A. Robson. London, 1952, p. 132

PICKSTOCK, F. *British Railways—the Human Problem*, Fabian Research Series No. 142. London, 1950

XXVII *Political Quarterly.* (January-March 1956) (Special issue on Trade Union Problems)

XXVII *Political Quarterly.* (July-September 1956) (Special issue on Employers and Labour Problems)

ROBERTS, B. C. As for Ch. XI

'Trade Unions and Nationalization', XLIV *Progress.* (1954-5), p. 114

ROBERTS, R. D. V., and SALLIS, H. 'Joint Consultation in the Electricity Supply Industry' 1949-59, XXXVII *Public Administration.* Summer 1959, p. 115

ROBSON, W. A. 'General Conclusions' in *Problems of Nationalized Industry*, ed. W. A. Robson. London, 1952, pp. 338 ff.

SAXENA, S. K. *Nationalization and Industrial Conflict.* The Hague, 1955
SOCIALIST UNION. *Twentieth Century Socialism.* Harmondsworth, 1956. Ch. X
STEWART, A. C., and WATKINS, W. P. *The Socialization of Coal Mining.* Co-operative Union. Manchester, 1951
STURMTHAL, A. 'Nationalization and Workers' Control in Britain and France', LXI *Journal of Political Economy.* February 1953
WHITE, E. *Workers Control?* rev. edn. Fabian Tract No. 271. London, 1951
Annual Reports of the Corporations under the heading 'Staff'

Governmental Reports

Report of the Committee of Inquiry into London Transport. London, 1955, Ch. XV
Joint Consultation in Industry. Supplement No. 3 to Industrial Relations Handbook. London, 1950

CHAPTER XIII: RESEARCH

BESKINE, J. M. 'Scientific Research makes big contribution to Railway Modernization', *Transport Age.* July 1958, p. 8
BURNS, J. *Presidential Address to The Institution of Gas Engineers.* Institution of Gas Engineers, London, 1958
CENTRAL OFFICE OF INFORMATION. *Nuclear Energy in Britain.* London, 1947
CHESTER, D. N. (ed.), and WILLSON, F. M. G. *The Organization of British Central Government* 1914–1956. London, 1957. Ch. VII
CROSSLAND, J. 'Scientific Aspects of the Work of the National Coal Board', CLXI *Nature.* (1948), p. 546
DEWS, E. 'Scientific Research and Nationalized Industry' in *Problems of Nationalized Industry,* ed. W. A. Robson. London, 1952, p. 208
EDWARDS, R. S. *Co-operative Industrial Research.* London, 1950
'The Future of Industrial Research and Development in Great Britain', *Lloyds Bank Review.* January 1952, p. 32
FEDERATION OF BRITISH INDUSTRIES. *Research and Development in British Industry.* London, 1952
Scientific and Technical Research in British Industry. London, 1947
HAWTHORNE, W. R. 'Can the Atom Solve our Fuel Problems?' *Westminster Bank Review.* May 1955, p. 1
HEATH, SIR H. F., and HETHERINGTON, A. L. *Industrial Research and Development in the United Kingdom.* London, 1946
JEWKES, J. 'The Sources of Invention', *Lloyds Bank Review.* January, 1958, p. 17
SAWERS, D., and STILLERMAN, R. *The Sources of Invention.* London, 1958
MEIER, R. L. 'The Role of Science in the British Economy', XVIII *Manchester School,* (1950), p. 101
RHODES, K. D. and DART, M. R. A paper on long welded rail track, VII *Proceedings of the Institution of Civil Engineers.* (1957), p. 344
ROBSON, W. A. 'General Conclusions' in *Problems of Nationalized Industry,* ed. W. A. Robson. London, 1952, pp. 361 ff.

SAYERS, R. S. 'The Peaceful Use of Atomic Energy', *Three Banks Review.* December 1951, p. 3

'The Springs of Technical Progress in Britain, 1919-39', LX *Economic Journal.* (1950), p. 275

SIMON, SIR F. 'Nuclear Energy and the Future', *Lloyds Bank Review.* April 1955, p. 1

STEELMAN, J. R. *Science and Public Policy.* Report of the President's Scientific Research Board. Government Printing Office. Washington, 1947

WILSON, T. 'Science and Industry', *Lloyds Bank Review.* October 1957, p. 34

Governmental Reports

Department of Scientific and Industrial Research Annual Report 1947-8, Cmd. 7761/1949. (S.15, 'Research and the Nationalized Industries')

Department of Scientific and Industrial Research Annual Reports

The Annual Report of the Advisory Council . . . for Scientific and Industrial Research, Cd. 8336/1916

First Annual Report of the Advisory Council on Scientific Policy, Cmd. 7465/1948

Treasury. Government Scientific Organization in the Civilian Field. 1951

Parliamentary Papers

Report of the Committee of Inquiry into the Electricity Supply Industry, Cmd. 9672/1956, pp. 120 ff. and Ch. XXII

Report of the Machinery of Government Committee, Cd. 9230/1918. Pt. II, Ch. IV. ('Research and Information')

Scientific Research and Development, Cmd. 6514/1944

Third Annual Report of the Advisory Council on Scientific Policy, Cmd. 7992/1950

Third Report of the Select Committee on Estimates, H.C. 132-I of 1946-7. 1946. (Expenditure on Research and Development)

Parliamentary Debates

395 H.C. Deb. 5s, cols. 216-311, April 19, 1944

474 H.C. Deb. 5s, cols. 2060-150, May 15, 1950

CHAPTER XIV: DEVELOPMENT

ABEL, D. 'British Conservatives and State Ownership', XIX *Journal of Politics.* (1957), p. 227

BESWICK, F. *Plan for the Aircraft Industry,* Fabian Research Series No. 176. London, 1955

BRITISH ELECTRICITY AUTHORITY. *Power and Prosperity.* 1954

The British Electricity System—Comments of the British Electricity Authority, Area Electricity Boards, and the National Joint Advisory Council of the Electricity Supply Industry on the U.S. Productivity Team Report. London, 1954

BRITISH TRANSPORT COMMISSION. *Modernization and Re-equipment of British Railways.* London, 1955

COLE, G. D. H. *Is this Socialism?* New Statesman pamphlet. London, 1954
DAVIES, E. A. J. *Problems of Public Ownership.* London, Labour Party, 1952, pp. 29 ff.
GAS COUNCIL. *Fuel for the Nation* (The Gas Industries Programme). London, 1954
GOLLAN, J. *Why Not Nationalize?* London, Communist Party, 1957
GOODMAN, E. *Forms of Public Control and Ownership.* London, 1951. Chs. V-VIII
HUGHES, J. *Plan for Steel Re-nationalization,* Fabian Research Series No. 198. London, 1958
JENKINS, C. As for Ch. IX
KELF-COHEN, R. 'Steel and the Labour Party' and 'Steel under Public Control', *Manchester Guardian.* September 23 and 26, 1958
LABOUR PARTY. *British Transport.* London, 1954
Public Enterprise. London, 1957. Chs. II, VIII and IX
LEWIS, R. *Industry and the Property Owning Democracy,* Bow Group. London, 1954
NATIONAL COAL BOARD. *Investing in Coal.* London, 1956
Plan for Coal. London, 1950
XXVI *Political Quarterly.* (1955). 'Notes and Comments: Nationalized Industry—a New Phase', p. 99
POWELL, J. E., and MAUDE, A. E. U. (eds.). *Change is Our Ally.* Conservative Political Centre. London, 1954. Pt. II
ROBSON, W. A. 'General Conclusions' in *Problems of Nationalized Industry,* ed. W. A. Robson. London, 1952, pp. 346 ff. and 365 ff.
SHORE, P. 'In the Room at the Top' in *Conviction,* ed. N. Mackenzie. London, 1958, p. 23
SINCLAIR, W. A. *Socialism and the Individual.* London, 1955. Ch. VII

Parliamentary Papers

The Future Organization of the United Kingdom Atomic Energy Project, Cmd. 8986/1953
Railway Reorganization Scheme, Cmd. 9191/1954
The British Transport Commission: Proposals for the Railways, Cmnd. 9880/1956
An exchange of Correspondence between the Minister of Transport and Civil Aviation and The Chairman of the British Transport Commission, Cmnd. 585/1958 (about the financial position and the future prospects of Railways)

CHAPTER XV: PERFORMANCE

ANGLO-AMERICAN COUNCIL ON PRODUCTIVITY. *The British Electricity System.* London, 1953
ARDANT, GABRIEL. 'The Measurement of Productivity in State Undertakings and Public Services', *Annals of Collectivist Economy.* Geneva, September 1953, pp. 79-96
BALDWIN, B. B. *Beyond Nationalization.* Harvard U.P., 1955

BEACHAM, A. 'Efficiency and Organization of the British Coal Industry', LV *Economic Journal.* (1945), p. 206

'The Present Position of the Coal Industry in Great Britain', LX *Economic Journal.* (1950), p. 9

BRITISH INSTITUTE OF MANAGEMENT. *Management Efficiency in Nationalized Undertakings.* London, 1950

Nationalized Audit Service. Conference Series No. 11. London, 1949

BRITISH PRODUCTIVITY COUNCIL. *The British Electricity System.* (Report of a Productivity Team from the U.S.). London, 1953

BURN, D. See *General*

CHESTER, D. N. 'The Nationalized Industries', *Three Banks Review.* December 1952, p. 24

KELF-COHEN, R. *Nationalization in Britain.* London, 1958

ELLIOT, SIR JOHN. 'Efficiency versus Cost in Public Transport', XXVII *Journal of the Institute of Transport.* London, (1958), p. 334

FEDERATION OF BRITISH INDUSTRIES. *A National Fuel Policy.* London, 1952 (Evidence submitted to the Committee on National Fuel Policy)

Nationalization. London, 1958

FLORENCE, P. SARGANT, and WALKER, G. 'Efficiency under Nationalization and its Measurement' in *Problems of Nationalized Industry,* ed. W. A. Robson. London, 1952, p. 199

GREENLAND, A. *Fuel for the Future.* London, Conservative Political Centre, 1956

HOULDSWORTH, SIR H. S. and others. *Efficiency in the Nationalized Industries.* London, 1952

LABOUR PARTY. *Success Story: the Nationalized Industries.* London, 1958

LATHAM, LORD. 'Efficiency in London Transport', II *British Transport Review.* London, (1952), p. 387

LOMAX, K. S. 'Cost Curves for Electricity Generation', XIX *Economica,* N.S. (1952), p. 193

NABARRO, G. D. N. *Ten Steps to Power.* London, 1952

and ALPORT, C. J. M. *Make Coal Work Harder.* London, Conservative Political Centre, 1951

NATIONAL COAL BOARD. *Investing in Coal* (Progress and Prospects under the Plan for Coal), London, 1956

NOEL-BAKER, P. J. *Coal.* London, Labour Party, 1950

NOTTAGE, R. As for Ch. IV

XXVII *Public Administration.* (1949), 'Tests of Efficiency', p. 67

Public Enterprise. Labour Party, (1957)

QUICK-SMITH, G. W. 'Road Haulage as a National Service', II *British Transport Review.* London, (1952), p. 199

RISK, W. S. 'Efficiency in Nationalized Industries', CXXIII *Accountant,* N.S. (1950), p. 56

ROBERTSON, GENERAL SIR B. 'The British Transport System'. A lecture published by the British Transport Commission, 1956

SPECTATOR STEEL INQUIRY. *The Spectator.* March 13, 1959, p. 359

TRIBE, SIR F. 'Efficiency in the Public Services', XXVII *Public Administration*. (1949), p. 159
WICKER, E. R. 'The Colonial Development Corporation (1948-54)', XXIII *Review of Economic Studies*. (1955-6), p. 213; see also a note by A. Hazlewood, *ib.*, p. 229
WHEATCROFT, S. *The Economics of European Air Transport*. Manchester, 1956
WILSON, R. H. 'Observations on the Process of Efficiency Audit', XXVII *Public Administration*. (1949), p. 76

Governmental Reports

Report of the Committee of Inquiry into London Transport. London, 1955. Ch. XIV

Parliamentary Papers

Report of the Committee on National Policy for the use of Fuel and Power Resources, Cmd. 8647/1952
The British Transport Commission—Re-appraisal of the Plan for the Modernization and Re-equipment of British Railways. Cmnd. 813/1959
Annual Reports of the Public Corporations

Parliamentary Debates

478 H.C. Deb. 5s, cols. 2795-1919 (October 25, 1950)
168 H.L. Deb. 5s, cols. 41-126 (July 5, 1950)
H.C. Deb., Standing Committees, 1947-8, vol. II, Standing Committee D., cols. 1971-86, May 12, 1948 (Gas Bill)

CHAPTER XVI: PUBLIC OWNERSHIP

ABEL, D. 'British Conservatives and State Ownership', XIX *Journal of Politics*. (1957), p. 227
ALBU, A. 'The Organization of Industry' in *New Fabian Essays*, ed. R. H. Crossman. London, 1952
BESWICK, F. *Plan for the Aircraft Industry*. Fabian Research Series No. 176. London, 1955
COLE, G. D. H. *Is This Socialism?* New Statesman pamphlet. London, 1954
CONSERVATIVE AND UNIONIST CENTRAL OFFICE. *The Campaign Guide*. London, 1951 and 1955
CONSERVATIVE AND UNIONIST PARTY. *United for Peace and Progress*. London, 1958
CO-OPERATIVE CONGRESS. *Report of the 89th Annual Congress*
CO-OPERATIVE PARTY NATIONAL COMMITTEE. *The People's Industry*. 1952
CROSLAND, C. A. R. *The Future of Socialism*. London, 1956
DUGDALE, J. 'The Labour Party and Nationalization', XXVIII *Political Quarterly*. (1957), p. 256
FEDERATION OF BRITISH INDUSTRIES. *Report on Nationalization*. London, 1958
GAITSKELL, H. T. N. *Socialism and Nationalization*. London, 1956
'The Economic Aims of the Labour Party', XXIV *Political Quarterly*. (1953), p. 6

GOLLAN, J. *Why Not Nationalize?* London, 1957

JAY, H. 'Public Capital and Private Enterprise', 28 *Fabian Journal*. July 1959

JENKINS, R. 'Equality' in *New Fabian Essays*, ed. R. H. Crossman. London, 1952

LABOUR PARTY. *Industry and Society. Labour's Policy on Future Public Ownership.* London, 1957

Forward with Labour. London, 1955

Report of the Annual Conference, 1957

Public Ownership. London, 1957

Challenge to Britain. London, 1953

Public Enterprise, Labour's Review of the Nationalized Industries. London, 1957

LEWIS, R. *Industry and the Property Owning Democracy*, Bow Group. London, 1954

ROBSON, W. A. 'Freedom, Equality and Socialism', XXVII *Political Quarterly*. (1956)

SOCIALIST UNION. *Twentieth Century Socialism*. London, 1956

STRACHEY, E. J. 'The Object of Further Socialization', XXIV *Political Quarterly* (1953), p. 68

TRADES UNION CONGRESS. 'The Public Control of Industry'. Report, 1950. App. D. London

Report of the 89th Annual Congress

Universities and Left Review. 'The Insiders.' Winter 1958

Index

For Product Safety Concerns and Information please contact our EU
representative GPSR@taylorandfrancis.com
Taylor & Francis Verlag GmbH, Kaufingerstraße 24, 80331 München, Germany

www.ingramcontent.com/pod-product-compliance
Lightning Source LLC
LaVergne TN
LVHW080113011026
849160LV00013B/1092

* 9 7 8 1 0 3 2 2 0 2 9 8 3 *